Lecture Notes in Computer Science   3232

Commenced Publication in 1973
Founding and Former Series Editors:
Gerhard Goos, Juris Hartmanis, and Jan van Leeuwen

Rachel Heery   Liz Lyon (Eds.)

Research and Advanced Technology for Digital Libraries

8th European Conference, ECDL 2004
Bath, UK, September 12-17, 2004
Proceedings

 Springer

Volume Editors

Rachel Heery
Liz Lyon
UKOLN, University of Bath, Bath BA2 7AY, UK
E-mail: r.heery@ukoln.ac.uk

Library of Congress Control Number: 2004111112

CR Subject Classification (1998): H.3.7, H.2, H.3, H.4.3, H.5, J.7, J.1, I.7

ISSN 0302-9743
ISBN 3-540-23013-0 Springer Berlin Heidelberg New York

Springer is a part of Springer Science+Business Media

springeronline.com

© Springer-Verlag Berlin Heidelberg 2004
Printed in Germany

Typesetting: Camera-ready by author, data conversion by Olgun Computergrafik
Printed on acid-free paper   SPIN: 11319139   06/3142   5 4 3 2 1 0

Preface

We are delighted to present the ECDL 2004 Conference proceedings from the 8th European Conference on Research and Advanced Technology for Digital Libraries at the University of Bath, Bath, UK. This followed an impressive and geographically dispersed series of locations for previous events: Pisa (1997), Heraklion (1998), Paris (1999), Lisbon (2000), Darmstadt (2001), Rome (2002), and Trondheim (2003).

The conference reflected the rapidly evolving landscape of digital libraries, both in technology developments and in the focus of approaches to implementation. An emphasis on the requirements of the individual user and of diverse and distributed user communities was apparent. In addition, the conference programme began to address, possibly for the first time, the associated themes of e-research/e-science and e-learning and their relationship to digital libraries. We observed increasing commonality in both the distributed information architectures and the technical standards that underpin global infrastructure developments. Digital libraries are integral to this information landscape and to the creation of increasingly powerful tools and applications for resource discovery and knowledge extraction. Digital libraries support and facilitate the data and information flows within the scholarly knowledge cycle and provide essential enabling functionality for both learners and researchers. The varied and innovative research activities presented at ECDL 2004 demonstrate the exciting potential of this very fast-moving field.

The 148 papers, 43 posters, 5 panels, 14 tutorials and 4 workshops submitted this year were once again of the highest quality. They covered a very wide range of topics and were submitted from many countries reflecting the standing and profile of this major European conference. Our international Programme Committee of 70 expert reviewers carried out an exacting peer-review process to assure continued quality standards and to generate an outstanding conference programme. We were able to accept 47 papers, 4 of which were short papers, which equates to a 32% acceptance rate. In addition we had three leading experts giving keynote presentations: Prof. Tony Hey (Director, UK E-Science Programme), Neil McLean (Director, IMS Australia), and Lorcan Dempsey (VP Research & Chief Strategist, OCLC). All information relating to the conference is located at http://www.ecdl2004.org/.

We recognize that there is a huge effort required to organize a successful major international conference and thanks are due to many individuals and organizations. In particular, we should like to extend our thanks to the Organizing Committee, the members of the Programme Committee, the additional referees, the conference Chairs, the invited speakers, panelists, all the presenters (panels, papers, posters, workshops and tutorials) and of course all the participants. We are grateful for the support of the University of Bath, Delos NoE, JISC, and MLA and for the helpful advice and guidance of many experts who willingly and freely gave their time and expertise for our collected benefit.

Finally we would like to extend our most sincere thanks to all our colleagues at UKOLN, who assisted and supported ECDL 2004 from conception to conclusion. Special thanks are due to Andy Powell, Greg Tourte and Richard Waller for their assistance in editing these proceedings.

July 2004   Rachel Heery
                                                                    Liz Lyon

Organization

General Chair

Liz Lyon, UKOLN, University of Bath, UK

Programme Chair

Rachel Heery, UKOLN, University of Bath, UK

Organization Chairs

James Davenport, University of Bath, UK
Michael Day, UKOLN, University of Bath, UK

Local Organizing Committee

Natasha Bishop, UKOLN, University of Bath, UK
Sarah Smith, UKOLN, University of Bath, UK

Workshop Chairs

Stefan Gradmann, Hamburg University, Germany
Lesly Huxley, University of Bristol, UK

Panel Chairs

Christine Borgman, University of California, USA
Stefan Decker, DERI, Ireland
Neil McLean, Macquarie University, Australia

Poster and Demonstration Chairs

Donatella Castelli, IEI-CNR, Italy
Heike Neuroth, Goettingen State and University Library, Germany

Tutorial Chairs

Jose Borbhina, National Library of Portugal
John MacColl, University of Edinburgh, UK
Tamara Sumner, University of Colorado, USA

Programme Committee

Hanne Albrechtsen, RISO National Laboratory, Denmark
Anders Ardö, Lund Institute of Technology, Sweden
Daniel Atkins, University of Michigan, USA
Ricardo Baeza-Yates, University of Chile, Chile
Thomas Baker, Fraunhofer-Gesellschaft, Germany
Dave Beckett, ILRT, University of Bristol, UK
Nick Belkin, Rutgers University, USA
Ann Blandford, UCL, UK
Gerhard Budin, University of Vienna, Austria
Lorna Campbell, University of Strathclyde, UK
Vittore Casarosa, National Research Council, Italy
Key-Sun Choi, KAIST, Korea
Sheila Corrall, University of Sheffield, UK
Fabio Crestani, University of Strathclyde, UK
David de Roure, Southampton University, UK
Marilyn Deegan, University of Oxford, UK
Lorcan Dempsey, OCLC, USA
Martin Doerr, ICS FORTH, Greece
Matthew Dovey, Oxford University, UK
Dieter Fellner, Technical University of Braunschweig, Germany
Ed Fox, Virginia Tech, USA
Norbert Fuhr, University of Duisburg-Essen, Germany
Carole Goble, University of Manchester, UK
Norbert Gövert, University Library of Dortmund, Germany
Jane Greenberg, University of North Carolina, USA
Juha Hakala, Helsinki University Library, Finland
Margaret Hedstrom, University of Michigan, USA
Debra Hiom, ILRT, University of Bristol, UK
Jane Hunter, University of Queensland, Australia
Pete Johnston, UKOLN, University of Bath, UK
Leonid Kalinicichenko, Russian Academy of Sciences, Russia
Stephen Katz, Food and Agriculture Organization of the United Nations, Italy
Jaana Kekalainen, University of Tampere, Finland
Kersten Kleese, CCLRC e-Science, UK
Traugott Koch, Netlab Lund University, Sweden
Harald Krottmaier, IICM, Austria
John Kunze, California Digital Library, USA
Carl Lagoze, Cornell University, USA
Mounia Lalmas, University of London, UK
Ray Larson, University of California, Berkeley, USA
Clifford Lynch, Coalition for Networked Information, USA
Michael Mabe, Elsevier Science, UK
Pier Giorgio Marchetti, European Space Agency, Italy
Gary Marchionini, University of North Carolina, Chapel Hill, USA

Additional Reviewers

Sponsors

Joint Information Systems Committee, UK

Table of Contents

Digital Library Architectures

Evaluation and Usability

User Interfaces and Presentation

New Approaches to Information Retrieval

Interoperability

Enhanced Indexing and Searching Methods

Personalisation and Annotation

Music Digital Libraries

Personal Digital Libraries

Innovative Technologies for Digital Libraries

Open Archives Initiative

New Models and Tools

User-Centred Design

Innovative Technologies for Digital Libraries

Dynamic Digital Library Construction and Configuration

David Bainbridge, Katherine J. Don, George R. Buchanan, Ian H. Witten,
Steve Jones, Matt Jones, and Malcolm I. Barr

Department of Computer Science, University of Waikato, Hamilton, New Zealand
Phone (+64) 7 838 4407, fax (+64) 7 858 5095
davidb@cs.waikato.ac.nz

Abstract. This paper describes a digital library architecture and implementation that is configurable, extensible and dynamic in the way it presents content and in the services it provides. The design manifests itself as a network of modules that communicate in terms of XML messages. All modules characterize the functionality they implement in response to a "describe yourself" message, and can transform messages using XSLT to support different levels of configurability. Traditional library values such as backwards compatibility and multiplatform operation are combined with the ability to add new collections and services adaptively. The paper describes the new design and shows how it can be used to build four different digital library systems. We conclude by showing how the design fits existing interoperability frameworks.

1 Introduction

This paper describes a digital library design that improves upon the Greenstone toolkit [7]. First, it provides more flexible ways of dynamically configuring the run-time system and adding new services to it. Second, it lowers the overhead incurred by collection developers when accessing this flexibility to organize and present their content. Third, it modularizes the internal structure and simplifies the addition of new modules. The design is based on widely-accepted standards such as XML, current software practices such as simple protocols (like SOAP), cross-platform development strategies (Java), and contemporary schemes for software modularization and dynamic updates. Most important of all, it is informed by our experience with the current Greenstone system and the problems and challenges faced by real users, international collection developers, and practicing librarians.

The structure of the paper is as follows. First we give some background out of which the requirements for the digital library software arose. Next we describe the new design, called Greenstone3, and discuss how it meets the identified needs. Fundamental to the approach is the use of XML throughout for data representation, combined with XSL Transforms to provide a flexible mechanism for adjusting the functionality of the runtime system without having to modify and recompile the source code. To promote cross-platform independence (which

R. Heery and L. Lyon (Eds.): ECDL 2004, LNCS 3232, pp. 1–13, 2004.
© Springer-Verlag Berlin Heidelberg 2004

has consumed inordinate human resources in the present Greenstone system) and facilitate the dynamic loading of services and other modules, the implementation uses Java.

Following this we describe four very different examples built using the new design. The first demonstrates backwards compatibility, and, in addition, operates within a distributed environment. The second augments text at display time, using an established software tool for text mining developed elsewhere, to show how functionality can be enriched through the introduction of a new service. The third is a map-based digital library that introduces two new services to support geographic functionality and, while still accessed through a web-based interface, is highly tailored to the specific domain of its source documents. The fourth is a radically different interface for the interactive viewing of search results as a hierarchically organized cluster of documents, and illustrates the versatility of the design in coping with fine-grained interaction. We conclude with a commentary on how the design fits existing interoperability frameworks, from which many valuable lessons have been learned.

1.1   Background

Over the years the Greenstone digital library software has been employed by many users internationally to develop a wide variety of digital libraries. In addition to operation over the Web, an early application, and still a major one, is collections of humanitarian information in the form of CD-ROMs that run on any Windows computer (including Windows 3.1). There are now over two dozen of these collections, and they have been distributed widely by the United Nations and other non government agencies [9].

Many other styles of collection have been developed under Greenstone. They range from numerous personal collections based around common document formats such as E-mail, photographs, Word, and PDF documents through to large-scale bibliographic catalogs such as the BBC radio and TV archives. There are mixed media collections involving text, images and audio drawn from data such as historic newspapers and oral history. Several demonstration music collections support direct content-based retrieval through "query by humming." Many customized and branded user interfaces exist, such as the New York Botanical Gardens, and many international collections in local languages created by institutions in China, India, Croatia, Russia and Israel.

The software is distributed in source form, and for convenience binaries are available for Windows, Linux and MacOS X. The user interface is available in 30 languages. A recent addition is a graphical interface for collection design and construction [2] which is also multilingual. A portfolio of demonstration collections is available at *www.nzdl.org*, and selected example collections built internationally can be found at *www.greenstone.org*.

1.2   Weaknesses

Many experimental interfaces have been built for Greenstone, some of which make use of a CORBA-based protocol to support distributed client-server interaction. These include a Venn diagram tool for formulating Boolean queries graphically, and a bibliographic visualization tool that plots matching citations on an x-y grid based on publication year and ranked relevance score to the query terms [1]. However, while perfectly functional, some of these variants are implemented inelegantly, exposing limitations caused by certain aspects of the design. For instance, the immutable nature of the index files generated during the building process makes incremental adjustments to a collection expensive. Another hindrance is the low level of functional customization supported by the runtime system. Although minor presentation tweaks are easy, more extensive changes involve modifying and recompiling the source code. The strongly typed nature of the CORBA protocol was also found to be overly restrictive in many practical situations.

1.3   Requirements

From these and other considerations arose the following requirements for an improved design.

Backwards compatibility. Naturally we wish to retain the existing system's strengths. This is accomplished by ensuring that the new design is backward compatible, which has the added benefit of providing existing developers and users with an easy migration path.

Levels of customization. To match the different categories of people involved in constructing digital libraries, different levels of customization are required. For instance, a content developer may wish to include source documents in a new format; a collection editor may seek influence over diverse issues of presentation.

Software modularity. To facilitate development and long-term management of the software, code modularization – a mantra of any software engineering approach – is essential. This is promoted by adopting off-the-shelf technology such as a database system, indexing tools, and page rendering software; and by the use of standards.

Service based. Basing a digital library around a set of services is another way to accomplish modularity – in this case, modularity of function.

Distributed architecture. A rich digital library infrastructure can only be supported by a distributed architecture, and the addition of an open protocol helps to foster interoperability.

Future compatibility. Libraries are long-term institutions with a mandate for preservation, and it is essential that old collections can be presented by future versions of the system. This is a more ambitious requirement than mere extensibility which, although an admirable quality in any design, does not necessarily ensure that future versions can safely interact with current ones.

Dynamic. Many aspects of the library should be dynamic, for example *content*, whereby documents and metadata can be added, revised and removed while a repository remains on-line, and *configuration*, where presentational issues can be adjusted and services added at runtime.

Integrated documentation. Large-scale software systems such as digital libraries benefit immensely from the use of an integrated documentation system.

Self-describing modules. This goes a stage further than the previous item: modules describe themselves in a machine-readable format so that other modules can interact with them without the need for explicit control.

Computer environment integration. A digital library should mesh well into a user's existing computer environment. Full integration makes a digital library become a seamless component of each user's work environment.

2 Software Design

The new software design has evolved from the requirements articulated above, our own experience of developing digital library systems, and studies of other open source software and research projects. This section provides an overview of modularity and inter-module communication, and then works through a simple, stand-alone example. The next section describes four very different examples built using the new design, to illustrate the general applicability of the approach.

2.1 Modularity

We decided that the best way to meet the challenges posed by the list of requirements was to reimplement Greenstone using a modular topology. In the design, a digital library manifests itself as a network of modules, and communication between them is expressed through an instantiation of XML. A mandatory requirement for a module – enforced through its base class definition – is that it handles "describe yourself" messages. What kinds of messages follow typically depend on the outcome of an initial "describe yourself". Modules have the ability to transform messages by applying an XSL Transform. This is a particularly useful mechanism for dynamically controlling levels of configurability – one of our requirements. Within the network of modules comprising a digital library, a set of services are defined that prescribe the functionality supported by that particular digital library configuration.

2.2 Communication

Modules communicate using synchronous request-response pairs. Fig. 1 shows an example XML exchange, where the TextQuery module in a collection called "demo" is asked to describe itself. It does this, providing information about the structure of the service as well as fragments of text to be used for display. These are returned in the language specified in the request. While the language used is structured and typed, it has been crafted in such a way that the information it contains can be open-ended. For example, in Fig. 1 the *paramList* structure allows other items to be included, such as whether stemming is on or off. In addition to supporting optional parameters, extensions can be introduced without

```
<request to='demo/TextQuery' lang='en' type='describe' uid='21'/>

<response from='demo/TextQuery' lang='en' type='describe'>
  <service name='TextQuery' type='query'>
    <displayItem name='name'>Search</displayItem>
    <displayItem name='description'>Full text search</displayItem>
    <displayItem name='submit'>Search</displayItem>
    <paramList>
      <param name='index' type='enum_single' default='stx'>
        <displayItem name="name">Index to search in</displayItem>
        <option name="dtx">
          <displayItem name="name">entire documents</displayItem>
        </option>
        <option name="stx">
          <displayItem name="name">chapters</displayItem>
        </option>
      </param>
      <param name='maxDocs' type='integer' default='10'>
        <displayItem name="name">Maximum hits to return</displayItem>
      </param>
      <param name="query" type="string">
        <displayItem name="name">Query string</displayItem>
      </param>
    </paramList>
  </service>
</response>
```

Fig. 1. A sample XML exchange as a request/response pair.

having to update the protocol's API, thereby avoiding the need to propagate code changes to the entire distributed network (which may require taking it off-line while the changes are made). For a more thorough technical description of the design, see the integrated documentation that is supplied with the Greenstone3 source code (available through SourceForge).

2.3 A Simple Stand-Alone Example

The simple stand-alone example shown in Fig. 2 encapsulates many of the design's key features. It comprises a "back end" server, termed a digital library *site* in our design, coupled to a "front end" that provides the user interface. The modules' names were chosen to emphasize the roles they play. The Receptionist's point of contact with the server is the MessageRouter (MR) module – all communication with the site occurs through this module. The configuration is designed to generalize to a distributed environment.

The digital library back end in Fig. 2 contains two collections, *demo* and *fao*, and a cluster of collection-formation services. *AddDocument* is a service that adds a document to a collection. *ImportCollection* imports into the system all documents associated with a collection, converting them where necessary from their original form. *BuildCollection* builds all indexes and browsing structures that are associated with a collection. *ActivateCollection* makes a newly-built collection active, so that it can be seen by digital library users. These services are all concerned with creating a digital library collection. Being related, they are grouped together into a "service cluster." In Fig. 2 the services just listed are accessed through the *CollectionFormation* service cluster module.

As far as the digital library user is concerned, a "collection" is a focused group of documents with a uniform means of access. For the system, it is a service clus-

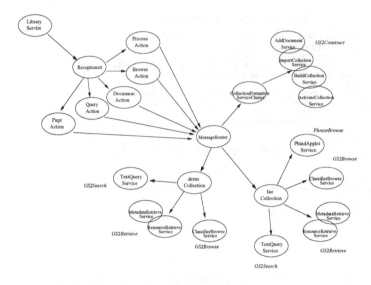

Fig. 2. A simple stand-alone site.

ter that groups a set of services that are related by the data they work on. For example, the *demo* collection towards the lower left of Fig. 2 contains three modules providing four services to the user. The modules are called "Search," which provides a *TextQuery* service, "Retrieve," which provides a document retrieval service *ResourceRetrieve* and a metadata retrieval service *MetadataRetrieve*, and "Browse," which provides a metadata browsing service *ClassifierBrowse*.

The Web-based front end at the upper left of Fig. 2 centers around the Receptionist, which is the point of contact for the interface generator. A servlet (labeled "Library Servlet") takes HTTP commands in the form of URLs and arguments and translates them into XML for the Receptionist. The Receptionist is capable of executing various different actions, each of which involves (usually) many calls to the digital library's MessageRouter (center of Fig. 2). The built-in ability for Receptionist modules to transform XML messages using XSLT is used – in conjunction with a style sheet – to generate the HTML that is finally presented to the user.

3 Examples

For pedagogical purposes, the example configuration in Fig. 2 is rudimentary. The front and back ends (receptionist and site server) are compiled together into a single executable process with a single MessageRouter handling all communication between them. However, the design supports a far richer infrastructure than this. MessageRouters have the capability to communicate across a distributed network with other MessageRouters and with Receptionists. Different implementations of the same service can be switched in and out to give a digital library site different algorithmic behavior (such as incremental building); and new services can be introduced and brought on-line, dynamically if necessary. The library can also have many different user interfaces.

We now describe four more interesting scenarios. The first emulates "classic" Greenstone to demonstrate backwards compatibility, with a distributed configuration a straightforward addition. The second augments text at display time, to show how functionality can be enriched through the introduction of a new service. The third and fourth utilize novel interfaces to enrich the interaction: the former is specialized for geographic maps, and the latter for text based collections.

3.1 Classic Greenstone, with Collections on Remote Sites

To provide backwards compatibility, a set of Greenstone3 services have been implemented that access index and database files generated by a Greenstone2 system. Indeed we have already seen these in Fig. 2. Moreover, using Cascading Style Sheets (CSS), the look and feel of the traditional interface has been matched one-for-one, so that the user's experience of the digital library remains the same. Of course with the more versatile design, more sophisticated internal structures can be built within the digital libary. For instance, because of the design decision that all communication be XML based, it is straightforward to arrange for the XML messages sent between modules to be seamlessly streamed across remote machines. For this we employ the Simple Object Access Protocol (SOAP), but any protocol that can process text can be used. To the user there is no disernable difference accessing collections this way. Backwards compatability is not the sole aim, however, and the structure allows increasingly interesting digital library designs – ones that do provide a distinctly different expierence for the user. We discuss three such examples next.

3.2 Dynamic Text Mining

The next example shows how a new Greenstone3 service can be provided that enhances documents for the reader, based upon the open source GATE system for text mining [5]. The motivation is that highlighting selected items in documents can make it easier for users to scan them for particular pieces of information. In this implementation, digital library documents, once located, are mined on the fly marking up entities such as keywords and place names before presenting them to the user [8].

Fig. 3(a) shows a section of a book on Butterfly Farming in Papua New Guinea (from the Humanity Development Library at *www.nzdl.org*) that the user is reading. The Annotate document menu at the top right calls the display-time text mining feature. When items on this menu are selected, text of the selected type is highlighted in the document displayed. In this case the user has selected Places and Organizations, and these are highlighted wherever they occur, in different colors (simulated by white-on-grey and black-on grey in the illustration).

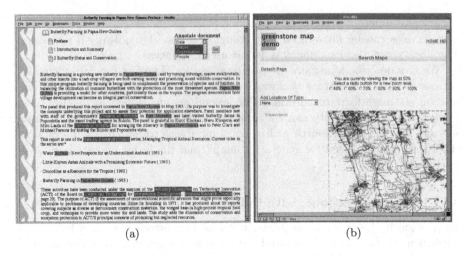

(a)   (b)

Fig. 3. Additional services to augment run-time functionally (a) text augmentation of place names; (b) a novel map-based interface.

The selectable items in Fig. 3(a) were identified and extracted by ANNIE, GATE's information extraction system. Whenever an annotation type is selected from the menu, Greenstone3 calls the information extraction module dynamically to identify items of that type. This incurs a delay that depends on the document's size but is usually short: the system processes text at the average rate of 15 Kb/sec on a typical workstation. In order to achieve this the software is loaded when the Greenstone3 server is executed and remains resident in memory thereafter, to avoid a start-up delay (of about 10 seconds) in which all the text processors are initialized and prepared for use.

In Greenstone3, GATE is encapsulated in a module as just another service. It takes messages with two parameters, the type of annotation and a document, and returns the document with relevant items marked up with XML tags. A style sheet in the server module chooses the colors in which the items are displayed.

In order to generate the menu in the figure, a "describe yourself" message is sent to the GATE module, which returns a list of the annotations that are available. Apart from this one module, the rest of the digital library system knows nothing of GATE. However, it does know about a general class of services, *Enrich*, that take a document and return the same document with some elements marked up. To add this text-mining ability to an existing Greenstone3 site dynamically the Java class files for the new service need to added to the correct folder on the DL site's file system, the site's configuration file updated to name the new service, and a "reconfigure" signal sent (which can be initiated through a web browser) to the DL site server.

3.3   Geographical Map Based Interface

Fig. 3(b) is taken from a site configured to support map searching based on a small collection of New Zealand maps drawn between 1770 and 1953, part

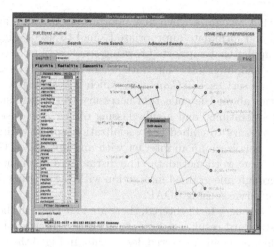

Fig. 4. Applet based Dendro visualization of clustered documents matching query.

of our university library's special collections. It shows the result of searching for "Rangiriri" – a township in the North Island of New Zealand and, on a hill nearby of the same name, the scene of a battle in 1863 between Maori and British soldiers. Two crosses (colored red when viewed online) have been overlaid on the map showing the position of the township and hill, and can be seen slightly above the center of the map.

The query interface and presentation of the results is similar to the traditional interface, except that against each matching item a thumbnail of the map containing the place name is given. Fig. 3(b) is the result of honing in on one such map appearing in the result set. Through the interface the user can change the level of magnification of the map and request that additional features such as cemeteries, bridges, and estuaries be marked.

This new functionality is provided by adding two new services, including geographic metadata with the collection's source documents (the maps), and a gazetteer of over 40,000 entries from Land Information New Zealand (LINZ). Searching is handled by the *MapQuery* service. For each place name query term that is located in the gazetteer, its longitude and latitude are checked against each map to see if it falls within its boundaries. Once all cross-referencing is complete, the list of maps with matching entries is sorted by the number of query terms on each map. Image manipulation and the results display are handled by the *MapRetrieve* service, which makes use of the open source ImageMagick toolkit for copying, annotating (such as placing a cross at an x, y location) and resizing images.

3.4 Cluster Visualizations

Fig. 3 shows a web-based interface, but there may be other forms, ranging from standalone applications and applets that display documents in different ways to alert services that recognize when new information becomes available in one of the collections and formulate appropriate E-mail to users. Fig. 4 is one such instance: a Java applet that supports browsing result sets as document clusters through a multiviewed, interactive interface [3]. To function it needs the addition of a new build-time service, *VisConstruct*, which is responsible for computing additional statistics about the collection necessary to perform subsequent document clustering operations, and a sub-classing of the *Applet* service, tailored for the HTML necessary to embed the visualization applet within a web page. Besides this, the visualization can interact with any text-based Greenstone collection that defines keyword metadata. The distinctly different interface behavior is achieved through fine-grained interaction with the existing *TextQuery* and *MetadataRetrieve* services using SOAP.

Derived from the query term entered, there are four views in the visualization. The first is the standard result list format; the other three are based around a shared model of hierarchically clustered documents. In Fig. 4 the user has entered the query term "recession" to a collection based on the Wall Street Journal and is viewing the result as a Dendro map – the circular arranged tree displayed in the main panel – which contains words like *slowing, slowdown* and *inflationary* around the circumference.

The size of nodes in the tree represents the number of documents clustered at that point in the hierarchy, and for reasons of space only 5 levels of the tree are shown at a time. Clicking on a node shows a popup menu with the precise number of documents in the cluster and the option of "drilling down" as shown in the figure. The consequence of choosing this option is for the tree to be redrawn with the selected node at the center of the map, thereby exposing more of the detail in that part of the hierarchy. While all this is going on, the left-panel displays the keywords relevant to the selected cluster, and the bottom panel lists the documents involved. Within the left panel, keywords can be activated or deactivated and the bottom panel dynamically filtered to reflect the changes.

4   Interoperability Frameworks

This modular, service-based and dynamically configurable approach to digital library architecture can be found in other designs and systems. Two key examples are the Extended Open Archives Initiative protocol (XOAI) proposed by Suleman and Fox [6] and the OpenDLib system of Castelli and Pagano [4].

The XOAI protocol, based upon XML and related technologies, builds upon the basic OAI Protocol for Metadata Harvesting. It is a modular protocol which represents each service as a different type of OAI request. This service-based approach is readily seen in Greenstone3's protocol, where each service has its own request and response format. Like OAI and XOAI, Greenstone3 uses XML for representing requests and responses; providing a gateway between Greenstone3 and XOAI servers and clients should be readily achievable.

The OpenDLib system also takes a modular approach to service communication and library construction. Many of its features are similar to those of XOAI and Greenstone3, and the handling of requests to the library map as readily as for XOAI. However, OpenDLib is centered upon a "manager" service that coordinates services, responding to the introduction of new services and alterations to existing ones. Coordination is achieved through a communication protocol between the manager and each service. Individual services, including each library in a federation, acquire data from the manager. The manager does not itself control or direct requests for searches, documents, and so on but instead coordinates between services to ensure consistency. Greenstone3 provides many of these features – for instance, service description requests – without requiring a centralized manager.

The similarity of protocols between Greenstone3, XOAI and OpenDLib echoes experience with the previous generation of DL protocols and augers well for interoperability. Greenstone's widespread adoption and free availability allows others to adopt it as a platform for experimenting with the service-centered design approach. It facilitates the addition of new digital library features which would have been hampered by the less open structures of Greenstone2 and its contemporaries. Greenstone3 retains and extends the lightweight configurability of its predecessor without requiring centralized management processes.

5   Conclusions

This paper has presented a new digital library design which is significantly different from the present Greenstone, but strongly rooted in past success. To meet a broad range of requirements a modular based topology is utilized to provide a flexible infrastructure. Written in Java to promote portability, dynamic loading of objects and internationalization, modules communicate by streaming XML messages between each other. Using SOAP this communication can be distributed across a network. All modules have the ability to describe themselves in a machine readable form, and to apply an XSLT to transform messages. The latter is instrumental in providing different levels of configurability, an important ability given the different types of people involved in the life-cycle of a digital library.

Several working examples have been given to convey the general applicability of the design. The first example demonstrated backwards compatibility to collections built with Greenstone2, and satisfies another of the identified requirements: to help minimize the migration path of existing developers and users. It also demonstrated the design functioning in a distributed environment. The second example augmented an existing DL site with text mining capabilities with the introduction of a new service. The third and fourth examples illustrated substantially different user interfaces: one specialized for maps that required two extra services to provide the necessary geographical functionality; the other provided an interactive visualization to search results through a Java applet that was applicable to a wider realm of text-based collections.

Numerous aspects of the design contribute to its dynamic configurability. The "describe yourself" feature allows receptionists to adapt to the facilities that a server presents. Through XSLT a corpus editor can exert significant control over the function and appearance of a digital library such as modifying the structure of a generated page, for example adding a transform that sorts the query results alphabetically by title rather than ranked score. Alternatively they may reformat the results according to OAI syntax in preparation for exporting. Previously such changes required editing the source code and restarting the digital library software after recompilation.

Implementing the design in Java has promoted dynamic attributes in the system, particularly through the ease in which modules can be loaded at runtime. The re-reading of configuration files is also straightforward to arrange and adds dynamic abilities that a digital library administrator can take advantage of. In addition to integrating the documentation with the software using JavaDoc and other techniques, usability of the software also benefits from the development of self-documenting collections that both demonstrate and describe particular aspects of design. The list of requirements is ambitious, however, and not all of them have been proven yet. For example, while none of the sample implementations demonstrate computer environment integration, the design is capable of supporting the idea through specialized receptionists. For future compatibility, more time is needed to establish if the design successfully meets such a criteria.

Acknowledgments

We gratefully acknowledge the stimulating research environment provided by the New Zealand Digital Library Project, and in particular Michael Dewsnip; Stefan Ruger and Daniel Heesch of Imperial College London; Valentin Tablan of the University of Sheffield, all of whom contributed to certain aspects of this work. This research is supported by the New Zealand New Economy Research Fund.

References

1. D. Bainbridge, G. Buchanan, J. McPherson, S. Jones, M. Mahoui, and I. H. Witten. Greenstone: a platform for distributed digital library applications. In *Proceedings of the European Conference on Digital Libraries*, pages 137–148, Darmstadt, Germany, September 2001.
2. D. Bainbridge, J. Thompson, and I. H. Witten. Assembling and enriching digital library collections. In *Proc. of the third ACM and IEEE joint conference on Digital Libraries*, pages 323–334, Houston, Texas, 2003.
3. M. Carey, D. C. Heesch, and S. M. Rüger. Info navigator: A visualization tool for document searching and browsing. In *Proc. of the Intl. Conf. on Distributed Multimedia Systems (DMS)*, September 2003.
4. D. Castelli and P. Pagan. A system for building expandable digital libraries. In *Proc. of the third ACM and IEEE joint conference on Digital Libraries*, pages 335–345, Houston, Texas, 2003.
5. H. Cunningham. GATE, a general architecture for text engineering. *Computers and the Humanities*, 36:223–254, 2002.

6. H. Suleman and E. A. Fox. Designing protocols in support of digital library compo-
    nentization. In *Proceedings of the European Conference on Digital Libraries*, pages
    568–582, Rome, Italy, 2002.
7. I. H. Witten and D. Bainbridge. *How to build a digital library*. Morgan Kaufmann,
    San Francisco, 2003.
8. I. H. Witten, K. J. Don, M. Dewsnip, and V. Tablan. Text mining in a digital
    library. *Journal of Digital Libraries*, 2003 (in press).
9. I. H. Witten, M. Loots, M. Fernandez-Trujillo, and D. Bainbridge. The promise of
    digital libraries in developing countries. *The Electronic Library*, 20(1):7–13, 2002.

Milos: A Multimedia Content Management System for Digital Library Applications*

Giuseppe Amato, Claudio Gennaro, Fausto Rabitti, and Pasquale Savino

ISTI-CNR, Pisa, Italy
{giuseppe.amato,claudio.gennaro,fausto.rabitti,pasquale.savino}
@isti.cnr.it

Abstract. This paper describes the MILOS Multimedia Content Management System: a general purpose software component tailored to support design and effective implementation of digital library applications. MILOS supports the storage and content based retrieval of any multimedia documents whose descriptions are provided by using arbitrary metadata models represented in XML. MILOS is **flexible** in the management of documents containing different types of data and content descriptions; it is **efficient** and **scalable** in the storage and content based retrieval of these documents. The paper illustrates the solutions adopted to support the management of different metadata descriptions of multimedia documents in the same repository, and it illustrates the experiments performed by using the MILOS system to archive documents belonging to four different and heterogenous collections which contain news agencies, scientific papers, and audio/video documentaries.

1 Introduction

Digital Library (DL) technology is today limited to manage specific types of digital objects and specific metadata description models. This implies that existing DL applications can be hardly adapted to different application environments and to different metadata description models. Indeed, many DLs were built having in mind a specific application and, in many cases, a specific document collection, thus resulting in an ad-hoc solution: all components of the DL – the data repository, the metadata manager, the search and retrieval components, etc. – are specific to a given application and cannot be easily used in other environments. Many of these systems guarantee inter-operability with other systems, by adopting standard protocols such as OAI, or Z39.50. However, their inter-operability is limited to the exchange (import/export) of data/metadata. In fact, there is no chance of reusing software components, to integrate functionality of other DLs,

* This work was partially supported by the ECD project (Extended Content Delivery) [12], funded by the Italian government, by the VICE project (Virtual Communities for Education), also funded by the Italian government, and by DELOS NoE, funded by the European Commission under FP6 (Sixth Framework Programme). We would like to thank Paolo Bolettieri, Franca Debole, Fabrizio Falchi, Francesco Furfari, and Bertrand Le Saux for their valuable contribution to the MILOS implementation.

R. Heery and L. Lyon (Eds.): ECDL 2004, LNCS 3232, pp. 14–25, 2004.

or to use digital contents (documents and metadata) compliant to other standards. This is mainly due to the lack of standard general purpose basic building components tailored to DL application design.

In this paper we propose an approach similar to that applied in the field of traditional database applications. In fact, database applications are generally built relying on a Database Management System (DBMS), a general purpose software module that offers all functions needed to build many different database applications (e.g., banking, corporate management, billing, etc.); these applications will use different types of data, and they will support many different types of retrieval. We intend to demonstrate that the same can be done in the DL field: it is possible to build a general purpose Multimedia Content Management System (MCMS) which offers functionalities specialized for DL applications. Different DL applications, can be built on top of such an MCMS, each supporting the management of documents of any data type, described by using different metadata description models, searchable in many different modes. This MCMS should be able to manage not only formatted data, like in databases, but also textual data, using Information Retrieval technology, semi-structured data, typically in XML, mixed-mode data, like structured presentations, and multimedia data, like images and audio/video.

In this paper we discuss the functionality that the MCMS should provide (Section 2) and we present the MILOS Multimedia Content Management System (Section 3), that we built according to those criteria. Finally we present several significant DL applications that were implemented by using MILOS, and we show the advantages of the proposed approach in building these specific DL applications, resulting in the simplicity of the implementation and in significant system performance (Section 4).

2   Motivations

Digital library applications are document intensive applications where possibly heterogeneous documents and their metadata have to be managed efficiently and effectively. We believe that the main functionalities required by DL applications can be embedded in a general purpose Multimedia Content Management System (MCMS), that is a software tool specialized to support applications where documents, embodied in different digital media, and their metadata are efficiently and effectively handled.

The minimal requirements of a Multimedia Content Management System are *Flexibility*, in structuring both multimedia documents and their metadata, *Scalability*, and *efficiency*. *Flexibility* is required to manage both basic multimedia documents and their metadata. The flexibility required in representing and accessing metadata can be obtained by adopting XML as standard for specifying any metadata (for example MPEG-7 [5] can be used for multimedia objects, or SCORM [11] for e-Learning objects). Requirements of *scalability* and *efficiency* are essential for the deployment of real systems able to satisfy the operational requirements of a large community of users over a huge amount of multimedia information.

A MCMS mainly supports the *storage and preservation* of digital documents, and their *efficient and effective retrieval* and *management*. This is provided with an appropriate management of documents and related metadata, by:

1. managing different documents embodied in different media and stored with different strategies;
2. supporting the description of document content by way of arbitrary, and possibly heterogeneous, metadata;
3. providing DL applications with custom/personalised views on the metadata schema actually handled.

Point 1) requires that no assumption should be taken on the types of media and encoding used to represent documents, and especially on the specific strategy used to store them. This allows applications to be unaware of the technical details related to multimedia document management. For instance, textual documents can be stored in the file system and served to the users using a normal web server. However, video documents might need to be maintained in a video server that uses various storage devices, as for example digital tapes stored in silos, optical disks, and/or temporary storage space on arrays of hard disks [21]. In addition, video documents might be served exploiting specific real-time continuous media streaming strategies to avoid hiccups during playback. The DL application should be designed independently from these issues, which should be managed transparently by the MCMS. For instance, changes in the storage strategies should be possible without changing the DL application software.

Point 2) states that a content management system should be able to deal with arbitrary metadata. This is required by the fact that different DL applications, according to their specific requirements, might need to use different metadata. Consider that existing archiving organizations have already their own metadata schemas, and hardly want to modify them to be compatible with a specific system. Therefore, a DL management system should be able to support any metadata schema without requiring metadata translation or restrictions on the functionality offered. There are also cases where the same application needs to deal with different metadata at the same time. These different metadata might be needed because the documents have redundant descriptions in terms of different metadata, or because the DL application is dealing with a document collection described with heterogeneous metadata. The last case might occur, for instance, in case of integration/merging of archives managed by different organization.

Point 3) makes it possible that the metadata schema seen by the DL application is different from the metadata schemas actually stored in the repository of the content management system. Suppose that an application was built to deal just with a specific metadata schema. The MCMS should be able to serve requests of such an application even if metadata stored in the repository comply to different schemas. Metadata schema independence can be obtained by exploiting techniques of schema mapping. This feature is especially useful in case of heterogeneous metadata available at the same time in the repository: the DL application will refer to just one metadata schema, relying on the multiple schema mapping performed on the fly by the MCMS. In addition, this feature allows different DL application, which require different metadata schemas, to share the same MCMS transparently.

3   The MILOS Multimedia Content Management System

We have designed and built MILOS (Multimedia dIgital Library Object Server), a MCMS that satisfies the requirements and offers the functionalities discussed in previous section. The MILOS MCMS has been developed by using the Web Service technology, which in many cases (e.g. .NET, EJB, CORBA, etc.) already provides very complex support for "standard" operations such as authentication, authorization management, encryption, replication, distribution, load balancing, etc. Thus, we do not further elaborate on these topics, but we will mainly concentrate on the aspects discussed above.

MILOS is composed of three main components as depicted in Figure 1: the Metadata Storage and Retrieval (MSR) component, the Multi Media Server (MMS) component, and the Repository Metadata Integrator (RMI) component. All these components are implemented as Web Services and interact by using SOAP. The MSR manages the metadata of the DL. It relies on our technology for native XML databases, and offers the functionality illustrated at point 2) above. The MMS manages the multimedia documents used by the DL applications. MMS offers the functionality of point 1) above. The RMI implements the service logic of the repository providing developers of DL applications with a uniform and integrated way of accessing MMS and MRS. In addition, it supports the mapping of different metadata schemas as described at point 3) above. All these components were built choosing solutions able to guarantee the requirements of flexibility, scalability, and efficiency, as discussed in the next sections.

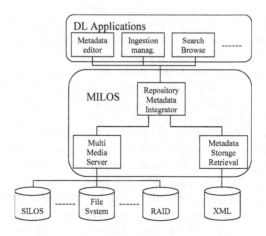

Fig. 1. General Architecture of MILOS.

3.1   Metadata Storage and Retrieval

A typical search in a DL is performed on metadata which describe the document content end their bibliographic information. Three different approaches have been adopted until now to support document retrieval in digital libraries: (a) use of relational databases; (b) use of information retrieval engines; (c) full sequential scan of metadata records. Unfortunately, these approaches did not prove to be effective for DL applications: designers had to face the problem of choosing the right compromise between efficiency of the search systems and complexity of the metadata schema. The result of this compromise is that in mostmany cases DLs use very simple and flat metadata schemas such as Dublin Core [2].

Solution (a) requires that metadata should be converted into relational schemas. This is easy for simple flat metadata schemas, such as Dublin Core, but it far more difficult for complex and descriptive metadata schemas, such as ECHO [14], MPEG-7 [5], IFLA-FRBR [10], P/META [13]. Moreover, a query on these metadata must be translated into complex SQL queries at relational level, resulting in many expensive joins to implement tree structure traversals. Thus, the resulting search performance is often unacceptable. However, even with flat metadata schemas, pure relational databases do not offer all functionalities needed for an effective retrieval, such as full text search.

Solution (b) uses full text search engines [22] to index metadata records. In this case the main emphasis is devoted to the textual information contained in metadata fields. Many text search engines offer the fielded indexing capability, where text contained in different fields is independently indexed. However, applications are limited to relatively simple and flat metadata schemas. In addition, it is not possible to search by specifying ranges of values.

Solution (c) is very trivial and inefficient. It is not practicable in applications that pretend to be more than toy systems. In this case no indexing is performed on the metadata and the custom search algorithms always scans the entire metadata set to retrieve searched information.

We successfully attempted a different approach: we have designed and implemented an enhanced native XML database/repository system with special features for DL applications. This is especially justified by the well known and accepted advantages of representing metadata as XML documents. Metadata represented with XML might have arbitrary complex structures, which allows to deal with complex metadata schemas, and might be easily exported and imported. Our XML database can store and retrieve any valid XML document. No metadata schema or XML schema definition is needed before inserting an XML document, except optional index definitions for performance boosting. Once an arbitrary XML document has been inserted in the database it can be immediately retrieved using XQuery. This allows DL applications to use arbitrary (XML encoded) metadata schemas and to deal with heterogeneous metadata, without any constraint on schema design and/or overhead due to metadata translation.

We decided not to use a commercial XML database system (e.g. Tamino [9]) because of our specific operational requirements:

1. Particular attention must be given to the performance of search and insert operations.
2. It is not necessary to enforce a database-like transactional mechanism, since update operations are quite rare compared to search operations. Editing of complex multimedia objects and their metadata, can be based on a sort of check-out/check-in mechanism.

Thus, our native XML database/respository system is simpler than a general purpose XML database system, but offers significant improvements in specific area: it supports standard XML query languages such as XPath [18] and XQuery [19], and offers advanced search and indexing functionality on arbitrary XML documents; it supports high performance search and retrieval on heavily structured XML documents, relying on specific index structures [15, 23], as well as full text search [22], automatic classification [20], and feature similarity search [17]. The system administrator can associate an index to a specific XML element. For instance, the tag `<abstract>` can be associated with a full text index and to an automatic topic classifier that automatically indexes it with topics chosen from a controlled vocabulary. On the other hand, the MPEG-7 `<VisualDescriptor>` tag can be associated with a similarity search index structure and with an automatic visual content classifier. The XQuery language has been extended with new operators that deal with approximate match and ranking, in order to deal with these new search functionality.

In our database every XML document is identified by an URN. Therefore, relationships and links among documents - even if they are stored in different repositories - can be easily and unambiguously represented.

3.2   Multi-media Server

Different DL applications may have different storage and access needs. For example, very small DLs might store documents on standard hard disks, while more mission critical applications might need to store documents on arrays of disks, possibly duplicating and distributing content on several sites. Digital libraries dealing with huge archives of video documents, might need to store them on digital tapes maintained in silos, and to have arrays of disks used as temporary storage for frequently used documents. In addition, we must consider that a DL may scale over time, when the number of documents grows over a certain limit or faster access is needed.

DL applications might also use different delivery strategies. For example, a small DL might serve documents using a normal web server, while heavily accessed DLs might need to use replication and load balancing strategies to guarantee high performance access to content. A video DL might use high performance video servers to stream videos in real time to users [21].

The MMS allows the programmers of the DL applications to be unaware of all these issues. The key idea is that the DL application should deal with documents in a uniform way, independently of the specific strategy used to manage them. Thus, the MMS identifies all documents with an URN and maintains a mapping table to associate URNs with actual storage locations. Applications use the URN to get or store documents from the MMS, which behaves as a gateway to the actual repository that stores the document. The system administrator can define rules that make use of MIME types, to specify how the MMS has to store a document of a specific type. For example, the rule may specify that an MPEG-2 video has to be be stored in a tape of a silos, while an image will be stored in an array of disks.

A special care is taken to deal with the actual access protocols offered to retrieve the documents. An application will refer a specific document always using its URN. However, the retrieval of the document should be done using an access protocol compatible with the storage and delivery strategy associated with the document. For instance, when the document is stored in a web server it will be retrieved with an HTTP request. On the other hand, suppose that a video document is served through a commercial video server such as the Helix Universal Server [4]; in this case the real time streaming of the video will be obtained using RTSP [6]. When an application requires to retrieve a document, the MMS will translate the given URN into a specific handle (for instance an RTSP URL) that the application will use to access the document.

3.3 Repository Metadata Integrator

The RMI manages the accesses to the document and metadata repositories and supports metadata mapping to guarantee metadata independence. The mapping of application requests into requests compatible to the metadata schema actually managed by the MCMS is accomplished by defining a set of schema mapping rules. The main purpose of this mapping is to translate application requests into XQuery queries compliant to the stored metadata. This mechanism allows the RMI to translate names of fields (such as Title, Author, etc.) known to the DL application, into requests to the MSR without the need of knowing the specific schema model adopted. When a new XML schema is introduced, the system administrator must specify the mappings for the new metadata.

Each mapping rule specifies how to translate the name of a metadata field, known to the application, into an XPath expression that specifies the XML path names that should be used to access that metadata field in the target metadata schema. A generic mapping rule has the following structure:

$metadataType[.Name]^* = <RE\_XPath>,<SE\_XPath>$ where

1. The *metadataType* field identifies the metadata model used by the application e.g. DublinCore, SCORM, MPEG-7 etc;
2. *Name* is the name of a metadata field requested by the application e.g., Title, Author, etc. If empty, it means that the rule applies to all metadata fields of the specified *metadataType*;
3. $<RE\_XPath>$ (Retrieved Element XPath) is the XPath corresponding to the XML element that will be retrieved with this field;
4. $<SE\_XPath>$ (Searched Element XPath) is the XPath, under $<RE\_XPath>$, of the element that contains the value of the metadata field used for searching.

As an example, let us consider a DL for e-Learning applications, where the Learning Objects in the repository have a complex metadata structure, based on SCORM [11]. Suppose that we want to search SCORM metadata trough Dublin Core. We can use the following mapping rules:

```
dc.title = /lom, general/title/langstring
dc.description = /lom, general/description/langstring
```

They specify that the Dublin Core metadata fields 'dc.title' and 'dc.description' can be searched in SCORM respectively by means of the XPath string `lom/general/title/langstring`, and `lom/genaral/description/langstring`. The whole `<lom>` element will be retrieved when `<langstring>` contains the desired value. Note that, the `<title>` and `<description>` SCORM XML elements do not contain the title text of the document, but the element `<langstring>`, which in turn contains the real text.

Let us now explain how the mapping directives are used by RMI to generate the XQuery query. The RMI allows applications to search on metadata by using the *findExactMatch* method:

> *findExactMatch*(**string** MetadaType, **vector of string** fields, **vector of string** values, **string** returnFields),

This method searches for a set of metadata records of the specified *MetadaType*. The *fields* parameter is a vector of (application known) names of metadata fields, of the *MetadaType*, to search for. The *values* parameter specifies the values that the fields must match (the different fields are searched by using the boolean connective **AND**). Finally, *returnFields* specifies the fields of the retrieved records (i.e. RE_XPath) that the application wants to know. The method translates the request into an XQuery query as follows:

1. for each triple $<MetadaType, value_i, field_i>$, specified in the *findExactMatch*, RMI searches the mapping rules matching $MetadaType.field_i$ to fetch the corresponding XPath strings RE_XPath_i and SE_XPath_i;
2. for each pair $<MetadaType, returnField_i>$, specified in the *findExactMatch*, RMI searches the mapping rules matching $MetadaType.returnField_j$ to fetch the corresponding XPath strings $RE\_XPath_{ret_j}$ and $SE\_XPath_{ret_j}$.
3. check that all the strings RE_XPath_i and $RE\_XPath_{ret_j}$ are the same string and call that string RE_XPath, otherwise fail and stop;
4. finally, combine the XPath strings RE_XPath, SE_XPath_i, and $SE\_XPath_{ret_j}$ to generate the XQuery query, as follows:

   for \$a **in** RE_XPath
   where $\$a/SE\_XPath_1 = value_1$ **and** ... **and** $\$a/SE\_XPath_n = value_n$
   return $\$a/SE\_XPath_{ret_1}$ ... $\$a/SE\_XPath_{ret_m}$

Example: Suppose that an application wants to use Dublin Core to search SCORM metadata having a specific title, and wants to have back the corresponding descriptions. In this case we have $MetadataType = dc$, $field_1 = title$, $returnField_1 = description$. Applying the previous mapping rules we obtain:

for a **in** /lom
where $a/general/title/langstring = value_1$
return $a/general/description/langstring

4   Field Trials

In order to verify and demonstrate the flexibility and efficiency of MILOS in managing different heterogeneous DL applications, we took four data sets used by four different existing DLs and we built the corresponding DL applications on top of MILOS. The data sets that we considered consist of documents and metadata of very different nature: the Reuters data set [7], the ACM Sigmod Record dataset [8], the DBLP data set [1], and the ECHO data set [14].

The DL applications that we built use the same MILOS installation and all data sets were stored together. The functionality of MILOS allows individual applications to selectively access data and metadata of their interest or to perform cross-library search. Each DL application consists of a specific search and browsing interface (built according to the data managed) and a bulk import tool. The search and browse interfaces were built as web applications using Java Server Pages (JSP). The bulk import tool was a simple Java application. On average, the effort required to build each application from scratch was one week of work of a single skilled person. This, we believe, is really a little effort compared to the cost that would have been required to build from scratch a DL, without general purpose tools, or the cost that would have been required to translate and adapt the data and metadata to cope with the requirements and restrictions of an existing DL system.

We built the browse and retrieval interface from scratch. However, we are currently working to develop a tool supporting the automatic generation of the browsing and retrieval interface according to data and metadata fields. This will contribute to a further reduction of the cost of building DL applications.

All applications resulted to be very efficient. We installed the system, the applications, and the data on a single computer equipped with a Pentium 1.8 GHz and 1 Gb of RAM, running Windows 2000 server. We have used JAX-RPC as SOAP application server to run MILOS. Applications have been tested by 30 users operating at the same time from remote workstations, and executing a predefined search intensive job. On average the response time of the system was below 1 second. Notice also that for more intensive uses of the system, the underlying Web Service technologies offer plenty of solutions to guarantee scalability exploiting techniques of replication, load balancing, resource/connection pooling etc.

The **Reuters data set** [7] contains text news agencies and the corresponding metadata composed of Reuters specific metadata including titles, authors, topic categories, and extended Dublin Core metadata. The data set contains 810,000 news agencies (2.6 Gb) with text and metadata both encoded in XML. We associated the full text index and the automatic topic classifier to the elements containing the body, the title, and the headline of the news. Other value indexes were associated with elements corresponding to frequently searched metadata, such as location, date, country. The search interface allows the user to perform integrated text, category, and exact match search.

Both the **ACM Sigmod Record** [8] and the **DBLP** data-sets [1] consist of metadata corresponding to the description of scientific publications in the computer science domain. The ACM Sigmod record is composed of 46 XML files (1Mb), while the DBLP data-set is composed of a sinlge large (187Mb) XML file. Their structure is completely different even if they contain information describing similar objects. For these two datasets we built one single DL application that allows one to access both. The MILOS mapping is used to translate application requests in the two schemas. We associated a full text index to the elements containing the titles of the articles, and we associated other value indexes to other frequently searched elements, such as the authors, the dates, the years, etc. The search and browse interface allows users to search for articles by various combinations full text and exact/partial match of elements. In addition it allows user to browse results by navigating trough links (and implicitly submitting new queries to MILOS) related to the author, journal, conference, etc.

The **ECHO data set** [14] includes historical audio/visual documents and the corresponding metadata. ECHO is a significant example of the capability of MILOS to support the management of arbitrary metadata schemas. The metadata model adopted in ECHO, based on IFLA/FRBR [10] model, is rather complex and strongly structured. It is used for representing the audio-visual content of the archive and includes among others, the description of videos in English and in the original language, specific metadata fields such as Title, Producer, year, etc., the boundaries of scenes detected (associated with a textual descriptions), the audio segmentation (distinguishing among noise, music, speech, etc.), the Speech Transcripts, and visual features for supporting similarity search on key-frames. The collection is composed of about 8,000 documents for 50 hours of video described by 43,000 XML files (36 Mb). Each scene detected is associated with a JPEG encoded key frame for a total of 21GB of MPEG-1 and JPEG files. Full text indexes where associated to textual descriptive fields, similarity search index where associated with elements containing MPEG-7 image (key frames) features, and other value indexes where associated with frequently searched elements. The search and retrieval interface (Figure 2) allows users to find videos by combining full text, image similarity, and exact/partial match search. Users can browse among scenes, and corresponding metadata. The original ECHO DL application [3], was built using a relational database, and translating all metadata in a relational schema. Even simple searches required several (up to 10 or more) seconds to be processed. With MILOS we had a dramatic improvement of performance, being able to serve requests in less than one second even with several users accessing the system.

5 Conclusion

This paper described the architecture of the MILOS Content Management System and the solutions adopted to obtain a system that is flexible in the manage-

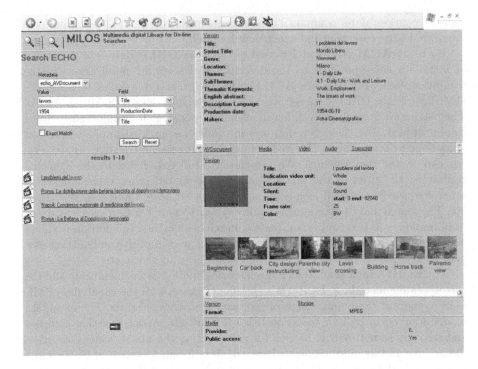

Fig. 2. The ECHO retrieval interface implemented in MILOS.

ment of documents with different types of content and descriptions, and that is efficient and scalable in the storage and content based retrieval of these documents. In particular, we described the approach adopted to support the management of different metadata descriptions of multimedia documents in the same repository. This goes towards the solution of the challenging problems of interoperability among different metadata descriptions. The proposed solution, based on the use of a mapping mechanism among the metadata fields of the different models, has been practically experimented by using the MILOS system to archive documents belonging to four different and heterogenous collections which contain news agencies, scientific papers, and audiovideo documentaries. The archiving of these documents was straightforward and it only required the creation of the mapping file and the development of the user interfaces to archive and to search the documents.

An evolution of this activity is foreseen in several directions: on one side we are working to improve the retrieval capabilities of the Metadata Storage and Retrieval component; on the other side, we are working with partners of the ECD [12] project on the automatization of the mapping between different metadata schemas, by using thesaurus and cross-language vocabularies [16].

References

1. DBLP computer science bibliography.
   http://www.informatik.uni-trier.de/~ley/db/.
2. Dublin Core Metadata Initiative. http://dublincore.org/.
3. Echo: European CHronicles On-line. http://pc-erato2.iei.pi.cnr.it/echo/.
4. Helix Universal Server.
   http://www.realnetworks.com/products/server/index.html.
5. Motion picture experts group. http://mpeg.cselt.it.
6. Real Time Streaming Protocol. http://www.rtsp.org/.
7. Reuters corpus. http://about.reuters.com/researchandstandards/corpus/.
8. Sigmod record, xml edition. http://www.acm.org/sigs/sigmod/record/xml/.
9. Tamino XML Server. http://www.softwareag.com/tamino/.
10. IFLA study on the functional requirements for bibliographic records, 1998.
    http://www.ifla.org/VII/s13/frbr/frbr.pdf.
11. Shareable content object reference model initiative (scorm), the xml cover pages,
    October 2001. http://xml.coverpages.org/scorm.html.
12. ECD - Enhanced Content Delivery, 2002. http://ecd.isti.cnr.it/.
13. P_META, the EBU metadata exchange scheme, 2003. http://www.ebu.ch/en/
    technical/publications/Tech_3000_series/tech3295/.
14. G. Amato, D. Castelli, and S. Pisani. A metadata model for historical documentary
    films. In J. L. Borbinha and T. Baker, editors, *Proc. of the 4th European Conference
    ECDL*, pages 328–331. Springer, 2000.
15. G. Amato, F. Debole, F. Rabitti, and P. Zezula. YAPI: Yet another path index
    for XML searching. In *ECDL 2003, 7th ECDL Conference, Trondheim, Norway,
    August 17-22, 2003*, 2003.
16. D. Beneventano and al. Semantic integration and query optimization of heteroge-
    neous data sources. In *OOIS Workshops*, pages 154–165, 2002.
17. C. Böhm, S. Berchtold, and D. Keim. Searching in high-dimensional spaces: Index
    structures for improving the performance of multimedia databases. *ACM Comput-
    ing Surveys*, 33(3):322–373, September 2001.
18. W. W. W. Consortium. XML path language (XPath), version 1.0, W3C. Recom-
    mendation, November 1999.
19. W. W. W. Consortium. XQuery 1.0: An XML query language. W3C Working
    Draft, November 2002. http://www.w3.org/TR/xquery.
20. N. Cristianini and J. Shawe-Taylor. *An Introduction to Support Vector Machines*.
    Cambridge University Press, 2000.
21. D. J. Gemmell, H. M. Vin, D. D. Kandlur, P. V. Rangan, and L. A. Rowe. Multi-
    media storage servers: A tutorial. *IEEE Computer*, 28(5):40–49, May 1995.
22. G. Salton and M. J. McGill. *Introduction to Modern Information Retrieval*.
    McGraw-Hill Book Company, 1983.
23. P. Zezula, G. Amato, F. Debole, and F. Rabitti. Tree signatures for xml querying
    and navigation. In *Database and XML Technologies, XSym 2003*, volume 2824 of
    LNCS, pages 149–163. Springer, 2003.

Designing an Integrated Digital Library Framework to Support Multiple Heterogeneous Collections

George Pyrounakis, Kostas Saidis, Mara Nikolaidou, and Irene Lourdi

Libraries Computer Centre, University of Athens
University Campus, 15784 Athens, Greece
forky@libadm.uoa.gr, {saiko,mara}@di.uoa.gr, elourdi@lib.uoa.gr

Abstract. Athens University recently initiated a digital collection development project to provide enhanced educational capabilities. Collections vary in terms of the material included and the requirements imposed by potential users. In order to simplify collection management and promote collection interoperability, a common Digital Library platform should be employed to support all collections. In order to deal with the extended requirements imposed, Athens University has decided to support an integrated Digital Library framework for multiple heterogeneous digital collections development. The most important requirements imposed by the University's collections are discussed in this paper, along with the characteristics of the Folklore Collection, one of the most complex and diverse ones. In order to evaluate available Digital Library systems, the Folklore Collection has been chosen as a guide for the development of two prototype implementations using Fedora and DSpace. Conclusions drawn from their comparison and the proposed integrated Digital Library architecture based on Fedora are also presented.

1 Introduction

Athens University initiated a digital collection development project to gather research material produced by its members in order to provide enhanced educational capabilities. The material belongs to collections developed by cataloguers and researchers working in University libraries, administered by the Libraries Computer Centre (LCC). Each collection has specific scientific or cultural significance, includes different types of material (e.g. text and manuscripts, music, photographs, videos), consists of either born-digital or digitized material and satisfies diverse user requirements in terms of object structure, metadata and presentation. For instance, most cultural collections are archival in nature and mainly contain digitized material, while most scientific collections are constantly updated and contain both digitized and born-digital material.

In order to simplify collection management and promote collection interoperability, it was decided to employ a common Digital Library (DL) platform to support all aforementioned collections. Among these collections, the Folklore Collection has been selected as a guide for the design of the DL system, representing one of the most complex collections of Athens University. Moreover its main characteristics and requirements are rather common in the majority of the other collections. Folklore Collection is described in detail in Section 2.

R. Heery and L. Lyon (Eds.): ECDL 2004, LNCS 3232, pp. 26–37, 2004.
© Springer-Verlag Berlin Heidelberg 2004

Libraries Computer Centre policy emphasizes in extending a fully customizable DL system, than using "out of the box" software. The basic prerequisites of this software are to be open-source and provide interoperable features, adequate preservation capabilities and support for both born-digital and digitized content. The detailed requirements, as imposed by LCC, are presented in Section 3. Based on these criteria, two systems were selected, namely *Fedora* [7] and *DSpace* [4], and their final evaluation, as presented in Section 4, has been based on a prototype version of the Folklore Collection developed on both systems. The results of this attempt lead to the integrated DL architecture designed to support Folklore Collection, as described in Section 5. Finally, a summary is provided in Section 6.

2 Folklore Collection Characteristics

The Folklore Collection is dedicated to local tradition and customs of several regions in Greece representing the way of living and thinking in these regions through the last two centuries. The Folklore Collection consists of hand-written travelling notebooks generated by the students of the Greek Literature Department. The same notebooks are further composed by notes and maps created by the author and lyrics or handcrafts related with a specific region. The lyrics and handcrafts included in a notebook must be treated both as parts of it and as independent objects belonging in a different sub-collection. Specifically the Folklore Collection is divided into:

a) Notebook sub-collection. Each notebook is a manuscript written by a student after local research and refers to a specific area or village. The notebook is separated into predefined chapters and sections and includes a table of contents. Most of the notebooks are accompanied by drawn maps, photographs of habitants and regions, artifacts (e.g. laces or doles) and sound recordings with songs and folk music.
b) Photographs sub-collection, consisted of the photographs that are inside the notebooks as accompanying material
c) Artifact sub-collection, exposed in the library and
d) Sound recordings sub-collection, consisting of local music, lyrics and tale recordings related to the notebooks.

In order to support the Folklore Collection, the following requirements should be satisfied:

Sub-collection Support
Due to the variety of material and the complex relations between Folklore Collection resources, the collection must be organized into sub-collections by unifying kindred resources according to specific criteria like the ones that Johnston and Robinson [10] have indicated: i) the topic coverage, ii) the specific usage or purpose that each resource has in the context of the collection, iii) the provenance, iv) the type of material, v) the specific spatial or temporal coverage and vi) the same category of object. The heterogeneity and the big amount of the resources warrant the need for separating the material into collections and sub-collections, as it is impossible to represent complex structures and to accredit rich semantics to any level by another way. By defining sub-collections the attributes inherited from the collection to sub-collections are identified and the overall collection can be easily navigated by users using various access points (date, subject, geographic area).

Collection-Level Description and Definition
High-level collection description is important in order to help the navigation, discovery and selection of cultural content [3]. The collection-level description simplifies the retrieval of information because the user can decide whether the collection is of his interest without getting into details about the objects and also contributes to better administration of large collections. Thus, it is required to offer a detailed collection and sub-collection level description with the appropriate metadata elements, after specifying the structure of the collection. Specifically, the Folklore Collection is described by the Dublin Core Collection Description Application Profile [6], while the schema is extended by local elements related to custom properties.

Representation of Composite Objects
Every notebook contains hand-written text separated into chapters and sections along with a table of contents. The notebook structure is based on a predefined list of headings that correspond to specific aspects of every day life, like dressing code, eating and religious customs. Furthermore each notebook is accompanied by artifacts, photographs and maps. In its written form, it is difficult to search for information inside the notebook. Notebooks should be represented as composite objects consisting of disparate parts (chapters and sections), which should be characterized individually by descriptive metadata.

Description of Existing Relations
It is necessary to represent all kinds of relations that exist inside and outside the collection throughout structural levels, in order to provide the users with all the information that is hidden in the collection. For example, the relation between the photograph referenced at a notebook page and the actual photograph belonging in the photographs sub-collection - probably in another format - should be identified (for example: "has format" or "is converted to" or "is the same with").

Appropriate Metadata Support
Due to the variety of Folklore Collection material, various metadata schemes, as Dublin Core (DC) [5] and Learning Object Metadata (LOM) [8], and local fields should be supported. This is a strong necessity in order to keep all the valuable information for preservation, authenticity and retrieval of information. It is important for the users to have many access points to the content of the Folklore Collection and to be able to search by date, subject, geographic domains and the type of objects. DC is adopted as the basic metadata scheme, while it is further extended to cover other aspects as i) the technique of digitization and the technical requirements ii) meta-metadata information because of the heterogeneous material and iii) the educational character and the purpose of every resource.

Selecting Folklore Collection as a Guide
The Folklore Collection has been selected as a guide for the development of the DL platform due to its complex and diverse nature, since it consists of interrelated manuscripts, photographs, maps, artifacts and audio. This material is not born-digital, so its digitization is required. This fact stands for the majority of Athens University Collections. Moreover, this digitized content imposes certain limitations regarding user's interactions (i.e. no free text search on the actual content is available), so there should

be provided alternate facilities for the user in order to enrich his/her capabilities. These enhancements will be targeted on the accurate representation of the physical relations and associations of the digitized content, along with its structure (chapters, sections, table of contents). Such entities and relations, if characterized with appropriate metadata, will eventually allow the user to acquire an enhanced view of the whole collection. Once again, such exploration of possibilities is better performed on the Folklore Collection, due to its complexity.

3 Criteria for Selecting a Digital Library System

This section discusses the DL System requirements imposed by LCC, covering storage / collection issues and design / implementation issues of the DL System.

Storage Capabilities / Collection Issues

- *BasicPreservationcapabilities* : The DL System should handle effectively preservation issues, by assigning persistent unique identifiers to digital objects and providing support for various file formats and versions for the storage of their content. It is also necessary to support the usage of technical metadata in order to describe the format of the files or the digitization process.
- *Multilingualsupport* : The system should support at least the Greek and English languages, with regard to both content and metadata storage and presentation.
- *EffectiveSupportforDigitizedContent* : As illustrated by the description of Folklore Collection, the system should provide the ability to handle digitized content effectively. Moreover, the majority of the Libraries collections considered for digitization in Athens University are sharing the similar dependence on digitized content support with the Folklore Collection (Byzantine music manuscripts, ancient papyrus, etc).
- *Supportformultiple, heterogeneouscollections* : The point described above depicts the requirement for the efficient handling of multiple, heterogeneous collections by a common centralized DL System.

Design / Implementation Issues

- *Interoperability support* : Interoperability between Athens University DL and other Academic DLs in Greece or worldwide is an important issue. The standard that should be supported to achieve interoperability of metadata is Open Archives Initiative Protocol for Metadata Harvesting (OAI-PMH)[11]. Furthermore, the system must support open standard file types, for the interoperability of the digital content.
- *Flexibility and Expandability* : The system should be flexible and expandable, allowing the addition of extra functionality in a straightforward manner. This issue suggests that the selected DL System should impose minimum restrictions regarding its usage patterns and scenarios.
- *Separationofcontentstorageandrepresentation/interfaces*   : The system should separate the representation logic from its core storage functionality in the highest possible degree. DL service must be included into an integrated web environment, the LCC portal, so it is of great importance to be supplied with the ability

to "program" the interface in arbitrary ways while the DL system handles the storage, preservation and content retrieval issues independently.

- *Implemented in Java* : The development of LCC portal has already been started using Java to integrate backend databases, the OPAC and collaboration software used by Library staff for every day activities. Usage of Java as the basic development language is an important issue in order to retain the integrated computing environment of the LCC.

The above requirements highlight the main DL System selection criteria. No existing DL system could be used "out of the box" to implement Folklore Collection, or other collections of the same diverse and complex nature. In order to develop an effective, usable and integrated DL, the University is focusing on settling a long run investment on the selected DL System. Under this perspective, another important requirement is added, which refers to the ability to freely extend and customize the selected system. In other terms, the selected DL System should be distributed under an Open Source License [14].

4 Digital Library System Comparison

A list of open-source institutional repository software supporting OAI-PMH is proposed in [13]. Based on the criteria presented in the previous section, two of them were chosen for further evaluation: Fedora and DSpace. From the seven systems included in this list, three of them are implemented using programming languages other than Java, so they were not considered for the final evaluation. From the remaining systems, two have no defined preservation strategy, which is a basic prerequisite for Athens University DL System. So we concluded to the further evaluation of Fedora and DSpace that are consistent to all basic requirements and already have a large number of installations worldwide. Fedora and DSpace are based on open and modular architectures. The first one is using Flexible and Extensible Digital Object and Repository Architecture (FEDORA) [15], while the second is based on a three-layered architecture and a data model influenced by the Open Archival Information Systems (OAIS) reference model [2]. The main modules of each system provide public APIs to access and manage metadata and digital content. Both of these systems support preservation issues, by providing many digital formats of the same content, using technical metadata and retaining a global unique identifier to access each digital object. They support digitized objects, more than other platforms that are oriented on born-digital material, mainly electronic documents. The systems are not restricted to specific file formats or digital content type.

In order to evaluate both systems, a prototype version of the Folklore Collection has been developed in each one. The goal was to explore each system capabilities to support the specific collection, using their built-in functionality. A brief description of each system along with the related comments and remarks of this attempt are reported in the following sections.

4.1 Fedora

Fedora is a java based open-source digital repository system [17] comprised of a flexible and extensible architecture. The basic entity of Fedora repository is digital object. A digital object is comprised of a persistent identifier (PID), system metadata, one or more datastreams and disseminators that associate datastreams to behaviors. Datastreams are used to represent metadata or digital content. Digital objects are stored internally as XML files based on an extension of Metadata Encoding and Transmission Standard (METS) schema [12]. There are three distinct types of digital objects: data objects, behavior definition objects and behavior mechanism objects. The first one represent entities that contain the content and metadata, while other two define and implement the methods that present or transform the content of digital objects. It provides two public APIs for the management services (API-M, API-M-Lite) and two for access services (API-A, API-A-Lite).

Collections are not natively supported by Fedora. In order to describe collections, it is practical to use a data object to represent each collection containing the appropriate collection description and rights metadata and the templates for the creation of data objects. Sub-collections can be defined in the same way and the relation between the parent and child collection can be described by specific structural metadata in both data objects. Sub-collection objects can inherit description and rights metadata from the parent collection. Additionally, a collection management module should be implemented that will communicate with the management API and control the aforementioned functionality.

A composite object, such as Folklore notebook, can be represented as a number of data objects. Some of the data objects represent logical entities of the physical object, as chapters or the whole notebook view. Others represent the physical entities, for example the pages of the notebook. The relations between those data objects comprise the structure of the composite object.

Relations are necessary to represent the structure of composite objects or to relate independent data objects that belong to the same or different collections. To support relations in Fedora, a special datastream can be used on each data object that will contain the structural metadata of it. A behavior object can be associated to the data object and describe the methods that will represent the relations in presentation level. These methods must be implemented in a general manner in order to support each relations special requirement. An extension module must also been developed over Fedora management API in order to manage the relations between data objects.

Every metadata model can be described and accessed in one or more datastreams of the digital object. The metadata model can be a local metadata set, a standard metadata set or an extension of Dublin Core metadata element set. The disadvantage is that Fedora supports indexing and searching services, only for Dublin Core metadata element set, so an external application should be used to index other metadata fields.

4.2 DSpace

DSpace is an open source digital repository system [16], implemented in Java and primarily focused on institutional and research material (reports, research papers and publications). It provides a solution for the problem of collecting, storing, preserving, indexing and distributing such material in digital form.

DSpace is based on a straightforward three-tier architecture, consisting of a storage layer, responsible for the storage of items (digital objects) and their metadata (qualified Dublin Core metadata scheme). Digital content is stored in the file system and associated to items in terms of bitstreams and bundles, allowing an item to contain various files. Business logic layer consists of a numerous components handling individual aspects of the DSpace system, such as browsing, searching, user/group management and authorization, workflow management, content management and administration. Finally, the application layer provides the end user interaction and interface functionality, in terms of web user interface, batch item importing facilities, OAI metadata providers and the like. Regarding preservation issues, DSpace provides support for CNRI handles, assuring the assignment of global persistent identifiers for its items. Moreover, by exploiting a simple and effective file format supporting scheme it provides "bit preservation" of the digital content, while "functional preservation" will be provided only for the "supported" file formats. DSpace information model is based on Communities, consisting of users and groups, containing Collections, which in turn contain items (the digital objects). Finally, an adequate for most purposes workflow model is provided along with a simple administration toolkit.

DSpace can be used "out of the box" for the generation of a digital repository in the case that content consists of independent digital documents. It provides simple, usable and effective resolutions of common problems, such as user and workflow management, persistence and indexing/searching. However, its aims do not include digitized content, interrelation schemes and custom metadata in a fine-grained manner (per collection or sub-collection, for instance). Its customization capabilities also refer to this context and mainly are related to:

- user interface arrangements
- installation wide modification of the qualified DC metadata element set
- custom workflow steps setup

Although, DSpace provides several built-in facilities that simplify and speed-up the development of a digital repository, these features are highly coupled with each other and, mainly, coupled to the underlying database schema. For example, DSpace natively supports collections and the database schema reflects it by providing a distinct Collection table, holding collection related information. Enriching this information, by adding more table fields is possible, easy to be accomplished and straightforward. The same stands for analogous issues, such as metadata support, sub-collections or relations since all could be potentially supported by performing the necessary database schema modifications. Nevertheless, two important issues arise by performing such modifications:

- Changes should be also made to the system "core" components. In order to perform significant modifications to its functionality, changes should be applied to both the database schema and relevant code.
- These changes, once made, break compatibility with future releases and the rest of DSpace installations, limiting the ability to benefit from future improvements, additions and extensions.

In simple cases, such as sub-collection support, the modifications or extensions required can be identified, designed based on current DSpace status and implemented in an adequately satisfying manner. In the case of more complex features, such as advanced collection management (i.e. support of heterogeneous collections with disparate metadata sets) the required modifications may become extremely complicated. The point is whether the current architecture of DSpace will stand in the way for the development of such features, not included in its initial design and development. Its database orientation indicates that this will be the case, practically deprecating its current form and design and requiring a re-implementation from the beginning.

4.3 DL System Selection

Based on the aforementioned remarks, LCC has selected to use Fedora for the development of Athens University Digital Library. Its XML-based digital object model provides the ability to support composite objects and preserve heterogeneous metadata of different categories (descriptive, technical, administrative or structural metadata). Furthermore, by using behaviors on each digital object it is feasible to dynamically implement collection-specific relations, in a unified and system-oriented fashion. It is also effective to support methods to create, edit or present digital objects, based on collection-specific templates. Collections can be represented as common digital objects, providing an elegant unified representation and management scheme at the programming level.

Finally, Fedora's extensible architecture provides the ability to develop additional external modules, which do not intervene with its core but communicate with it through its public APIs. This characteristic enables the development of a DL system on top of Fedora, which can operate in an independent manner regarding its business logic, custom metadata elements and semantics, while preserving the ability to benefit from new versions of the "Fedora core".

5 Extending Fedora to Support Folklore Collection

Based on the experiences gained from the prototype collection implementations, a set of modeling customizations and system extensions were considered, in order to support Folklore Collection advanced features. The proposed architecture (presented in Figure 1) may be used to host other collections with similar features as well. The Object management and Collection management modules are used to reflect the advanced object and collection management requirements imposed by the Folklore Collection. An external module is used to extend the indexing and searching capabilities of the Fedora core system over additional metadata sets. These three modules utilize the Fedora APIs, so there is no need to intervene with the internal Fedora Repository System. They act as an intermediate level between the applications that will be developed (providing administrator, cataloguers and user presentation services) and the underlying Fedora system.

The main modeling conventions adopted for Folklore Collection special features are discussed below. The main modules extending Fedora's functionality are also described.

Collection and Sub-collection Definition and Description
Each collection object is represented as a common Fedora digital object, containing a datastream holding collection description and rights metadata and a datastream holding the templates of the common data objects that will be created in the context of this collection. All datastreams are implemented as inline XML content.

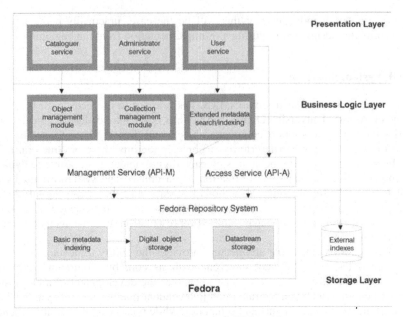

Fig. 1. The proposed integrated DL architecture

The main reason for defining templates per collection is to provide guidelines for the creation and management of all collection data objects in a unified manner. A different template is used for each distinct type of data object (i.e. notebook, photograph, map). This template contains the definition of metadata fields for the data object and their attributes (repeatable, mandatory, indexed, etc), the description of files that represent digital content, the proper relations and the behaviors associated to disseminate content and metadata.

An example of a digital object template from the Folklore Photographs subcollection is presented in Figure 2. The template for the "photograph" data object type contains the following tags:

- *<field>*: defines the fields of the metadata set used by the data object type. When a data object is created, all these metadata fields are inserted in a datastream.
- *<file>*: defines the necessary file formats for the data object. Each file is associated with a datastream.
- *<relation>*: defines the permitted relations in which the data object is able to participate. In the data object, the relations will be stored in a separate datastream.
- *<disseminator>*: defines the disseminators supported by this object type. A disseminator associates a behavior definition object (bdef) and a behavior mechanism object (bmech) with a specific datastream of the data object.

An external module manages collections using Fedora's management API (API-M). The main role of this module is to create collections and sub-collections, edit collection description metadata and import templates for the creation of data objects. When creating a sub-collection the description and rights metadata are copied from the parent to the child collection. The persistent id of the parent collection is denoted on the content model type identifier (contentModelID) in data object's system metadata.

```
<dobj type="photo">                        <file>
  <field>                                    <name>THUMB</name>
    <name>dc:title</name>                    <type>image/jpeg</type>
    <indexed>true</indexed>                  <label lang="eng">Photo thumbnail
    <mandatory>true</mandatory>              </label>
    <repeatable>false</repeatable>         </file>
    <viewable>true</viewable>             <relation>
    <label lang="eng">Photo itle</label>    <name>page</name>
  </field>                                   <label lang="eng">Notebook page
  <field>                                    </label>
    <name>dc:subject</name>                  <target_type>uoadl:10.page
    <indexed>true</indexed>                  </target_type>
    <mandatory>false</mandatory>           </relation>
    <repeatable>true</repeatable>         <disseminator>
    <viewable>true</viewable>               <name>goToPage</name>
    <label lang="eng">Subject</label>       <label lang="eng">View notebook page
  </field>                                   </label>
  <file>                                     <datastream>STRUCT</datastream>
    <name>PHOTOHQ</name>                     <bdef>uoadl:20</bdef>
    <type>image/tiff</type>                  <bmech>uoadl:21</bmech>
    <label lang="eng">High quality photo   </disseminator>
    </label>                              </dobj>
  </file>
</file>
```

Fig. 2. Data object template from Folklore Photographs sub-collection

Composite Objects

The folklore notebook is represented as a set of data objects that belong to three different types: main, chapter and page. Every type corresponds to a data object template, which is defined on the appropriate collection. Type is defined in the *content-ModelID* field of the digital object in the form *collection_pid.object_type (.e. uoadl:10.chapter)* and it is pointing to the specific data object template. Main and chapter objects contain descriptive metadata specific to the notebook and the chapter respectively, together with structural metadata. Page objects contain the digital content (the page image in different formats) without descriptive metadata, together with structural metadata. Descriptive metadata, structural metadata and digital content are implemented in Fedora as separate datastreams of a data object.

The objects management module creates data objects of specific types based on the templates defined on the collection. The basic methods provided are: retrieve template guidelines, edit metadata, add files, create disseminators and relate data objects using the appropriate relations. All these actions are restricted from the guidelines given by the data object template.

Digital Object Relations

Relations are necessary to represent the structure of composite objects or to relate independent data objects belonging to the same or different collections. To implement relations, a special datastream is used on every data object. This datastream contains structure metadata, of the form:

```
<relation type= 'relation_type'>pid</relation>
```

The value *relation_type'* denotes the type of the relation between the current data object and the one with the specified *pid*. The permitted relations for a data object are specified at collection level. The meaning of every relation is defined by the data object's disseminators. The relation types for the notebooks collection digital objects are: *previous'* and *'next'* to navigate between pages, *'chapter'* and *'main'* to define current data object's chapter and main object, and *'photo'* to retrieve the photograph attached to the current page object. To extend navigation functionality in a notebook, a table of contents is used in each main digital object. This table is generated from the structural metadata of every data object connected to the specified notebook, by the 'main' relation. Table of contents is represented in main digital objects as an XML content datastream.

Although standard relation metadata can be used, such as Dublin Core relation element refinements (i.e. isParentOf, isReference, etc), a local metadata set was used, since it is more helpful to manage the structural metadata in a separate datastream, and more flexible to define specific relations depending on the collection needs, than using standard relation types. For example, the 'next' and 'previous' types have a special meaning in the notebook collection, helping the user to navigate between pages. In order to support interoperability with other digital repositories, we use a mapping of these metadata to DC element refinements. In order to facilitate the defined relations in the presentation level, specific web services are implemented and associated with behavior objects. Thus, end-user service communicates directly with Fedora Access API, in order to retrieve and use the appropriate behavior methods.

Extended Metadata Support

Every metadata model can be described in one or more datastreams of the digital object. Fedora supports indexing and searching methods, only for Dublin Core metadata element set ('DC' datastream) and digital object's system metadata. An external indexing application supports indexing and searching of other metadata sets using Fedora's management API. Separate indexes must be created for every collection. Two open-source indexing applications that may be suitable for this purpose are Jakarta Lucene [9] and Apache Xindice [1].

Summary

Athens University must support an integrated Digital Library framework for multiple heterogeneous digital collection development. The most important requirements imposed by the University's collections were discussed in this paper, along with the description of the Folklore Collection. In order to evaluate available Digital Library systems, the Folklore Collection was chosen as a guide. A prototype implementation of Folklore digital Collection was developed using Fedora and DSpace. Based on the comparison results, it was decided to develop the integrated Digital Library platform on Fedora, accompanied with a proposed extension that better fits Athens University's special needs. While DSpace provides an enhanced "out of the box" solution to develop institutional collections that include digital material, Fedora's architecture is preferred due to its extensibility.

References

1. Apache Xindice, [http://xml.apache.org/xindice/]
2. Consultative Committee for Space Data Systems (CCSDS), Reference Model for an Open Archival Information System (OAIS). Blue Book, Issue 1, January 2002.
3. Dempsey, L., Scientific, Industrial, and Cultural Heritage: a shared approach. Ariadne Issue 22, 1999, [http://www.ariadne.ac.uk/issue22/]

4. DSpace Federation, [http://www.dspace.org/]
5. Dublin Core Metadata Initiative: Dublin core Metadata Element Set, Version 1.1: Reference Description, [http://www.dublincore.org/documents/dces]
6. Dublin Core Collection Description Application Profile, [http://www.ukoln.ac.uk/metadata/dcmi/collection-application-profile/2003-08-25/]
7. Fedora Project, [http://www.fedora.info/]
8. IEEE (2002), IEEE P1484.12.1/D6.4 Draft Standard for Learning Object Metadata, [http://ltsc.ieee.org/doc/wg12/LOM_WD6_4.pdf]
9. Jakarta Lucene, [http://jakarta.apache.org/lucene]
10. Johnston, P. and Robinson, B., Collections and Collection Description. Collection Description Focus, 2002, [http://www.ukoln.ac.uk/cd-focus/briefings/bp1/bp1.pdf]
11. Lagoze, C. and Van de Sompel, H., The Open Archives Initiative: Building a low-barrier interoperability framework. JCDL '01, June 2001
12. Metadata Encoding and Transmission Standard, [http://www.loc.gov/standards/mets/]
13. Open Society Institute, A Guide to Institutional Repository Software. 2nd Edition, January 2004.
14. Open Source Initiative, [http://www.opensource.org/]
15. Payette S. and Lagoze C., Flexible and Extensible Digital Object and Repository Architecture (FEDORA). ECDL '98, LNCS 1513, pp. 41-59, 1998.
16. Smith, M. et al., DSpace: An Open Source Dynamic Digital Repository. D-Lib Magazine, 9(1), January 2003.
17. Staples, T., Wayland, R. and Payette S., The Fedora Project: An Open-source Digital Object Repository Management System. D-Lib Magazine, 9(4), April 2003.

DSpace: A Year in the Life
of an Open Source Digital Repository System

MacKenzie Smith[1], Richard Rodgers[1], Julie Walker[1], and Robert Tansley[2]

[1] MIT Libraries, 77 Massachusetts Ave, Cambridge, MA 02139
{kenzie,rrodgers,jhwalker}@mit.edu
[2] Hewlett-Packard Laboratories, One Cambridge Center, Cambridge, MA 02142
robert.tansley@hp.com

Abstract. The DSpace™ digital repository system was released as open source software in November of 2002. In the year since then it has been adopted by a large number of research universities and other organizations world-wide that need a digital repository solution for a number of content types: research articles, gray literature, e-theses, cultural materials, scientific datasets, institutional records, educational materials, and more. The DSpace platform and its various applications are becoming better understood with experience and time. As one result of a recent meeting of the DSpace user community, we are now venturing into the territory of broad, community-based open source development and management, and gaining insights from the experience of the Apache Foundation, Global Grid Forum, and other successful open source projects about how to build open source software for the digital library domain.

Introduction

DSpace™ is a free, open source software platform for building repositories of digital assets, with a focus on simple access to these assets, as well as their long-term preservation (to help ensure access over very long time frames) [1]. It was originally designed with a particular service model in mind: that of institutional repositories of research material, and particularly research articles, which are produced by academic research institutions [2]. The idea was that institutions of all kinds could and should accept stewardship responsibility for their intellectual research output, for its widespread and long-term access. This is related to, but not synonymous with, the Open Access movement[1], since while many of the institutions using DSpace have free access to their assets as a goal, the platform itself does not assume that assets it stores will be made available for free.

DSpace was originally designed by developers at the MIT Libraries and HP Labs to be a breadth-first system with functionality to capture, describe, store, and preserve digital content, which adopters could download and install with minimal configuration and customization [3]. This decision was made for two reasons: to test the value of archivally-oriented digital asset management systems to the research university community without the need for extensive technical development, and to get a system

---

[1] E.g. the Budapest Open Access Initiative. http://www.soros.org/openaccess/initiatives.shtml

R. Heery and L. Lyon (Eds.): ECDL 2004, LNCS 3232, pp. 38–44, 2004.

out to the open source development community that was "good enough" to get things going and foster wider debate about the many technology choices involved.

Since its launch as an open source project in November of 2002, DSpace has undergone widespread adoption in several communities, and is starting to undergo active development by an open source developer community. This process of going from research to a public production release 1.0 on SourceForge, and then to a platform that is being developed by a large group of software developers representing both the original target audience and others who were not foreseen is an interesting story. It is our belief that the academic research community who often create open source projects for very good reasons don't necessarily understand the implications of the open source model or the long-term issues it raises. Our experience with DSpace is both atypical of many of the successful open source projects and also instructive to other research projects with a goal of becoming successful open source projects as their long-term business plan.

As a research project, it was the goal of the MIT Libraries or HP neither to productize DSpace, nor to continue to provide sole support and development of the platform going forward. Both organizations continue to work on the platform, in different areas and for different reasons, and we are committed to making sure that the platform has a viable and sustainable model for its ongoing development and adoption. That means ceding a large degree of control in order to gain the long-term vision of a self-sustained tool that we can all leverage to our best advantage.

This article attempts to provide enough context for DSpace to explain its origin and goals, to report on what has happened during the first year of its life as an open source project, and to attempt to divine the future of its transition to the next phase.

Background

The DSpace project was born out of a need voiced by faculty to the MIT Libraries to create a scalable digital archive that preserves and communicates the intellectual output of MIT's faculty and researchers. At the Institute, there is a growing body of digitally born materials representing significant intellectual assets that require stewardship. In addition to the more traditional text-based research output such as preprints and working papers, these assets include audio files, videos, datasets, software simulations and more. Faculty members often post their work on personal or departmental websites, but increasingly have become concerned about the sustainability of that solution. DSpace offers faculty and researchers a professionally managed archive that allows easy accessibility to their scholarly work.

Recognizing that the problems DSpace seeks to address are not unique to MIT, the MIT Libraries and HP Labs envisioned a federated repository based on a common set of institutional repository standards for interoperability. Interoperability would make available the collective intellectual resources of the world's leading research institutions. Further, we opted from the beginning to make the software entirely open source with the hope that a community of users and developers would emerge beyond the original MIT and HP team to contribute to the maintenance and enhancement of the code base over the long term.

The DSpace Federation

In January 2003, the MIT Libraries embarked on a project funded by the Andrew W. Mellon Foundation to work with seven other research universities to begin the process of building a collaborative federation of institutions running DSpace. Each of the seven universities installed DSpace and tested the adaptability of the system to their university environment. Our goal was to learn from these implementations and to share lessons learned with a wider DSpace Federation.

From the time the system was released as open source in November of 2002, uptake of the system has extended well beyond the original Federation project partners. DSpace has been adopted by a large number of research universities and other organizations that need a digital repository solution for a number of content types. These universities have evaluated DSpace's functionality and are further developing it to meet their needs. As the moment the software has been downloaded nearly 10,000 times; over 125 universities are investigating it for use in their university environment; and at least 20 universities are running production DSpace systems.

With interest in and use of DSpace mounting far more quickly than was originally anticipated, the set of institutions participating in the DSpace Federation project made the strategic decision to expand the final project meeting to include all institutions currently using DSpace and shift the purpose of the gathering to an open user group meeting, which was held on March 10-11, 2004. Approximately 120 people attended the sold-out meeting, representing 50 institutions, including universities, government agencies, and corporations, from 10 different countries. Members of the user community shared their DSpace experiences and plans, through which we learned that the DSpace platform is being put to a variety of uses: primarily to create institutional repositories of research publications and other material, but also for other applications (e-thesis repositories, learning object repositories, e-journal publishing, cultural material collections, electronic records management, and so on).

Within the UK, we already are beginning to see the diversity of purposes to which DSpace can be applied. The DSpace@Cambridge project, a joint collaboration between Cambridge University Library and MIT Libraries, aims to implement an institutional repository for scholarly research, but also is exploring the use of DSpace for administrative records and learning objects. Edinburgh University chose the DSpace platform for its Theses Alive! project, which aims to produce an OAI-compliant repository for the creation and management of e-theses and pilot it as a national service. Programmers at Edinburgh have developed an add-on module for DSpace that includes a supervised workspace for theses creation, supervision administrative tools, and a submission system for theses metadata collection. Glasgow's DAEDALUS project is piloting several open source institutional repository solutions and has opted to deliver a range of distinct open access services supported by complementary software platforms (one of which is DSpace) that optimally meet Glasgow University's needs for specific collection and digital content types. For the international community, it is also relevant to note the work done by the Université de Montréal's Érudit project to translate DSpace into French, work that has provided important lessons for customizing DSpace for local language. Other institutions in non-English speaking countries are now working to translate the system into local languages, and have identified general internationalization as an important goal for the future.

DSpace, and institutional repositories in general, are proving to be a high-value, long-term vision, but are still very much works in progress. Universities are setting their own policies to define what an institutional repository service means in the context of their university environment. Seemingly straightforward questions such as what types of file formats or content will be accepted and who is authorized to submit materials to DSpace quickly become complex when long-term implications for digital preservation and stewardship are considered.

Building collections of digital content, particularly scholarly research content, has proven to be another challenge universities consistently grapple with when implementing institutional repositories. Many of the DSpace projects around the world are grant funded or have limited resources and are under pressure to prove the value of the service, often measured (rather simplistically) through the number of items in the repository. DSpace was designed with a decentralized web submission interface that allows research communities to contribute their own items and metadata. This paradigm shift has been a novel and attractive aspect of the service but has meant that library staff has had to become proficient marketers, carefully positioning the service to meet user needs. Publicity and promotional activities help raise initial awareness among potential users but targeted communications with highly tailored marketing messages often are what persuade them to become submitters.

Open Platform – First Steps

The DSpace software released as version 1.0 into open source embodied use-cases derived from an analysis of needs within the MIT scholarly community viewed through the lens of the library. Yet this begged an important question: to what extent did these use-cases reflect the needs of institutional repositories generally? Rather than undertake a systematic survey or study, the expectation was that those who evaluated or adopted the software would provide an answer in the form of reworking the software itself to suit local purpose. The evolution of the DSpace platform would then consist of a rational assimilation of this work into the centrally managed code repository. Our biggest concern was the possibility of fragmentation or 'centrifugal' dissipation: that the platform would be pulled in too many directions, asked to do too many things, so that none could be done well. To prevent this, procedures were instituted to subject proposed contributions to a closely managed review process. Those of sufficient technical merit and deemed consistent with the vision of DSpace would be incorporated; the rest would reside as localizations of the platform outside its management.

The first year produced relatively few contributions, given the size and interest level of the adopter community. This was not due to a shortage of ideas, however: the mail lists and other forums were filled with use-cases and other expressions of need exceeding the 1.0 platform capability. Analysis of this situation revealed several factors at work: (1) The process of adopting DSpace could be lengthy and involved, and technical rework was often put behind such tasks as formulating a sustainable business model, developing service guidelines, or building awareness and buy-in from depositors. This had the effect of pushing software development considerations out of an early time frame. (2) Many of the potential adopter institutions lacked the technical resources required to undertake significant software development. (3) Architectural limitations in the implementation of the platform made certain kinds of modification difficult to do. (4) Perhaps most interesting, however, was the perception that the platform, although distributed freely in source code form, was an immutable offering, much like commercial software product offering. There are many reasons why this perception took root, including the fact that its initial development cycle was 'closed', and that in order to build awareness of the platform it was 'branded' as an MIT/HP-sponsored effort, rather than an outgrowth of a community-driven process.

To address this perception, DSpace development was deliberately steered in the direction of the needs of the nascent community of users. The functional requirements of the next major release of the platform, 1.2 (1.1 basically represented the completion of the original research project agenda) were culled from postings to the DSpace lists, and from other discussions and surveys eliciting adopter feedback. In this way we hoped both to realize and to convey the community-centric nature of the DSpace platform. And to the degree that this additional functionality will remove barriers to adoption, the plan is proving successful. Yet since the bulk of the development effort was still concentrated within MIT/HP, it also is having the opposite effect – that of reinforcing the vendor/consumer dichotomy it was intended to overcome.

On the technical architecture front, the analysis of limitations has produced a roadmap for a new design direction, DSpace 2.0, which will address several key shortcomings of the current architecture: (1) Functional modularity coupled with the use of stable, well-defined APIs for their use will promote the development of independent implementations by DSpace adopters. This will substantially alter the concept of DSpace as a closed body of code, replacing it with the concept of a software framework, within which myriad implementations may coexist. (2) A refactoring of the presentation layer will enable much simpler alteration of UI without complications elsewhere in the code. (3) A much cleaner representation of content and associated metadata as a self-contained archival information package (AIP) will facilitate interoperability and maintenance of a DSpace repository.

From Code to Community

One important lesson we learned was this: to build an open source community, it is insufficient merely to publish a body of code as open source, even on commercially-friendly licensing terms (BSD[4]), and wait for a community to coalesce. Achieving true community requires the transformation of users who are initially consumers into stakeholders. We are examining several successful open source initiatives, such as the Apache Software Foundation, the Global Grid Forum, and the Eclipse Foundation, and, together with the user community, are formulating a plan for the DSpace platform. Among short-term objectives are: (1) expansion of the core set of developers to include those outside the initial circle of researchers. (2) Articulation of a clear process to encourage further enlargement of the developers' group. In most open source models, the existing group invites new developers, and functions as a project management board. (3) Recruitment of contributors to the platform on many other levels, from requirements definition to documentation, testing – indeed all aspects of platform maintenance and evolution. (4) Improved communication channels. Two goals are involved here: first, to produce greater *transparency* in the process of platform development we will need better ways to expose the deliberative steps involved. A developer-focused mailing list is one frequently adopted technique to achieve this.

Second, there need to be more flexible and accessible opportunities to become involved in development issues. Wikis and other semi-structured discussion tools can serve this purpose.

In the longer term, it will be important to establish or join forces with an independent not-for-profit entity (e.g. a 501(c)(3) corporation[5]) to be charged with stewardship of the software, and to possibly assume ownership of the intellectual property (copyright, trademark, license, etc.). Issues of financial support and governance models will be foremost in choosing a model – e.g. does financial contribution confer special privileges with respect to platform development? We hope to address these issues carefully, while proceeding quickly on the short-term agenda. Throughout this process, what is paramount to communicate to the greater body of adopters is that the continued evolution and in fact the very existence of the platform will depend upon a collective effort, not on the beneficence of the founding institutions.

Conclusion

As stated earlier, while it is not the current aim of the MIT Libraries or HP to build a commercial product with DSpace, neither was it our aim to prevent that from happening at all. We wanted to understand what it would take to build a useful digital archival repository: to test the technologies involved, to have a platform to explore service models like institutional repositories, and to have a platform for ongoing research in important areas such as digital preservation, Semantic Web techniques for metadata management, persistent identification schemes, and open access-friendly DRM systems.

In order to achieve our goals for the DSpace platform it is vital that it become a successful open source project with an active community of developers far beyond MIT or HP. That can only happen if the platform is useful to a critical mass of organizations that can provide the resources to do this work. We also expect that development of the platform will reveal a range of necessary standards – for interoperability, for rights managements, for identification of content and the people accessing it, for content discovery and preservation, for the metadata to support all of this, and more. The future DSpace Federation organizational home will provide the governance to make sure that everyone's goals for the platform are met, and hopefully to foster its adoption by a range of organizations in many sectors. The research community who we represent is but one potential adopter of this technology, and we believe that by leveraging the expertise and resources of other sectors, ours will ultimately benefit in ways that have proved elusive in the past.

The promise of open source for projects like DSpace to the digital library community are obvious, if it's successful. But there are some barriers to success. Many institutions lack the resources to deal with complex applications like DSpace on a technical level – they require support to install, configure and customize it for their local needs, and to maintain it over time. The open source world, with a few exceptions (most notably Red Hat for the LINUX operating system), doesn't provide models for such support and assumes that adopters have the necessary local expertise. The second barrier to success is in sustaining the developer community that will ensure the platform's continued usefulness over time. The research library community, who have been the primary adopters of the DSpace platform so far, do not, by themselves, have the resources themselves to sustain DSpace indefinitely. They have technical expertise, to be sure, but it is typically over-stretched. They often cannot dedicate programmers to work on an open source platform without external support (usually for a grant-funded project of a year or two). It is possible that DSpace could survive on that basis, but risky. If the digital library community can share control of the platform with other sectors, particularly commercial and governmental sectors, then many more resources can be brought to bear to the problem.

So why are research libraries motivated to get involved in open source projects like DSpace? To learn more about how it really works, to better fulfill their mission, because commercial offerings are too expensive and often inadequate. Why are research libraries not getting involved? There is a noticeable tendency among managers to treat open source software as if it was commercially supplied. The owning organization is the "vendor" and the "products" can be comparatively evaluated and judged good or bad accordingly. The problem with this approach is that where open source software is concerned we are all, collectively, "the vendor". Or rather, there is no vendor to negotiate with, and if the product doesn't meet local needs then it can be made to do so. There is a corresponding tendency among library adopters of open source software to feel faint obligation back to its source – the software is just a product that happens to be free. But open source software certainly does cost its adopters something: the staff time to configure and maintain it without a formal support contract (typically), and the more nebulous moral obligation to provide some value in return for this free good. If open source software works at all then it's because those who benefit from it also contribute to it in some way: functionally, technically, or monetarily. Our community has much to learn about ways in which is can contribute to these efforts other than as grateful, but silent, adopters.

We have looked for inspiration to existing open source projects and organizations: obviously LINUX and the Apache Foundation, but also the Global Grid Forum and CNRI. Each of these organizations has some model for sustaining open source software but they're all different. Undoubtedly there are many others that we have not yet had time to identify and investigate. Which one is the most relevant to applications like DSpace? Which to the communities that created it? Which to the communities who are now adopting and improving it? Clearly there are many, many issues still to be addressed, and we hope that our experience in some way informs the understanding of the open source promise to and contract with the digital library community.

References

DSpace: An Open Source Dynamic Digital Repository. Smith, et al. D-Lib Magazine 9:1, January 2003. http://www.dlib.org/dlib/january03/smith/01smith.html
Institutional Repositories: Essential Infrastructure for Scholarship in the Digital Age. Clifford Lynch. ARL Bimonthly Report 226, February 2003.
http://www.arl.org/newsltr/226/ir.html
DSpace Internal Reference Specification. Bass, et al. March 2002.
http://dspace.org/technology/functionality.pdf
BSD is the "Berkeley Software Distribution" license originally written in 1979 at the University of California, Berkeley for their open source unix software
http://www.opensource.org/licenses/bsd-license.php. It is considered one of the "classic" open source software licenses, and the most commercial-friendly since it allows commercial development using the open source code.
501(c)3 organizations in the U.S. are legally-recognized, registered non-profit organizations

Spatial Ranking Methods for Geographic Information Retrieval (GIR) in Digital Libraries

Ray R. Larson[1] and Patricia Frontiera[2]

[1] School of Information Management and Systems
ray@sherlock.berkeley.edu
[2] College of Environmental Design
University of California, Berkeley
Berkeley, California, USA, 94720
pattyf@regis.berkeley.edu

Abstract. This paper presents results from an evaluation of algorithms for ranking results by probability of relevance for Geographic Information Retrieval (GIR) applications. We review the work done on GIR and especially on ranking algorithms for GIR. We evaluate these algorithms using a test collection of 2500 metadata records from a geographic digital library. We present an algorithm for GIR ranking based on logistic regression from samples of the test collection. We also examine the effects of different representations of the geographic regions being searched, including minimum bounding rectangles, and convex hulls.

1 Introduction

Geographic data are an extremely important resource for a wide range of scientists, planners, policy makers, and analysts who study natural and planned environments. Notably, the landscape of geographic analysis has been changing rapidly from data and computation poor to data and computation rich [15]. Developments in digital electronic technologies, such as satellites, integrated GPS units, digital cameras, and miniature sensors, are dramatically increasing the types and amounts of digitally available raw geographic data and derived information products [17]. At the same time, advances in computer hardware, software and network technologies continue to improve our ability to store and analyze these large, complex data sets.

These factors are contributing to a growing political, social, scientific and economic awareness of the value of geographic information and driving new applications for its use. In response to this, geographic digital libraries are growing in number, collection size, and sophistication. Moreover, mainstream digital libraries, i.e. those that deal with primarily text materials, are increasingly considering geographic access methods for information resources that have important geographic characteristics. Simply stated, most of the objects in digital libraries are, to a greater or lesser extent, about, or related to, particular places on or near the surface of the Earth.

R. Heery and L. Lyon (Eds.): ECDL 2004, LNCS 3232, pp. 45–56, 2004.
© Springer-Verlag Berlin Heidelberg 2004

One common approach in digital libraries is to use place names as a geographical search surrogate. However, place names have well-documented lexical and geographical problems [13]. Lexical problems include lack of uniqueness, variant names or spellings, and name changes. Geographical problems include boundaries that change over time and geographic features or areas without known place names. Geographic coordinates, on the other hand, provide an unambiguous and persistent method for locating geographic areas or features. However, the use of coordinates presents many challenges in terms of storage, indexing, processing and user interface design that only recently have begun to be investigated in the context of geographic information retrieval (GIR) for digital libraries.

One key question for GIR is what level of detail should be used to encode coordinate information? Gazetteer research cautions that complex spatial objects present enormous data storage and performance problems for online geographic digital libraries [1, 11], which provide, at best, extremely limited GIS functionality. The decomposition of complex spatial objects into approximate representations is a common approach to simplifying coordinate representations. Early work in this area by Hill [10] suggests that minimum bounding rectangles can sufficiently represent geographic objects for information retrieval applications. Other research [1, 12] indicates that even single point representations can be used effectively when combined with innovative retrieval and ranking methods.

In this paper we explore these issues and present some new algorithms for ranked retrieval of georeferenced objects in digital library collections. We discuss the characteristics of georeferenced information and its use in digital libraries. The next section describes the primary components for GIR within digital libraries and describes the characteristics of GIR in a digital library context. Subsequent sections examine indexing and access creation for geo-referenced sources. We then examine the retrieval effectiveness of several GIR algorithms using a test collection of geospatial metadata from the California Environmental Information Catalog (CEIC – http://ceres.ca.gov/catalog).

2   Geospatial Metadata

Geographic digital libraries typically use geospatial metadata to provide surrogate representations of geographic resources that encode the structure and content of digital geographic data to support identification, discovery, evaluation, and understanding. This metadata is vital for most geographic data because, as non-textual, abstract representations of complex phenomena, they cannot be effectively and appropriately used without it.

Geospatial metadata specifically addresses the encoding of coordinate representations of geographic objects. There are geospatial metadata standards in most EU countries. In the U.S., it is usually created in accordance with one of two metadata standards: 1) the Dublin Core (DC) [6]; or 2) the Federal Geographic Data Committee's Content Standard for Digital Geospatial Metadata (FGDC) [8]. The only geographic element in the base DC is the Coverage element. This element can be used to specify a place name, place code (e.g. zip

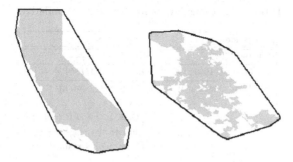

Fig. 1. Minimum Bounding Rectangles (thin lines) and Convex Hulls for the State of California and the City of San Jose.

code), or the geospatial coordinates of a point, bounding rectangle, or irregular polygon that locates the resource being described.

The FGDC Standard was created specifically to describe digital geospatial data, but is also applied to paper maps, air photos, atlases, environmental impact statements, and other geographically related materials. It provides elements that address the geospatial characteristics of the data, including: *Spatial domain* (geographic coordinates defining the data's extent), *Place names* (qualitative descriptors of the geographic extent), *Spatial reference system* (projection and coordinate system information, *Spatial Representation model* (vector, raster), *Spatial features* (type and quantity) and *Spatial data quality* (accuracy, completeness, lineage, and sources). The FGDC Standard *requires* only a coordinate pair defining a Minimum Bounding Rectangle (MBR) for the object, but allows more complex descriptions also.

As can be seen in Figure 1, MBRs provide a compressed, abstract approximation of a spatial object. The representation is conceptually powerful because it evokes a printed map. Its simplicity, computational efficiency, and storage advantages make it the most commonly used spatial approximation [4]. Yet, the MBR has obvious weaknesses when representing diagonal, irregular, non-convex, or multi-part regions [18]. MBRs over-estimate area, misrepresent shape, and fail to capture the distribution of the data within themselves, leading to "false positives" in GIR matching.

3   Geospatial Search and Ranking Methods

Other spatial approximations, such as the minimum bounding ellipse, minimum bounding N-corner convex polygon, and convex hull, have been investigated in the context of spatial databases and GIS applications, but not for GIR, where the MBR still represents the state of the art. In searching, a query region representing the user's area of interest may be defined by 1) Entering geographic coordinates for a point or bounding box, 2) Using a graphical map interface to zoom in to, click on, or draw a polygon, typically a bounding box, around the area of interest and 3) Entering a place name or selecting it from a list.

Table 1. Methods for computing spatial similarity.

Reference	Formula
Hill, 1990 [10]	$Range = 2\frac{O}{Q+C}$
Walker et al, 1992 [19]	$Range = MIN\left(\frac{O}{Q}, \frac{O}{C}\right)$
Beard and Sharma, 1997 [3]	Case 1: Q contains C $Range = \frac{C}{Q}$ Case 2: Q and C overlap $Range = \frac{O/Q\%}{(1-O/C\%)+100}$ Case 3: Q contained in C $Range = \frac{Q}{C}$
Where: Q = area of query region C = area of candidate GIO O = area of overlap for G, C	Range (for all): 0 = no similarity 1 = identical

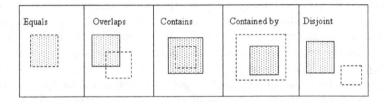

Fig. 2. Spatial relationships between overlapping regions.

The first two methods result in the delineation of a coordinate-based query region. The third uses a digital gazetteer to obtain coordinate representations for named places. Regardless of the method used, a query region is often represented internally as a simple bounding rectangle [11]. For geospatial searches, the query region is compared with MBRs of all candidate geographic information objects (GIOs) in the digital library using polygon-polygon geometric operations. If there is overlap between the query and the GIO regions, the GIO is considered a match. Possible relationships between two overlapping regions are illustrated in Figure 2. This is a simplified subset of the 9 intersection topological model for spatial relations [7]. Proximity relationships (such as near or adjacent) are not considered matches.

GIR ranking methods are based on quantifying the similarity between the query and a GIO in the collection. This similarity "score" can be interpreted as an estimate of the relevance, or utility, of a candidate GIO for a user's information need. Retrieved items are ranked and presented to the user in descending order of these scores. While traditional IR scores and rankings are based on the statistical properties of terms in a collection, GIR relies on spatial scores and rankings based on geospatial characteristics such as size, shape, location, and distance. There are three basic approaches to spatial similarity measures and ranking:

Method 1: Simple Overlap. Candidate geographic information objects (or GIOs) that have any overlap with the query region are retrieved.

Method 2: Topological Overlap. Spatial searches are constrained to only those candidate GIOs that: a) are completely contained within, b) overlap, or c) contain the query region. Each category is exclusive and all retrieved items are considered relevant.

Method 3: Extent of Overlap. A spatial similarity score is derived from the extent of overlap between a candidate GIO and the query region. The greater the overlap, the greater the assumed relevance of the candidate GIO to the query. A variety of spatial scores based on overlap are discussed in the literature (Hill, 1990; Walker et al, 1992; Beard and Sharma, 1997) and presented in Table 1.

The simple and topological overlap approaches are most commonly used in digital libraries where the geographic objects of interest are represented by MBRs. Retrieval algorithms based on MBRs are easy to implement and are supported by the GEO profile of the Z39.50 information retrieval protocol [16]. However, the Boolean matching criterion does not allow for spatial ranking and thus inhibits good retrieval performance [2](p. 26), especially as result sets grow in size. Classifying retrieved candidates based on topological relationships (e.g., contains, overlaps, contained within), as in method 2, is a first step in discriminating among the results, but it doesn't speak directly to the issue of relevance. Moreover, the burden is on the user to understand these relationships and how they impact a geospatial search. There has been very limited research on the effectiveness of spatial ranking with Hill [10] presenting the only empirical data and evaluation.

3.1   Probabilistic Spatial Ranking

Maron and Kuhns [14] first introduced the idea that, given the imprecise and incomplete ways in which a user's information need is represented by a query and an information object by its indexing, relevance should be approached probabilistically. This is especially true for geographic information retrieval since all geographic information objects are abstract, compressed representations of real world phenomena that contain some degree of error and uncertainty [9].

In the Logistic Regression (LR) model of IR [5], the estimated probability of relevance for a particular query and a particular record in the database $P(R \mid Q, D)$ is calculated as the "log odds" of relevance $\log O(R \mid Q, D)$ and converted from odds to a probability. The LR model provides estimates for a set of coefficients, c_i, associated with a set of S statistics, X_i, derived from the query and database, such that:

$$\log O(R \mid Q, D) = c_0 + \sum_{i=1}^{S} c_i X_i \qquad (1)$$

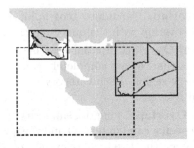

Fig. 3. Search Query (dashed rectangle) and MBRs and Polygon Representations of Marin (NW) and Stanislaus (E) Counties.

where c_0 is the intercept term of the regression. The spatial ranking, or probability of relevance, can then be given as:

$$P(R \mid Q, D) = \frac{e^{\log O(R|Q,D)}}{1 + e^{\log O(R|Q,D)}} \qquad (2)$$

For this study, the geospatial characterics, i.e. explanatory statistics or feature variables, explored in the logistic regression model are:

$X_1 =$ area of overlap(query region, candidate GIO) / area of query region
$X_2 =$ area of overlap(query region, candidate GIO) / area of candidate GIO
$X_3 = 1 -$ abs(fraction of query region that is onshore – fraction of candidate GIO that is onshore)

Like the spatial similarity measures presented in Table 1, X_1 and X_2 are based on the extent of the area of overlap and non-overlap between the query and candidate GIO regions. X_3 requires a bit more explanation. As noted in Hill [10] geographic areas that are near a coastline can be problematic when approximated by simplified geometries like the MBR. The MBR for an offshore region may necessarily include a lot of onshore area, and vice versa. We define X_3 as a "shorefactor" variable that captures the similarity between the fraction of a query region that is onshore compared to that of a candidate GIO region. For example, if a query region is 20% onshore and a candidate GIO region is 75% on shore, then the shorefactor is $1 - abs(.20 - .75) = .45$. Calculating shorefactor is illustrated in Figure 3. Marin County is 70% onshore, while Stanislaus County is 100% onshore. The dashed query box in Figure 3 is 45% onshore. Thus, the shorefactor for Marin is $1 - abs(.45 - .70) = .75$ while for Stanislaus it is $1 - abs(.45 - 1) = .45$. A shorefactor of 1 indicates that both regions are either offshore or onshore. A shorefactor approaching 0 indicates that one region is almost completely onshore and one is almost completely offshore, thus it allows geographic context to be integrated into the spatial ranking process. The shorefactor was computed by intersecting both the query and GIO regions with a very generalized polygonal representation of the Western USA.

4 Evaluation Approach

We applied our logistic regression method and the three spatial ranking methods presented in Table 1 to a test collection of geospatial metadata. The research questions were: 1) How effectively can the geographic relationship between a query region and the region of a candidate information object be evaluated and ranked based on the overlap of the geographic approximations of these regions? and 2) How do different geographic approximations affect the rankings? To examine question one, the results of the different ranking methods were summarized and compared using two standard retrieval performance evaluation measures: average precision at 11 standard recall levels and the mean average query precision.

In response to the second question, we applied and compared the results of these ranking methods for both MBR and convex hull approximations of the candidate GIOs. The convex hull is the minimum convex polygon that contains a geometric object (i.e. collection of points). It can be visualized as a rubber band around a geographic polygon to approximate its extent (see heavy lines in Figure 1). The convex hull is widely used as a geometric approximation in GIS and it provides the best approximation quality of conservative (i.e., encloses all points of the original) convex representations [4]. Because a convex hull is a better approximation of the original spatial object than an MBR, it will retrieve fewer false positives when used for GIR.

We assumed that candidate GIO regions that overlap the query region are relevant and regions that do not overlap are not relevant. Given that all regions are represented by conservative approximations, all relevant items will be retrieved (i.e. 100% recall). However, not all *approximations* that overlap will be relevant because the regions they represent may *not* overlap [18].

4.1 Test Collection Overview

The test collection for this study was a subset of metadata records from the California Environmental Information Catalog (CEIC), (`http://ceres.ca.gov/catalog`). The CEIC collection includes a wide variety of different types of geographic information resources, including: vector and raster geospatial data, maps, databases, documents, reports, websites, models, etc. These resources are documented with metadata prepared in accordance with the FGDC standard. For this study, approximately 2500 metadata records in XML format were selected from the total collection of about 4000 (as of August 2003). These records can be divided into two main categories: 1) those that refer to known, named geographic regions within the state; and 2) user defined areas (UDAs) – those regions that are specific to the person or organization that created the GIO described by the metadata. An important distinction between these two categories is that the geographic regions associated with the CA places are typical of those found in gazetteers and place name thesauri. Moreover, these regions can be traced, via their names, to geographic data containing more precise geographic representations, which we used in calculating the "shorefactor" described above.

For the UDA regions, which seldom have accurate or complete data available, we assume that both the convex hull and complex polygon representations of the geographic extent are equal to the MBR approximation. The MBRs and convex hulls were pre-processed in the ESRI ArcView software and then loaded into Postgres 7.4, with the PostGIS 0.8 and GEOS 1.0 extensions, where the analysis was done.

5   Results

This research considers the test collection in two parts. In the first part, the issues of spatial representation and ranking are considered for the metadata indexed by CA places. The second part considers the entire collection, both CA places and UDAs.

Our first set of tests considered only the 2072 test metadata records, or GIOs, that were indexed geospatially by known CA places. The 42 CA counties referenced in these GIOs were used, each in turn, as query regions. MBR and convex hull approximations of all CA places referenced by these metadata were treated as candidate GIO regions.

The first task was to determine the reference set of candidate GIO regions relevant to each county query region. This was done using the complex polygon data to select all CA place regions that overlap, contain, or are contained within the query region. All retrieved regions were reviewed (semi-automatically) to remove sliver matches, i.e. those regions that only overlap due to inconsistencies in the data. This process resulted in a master file of CA place regions relevant to the 42 CA county query regions. Queries for ten county regions were used to train the logistic regression models. LR Equation 3 was used for the MBR rankings and LR Equation 4 for convex hulls:

$$\log O(R \mid Q, D) = -5.040 + 6.5154 \cdot X_1 + 5.7729 \cdot X_2 \tag{3}$$

$$\log O(R \mid Q, D) = -3.4767 + 7.4536 \cdot X_1 + 5.7569 * X_2 \tag{4}$$

Queries for the other 32 county query regions were run against the MBR and convex hull approximations of the candidate GIO regions. We then applied all four spatial ranking methods to the result sets and calculated precision-recall summary statistics.

Tables 2 and 3 show the evaluation results of the four spatial ranking methods on the CA places subset of the test collection. These tables show that: 1) the values for the non-logistic regression ranking methods are extremely similar; 2) the logistic regression method performed better than the other methods on this test collection; 3) for all methods, rankings based on the convex hull representations performed better than those based on the MBR representations. Yet, it is interesting to note that the non-logistic regression spatial ranking methods applied to the convex hull approximations do *not* perform better than the logistic regression method applied to the MBRs. An important implication of this is that it is worth investigating more effective spatial ranking methods before adopting

Table 2. Mean Average Query Precision for Named Places.

Ranking method	MBRs	Convex Hulls
Hill, 1990	0.7193	0.8097
Walker, et al., 1992	0.7025	0.8006
Beard and Sharma. 1997	0.7094	0.8116
Logistic Regression	0.9389	0.9973

Table 3. Average Precision at 11 Standard Recall Levels for Named Places using Minimum Bounding Rectangles and Convex Hulls.

	Minimum Bounding Rect.				Convex Hulls			
Recall Level	Hill	Walker	Beard	Logistic	Hill	Walker	Beard	Logistic
0.00	1.0000	1.0000	1.0000	1.0000	1.0000	1.0000	1.0000	1.0000
0.10	0.8668	0.8660	0.8717	0.9777	0.9232	0.9248	0.9277	1.0000
0.20	0.8409	0.8362	0.8430	0.9663	0.9152	0.9049	0.9083	1.0000
0.30	0.8101	0.8109	0.8214	0.9651	0.8708	0.8775	0.8813	1.0000
0.40	0.8017	0.7985	0.8073	0.9651	0.8705	0.8669	0.8746	1.0000
0.50	0.7940	0.7972	0.8068	0.9651	0.8661	0.8658	0.8735	1.0000
0.60	0.7919	0.7951	0.8039	0.9651	0.8660	0.8658	0.8735	1.0000
0.70	0.7919	0.7951	0.8039	0.9643	0.8623	0.8658	0.8698	0.9997
0.80	0.7919	0.7951	0.8039	0.9520	0.8623	0.8658	0.8698	0.9983
0.90	0.7914	0.7947	0.8035	0.9477	0.8621	0.8656	0.8696	0.9882
1.00	0.7613	0.7684	0.7881	0.9114	0.8243	0.8274	0.8291	0.9648
Avg Prec	0.8220	0.8234	0.8321	0.9618	0.8839	0.8846	0.8888	0.9955

more complex spatial approximations. Average precision at 11 standard recall levels (Table 3) gives one an idea of how an algorithm performs over the course of retrieving all relevant GIOs. Mean average query precision is a measure that favors systems that rank relevant documents early in the results (Table 2). It averages precision values after each new relevant document is observed in the ranked list and presents a summary statistic of overall performance. However, it may not indicate if an algorithm has poor recall [2](p. 80). But, these characteristics make it a good fit for spatial ranking algorithms because poor recall is very rarely an issue and high precision is desireable. Moreover, the metric is insensitive to differences in the number of items indexed to the same geographic region. This latter is not true of average precision at standard recall levels, therefore the values for average precision (Table 3) are lower than those for mean average query precision (Table 2). Interestingly, the difference between these values for the logistic regression method does not differ as much as for the non-logistic regression ranking methods.

The second part of our study considers the test collection metadata as a whole: both those metadata indexed by CA places and those indexed by user-defined areas (UDAs). As with the tests in Part I, the 42 CA counties referenced in the GIOs were considered query regions and the MBR and convex hull representations for all geospatially indexed areas were treated as candidate GIO regions.

Table 4. Mean Average Query Precision for Full Collection.

Ranking Method	MBRs	Convex Hulls
Ranking Method	MBRs	Convex Hulls
Hill, 1990	0.6722	0.7936
Walker et al., 1992	0.6509	0.7810
Beard and Sharma, 1997	0.6523	0.7778
Logistic Regression 1	0.8141	0.9099
Logistic Regression 2	0.8819	0.9238

The reference set of UDA regions relevant to each county query region was determined through a manual review of the UDA metadata. This process could not be automated because, unlike the CA place regions, there are no reference data sets of complex polygons that delineate the UDA regions.

As in Part I, queries for ten county query regions were used to train the logistic regression models. Because 88% of the UDAs represent coastal or offshore regions, an additional logistic regression model was tested that includes the shorefactor variable. LR equations 5 and 6 were used for MBRs and equations 7 and 8 were used for convex hulls.:

$$\log O(R \mid Q, D) = -1.6747 + 1.9871 \cdot X_1 + 3.2976 \cdot X_2 \qquad (5)$$

$$\log O(R \mid Q, D) = -2.1303 + 1.9138 \cdot X_1 + 3.2157 \cdot X_2 + 0.7451 \cdot X_3 \qquad (6)$$

$$\log O(R \mid Q, D) = -1.2123 + 1.4471 \cdot X_1 + 5.4585 \cdot X_2 \qquad (7)$$

$$\log O(R \mid Q, D) = -1.2825 + 1.4341 \cdot X_1 + 5.4096 \cdot X_2 + 0.1267 \cdot X_3 \qquad (8)$$

The evaluation results are presented in Tables 4 and 5. These show a similar pattern to the results presented in Part I. The logistic regression rankings perform better than non-logistic regression methods and the convex hull approximations also perform better than the MBRs. Again, the logistic regression rankings for MBRs perform as well as or better than the non-logistic regression rankings for convex hulls, although by a smaller margin than when just the CA place regions were considered.

The addition of the UDA regions significantly degrades the retrieval performance for all algorithms, even though these regions only index 19% of the total metadata records. The majority of the UDA regions are for coastal or near-coastal offshore areas which, when approximated by either MBRs or convex hulls necessarily overlap with onshore regions, thus generating more false-positive retrievals. The logistic regression model (LR2) that incorporates the shorefactor variable is meant to address this problem, yet this method shows only a small (but significant) improvement over the other logistic regression model (LR1), especially for the convex hull approximations. T-tests for paired samples of LR1 and LR2 results gave results ranging from -3.028 to -4.144 with 0.005 or less probability of random occurrence.

Table 5. Average Precision at 11 Standard Recall Levels for the Full Collection using Minimum Bounding Rectangles and Convex Hulls.

Recall Level	Minimum Bounding Rect.					Convex Hulls				
	Hill	Walker	Beard	LR1	LR2	Hill	Walker	Beard	LR1	LR2
0.00	1.0000	1.0000	1.0000	1.0000	1.0000	1.0000	1.0000	1.0000	1.0000	1.0000
0.10	0.8384	0.8453	0.8562	0.9174	0.9529	0.9099	0.9146	0.9188	0.9715	0.9781
0.20	0.7983	0.7782	0.7885	0.9114	0.9413	0.8905	0.8827	0.8874	0.9676	0.9746
0.30	0.7575	0.7729	0.7871	0.8898	0.9395	0.8484	0.8634	0.8686	0.9560	0.9641
0.40	0.7402	0.7460	0.7570	0.8785	0.9310	0.8428	0.8482	0.8585	0.9534	0.9635
0.50	0.7377	0.7450	0.7570	0.8767	0.9291	0.8406	0.8481	0.8583	0.9534	0.9625
0.60	0.7350	0.7420	0.7538	0.8742	0.9291	0.8406	0.8481	0.8583	0.9534	0.9625
0.70	0.7350	0.7420	0.7538	0.8742	0.9291	0.8403	0.8481	0.8548	0.9505	0.9579
0.80	0.7350	0.7420	0.7538	0.8631	0.9182	0.8371	0.8481	0.8548	0.9412	0.9539
0.90	0.7344	0.7416	0.7534	0.8631	0.9018	0.8312	0.8478	0.8544	0.9342	0.9432
1.00	0.7067	0.7139	0.7311	0.7715	0.7743	0.7819	0.7782	0.7787	0.8340	0.8272
Avg Prec	0.7744	0.7790	0.7902	0.8836	0.9224	0.8603	0.8661	0.8721	0.9468	0.9534

6   Conclusions

In GIS and spatial database technologies, geometric approximations, primarily the MBR, are used as a first step to filter possible matches. Then, a refinement step examines the actual complex spatial objects to determine the final result set. However, in a geographic digital library environment, the end-user is the refinement step. For this reason, both high-quality approximations that limit the number of false matches and spatial ranking strategies that present best matches first are extremely important in GIR. We have shown that a logistic regression based spatial ranking algorithm can provide significant improvements for geographic information retrieval, even when the simplest regional approximations (MBRs) are used. We have also shown that taking into account the portion of offshore areas included in a geographic representation can improve GIR performance even further.

Acknowledgments

Work on geographic information retrieval was supported in part by the National Science Foundation and Joint Information Systems Committee(U.K) under the *International Digital Libraries Program* award #IIS-9975164. Addition support was provided by a grant from the Institute of Museum and Library Services (IMLS) entitled "Going Places in the Catalog".

References

1. H. Alani, C. B. Jones, and D. Tudhope. Voronoi-based region approximation for geographical information retrieval with gazetteers. *Internation Journal of Geographical Information Science*, 15(4):287–306, 2001.

2. R. Baeza-Yates and B. Ribeiro-Neto, editors. *Modern Information Retrieval*. Addison Wesley, New York, 1999.
3. K. Beard and V. Sharma. Multidimensional ranking for data in digital spatial libraries. *International Journal of Digital Libraries*, 1(2):153–160, 1997.
4. T. Brinkhoff, H. P. Kriegel, and R. Schneider. Comparison of approximations of complex objects used for approximation-based query processing in spatial database systems. In *Proceedings of 9th International Conference on Data Engineering*, 1993.
5. W. S. Cooper, F. C. Gey, and D. P. Dabney. Probabilistic retrieval based on staged logistic regression. In *15th Annual International ACM SIGIR Conference on Research and Development in Information Retrieval, Copenhagen, Denmark, June 21-24*, pages 198–210, New York, 1992. ACM.
6. Dublin Core Metadata Initiative. Dublin core metadata element set, version 1.1: Reference description, 2003-02-04.
   Available as: http://dublincore.org/documents/2003/02/04/dces/.
7. M. Egenhofer and R. Franzosa. Point-set topological spatial relations. *International Journal of Geographical Information Systems*, 5(2):161–174, 1991.
8. Federal Geographic Data Committee. Content standard for digital geospatial metadata,csdgm version 2 – fgdc-std-001-1998. Available as: http://www.fgdc.gov/standards/documents/standards/metadata/v2_0698.pdf.
9. M. Goodchild. Future directions in geographic information science. *Geographic Information Science*, 5(1):1–8, 1999.
10. L. L. Hill. *Access to Geographic Concepts in Online Bibliographic Files: effectiveness of current practices and the potential of a graphic interface*. PhD thesis, University of Pittsburgh, Pittsburgh, 1990.
11. L. L. Hill. Core elements of digital gazetteers: placenames, categories, and footprints. In J. Borbinha and T. Baker, editors, *Research and Advanced Technology for Digital Libraries : Proceedings of the 4th European Conference, ECDL 2000 (Lisbon, Portugal, September 18-20, 2000)*, pages 280–290, Berlin, 2000. Springer.
12. C. B. Jones, H. Alani, and D. Tudhope. *Geographical Terminology Servers – Closing the Semantic Divide*, chapter 11, pages 205–222. Taylor and Francis, London, 2003.
13. R. R. Larson. Geographic information retrieval and spatial browsing. In L. Smith and M. Gluck, editors, *GIS and Libraries: Patrons, Maps and Spatial Information*, pages 81–124. University of Illinois at Urbana-Champaign, GSLIS, Urbana-Champaign, 1996.
14. M. E. Maron and J. L. Kuhns. On relevance, probabilistic indexing and information retrieval. *Journal of the ACM*, 7(3):216–244, 1960.
15. H. J. Miller and J. Han. *Geographic Data Mining and Knowledge Discovery: An Overview*. Taylor & Francis, New York, 2001.
16. D. D. Nebert. Z39.50 application profile for geospatial metadata or 'GEO', version 2.2, 27 may 2000. Available as:
   http://www.blueangeltech.com/Standards/GeoProfile/geo22.htm.
17. S. Openshaw. Geographical data mining: key design issues. In *GeoComputation'99*, 1999.
18. D. Papadias, Y. Theodoridis, T. Sellis, and M. Egenhofer. Topological relations in the world of minimum bounding rectangles: a study with r-trees. In *Proceedings of the ACM SIGMOD Conference, San Jose, California*, 1995.
19. D. Walker, I. Newman, D. Medyckyj-Scott, and C. Ruggles. A system for identifying datasets for gis users. *International Journal of Geographical Information Systems*, 6(6):511–527, 1992.

Evaluation of an Information System
in an Information Seeking Process

Lena Blomgren[1], Helena Vallo[2], and Katriina Byström[3,*]

[1] Stockholm Public Library, SE-113 80 Stockholm
[2] FOI – Swedish Defence Research Agency, SE-172 90 Stockholm
[3] The Swedish School of Library and Information Science, University College of Borås,
SE-501 90 Borås, Sweden,
katriina.bystrom@hb.se

Abstract. This paper presents a holistic evaluation of an operational information system that employs the Boolean search technique. An equal focus is laid
on both the system (system perspective) and its users (user perspective) in the
actual environment where the system and its users are functioning (contextuality). In addition to these research objectives, the study has a methodological objective to test an evaluation approach developed by Borlund [1] in a real life
setting. Our evaluation methodology involves triangulation (pre-search questionnaires; search log; post-interviewing) as well as novel interactive performance measures, such as the Ranked Half-Life measure and the Satisfaction and
Novelty perception by users supplementing the traditional Precision. The study
confirms the finding of earlier research and reveals the discrepancy between the
evaluation results according to the system and the user perspectives. More specifically, the system performed better when evaluated from the user perspective
than from the system perspective.

1 Introduction

The evaluation of information systems has traditionally been conducted in laboratory
settings, and focused on the objective performance of information systems. Classical
information retrieval research aims at developing more advanced and exact algorithms for retrieval purposes. However, it does not focus on the evaluation of the
systems from a user perspective. This has been compensated during recent years by
more user-oriented information retrieval studies, but these suffer unfortunately from
the lack of standardised tools for analysis. Findings are thus seldom possible to gener-
alise and difficult to compare. In the light of these difficulties, the evaluation of information systems outside laboratory settings is therefore a necessary challenge to
meet.

This paper presents an experimental study that aims to conduct a holistic evaluation of an operational information system. By holistic evaluation we mean that an
equal focus is laid on both the system (system perspective) as well as its users (user
perspective) in the actual environment where the system and its users are functioning
(contextuality). We report the research findings on the use, the efficiency and the
effectiveness of the information system. First, an information system for newspaper

---

* Corresponding Author.

R. Heery and L. Lyon (Eds.): ECDL 2004, LNCS 3232, pp. 57–68, 2004.
© Springer-Verlag Berlin Heidelberg 2004

articles was tested by comparing algorithmic relevance judgements [2, 3] with situational relevance judgements [4, 3] by a journalist performing a journalistic task. Second, the system was evaluated as a resource among other available information sources. In addition to these research objectives the study had a methodological objective to test a new research approach, which was originally developed in an experimental setting [1], in a real life environment. The paper begins with a presentation of the theoretical framework and related research findings. The research methods and data are then described. This is followed by an analysis of the results. The paper concludes with a discussion of the findings.

2   Information Retrieval for Work Task Completion

In the present study we aim to evaluate an operational information retrieval system from a holistic perspective. The focus is on three dimensions. First, we consider the effectiveness of the system in responding to the search query (system perspective). Second, we consider the usefulness of the search results for the information need (user perspective). Third, we also consider the role of the system among other available information resources (contextuality).

This paper addresses the following research questions: What role does the IR system play for its users, as a resource among other available information sources? How well do the relevance assessments of the IR system (algorithmic relevance) correspond with those of the users (situational relevance)? And: Is the evaluation method applied well suited for evaluations of operational IR systems in real-life settings?

This research setting uses the cognitive model of the IR interaction by Ingwersen [5, 6] as a starting point. He suggests that research on information retrieval needs to acknowledge the context (a work task or an interest as well as the social environment). In addition to the "cognitive context" - or as a specific result of it [7], the actual resources available are likely to affect the perceived usefulness of an information system. We argue that real-life information retrieval is an integrated part of information seeking in general and that both of these processes are seldom separable from the overall situation where the information is sought and used [8]. In the present study, we consider information retrieval in the context of work task performance conducted among other information seeking activities in order to accomplish the task at hand.

In order to combine a system perspective and a user perspective, we have chosen to base the evaluation on algorithmic relevance and situational relevance [2, 3]. Algorithmic relevance is an objective relevance criterion that is determined through the match between a query and the document (used here in a broad meaning: carrier of information) representation. These relevance judgements are stable in the sense that as long as the query does not vary, neither do the relevance values of the documents. This is a common method for ranking search results in information systems. The situational relevance criteria depend on the situation where information is used [3, 9, 10, 11, 19]. This means that the same document, even as a result of the same query, may have different relevance values depending of the user and the task process. Relevance is determined according to the task performer's perception of the usefulness of the document for his/her work task. As algorithmic relevance focuses on the matching of the query and the document (mathematical relevance measurement), situational relevance focuses on the match between the perceived information need and the perceived value of the document content (intellectual relevance measurement).

To increase the holistic nature of the present evaluation, the system was evaluated as an resource among other available sources. To our knowledge, this is an evaluation aspect that is neglected in IR studies, where information systems are evaluated as the only source of information. Since operational information systems are functioning in environments where there are several different kinds of information sources available, it is important to recognise that the usefulness of an information system is determined in relation to the other available information sources in real-life environments. This is an important consideration, since research has shown that people look for different types of sources [12]. Similarly, people match communication channels with the type of communication matter. [13] Therefore, it is likely that the tack performer is not asking the information system to cover all of the information needed for the work task completion but certain parts of it [8].

3   Research Method and Data

The research method used in this study is inspired by Borlund's [1] approach to the evaluation of (interactive) information (retrieval) systems, the IIR evaluation package, which was created as an alternative to the traditional, system-oriented approach. The main advantages of her approach are that it combines the system perspective with a user perspective, and that it ensures both realism and control. It also proposes alternative performance measures, which allow non-binary relevance assessments.

The IIR evaluation package contains three components that focus on (1) an appropriate research setting, (2) empirical recommendations for simulation and (3) alternative relevance measures. In order to fulfil the conditions for an appropriate research setting, the participants need to be potential users with both individual, (potentially) dynamic information needs and relevance judgements (based on an authentic or simulated situation). Borlund [1] provides several empirical recommendations. She suggests that both an information need from a simulated situation and from an authentic situation ought to be studied. Furthermore, the simulated situation needs to be tailored for the test persons (easily identifiable, interesting, relevant and sufficiently informative). The order of the simulated and authentic situation ought to be varied in order to avoid (possible) learning effects. Finally, she recommends a pilot test. For alternative relevance measures, the measure of RR (Relative Relevance) and the RHL (Ranked Half-Life) are proposed.

3.1   Setting

The participants of the study were newspaper journalists who at the time were employed at the second largest newspaper in Scandinavia; Göteborgs-Posten (GP). Twenty out of a total of 280 journalists were selected. They represent different genders, ages and several different editorial departments. The information system, NewsLink, is a manually indexed full-text database containing all articles published in GP since 1994 and a selection of articles from 1992-93. The system employs the Boolean search technique and offers a choice between showing the retrieved result ranked by date or relevance.

3.2 Data Collection

The setting of our study corresponds to Borlund's approach by involving real users as test persons and by using both simulated and real work task situations as a trigger for information search. A simulated work task situation is a short "cover story" to frame the information search, which is common for all participants. This ensures experimental control across the tested system and across the participants in the study. The setting allowed the collection of both traditional system-oriented data on system performance and user-oriented data on the behaviour and perceptions of the participants. Borlund [1] used four simulated work task situations and one personal situation per participant in her study. Since our participants were real users with pressuring time constraints, we decided to settle with one of each. We used the following simulated work task situation:

> The Terror Attacks in USA September 11th
> Some time has passed since the terror attacks in USA. GP is now planning a follow-up and a summarizing series of articles on the subject, which will illustrate how different areas have been affected and the long term consequences. You have been asked to write an article that will illustrate this issue from your particular subject field.

The data collection methods used were: (1) questionnaires on the demographics and searching experience of the participants in the study; (2) search protocols (combined with observation) designed for the purpose of collecting information on the participants' original and modified query formulations, their non-binary relevance assessments (based either on title or full-text) as well as the algorithmic rank order, by date and relevance respectively, and information about whether or not a document was known to the user; (3) a post-search interview considering the practical use of the system, and its role for the users as a resource among other available information sources. It was also a way to gain additional information about the participants' relevance assessments and level of satisfaction. During the course of our study, we found a discrepancy between the editorial departments in the usage of NewsLink. Because of this, we gathered complementary information by means of a web form directed to all journalists at GP. The information we requested focused on their main information sources as well as how often and for what purposes they use NewsLink. Both the questionnaires, the interview and the web form included questions on the users' information behaviour in a broader sense, which were not included in Borlund's study. This aspect was added to enable a holistic evaluation of the system and its users.

3.3 Analysis

The performance measures used in the analysis were RHL (Ranked Half-life), Precision, Satisfaction and Novelty. As opposed to Borlund (2000), we did not use the RR measure, partly due to technical obstacles and partly to reduce the demands on the participants' time and effort. As a consequence of this no expert panel was used. We concluded that the RHL measure provides sufficient data. The Satisfaction [14] and Novelty [15] measures were added, as we anticipated these to be noteworthy factors affecting the users' relevance judgements.

Precision was calculated at DCV (Document Cut off Value) 15, which is common in IR evaluations. It measures the number of relevant articles the system retrieves and places among the top 15 documents. Precision was calculated on the respondents' situational relevance assessments made on a non-binary scale. Precision may therefore be more correctly called perceived precision.

RHL was used as a complement to (perceived) precision. It shows the ability of the system to place relevant documents high in the ranked list of retrieved documents, that is, its capability of ranking its output according to the end users' situational relevance assessments. The RHL measure is based on the common formula for the median of grouped continuous data [1, 16]. The RHL value is the median case of the continuous data. Each document in the algorithmically ranked list represents a class of grouped data where the frequency equals the assigned relevance value. The lower the RHL value, the higher the relevant documents are placed in the ranked output, i.e. the better the retrieval engine [1].

$$RHL = L_m + \left(\frac{n/2 - \sum f2}{F(med)} \times CI \right)$$ (1)

L_m: Lower real limit of the median class, i.e. the rank position of the lowest positioned information objects above the median class

n: Number of observations, i.e. the total sum of the assigned relevance values

$f2$:   Cumulative frequency (relevance values) up to and including the class preceding the median class

$F(med)$:   The frequency (relevance value) of the median class

CI: Class interval, commonly in IR = 1[1]

In order to make the RHL value more comparable, it can be recalculated into an RHL index value. This is done by normalising it against a predefined Precision value (Precision = 1). This Precision value is divided by the calculated Precision value. The quotient is then multiplied by the calculated RHL value, thus resulting in the RHL index value [1]. Below is the formula for calculating the RHL index, where the predefined Precision value is equal to 1.

$$= - \times$$ (2)

P: Calculated Precision value
R: Calculated RHL value

Table 1 shows an example from one of the searches made by a participant in our study. Below the table are calculations on the RHL and RHL index, to facilitate the understanding of them. The values in the columns for Ranking by Date and Relevance

[1] The highest relevance value (upper real limit) 1 minus the lowest (lower real limit) 0 = 1.

Table 1. Values for relevance assessments made in ranking by date and algorithmic relevance

Ranking by Date	User's assessment		Ranking by Relevance	User's assessment	
1	1	(1)	1	0	(0)
2	1	(2)	2	1	(1)
3	1	(3)	3	1	(2)
4	0.5	(3,5)	4	1	(3)
5	1	(**4,5**)	5	0	(3)
6	1	(5,5)	6	0	(3)
7	1		7	1	(4)
8	0.5		8	0	(4)
9	0		9	1	(5)
10	1		10	1	
11	1		11	1	
12	1		12	0	
13	0		13	1	
14	0		14	1	
15	0		15	1	
Sum	10	10/2= **5**	Sum	10	10/2= **5**
Precision	**0.67**		Precision	**0.67**	
RHL	**5.5**		RHL	**9**	
RHL index	8.21		RHL index	13.43	

represent the non-binary relevance assessments made by the respondent; *not relevant* = 0, *partly relevant* = 0,5, *very relevant* = 1. The figures used in the calculations are stressed in bold.

$$RHL = 5 + \left(\frac{5-4,5}{1} \times 1 \right) = 5,5 \qquad RHL = 8 + \left(\frac{5-4}{1} \times 1 \right) = 9$$

$$RHL\,index = \left(\frac{1}{0,67} \times 5,5 \right) = 8,21 \qquad RHL\,index = \left(\frac{1}{0,67} \times 9 \right) = 13,43$$

(3)

This example shows how RHL can distinguish between the results even if the Precision values are exactly the same. In the ranking made by date, half of the Precision value is obtained by going through just over five documents, while nine documents are scrutinised in ranking by algorithmic relevance. The RHL index value makes the results comparable by normalising the RHL values to Precision = 1.

Novelty [15] was calculated and used in combination with the interview questions on the same topic, to give an idea of whether the situational relevance assessments were effected by the document being previously known by the user. Satisfaction [14] is a measure of the level of satisfaction the respondents feel after completing their search task.

4   Results

The results focus on the comparability of the relevance judgements assessed by the system and by the users. The aim was to determine how well the system serves the end users attending their work tasks. The results also focus on the estimated value of the system as an information source among other available sources, both in general and in relation to the task at hand.

We placed our respondents in categories based on editorial departments, gender and age to facilitate comparisons concerning the usage of NewsLink. As we found no discrepancies in the gender age categories, we present the editorial categories: Feature group – editorial departments writing longer reports (six respondents); Specialists' group – editorial departments with a more specific direction (five respondents); and Local news group – editorial departments writing about domestic and local matters (nine respondents). 63 journalists of the total of 280 filled in the web form. Their answers correspond with our findings from the rest of the study.

4.1   The Role of the System Among Other Information Sources Available

The overall most important information sources are oral sources and the Internet. NewsLink and other media are also among the top sources. Oral sources and the Internet are generally used daily, while NewsLink is used on a weekly basis. There are some differences between the editorial categories. The Local news group uses NewsLink most of all, stating that they use the system either daily or weekly. None of the respondents in either feature group or in the specialists' group use NewsLink daily.

Our findings show that NewsLink is an important information source but is often used in combination with other sources. NewsLink is mainly used for checking what has been written in GP, for finding specific information and avoiding duplicate articles.

The majority of the participants considered themselves as knowledgeable about the system. When it comes to search functions, they all stated they have a good grasp of free text search, while more than half of them stated that they need more education in truncation and Boolean search logic. Our data did at the same time reveal a need for end user education. For example, the respondents required already existing functions that they were not aware of.

4.2   The Relevance Assessments by the System and Its Users

The results for both the Precision and RHL index show that the system performs best on the real work tasks, as seen in tables 2 and 3.

Table 2. Measures of central tendency and measures of variation for Precision at DCV 15

Precision DCV 15	Simulated work task		Real work task	
	Date	Relevance	Date	Relevance
Mean	0.25	0.27	0.3	0.38
Standard deviation	0.156	0.146	0.123	0.162
Median	0.21	0.28	0.33	0.38

Table 2 shows the average Precision values at DCV 15. The median and the mean do not differ much. As all mean values for Precision are below 0.5 (the optimal being

1.0), the system is not especially efficient. The standard deviation shows that the values are relatively coherent. The results were somewhat better for the respondents' real work task, with values generally between 0.18–0.42 as ranked by date and 0.22–0.54 as ranked by algorithmic relevance. For the simulated work task the Precision values for ranking by date were normally between 0.09–0.41, and ranking by algorithmic relevance had values between 0.12–0.42. Only as ranked by relevance for the real work task, we found values over 0.42.

Table 3. Measures of central tendency and measures of variation for RHL index at DCV 15

RHL index DCV 15	Simulated work task		Real work task	
	Date	Relevance	Date	Relevance
Mean	26.14	19.29	15.29	15.59
Standard deviation	15.951	12.761	9.360	9.306
Median	25.17	18.27	13.3	11.6

Table 3 shows some differences between mean and median, especially for the real work task (as ranked by relevance). This is also visible in the relatively widespread values. For the simulated work task, it was necessary to go to places 10.19 to 42.09 to find enough relevant documents as they were ranked by date, while when ranking by algorithmic relevance they were found at places 6.53 to 32.05. The corresponding values for the real work task was 5.93–24.65 as ranked by date and 6.28–24.9 as ranked by algorithmic relevance.

The results from the precision and RHL index show that the system generally performs better in relation to real work tasks than for simulated work tasks. One explanation might be that the participants are familiar with the requests of the work task and more motivated to obtain useful results [8]. As for the simulated work task, the width of the topic made it applicable to all the different editorial departments, but it may also have made relevance assessments more perfunctory. The topic was somewhat difficult to place in time, which may have favoured the ranking by relevance.

Table 4. Value of Satisfaction for the editorial categories respectively, with reference both to the real and the simulated information need

	Feature group		Specialists' group		Domestic group		Total	
	Real	Sim.	Real	Sim.	Real	Sim.	Real	Sim.
Yes	6	4	4	1	6	2	16	7
In part	0	0	0	2	0	2	0	4
No	0	2	1	2	3	5	4	9
Total	6	6	5	5	9	9	20	20

Our results for Novelty and the post-search interview show that the relevance assessments are usually affected by whether or not a document is new to the user depending on the work task at hand. As for Satisfaction (see table 4), there is a significant difference between the editorial categories. In the Feature group, a majority of the respondents were satisfied with their search results for both work tasks, while in the other categories a majority were only satisfied with the real work task.

5   Discussion

5.1   Conclusions of the System Evaluation

The effectiveness of the system in responding to the search query was measured using the Precision and RHL index. Our results show that NewsLink often performs poorly on relevance values for the documents. On the other hand, we found the system to be effective from a user perspective, as shown by the results for Satisfaction. Findings from earlier research indicate that relevance ranking by system and by users often do not correspond [17, 18]. This is an important aspect of system evaluation from a user perspective and especially interesting since the evaluated system is manually maintained, thus requiring higher maintenance costs.

Our results revealed a discrepancy between the results for the system-oriented and the user-oriented measures. Some of the respondents retrieved only one document, but this was the one relevant document required, while others wanted to make sure that there were no earlier articles on the subject in GP, (i.e. for them no retrieved relevant documents was optimal). Both examples resulted in high satisfaction but very poor Precision and RHL-index values. In addition, the involvement of real end users led to dynamic information needs (cf. [11, 19]) also affecting the values for Precision and RHL. The Novelty measure shows that as the respondents retrieved two or more documents about the same subject, only the first one was judged relevant (cf. [20]). Measures of effectiveness, such as Precision and RHL index, judges such documents equally relevant.

Our findings show that although NewsLink is important for the journalists in their daily work, it does not function as their only or primary information source. A majority of the respondents stated oral sources as being the most useful, turning to NewsLink mainly for background material. There was a strong correlation between the journalistic task at hand and the use and role of the system. The Local news group uses NewsLink most and, contrary to the other groups, value oral sources more than the Internet. Also in this respect our findings correspond to other studies on journalists' seeking behaviour (cf. [21]).

It is of major importance that the system is well suited to its (potential) users. Otherwise, it may as well be useless, no matter how well it performs according to effectiveness. The system evaluated in this study, NewsLink, seems to be adapted for the journalists working at Göteborgs-Posten. The system is experienced as effective from the users' point of view and judged as an important information source among others. Our general conclusion is that the study reported here highlights how difficult an evaluation of an operational IR system is. Our results for Satisfaction and Novelty confirm how important it is to consider qualitative measures as well as quantitative performance measures such as Precision, especially when it comes to evaluations in real life settings. Even when NewsLink was performing poorly, its real users were satisfied with it. Whether the reason for this is that the users had become used to the system or that the system is performing "well enough" or something else, it is still clear that knowing the users and their context is a key factor in successful system design.

5.2 Conclusions of the Method Evaluation

The methodological objective of the study was to test Borlund's "IIR evaluation package" in a real life setting. We found that the simulated work task situation functioned well in many respects. It did not control the participants in detail. Less than a third of the words used in the queries were directly from the description of the simulated work task situation. They used "terror" in different combinations and "September". However, we became aware that composing a simulated work task situation that offers a sufficient level of reality for all participants, must be done with great care. Moreover, the importance of using at least one real work task cannot be overvalued. The familiarity of the task requirements and a higher motivation lead to better values for Precision, RHL index and Satisfaction than they did in relation to simulated work tasks.

The performance measures we used were chosen because they consider both the system and its users. We found our results for RHL and Precision to be very similar. The reason for this is that both measures are depending on the values of the relevance assessments. In spite of this, they both provide complementary information. Our example (3) shows that the RHL measure can indicate which system is most effective even where the Precision values are identical. When only the top fifteen documents are taken into consideration, the difference in effectiveness will be marginal, but when it comes to larger amounts of documents, the placing of relevant documents may be of great importance. Precision is a measure of the proportion of retrieved documents that are relevant, but it reveals nothing of where the relevant documents can be found. This is highly relevant for the users though, as they seldom are interested enough to look through large amounts of documents. Since the RHL-indicator may be somewhat misleading it ought to be normalised into an RHL index value to produce more easily interpreted and comparable results.

Applying a holistic approach to IR evaluation has major advantages. Several factors in our study prove the importance of involving the real users of the system. Respondents were satisfied with their search results despite poor results according to the effectiveness measures, mainly because the documents, instead of being judged in isolation, were valued in an authentic search situation. This points to the fact that using Precision and other system oriented measures in this kind of evaluation is debatable. Journalists need few but highly relevant documents placed in top positions in the ranked list, thus enabling swift access to them. Since they constantly work under time pressure it is difficult, if not impossible for them to look through huge amounts of documents. These working conditions are now becoming increasingly common within several professions, which means that evaluations in general should include the users of the system and user-oriented measures as a complement to the system-oriented ones.

We were also able to determine the type of information that was retrieved from the system. These kinds of results are novel in evaluation context, but nonetheless very important for making a correct evaluation of an information system. If the users deliberately use different sources for different kinds of information as indicated by findings of Byström [12], the system may still be highly satisfactory to its users even if it only provides them with certain kinds of information. Calculating Precision from dynamic situational relevance assessments made on a non-binary scale improves the significance of the measure, but Precision values can not tell whether or not the users are satisfied and have achieved work task fulfilment. Combining both user- and system-oriented measures and adding post search interviews, enables a fuller and more accurate picture of the system, its users and context.

To sum up, we mean that the evaluation method used in this study is well suited for evaluations of operational systems, covering system, user and context. It aims to provide an overall view of how well the system suits its users and the system's role among other available information sources. The approach as such has functioned well and provided a solid methodological base. The measures used have yielded valuable information about the system from a users' point of view. These different measures functioned well and generated different types of information to complete each other. We look forward to developing and testing the methodology in additional studies.

References

1. Borlund, P. (2000). Evaluation of interactive information retrieval systems. Åbo: Åbo Akademi University Press.
2. Cooper, W.S. (1971). A definition of relevance for information retrieval. Information Storage and Retrieval, 7(1), 19-37.
3. Saracevic, T. (1996). Relevance reconsidered '96. In: Ingwersen, P. & Pors, N.O., eds. *Information Science: Integration in Perspective. (CoLIS2)*. Copenhagen: Royal School of Librarianship, 1996, pp. 201-218.
4. Wilson, P. (1973). Situational relevance. *Information Storage and Retrieval*, 9, 457-469.
5. Ingwersen, P. (1996). Cognitive perspectives of information retrieval interaction: elements of a cognitive IR theory. Journal of Documentation, 52(1), 3-50.
6. Ingwersen, P. (2001). Users in Context. In: Agosti & Crestani & Pasi (eds.) *Lectures on Information Retrieval*. Bonn: Springer Verlag, 157-178.
7. Taylor, R.S. (1991). Information use environments. In: Dervin, B. & Voigt, M. (Eds.) *Progress in communication sciences*, pp. 217-255. Norwood, NJ: Ablex.
8. Byström, K. & Hansen, P. (2002) Work tasks as units for analysis in information seeking and retrieval studies. In (eds.) Bruce, H., Fidel, R., Ingwersen, P. & Vakkari, P. Emerging Frameworks and Methods. Libraries Unlimited: Greenwood Village, CO. pp. 239-251.
9. Mizzaro, S. (1998). How many relevances in information retrieval? *Interacting with Computers*, 10, 303-320.
10. Reid, J. (2000). A task-oriented non-interactive evaluation methodology for information retrieval systems. *Information Retrieval*, 2(1), 113-127.
11. Schamber, L. (1994). Relevance and information behavior. In Williams, Martha 0E., ed. *Annual Review of Information Science and Technology (ARIST)*, vol. 29, pp. 3-48.
12. Byström, K. (2002). Information and information sources in tasks of varying complexity. Journal of American Society of Information Science and Technology, 53(7), 581-591.
13. Webster, J. & Trevino, L.K. (1995). Rational and social theories as complementary explanations of communication media choices: Two policy-capturing studies. *Academy of Management Journal*, 38(6), 1544-1572.
14. Harter, S. & Hert, C (1997). Evaluation of Information Retrieval Systems: Approaches, Issues, and Method. Ingår i Williams, Martha E., ed. *Annual Review of Information Science and Technology (ARIST)*, vol. 32, pp. 3-94.
15. Baeza-Yates, R. & Ribeiro-Neto, B. (1999). Modern Information Retrieval. Addison-Wesley.
16. Stephen, P. & Hornby, S. (1997) Simple statistics: for library and information professionals. 2nd edition. London: Library Association Publishing.
17. Kekäläinen & Järvelin (2002). Evaluating Information Retrieval Systems under the Challenges of Interaction and Multi-Dimensional Dynamic Relevance. Ingår i Bruce, Harry, Fidel, Raya, Ingwersen, Peter & Vakkari, Pertti, eds. Proceedings of the 4 th CoLIS Conference. Greenwood Village, CO: Libraries Unlimited. s. 253-270.

18. Robertson & Hancock-Beaulieu (1992). On the Evaluation of IR Systems. Information Processing and Management, vol. 28, nr 4 s. 457-466.
19. Schamber, L., Eisenberg, M. & Nilan, M. (1990). A re-examination of relevance: Toward a dynamic, situational definition. Information Processing & Management, vol. 26, nr 6 pp. 755-776.
20. Vakkari, P. (2001). A Theory of the Task-based Information Retrieval Process. Journal of Documentation, vol. 57, nr 1, s. 44-60.
21. Nicholas, D. & Martin, H. (1993). Should journalists search themselves? (And what happens when they do?). In Raitt, David I. & Jeapes, Ben, eds. Online information 93 : 17th International Online Information Meeting, London 7-9 december 1993 : proceedings. Oxford : Learned Information. pp. 227-234.

Fiction Electronic Books: A Usability Study

Chrysanthi Malama, Monica Landoni, and Ruth Wilson

Dept. of Computer and Information Sciences
University of Strathclyde
UK G1 1XH
monica.landoni@cis.strath.ac.uk

Abstract. This paper focuses on fiction electronic books and their usability. Two complementary studies were drawn together in order to investigate whether fiction e-books can successfully become part of people's reading habits: the Visual Book project, which found that electronic texts which closely resemble their paper counterparts in terms of visual components such as size, quality and design were received positively by users, and the EBONI Project which aimed to define a set of best practice guidelines for designing electronic textbooks. It was found that the general guidelines for the design of textbooks on the Internet that have been proposed by the EBONI project can also be applied to the design of fiction e-books. Finally, in terms of the electronic production of fiction e-books, this study suggests that concentrating on the appearance of text, rather than the technology itself, can lead to better quality publications to rival the print version of fiction books.

1 Introduction

This paper describes a study into the usability of fiction e-books while verifying the applicability/portability of some of the findings reported on educational e-books across literature genres.

The study is based on two relevant projects:

- The Visual Book project [1], which investigated how to produce better quality electronic publications by focusing on the impact of appearance of information, and
- The EBONI project [2], which investigated the importance of considering the user in the design of electronic books.

Both studies focused on educational material, with the Visual Book restricted to scientific texts and EBONI considering e-textbooks across disciplines in higher education. Previous work suggests that consulting an e-book for study or reference is a very different experience to reading for pleasure, in which the process is much closer to that of reading a paper book [3]. This paper reports on an experiment devised at studying whether principles for designing the visual components of electronic textbooks can be transported into the fiction genre. Will a fiction e-book presented in accordance with EBONI's design guidelines increase user satisfaction and usability?

R. Heery and L. Lyon (Eds.): ECDL 2004, LNCS 3232, pp. 69–79, 2004.

1.1   The Fiction e-Books

In order to determine whether the EBONI project's guidelines can further the purposes of the Visual Book project, a fiction e-book in three different formats was considered: *The Adventures of Gerard,* by Sir Arthur Conan Doyle.

The three versions of the specific electronic book were chosen in terms of format, functionality and availability. The book is available free on the Internet, and users are allowed to include it in personal Web sites.

The three versions of the e-book were evaluated with respect to usability and subjective satisfaction issues:

- Scrolling Book
- Portable Book with software applications (Adobe Ebook Reader$_R$ PDF)
- Portable Book with software applications (Microsoft Reader)

The purpose was to determine whether the PDF and the MSReader versions of the text, that share many of the characteristics of EBONI's guidelines for designing e-books, would perform better than the "Scrolling" version of the fiction e-book.

The aims of this study, therefore, were:

- To study whether the presentation of a fiction book in electronic format that shares the EBONI project's guidelines in terms of visual components (such as size, quality and design) increases satisfaction and usability.
- To compare the results of this study with the results of the EBONI project which focused on the design of learning and teaching material on the Internet.

Note that it was not within the scope of this study to examine ebook hardware (portable ebook) issues. These were previously investigated by EBONI and the findings have been reported [4, 5].

1.2   The Visual Book and the Web Book Experiments

The Visual Book experiment, conducted between 1993 and 1997, was part of a more general project called *SuperLibrary* and highlighted the importance of appearance in the design of electronic textbooks [1].

The Visual Book project started from the observation that,

> the appearance of information contributes positively to its overall value and that because there is an almost infinite number of possible ways to represent various kinds of information, it is very important to find the one which is going to be the most effective and which conveys as much of the value of the original information [1].

The idea was that, because people know how to read books and use tables of contents and indexes, maintaining the same model on screen would facilitate access to electronic information. The experiment concluded that the book metaphor is an important aspect in defining guidelines for the design of electronic books.

In general, the results of the evaluation of the Visual Book, which were supported by the findings of a similar project, the Hyper-Book [6], showed that the book metaphor was both accepted and understood by its evaluators. Furthermore, the results highlighted the need for a new role in electronic publishing: "the designer of electronic books, as the person in charge of final appearance" [7].

The Web Book project investigated this issue with respect to the production of books on the Web" [7]. Despite the fact that the experiment was conducted on a small scale, the results indicated that making texts on the Web more scannable (according to Morkes and Nielsen's Guidelines [8]) has a positive effect on their usability.

1.3 EBONI Project

EBONI built on the work of the Visual Book and the Web Book. The aim of the project was to compile a set of guidelines for the publication of electronic textbooks, reflecting the usability requirements of the UK higher education community [9].

The following were among the evaluations which applied a specific methodology developed for EBONI [2]:

- An evaluation of three textbooks in psychology, all of which had been published on the Internet by their authors. The three textbooks were evaluated by second, third and fourth year psychology undergraduates in UK higher education.
- An evaluation of *Hypertext in Context* by McKnight et al [10]. The textbook was compared in three formats: print, the original electronic version on the Web, and a second electronic version revised according to Morkes and Nielsen's guidelines for "scannability" [8].
- A comparison of three electronic encyclopedias: *Encyclopedia Britannica, The Columbia Encyclopedia,* and *Encarta.*
- A comparison of a title in geography by second year geography undergraduates that is available in three electronic formats: MobiPocket Reader, Adobe Acrobat Ebook Reader, and Microsoft Reader.
- A study into usability issues surrounding portable electronic books. Lecturers and researchers at the University of Strathclyde evaluated five devices in order to determine which elements enhance and which detract from the experience of reading an electronic book.

The results of these studies were then re-elaborated to form a set of Electronic Textbook Design Guidelines (http://ebooks.strath.ac.uk/eboni/guidelines/).

2 Methodology

In order to be able to compare results of the fiction e-book study with a previous corpus of findings, the evaluation methodology developed by the EBONI project [2] was adhered to as closely as possible, and the content of the questionnaires used in this study was replicated with few adjustments.

Since this research involved a fiction book, rather than the textbooks used in the EBONI experiments, a number of differences in procedure were observed.

First of all, the specific nature of fiction made completing a series of tasks while reading a book impractical, and participants were left to decide how they would explore the book – whether they would simply choose to read a chapter, browse through it, or even read all the chapters. Participants had only to complete three questionnaires (one for every version of the book) after reading the book, so that their responses were informed and based on experience.

Further, several of the items in the questionnaire used in the EBONI experiments were omitted due to their inapplicability in assessing the usability of a fiction electronic book. For example, the words "concise", "frustrating", "interesting", "likeable", and "useful" were removed and replaced with direct questions such as: "Was the text easy to read?", "Was the book easy to navigate?", "How frustrated did you feel by the appearance of the book?", and "What did you like or dislike about reading the specific version of the e-book?"

2.1 Participants

Twenty-five subjects comprising respondents to emails sent to the wider public, and to lecturers and Postgraduate students in Computer and Information Science at Strathclyde University participated in this experiment. A level of Internet experience was assumed, because participants were contacted by email and the experiment, which involved reading a book and filling out a form, was conducted entirely on the web.

2.2 Selection of Material

The text selected for use in the study was *The Adventures of Gerard* by Sir Arthur Conan Doyle. This was chosen not only because it was one of the limited titles available in the desired three versions (Scrolling Book, PDF format, and MS Reader), but also because it was thought that the story would provide enough interest to ensure that participants would enjoy reading it. Three versions of the text were used in the study:

Scrolling Book: Provided by Project Gutenberg (http://gutenberg.net/index.html), the book is very simple in format and is presented according to a scroll metaphor. The first part of the text includes information about Project Gutenberg and copyright issues. The main part of the text contains the book by Sir Arthur Conan Doyle. The e-book is not divided into pages and the text scrolls almost without any physical limitation. The information is presented according to a book style hierarchy, made of chapters, subchapters, paragraphs and sections, but everything is displayed on the same page.

The next two versions are software applications, also known as e-book readers. These provide extra functionalities such as annotations, bookmarks, different fonts and colors to help users in their reading/scanning process.

Adobe Ebook Reader: This version of the book was provided by Nalanda Digital Library in India (http://www.nalanda.nitc.ac.in/index.html). It has the typical PDF format and provides a series of functionalities to the reader such as bookmarks, thumbnails, and the ability to change fonts and size. The text has the physical look of a book, with a single numbered page appearing on the screen at any time. More specifically, some of the functionalities that it offers are as follows:

- *Adjust size*: allows readers to adjust the size of the book (actual size, fit in window, or fit width).
- *Bookmarks*: readers can mark the last part of the book that was visited and return to it later.
- *Find*: helps readers to search for words or phrases quickly and easily.

- *Go to previous/next view:* takes readers to the part of the book that was visited previously.
- *Graphics/text select tool:* allows readers to select and process specific parts of the text.
- *Move first/previous page:* readers can navigate through the pages themselves.
- *Print:* readers can download and print the e-book.
- *Rotate text:* allows readers to change the orientation of the text on the screen.
- *Thumbnails:* allows readers to view all pages of the book on the left side of the screen.
- *Zoom in/out tool:* readers can use this facility to get a close-up view of text and graphics.

MS Reader: The third version of the book was provided by the Virginia Digital Library (http://etext.lib.virginia.edu/ebooks/Plist.html) and can be read with Microsoft Reader. This is the most complicated version of the book and offers a plethora of functionalities. Some of these functionalities are described below:

- *Clear type:* improves the clarity of text on standard LCD screens, delivering a print-like display.
- *Navigation:* the "Riffle Control" allows readers to easily turn pages or skip to another page in the book using their keyboard or mouse.
- *Font size:* allows readers to increase or decrease font size from the settings page.
- *Find:* helps readers to search for words or phrases quickly and easily.
- *Pan and zoom graphics:* readers can use this facility to get a close-up view of graphics and pictures. After zooming in, they can pan around the graphic to take a closer look at any area.
- *Bookmarks:* always appear in the page margin and they are filled when readers are on the bookmarked page, otherwise only their outline is shown. Readers can also change the color of bookmarks to suit their preferences.
- *Library:* all the books and other content that readers acquire are stored in the library. Readers can organise items in their library to appear by title, author, last read, e-book size, or date acquired.
- *Notes:* readers can use their keyboard to add written comments to any page.
- *Drawings:* readers can choose from a wide range of colors to circle words, underline text, or add any other type of mark to a page.
- *Annotations:* personal annotations – highlights, bookmarks, notes, and drawings – are stored in one location and can be easily organised.
- *Highlights:* readers can call attention to a word or passage by highlighting it with a stroke of the mouse, as they would do with a highlighter in a paper book.
- *Dictionary:* allows readers to look up word meanings through the built-in Lookup functionality.

2.3 Procedure

Every stage of this experiment was carried out over the Internet. Emails inviting participation in the study were sent to the wider public, to students who had studied Information and Library Studies at Strathclyde University, and to lecturers in the Department of Computer and Information Sciences at the University. The emails explained briefly the purpose of the study, told potential respondents it would involve visiting a Web site, reading three versions of a fiction electronic book and answering some questions, and directed them towards a URL to begin the survey.

On visiting the URLs, participants were first asked to complete some details about themselves. They were asked about their age, gender and occupation and, to judge their degree of familiarity with fiction e-books, the questions:

1. Prior to this study, had you read a fiction e-book?
2. If you are not currently using fiction e-books is it because:
   - generally you have not considered them
   - you consider that they offer no advantages over print
   - you think that you would experience access problems
   - you think that they are difficult to use
   - you think that they are difficult to find

To minimise learning effects, participants were then asked to read the three versions of the book in any order. In the Subjective Satisfaction questionnaire participants were asked to describe how easy it was to learn to use the book, read through it, and navigate. The first part asked them about specific aspects of working with the book, while the second part asked them to rate a list of adjectives according to how well they describe it. Finally, respondents were asked to add any comments about the experience of reading a fiction book in an electronic format, and whether they would read fiction e-books in the future.

2.4 Measurement of Results

The subjective satisfaction index was the mean score of the following two indices:

- **Ease of use.** This part included four questions: "Compared to what you expected, how quickly did you learn to use the e-book?", "Was the text easy to read?", "Was the book easy to navigate?", and "How frustrated did you feel by the appearance of the book?"
- **Quality.** The first question consisted of four adjectives that described the book: annoying, engaging, helpful and unpleasant. The second question asked readers to rate the various functionalities offered by each version of the book on a scale from "very helpful" to "not very helpful".

To judge whether participants liked or disliked reading an e-book, they were asked to summarise their views by answering the following questions:

- What did you like about reading the specific version of the book?
- What did you dislike about reading the specific version of the book?

Finally, respondents were asked to respond with a simple "yes" or "no" to the following question: "Would you read a fiction e-book in the future?"

3 Results

Results are presented in terms of ease of use and quality in Table 1.

Table 1. Mean scores for the two major measures, on a scale from one to 10

	Ease of use	Quality
Scrolling Book	6.9	5.3
Adobe Ebook Reader	7.1	6.8
Microsoft Reader	5.8	5.8

Next, the overall subjective satisfaction score for each version of the fiction e-book was calculated, by adding the mean scores of the two measures (ease of use and quality). These results are presented in Table 2.

Table 2. Mean scores for the two major measures, and overall usability

	Ease of use	Quality	Overall Subjective Satisfaction
Scrolling Book	6.9	5.3	6.1
Adobe Ebook Reader	7.1	6.8	7
Microsoft Reader	5.8	5.8	5.8

3.1 Users' Comments

In accordance with the results of the questionnaire, users' comments about the Scrolling version of the book were generally negative, while comments about Adobe Ebook Reader and Microsoft Reader were more positive.

Users of the Scrolling version liked the fact that the book was easy to download without having to first of all install any special programs. One user noted that it was "fairly easy to access, and because it was plain text, it would be very easy to copy and paste sections". Overall, respondents were satisfied with the fact that the text was easy to download and quite simple in format. However, they elaborated more on their answers when they were asked to describe what they disliked.

A lack of user-friendliness was commented on twice, with one user complaining that he/she found it "very user-unfriendly because it was hard to work out where the book actually started – there was a lot of additional information at the beginning which I was not interested in reading" and another stating that, "Scrolling made it hard to read easily. The font and layout was also a bit unfriendly". One user described the book as "monotonous and quite confusing", and another stated that it was "not the most inspiring format, and having to scroll down through the whole document instead of jumping to a particular chapter was annoying". Another participant reported that, "the scrolling sometimes jumped more lines that I wanted so I had to go back to read the start of each paragraph". Two participants were dissatisfied with navigation: one reported "too much preamble at beginning. Not able to see how far you have got, i.e. pages read and pages to go", while another noted, "the typeface is unattractive and the page looked crowded. It felt as if you could easily get lost reading it (especially if you were a bit tired) because of the type of text - unclear layout".

Adobe Ebook Reader version elicited more positive responses. "Clear, well-spaced typeface, easy to resize and attractive to look at", wrote one participant, and another commented that the book was "colourful, interesting, easy to use and quick to navigate". One user reported that it was "much more attractive than the Scrolling version". Another stated, "It was like reading a book, unlike the scrolling version, you don't have to move your hand until you find the right page". A third user reported that it was "Much more user-friendly in comparison to the first version. Much more 'book-like' format/layout". Two participants liked the appearance of the book, with one user stating, "I liked the fact that it looked like a book. It was easy to read and you could make changes to its appearance", and another observing that "The design of the e-book actually looked like the pages of a real book, which made it much more pleasant to read".

Seven out of the 25 respondents commented that there was nothing they disliked in the Adobe Ebook version, with one user noting, "I don't think there was anything I didn't like. I am a great fan of .pdf files" and another reporting, "[I disliked] nothing, it was very pleasant to read". However, four participants commented on the fact that it takes a while to download the text. A couple of participants also complained about the highlight facility: "If you want to underline, that's not really possible with a PDF file". There were also few comments about the overall appearance of the book. One participant, although he/she liked the particular version, still did not like the representation of the book in an electronic format: "Did not dislike anything, but would still be unlikely to read it. Still prefer an actual physical book". "I disliked the fact that although it looked like a book it did not feel like one", wrote another user.

Users also made some positive remarks about Microsoft Reader. Six participants commented on navigation and the extra features offered by the Microsoft Reader; one wrote, "it was easier to navigate than the other two formats" and another noted, "I liked the format of the text and the extra features the MS-Reader offers". A couple of readers liked the fact that they could interact with the book, and one commented, "I liked everything about it. It looked and felt like a real book. I could not believe that you could draw inside the text, and that you could also make notes or highlight".

Even though the majority of participants liked the overall appearance of the text and the extra features, they were very critical when they had to add their own remarks on what they disliked about reading this version. A lack of good navigation features was commented on twice, with one user complaining about "lack of icons and not so good navigation features as the PDF". Several users had problems in downloading Microsoft Reader or even get the program to run. "I disliked the fact that I had to download a program", one participant wrote, while another reported, "Sorry, after downloading Microsoft Reader I downloaded the book 3 times but still could not get it to work – despite help menu: it seems very technical and difficult to use and I have given up on it for the time being". Also, eight participants reported that they would prefer not to have to download extra software in order to read the book: "[I disliked] having to download specific software. I think e-books will only increase in popularity when people can read them with absolutely no extra effort ... people tend to have a low patience threshold when it comes to computers!".

3.2 Analysis and Discussion

The purpose of this study was to explore whether the presentation of a fiction book in electronic format that adheres to the EBONI project's guidelines in terms of visual components (such as size, quality and design) increases users' satisfaction and overall usability of the text.

The results of the experiment have shown that users of Adobe Ebook Reader, which adheres closely to the guidelines, reported highest subjective satisfaction. In particular:

- Users of the Adobe Ebook Reader and Scrolling Book reported a higher score when it comes to **ease of use** of the site.
- Users of the Adobe Ebook Reader and Microsoft Reader reported a higher score when it comes to **quality** of the site.
- When combined into an overall satisfaction score, Adobe Ebook Reader has the highest score.

However, although Adobe Ebook Reader scored highly, Microsoft Reader was found to be more difficult to use than the Scrolling Book, despite also adhering to the design guidelines, and this requires further investigation. Participants' comments and their ratings of quality were positive, but they thought it quite difficult to use. On the contrary, the Scrolling version achieved a high score (6.9/10) for ease of use and, although it had the lowest score for quality, it still managed to perform better than Microsoft Reader in the overall subjective satisfaction score.

It is unlikely that users read the entire book in three different formats, and this may have affected scores. Users are already familiar with the scrolling metaphor and with PDF, but are less familiar with ebook software. When using the books for only a short time, it seems likely that this unfamiliarity with Microsoft Reader software may have had a negative impact on reported ease of use.

In terms of the electronic production of fiction books in general, this study provides an example of how concentrating on the appearance of text, rather than the technology itself, can lead to better quality publications to rival print versions.

Therefore, the general guidelines for the design of textbooks on the Internet as proposed by the EBONI project can also be applied to the design of fiction e-books. In both studies, analysis of the results has indicated that adherence to the book metaphor increases users' subjective satisfaction and overall usability of the book.

In particular, participants confirmed the importance of the following guidelines for the design of fiction e-books:

Tables of Contents. Tables of contents are an essential feature in both print and electronic media, used by readers to skim the contents of an unfamiliar book to gain an idea of what can be found inside. They also provide the reader with a sense of structure, which can easily be lost in the electronic medium, and can be an important navigation tool. In the words of one participant, "I liked that it looked like a usual book and the fact that I could find any chapter I wanted easily simply by using the table of contents".

Fonts. Fonts should be large enough to read comfortably for long periods of time. If possible, readers would like to choose a font style and size to suit their individual preferences, thereby satisfying the needs of those with perfect vision and those with low vision or reading difficulties. Fonts which include specific special characters such as italics should be used, and a colour that contrasts sufficiently with the background should be chosen. As one participant in the experiment noted, "change of font is a welcome facility".

Search Tool. Tables of contents offer access points for browsing. These can be supplemented by search tools which provide another method of finding information in an electronic text, and are appreciated by readers. A choice of simple searches (searching the whole book, a chapter, or a page for a keyword) should be offered to suit different levels or reader. As one participant noted, "I did not like the fact that I could not perform a search in the Scrolling version of the fiction book".

Navigation Icons. Participants strongly valued the fact that they could make use of a set of navigation buttons that enabled them to move forward and back in the book, skip chapters, and choose particular parts of the text. However, the function of any navigation icons should be explicit. As one participant noted, "the navigation menu was sometimes difficult to follow".

Bookmarks. Participants expressed a desire to have bookmarking facilities, which they would like to be straightforward and quick to use.

Highlight Facility. Participants also expressed a desire to have a highlight facility, which is not always provided in e-books. Readers appreciated the highlight facility available in the Microsoft Reader version of the book because it allowed a degree of interaction. In the words of one reader, "[I] liked the highlight and drawing facilities offered by the MS Reader – allowed you to interact with the book. Made it feel more real".

Participants also found it difficult and unpleasant to read long streams of text on screen. "Not the most inspiring format, and having to scroll down through the whole document instead of jumping to a particular chapter was annoying" one participant noted, while another one reported "I disliked the feeling that there were no pages and the continuous format was very tiring". These comments were provided for the Scrolling version of the book and it illustrates that it is important to divide the book into short chapters, with short pages, and short paragraphs.

Readers gain a sense of their place in a printed book via the page numbers and by comparing the thickness and weight of the pages read against the thickness and weight of the pages still to be read. Participants complained that they did not have this option while reading the Scrolling version of the book and one of them noted "Too much preamble at beginning. Not able to see how far you have got, i.e. pages read and pages to go".

Participants also expected the background of the book to be in colour. As was suggested in EBONI, colour makes the book more appealing and interesting. Readers in this experiment preferred to read the book by having more interesting colours in the background than grey and black.

4   Conclusions

The study described in this paper looked into a specific type of e-books, fiction e-books, and provides an indication of future steps which could be taken to make them easier and more enjoyable to read, and of course more suited to the needs of the wider public. As noted by Rao [11], for e-books to change people's reading habits, the incongruence with user expectations about how books are handled needs to be investigated and overcome.

This experiment was conducted on a small scale, and so the results are just indications of the potential effect of altering the appearance of fiction e-books to make them more attractive and practical to use. Nonetheless, these indications are positive and in tune with the findings of previous studies, which formed the background to the experiment.

Another issue is that the experiment took place over the Internet and thus it could be assumed that all participants are computer literate and have at least a basic knowledge of how to use the Web. However, it would be interesting to carry out a study with participants who have little or no computer experience to determine to which version of electronic books they can adapt more easily. Thus, researchers and developers of electronic books will have a clearer view about the needs of the wider population and not only of the academic community. Finally, it would be meaningful to allow users to pick their favourite titles and provide them with a real choice so that their reactions and motivations would be more realistic.

Indeed, most academic libraries already include a certain number of e-books in their stock, and some public libraries are experimenting with offering e-books to their readers by circulating dedicated portable readers. It therefore seems that much research on the introduction and use of electronic books could be undertaken within libraries.

References

1. Landoni, M. *The Visual Book system: a study of the use of visual rhetoric in the design of electronic books*. Glasgow: Department of Information Science, University of Strathclyde (PhD Thesis), 1997.
2. Wilson, R., Landoni, M. and Gibb. F. The WEB Book experiments in electronic textbook design. *Journal of Documentation*. 59 (4), 2003.
3. Schcolnik, M. A study of reading with dedicated e-readers. Unpublished dissertation. Florida: Southeastern University, 2001.
4. Wilson, R. Ebook readers in higher education. *Educational Technology and Society*. 6 (4), October 2003.
5. Wilson, R. and Landoni, M. Evaluating the usability of portable electronic books. *18th ACM Symposium on Applied Computing (SAC 2003)*. Florida Institute of Technology, USA, 2003.
6. Catenazzi, N. *A Study into electronic book design and production: Hyper-Book and Hyper-Book Builder*. Glasgow: Department of Information Science of the University of Strathclyde (PhD Thesis). 1994.
7. Landoni, M., Wilson, R. and Gibb, F. From the Visual book to the Web book: the importance of design. *The Electronic Library*. 18 (6), 2000.
8. Morkes, J. and Nielsen, J. *Concise, SCANNABLE, and objective: how to write for the Web. 1997*. Available: URL http://www.useit.com/alertbox/980726.html
9. Landoni, M., Wilson, R. and Gibb, F. A user-centred approach to e-book design. *The Electronic Library*. 20 (4), 2002.
10. McKnight, C., Dillon, A. and Richardson, J. (eds.), *Hypertext in Context,* Cambridge: Cambridge University Press. 1991.
11. Rao, S. Electronic books: a review and evaluation. *Library Hi Tech*. 21 (1), 2003.

Interoperable Digital Library Programmes?
We Must Have QA!

Brian Kelly

UKOLN, University of Bath, Bath, BA2 7AY, UK
B.Kelly@ukoln.ac.uk

Abstract. Digital library programmes often seek to provide interoperability through use of open standards. In practice, however, deployment of open standards in a compliant manner is not necessarily easy. The author argues that a strict checking regime would be inappropriate in many circumstances. The author proposes deployment of quality assurance (QA) principles which provide documented policies on the standards and best practices to be implemented and systematic procedures for measuring compliance with these policies. The paper describes the work of the QA Focus project which has developed a QA methodology to support JISC's digital library programmes. A summary of the application of the methodology to support selection of standards and the deployment of deliverables into service is given. The author argues that similar approaches are needed if we are to provide interoperability across digital library programmes.

1 Introduction

The need for open standards in order to provide interoperable digital library services is widely acknowledged. In addition to use of open standards there is also a need to make use of agreed best practices in the provision of digital library services.

Although such principles are widely accepted in the digital library community, in practice appropriate standards and best practices are not always used. This can happen for a number of reasons, some of which are legitimate (immaturity of open standards, a lack of tools, etc.) However a failure to use appropriate solutions may be due to inertia on the part of the developer, a failure to understand the need for open standards, a failure to appreciate appropriate architectures for open standards, lack of agreement on a definition of 'open standards' or a mistaken impression that open standards are being used. There is therefore a need to provide a model which seeks to exploit the potential of open standards, but is capable of addressing the challenges this can provide in a flexible manner.

This paper reviews the quality assurance methodology and support materials developed by the JISC-funded QA Focus project which aims to ensure that JISC's digital library programmes are functional, widely accessible, interoperable and can be deployed easily into a service environment. Particular emphasis is given to the application of the quality assurance framework in the selection of standards and the deployment of project deliverables into a service environment.

R. Heery and L. Lyon (Eds.): ECDL 2004, LNCS 3232, pp. 80–85, 2004.

2   Traditional Approach to Support

2.1   Background

NOF-digitise is a digital library programme in the UK supported by public funding of about £50 million. The programme funds universities, museums, libraries, etc. to digitise materials from their collections and archives in order to make this cultural heritage available online.

Although organisations with proven expertise in digitisation work were funded, a number had little experience of large-scale digitisation activities. The programme provided a valuable opportunity for public sector bodies to enhance their expertise in this area; expertise which would be valuable in supporting in-house development activities.

The importance of open standards was emphasised from the start. It was a requirement that the projects addressed the need for potential reuse of the resources. In order to support over 150 projects the NOF-digi Technical Advisory Service (NOF-TAS) [1] was established. Early activities of NOF-TAS included producing the NOF-digi *Technical Standards and Guidelines* document [2] and organising workshops to support the projects. This was complemented by an email support list and a series of FAQs.

NOF-TAS was not responsible for monitoring projects' compliance with the standards. This work was carried out by BECTa. NOF-TAS worked with BECTa in developing a self-assessment reporting procedure. A reporting template was used to allow projects to report on compliance with standards. Projects were expected to document areas in which they were failing to make use of appropriate open standards. It was recognised that there were areas in which open standards would be difficult to implement: e.g. areas in which the standards were immature, with limited availability of authoring tools and poor support for viewers. For example in the area of synchronised multimedia the preferred open standard is SMIL (Synchronized Multimedia Integration Language); however this format is not yet ready for mainstream use. The proprietary alternative many projects preferred was Flash.

In response to such challenges the reporting procedure required projects to document:

- Reasons why they intend to make use of a proprietary format.
- Reasons why open standards could not be used.
- The scope of their proposed use of proprietary solutions.
- Migration strategies to open standards if they become more readily available.
- Indications of funding issues to support the migration.

It was permissible, for example, to develop an interactive game using Flash; however it would not be permitted to produce an entire Web site in Flash or use Flash to provide site navigation or to use it simply because of availability of in-house expertise in the format. The process is described in a NOF-TAS FAQ [3].

2.2   Limitations of This Approach

Although the work of NOF-TAS was highly appreciated by the projects and the funders the support model used by the service did have limitations:

- There is a danger that projects may regard open standards as something imposed upon them. Organisations which carried out the project work will not necessarily have embedded a standards-based approach throughout their organisations.
- Projects may regard checking compliance as something carried out by external bodies and may not have developed in-house checking procedures.
- A formal compliance checking regime may not be well-suited in other development environments.
- It has not been possible to maintain the standards document, support materials, etc. following the end of the project funding.

3 The QA Focus Approach

QA Focus has been funded by the JISC to support JISC's digital library programmes. QA Focus began its work in January 2002 with funding initially for two years (subsequently extended by 7 months). QA Focus, along with NOF-TAS, is provided by UKOLN and the AHDS (Arts and Humanities Data Service). However QA Focus takes a different approach to NOF-TAS. Rather than providing technical support directly to projects QA Focus has developed a quality assurance methodology to be deployed by the projects themselves. This approach is based on self-assessment; unlike the NOF-digi programme no compliance checking is provided by third parties. The quality assurance methodology is described in section 4.

The QA framework is complemented by its support materials consisting of briefing documents and case studies, together with an online 'toolkit'. Over 60 briefing documents are available which provide focussed advice in various technical areas. The documents provide advice on why particular standards are needed, the advantages and disadvantages of various implementation approaches, common problems and approaches for ensuring compliance with standards or best practices.

The case studies, which are written by projects themselves, help in community-building by allowing projects to share implementation experiences. In order to avoid projects using the case studies as a publicity vehicle a template is provided which requires authors to give a description of their project, the problem being addressed in the document, the solution used and problems experienced or lessons learnt.

Other important areas which have been addressed include the selection of standards for use by projects and the deployment of project deliverables into service. These areas are summarised in sections 5 and 6.

In addition a series of online toolkits have been developed which provide interactive self-assessment of use of appropriate standards and best practices and a series of surveys of Web sites has been carried out using a variety of testing tools.

Further information on these resources and on the QA Focus project is available from the QA Focus Web site [4].

4 QA Methodology

At the core of the work of the QA Focus project is its quality assurance (QA) methodology. The work is based on well-established QA principles. We feel that in order to provide functional, widely accessible and interoperable deliverables projects need to document their technical policies and implement systematic procedures which ensure that the policies are being implemented correctly. We acknowledge that projects often have limited resources and are subject to tight timescales, so we have developed a lightweight QA methodology.

An example of a technical policy is illustrated below.

Area: Web Access
Standards: XHTML 1.0
Exceptions: Resources derived from MS Office applications may not comply with HTML standards due to the limitations of Microsoft's conversion program.
Implementation Architecture: The Web site uses PHP scripts for processing metadata, navigational bars, etc. PHP template files will comply with XHTML 1.0. Content fragments will be edited with an XHTML-aware authoring tool.
Compliance Checking: When pages are created or updated the author is responsible for running the ,validate tool to ensure XHTML compliance. A batch check of the Web site will be carried out quarterly. W3C's Web Log Analysis tool will run monthly to detect the most widely accessed pages which are non-compliant.
Audit Trails: Reports of the Web Log Analysis tool and batch audits will be kept.
Addressing Non-Compliance: Page authors are responsible for ensuring their pages are compliant.
Responsibilities: The project manager is responsible for enforcing this policy.

Fig. 1. Example of a Technical Policy Statement

This policy and related policies on CSS standards and link checking have been implemented for the QA Focus Web site. As can be seen such policies need not be onerous to develop. As well as documenting the standards to be used, the implementation architecture is also described. This will help ensure that an appropriate architecture is used. The compliance checking regime is documented, and, in recognition of real-world complexities, details of permitted exceptions are given.

It should be noted that we have implemented a lightweight technique to simplify compliance checking procedures. In particular appending ,validate to the end of any URL on the UKOLN Web site will run the W3C validation program on the page. Similarly appending ,cssvalidate will run a CSS validator, appending, rvalidate will validate the current pages and pages beneath it, appending, checklink will run a link checker on the page and appending, rchecklink will run a link checker on the page and pages beneath it. This simple interface to a range of testing services can be implemented using a simple update to a Web server's configuration file as described at [5].

5 Selection of Standards

Although the merits of open standards are widely acknowledged deployment of open standards is not always easy. There will be times when open standards are immature, with limited availability of authoring tools and viewers, or open standards fail to reach critical mass. Even in areas in which open standards are mature we do not always see open standards being used correctly: for example many Web sites are not compliant with the HTML standard. A more complete review of the difficulties experienced in using open standards within digital library programmes is given in [6].

In light of such issues there is a need for a methodology for selecting standards. It would clearly be inappropriate to abandon a commitment to the philosophy of open standards, and yet more forceful mandating of use of and compliance with open standards may well prove counter-productive. The approach taken by QA Focus is the use of a checklist for the section of standards. We have developed a checklist which illustrates the range of factors which should be considered when initially selecting the standards to be used within a project, as illustrated below.

Table 1. Checklist for Choosing Standards

Area	Issues
Ownership	Is standard owned by a recognised open standards body?
Development process	Is there a community process for developing the standard?
Availability	Has the proprietary standard has been published?
Viewers	Are viewers (a) available for free, (b) available as open source and (c) available on multiple platforms?
Authoring tools	Are authoring tools (a) available for free, (b) available as open source and (c) available on multiple platforms?
Fitness for purposes	Is the standard appropriate for the purpose envisaged?
Resource issues	What are the resource implications in using the standard?
Complexity	How complex is the standard?
Interoperability	How interoperable is the standard?
Service deployment	How easy will it be to deploy the deliverable into service?
Preservation	Is the standard suitable for long term preservation?
Migration	What approaches can be taken to migrating to more appropriate standards in the future?
Measuring compliance	What approaches can be taken to measuring compliance?

We envisage that projects would complete a checklist and use this to aid the discussions of the standards to be deployed. A record of the issues and decisions made should be kept, which could require approval by an external body but, in other cases, may be documented in project reports without the need for external approval.

6   Service Deployment

Many project deliverables will be expected to be deployed into service. However an easy transition into service cannot always be guaranteed for a number of reasons:

- Software, resources or expertise may not be available in the target service.
- Project deliverables may not fit in with the service's strategic aims.
- Concerns over technical quality, costs or legal issues in deploying the deliverables.

We recommend that projects should provide information about the technical environment, identify potential service environments and have an understanding of issues of concern to services. Projects should make their QA policies available to potential service providers in order to help address possible concerns and facilitate the deployment of project deliverables.

7 Conclusions

This paper has argued that in order to enhance the interoperability of digital library projects there is a need to deploy quality assurance. QA Focus has developed a pragmatic lightweight QA framework which acknowledges the resource and deployment pressures faced by projects.

We feel the approaches described in this paper will be of interest to other digital library programmes. We welcome the opportunity to explore possibilities of working with other digital library programmes. To support this we are exploring the possibilities of making our resources available with a Creative Commons licence [7].

Acknowledgements

The author would like to acknowledge the contributions made by members of the QA Focus team (Marieke Guy and Amanda Closier, UKOLN and Hamish James and Gareth Knight, AHDS), by Karla Youngs and Ed Bremner, ILRT in the early days of the project and to the JISC for funding this work.

References

1. NOF-digitise Technical Advisory Service, UKOLN, http://www.ukoln.ac.uk/nof/support/
2. NOF-digitise Technical Standards And Guidelines, NOF-digitise Technical Advisory Service, UKOLN, http://www.peoplesnetwork.gov.uk/content/technical.asp
3. FAQs: Web Sites, NOF-digitise Technical Advisory Service, UKOLN, http://www.ukoln.ac.uk/nof/support/help/faqs/website.htm#migration
4. QA Focus, UKOLN, http://www.ukoln.ac.uk/qa-focus/
5. A URI Interface To Web Testing Tools, QA Focus, UKOLN, http://www.ukoln.ac.uk/qa-focus/documents/briefings/briefing-59/
6. Kelly, B., Dunning, A., Guy, M. and Phipps, L., Ideology Or Pragmatism? Open Standards And Cultural Heritage Web Sites, ichim03 Conference (CDROM), http://www.ukoln.ac.uk/qa-focus/documents/papers/ichim03/
7. Creative Commons, http://creativecommons.org/

Next Generation Search Interfaces – Interactive Data Exploration and Hypothesis Formulation

Jane Hunter[1], Katya Falkovych[2], and Suzanne Little[3]

[1] DSTC, Brisbane, Australia 4072
jane@dstc.edu.au
[2] CWI, Amsterdam, Netherlands
katya@cwi.nl
[3] ITEE, The University of Qld, Brisbane, Australia 4072
slittle@dstc.edu.au

Abstract. To date, the majority of Web search engines have provided simple keyword search interfaces that present the results as a ranked list of hyperlinks. More recently researchers have been investigating interactive, graphical and multimedia approaches which use ontologies to model the knowledge space. Such systems use the semantic relationships to structure the assimilated search results into interactive semantic graphs or hypermedia presentations which enable the user to quickly and easily explore the results and detect previously unrecognized associations. More recently, the proliferation of eResearch communities has led to a demand for search interfaces which automate the discovery, analysis and assimilation of multiple information sources in order to prove or disprove a particular scientific theory or hypothesis. We believe that such semi-automated analysis, assimilation and hypothesis-driven approaches represent the next generation of search engines. In this paper we describe and evaluate such a search interface which we have developed for a particular eScience application.

1 Introduction

Traditionally Web search engines have provided simple keyword search interfaces which retrieve relevant documents and present the results as a list of hyperlinks which the user has to click through one at a time [1]. The Semantic Web [2] is beginning to enable more interactive, graphical and multimedia search-and-browse interfaces which leverage semantic relationships between retrieved information objects. Technologies such as machine-processable semantic annotations, ontologies and semantic inferencing rules and engines are enabling automated reasoning about complex relationships and a shift towards automated integration and analysis of retrieved documents and data. Researchers are developing systems that can assimilate, structure and present large amounts of mixed-media, multi-dimensional data and information as interactive semantic graphs or hypermedia presentations – greatly enhancing the capacity of domain analysts to process information and mine new knowledge.

In addition, the recent proliferation of eScience communities has led to a demand for more sophisticated search interfaces which assist users to interpret experimental

R. Heery and L. Lyon (Eds.): ECDL 2004, LNCS 3232, pp. 86–98, 2004.

data in order to prove or disprove a particular scientific theory or hypothesis. We believe that eScience will drive the next generation of search engines – interactive 'hypothesis refinement' interfaces which automatically retrieve, process, assimilate and present relevant information in such a way that the user can see whether there is sufficient evidence to corroborate their hypothesis or if it needs refinement. Assuming the hypothesis refinement process does produce promising results, the next requirement is to be able to capture and store the hypothesis and its associated provenance data and body of evidence. This will enable future collaborative sharing, discussion and defense of new theories and help prevent duplication of analytical or experimental activities.

The research that we describe in this paper, focuses on the design, prototyping and evaluation of a data exploration and hypothesis-driven search interface called FUSION, that supports indexing and querying of complex semantic relationships and is driven by notions of information trust and provenance and the interactive investigation, development and capture of hypotheses. Although we have developed FUSION for a particular eScience application, the optimization of fuel cells by fuel cell experts, the research described here is applicable across any domains (e.g., science, engineering, homeland security, social sciences and health) that are attempting to solve complex problems through the analysis and assimilation of large-scale, mixed information and data sets.

The remainder of this paper is structured as follows. The next section describes related work, the background and objectives. Section 3 describes the architectural design of the system and the motivation for design decisions that were made. Sections 4 and 5 describe the interactive data exploration and hypothesis generation interfaces respectively. Section 6 describes the results of evaluating the system on real fuel cell data and images. Section 7 contains concluding remarks and plans for future work.

2   Related Work and Objectives

Hypothesis formulation involves finding local interrelations (hypotheses) among attributes within large databases of high dimensionality [3]. Since finding all possible interrelations is an infeasible task for many such databases, current research is concerned with the problem of finding potentially promising hypotheses, which can be further verified. This problem is tackled by a number of technologies including statistical data mining [4], data visualization, clustering and image processing of visualized data. In this paper we focus on a novel interactive visualization approach.

Visualization of large data sets is not new – a large amount of research has been undertaken on the application of visualization to data mining and knowledge discovery. Visualization can provide a qualitative overview of large and complex datasets, summarize data, find patterns, correlations, clusters or exceptions in data sets and greatly assist with exploratory data analysis. A comprehensive overview of data visualization techniques can be found in [5]. These approaches mainly apply to purely numerical data, do not support heterogeneous data and mixed-media objects (e.g., images, audio, video, text) and don't employ Semantic Web technologies to infer or visualize semantic associations.

Systems like Flamenco [6], Topia [7], CS AKTive Space [8] are examples of early efforts at blending specific information exploration goals with well-associated contextual information. Information from multiple heterogeneous sources are combined and presented to provide an integrated view of a multi-dimensional information space. Polyarchy visualizations [9] and mSpaces [10] are two formalisms recently employed to visualize semantic relationships between multiple information objects. Other examples include work by researchers at DSTC [11] and CWI [12] who have been working on automatic generation of multimedia presentations based on the semantic relationships between mixed-media information objects. The common objective of all of these systems is to provide interactive browsers which present semantically-associated information visually. The methods for visualizing relationships between database attributes or information objects varies depending on the nature (i.e., types, formats, size, granularity, dimensionality and subject) of the data and information objects. These information objects may be spatial, temporal, spectral, visual, audio, textual, 3D, numerical, arrays, matrices, web pages or scholarly publications. Graphs (2D and 3D), animations, virtual reality, hypermedia, map interfaces and combinations of these, have all been employed to visually represent knowledge bases or information structures.

The objectives of our work are to enable scientists to solve particular scientific or engineering problems by presenting the relevant data in an integrated, synchronized and coherent way that facilitates the discovery of new relationships or patterns that would not be possible through traditional search interfaces. More specifically we wanted to develop a system that combines visualization techniques with semantic inferencing and applies them to both multimedia information and multi-dimensional data. Consequently our objectives were to:

- Provide a search, browse and data exploration interface which allows users to interactively formulate hypotheses.
- Enable users to define their own mappings from semantic relationships between objects and data to preferred spatio-temporal presentation modes.
- Provide a hypothesis testing interface which allows users to quickly and easily specify their hypotheses, see whether there was any evidence to support this theory and modify or refine it based on the visual/graphical feedback
- Determine standardized methods for defining, recording and exchanging hypotheses (e.g., RuleML) and their associated, corroborative, evidential and provenance data which have been aggregated within a multimedia object (e.g., SMIL + 3D).
- Enable storage, search and retrieval of past hypotheses. This captures domain expert knowledge, enables its re-use and refinement, reduces duplication and provide evidence and provenance for experimental results.
- Enable annotations of stored presentations – particularly those that reveal new or interesting trends. Semantic annotations (based on domain-specific ontologies) of presentations enable their retrieval and re-use for further knowledge mining.
- Test and evaluate the system within the context of a particular eScience application. In our case, we have chosen 'fuel cell optimization' because it is a typical scientific problem involving a large number of variables and data types.

2.1   eScience Example Scenario

Fuel cells offer an alternative, clean, reliable source of energy for residential use, transport and remote communities. Their efficiency is dependent on the internal structure of the fuel cell layers and the interfaces between them. Electron microscopy generates images of cross-sectional samples through fuel-cell components that reveal complex multi-level information. Simple macro-level information such as the thickness of the cell layers, surface area, roughness and densities can be used to determine gas permeation of the electrode materials. Nano-level information about the electrode's internal interface structure provides data on the efficiency of exchange reactions. Figure 1 illustrates the range of image data obtainable.

Fig. 1. Microscopic images of a fuel cell at 3 different magnifications

By digitising the images and applying image processing techniques (MATLAB) to them, the amount of information expands even further to levels where human processing is not possible and more sophisticated means of data mining are required. In addition to the microstructural information revealed by the images, there are the manufacturing conditions and processing parameters used to produce the cell configurations. Finally, for each cell configuration, performance data is available and the crux of the project is to marry the microstructural data with manufacturing and performance data to reveal trends or relationships which could lead to improvements in fuel cell design and efficiency. Table 1 shows the range of parameters we are dealing with, in addition to the fuel cell images captured at different magnifications.

Table 1. Fuel Cell Parameters

Fuel cell characteristics	Performance	Manufacturing
Layer thickness	Strength	Wt% Y2O3 - ZrO2
Composition	Density	Wt% Al2O3
Density	Conductivity graph	Wt% Solvent
Particle Size and Shape	Efficiency	Solid Content
Nearest neighbors	Lifetime	Viscosity
Surface area		Tape Speed and Thickness
Porosity		Drying Temperature and Time
Surface roughness		Cost

The aim of the work described here was to build and test an interactive interface which will enable fuel cell experts to quickly and easily explore the fuel cell images and data in order to determine associations or patterns between parameters, formulate and validate hypotheses, and save hypotheses and associated corroboratory evidence to share with others and keep as a historical record that tracks past investigations.

3   System Architecture

Figure 2 illustrates the overall architecture and major components of the FUSION system.

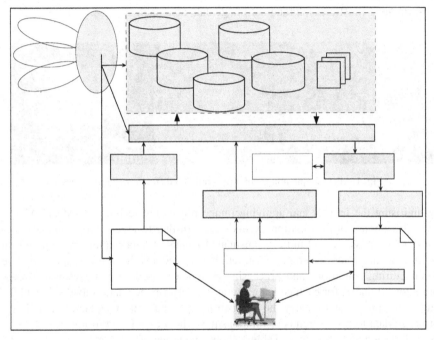

Fig. 2. System Architecture

Users access multiple distributed repositories through a Web browser (Microsoft Internet Explorer) and an ODBC interface – no specialized software is required on the client side except IE 5.5 or higher and an SVG plug-in. The Microsoft implementation of SMIL, HTML+TIME [13], is used to build the multimedia presentations. It allows spatio-temporal relationships between information objects as well as visual effects (such as fading between images) to be implemented. Dependencies between values are represented graphically using SVG [14]. Presentations and graphs are dynamically generated using Python scripts. The HTML forms and pull-down menus presented to the user are generated from domain-specific (OWL[15]) ontologies, described in earlier work [16] and which are specified during system configuration. The architecture is extremely flexible and can quickly and easily be adapted to any domain by connecting to different backend ontologies and knowledge repositories.

The two main system components, that are described in the next two sections, are:
1. Data Exploration;
2. Hypothesis Formulation.

3.1 Data Exploration

The data exploration process consists of four stages, as shown in Figure 3.

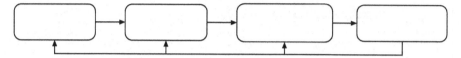

Fig. 3. Four stages of the data exploration process

Initially, the user chooses the aspects of the fuel cell data which they are interested in by selecting the parameters from the data set to be viewed. For example, *porosity*, *efficiency* and *cost*. The Query Interpreter (Figure 2) transforms the user's selection from the HTML form into a format that the Data Interface can process. The Data Interface refers to the metadata structure (harmonized ontologies) to determine which knowledge repositories should be queried. In this example, the performance and manufacturing data repositories are queried. The retrieved results include the unique IDs for the fuel cells matching the query. A request is sent to the image database to retrieve images of the fuel cells matching these IDs. The results of the search are submitted to the HTML interface for the execution of stages 2 and 3.

The HTML interface allows users to specify his/her preferences for displaying the retrieved results. Users can specify the following display preferences:

• an ordering parameter for structuring and presenting the results;
• selection of any additional parameters to be displayed;
• the type of presentation mode required (time-based or static);
• preferred data presentation formats (values displayed graphically, or in a list);
• any special effects to be applied to the presentation (e.g., fading etc.).

Figure 4 shows the user interface in which the user has specified that they wish to "order retrieved fuel cell data by increasing efficiency" and "also display values for porosity and cost". These additional specifications are submitted to the Query Inter-preter, which reformulates the request to the Data Interface ("for previously retrieved fuel cell IDs retrieve corresponding values for efficiency, porosity and cost"). The results of the reformulated query are processed by the Data Interpreter, which trans-forms them into the necessary format for the Presentation Generator. The Presenta-tion Generator makes decisions about the spatio-temporal layout of the result sets based on the users' preferred presentation mode, format and any special effects.

Figure 5 shows the user interface for specifying presentation preferences. There are three possible presentation modes to choose from: a time-based mode (slide-show) or one of two possible static modes – interactive and thumbnail views. When a large number of images are retrieved as a result of a search, the slide-show mode will display the images automatically without the need to click the next button. The default speed for a slide-show is 2 seconds per screen, but this can be adjusted. Alternatively, a static mode (interactive or thumbnail tiled view) can be selected to allow viewing of the results without any time restrictions. The interactive mode requires the users to press the next button to move to the next fuel cell image.

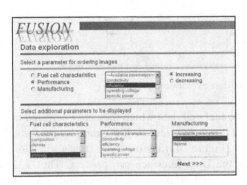

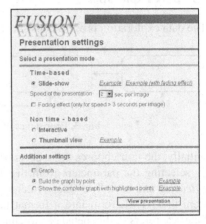

Fig. 4. Data Organization   **Fig. 5.** Presentation Settings

The slide-show mode also displays an animated graph together with the images and any additional parameter values chosen by the user. The SVG graph plots one or more parameter values against time, and is generated dynamically in synchronization with the fuel cell images. This enables users to relate visual features in the images to manufacturing and/or performance data. In addition, fading effects can be applied to the images in the slide-show. This is helpful for distinguishing differences across sequential images.

The thumbnail presentation mode lays out thumbnail images for all of the retrieved fuel cells in a tiled structure ordered by the chosen parameter. In addition any requested parameter values are displayed below each corresponding thumbnail. Users can click on a thumbnail image to view it in full-size with all requested parameters and values listed below it.

Figure 6 illustrates the results of a slide-show presentation – the final stage of the data exploration process. The data exploration interface has been designed to enable a user to interactively explore large mixed-media, multidimensional data and information sets. By enabling users to choose the presentation style which best suits them, and to focus on the range and scope of data sets that most interest them, the system maximizes the potential and speed at which domain experts can discover new interdependencies or trends within the data or develop hypotheses. If the user finds an interesting pattern or association they can save the HTML+TIME+SVG presentation, together with the associated metadata (Unique ID, Date/Time, Creator, Settings, Objective) or move on to the next stage, the hypothesis testing interface, which is described in the next section.

All screenshots in this paper are also available at [17].

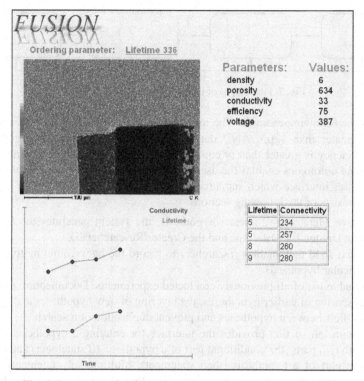

Fig. 6. Screenshot of a slide-show presentation with animated graphs

3.2 Hypothesis Testing

The design of the data exploration interface was based on a user-needs analysis and user feedback, as well as certain assumptions regarding the usefulness of particular features and presentation modes for displaying large amounts of heterogeneous data and information. The design of the hypothesis testing interface, however, was based on an analysis of the cognitive process of hypothesis testing and scientific discovery. Hypothesis formulation does not occur spontaneously but is an interactive, evolutionary process which grows out of background experience and assumptions which lead to ideas about relationships within the data, which the scientist wants to verify. Research into the process of conducting tests and experiments has shown that the hypothesis formulation workflow depends on whether results are expected or unexpected [18, 19]. If results conform to a particular hypothesis, then the work continues forward with the verification of further hypotheses. If an unexpected result occurs, further testing is done in order to explain the result. An unexpected result may occur due to an erroneous primary assumption or methodological errors. Otherwise, unexpected results may lead to a new discovery. Taking this into account, we developed an interface that enables users to specify their hypotheses, define prerequisites for validating and testing hypotheses and attach explanations to the results which are obtained. The workflow for the hypothesis testing process is shown in Figure 7.

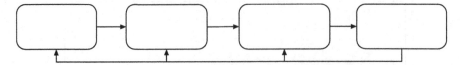

Fig. 7. Four stages of the hypothesis testing process

Consider the following example. The user wants to test the hypothesis: "IF substrate width is greater than 12μm AND density value lies between 5–10 particles/μm^2 THEN efficiency is greater than or equals 80%". A HTML interface generated from the back-end ontologies enables the user to specify such a hypothesis. Figure 8 illustrates the user interface which supports the first and the second phases in Figure 7. Figure 8 consists of the following sections:

- Descriptive Metadata – for each hypothesis, the system generates the following metadata: Unique ID, Date/time and the Creator/Researcher ID.
- A free text field that enables researchers to record the background motivation for this particular hypothesis.
- A searchable list of all previously conducted experiments. Documenting past work enables sharing of earlier hypotheses, the layering of new hypotheses and helps reveal conflicts between hypotheses and prevent duplication of research.
- The bottom left section provides the interface for entering a hypothesis. It is divided into two parts: the conditional part of a hypothesis (if statement) and the consequence part of a hypothesis (then statement). Multiple sub-statements can be combined within the if or then statements using logical connectors (AND/OR). The bottom right part of the window contains dynamically filled lists of then statements that match the specified if statement on the left hand side. This mechanism helps to indicate dynamically, whether a hypothesis with the same if statement has previously been tested and what the outcome of this investigation was. If a matching previously-tested hypothesis is found, then the user can click on the then statement and retrieve a complete record of the results of that investigation.

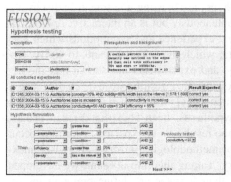

Fig. 8. Hypothesis specification

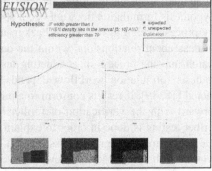

Fig. 9. Results of Hypothesis testing

The process of translating a hypothesis into a set of queries and retrieving the relevant data is identical to the process described in Section 3.1. The values/ranges that are retrieved for the specified parameters are sent to the Hypothesis Testing component, which attempts to verify or refute the hypothesis. The verification results together with the hypothesis itself, are passed through the Data Interpreter and Presentation Generator to produce a presentation. Dependencies between specified parameters are displayed within dynamically-generated SVG graph(s). The hypothesis itself is transformed into RuleML [20] format that users can choose to save to a Xindice [21] repository of stored hypotheses.

Figure 9 illustrates a presentation that was generated following the specification and submission of a hypothesis to the knowledge repository. The hypothesis statement is displayed at the top of the screen. The set of graphs displayed beneath the hypothesis statement, depict the dependencies between parameters specified in the hypothesis and provide feedback to the user on whether or not there is any evidence to support their hypothesis. For the example hypothesis given above, two graphs are generated. One plots density against substrate width. The other plots efficiency against substrate width. Users are able to either save this hypothesis (with an explanatory annotation) or go back and make changes to the original hypothesis and resubmit this to the knowledge base. A complete record of the saved experiment/hypothesis consists of:

- The metadata for the hypothesis: unique ID, date, and author;
- The motivation or background for the hypothesis;
- The hypothesis itself in the form of an if-then statement;
- The results of applying the hypothesis to the knowledge repository – an HTML+TIME+SVG presentation;
- An outcome attribute specifying whether the results were positive or negative;
- An annotation field, entered by the user, which contains a possible explanation for the results that were obtained.

An XML metadata record and the RuleML representation for the example hypothesis given at the start of this section can be found at [17].

4 Evaluation

User testing of the system has been carried out by fuel cell scientists from The University of Queensland's Centre for Microscopy and Microanalysis. Feedback from the users to date has indicated the following:

- The user interface design and incorporation of domain-specific ontologies [16] allowed users with little knowledge of the domain, to quickly and easily explore the data and gain an understanding of the knowledge space;
- Different users carry out research activities differently. Being able to customize or personalize the mode, scope and focus of the assimilated data presentations and the hypothesis refinement process was very beneficial for individual productivity;

- The different presentation modes enabled faster processing and interpretation of large data sets and images by the fuel cell scientists than was possible manually and expedited the hypothesis generation and refinement process;
- Slide shows of images synchronized with animated graphs that plot corresponding requested parameter values, were the most popular method of data exploration and hypothesis formulation;
- The fading effect was useful for detecting subtle image differences;
- Static presentations and graphs can be incorporated directly into scholarly publications, reducing the time required to disseminate research results;
- Being able to record, browse and retrieve past investigations and hypotheses, reduced duplication and enabled existing hypotheses to be refined or new hypotheses to be developed based on past work. It also provides a way of capturing and sharing tacit domain expert knowledge, explicitly, in the form of rules;
- Existing automatic hypothesis testing techniques (e.g., statistical analysis) only work on quantitative data. A major advantage of The FUSION system's approach is that it applicable across a range of data and media types.
- The saving of evidential and provenance data with hypotheses, enables the validity of earlier hypotheses or assumptions to be assessed by other scientists – who are able to attach their own opinions in the form of annotations;
- The use of semantic web technologies such as ontologies, annotations and inferencing rules, provide a consistent, machine-processable way for describing, capturing, re-using and building on the domain knowledge. It also enables better collaboration between distributed research laboratories and industry through improved sharing of knowledge and data.

An on-line demonstration of the prototype system is available at [22]. Users need to be using IE 5.5 or higher and an SVG plug-in, such as Adobe's plugin [23].

5   Conclusions and Future Work

In this paper we describe a search interface that enables scientists to interact with a knowledge base through a hypothesis-driven approach that combines data exploration, integration, search and inferencing – enabling more complex analysis and deeper insight. We believe that such interfaces represent the next generation of search engines and that they are will be increasingly in demand and applied across many domains including science, engineering, homeland security, social sciences and health, to solve complex problems and provide decision support tools based on the analysis and assimilation of large-scale, mixed-media, multi-dimensional information and data sets.

Plans for future work include:

- Further testing and refinement of the system, particularly within a real-world industrial environment. We plan to deploy it within a fuel-cell manufacturing company to facilitate the exchange of knowledge between university research and industry organizations in this domain;

- Integrating statistical data analysis methods and applying them to hypotheses formulated through our system, to fit more precise mathematical models to relationships between parameters;
- Investigating how the empirical modeling approach described here can be combined with the physical modeling approach to generate a more accurate predictive model for simulating fuel cell behaviour.
- Testing the portability, flexibility and scalability of the system by applying it to other domains, such as environmental modeling and bioinformatics.

Looking even further into the future, we envisage that instead of users interactively submitting hypotheses to such a system, there will be pro-active systems which are: constantly dynamically assimilating new information; using existing, stored hypotheses to automatically detect anomalies, problems, or exceptional events; inferring new hypotheses and knowledge; and notifying users by returning actionable information. But we still have a long way to go before such intelligent or sophisticated systems become widely available.

Acknowledgements

The work described in this paper has been funded by the Cooperative Research Centre for Enterprise Distributed Systems Technology (DSTC) (through the Australian Government's CRC Programme) and through a University of Queensland Development Grant. Thanks to CWI for supporting Katya's secondment to DSTC and to John Drennan and the University of Queensland's Centre for Microscopy and Microanalysis for providing the fuel cell images and data and for their valuable user feedback.

References

1. Google, (http://www.google.com).
2. Hendler, J., Berners-Lee, T., and Miller, E., Integrating Applications on the Semantic Web. Journal of the Institute of Electrical Engineers of Japan. Vol 122(10): p. p. 676-680., 2002.
3. Amir, A., Kashi, R., and Netanyahu, N. S. "Efficient Multidimensional Quantitative Hypotheses Generation." in Proceedings of the 3rd IEEE International Conference on Data Mining (ICDM). Melbourne, Florida, USA, November 19-22, 2003.
4. Smyth, P., Data Mining at the Interface of Computer Science and Statistics, Invited Chapter in Data Mining for Scientific and Engineering Applications. 2001, Kluwer. p. 35-61.
5. Fayyad, U., Grinstein, G. G., and Wierse, A., Information Visualization in Data Mining and Knowledge Discovery. 2001: Morgan Kaufmann.
6. Hearst, M., et al., Finding the Flow in Web Site Search. Communications of the ACM. 45(9): p. pp.42-49., 2002.
7. Topia, (http://topia.demo.telin.nl/).
8. Shadbolt, N. R., et al., CS AKTive Space or how we stopped worrying and learned to love the Semantic Web. IEEE Intelligent Systems. 2004.
9. Robertson, G., et al. "Polyarchy visualization: visualizing multiple intersecting hierarchies", in Conference on Human Factors in Computing Systems. Minneapolis, Minnesota, USA.

10. Gibbins, N., Harris, S., and Schraefel, M. "Applying mSpace Interfaces to the Semantic Web", in Submitted to Proceedings of World Wide Web Conference 2004. New York, USA.

11. Little, S., Geurts, J., and Hunter, J. "The Dynamic Generation of Intelligent Multimedia Presentations through Semantic Inferencing", in ECDL2002. Rome, Italy, September 2002.

12. Geurts, J., et al. "Towards Ontology-Driven Discourse: From Semantic Graphs to Multimedia Presentations", in International Semantic Web Conference (ISWC2003). Sanibel Island, Florida, USA, October 2003.

13. Microsoft, HTML+TIME 2.0 Reference, (http://msdn.microsoft.com/workshop/author/behaviors/reference/time2_entry.asp).

14. W3C, Scalable Vector Graphics (SVG) 1.1 Specification, W3C Recommendation, 14 January 2003, Edited by Jon Ferraiolo and Fujisawa Jun and Dean Jackson, (http://www.w3.org/TR/SVG/).

15. W3C, OWL Web Ontology Language Reference, W3C Candidate Recommendation, 18 Aug 2003, Edited by Mike Dean and Guus Schreiber, (http://www.w3.org/TR/owl-ref/).

16. Hunter, J., Drennan, J., and Little, S., Realizing the Hydrogen Economy through Semantic Web Technologies. IEEE Intelligent Systems Journal - Special Issue on eScience. 2004.

17. Falkovych, K., Little, S., and Hunter, J., Appendices and Examples Screenshots, (http://metadata.net/sunago/fusion/visualisation/ecdl2004.html).

18. Dunbar, K., How Scientists Build Models InVivo Science as a Window on the Science Mind, in Model-Based Reasoning in Scientific Discovery, L. Magnani, N.J. Nersessian, and P. Thagard, Editors. 1999, Kluwer Academic/Plenum Publishers: New York. p. 85-99.

19. Okada, T. and Simon, H. A. "Collaborative Discovery in a Scientific Domain", in Proceedings of the 17th Annual Conference of the Cognitive Science Society, 1995.

20. Boley, H., Tabet, S., and Wagner, G. "Design Rationale of RuleML: A Markup Language for Semantic Web Rules", in Semantic Web Working Symposium (SWWS), 2001.

21. Apache Software Foundation, Apache Xindice, (http://xml.apache.org/xindice/).

22. Falkovych, K., Little, S., and Hunter, J., Scientific Data Exploration and Hypothesis Testing OnLine Demo, 2004, (http://metadata.net/sunago/fusion/visualisation/intro.html).

23. Adobe, Adobe SVG plugin, (http://www.adobe.com/svg/).

Ontology Based Interfaces to Access a Library of Virtual Hyperbooks

Gilles Falquet, Claire-Lise Mottaz-Jiang, and Jean-Claude Ziswiler

University of Geneva
CUI – Department of Information Systems
24, rue Genénéral-Dufour, CH-1211 Genève 4, Switzerland
{Gilles.Falquet,Claire-Lise.Mottaz,Jean-Claude.Ziswiler}@cui.unige.ch

Abstract. A virtual hyperbook is a virtual document made of a set of information fragments linked to a domain ontology and equipped with selection and assembly methods or rules. In this paper, we study the problem of accessing and reading in a digital library of virtual hyperbooks. In this case it is necessary to generate hyperdocuments that present information and knowledge originating from several hyperbooks. Moreover, these hyper-documents must fit with the reading objectives or specific point of views of readers. Our approach is based on the integration of domain ontologies and the re-use of interface specifications.

1 Introduction

A virtual document is a set of information fragments associated with filtering, organisation and assembling mechanisms. Depending on a user profile or user intensions, these mechanisms will produce different documents adapted to the user needs. The idea of virtual document has emerged from research on 'pre-Web' hypertext systems, such a MacWeb [20] and, more recently, on adaptive and personalized hypertext systems. Given the rapid development of theoretical and practical tools in this domain, it is reasonable to think that digital libraries will incorporate virtual documents in addition to traditional electronic documents.

It is thus interesting to explore the new accessing and reading possibilities that a library of virtual documents can provide. The main distinction between a traditional digital library and a virtual document library is the disappearance of the monolithic character of a book or an article. The ability to select and assemble informational fragments coming from various virtual documents opens new perspectives on the reading action, but it also raises important questions. In a digital library of virtual documents, a document reading system should be able to compose new documents from all the available informational fragments of the library, according to the readersi objectives. For instance, a reader wishing to obtain some information about the concept of recursion should get a document containing a definition of this term, eventually other definitions that represent alternative point of views, examples and exercises drawn from various virtual documents, historical notes, etc. We can also consider that a virtual book, once

R. Heery and L. Lyon (Eds.): ECDL 2004, LNCS 3232, pp. 99–110, 2004.
© Springer-Verlag Berlin Heidelberg 2004

inserted into a library, will automatically enrich itself by connecting to fragments of other books (new examples and exercises, new comments about several concepts, etc.).

In these two cases it is obviously necessary to check the semantic compatibility of the fragments before re-using them. The objective is to deliver to the reader new documents that are semantically coherent. For this, we propose an approach based on ontology integration and on reusability of virtual document interface specifications.

1.1 Hyperbooks and Virtual Documents

For several years, the concept of virtual document has been studied in different contexts and from different perspectives. Research on hypertexts has tackled several problem areas that are related to our study. Systems like Intermedia [14] or Storyspace [2] were developed essentially for producing hypertext literature, others like KMS [1] or MacWeb [20] have aimed at the management and sharing of knowledge. Concepts like links, anchors, composition of nodes, etc. were studied in detail. This led, among other results, to the definition of the Dexter reference model [16]. Various models and systems have also been proposed for the integration of books and electronic documents into hyperbooks. This concerns the transformation of paper books into hypertext [22] or into electronic books [19], writing directly in electronic form (hypertext) [11] or also integrating existing electronic documents [3]. The hypertext personalization problem led to the definition of models and techniques for adaptation and adaptivity [7], [4]. The capacity of adaptation corresponds to the presentation of different or differently organized contents, depending on a user profile. Adaptivity consists in automatically updating the user profile according to his or her behaviour. A well-known example of the adaptability is the change of colors of the links leading to already visited web pages. In [25], the authors propose a model of adaptive hypertext which includes a domain model, a user model and adaptation rules. The domain model is a semantic network consisting of domain concepts and relations between concepts. This model serves essentially to define adaptation rules, depending, for instance, on the concepts known or appropriated by the user. More recently, a research field has emerged that concentrates on the concept of personalizable virtual documents [6], [13]. Personalizable virtual documents are defined as sets of elements (often called fragments) associated with filtering, organization and assembling mechanisms. According to a user profile or user intensions, these mechanisms will produce different documents adapted to the user needs. For instance, in [5] Crampes and Ranwez define pedagogical virtual documents. Garlatti and Iksal [17] proposed a comprehensive and detailed model of virtual documents based on several ontologies.

There is presently no consensus on a common virtual document model. Nevertheless, most of the proposed models are comprised of (at least) a domain ontology and a fragment base. These model generally differ on the user interface part, i.e. how to specify the production of user-readable documents. Existing models use declarative languages, pedagogical or narrative ontologies, inference rules, or other mechanisms.

1.2   Ontology Integration

The integration and re-usability of ontologies plays a major role in the domain of virtual books and a fortiori in the domain of virtual libraries. If we suppose that each virtual book has its own domain ontology, we need an integration technique to create a semantically coherent virtual library. It is important to note here that it is not realistic to suppose that all the virtual books will refer to the same (global) ontology, because either such an ontology does currently not exist or, even if it existed, it would contain only stable and well established concepts (thus it would not be convenient for books on new and advanced topics).

The literature about ontology integration is indeed very heterogeneous. As a starting point, we can refer to [21] and [18] for drawing a typology of the principal methods of integration. There are two major approaches to ontology integration, namely, alignment and fusion.

Alignment techniques try to bring two ontologies into mutual agreement by establishing correspondence links between the concepts of the two ontologies [18]. As a subcategory, mapping techniques intend to relate corresponding concepts or relations by an equivalence relation. In both cases, the existing ontologies will persist. This integration process is often chosen if the ontologies cover complementary domains.

The fusion of ontologies consists in creating a new coherent ontology by merging or matching concepts. This process is often quite complex because it may require, among others, the creation of new concepts in order to relate concepts from the two ontologies. It is thus very difficult to automate. Nevertheless, there exists environments and tools, like Chimaera [15], to help merging and diagnosing multiple ontologies.

In our particular case of digital libraries, we should take into account the fact that such a library can be very evolutionary. The arrival of new documents will require a constant process of integration so that the ontology remains adapted to the digital library. Thus, the fusion approach is probably not adequate for integrating hyperbooks in a digital library. Hence, the approach we propose is based on alignment and mapping.

In the rest of this paper, we first propose, in section 2, a simple model for virtual documents (virtual hyperbooks). Next, we describe in section 3 our multi-point of view approach of ontologies and the integration process of hyperbooks into digital libraries. In section 4, we will show how to use the model to define documents for 'global' reading in an integrated library. The conclusion briefly presents the implementation techniques for realizing prototypes of digital libraries.

2   Virtual Hyperbook Model

The hyperbook model we use is comprised of a fragment repository, a domain ontology, and an interface specification, as shown in Fig. 1. The fragments and the ontology, together with their interconnecting links, form the structural part

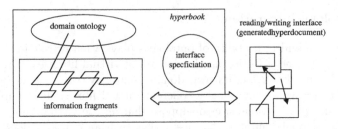

Fig. 1. Components of the virtual hyperbook model and the reading/writing interface.

of the hyperbook. The interface specification specifies how to assemble the information fragments, with the help of the domain ontology, to produce a hypertext that constitutes the hyperbookis user interface.

2.1   Structural Part of a Hyperbook

The hyperbook structure is shown in Fig. 2 as a set of classes and associations (expressed in UML). The structural part of a particular hyperbook is a set of objects that are instance of these classes. Classes *OF_Link* and *FF_Link* are associative classes that represent the links between the domain ontology and the fragments and between fragments. Links between fragments can have different natures, such as: structural links (from fragments to sub-fragments); argumentative links (arguments, positions, contradictions, ...); narrative or rhetoric links (elaboration, summary, reinforcement, ...). The domain ontology is a set of concepts connected through semantic relations that have a type and possibly restrictions (such as number restrictions). Every concept is connected to one or more terms.

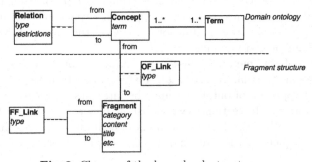

Fig. 2. Classes of the hyperbook structure.

The domain ontology plays two roles. On one side it describes the concepts of the domain. On the other side, it serves as a reference to describe the information content of the fragments. By establishing typed links from fragments to concepts, one can qualify not only what the fragment is about but also what relationship it has with the domain concepts. Typical link types are:

- instance, example, illustration: the fragment describes a particular instance of the referred concept
- definition: the fragment contains a textual (or audio, or graphical) definition of the concept
- property: the fragment describes a property of the concept
- reference, use, required: the fragment refers to the concept (it is necessary to know the concept to understand the fragment)

2.2   Interface Specification

The interface of a virtual hyperbook is a (real) hypertext, made of nodes and links, derived from the informational structure according to an interface specification. An interface specification is a set of node schemas, the instantiation of which produces the real nodes (XML documents) and links of the interface. A node schema is an expression of the form

> **node** *name* [*parameters*]
>   *content and_link_specification*
> **from** *selection_expression*

A selection expression is a path expression with attribute conditions. A path expression is a sequence $E_1, \ldots, E_n$ where each E_i is a path element is of the form *class_name variable* [condition] or of the form -(*association_name variable* [condition])->. The evaluation of such an expression yields an n-tuple of interconnected objects that belong to the classes of the hyperbook structure (fragments, concepts, ontology-fragment links, etc.) and that satisfy conditions on their attributes. For instance, the expression

`Concept c -(OF_Link k [type="example"])-> Fragment f`

specifies the set of triples (c, k, f) such that c is a *Concept*, k is an *OF_Link* with k.type = *example*, f is a *Fragment*, and k.from = c and k.to = f. In other words, it selects all the concepts and fragments that are connected through an ontology-fragment link of type *example*. The path expressions can be abbreviated by omitting the associative class names when there is no ambiguity. Moreover, when the condition has the form type = *type_name*, we will simply write *type_name*. Hence, the above path expression will be written as

`Concept c -"example"-> Fragment f`

The content specification of a node is a list of XML elements that may contain string constants, object attributes, or expressions with string or arithmetic operators.

Example 1. The following node schema selects all the fragments that are linked to a given concept C. The content of a node instance is comprised of

- a title element that contains the main term associated to concept C
- for each fragment F connected to C through a link L: the link type and the fragment's title and content

```
node connected_fragments[C]
    <title> Fragments connected to, C.term </title> ,
    { <subtitle> L.type, : , F.title </subtitle>
      <text> F.content </text>
    }
from Concept C -(L)-> Fragment F
```

(The content specification between { and } is repeated for each selected n-tuple
of objects)

The actual presentation of a node instance of this schema will be determined by
XSLT or CSS style sheets.

2.3   Ontology and Link Inference

The links between the ontology and the fragments play a crucial role to establish
relevant links between fragments and to generate interface documents. The idea
is to replace direct linking between fragments (often called horizontal linking) by
inferred links that correspond to paths starting from a fragment, going through
one or more ontology concepts, and ending on another fragment. Inferred links
are preferred to direct links because users (authors) are generally able to establish
correctly typed links from the fragments they write to the relevant concepts.
But when they are asked to link their fragments directly to other fragments
they have difficulties finding relevant fragments to link to and deciding on what
type of links to establish. Since the ontology has a graph structure, semantically
meaningful links can be obtained by simple inference rules that consist in path
expressions. For instance, Fig. 3 shows two derived links (1) and (2) obtained by
going up into the domain ontology and then down to another fragment. In the
next section we will present the path expression language.

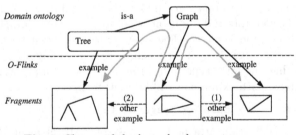

Fig. 3. Classes of the hyperbook structure.

Example 2. The following node schema has a selection expression that corresponds to the above-mentioned link inference path (1). An instance of this
schemas will display the content of the fragment *Ex* and a list of hypertext
links (href) to nodes (showFragment) that display other examples of the same
concept *C*. The titles of the other examples are used as anchor text for the
hyperlinks (OtherEx.title).

```
node exampleAndOthers[Ex]
   Ex.content , + ,
   "Other examples of concept ", C.term ,
   {
      href showFragment[OtherEx] ( OtherEx.title )
   }
from Fragment Ex <-"example"- Concept C
   -"example"-> Fragment otherEx
```

This same link inference mechanism will be used to generate links accross hyperbooks. In addition to the standard hyperlinks shown on the previous example, the interface specification language also provides inclusion links. Inclusion links enable the interface designer to create complex contents that show several fragment contents together in a single hypertext node. Had we used inclusion in this example, we would have obtained a single node (document) showing an example together with all the other examples.

3 A Multi-point of View Approach to Hyperbook Integration

With the objective of creating interface documents for reading not only virtual documents, but also for accessing a whole library, we could choose a very direct approach that consists of integrating all hyperbooks into one large hyperbook. In this case, we must create a global ontology from the available hyperbook ontologies. However, this approach is very limited because:

- It forces to strongly unify the concepts that does not conduct to a problem for the well established terminology of a domain, but which might be problematic when concepts have vague environments or when there remains divergent and contradictory interpretations.
- It does not reflect the fact that each book represents the point of view of an author on a subject. This diversity of point of views would be lost.
- It loses the diversity of narrative styles (reflected in the interface documents) adopted by the different authors. This is why we propose an approach based on multi-point of view ontologies [8, 9].

3.1 Concept Conflicts and Point of Views

Gaines and Shaw [12] propose a methodology to compare conceptual systems of several domain experts. This method is based on analyzing domain entities (concepts), terms used to design them, and their attributes. The aim is to highlight the divergences between experts in order to facilitate the discussion to obtain a consensus. This analysis can lead to four different situations:

Consensus. The experts use the same term for describe the same concept.
Correspondence. Different terms are used for the same concept.

Conflict. The same term is used for different concepts.

Contrast. The experts identified different concepts and use different terms to name them.

In a situation of conflict the domain experts must work together to reach a consensus, i.e. to define a single concept that correspond to the term in question. In a multi-point of view approach, the resolution of conflicts is carried out differently, by considering that there can exist several concept definitions associated to the same term, provided they belong to different point of views on the domain. When integrating hyperbook ontologies we will consider that each hyperbook represents a point of view on its domain. Since the hyperbooks may belong to completely different domains, we will find the following three situations:

- Two concepts designated by the same term do not belong to the same semantic domain. For example, the concept 'table' of the furniture ontology and the concept 'table' of a ontology about databases.
- Two concepts effectively belong to the same domain, but they have different definitions. The two definitions represent different point of views of this concept.
- The definitions of the two concepts are considered to be equivalent. The point of views of the two hyperbooks coincide for this concept.

3.2   Ontology Integration for Virtual Documents

Since the objective of the integration process is to lead to a multi-point of view ontology and not just to a "monolithic" ontology, the most appropriated integration techniques are those which establish links between concepts (mapping of ontologies).

For this, we propose to use an extension of the technique of Rodríguez and Egenhofer [23]. There, the similarity between two concepts is the weighted sum of three measurements: similarity of the terms (set of synonyms), similarity of the attributes (set of values) and similarity of the semantic neighbourhood (set of the concepts close to the semantic links in the graph). Moreover, the similarity function takes into account the difference of depth of the concepts (relative to their respective ontologies).

In the case of virtual documents, we make use of additional information to evaluate the similarity between concepts thanks to the fragments related to each concept. If two concepts A and B are bound by links of the same type t to sets of fragments $t(A)$ and $t(B)$ respectively, the similarity between $t(A)$ and $t(B)$ can be taken into account in to compute the similarity between A and B. The similarity between $t(A)$ and $t(B)$ can be obtained with well-known document similarity measures (for instance, the cosine between the *tf-idf* vectors representing the documents in the space of terms [24] or the Kolmogorov distance). Then, we define the similarity between $t(A)$ and $t(B)$ based on the similarities between documents (for example by taking the maximum similarity found between all the fragments of $t(A)$ and $t(B)$). The similarities obtained for all types of links will then be added up to the similarity measure computed at the conceptual level. It is important to remark that link typing is crucial here. Indeed, the comparison makes sense only if the compared fragments play the same role with respect to a concepts. If, for instance, fragment a is an example of concept A whereas b is a counter-example of B, a strong similarity between a and b does not imply a strong similarity between A and B, on the contrary.

4   Generation of Interface Documents for Libraries

An interesting characteristic of the virtual hyperbook model and of the integration model is the possibility of re-using specifications of virtual interface documents to create global reading interfaces.

A first technique for building a global interface consists in re-using the specification of a hyperbook interface, but to apply it to the whole information space of the library, i.e. to the fragments and ontologies of all the hyperbooks and their interconnections through similarity links. A new, extended, version of each node schema of the interface is derived by extending its selection expression as follows:

Each element of the form

$$\texttt{Concept c}$$

is replaced by

$$\texttt{Concept c [hybook = L] - ("sim") -> Concept c'}$$

Thus every path through c can now "jump out" to another hyperbook as shown in Fig. 4.

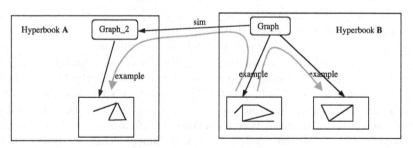

Fig. 4. Selection path to another hyperbook.

The initial book is thus enriched with other point of views of the subject. The following node schema is the extension of the schema shown in Example 2.

```
node Extended_exampleAndOthers[Ex, threshold]
    Ex.content , + ,
    "Other examples of concept ", C.term ,
    { href Fragment[OtherEx, R.value] ( OtherEx.title }
```

```
from Fragment Ex <-"example"- Concept C
    -(R [type="sim" and value>threshold])-> Concept C2
    -"example"-> Fragment otherEx
```

By adjusting the threshold value, the user can define the type of extension he or she desires. A very high threshold corresponds to an extension with very close point of views while a lower threshold accepts dissimilar point of views. A second way to re-use an interface specification consists of applying the interface specification of a hyperbook to another one. In this case, we will see the informational content of one hyperbook with the interface of another. If we consider that the interface of a hyperbook represents its narrative style, we obtain a vision of the content of a hyperbook in the style of another one. This kind of re-use does not require any rewriting of node schemas, but it implies that the hyperbook ontologies use the same types of relations.

It is also possible to define a completely new reading interface on the whole library. In this case, we suppose that an author wants to create a new book starting from information already existing in the library. This is a second level author, who will not create information, but invent new narrations and presentations. This task can be achieved either by creating new node schemas, or by re-using schemas of different hyperbooks. As we have already seen, each node schema can be applied to any hyperbook. As a consequence, a second level author can create new schemas that include or refer to existing schemas, without having to modify the latter.

5   Conclusion and Future Work

In this paper, we have presented a virtual hyperbook model and an ontology integration approach adapted to the reading of hyperbooks in a digital library environment. Each hyperbook has its own domain ontology and hypertext interface specification. Our approach to 'globally' reading in a library of virtual hyperbooks is based on the idea that each hyperbook corresponds to a point of view on a domain. By applying integration techniques to the hyerbookis ontologies, we can create a multi-point of view ontology that describes a set of hyperbooks. A hypertext interface specification language can use this ontology to infer semantic relations between informational fragments and to construct new semantically and narratively coherent documents that are based on the content of several hyperbooks. Thus, a user will read something that is more than each individual book in the library. We have created various implementations of hyperbooks using techniques of hypertext views on databases. The domain ontology, the hyperbook ontology and fragments are stored in a relational database (the class diagram of Fig. 3 can be readily translated into a relational database schema). The node schemas of the interface are specified in the Lazy language, which is a declarative language to specify hypertext views on relational databases [10]. This language corresponds to the node schema specification language presented in this paper. With this technology, we have developed a hyperbook management system for courses. Every course has its own hyperbook. The reading interface provides the user with different views to help him or her grasp the meaning of concepts and see the direct or indirect interconnections between the courseis concepts. We are currently using the integration techniques described here to define global reading interfaces for these hyperbooks. We plan to implement different similarity measures and compare them on hyperbooks in different domains.

References

1. Akscyn R., McCracken D., Yoder E.: KMS: a distributed hypermedia system for managing knowledge in organizations. Communications of the ACM, vol. 31, July 1988, 820–835.
2. Bernstein M.: Storyspace. Proceedings of the thirteenth Conference on Hypertext and Hypermedia, 2002, College Park, Maryland, 2002, 172–181.
3. Brusilovsky P., Rizzo R.: Map-Based Horizontal Navigation in Educational Hypertext. Proceedings of the ACM Hypertext 2002 Conference, College Park, Maryland, 2002.
4. Brusilovsky, P.: Methods and techniques of Adaptive Hypermedia. User Modelling and User-Adapted Interaction. Adaptive Hypertext and Hypermedia, Kluwer, 1998, 1–43.
5. Crampes, M., Ranwez, S.: Ontology-Supported and Ontology-Driven Conceptual Navigation on the World-Wide Web". Proceedings of the ACM Hypertext 2000 Conference, San Antonio, USA, 2000.
6. Crampes M.: User Controlled Adaptivity versus System Controlled Adaptivity in Intelligent Tutoring Systems. Proceedings of the Artificial Intelligence in Education Conference, Le Mans, France, July 1999, 173–180.
7. De Bra P., Calvi L.: Creating Adaptive Hyperdocuments for and on the Web. Proceedings of the AACE Web-Net Conference, Toronto, 1997, 149–155.
8. Falquet G., Mottaz Jiang C.-L.: A Model for the Collaborative Design of Multi-Point of View Terminological Knowledge Bases. In R. Dieng R., Matta N. (Eds) Knowledge Management and Organizational Memories, Kluwer, 2002.
9. Falquet G, Ziswiler, J.-C.: A Virtual Hyperbook Model to Support Collaborative Learning. Supplemental Proceedings of the Artificial Intelligence in Education Conference, Sydney, Australia, July 2003.
10. Falquet G., Mottaz Jiang C.-L.: A Framework to Specify Hypertext Interfaces for Ontology Engineering. Proceedings of the Knowledge Management and Organizational Memories workshop on the 18th IJCAI Conference, Acapulco, Mexico, 2003.
11. Fröhlich P., Nejdl W.: A Database-Oriented Approach to the Design of Educational Hyperbooks. Proceedings of the Workshop on Intelligent Educational Systems on World Wide Web, 8th World Conference of the AIED Society, Kobe, Japan, 1997. 18–22.
12. Gaines, M., Shaw, B.: Comparing Conceptual Structures: Consensus, Conflict, Correspondence and Contrast. Knowledge Science Institute, University of Calgary, 1989.
13. Garlatti, S., Iksal, S.: Revisiting and Versioning in Virtual Special Reports. Proceedings of the Hypertext 2001 conference, Arhus, Denmark, 2001.

14. Garret L. N., Smith K. E., Meyrowitz N.: Intermedia: Issues Strategies and Tactics in the Design of a Hypermedia Document System Proceedings of the Computer Supported Collaborative Work Conference, Austin, Texas, 1986.
15. McGuinness D. L., Fikes R. Rice J., Wilder S.: An Environment for Merging and Testing Large Ontologies. Proceedings of the Seventh International Conference on Principles of Knowledge Representation and Reasoning (KR2000), Breckenridge, Colorado, April 2000.
16. Halasz F., Schwartz M.: The Dexter hypertext reference model. Communications of the ACM, vol. 37, no 2, 1994, 30–39.
17. Iksal, S., Garlatti, S., Tanguy P., Ganier F.: Semantic Composition of Special Report on the Web: A Cognitive Approach. Proceedings of the H2PTMi01 conference, Valenciennes, France, 2001.
18. Klein M.: Combining and relating ontologies: an analysis of problems and solutions. Proccedings of the IJCAI2001 workshop on Ontologies and Information Sharing, Seattle, 2001.
19. Landoni M., Crestani F., Melucci M.: The Visual Book and the Hyper-Textbook: Two Electronic Books One Lesson? Proceedings RIAO Conference, 2000, 247–265.
20. Nanard J., Nanard M.: Should Anchors be Typed Too? An Experiment with MacWeb. Proceedings of ACM Hypertext i93 Conference, 1993, 51–62.
21. Pinto, H. S., Gómez-Pérez, A., Martins, J. P.: Some Issues on Ontology Integration. Proceedings of the IJCAI-99 workshop on Ontologies and Problem-Solving Methods (KRR5), Stockholm, Sweden, 1999.
22. Rada R.: Hypertext writing and document reuse: the role of a semantic net. Electronic Publishing, vol. 3, no. 3, 1990, 125–140.
23. Rodríguez M. A., Egenhofer.M. J.: Determining Semantic Similarity among Entity Class from Different Ontologies. IEEE Transactions on Knowledge and Data Engineering, Vol. 15, No. 2, March/April 2003.
24. Salton, G.: *Automatic Text Processing: The Transformation, Analysis, and Retrieval of Information by Computer.* Addison-Wesley, 1989.
25. Wu H., de Kort E., De Bra P.: Design Issues for General-Propose Adaptive Hypermedia Systems. Proceedings of the ACM Hypertext 2001 Conference, Aarhus, 2001, 141–150.

Document Icons and Page Thumbnails: Issues in Construction of Document Thumbnails for Page-Image Digital Libraries

William C. Janssen

Palo Alto Research Center
3333 Coyote Hill Road
Palo Alto, California, USA
janssen@parc.com

Abstract. Digital libraries are increasingly based on digital page images, but techniques for constructing usable versions of these page images are largely folklore. This paper documents some issues encountered in creating various kinds of renderings of page images for the UpLib digital library system, and suggests approaches for each, based on both problem analysis and user feedback. Several factors important in determining useful sizes for small visual representations of the documents, called *document icons*, are discussed; one algorithm, called *log-area*, seems most effective.

1 Introduction

The UpLib personal digital library system provides a secure long-term storage and retrieval system for a wide variety of personal documents such as papers, photos, books, clippings, and email. It is suitable for collections comprising tens of thousands of documents, and provides for ease of document entry and access as well as high levels of security and privacy. It is highly extensible through user scripting, and is also intended to be useful as a platform for further research into digital libraries and computer-augmented reading. The general architecture and design of UpLib is more fully described in [6] and [5].

UpLib creates a searchable repository accessed through an active agent via a Web interface. This interface is highly visual, displaying documents as *document icons* (figure 1), laid out in a two-dimensional space, for the user to select from. The built-in reader application also uses thumbnail images of each page (figure 5), in two sizes, for various purposes, but primarily for reading. Other applications, such as the corpus browser discussed in [2], also use the thumbnails in their interfaces. In the process of designing these interfaces for UpLib, a number of issues arose regarding effective generation of document icons and page thumbnails. The rest of this paper presents these issues, and discusses our approach to resolving them.

R. Heery and L. Lyon (Eds.): ECDL 2004, LNCS 3232, pp. 111–121, 2004.

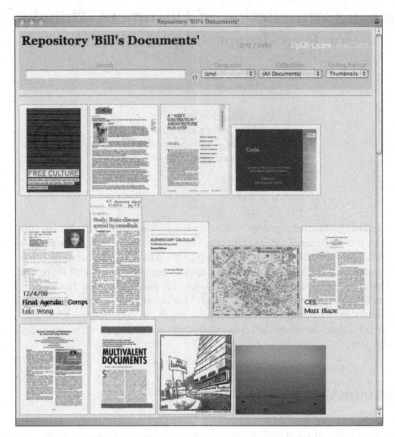

Fig. 1. Document icons in an UpLib overview. These icons are generated using a *constant-area* algorithm, which allocates the same amount of area to each thumbnail, regardless of orientation. In this interface, clicking on an icon opens that document in a reader program.

2   Document Icons

In the user interfaces of many digital library systems, when a selection of documents is shown to the user, it is presented as lines of text [12], [11]. Sometimes these lines contain document titles, sometimes they contain descriptions of the documents, sometimes they include information such document size or owner or creation date. In many systems, these description lines also include small icons, typically indicating the document format or genre, such as "folder" or "Word document" or "web page". This is also the presentation system used on Windows and MacOS desktops, for Google search results, and for many other multi-document systems. The SOMLib system uses generic icons of books, colored to indicate genre, but otherwise connected to the content of each icon only with textual labels on the icons [8].

In the UpLib system, however, the primary display mode for a selection of documents is as as a set of graphical *document icons*, as shown in figure 1. These icons are not genre icons; rather, they are intended to remind the user of the source document, in terms of appearance, shape, and size. They are small but compelling visual representations of the documents they represent. In contrast to more general-purpose digital library systems, UpLib is intended for personal use by an individual; almost all the documents in any collection have already been seen (and often handled) by the user of the system. This reinforces the ability of visual representations to remind the user of the content of the associated document. The use of document icons also capitalizes on the human perceptual preference for pictures over words when locating an item amidst a number of other similar items [7].

2.1   Computing Document Icon Size

To visually represent the physical document in the digital space, it is usually necessary to scale the size of the document page to a thumbnail representation. It is customary to anti-alias the scaled image, and to preserve the aspect ratio of the image. However, it is less clear what an appropriate size for the icon should be.

In UpLib, page thumbnails are generated for each page of a document (see section 3.1). These are typically constrained to fit in a particular rectangular region, as part of the reading system showin in figure 5. In the first implementation of UpLib, no special document icons were generated; the page thumbnail for the first page of the document was used as its iconic representation. This posed some interesting problems, and led to a series of algorithms for determining icon sizes.

Figure 2 shows seven representative documents arranged in four rows, each row illustrating a particular icon sizing algorithm. From left to right, the documents are a scanned store receipt, actual size 63.8x82.8 mm; an A4 technical paper, actual size 210x297 mm; a US-letter saved Web page, actual size 216x279.4 mm; a Powerpoint presentation, actual size 279.4x216 mm; a map, actual size 355.6x279.4 mm; a scanned newspaper clipping, actual size 99.1x222.7 mm; and a photograph, actual size 162.6x121.9 mm. The top row of the figure shows the effects of the original algorithm, using page thumbnails. While this algorithm worked well for the pages of a single document, all of which were the same size, it does not perform particularly well for a juxtaposed assortment of documents of different sizes. In particular, landscape-oriented documents were shortchanged in the display, when arranged near portrait-oriented documents.

The second row of the figure shows our first attempt at rectifying this problem. A special "document icon" was generated for each document, instead of simply using the thumbnail of the first page. Instead of using a portrait-oriented rectangle to size the icon, we use a square. You will note that the Powerpoint document now receives as much display area as the paper to its left.

However, this algorithm fails to preserve some salient physical differences. Users complained that they were unable to distinguish A4 papers from US-

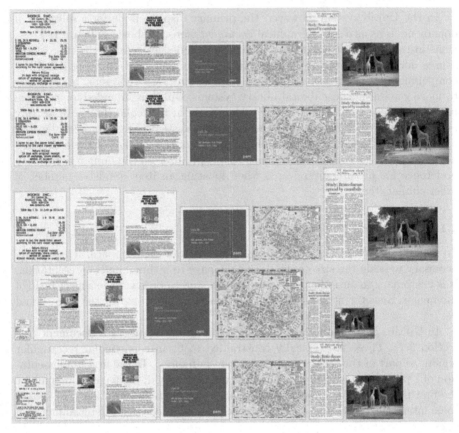

Fig. 2. This figure illustrates five possible icon size generation strategies. At the top is *constant-rectangle*, which attempts to scale each icon to fit in a constant-size rectangle. The second row illustrates *constant-square*, a version of constant-rectangle which provides parity for landscape and portrait mode documents. Both of these suffer from the inability to quickly distinguish US-Letter from A4 documents by their primary distinguishing characteristic, height. This problem is addressed by the *constant-area* algorithm shown on the third row, which allocates the same amount of area to each document icon. However, this algorithm tends to distort the relative sizes of documents. The fourth row illustrates the *linear* algorithm, in which each icon has the same size relative to the others as the physical document would. With this algorithm, large documents such as maps, posters, or blueprints dominate the display. Finally, the *log-area* algorithm in the bottom row provides the same amount of area as the linear algorithm for an US-Letter document, but allocates more area (about four times more) to the small receipt, and somewhat less area to the large map (about two-thirds of the linear algorithm).

Letter papers, even though the A4 document icon shown is somewhat "thinner" than the US-Letter icon. Apparently, the memorable characteristic of the A4 page size is that it is somewhat "taller" or longer than US-Letter; our iconic representation did not preserve that relationship.

The third row of figure 2 illustrates a different algorithm that gives each document icon an equal amount of display area, while preserving the document's aspect ratio. The A4 document can be clearly distinguished from the US-Letter document by height. However, this still masks other relative differences in size. The small sales receipt and small photograph seem to be as large as the US-Letter document. The large map seems to be the same size as the Powerpoint presentation, while the relatively small newspaper clipping towers above the other icons.

To address these issues, we looked for a sizing algorithm that would preserve some elements of the relative sizes of the documents. A strict linear reduction in size, shown in the fourth row of figure 2, would be problematic, as it would tend to make very large icons for very large documents, and vanishingly small ones for very small documents. We decided to use a smooth non-linear function of the area of a document to calculate the icon size. To increase the size of small documents, and reduce the size of very large ones, we chose a function relatively linear around the area of a US-Letter document, which would still reveal small differences, such as those between A4 and US-Letter, but which would still result in smaller icons for smaller documents, and larger ones for larger documents.

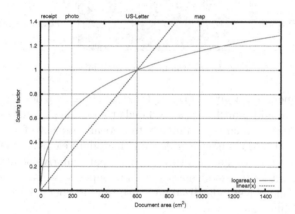

Fig. 3. The *linear* and *log-area* scaling functions.

The graph in figure 3 shows this function, which has the following formula:

$$factor = \sqrt{\ln\left(\frac{area_{document}(e-1)}{area_{US-Letter}} + 1\right)} \qquad (1)$$

To calculate the amount of area to allot to each icon, this factor is multiplied by the amount of area that would be given to the icon for a US-Letter document. The bottom row of figure 2 shows the result of sizing the document icons in this manner, which we call *log-area*. While this scaling algorithm seems preferable to the others, all five are available in the current UpLib system, and user-selectable via the configuration mechanism.

2.2   Document Icon Decoration

Enhancement of document icons used in task-oriented applications has been examined by Woodruff et. al., [13]. That application constructed custom document icons to display search engine results to users. Each icon was a rendering of the result Web page, and text items that matched the query terms were exaggerated. This differs from the use of icons in UpLib in several ways: the rendering was only one of many possible renderings of the same Web page, the user may never have encountered that page before, and the text labels exaggerated on the page were specific to that search. However, the general idea of using exaggerated text on document icons to improve recognizability seems a useful one.

Fig. 4. Document icons with labels.

UpLib document icons support colored text labelling, in a deliberately limited fashion. Users can add multiline colored labels to document icons using a single size of a single font (chosen to be unlikely to appear similar to fonts in common use), by defining the "document-icon-legend" metadata element. Figure 4 shows an example of this type of document icon. This is particularly useful for technical papers using small fonts, email messages, newspaper web pages, or any other document that follows a standardized layout so that all documents in that layout appear quite similar.

This approach can also be extended to non-text labels. The rightmost icon in figure 4 shows a mockup of an icon for an email message in an UpLib repository. A picture of the sender has been located in a "biff" library of email senders, and pasted into a whitespace area of the original page image. In addition, a label has been automatically calculated for the mail message from information in the mail headers.

E-mail raises some questions about the appropriate granularity of documents. Is it a good idea to make each mail message a separate document, or is it more useful to compose a single document from all of the messages that make up a thread in an email discussion? If so, an appropriate document icon may consist of a graph of the thread tree, rather than a picture of the first sender. Similarly, a related series of photographs might be stored as a single document, with concomitant considerations for the document icon. A document similar to the

WebBook proposed by Card et. al. [4] could be built from a set of Web pages traversed in a single browsing session; an icon for such a book might be a graph of the session, similar to the "Web behavior graphs" discussed in [3]. The Web caricatures work [14] developed a feature analysis of a Web page, then used that analysis to drive construction of an iconic representation for that page.

Other icon decoration possibilities are possible. The DocuWorks system [1] incorporates cartoon decorations related to the desktop metaphor. Multi-page documents are distinguished from single-page documents with a small binder clip cartoon in the upper left corner. Multiple documents "bound" together are distinguished from individual documents by the addition of the cartoon of a spiral binding on the left side of the document. These decorations typically act as active controls; for example, the binder clip has left and right arrows that allow you to page through the page thumbnails of the document, and clicking the clip itself will fan out the pages of the document.

3   Page Images

The UpLib document reading subsystem makes certain assumptions about the economics of the computing environment. It assumes that disk storage on the order of gigabytes is very cheap (though not free, due to the overhead cost of backups); that the average communications speed is relatively fast, at least 802.11b speeds; and that display screens are fairly tall, at least 1024 pixels in height. A tablet-PC, for example, in portrait mode has a screen that is at least 768 pixels wide and 1024 pixels high. These assumptions are partially due to Up-Lib's design for personal use: a personal library will have fewer documents than a community library, reducing storage requirements; the document repository will frequently reside on the machine the user is using it on, reducing communication overhead.

As a result of this calculation, the reading subsystem uses page images as the primary presentation form of the document (figure 5). These are anti-aliased reduced-resolution versions of the document's page images, sized to fit on the screen, and optimized for reading. In addition, a small thumbnail version of each page is generated, for use in document overviews. This thumbnail also contains an oversized page number for that page. This section discusses appropriate generation of these two types of document page images.

3.1   Page Thumbnails

Small page thumbnails are used to show an overview of the pages of the document. Examples of this usage are shown in figures 5 and 6. They allow a user to locate graphically distinctive pages, containing diagrams, maps, or photographs, easily. They can also be used to provide some context for the particular page the reader is on. They are sized to be significantly smaller than document icons. This allows more of them to be presented to the reader without scrolling. For most slideshows or technical papers, all of the document's page thumbnails can be presented without scrolling in a display such as that shown in figure 6.

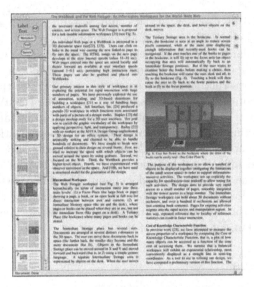

Fig. 5. An "open" document in an UpLib viewer. The small page icons on the left-hand side provide direct access to that page; when used on the 768 × 1024 pixel screen of a Tablet PC, they are partially occluded on the right side, but the page numbers are still visible.

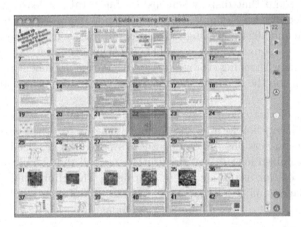

Fig. 6. The small page thumbnails are used for overviews of a document, as shown here and in figure 5. The highlighted thumbnail shows that the current page is page 22. Gross graphical detail on other pages is discernible.

Each page thumbnail is numbered on the left top of the image. In a frame-based display such as that shown in figure 5, this allows the frame to be dragged to the left, occluding the right side of the page thumbnail, but providing more space for the main page image, and still showing the page number on the page thumbnail.

3.2   Large Images

UpLib uses "large thumbnails" in its primary reading interface. These are anti-aliased versions of the original high-resolution page images, scaled to fit on a typical display. The actual display size is user-configurable; by default, each large thumbnail is constrained to fit in a 680x880 pixel rectangle. This allows display on the 768x1024 pixel screen of a tablet-PC in portrait mode. The image format is also important for readability. A text page scaled to size and stored as either PNG (compression level 8) or JPEG (quality 75%) will be about the same size, but the JPEG version will exhibit ghosting effects around the characters, making it harder to read.

Human response times must be considered for Web-based user interfaces. Typically, actions that complete within about 100 msec are seen as instantaneous, and users become impatient if actions do not complete within about 700-1000 msec (see [10], [9]). If we assume a transfer rate of about 2Mbps (a reasonable average for 802.11b), and a maximum allowable user delay of 700 msec, the page image should be no larger than about 170 KB. Allowing for decompression overhead, a top size of about 150 KB is a good target. Faster transfer speeds and user-side caching can be used to increase this limit.

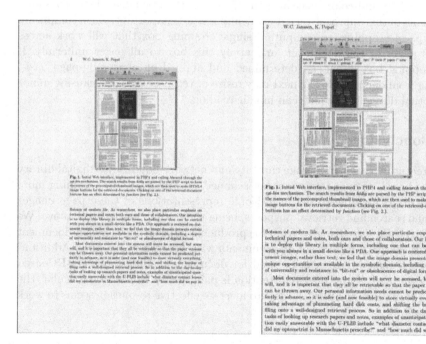

Fig. 7. A page from a paper, before and after whitespace cropping. Both versions are scaled to fit in a 680x880 pixel rectangle, but the one on the right is significantly more readable.

Another concern is the relationship of the presented document size to the original document size. Our original implementation scaled each document to fit within a fixed 680x880 rectangle. This had the unforeseen effect of blowing up small documents, such as the cash register receipt shown in the first column of figure 2, to very large scales, so large that pixelization of the image impaired its readability. In addition, users had difficulty recognizing it for what it was, since they were used to the small size of the physical artifact. To counteract this effect, a sizing governor was used to limit the maximum size for a document. This governor assumes a display resolution of about 100 ppi, and scales documents for display at that resolution, if possible, or for a lower resolution if necessary. This means that the large thumbnail of a document 5cm on a side, scanned at 300dpi, would be only about 197 pixels on a side rather than 680 pixels; that is, it would be rendered at about its normal size on a 100 ppi display.

Larger documents are of course reduced more to fit in the bounding rectangle. For a letter-size document, there are about 80 ppi to work with. For 9-point text, this is about 10 pixels per line. With clean text, this is often good enough. However, since ppi is a ratio of total pixels to document size, it is possible to increase the apparent resolution not only by increasing the number of pixels, but also by decreasing the document size. We take the latter approach, by trimming excess background-color space around the text of the document. Figure 7 shows the results of this approach on a document page. It is important, when computing this type of cropping, to compute a single cropping box that will work across all the pages of the document, and apply this box to all pages uniformly. If the cropping box is instead determined and applied on a page-by-page basis, flipping from one page to the next may resize or recenter the text, causing minor perceptual dissonance which can impair reading.

4   Conclusion

With recent increases in storage capacity and network bandwidth, digital library systems based on page images, either scanned or generated, are becoming more popular. It is possible to optimize iconic representations of these page images for visual search and retrieval purposes, using the techniques outlined above. We recommend the *log-area* algorithm for producing appropriately scaled document icons for selection from a set of documents with heterogeneous sizes. Additionally, scaled page images can be used for document reading on tablet-PC-sized display surfaces, if appropriate attention is paid to size issues. In particular, the technique of removing page borders to increase effective resolution seems to work quite well.

Acknowledgements

The UpLib system itself is the result of joint work with Kris Popat at PARC. Many of our colleagues at PARC have contributed generously to our work on this project, notably Eric Bier, Jeff Breidenbach, and Lance Good.

References

1. See http://www.fujixerox.co.jp/soft/docuworks/.
2. E. Bier, L. Good, K. Popat, and A. Newberger. A document corpus browser for in-depth reading. In *Proceedings of the Fourth ACM/IEEE Joint Conference on Digital Libraries (JCDL 2004)*, pages 87–96, June 2004.
3. S. K. Card, P. Pirolli, M. Van Der Wege, J. B. Morrison, R. W. Reeder, P. K. Schraedley, and J. Boshart. Information scent as a driver of web behavior graphs: results of a protocol analysis method for web usability. In *Proceedings of the SIGCHI conference on Human factors in computing systems*, pages 498–505. ACM Press, 2001.
4. S. K. Card, G. G. Robertson, and W. York. The WebBook and the Web Forager: An information workspace for the World-Wide Web. In *Proceedings of the Conference on Human Factors in Computing Systems CHI'96*, 1996.
5. W. C. Janssen. Collaborative extensions for the uplib system. In *Proceedings of the Fourth ACM/IEEE Joint Conference on Digital Libraries (JCDL 2004)*, pages 239–240, June 2004.
6. W. C. Janssen and K. Popat. UpLib: a universal personal digital library system. In *Proceedings of the 2003 ACM symposium on Document Engineering*, pages 234–242. ACM Press, November 2003.
7. A. Paivio and I. Begg. Pictures and words in visual search. *Memory & Cognition*, 2(3):515–521, 1974.
8. A. Rauber and D. Merkl. The SOMLib digital library system. In *Proceedings of the 3rd European Conference on Research and Advanced Technology for Digital Libraries*, number 1696 in Lecture Notes in Computer Science, pages 323–342, September 1999.
9. G. G. Robertson, S. K. Card, and J. D. Mackinlay. The Cognitive Co-Processor architecture for interactive user interfaces. In *Proceedings of the ACM Conference on User Interface Software and Technology (UIST '89)*, pages 10–18. ACM Press, 1989.
10. G. G. Robertson, S. K. Card, and J. D. Mackinlay. Information visualization using 3D interactive animation. *Communications of the ACM*, 36(4):57–71, April 1993.
11. R. Wilensky. Personal libraries: Collection management as a tool for lightweight personal and group document management. Technical Report SDSC TR-2001-9, San Diego Supercomputer Center, 9500 Gilman Drive – La Jolla, CA 92093-0505, 2001.
12. I. H. Witten, R. J. McNab, S. J. Boddie, and D. Bainbridge. Greenstone: A comprehensive open-source digital library software system. In *Proceedings of the Fifth ACM International Conference on Digital Libraries*, 2000.
13. A. Woodruff, A. Faulring, R. Rosenholtz, J. Morrsion, and P. Pirolli. Using thumbnails to search the web. In *Proceedings of the SIGCHI conference on Human factors in computing systems*, pages 198–205. ACM Press, 2001.
14. M. Wynblatt and D. Benson. Web page caricatures: Multimedia summaries for WWW documents. In *Proceedings of the IEEE International Conference on Multimedia Computing and Systems*, June 1998.

Citiviz: A Visual User Interface to the CITIDEL System

Nithiwat Kampanya, Rao Shen, Seonho Kim, Chris North, and Edward A. Fox

Department of Computer Science, Virginia Tech,
Blacksburg, VA 24061 USA
{nkampany,rshen,shk,north,fox}@vt.edu

Abstract. The Digital Library (DL) field is one of the most promising areas of application for information visualization technology. In this paper, we propose a visual user interface tool kit for digital libraries, to deliver an overview of document sets, with support for interactive direct manipulation. Our system, Citiviz, employs a dynamic hyperbolic tree to display hierarchical relationships among documents, based on where their topics fit into the ACM classification system. Also, Citiviz provides an interactive, animated 2-dimensional scatter plot. With it, users may gain insight by changing various parameters, or may directly jump to a particular document based on its label or location. According to a preliminary evaluation, our system shows advantages in performance and user preference relative to traditional text based DL web interfaces.

1 Introduction

The Computing and Information Technology Interactive Digital Educational Library (CITIDEL, http://www.citidel.org), part of the NSDL (National Science Digital Library, http://www.nsdl.org), uses OAI-PMH (the Open Archives Initiative Protocol for Metadata Harvesting) to harvest resource metadata from its member collections. Those member collections are other digital libraries (DLs) that share their resources with CITIDEL, which provides integrated browsing and searching services. Users can browse separately through each member collection, or can browse through the union collection using any of four different classification schemes. Nevertheless, the primary means to access CITIDEL is through searching. Unfortunately, if users are unfamiliar with the topic of their search, or lack experience regarding search tactics, relevant documents may only appear frustratingly far down in a ranked list of search results. Fortunately, visual interfaces to DLs apply powerful data analysis and information visualization techniques to generate visualizations of document collections in DLs, with possible beneficial effect on browsing and searching. Thus, we have integrated text mining and information visualization to develop a visual interface to CITIDEL.

Visualization techniques of one broad category consider predefined document attributes, such as author or date, and query relevance. One example is the Envision interface [14, 22]. It can organize search results according to metadata along the X and Y-axes, and show values for attributes associated with retrieved documents within each cell. However, the view provided by the original version of the Envision interface gave few cues about how the documents are related to each other in terms of their content and meaning.

R. Heery and L. Lyon (Eds.): ECDL 2004, LNCS 3232, pp. 122–133, 2004.

Visualization techniques of another category do not make assumptions regarding document attributes. They automatically derive a collection overview through unsupervised learning, which usually is based on inter-document similarities. Scatter/Gather [3, 7] is such a system that applied document clustering approaches to browsing and searching. However, the representation of document clusters by Scatter/Gather is textual, not graphical.

Reflecting upon the above two different types of visualization techniques has led us to the following research questions:

1. How should we combine the two different types of visualization techniques to develop a visual interface to CITIDEL for post-retrieval analysis?
2. What text mining technology should we use to explore the inter-document similarities for online document collections that are dynamically created, such as the set of retrieved documents from a search engine?
3. What are the insights supported, and how are they supported?
4. What interaction and navigation strategies should we use to facilitate visual browsing and analysis?

To address the above questions, we

1. Developed clustering components to discovery document relationships and to identify subject categories for retrieved documents.
2. Developed a visual interface, called Citiviz (http://feathers.dlib.vt.edu/ CitiViz/), for post-retrieval analysis, initially for CITIDEL, following the guiding principles of Resnikoff [18] and Shneiderman [20]. Resnikoff observed that the human eye and other biological systems process the vast amounts of information available in the real world by smoothly integrating a focused view, for details, with a general view, for context. Shneiderman advocated an interaction model in which the user begins with an overview of the information to be worked with, then pans and zooms to find areas of potential interest, and then views details. The followings are interaction and navigation methods we implemented.

- Use aggregation by document clustering as an overview strategy.
- Use the "focus + content" (fisheye) scheme to visualize a hierarchical graph of a concept map representing subject categories of retrieved documents.
- Combine tree graphs with scatter plot graphs. Documents attached to nodes of a tree graph can be visualized in a 2D space.
- Integrate a 2D scatter plot graph with a network of citations. Documents of selected clusters are scatter plotted in a 2D space and connected by citation relationships.
- Apply the aggregate towers technique [16] to solve occlusion problems of documents visualized in the scatter plot graph.

2   Related Works

Visual interfaces to DLs apply powerful data analysis and information visualization techniques to manage document collections in DLs. They exploit human vision and spatial cognition to help humans mentally organize and electronically access and manage large, complex information spaces [1]. They have common usage scenarios supporting searching and browsing for DLs. Further, visualization of search results has much in common with gaining an overview of the coverage of a DL to facilitate browsing. Both enable the user to become oriented, and to find relevant information. They differ mainly in two respects. First is the origin of the document sets (a pre-existing static collection, or result set dynamically retrieved from a search engine). Second is the information available that relates documents to user information needs.

Thus, first, we consider visualization based on predefined document attributes such as author or date, along with query relevance. In Section 1 we discussed Envision [14, 22]. Here we broaden the discussion to include semantic information. Cougar [5] and Cat-a-Cone [6] display semantic information (categories assigned to each document) to users. Categories also can be visualized as a Hyperbolic tree [12] or a SpaceTree [15] as well as through a traditional node-link representation of a tree. Cat-a-Cone used ConeTree [19] to display the category labels of the documents retrieved, while the retrieved documents are organized as pages in a WebBook [2]. Another example is Map.net (http://map.net/start). It provides hierarchical (multilevel/categorical) information maps for browsing over two million Web sites from the Open Directory Project (http://dmoz.com). Rather than using conventional search engine technology to navigate the Web, it creates a landscape that spatially represents data relationships, though in a very abstract, geometric fashion. Size and position of areas on the map indicate number of documents in respective categories and mutual relations between them. Users of this kind of interface gain an immediate overview of available categories and the number of documents these categories contain.

Document-query relevance was visualized in TileBars [4] and VIBE [11]. TileBars showed how query terms appear within individual documents, while VIBE displayed an overview of the retrieved documents according to which subset of query terms they contain.

Often there are more than two predefined document attributes. Visualizing multi-attribute sets can be seen as visualizing multidimensional data sets. Techniques for visualizing multidimensional data include pixel-oriented, geometric projection, icon-base, hierarchical, and graph-based techniques [9]. The basic idea of pixel-oriented techniques is to map each data item to a colored pixel, while icon-based techniques map each data item to an icon. A well-known representative of hierarchical techniques is Treemaps [8]. Graph-based techniques effectively present a large graph using specific layout algorithms, query languages, and abstraction techniques.

Visualization techniques in the second category introduced at the start of this section do not make assumptions regarding document attributes. They automatically derive a collection overview via the use of text mining, often through document clustering or neural networks. Examples are Scatter/Gather [3, 7], Grouper[24-26], Galaxy of News [17], Vivisimo (http://vivisimo.com), Kartoo (http://kartoo.com), Highlight (http://highlight.njit.edu/technology.htm), SOM [10, 13], ThemeScapes [23], and Mooter (http://mooter.com:8080/moot).

Occlusion is one of the important issues in information visualization. The Envision system [14, 22] solves this problem by using a flexible table that resizes its cells appropriately. On the other hand, the aggregate tower technique [16] avoids occlusion of objects by stacking objects together, creating towers of objects.

Grouper was a dynamic clustering interface to web search results. It introduced the Suffix Tree Clustering (STC) algorithm. Vivisimo is a web search clustering interface. Its algorithm is based on an old artificial intelligence idea: a good cluster or document grouping is one that possesses a good, readable description. Kartoo is a web interface organizing search results retrieved from relevant web search engines by topics that displays them on a 2-dimensional map. Theoretically, Kartoo provides a node-link graph. A document (Web page) node is presented by a ball. The size of the ball corresponds to the relevance of the document to the query. Links are labeled with sets of keywords shared by related documents. Another example of visualization techniques of this category is self-organizing map (SOM). SOM is a neural network algorithm that takes a set of high-dimensional data and maps them onto nodes in a 2D grid. Shifting to 3D, the ThemeScapes view imposes a three-dimensional representation on the results of clustering. The layout makes use of "negative space" to help emphasize the areas of concentration where the clusters occur.

Combining visualization with text mining could lead to novel discovery tools [21] Examples are commercial tools such as SAS JMP (http://www.sas.com), Spotfire (http://www.spotfire.com), and SPSS Diamond (http://www.spss.com).

3   System Design

To address the research questions raised in Section 1, and building upon related work (Section 2) and our prior work with CITIDEL and Envision, we have developed Citiviz, according to a component based design. Communication between components is XML based. There are three types of components. They are Data Source Components, Clustering Component, and Visualizing Component. The first two were implemented and then wrapped into Java servlets to enable web access. The Visualizing Components, also implemented in Java, communicate with those servlets in XML.

3.1   Data Source Components

Data Source Components send queries to CITIDEL or other DLs, and parse the retrieved HTML pages into XML files, conforming to XML schemas we developed. Those XML files are then transmitted to the Clustering Components for processing.

3.2   Clustering Component

Clustering Components are implementations of different document clustering algorithms. We developed a new clustering component to supplement the clustering components of Carrot2 [26] that have been incorporated into our system.

3.3   Visualizing Component or Citiviz

Citiviz applies two major visualizing techniques – a hyperbolic tree of a hierarchical concept map and a 2D scatter-plot graph. The initial interface is shown in Figure 1.

The top right of the screen is a hyperbolic tree based on the ACM Computing Classification System (1998 Version, CCS1998, http://www.acm.org/class/1998/). On

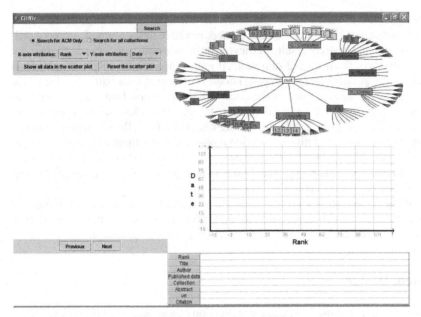

Fig. 1. Initial Interface of Citiviz

the top left is a query box. By default, a user will retrieve results from a member DL (e.g., "ACM DL") of CITIDEL. A user also has an option to retrieve results from all CITIDEL member DLs. In the middle right of the screen, there is a 2D scatter-plot. At the bottom right, there are fields for details of the attributes of a selected document. Citiviz supports exploring to gain insights, as is illustrated in the following three example scenarios.

Examples of Insights Sought

1. How are the retrieved documents clustered according to the ACM Computing Classification System?
2. How are the retrieved documents clustered according to inter-document similarity?
3. Which cluster has the largest portion of the document collection?
4. To what category does the 1st ranked document belong?
5. Which document is cited most among the selected clusters of documents?
6. Which documents cite a selected document?
7. What's the most recently published paper by a particular author?
8. To what topics does a document belong?

Scenario 1: Show Me the Retrieved Results from ACM DL

A user inputs query "Information Visualization". By default, Citiviz provides retrieved results from the CITIDEL member DL named "ACM DL". A hierarchical concept map organized according to the ACM Computing Classification System then is displayed as a hyperbolic tree on the top right of the screen. The node name represents a category, and a bubble attached to a node represents a document collection belonging to that category. The size of a bubble attached to a node indicates the size of the document collection clustered in that category. The hyperbolic tree supports "focus + context" navigation. After the user clicks "Show all data in the scatter plot" button, all the retrieved documents from ACM DL are scatter plotted in the 2D space as shown in Figure 2.

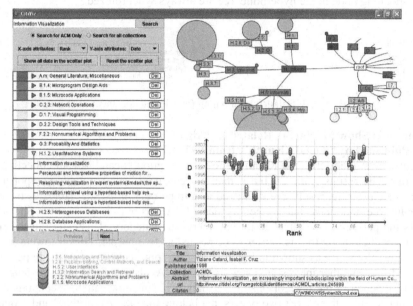

Fig. 2. Visual Results of Scenario 1

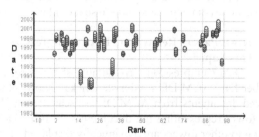

Fig. 3. Towers of documents

Each document is visually mapped to a tower of cylinders (see Figure 3). Each level of a tower represents a cluster to which a document belongs. The taller a tower is, the more categories the document belongs to. Moreover, clicking on a tower allows users to see detailed information for the selected tower, as shown in the bottom of the screen. (See Figure 2 and Figure 4.). On the left of the screen, there is a list of colored bars representing the categories that those retrieved documents belong to. Clicking on a bar allows users to see a list of documents belonging to the cluster represented by the clicked bar. Moving the mouse over a bar invokes an animation of blinking towers in the 2D scatter plot space. Those blinking towers represent documents belonging to the category visually mapped to a colored bar selected with the mouse. Towers in the

2D space can be arranged according to attributes of rank, date, and citations. The colors of the levels of a tower correspond to those categories to which a document belongs. A user can change the color of a bar to distinguish different categories. The color of a bar, the color of its corresponding level in all towers, and the color of its corresponding node in the hyperbolic tree are always synchronized.

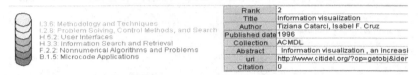

Rank	2
Title	Information visualization
Author	Tiziana Catarci, Isabel F. Cruz
Published date	1996
Collection	ACMDL
Abstract	Information visualization , an increasi
url	http://www.citidel.org/?op=getobj&ider
Citation	0

I.3.6: Methodology and Techniques
I.2.8: Problem Solving, Control Methods, and Search
H.5.2: User Interfaces
H.3.3: Information Search and Retrieval
F.2.2: Nonnumerical Algorithms and Problems
B.1.5: Microcode Applications

Fig. 4. Detailed information for selected document

Scenario 2: Show Me Papers Related to "Algorithm Analysis" and Published by "Donald Knuth", from CITIDEL

A user inputs query "Donald Knuth". She selects option "Search for all collections". The retrieved results from CITIDEL then are clustered, using suitable components. After the clustering, results are displayed as a hyperbolic tree. She navigates the hyperbolic tree and finds that a category named "Algorithm" is of interest. She then clicks the purple bubble attached to that interesting category. This cause all the five documents belonging to this cluster to be plotted as five purple, 1-level towers in the 2D scatter plot space as shown in Figure 5(a). She continues browsing the hyperbolic tree and finds another interesting category named "Analysis". She clicks the magenta bubble attached to the category named "Analysis". This new category contains nine documents. Since there exist two papers that belong to both "Algorithm" and "Analysis" categories, the interface shows seven 1-level magenta towers and two 2-story towers consisting one purple story and one magenta level as shown in Figure 5(b), instead of adding nine new 1-level towers into the scatter plot.

Scenario 3: Show Me All Papers Related to "Data Compression" That Are Cited by This Paper

A user inputs query "Data Compression". By default, she gets retrieved results from the CITIDEL member DL "ACM DL". After she clicks "Show all data in the scatter plot", all the retrieved documents from ACM DL are scatter plotted in the 2D space. When she clicks a tower representing the document with title "Data Compression", citation links pointing to other towers are dynamically displayed on demand as shown in Figure 6. A link connecting two towers indicates a citation relationship between the two papers. That is, a pointed to paper is cited by a pointing paper. She then follows the link to get detailed information for the cited papers.

4   Evaluation

To evaluate the interface, we conducted a small usability study to suggest further improvements and determine whether or not the combination of the hyperbolic tree and the scatter plot helps users find a document easier and faster than using traditional, web-based interfaces. Four Computer Science graduate students participated in this evaluation.

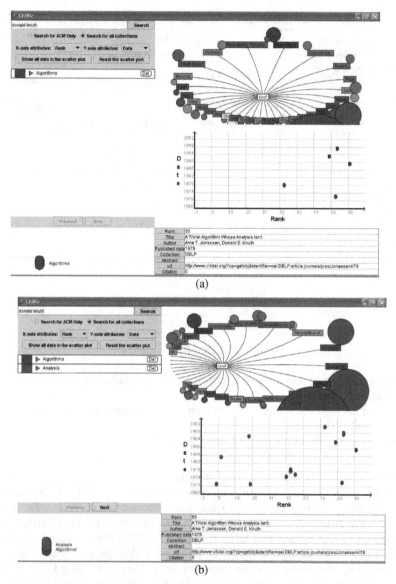

Fig. 5. a) Top, a 1-level document is selected. b) Bottom, where results for two categories are shown, the document selected has 2 levels

The test consists of three sections. Each section was designed to measure different tools: Citiviz using ACM classification, Citiviz using Citiviz clustering component, and CITIDEL (www.citidel.org). In each section, participants were asked to complete four tasks. The tasks were designed such that they could be completed using any of the tools. During the test session, the order of tool use was permuted to avoid bias. The participants were asked to perform each of the following tasks:

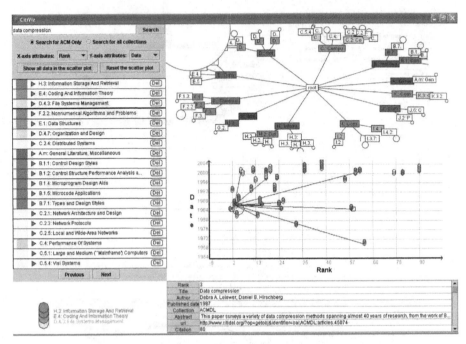

Fig. 6. Scatter Plot shows Citations

1. Given an author and a topic, find a document published by that author and belonging to that topic.
2. Given an author and a publication year, find a document published by that author and in that year.
3. Given a title, find a document having that title.
4. Find the most recently published paper.

The results of the study are summarized in Figure 7.

From the study, there is no significant difference between Citiviz (ACM classification) and Citiviz (Citiviz clustering) when users browse search results for a paper based on topic or title information (tasks 1 and 3). However, Citiviz (Citiviz clustering) helps users find a document faster than Citiviz (ACM classification) when users browse search result for a paper based on publication date (tasks 2 and 4). Based on our observations, the reason that users perform tasks faster when using Citiviz (Citiviz clustering) is that several users were confused by the concept of aggregate tower. As a result, it might be more difficult for users to identify documents in Citiviz (ACM classification), where documents usually are in towers consisting of several levels.

In contrast to Citiviz using the ACM classification scheme, documents visualized using Citiviz's clustering component usually have one level. Thus, it is relatively easy for users to identify the publication date of a document.

Unsurprisingly, Citiviz helps users find a document faster than CITIDEL, when users browse search results for a paper based on topic and publication date (tasks 1, 2, and 4). Citiviz is designed to visualize topic and publication date information graphically by using a hyperbolic tree and a scatter plot. These features allow users to gain more insight about document relationships based on topic and publication date information. In contrast, CITIDEL displays this information textually and individually. Users cannot see quickly the relationships among documents. However, CITIDEL helps users find a document faster than Citiviz when users browse search result for a paper based on title (task 3) because, in contrast to Citiviz, CITIDEL displays search result as a list of titles. As a result, finding a paper with a certain title is quite easy in CITIDEL. Accordingly, in a future version of Citiviz, we will add features to better support this type of task.

After users completed all tasks, they were asked to fill out questionnaires. It appears users believe that Citiviz is easy to use and helps them find documents easier and faster than would a traditional tool. Users also think the scatter plot and the hyperbolic tree are helpful, although some users think that the hyperbolic tree for the ACM classification scheme is too big and too complex.

The hyperbolic tree of the ACM classification scheme usually has three levels (depth-oriented). If users know the exact topic, it is still difficult to locate the topic in the hyperbolic tree. Unlike Citiviz using ACM classification scheme, the hyperbolic tree of Citiviz clustering component usually has one level (breadth-oriented). If users know the exact topic, it is easy to locate the topic in the hyperbolic tree and to find the document.

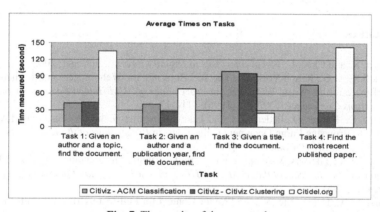

Fig. 7. The results of the user study

5 Conclusion

The result of our work is a DL visual interface tool kit combining text mining and information visualization. It uses a 2D scatter plot to visualize document attributes (e.g., rank, date) as did Envision [17, 25]. Unlike Envision, the 2D scatter plot space also integrates a network of citations to show the document relationships. A further difference of our work from Envision is that we integrate document clustering and information visualization to show the insight of similarity among documents as well as predefined document attributes. Though some approaches such as ThemeScapes [27] show the inter-document similarities, they display data in a completely flexible manner and do not provide an overview of document attributes.

The visual interface provides overviews of retrieved results from CITIDEL. The overview strategy of aggregation by document clustering provides users insights of how similar documents are clustered. The overview of a hierarchical concept map displayed as a hyperbolic tree supports "focus + context" navigation. "Focus + context" navigation provides direct manipulation and high interaction, and therefore a balance of local detail and global context. The overview of document attributes such as query relevance shown in the 2D scatter plot space allows users to understand why a document is retrieved. Integrating the 2D scatter plot space with a network of citations shows users document citation relationships. All these address the last two questions mentioned in Section 1.

The componentized and XML based architecture of our project makes the tool kit reusable for different DLs. The Data Source Component we developed provides a data source from CITIDEL, which serves as a portal to its member DLs such as the ACM DL. So, in addition to being a visual interface to CITIDEL, the result of our project is also to provide a visual interface to its member DLs. Connecting our tool kit to another different DL can be completed easily by implementing a Data Source Component for that DL. Accordingly, after some small improvements identified in this study are made to Citiviz, we plan to deploy it for larger scale testing with CITIDEL, CITIDEL-member DLs, and other DLs such as NDLTD (www.ndltd.org).

References

1. Börner, K. and Chen, C. *Visual Interfaces to Digital Libraries*. Springer, 2002.
2. Card, S.K., G.G., R. and York, W., The WebBook and the WebForager: an Information Workspace for the World Wide Web. in *Proceedings of ACM Human Factors in Computing Systems Conference (CHI'96)*, (1996), 111-117.
3. Cutting, D., Karger, D., Pedersen, J. and Tukey, J., Scatter/Gather: A Clusterbased Approach to Browsing Large Document Collections. in *Proceedings of the 15th Annual International ACM/SIGIR Conference*, (1992), 318-329.
4. Hearst, M.A., TileBars: Visualization of Term Distribution Information in Full Text Information Access. in *Proc. of the ACM SIGCHI Conference on Human Factors in Computing Systems*, (1995), 59-66.
5. Hearst, M.A., Using Categories to Provide Context for Full-text Retrieval Results. in *Proceedings of the RIAO'94*, (1994).
6. Hearst, M.A. and C., K., Cat-a-Cone: An Interface for Specifying Searches and Viewing Retrieval Results Using a Large Category Hierarchy. in *Proceedings of the 20th International ACM SIGIR Conference on Research and Development in Information Retrieval (SIGIR'97)*, (1997).
7. Hearst, M.A. and Pedersen, J.O., Reexamining the Cluster Hypothesis: Scatter/Gather on Retrieval Results. in *Proceedings of the 19th International ACM SIGIR Conference on Research and Development in Information Retrieval (SIGIR'96)*, (1996), 76-84.
8. ohnson, B. and Shneiderman, B., Treemaps: A Space-filling Approach to the Visualization of Hierarchical Information Structures. in *Proc. of the 2nd International IEEE Visualization Conference*, (San Diego, USA, 1991), 284-291.
9. Keim, D.A. and Kriegel, H.-P. Visualization Techniques for Mining Large Databsaes: A Comparison. *IEEE Transactions on Knowledge and Data Engineering, 8*. 923-938.
10. Kohonen, T., Exploration of Very Large Databases by Self-organizing Maps. in *Proceedings of the IEEE International Conference on Neural Networks*, (1997), 1-6.

11. Korfhage, R.R., To See or Not to See - Is That the Query? in *Proc. of the 14th Annual Int. ACM SIGIR Conference*, (Chicago, USA, 1991).
12. Lamping, J. and Rao, R., Laying Out and Visualizing Large Trees Using a Hyperbolic Space. in *Proceedings of the ACM Symposium on User Interface Software and Technology*, (1994), 13-14.
13. Lin, X., Visualization for the Document Space. in *IEEE Vis*, (1992).
14. Nowell, L.T. Graphical Encoding for Information Visualization: Using Icon Color, Shape, and Size To Convey Nominal and Quantitative Data *computer science*, Virginia Tech, Blacksburg, (1997), 84.
15. Plaisant, C., Grosjean, J. and Bederson, B.B., SpaceTree: Supporting Exploration in Large Node Link Tree, Design Evolution and Empirical Evaluation. in *INFOVIS 2002. IEEE Symposium on Information Visualization, 2002*, (2002), 57 -64.
16. Rayson, J.K. Aggregate Towers: Scale Sensitive Visualization and Decluttering of Geospatial Data. *Information Visualization, INFOVIS*, (1999), 92-99.
17. Rennison, E., Galaxy of news: An Approach to Visualizing and Understanding Expansive News Landscapes. in *Proc. of UIST'94, ACM Symposium on User Interface Software and Technology*, (New York, USA, 1994), 3-12.
18. Resnikoff, H.L. *The illusion of Reality*. Springer-Verlag, New York, 1989.
19. Robertson, G.G., Card, S.K. and Mackinlay, J.D. Information Visualization Using 3D Interactive Animation. *Communications of the ACM, 36(4).* (1993), 57-71.
20. Shneiderman, B., The Eyes have it: A Task by Data Type Taxonomy. in *Proc. of IEEE Symp. Visual Languages 96*, (1996), 336-343.
21. Shneiderman, B. Inventing Discovery Tools: Combining Information Visualization with Data Mining. *Information Visualization, INFOVIS*, (2002), 5-12.
22. Wang, J., Agrawal, A., Bazaza, A., Angle, S., Fox, E.A. and North, C., Enhancing the ENVISION Interface for Digital Libraries. in *Second ACM/IEEE-CS joint conference on Digital libraries*, (Portland, Oregon, USA, 2002), ACM Press, 275-276.
23. Wise, J.A., Thomas, J.J., Pennock, K., Lantrip, D., Pottier, M. and Schur, A., Visualizing the Non-visual: Spatial Analysis and Interaction with Information from Text Documents. in *Proc. of the Information Visualization Symposium 95*, (1995), IEEE Computer Society Press, 51-58.
24. Zamir, O. Clustering Web Algorithms: A Phrase-Based Method For Grouping Search Engine Results, University of Washington, 1999.
25. Zamir, O. and Etzioni, O., Grouper: A Dynamic Clustering Interface to Web Search Results. in *WWW8 / Computer Networks*, (1999).
26. Zamir, O. and Etzioni, O., Web Document Clustering: A Feasibility Demonstration. in *SIGIR 1998*, (Melbourne, Australia, 1998).

System Support for Name Authority Control Problem in Digital Libraries: OpenDBLP Approach

Yoojin Hong[1], Byung-Won On[1], and Dongwon Lee[2]

[1] Department of Computer Science and Engineering, The Pennsylvania State University
{yohong,on}@cse.psu.edu
[2] School of Information Sciences and Technology, The Pennsylvania State University
dongwon@psu.edu

Abstract. In maintaining Digital Libraries, having bibliographic data up-to-date is critical, yet often minor irregularities may cause information isolation. Unlike documents for which various kinds of unique ID systems exist (e.g., DOI, ISBN), other bibliographic entities such as author and publication venue do not have unique IDs. Therefore, in current Digital Libraries, tracking such bibliographic entities is not trivial. For instance, suppose a scholar changes her last name from A to B. Then, a user, searching for her publications under the new name B, cannot get old publications that appeared under A although they are by the same person. For such a scenario, since both A and B are the same person, it would be desirable for Digital Libraries to track their identities accordingly. In this paper, we investigate this problem known as *name authority control*, and present our system-oriented solution. We first identify three core building blocks that underlie the phenomenon, and show taxonomy where different combinations of the building blocks can occur. Then, we consider how systems can support the problem in two common functions of Digital Libraries – *Update* and *Search*. Finally, our test-bed called OpenDBLP is presented where the suggested solution is fully implemented as a proof of the concept.

1 Introduction

A bibliographic Digital Library (DL) such as DBLP [3], CiteSeer [9] or e-Print arXiv [10] archives a collection of articles and their citation data in a certain domain. Often, such a DL is a starting place for researchers to locate relevant works, and a good test-bed for various citation analysis studies. A *citation* or *reference* consists of various bibliographic fields (e.g., author, title, conference/journal name or year), which we refer to as *Bibliographic Entity* in this paper. Often, documents have ways to track their identity. For instance, similar to the case where ISBN can serve as a unique ID for books, Digital Object Identifier (DOI) [11] can provide a persistent ID for digital documents. Therefore, even if two citations are slightly different in format, if their associated DOIs are identical, then one knows two citations in fact refer to the same object in the real world. As DLs evolve over the time, bibliographic entities change too. Especially, due to data-entry errors or different formats used in references, DLs often contain a large variety of values referring to the same objects. For instance, Figure 1, inspired from [14], is the screen-shot of a search session in CiteSeer, looking for a book "Artificial Intelligence: A Modern Approach" by Russell and Norvig. Note that CiteSeer currently lists "23" citations as different, but all of them refer to the identical book, thus must be consolidated into a single citation.

R. Heery and L. Lyon (Eds.): ECDL 2004, LNCS 3232, pp. 134–144, 2004.
© Springer-Verlag Berlin Heidelberg 2004

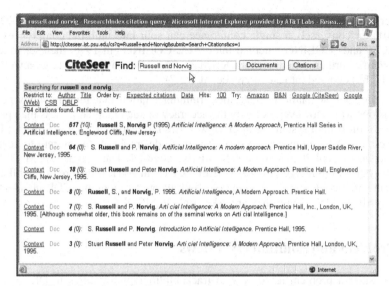

Fig. 1. Search results showing name authority control problem.

This so-called *Citation Matching* problem (or more generally known as *Record Linkage* [13] or *Identity Uncertainty* [14]) is mainly due to different formats people use on the Web or in publications. Toward this problem, people have devised various methods to automatically detect duplicate or similar bibliographic entities that refer to the same object (e.g., [13][14][8]). For instance, using Levenstein edit distance or Jaro distance, one may detect that "S. Russell" and "Russell, Stuart" are the same person. However, to our best knowledge, there has been little work as to how systems can support updating and searching duplicates, once such matches are identified. Furthermore, previous research tends to focus on irregularities caused by errors (e.g., misspell, data-entry error). However, there are also "semantic" irregularities that are legitimate but unavoidable (e.g., a person changes last name after marriage). Therefore, in this paper, we investigate how to support maintenance of DLs once various semantic irregularities are identified. We especially focus on tracking two bibliographic entities – *author* and *publication venue*. First, let us consider various semantic irregularities of two entities that may occur in DLs:

- **Author:** Since the identity of a person is often determined by the name, if person's name changes over time, system cannot keep track of the person's bibliographic records uniformly. For instance, when an author "Alon Levy" becomes "Alon Halevy" after marriage, DLs view two authors as different persons. Likewise, when two scholars share the same name, system cannot differentiate them. For instance, DBLP views two "Wei Wang"s, one at U. North Carolina and the other at HKUST but both are database researchers, as one person. Another case is that DL cannot recognize different varieties of a name. For instance, "Lee D. Coraor" and "Lee Coraor" are treated as two different persons although both refer to the same professor at Penn State.

- **Publication Venue:** Similarly, the identity of publication venue such as conference/journal/publisher is also determined by the name in DLs, but the name can be dynamic. For instance, multiple conferences may merge into a single conference over time (e.g., "ACM DL" and "IEEE ADL" merged into "ACM/IEEE JCDL" in 2001), or conversely a single conference can split into multiple conferences (e.g., "ACL" and "COLING" merged into "ACL-COLING" in 1998, then separated afterward). Furthermore, the characteristics of a venue may change (e.g., a workshop "ML" has evolved into a conference "ICML").

To handle such semantic irregularities, running citation matching methods periodically is one way. However, not only the accuracy of such methods is less than perfect, it is wasteful from a system point of view. Once DL learns that both "S. Russell" and "Russell, Stuart" are the same person, it is more desirable for the system to keep that knowledge to exploit it in future. Similarly, after DL learns that "ACM DL" and "IEEE ADL" were merged to "ACM/IEEE JCDL" in 2001, it may return publications from all three conferences for a query "find all publications in JCDL about Digital Identity after 1995" even if they are asked only to "JCDL."

2   Problem and Solution Overviews

We consider a problem as to how to track bibliographic entities in DLs, typically known as *Name Authority Control problem*. Formally, we solve the problem:

When bibliographic entities (i.e., author and publication venue) of citations change over time in Digital Libraries, devise a system support such that DLs can update and search the changes properly.

Toward the problem, we first present three core elements – linear change, split, and merge – as basic building blocks, and discuss how systems can support those. More specifically, we discuss how UPDATE and SEARCH functions of DLs are changed to track bibliographic entities. Then, we present a proof of the concept, fully implemented in a test-bed, called OpenDBLP [1].

3   Related Work

Citation matching problem has been extensively investigated under various names in various disciplines. For instance, it bears a great relevance to problems known as record linkage [13], identity uncertainty [14], merge-purge [2], etc. However, none of them concerns issues related to "system support" once matching citations are identified. Furthermore, we are interested in individual bibliographic entities – author and publication venue. Works done in [4][8] aim at detecting name variants automatically using data mining or heuristics techniques. Our work is complementary to them since we focus on system support issues once such variants are (semi-)automatically identified. Similarly, [5] introduces a method to find matching variants of named entity in a given text such as project name (e.g., DBLP vs. Data Base and Logic Programming). DOI [11] provide means to specify a persistent ID for digital objects. However their full acceptance is far from reality. Similarly, [6] discusses an effort to standardize author names using a unique number, called INSAN. [7] is a recent implementation for name authority control, called HoPEc, which bears some similarity to our approach. The detailed comparison between our OpenDBLP vs. [6][7] is summarized in Table 1.

Table 1. Comparison between OpenDBLP vs. INSAN [6], HoPEc [7].

4 Our Approach

Although many variations seem to exist in the name authority control issues, at the bottom, there are only three core elements as follows:

1. **Linear change (A→B).** A bibliographic entity A is changed to B. For instance, an author or a conference/journal name is changed over the time.
2. **Split (A→{A$_1$,A$_2$}).** A bibliographic entity is split into multiple ones. For instance, a conference can be broken into two or the publications of two scholars whose names have the same spelling can be split.
3. **Merge ({A$_1$,A$_2$}→A).** Conversely, multiple bibliographic entities are merged into one. For instance, two variants of a person's name may be merged into one authoritative one.

We first discuss how two common functions of DLs, Update and Search, can be changed to support three core elements.

4.1 UPDATE Function

Once name variants are identified (manually by a librarian/author or automatically by algorithms), the findings must be inserted into DLs to solve the name authority control. For instance, suppose an author "Wei Wang" realizes that her publication list is mixed with another person whose name has the same spelling as hers. Then, she may need to specify which of the publications in the DL belong to her and which does not. Or, if a librarian finds that publications under both "Lee Coraor" and "Lee D. Coraor" are by the same physical person, he probably wants to merge two publications lists into one by informing the DL all the name variants.

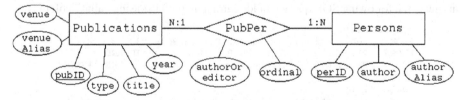

Fig. 2. One possible ER diagram for bibliographic digital libraries.

Imagine a DL built on RDBMS with three tables shown in Figure 2: (1) *Publications* table contains citations of each publication, except their author names, (2) *Persons* table contains author-related information, and (3) *PubPer(pubID, perID, ...)* tells which publication is authored by which person. Since a publication can be authored by many co-authors together, to avoid 1NF violation, separate *Persons* table is needed. Also, note that there are placeholders to store the "alias" name variants, for both author name (*authorAlias*) and publication venue (*venueAlias*).

1. **Linear change.** When an entity A is changed to B, the system sets A as an alias (either in the *authorAlias* or *venueAlias* column), and sets B as the current name (either in the *author* or *venue* column). Further, A's publications are moved to B by changing (*pubID,perID*) pair in *PurPer* table.
2. **Split.** Suppose an entity A needs to be split into B and C. Then, the system needs to know not only new names of A, (i.e., B and C), but also which of the A's publications belong to either B or C. Then, the system creates a new unique ID, *perID*, for both B and C and moves their corresponding publications accordingly. Note that B and C can be the same name. For instance, when originally the publications of two "Wei Wang"s were incorrectly mixed, separating them out is the case of split as in WeiWang → {WeiWang, WeiWang}.
3. **Merge.** When name variants, A and B, are merged into C, the system sets both A and B as aliases of C. Since all of A, B, C still have unique ID, *perID*, in the system so that when users want, he/she can still search using old name variants A and B.

4.2 SEARCH Function

Once duplicates are identified and put into the system, those knowledge can be exploited in searching. Suppose a user is looking at all publications about XML by "Alon Halevy," a database researcher at U. Washington, USA. When he submits two words "Alon Halevy" in the search box of DLs, internally, an SQL query similar to the following (assuming the schema of Figure 2) will be issued:

```
SELECT  P1.*
FROM    Publications P1, PubPer P2, Persons P3
WHERE   P1.pubID=P2.pubID AND P2.perID=P3.perID AND
        P3.author = 'Alon Halevy' and P1.title LIKE '%XML%'
```

However, what this user did not know is that DL keeps a separate list of publications by the same physical person, but under different name "Alon Levy". When such related information is updated by the previous function, now the system can do return merged list or display a link to publication lists under related name variants, etc. For instance, the following SQL query would return a merged list using "alias" columns:

```
(SELECT P1.*
FROM    Publications P1, PubPer P2, Persons P3
WHERE   P1.pubID=P2.pubID AND P2.perID=P3.perID AND
        P3.author = 'Alon Halevy' and P1.title LIKE '%XML%')
UNION
(SELECT P1.*
FROM    Publications P1, PubPer P2, Persons P3, Persons P4
WHERE   P1.pubID=P2.pubID AND P2.perID=P4.perID AND
        P3.author = 'Alon Halevy' AND P1.title LIKE '%XML%' AND
        P3.authorAlias = P4.author)
```

According to three core elements, over the time dimension, there are various strategies on how DLs can react to such a search function. Suppose conferences, C1 to C8, have evolved as follows: C1→C2 (i.e., name change), C3→{C4,C5} (i.e., conference split), and {C6,C7}→C8 (i.e., conference merge). Three possible strategies for searching conferences after the name evolutions are illustrated in Table 2. Both *"backward"* and *"forward"* schemes are temporal strategies where the system searches related conferences toward backward or forward on a temporal dimension. For instance, in the backward strategy, when a user searches for C2, system shows C2 as well as all its predecessors, C1, as answers. Another possible strategy is the *"semantic"* search, where all semantically related results are returned, regardless of the temporal aspect. That is, the semantic strategy is equal to the union of both backward and forward strategies. For instance, since C3 is broken into C4 and C5, whenever browsing C3 occurs, it is expanded to all conferences related to C3, thus C4 and C5. Note, however, that browsing C4 is not expanded to C5.

Table 2. Various searching strategies when name authority control is considered.

Search	Return
C1	C1
C2	C1,C2
C3	C3
C4	C3,C4
C5	C3,C5
C6	C6
C7	C7
C8	C6,C7,C8

(a) Backward

Search	Return
C1	C1,C2
C2	C2
C3	C3,C4,C5
C4	C4
C5	C5
C6	C6,C8
C7	C7,C8
C8	C8

(b) Forward

Search	Return
C1	C1,C2
C2	C1,C2
C3	C3,C4,C5
C4	C3,C4
C5	C3,C5
C6	C6,C8
C7	C7,C8
C8	C6,C7,C8

(c) Semantic

4.3 Taxonomy of Name Authority Control

By combining the three core elements as basic building blocks, one can cover various real patterns found in most DLs. Suppose two elements can be concatenated by "*", the concatenation operator (e.g., *split * merge*). We have analyzed DBLP thoroughly and uncovered various cases where concatenations of two elements need to be supported. Table 3 shows the taxonomy, where (1)   ...

...

Table 3. Taxonomy of name authority control for three core elements.

	→ →	→ →	→ →
	→ →	→	→ → →
	→ →	→ →	→ →

*Case 1 (Linear * Linear).* An author happens to change his name twice over the time. After applying a solution of *Linear* twice, a name A is changed to C.

*Case 2 (Linear * Split).* An author changes name from A to B, but there is the same name B already, mixing two publications together. To avoid the mixture, *split* is applied to B, yielding two name variants B_1 and B_2.

*Case 3 (Linear * Merge).* At time t_0, an author used A as the name, but later at time t_1, he changed A to B. However, due to data-entry error, C was used to refer to B as well. To fix this, *merge* is applied to B and C, making B as the authoritative name.

*Case 4 (Split * Linear).* An author A_1 wants to change his name to B, but currently his records are mixed with another name A_2.

*Case 5 (Split * Split).* When three authors' publications are mixed under the one name, A, then two *split* operations are applied in a row.

*Case 6 (Split * Merge).* An author A_1 found that his publication records are mixed with other name A. Also, he also found that B is his alias. Therefore, he wants to separate his records from A first, and consolidate them with B's records. Furthermore, he likes to use A_1 as the authoritative name.

*Case 7 (Merge * Linear).* An author A wants to merge his publications registered with his name variety B to his. Also, he wants to change his name to C. Since the name A and B cannot be changed to completely different name C at once by using 'Merge my profiles', they firstly merged to the name A. Then, the name A can be the name C.

*Case 8 (Merge * Split).* At time t_0, two conference names, A and B, are merged into A, but later at time t_1, A is changed to C.

*Case 9 (Merge * Merge).* When an author has many name variants (e.g., "Jeffrey Ullman," "J. Ullman," and "Ullman, Jeffrey D."), multiple consecutive *merge* operations can be applied.

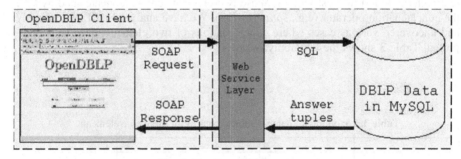

Fig. 3. The OpenDBLP system.

5 System Implementation

5.1 Overview of the OpenDBLP

Since the proposed solution is implemented in a test-bed, called OpenDBLP, in this section, we give a brief overview, as shown in Figure 3. The OpenDBLP is a rejuvenated version of the popular DBLP digital library with a few novel improvements: (1) fully DBMS-based storage system, supporting ranked and approximate query processing, (2) web service based programmable interface (box in Fig. 3) to the contents of DBLP, and (3) a web client program that faithfully mimics the original FORM interface of the DBLP. Especially, this program fully implements old "Browse" and "Search" interfaces using only web services.

The prototype system is accessible at **http://opendblp.psu.edu/**.

5.2 UPDATE Function in OpenDBLP

Here, we briefly show how three core elements are implemented in OpenDBLP. Users can update his/her records (after manually or automatically finding some semantic irregularities) using one of the tree menus shown in Fig 4.

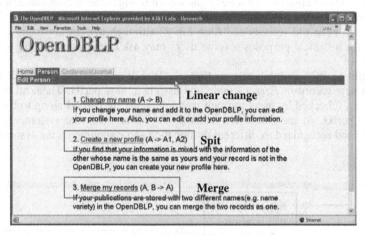

Fig. 4. OpenDBLP UPDATE menus.

Figures 5–7 demonstrate (1) the "Alon Levy" case of *linear change*, (2) "Wei Wang" case of *split*, and (3) "Lee Coraor" case of *merge*, respectively.

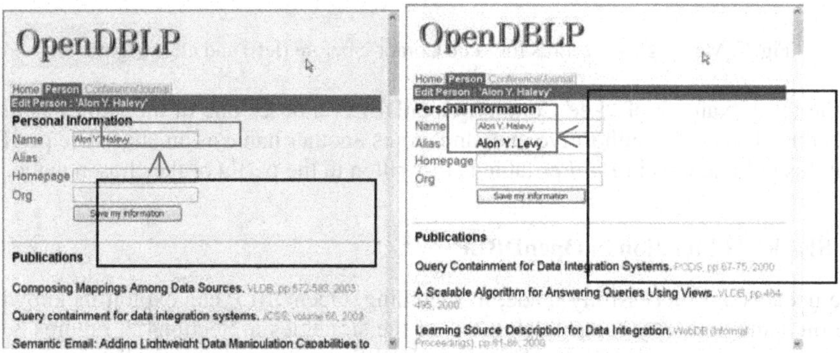

Fig. 5. Changing a name for "Alon Levy": before (left) and after (right).

Fig. 6. Creating a new profile for "Wei Wang": before (left) and after (right).

For the name change of "Alon Levy" as shown in Fig 5, the person name in *Person* table is changed to the new name and the old name is stored as an alias. Note that it is important to keep old records of "Alon Levy" although his current name is "Alon Halevy" for historical purposes – some users may ask queries specifically using his old name.

For spliting bibliographic information of "Wei Wang" in HKUST, OpenDBLP creates a new record in *Persons* table and assigns a new perID. Then, all the right publications (checked by users through web interface) are carried along to the newly generated perID. At the end, there are two "Wei Wang"s in the system, each kept separately and recognized as different despite their same spelling by the system.

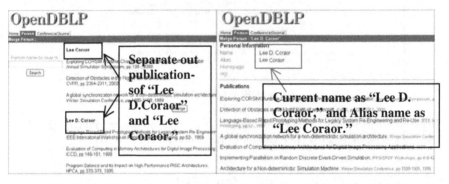

Fig. 7. Merging two records for "Lee Coraor": before (left) and after (right).

For the third example of "Lee Coraor", OpenDBLP chooses one of the names as his current name (i.e., the authoritive one) and stores another name as an alias. The perID for all his publications in *PubPer* table is re-written to the perID of the chosen name.

5.3   SEARCH Function in OpenDBLP

Once updates are successfully made, in searching, OpenDBLP can exploit its knowledge on name authority control using one of the strategies in Section4.2. Figures 8 – 10 illustrates the improved search in OpenDBLP that can automatically show, for instance, current as well as "old-but-relevant" authors or publication venues.

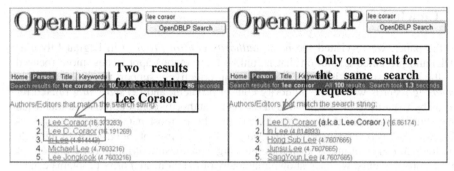

Fig. 8. Search result for "Lee Coraor" after update: before (left) and after (right).

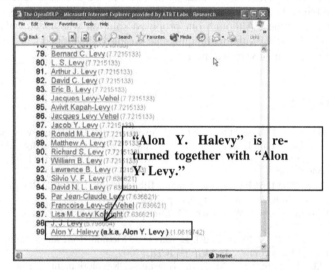

Fig. 9. Search result for "Levy" after update.

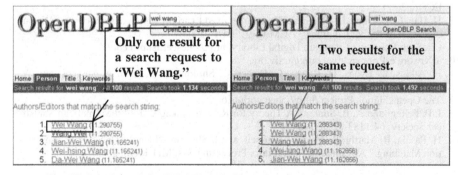

Fig. 10. Search result for "Wei Wang" after update: before (left) and after (right).

6 Conclusion

In the paper, we re-visited the *name authority control problem* in Digital Libraries (DL) and presented a solution that is, unlike the previous approaches, more focused on the system-support issues of how DLs can effectively support the problem in (1) *updating* records with name authority control problem, and (2) *searching* related records by exploiting the knowledge about name authority control. We have identified that three are mainly three core elements that lie in most name-related changes as follows: (1) *linear change* of entity from A to B; (2) *split* of an entity A to multiple entities; (3) *merge* of multiple entities into single one. Using different combinations of these core elements, we have shown that many of the name authority problems can be expressed and thus solved. Finally, all the proposed solutions are fully implemented in a test-bed, OpenDBLP system, so that two of the common functions of DLs, Update and Search, can fully track down the right bibliographic entities despite the usage of different values. Although our proposed solution was tested only on a particular domain (i.e., DBLP), the techniques that we have developed can be applied to other DLs in a straightforward manner.

References

1. Y. Hong and D. Lee. "OpenDBLP: Rejuvenating the DBLP into Web Service Based Programmable Digital Library." Technical report, Penn State University, 2004
2. M. A. Hernandez and S. J. Stolfo. "The Merge/Purge Problem for Large Databases," ACM SIGMOD, 1995.
3. M. Ley. "The DBLP Computer Science Bibliography: Evolution, Research Issues, Perspectives". *SPIRE*, Lisbon, Portugal, Sep. 2002.
4. J.W. Warnner and E.W. Brown. "Automated Name Authority Control". ACM/IEEE JCDL, 2001.
5. P. T. Davis, D. K. Elson, and J. L. Klavans. "Methods for Precise Named Entity Matching in Digital Collections". ACM/IEEE JCDL, 2003.
6. M. M. M. Synman and M. J. van Rensburg. "Revolutionizing Name Authority Control". ACM DL, 2000.
7. J. M. B. Cruz, N. J. R. Klink, and T. Krichel. "Personal Data in a Large Digital Library". ECDL, 2000.
8. H. Han, C. L. Giles, H. Zha et al. "Two Supervised Learning Approaches for Name Disambiguation in Author Citations," ACM/IEEE JCDL, 2004.
9. CiteSeer: Scientific Literature Digital Library, http://citeseer.ist.psu.edu/
10. arXiv.org e-Print archive, http://arxiv.org/
11. H. Atkins, C. Lyons, H. Ratner, C. Risher, C. Shillum, D. Sidman, A. Stevens, and W. Arms. "Reference Linking with DOIs: A Case Study," D-Lib Magazine, 2000.
12. The Open Citation Project. http://opcit.eprints.org/
13. I. P. Fellegi and A. B. Sunter. "A Theory for Record Linkage," J. of the American Statistical Society, 64:1183-1210, 1969.
14. H. Pasula, B. Marthi, B. Milch, S. Russell, and I. Shpitser. "Identity Uncertainty and Citation Matching," Advances in Neural Info. Processing Sys. MIT Press, 2003.

NLP Versus IR Approaches
to Fuzzy Name Searching in Digital Libraries

Paul Horng-Jyh Wu[1], Jin-Cheon Na[2], and Christopher S.G. Khoo[2]

[1] Mustard Technology Pte Ltd, 9 Jurong Town Hall Road
Paulwu@mustardtech.com
[2] Divison of Information Studies, School of Communication & Information,
Nanyang Technological University, 31 Nanyang Link, Singapore 637718
{TJCNa,assgkhoo}@ntu.edu.sg

Abstract. Name Search is an important search function in Digital Library systems and various types of information retrieval systems, such as directory search systems, electronic phonebooks and yellow pages. The paper discusses two main approaches to fuzzy name matching – the natural language processing (NLP) approach and the information retrieval (IR) approach – and proposes a hybrid approach. Person names can be considered a (sub-)language, in which case a name search system will be developed using Natural Language Processing apparatus including dictionary, thesaurus and grammatical schema. On the other hand, if names are perceived as (free) text, then an entirely different system may be built incorporating indexing, retrieving, relevance ranking and other Information Retrieval techniques. These two schools of thought, NLP and IR, have somewhat different sets of techniques originating from different theoretical concerns and research traditions. A selective combination of their complementary features is likely to be more effective for fuzzy name matching. Two principles, *position attribute identity (PAI)* and *position transition likelihood (PTL)*, are proposed to incorporate aspects of both approaches. The two principles have been implemented in an NLP- and IR-hybrid model system called Friendly Name Search (FNS) for real world applications in multilingual directory searches on the Singapore Yellowpages website.

1 Introduction

Name Search is an important search function in digital library and various types of information retrieval systems, such as online library catalogs, bibliographic retrieval systems, and yellowpages. A person's name can exhibit many variations and forms in published documents, and users searching for a name may enter a variant form not found in the documents and text, or not matching the form indexed in the system. Yet few systems offer fuzzy name matching to help users retrieved records with variant person names. For example, a user issuing an author name search as "Lee Kuanyew" is likely to miss a record indexed as "Lee, Harry Kuan Yew" although both refer to the same person – the first Prime Minister of Singapore. Similar instances involving slight mis-spelling or mis-ordering in the queries will result in fruitless name searches.

R. Heery and L. Lyon (Eds.): ECDL 2004, LNCS 3232, pp. 145–156, 2004.

Name searches fail not only because of errors in the users' search query, it is also because names have numerous acceptable variants. For instance, the name "Harry Kuan Yew Lee" is a Chinese name with native and adopted name tokens, where "Lee" is the surname, "Kuan Yew" the given name, and "Harry" the adopted name. Similarly, "Nurdini Abu Bakar Aljunied" is a Malay name with an adopted (Arabic) surname "Aljunied." To illustrate this, different forms of a name are listed in Table 1 according to five types of variations: Name Alternation (NMA), Sound-alike (SAL), Abbreviation (ABB), Short-hand (SHH), and Contraction (CON). To further quantify the fuzziness of the name, the number of variants is also included in the table.

Table 1. Possible Variations of Person Names

Type of Variation	Name Instances	Estimated number of variants
Name Alternation (NMA)	*Harry Kuan Yew Lee* or *Kuan Yew Harry Lee*	$(N-1)!$
	Nurdini Abu Baker Aljunied or *Aljunied, Nurdini Abu Baker*	where N is the number of name tokens (=6, when N=4)
Sound-alike (SAL)	*Harry Kuon You Lee* or *Harrie Kuan Yew Lee*	$\prod \begin{matrix} = \\ = \end{matrix}$ $\quad \cdot \quad -$
	Noordini Abu Baker Aljunie or *Nurdini Abu Baker Aljuneid*	$= \quad \cdot \quad =$
Abbreviation (ABB)	*Harry K Y Lee* or *H. Kuan Yew Lee*	$(2^{N-1} - 1) \cdot (N-1)!$
	Nurdini A. B. Aljunied or *Nurdini Abu Baker A.*	$(= 42,$ when $N = 4)$
Short-hand (SHH)	*Hari Kuan Yew Lee* or *Har Kuang Yew Lee*	Similar to SAL
	Dini Abu Barker Aljunied or *Nur Abu Baker Aljunied*	$(=\sim 1536$ assuming $|W_i| = 4)$
Contraction (CON)	*Harry Kuanyew Lee*	Similar to NMA
	Nurdini Abubaker Aljunied	$(=6$ when N=4$)$

Many Natural Language Processing (NLP) and Information Retrieval (IR) techniques have been applied in search systems that can handle the complexity demonstrated in Table 1 (e.g., Keen, E.M., 1992). Fundamentally, they are motivated by distinct theories of the nature of names, namely:

(NAL): Person names follow a conventional style of writing – a kind of grammar. More specifically, names can be parsed into components such as surname, given names and other limited number of name attributes.

(NAT): Person names are a text consisting of tokens as indexing features. More specifically, methods such as relevancy ranking and query expansion can be applied to rank name search results and accommodate name variants.

In Section 2, we discuss the Name-As-Language (NAL) view through a review of NLP techniques applicable to automatic name search systems. The principle of *attribute-position-identity* is proposed to reflect the Name-As-Language perspective. In Section 3, the Name-As-Text view and IR techniques are discussed, and the principle of *position-transition-likelihood* is proposed to reflect the Name-As-Text perspective. Some name search systems are reviewed in Section 4, and a hybrid model of an automatic name search system called Friendly Name Search is introduced in Section 5.

2   Name-as-Language (NAL) - The Deep Structure of Names

Adopting the generative grammar perspective in linguistics, we assume that names, like sentences and other text units, can be generated in a rule-governed fashion by a name grammar. A relevant question is:

> What is the "deep structure" of a name, in terms of the "form" and "sound," that remains *constant* throughout its conventional variants?

Technologists with this view would build name search systems based on the *normalization* of names aiming at recovering the deep structure that is constant across its variants. After normalization, the search process becomes a relatively straightforward template matching of attributes and values. However, the challenge is to compute the deep structure. This will require a native-speaker's language intuition. For example, to recognize names such as, "Harry Kuan Yew Lee" (Chinese), "James Hla Gyaw" (Burmese), and "Savar Sankaran Narashimhalu" (Indian), the attribute-value templates that need to be computed are as shown in Table 2.

Table 2. Chinese, Burmese and Indian Name Structures

Name Attributes	Harry Kuan Yew Lee	James Hla Gyaw	Savar Sankaran Narasimhalu
Surname (SN)	Lee	-	-
Native Given Names (GN)	Kuan Yew	Hla Gyaw	Narasimhalu
Acquired Name (AN)	Harry	James	-
Father's Name (FN)	-	-	Sankaran
Place Name (PN)	-	-	Savar

As demonstrated in Table 1, the surface form of the names has many variants. As a result, a regular grammar with disjunctive operators is needed to describe all potential forms of the names. A partial grammar for Indian names is illustrated in Table 3.

Table 3. Indian Name Structures

IN Type 1	GN [FN] SN	*Vimol Goel* (Hindi names)
IN Type 2	[FN | PN] + GN	*Savar Sankaran Narasimhalu* (e.g., Tamil)

The deep phonetic structure of a name token is simply its phonemes. However, name transliteration increases the complexity of the problem. For example, there is likely only one Arabic spelling in Arabic script for a name like "Sulayman." However, there are many Sound-alike (Spell-alike) versions in romanized forms such as "Suliman", "Seleiman", and "Solomon". The same phenomenon is observed in Chinese names where "Zhi," in standard Hanyu Pinyin, can be spelt as "Jih", "Jyh", "Ji", "Chi", "Chih" and so on. This is shown in Table 4.

Table 4. Arabic and Chinese Name Structure (Sound)

Surface Names	Phonetic Transcription
Sulayman, Suleiman	s.u.l.ey.m.ax.n
Salayman, Seleiman, Sylayman	s.ax.l.ey.m.ax.n
Suliman	s.u.l.ih.m.ax.n
Solomon	s.ao.l.ao.m.ao.n
Zhi, Jih, Jyh, Ji	zh.i
Chih, Chi	ch.i

Note: The transcription is based on the DECtalk system described in (Conroy, et. al., 1992).

2.1 Challenges to Name-as-Language-Based Name Search Systems

The grammatical formulation of person names has the advantage of being precise. The disadvantage is that it needs to be exhaustive. One such example is the Anapron system developed by Golding (1991) to pronounce names of different ethnic origins. The system contains 90 language identification rules, 205 morpheme rules, 619 transcription rules, and several hundred rules on syllable and stress structure assignments. Even with all this effort, the system only covers the sound variants. More rules will be needed to cover the form variants shown in Table 1.

An alternative to the grammar-rule-based approach is the Hidden Markov Model-based grammatical tagging systems (Church, 1988; DeRose, 1988). The task of assigning name attributes to name tokens can be seen as similar to that of assigning grammatical tags to words. This empirical approach requires a tagged corpus to develop the model. Such a corpus is easier to construct compared to dictionaries and grammatical rules for names. Another advantage is that this approach is nondeterministic, i.e. more than one plausible processing result can be computed, which allows further spelling disambiguation to be applied in the case of uncertainty. In fact, one such real world example for normalizing other types of phrasal units, such as addresses, has been developed using the same approach as grammatical tagging (Wang and Chuah, 1994).

Similarly, the sound aspect of names can equally be addressed through an empirical NLP perspective. For example, Bosch and Daelemans (1993) described a data-oriented method for grapheme-to-phoneme conversion, whereby a statistical measure, *Information Gain,* is applied to induce rules for transcribing Dutch words.

2.2 Position-Attribute-Identity (PAI) Principle

Whether it is a rule-based or an empirical approach, an NLP-based name search system requires much manual effort and time, to build the dictionary, thesaurus, schema/grammar rule, and linguistic tagging resources, which most likely will render an NLP-based approach infeasible.

We propose a resource economical approach called the *position-attribute-identity* principle, which is simply:

Name positions are literally taken as attributes for the name structure.

With positions as the attributes/tags and using a dynamic programming-like constraint checking process, the most plausible positions for each name token is identified and used as the basis for ranking and retrieving actual name records. More details are given in Section 5 of the paper.

Since the positional information of a name token can be readily accessed from a name database, no additional manual tagging is necessary during this process. That the *position-attribute-identity* principle is plausible can be seen from the fact that in a fully normalized name database, controlled by cataloging rules, the position corresponds exactly to the attribute of the name tokens. For instance, the first token for both Chinese and English names is the surname.

Taking the surface structure literally as the deep structure reduces resource overhead. This approach can also be applied to the sound aspect of names. In fact, Bosch and Daelemans (1993) used a straightforward table look-up method to transcribe the sounds of a Dutch name, outperforming statistical approaches such as those based on Information Gain.

In summary, what are gained by examining the Name-As-Language view of name search systems are the following:

1. Recovering the deep structures of the form and sound aspects of names makes name search systems more effective. But the resource required by the normalization process can be a serious constraint.
2. To overcome resource overhead, it is necessary to take readily available information from the name data as the basis for language modeling. The *position-attribute-identity* principle is proposed.

3 Name-as-Text (NAT) – The Feature and Similarity of Names

From a Name-As-Text perspective, names are seen as sets of characteristic features. For example, in a name database consisting of "Harry Kuan Yew Lee", "Harry Hui Kuan Deng", "Jack Yew Hui Lee" and "Peter Wu," nine distinct features are identified: (1) "Harry," (2) "Kuan," (3) "Lee," (4) "Hui," (5) "Deng," (6) "Jack," (7) "Yew," (8) "Peter," (9) "Wu," as shown in Table 5.

The order of the name tokens is significant for distinguishing names. However, a name can have more than one correct order, as illustrated earlier in Table 1. A name like *Harry Lee Kuan Yew,* represented as $< 1, 3, 2, 7>$, is the same as *Harry Kuan Yew Lee* ($<1, 2, 7, 3>$), while *Harry Yew Kuan Lee* ($<1, 7, 2, 3>$) is a different name. To measure the similarity between different name order precisely is a challenge.

Table 5. Name Records and Feature Representations

Name Records	Feature Representation
Harry Kuan Yew Lee	<1, 2, 7, 3>
Harry Hui Kuan Deng	<1, 4, 2, 5>
Jack Yew Hui Lee	<6, 7, 4, 3>
Peter Wu	<8, 9>

Considering "Sound-alike" variants of names from the viewpoint of NAT, is contrasted with the IR research focus on "Meaning-alike," where queries are expanded with synonymous terms using a thesaurus. In IR, if the system can judge the similarity between terms accurately, then "Meaning-alike" expansion with synonymous terms will increase the retrieval effectiveness (Qiu and Frei, 1993). However, this same principle cannot be applied literally to "Sound-alike" expansion.

3.1   Challenges in Name-as-Text-Based Name Search Systems

Most IR approaches rank relevance based on term frequency *(tf)* and inverse-document frequency *(IDF)*. The less frequently a particular token i appears across the collection (i.e. the lower the document frequency, and the higher the inverse document frequency, IDF_i) the more characteristic the token is to the name record. Similarly, the more frequent a token occurs in a name record (term frequency), the more characteristic the token is to the name. However, *IDF* and *tf* overlooks the attribute aspect of the token treated in the Name-As-Language view. For example, in the example "Robert Kong Kong Tan," "Kong" can be a surname ("Robert Kong Kong Tan") or a given name ("Robert Kong Kong Tan"), in which case the surname is "Tan." If the target record is "Robert Kong Kong Tan" (with "Kong" as the surname), then a retrieved record "Robert Kong Kong Tan," (surname "Tan") is actually not as relevant a record as "Robert Kew Chong Kong" (surname "Kong").

Furthermore, *phrase* and *proximity* operators, such as adjacency, window size and directed window, widely used in traditional IR systems fail to tackle finer grained relevancy ranking among positional variations because these operators are Boolean operators giving binary relevance results: either satisfied or failed (Keen, 1992).

There are essentially two approaches to ranking the relevance of records retrieved:

1. the expanded tokens can be combined with the original tokens, upon which the accumulation of postings is done for each token in the combined query. We refer to this as the +-combination.
2. postings in each of the *Cartesian* product of the expanded tokens can be accumulated. We refer to this as the ×-combination

Most query expansion techniques adopt the +-combination type (e.g. Qiu & Frei, 1993). However, in the case of "Sound-alike" type of name variation, the distinction in dimensionality cannot be maintained by just a simple +-combination. For example, given the expansion groups {"Kon", "Kong", "Khon"} and {"Yan", "Yen", "Yang"} and the +-combination, a query string "Kon Yang Kong," targeting the name "Kon Yang Khon", can be expanded into {"Kon", "Kong", "Khon", "Yan", "Yen", "Yang",

"Kon", "Kong", "Khon"}. Positional information is not maintained. Thus, a name such as "Kon/SN Yang/GN Chee/GN"[1] (not the targeted name) will be retrieved with an equal relevancy score as "Kon/SN Yang/GN Khon/GN" (the targeted name), both getting 4/9 from Dice's coefficient[2]. This is because the dimensionality of "Kon", a surname, and "Khon", a given name, are collapsed into an indistinguishable group in the +-combination process.

In order to avoid the drawbacks described above, the ×-combination of query expansion has to be adopted. However, computationally, the ×-combination leads to combinatorial explosion. For example, if a name has m tokens $<A_1,...,A_m>$, and each yields $|A_i|$ tokens after query expansion, the commonly used +-combination will result in $\sum$ query expanded tokens, whereas the ×-combination will yield $\prod$ tokens. How to overcome this serious constraint is the topic of the next section.

3.2 Position-Transition-Likelihood (PTL) Principle

To restrict the combinatorial expansion in the ×-combination query expansion, one approach is to incorporate a filtering mechanism while maintaining the same dimensionality. We propose the *position-transition-likelihood* principle:

> The likelihood of a transition between a pair of name tokens, in terms of their positions, is used to filter the expanded queries in ×-combination.

Using this principle, out of the 27 results from the ×-combination of the expanded "Kon Yang Kong," only one (the correct one) is plausible – "Kon Yan Khon," whose position transition, $Kon_{pos1}->Yan_{pos2}$ and $Yan_{pos2}->Khon_{pos3}$, was found to be highly probable.

In summary, our analysis of the Name-As-Text view results in the following:

1. Traditional measures of similarity and relevancy in IR are not sufficient for automatic name search systems, although the lead time to an operational Name-As-Text-based system can be shorter than a Name-As-Language-based one.
2. Overcoming the combinatorial explosion for more precise retrieval is crucial. As such, the *position-transition-likelihood* principle is proposed for filtering out unlikely combinations.

4   Previous Work on Name Search

Systems which deal directly with the task of automatic name search include the *Synoname* system (Siegfried and Bernstein, 1991; Borgman and Siegfried, 1992), developed by a team under the Getty Art History Information program to archive art works by around 6,000 artists. When museums exchange cataloging information, without a proper name matching procedure, artworks by the same artist may be cataloged under

---

[1] As shown in Section 2, SN stands for Surname and GN, Given Name.
[2] $\cap$

different names. The system's engine for name matching includes 12 comparison techniques: (1) Exact match, (2) Omission of one character, (3) Substitution, (4) Transposition, (5) Difference in punctuation, (6) Initials, (7) Extended name, (8) Inclusion of names within names, (9) No first name, (10) Word approximation, (11) Confusion of dividing names, and (12) Character approximation.

The first 4 techniques concern fuzzy string matching within 1-Levenshtein distance (Hall and Dowling, 1980). Techniques (7), (8), (9) and (11) are easily handled by an IR system, since they just mean the set of features in the query string is a subset of those of the name record. Technique (10) presents a challenge which can be covered under our considerations of Sound-alike (SAL) variants. Technique (6) is exactly the same as those treated in Abbreviation-type (ABB) variants. This leaves only technique (12), which is character approximation. For example, "Backhuyzen, Ludolf" is related to "Bakhuysen, Ludolf," and "D'Espagnat, George" to "Espagnat, George d'". These examples show that even strings with two Levenshtein distances away still need to be regarded as a match. Thus, technique (12) is just a generalization of techniques which handle cases of only 1-Levenshtein distance. In general, with the capability for handling NMA-, SAL-, ABB-, SHH-, and CON-types of name variation, our approach can have the same flexibility in name matching as Synoname.

Another interesting study on Name Search is a Ph.D. research by Hermansen (1985), who investigated the "New York State Identification and Intelligence System." The two important aspects of names, form and sound (identified as "name structure" and "transliteration" in the thesis), was argued to be crucial for automatic name search systems. However, no system implementation was involved in the study. Also, as it was a rather early work, no reference to modern NLP or IR techniques were made. On the other hand, many aspects of the ad hoc name search algorithms were examined, providing a good review for the technologies available up to the mid 80's. These ad hoc techniques are: sound-based similarity (Moore, 1965; Roughton and Tyckoson, 1985), n-gram entropy (Fokker and Lynch, 1974; Fokker, 1974), name subsetting (Taft, 1970), and record linkage (Moore, 1965). Pfeifer et al (1996) performed experiments for measuring retrieval effectiveness of various proper name search methods. They argue that phonetic similarity (PHONDEX) works as well as typing errors (Damerau-Levenstein metric) and plain string similarity (n-grams), and the combinations of these different techniques perform much better than the use of a single technique.

Beli and Sethi (2001) discussed potential matching algorithms for patient identification resolution for use with a massively distributed Master Patient Index, which is a facility to make all patients' medical records in the U.S. accessible to care providers. The patient identification resolution considers additional attributes in addition to name, such as address, telephone, social security number, and date of birth. Name searching is also important in the fields of machine translation and cross-lingual information retrieval. Stalls and Knight (1998) and Virga and Khudanpur (2003) worked on translating names and technical terms using phonetic translation (e.g., from English to Mandarin). Pirkola et al. (2003) investigated a fuzzy cross-lingual translation of proper names and technical terms, but no phonetic elements were included in the techniques.

In summary, existing name searching systems use mostly ad hoc techniques originating from disparate fields of study, such as fuzzy string matches, rule-based pattern matching, record-linking, and soundex schemes. In contrast, our system, the Friendly Name Search system adopts a theory-driven alternative for automatic name search system development. However, it is acknowledged that the form and sound aspects of names across the world are largely still an ad hoc phenomenon. Thus, in an operational environment, ad hoc methods may still be required to address certain peculiarities.

5   Friendly Name Search (FNS) –
Towards a Theory-Driven Automatic Name Search System

Human Logic iSearch is a name search solution from Mustard Technology.[3] The core technology called Friendly Name Search (FNS)[4], aspects of which are patented by Kent Ridge Digital Lab, of which Mustard Technology was a spin-off. The architecture of the current FNS system is shown in Fig. 1. The database name goes through a tokenization process before being indexed. During the process, a domain specific name thesaurus and metadata are incorporated in the name modeler to produce information based on the Position-Attribute-Identity (PAI) and Position-Transition-Likelihood (PTL) principles. A Fuzzy Name Index is produced at the end of the indexing process.

The query names are transformed and processed similarly as the names in the database, which are then matched, scored and ranked based on the fuzzy name indices to produce the search results.

Both the PAI (position-attribute-identity) and PTL (position-transition-likelihood) principles concern the overall collection, instead of individual postings. Fig. 2 demonstrates the case where three query tokens, A, B and C, are expanded. The first token is expanded into 4 tokens, Al to A4, and similarly for B and C. Each expanded token has frequency counts on different positions. For example, the first expanded token Al has frequency counts represented by A1.1 and A1.4, for positions 1 and 4; while A2 has A2.1, A2.2 and A2.4, for positions 1, 2, and 4. (In Fig. 2, these are sorted in position order.) Thus, a potential result from the ×-combination of the expansion is {A1.1, B1.2, C1.3}; on the other hand, {A2.1, B3.1, C1.1} is illegal, since in this case, all of A2, B3 and Cl are in position 1 of a name, which is not allowed. Thus it is pruned away from the final result.

For each legal result $\{X_i, i=1$ to $m\}$, where X_i is the name token at position i, the score is calculated as:

$$= \overset{-}{=} \qquad + \qquad + \quad \times \qquad + \tag{1}$$

---

[3] Mustard Technology's website URL: http://www.mustardtechnology.com
[4] "A System of Organizing Catalog Data for Searching and Retrieval" Patent No: US 6,381,607 B1 on 30 Apr 2002.

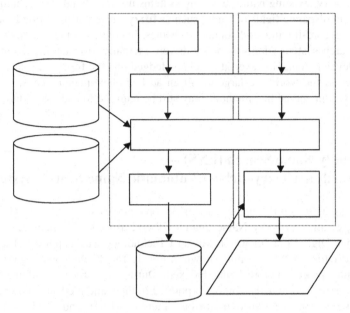

Fig. 1. Flow Diagram of Friendly Name Search

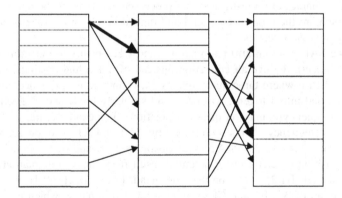

Fig. 2. Illustration of PAI and PTL principles in Name Modeler

The rationale is that the more frequent a position is associated with a token and a position transition is associated with a token pair, the more likely is a result containing the tokens and token pair is to be relevant. And the similarity is proportional to the frequencies of the occurrences of such tokens and pairs in the name. The actual accumulation of postings still needs to be executed to enumerate the matching records.

Computationally, a further advantage is noted from applying the principles. The process demonstrated in Figure 2 actually prunes away those illegal results whose postings need not be accumulated, saving index access time. The reduction gained is generally in the order of the difference between $\underline{\hspace{2cm}}$ and $\prod\limits_=^=$, where N is the potential positions (usually less than 10), M is the token length of the query name, and $|A_i|$ the sizes of each of the expanded token set.

A version of the Friendly Name Search has been deployed in a website, called *Singapore Yellowpages,* located at http://www.yellowpages.com.sg. The site contains millions of records and is among the most accessed website in Singapore.

6 Conclusion

Technologists building theory-driven name search systems are confronted with two seemingly different alternatives: the Name-as-Language (NAL) and the Name-as-Text (NAT) approaches. The NAL-based approach treats names as word sequences generated by rule-governed grammar. As an alternative to the NAL view, the NAT-based approach assumes names are just records consisting of features derivable from name tokens. Based on NAL, a more data-driven method, called Position-Attribute-Identity (PAI) principle, is proposed. The PAI principle regards name positions as attributes in name structures. The position-transition-likelihood (PTL) principle, which is motivated by NAT, together with the PAI principle, is introduced to prune and verify the query expansion process. Thus, a theory-driven name search system, called Friendly Name Search (FNS), is built by combing the complementary advantages of both the NAL and NAT approaches to achieve effectiveness both in system development and quality of search. FNS has been applied to real world application in Singapore Yellowpages and many organizations in the public, banking and telecommunications sectors.

References

1. Beli, G. B., & Sethi A. (2001). Matching Records in a National Medical Patient Index, *Communication of the ACM, 44*(9), 83-88.
2. Borgman, C.L., & Siegfried, S.L. (1992). Getty's Synoname and Its Cousins: A Survey of Applications of Personal Name-Matching Algorithms. *Journal of the American Society for Information Science, 43*(7), 459-467.
3. Bosch, A., & Daelemans, W. (1993). Data-Oriented Methods for Grapheme-to-Phoneme Conversion. In *Proceedings of the Sixth Conference of the European Chapter of the ACL, Utrecht, April, 1993.*
4. Church, K. (1988). A Stochastic Parts Program and Noun Phrase Parser for Unrestricted Text. In *The Second Conference on Applied Natural Language Processing, ACL, Austin, Texas.*
5. Conroy, D., Vitale, T., & Klatt, D.H. (1992) DECtalk DTC03 Text-to-Speech System Owner's Manual (Educational Services of Digital Equipment Corporation, P.O. Box CS2008, Nashua, NH 03061. Document number EK-DTC03-0M-001).

6. Davidson, L. (1962) Retrieval of Misspelled Names in an Airline Passenger Record System. *Communication of the ACM* 5:169-71
7. DeRose S. (1988) Grammatical Category Disambiguation by Statistical Optimization. *Computational Linguistics, 14*(1).
8. Fokker, D.W., & Lynch, M.F. (1974). Application of the Variety-Generator Approach to Searches of Personal Names in Bibliographic Database-Part 1. Microstructure of Personal Authors' Names. *Journal of Library Automation, 7*(2), 105-118.
9. Fokker, D.W. (1974). Application of the Variety-Generator Approach to Searches of Personal Names in Bibliographic Database-Part II. Optimization of Key-Sets, and Evaluation of Their Retrieval Efficiency. *Journal of Library Automation, 7*(3), 201-215.
10. Golding, A. (1991). *Pronouncing Names by a Combination of Rule-Based and Case-Based Reasoning.* Ph.D. Thesis, Stanford University.
11. Hall, P.A., & Dowling, G.R. (1980). Approximate String Matching. *Computing Surveys, 12*(4), 381-402.
12. Hermansen, J.C. (1985). *Automatic Name Searching in Large Data Base of International Names.* Ph.D. Thesis, Georgetown University.
13. Keen, E.M. (1992). Some Aspects of Proximity Searching in Text Retrieval Systems. *Journal of Information Science, 18*, 89-98.
14. Moore, G.J. (1965). Mechanizing a Large Register of First Order Patient Data. *Methods of Information in Medicine, 4*(1), 1-19.
15. Pfeifer, U., Poersch, T., & Fuhr, N. (1996). Retrieval effectiveness of proper name search methods. *Information Processing & Management, 32*(6), 667-679.
16. Pirkola, A., Toivonen, J., Keskustalo, H., Visala, K., & Järvelin, K. (2003). Fuzzy Translation of Cross-Lingual Spelling Variants. In *SIGIR'03, July 28-August, Toronto, Canada* (pp. 345-352).
17. Qiu, Y., & Frei, H.P. (1993). Concept Based Query Expansion. In *Proceedings of the Sixteenth Annual International ACM SIGIR Conference, Pittsburgh, PA, USA, June-July, 1993.*
18. Roughton, K.G., & Tyckoson, D.A. (1985). Browsing with Sound: Sound-Based Codes and Automated Authority Control. *Information Technology and Library, 4*, 130-136.
19. Siegfried, S.L., & Bernstein, J. (1991). Synoname: The Getty's New Approach to Pattern Matching for Person Names. *Computers and the Humanities, 25*, 211-226.
20. Stalls, B., & Knight, K. (1998). Translating names and technical terms in Arabic text. In *Proceedings of the COLING/ACL Workshop on Computational Approaches to Semitic Languages.*
21. Taft, R.L. (1970). *Name Search Techniques.* Albany: New York State Identification and Intelligent System.
22. Wong, W.S., & Chuah, M.C. (1994). A Hybrid Approach to Address Normalization. *IEEE Expert, 9*(12).
23. Wu, P.H.J., Shen, Z.Q., Guo, S., Lim, P.S., Chng, T.J., Chong, C.J., & Low, H.B. (1997). Technologies in Meta-Information Management and Service. In *Proceedings of the joint Pacific Asian Conference on Expert Systems and Singapore International Conference on Intelligent Systems, Singapore* (pp. 711-720).

From Abstract to Virtual Entities: Implementation of Work-Based Searching in a Multimedia Digital Library

Mark Notess[1], Jenn Riley[1], and Harriette Hemmasi[2]

[1] Digital Library Program, Main Library, Indiana University
Bloomington, Indiana, USA 47405
{mnotess,jenlrile}@indiana.edu
[2] Executive Associate Dean, Indiana University Libraries, Indiana University
Bloomington, Indiana, USA 47405
hhemmasi@indiana.edu

Abstract. Libraries of digitized multimedia content provide access to virtual entities. In the case of music, where there are frequently many different performances, editions, and arrangements of a given work, the Variations2 metadata model, links all instances of a work to an abstract work record, thus yielding superior search capabilities to digital library users. This paper summarizes the motivation for addressing the music metadata problem and describes the Variations2 search user interface, which is based on our work-centric, FRBR-like metadata model.

1 Introduction

The Variations2 Indiana University Digital Library is a large test-bed development and research project funded in part by Phase 2 of the Digital Libraries Initiative, with support from the National Science Foundation and the National Endowment for the Humanities [1]. This paper reports on the state of the Variations2 test-bed software, describing in particular the search user interface. We begin by reviewing the motivations for attempting an improved environment for music search. Some of these motivations are common to other digital library efforts; others are specific to issues associated with music. We then describe our implementation of a search user interface and the current state of our system.

2 Background

Motivations for the Variations2 approach to searching come from at least two directions. First, Variations2 shares in larger library and digital library issues associated with virtualization. Second, music information offers unique challenges, challenges which have not always been met well by existing solutions.

2.1 Virtualization, Abstraction and New Metadata Models

This paper springs from the junction of two simultaneous developments: library virtualization and catalog entity abstraction.

R. Heery and L. Lyon (Eds.): ECDL 2004, LNCS 3232, pp. 157–167, 2004.
© Springer-Verlag Berlin Heidelberg 2004

Digital libraries provide a level of disembodiment of library materials. Digital materials have a reduced physicality in at least three respects. First, patrons cannot pick a digital item off a shelf and hold it in their hands. Digital library contents are less tangible. Second, the collocation of items in a collection need no longer be spatial in a physical sense. Hence the term *virtual*, while not synonymous with *digital*, is often used to describe digital libraries. Third, reduced reliance on physicality also becomes evident as users seek content (i.e., works) rather than containers (e.g., the "red book," the "CD with a picture of a dog"), influenced at least in part by the MP3 phenomenon where users tend to think in terms of "tracks" or individual works. Effective metadata for resource discovery thus becomes even more important as physical browsing is no longer possible in digital library environments.

Over the last several decades, librarians have been reconsidering cataloging models. To a large extent, reconsideration has been driven by the development of cooperative cataloging and the consequent need for common practices brought about by such systems as OCLC's WorldCat [2] and RLG's Union Catalog [3]. Such efforts also afford opportunity beyond mere consistency towards fundamental improvements to the overall model. One such improvement effort is the Functional Requirements for Bibliographic Records (FRBR) effort from the International Federation of Library Associations and Institutions (IFLA) [4].

FRBR seeks to improve upon the existing paradigm of MAchine Readable Cataloging (MARC, [5]) bibliographic and authority records, the paradigm used by cooperative cataloging efforts such as OCLC's. The MARC-based paradigm stores information about the physical item in a bibliographic ("bib") record. It also has authority records for such information as work titles, people's names, and subject headings which help ensure consistent and unique naming. However, MARC-based implementations often provide no *linking* between the record types. For example, a cataloger will find the name authority record for a book's author but may not have any way to reference that authority record explicitly within the bib record or enact global changes across the system. Instead, the authoritative name for the author is copied separately into each bib record.

In contrast to MARC, FRBR uses an entity-relationship approach to provide strong linking between records. For example, in FRBR, an *item* (e.g., a copy of a book) is an exemplar of a *manifestation* (e.g., all books with the same ISBN), which embodies an *expression* (edition) of a *work* (the abstract entity representing the original intellectual or creative content). This strong linking can be used to provide both collocation and a coherent disambiguation path for users.

The FRBR specification has been used as the basis for some system development. FRBR-based projects include FRBR support within the VTLS Virtua system [6], the AustLit Australian Literature Gateway [7], RLG's RedLightGreen [8], and OCLC WorldCat's Fiction Finder [9].

When the Variations2 Indiana University Digital Music Library project began more than three years ago, we determined to develop a metadata model that would support a greatly improved search interface for music [10]. The weaknesses of MARC-based music cataloging are well documented (see, e.g., [11]; we review them briefly in the next section). While not based directly on FRBR, the Variations2 metadata model nonetheless bears a strong resemblance (Table 1).

Like FRBR, our system is *work*-centric, being influenced by the work of both Velucci [12] and Smiraglia [13]. We have implemented a digital music library, Variations2, based on that metadata model, have deployed the system in our music library, and have seen increasing usage over the past year and a half.

Table 1. Variations2 and FRBR Compared

Variations2		FRBR *Rough* Equivalent
Entity	**Description**	
Work	abstract concept of a musical composition or set of compositions	Work
Instantiation	recorded performance of a work (audio) or edition of a work (score)	Expression[1]
Container	physical item or set of items within which one or more instantiations are present (e.g., a CD or CD set, a score)	Manifestation[2] (physical embodiment of an expression, e.g., release, edition)
Media Object	digital sound file(s) or score image(s)	Item[3] (an actual copy of a manifestation)
Contributor	individuals or groups related to a work, instantiation, or container (e.g., composers, performers, conductors, producers, ensembles)	Two Entities: – Person – Corporate Body
Notes:		

Notes:
1. In FRBR an expression can be manifested multiple times; in Variations2, instantiations are unique to a container, even if two containers reflect the same performance.
2. "A manifestation may embody one or more than one expression" [7, p. 13]. The Variations2 Container, however, is less abstract, having some amount of item-level descriptors.
3. The FRBR item refers to a copy in a collection; the Variations2 media object is a digitization of a container. Thus in FRBR, there are potentially many items for a manifestation; in Variations2, there is only digitization of a container, even if multiple media objects are needed to capture all the container's content.

2.2   Finding Music in a MARC-Based OPAC

Online Public Access Catalogs (OPACs) are the primary means by which library users access library collections. OPACs offer searching of bibliographic records (almost always) in the MARC bibliographic format, and under certain circumstances provide to the user a list of authorized and unauthorized (i.e., cross-referenced) names, titles, or subjects from MARC authority records. Despite many advances that have been made to OPACs since library catalogs first went online, searching for musical materials in OPACs can still be problematic, due to both OPAC design and to the structure and contents of the MARC bibliographic record itself.

Library catalog records are created by a convergence of a number of different standards. The MARC Bibliographic format prescribes the fields, subfields, and indicators used to mark what type of information is being recorded. The basic descriptive information that is contained in the MARC record is copied from the item being cataloged and is formatted according to the Anglo-American Cataloguing Rules (AACR2 [14]). "Access points" – other descriptive information formatted in a standard way, not directly copied from the item being cataloged – are similarly selected and formatted according to AACR2 rules. Subject headings are chosen from controlled lists, most often the Library of Congress Subject Headings (LCSH).

The MARC format and its associated data content standards provide precision to bibliographic data. Encoding of information in bibliographic records, for example, allows the distinction between works *by* a person and works *about* a person, while still providing for a connection to be made between them by using the same form of the name in both places. The catalog of MARC records provides both a *descriptive* function – reproducing exactly what is on a physical item allowing users to access titles or authors they've seen – and a *collocating* function – grouping bibliographic items representing the same authors, subjects, and, to some extent, works.

One challenge to music searching is the MARC record's focus on a "static physical artifact" [11, p.2]. The data in a MARC record describe a bibliographic item as a whole, not necessarily any specific part of it. This is problematic because items held in a music library, especially sound recordings, often contain multiple works. Thus there is often no way for a user to know, for example, which of the performers listed in a record is connected with a given piece on the recording being described.

The Nature of an OPAC. The OPACs in use in libraries of all sizes today are typically one part of large Integrated Library Systems (ILSs) used for automation of many library services, including acquisitions, cataloging, circulation, and patron billing. OPACs from different vendors also have vastly different native functionalities, and are customizable by the library implementing them. Search and browse success in an OPAC relies heavily on the design and implementation decisions for an individual installation in addition to the nature and structure of the bibliographic data in the MARC records it contains.

Indiana University's IUCAT, based on the Sirsi Unicorn Integrated Library System (ILS), is a fairly typical example of a modern OPAC. Keyword searching in a large number of fields from the MARC bibliographic record is available, as is browsing and searching on fields (actually groups of fields from the MARC record) labeled as author, title, subject, series, periodical title, and medical subject. Basic Boolean operators and term truncation are available. The OPAC performs reasonably well for simple "known-item" bibliographic searches such as for author or title, but less well for more specialized queries essential to music searches, such as for discovery of pieces with specific instrumentation. Cataloging rules place names of instruments in multiple fields within the MARC record. But these fields do not use terms for instrumentation in a consistent manner, so a keyword search of the entire record on instrument names will not find all relevant records in the catalog, and will at the same time add many irrelevant records. One partial solution was the creation of a dedicated field in the MARC record for instrumentation, but this field is rarely used, due in part to the amount of time it takes to add this information to bibliographic records, but also largely due to the fact that almost no OPACs, including Indiana University's, index this field for searching or display it to users.

Collocation by Work. Collocation by *work* is one of the functions of cataloging wherein OPAC designers and consequently OPAC users often do not succeed. MARC and AACR2 provide basic work collocation through a mechanism called the *uniform title*. All records describing the same musical piece, whether in score or recording, have the same uniform title. There are also additions to music uniform titles that indicate, among other things, whether a record is for an arrangement of a musical work, a part of a musical work, or a musical setting of a textual work. This in theory allows connections to be made between multiple versions of the same work and its variations. For example, a score or recording of Bach's complete 2-book Well-Tempered Clavier would have the uniform title Wohltemperierte Klavier, the Prelude and Fugue #1 from Book 1 would have Wohltemperierte Klavier, 1T, Nr. 1, and an arrangement for guitar of the entire work would have Wohltemperierte Klavier, Arr.

But this work collocation function is often not readily available to the average library catalog user. First, uniform titles are not present in all bibliographic records. Cataloging rules governing appropriate use and the presence of records created before the uniform title achieved its present form are among the reasons a uniform title may be missing from a given record. Second, many OPACs don't make full use of the uniform title for display purposes. Many catalogs provide basic grouping capability on the first part of the uniform title (the actual name of the work), but then fail to meaningfully use the other parts of the uniform title that indicate format, arrangement or selection, and the like. Similarly, most library systems do not use the semantic links between whole works and their parts that uniform titles provide [11, p.4]. Current OPACs on the whole do not recognize this link, and thus fail to retrieve the larger work when a part is searched.

3 Implementation

In this section, we describe the current (version 2.1.1) Variations2 search user interface, including the options available on each of the four tabs (basic, advanced, keyword, and browse). We also describe how the disambiguation process varies depending both on what fields the user fills in and the actual content of the digital library.

The Variations2 software is cross-platform (Windows and Macintosh), implemented as a Java application. While the search interface could have been implemented in a web browser, the other features of Variations2 (audio player, score viewer, etc.) would not have worked as well within a browser window, so we decided to implement the entire application as separate Java windows. The technical architecture of Variations2 is beyond the scope of this paper, but a description may be found in [15].

3.1 Search Tabs

The Variations2 search window (Figure 1) is the default initial window displayed by the application after users log in. The search window is divided into two sections: the search tabs, where users specify their search criteria, and the results pane, where the results of the search are displayed. The results pane has a row of controls above it for forward/backward navigation, canceling a search in progress, or changing the display of the results by sorting or filtering.

Basic Tab. The search window defaults to the Basic tab, which provides five fields for search criteria specification.

- Creator/Composer (like *author*, but music is different)
- Performer/Conductor (critically important for music)
- Work Title (often different from the name of the container)
- Key (two drop-down lists: key letter and mode, e.g., A, minor)
- Media format (drop-down list with various types of recording and score formats)

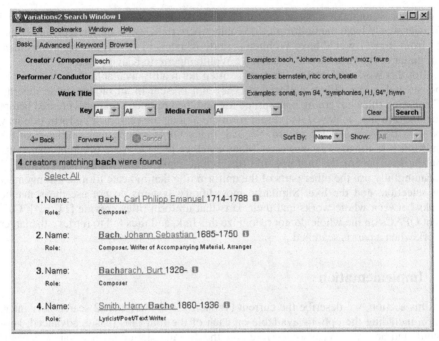

Fig. 1. Search Window, Basic Tab

In all of the text entry fields in the search interface, the following properties apply.

– Case insensitivity
– Partial words are matched by default, e.g., "beeth" will find Beethoven
– Quotation marks permit searching for the exact word or phrase
– Other punctuation and diacritics are ignored

Advanced Tab. The advanced tab offers the same fields as the basic tab, with the following additions.

– Recording/Score Title (i.e., container title)
– Other Contributor (e.g., arranger, producer)
– Publisher
– Subject Heading

Keyword Tab. The keyword tab offers two fields.

– Keywords(s) – accepts parentheses and the Boolean operators *and*, *or*, and *not*
– Media format (drop-down list with various types of recording and score formats)

Browse Tab. The browse tab (Figure 2) offers browsing of the entire collection. Users select one of the following "browse by" options.

– Creators (composers, poets, lyricists, etc.)
– Works

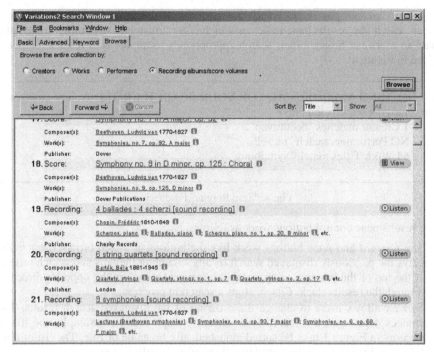

Fig. 2. Search Window, Browse Tab

– Performers
– Recording albums/score volumes

Users can initiate a search either by pressing the Enter key on their keyboards while they are in one of the text fields, or by clicking on the *Search* button.

3.2   Results Display and Interaction

The results display area uses a Java Swing component to render HTML. Descriptive text is black, hyperlinks are blue, and there are also buttons of various colors. Figure 3 shows a part of the Figure 1 results display. In the gray box at the top of each result set is a description of the results that follow. The main entry (first line) for each result is in a larger font, and the matching part of the string (if any) is bolded. The ■ iconic button indicates detailed information is available.

Fig. 3. Search Results Detail

Results are not paged: all results are returned. If there are not any results for a given search, the results pane indicates which criteria matched something in the database so users can broaden their search appropriately. Sample "zero results" output is given in Figure 4.

NOTHING MATCHED ALL OF YOUR SEARCH CRITERIA. Try changing or removing search elements.
- 1 Creator matches "beethoven".
- NO Performers match "mazel".
- 64 Work Titles match "symphony".

Fig. 4. "Zero Results" Feedback

The results pane control buttons work as follows.

- The *forward* and *back* buttons work like the buttons in a web browser: *back* displays the previously displayed search results, changing the tabs and search criteria at the top of the window as appropriate. *Forward* moves in the opposite direction through the results stack. *Cancel* stops a search in progress.
- *Sort By* allows users to change the ordering of the displayed search results. The choices depend on the record type currently displayed. For example, the list of creators in Figure 1 may be sorted alphabetically by name or role. The list of containers in Figure 2 may be sorted by title or (first listed) composer.
- *Show* allows filtering of containers by media type (score or recording).

Whenever a View or Listen button is present in the search results, clicking that button, or clicking the title on that same line, will launch the Variations2 score viewer or audio player, as appropriate.

An alternative navigation mechanism is available from a right-click popup menu (Figure 5). In this example, right-clicking on the score name offers two choices: opening the score in the score viewer (the default behavior had the link been clicked) or viewing detailed information about the score.

Fig. 5. Right-Click Menu Navigation

Right-clicking on "Vivaldi, Antonio" in Figure 5 also gives two options: getting detailed information about Vivaldi, or launching a new search for works by Vivaldi.

Viewing Record Details. Users may request record details either by using the popup menu or by clicking on the ■ button. Record details are displayed in a separate window, also using HTML and having both internal and external links. Internal links allow convenient navigation within a container record. External links provide record details for referenced records, bring up an audio player or score viewer, or provide links to external resources.

Disambiguation. The search logic in Variations2 provides step-by-step disambiguation during searches. Disambiguation steps are inserted in the search process when all of the search criteria can be satisfied by a variety of results, but

- a name used as search criteria matches more than one individual or collective name in the database, *or*
- a work title used as search criteria matches more than one work title in the database.

There is a set sequence to the disambiguation. In the "worst" case, a user specifies an ambiguous *creator, performer, work title,* and *other contributor.* First the user is presented with search results listing all the matching creators where the other criteria also have matches. After selecting the desired creator, the user is presented with the list of all matching performers who perform works by the selected creator, the other criteria still matching, etc. In this worst-case scenario, the user is not presented with media links until the fifth set of search results. Typically, however, only one or two disambiguation steps are required. If, at any disambiguation step, users want to see all the results without having to disambiguate, they can click the "Select All" link (Figure 3).

3.3 Current State

Cataloged content in Variations2 is somewhat limited at present. In March 2004, the digital library contained records for 1500+ works, 1300+ contributors, in support of 282 containers (262 recordings and 20 scores). The collection grows in response to pilot project needs, development team testing needs, and an overall goal of broadening the collection.

Variations2 is installed on approximately 120 computers in the music library. Any person with an IU login can come to the music library and use Variations2. While the primary mechanism for online access to music at IU is still IUCAT and Variations (our previous-generation digital music library [16]), Variations2 is available for general use.

4 Conclusions and Future Work

This paper documents the current Variations2 digital music library search user interface as a user-centered, FRBR-like alternative to traditional MARC-based OPACs as mechanisms for finding music. We have carried out multiple lab-based and field-based evaluations; results will be published separately. The short summary of our evaluation results is that we found no fundamental flaws with the user interface or the design of the metadata model. Such problems as were uncovered seem addressable by relatively non-invasive user interface improvements.

Variations2 is a continuing research project. Among the search-related features planned for future releases are the inclusion of themes and incipits in the search interface, initially as a means for users to distinguish works but eventually as a mechanism for limited content-based searching of music. We also plan on adding search fields for instrumentation, genre (e.g., jazz, pop, rock), musical form (e.g., song, symphony, opera), and style (e.g., baroque, romantic). To the current audio recording and scanned score formats we plan to add encoded scores. We are also considering implementing a web-browser-based search interface.

Variations2 is designed as a distributed solution, for use by multiple institutions. The current implementation is more monolithic, based on the collection of a single institution. As we evolve Variations2 to fulfill its distributed promise, we will have to consider how a distributed "union" catalog can be used within the search interface (while ensuring only authorized access to the digital content!). Only by addressing barriers to distributed deployment can we develop the cooperative cataloging community necessary to support re-cataloging and thereby a future existence for our metadata model and software.

Acknowledgements

We wish to acknowledge Mary Wallace Davidson for her contribution to the Variations2 metadata model, as well as Don Byrd, Jim Halliday, and Ryan Scherle for designing and implementing the search functionality. The authors also thank Don Byrd, Mary Wallace Davidson, Jon Dunn, and Jim Halliday for their helpful reviews of this paper. This material is based upon work supported by the National Science Foundation under Grant No. 9909068. Any opinions, findings, and conclusions or recommendations expressed in this material are those of the authors and do not necessarily reflect the views of the National Science Foundation.

References

1. Variations2: the Indiana University digital music library project.
   http://variations2.indiana.edu/.
2. OCLC WorldCat web site. http://www.oclc.org/worldcat.
3. Research Libraries Group (RLG) web site. http://www.rlg.org.
4. IFLA Study Group on the Functional Requirements for Bibliographic Records. Functional requirements for bibliographic records. K.G. Saur, Munich, 1998.
5. Library of Congress. MARC Standards web site. http://www.loc.gov/marc.
6. VTLS announces first FRBR user. Biblio Tech Review (24 January 2003).
   http://www.biblio-tech.com/btr11/S_PD.cfm?ArticleID=496&DO=A.
7. Ayres, M., Kilner, K., Fitch, K., & Scarvell, A. Report on the successful AustLit: Australian Literature Gateway implementation of the FRBR and INDECS event models, and implications for other FRBR implementations. International Cataloguing and Bibliographic Control, 32 1 (January/March 2003), 8-13.
8. Revolutionizing the catalog: RLG's RedLightGreen project.
   http://www.rlg.org/redlightgreen/
9. FictionFinder: a FRBR-based prototype for fiction in WorldCat.
   http://www.oclc.org/research/projects/frbr/fictionfinder.htm
10. Minibayeva, N., and Dunn, J.W, A digital library data model for music. In Proceedings of JCDL '02 (Portland, Oregon, 13-17 July 2002). ACM Press, New York, NY, 2002, 154-155.
11. Hemmasi, H. Why not MARC? In Proceedings of ISMIR 2002: The Third International Conference on Music Information Retrieval (Paris, France, 13-17 October 2002). IRCAM – Centre Pompidou, Paris, France, 2002, 242-248.

12. Velucci, S. L. Bibliographic relationships in music catalogs. Scarecrow Press, Lanham, MD, 1997.
13. Smiraglia, R. P. The nature of "The work." Scarecrow Press, Lanham, MD, 2001.
14. Anglo-American cataloguing rules, 2nd ed., 2002 revision. American Library Association, Chicago, 2002.
15. Variations2 Development Team. Variations2 system architecture: report for the project midterm review. Technical report. http://variations2.indiana.edu/html/v2-architecture-findings-nov2002.
16. Variations website. http://www.dlib.indiana.edu/variations.

Approaching the Problem of Multi-lingual Information Retrieval and Visualization in Greek and Latin and Old Norse Texts

Jeffrey A. Rydberg-Cox[1], Lara Vetter[1], Stefan Rüger[2], and Daniel Heesch[2]

[1] Department of English, University of Missouri Kansas City, Kansas City, MO 64110 USA
{rydbergcoxj,vetterl}@umkc.edu
[2] Department of Computing, Imperial College, London SW7 2BZ
{s.rueger,daniel.heesch}@imperial.ac.uk

Abstract. In this paper, we explore approaches to multi-lingual information retrieval for Greek, Latin, and Old Norse texts. We also describe an information retrieval tool that allows users to formulate Greek, Latin, or Old Norse queries in English and display the results in an innovative clustering and visualization facility.

1 Introduction

Cross-lingual information retrieval is a particularly intriguing technology for students and scholars of Ancient and Early-Modern Greek and Latin or Old Norse. Works written in these languages are extremely important for understanding our literary, scientific, and intellectual heritage, but these languages are difficult and few people know them well. In particular, this technology can be extremely useful for non-specialist scholars and students who are somewhat familiar with these languages, but who do not know enough to form a mono-lingual query for a search engine. Students of Ancient Greek literature, for example, might want to know more about the quality of 'cunning intelligence' that is admired and exemplified in the character of Odysseus in Homer's *Odyssey*. Because this quality is multifaceted, it would be very difficult for readers to formulate a query for this type of passage if they were working only with an English translation of the text; they must rely on the consistency of the translator. A cross-lingual information system, on the other hand, would help students identify words or key phrases – such as the Greek word for cunning intelligence, *'metis'* – and then study passages where they appear.

Such a system is, of course, only the beginning. At best, it can identify passages that need further study and translation since a user who cannot formulate a query probably cannot easily read the text in its original language either. While a great deal of work has been done on these sorts of systems in venues such as the Cross Lingual Evaluation Forum *(CLEF)* and the Translingual Information and Detection program *(TIDES)*, their focus has largely been on business journals, newswires, and national security applications. Our work has focused on evaluating how the needs of students and scholars in the humanities differ from those in other domains and developing a system to meet these needs.

R. Heery and L. Lyon (Eds.): ECDL 2004, LNCS 3232, pp. 168–178, 2004.

2 Context and Testbeds

The work described in this paper takes place in the context of the Cultural Heritage Language Technologies consortium (http://www.chlt.org), a jointly funded project of the National Science Foundation and European Commission Information Society Technologies Program. This project is a collaborative effort of eight partner institutions located in both the United States and Europe. Many of these partners have contributed corpora and core technologies that we have relied on in our work. Our testbeds for this project include the six million words of Greek and four million words of Latin with parallel translation from the Perseus Digital Library (http://www.perseus. tufts.edu); more than one million words of Latin drawn from early printed works in the history of science from Special Collections department at the Linda Hall Library in Kansas City (http://www.lindahall.org); a 750,000 word corpus of Early-Modern Latin from the Stoa consortium at the University of Kentucky (http://www.stoa.org); a corpus of Isaac Newton's alchemical, theological, and chemical papers from the Newton Project at Imperial College (http://www.newtonproject.ic.ac.uk/); and a corpus of Old Norse sagas from the University of California at Los Angeles. In addition to these textual testbeds, the Perseus Project has also provided its parsers and machine-readable dictionaries for Greek and Latin while the group at UCLA is creating comparable resources under the aegis of this project.

3 Approaches to the Problem

The problem of multi-lingual information retrieval is essentially one of machine translation on a very small scale. There have been two dominant approaches to this problem: 1) dictionary translation using machine-readable multi-lingual dictionaries and 2) automatic extraction of possible translation equivalents by statistical analysis of parallel or comparable corpora[1].

Dictionary translation is a low-cost search technology that translates queries by substituting each word in a query with translations automatically derived from the machine-readable dictionary. This approach by itself is not very good, achieving results that are only 40-60% as effective as a mono-lingual search ([4-6]). The primary problems of this approach are related to the introduction of extraneous words and ambiguity into the query due to the multiple senses contained in most dictionary entries, the failure of most machine-readable dictionaries to account for technical terms in a consistent way, and the loss of important fixed phrases.

Automatic extraction of translation equivalents from parallel or comparable corpora introduces similar sorts of ambiguity and carries two additional problems: 1) these corpora can be extremely expensive to produce, and 2) these automatically extracted translation equivalents are most effective in restricted domains ([7-9]).

---

[1] There are, of course, other approaches. [1] points out that it is also theoretically possible to machine-translate target documents, but this technology is not yet feasible for most modern languages, let alone Greek, Latin, or Old Norse. See also [2] and [3] for an innovative approach based on topic modeling.

The needs and nature of our user community of students and scholars in a humanities digital library suggest that we can profitably adopt both of these approaches if we take appropriate steps to reduce query ambiguity. The nature of the corpus of Ancient Greek and Latin and Old Norse texts makes it ideal for this project, as it is highly domain specific within some broad parameters[2]. Further, the corpus itself is very stable, so the cost of creating a parallel corpus is finite and the investment, once made, would have lasting value for students and scholars in its field. At the same time, these ancient languages have been highly studied and thus can benefit from the work of scholars who have developed comprehensive 'unabridged' lexica as well as domain specific dictionaries for both fields of discourse and specific authors.

The information-seeking behaviors of the people who use digital resources in these languages also inform our approach. Students and scholars of ancient languages are almost a 'hyper-fit' for the profile of a user of a multi-lingual information retrieval facility. Very few specialists are trained to write and speak Greek, Latin, or Old Norse; advanced training – for the most part – focuses on reading these languages. This focus on reading, however, means that the user community is trained in a philological approach that focuses on the use of small families of words and that is attuned to the shades of overlapping meanings of different words. The example in the introduction of a scholar studying 'cunning intelligence' is not random but drawn from a book-length study of the word *metis* ([11]). Further, even the most skilled readers of ancient languages are well versed in the use of reference works such as grammars and dictionaries and are accustomed to using them regularly as they read. Classicist Martin Mueller describes the user community as follows: "Very few readers know ancient Greek well enough to read it without frequent recourse to a dictionary or grammar, and because of their highly specialized interests, the few readers who can do so are likely to be particularly intensive users of such reference works" ([12]).

The nature of our users means that they are well equipped to help translate their query into the target language as long as they are provided with tools to help them in this process. In 1972, Salton demonstrated that with carefully constructed query expansion thesauri, multi-lingual information retrieval tools could be as effective as mono-lingual tools ([13]). The information retrieval community has, however, eschewed Salton's arguments for hand-constructed query expansion thesauri in favor of solutions that are more general and domain independent (i.e. [5], [8]). Salton's carefully constructed thesauri are still expensive but this is an expense that can reasonably be shifted to each end user at query time for humanities applications. A tool that helps them give feedback during the query translation process allows users to construct their own *ad hoc* query expansion thesauri, thus facilitating the construction of a query that is most useful for their needs. This approach does not preclude automatic disambiguation methods; as we will demonstrate below, we have developed a user feedback mechanism with tools to help end-users translate queries including easy access to machine readable dictionaries and several query-specific statistical measures that assist users' identification of relevant search terms.

---

[2]   In fact, the *Thesaurus Linguae Gracae* already defines 86 restricted domains for the surviving corpus of more than 71 million words written in Ancient Greek (see [10] and http://www.tlg.uci.edu).

4 Query Formation

4.1 Query Translation

The search facility begins with a simple interface that allows users to enter search terms in English, to select the sources that will be used for query translation, and to restrict their results to words that appear in works written by a particular author.

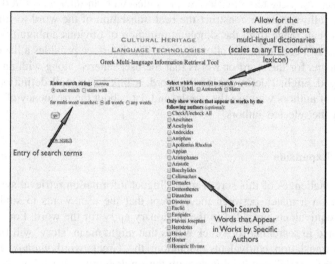

Fig. 1. Query Entry Screen

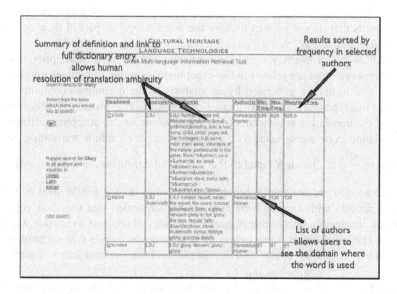

Fig. 2. Query Translation Screen

Several of the options presented to the user in this phase are integrated with the larger digital library system and designed to scale up as new texts and reference works are added. The system for dictionary translation is based on a piece of middleware with a modular design that automatically extracts translation equivalents from any SGML or XML dictionary tagged in accordance with the guidelines of the Text Encoding Initiative or any other user-defined DTD. The author list restrictions are generated from the cataloging metadata from the digital library.

After entering query terms, users are presented with an interface with detailed information to allow them to construct the best translation of the word for their needs. This process can range from the simple elimination of obvious ambiguities and mistakes to a careful consideration of every term. The interface provides a list of translation equivalents for the word or words that the user entered along with an automatically abridged English definition of the word, a link to the full definition for each word, a list of authors who use the words, and data about the frequency of each word in works by the selected authors.

4.2 Query Expansion

One of the challenges of this sort of multi-lingual information retrieval system is the dependence on a match between the concept that the user wants to study and the translation equivalents provided in the dictionary entry for the word. For example, a user interested in searching for Greek words that might mean 'story' will find several very good translation equivalents, including the Greek word *muthos* that means "speech, story or tale" and is cognate with the English word 'myth,' as well as other words such as *ainos*, meaning "tale or story," and *polumuthos*, a compound word meaning "much talked of, famous in story". The first phase will, however, miss other related words that do not happen to have the word 'story' as part of their definition, such as *epos*, defined as *"that which is uttered in words, speech, tale."*

To address this problem, we provide users with a query expansion option that suggests other words that are related to the exact matches returned by their initial query. These related terms are generated by an analysis of the definitions contained in the electronic machine-readable multi-lingual dictionaries. This process involves extracting all of the translation equivalents from the dictionaries and stripping suffixes from the translation equivalents using Porter's algorithm. We exclude translation equivalents where $\dfrac{df_1}{N} \geq .5$ with N equal to the number of definitions in the dictionary. The terms themselves are assigned a binary weight rather than a weight such as *tf x idf*. Our experiments with various weighting schemes revealed that they had very little impact on the results because documents were very short (just over four words on average). Having developed this index, we determine the entries that are most similar to each other using a simple Dice similarity coefficient ($sim(def_i, def_j) = \dfrac{2|def_i \cap def_j|}{|def_i| + |def_j|}$). The five words with the highest correlation coefficient are then included in the results for the query translation phase of the process.

In many cases – as in the above example of a search for the word 'story' - this process enhances what are already very good search results. By its nature, this process expands recall at the expense of precision, thus running the risk of presenting the user with too much irrelevant information in the query translation phases. Therefore, a user seeking a more precise query can switch off the query expansion function.

4.3 Sources of Translation Equivalents

Our current research is focused on determining whether the work of Church and Gale for the *Oxford English Dictionary* [14] can be applied to our parallel corpora of Greek texts with English translations and Latin texts with English translations. Church and Gale argue that a χ^2 test can be used to determine translation equivalents in parallel corpora aligned at the sentence level. They posit a null hypothesis that words occur in parallel sentences independently or by chance. This null hypothesis is then compared with the actual count of term co-occurrence across parallel corpora block using the following equation:

$$x^2 = \frac{(O-E)^2}{E}$$ with O equal to the number of times that a word pair appears

together and E equal to the average number of times that the terms would appear together if they were evenly distributed across the entire corpus. Our hope is that we will be able to generate a dynamic thesaurus of translation equivalents based on our corpora and offer this thesaurus to our users alongside the machine-readable dictionaries that we are currently using in this interface.

Church and Gale's results are intriguing, but we need to determine if they can be applied to texts written in Greek and Latin. We are focusing our investigations in three key areas.

First, Church and Gale worked on business documents written in English and French drawn from the Union Bank of Switzerland corpus. Greek and Latin have much more complex morphological structures and very free word order, so it is necessary to study the impact of these linguistic differences when applying this algorithm.

Second, our corpora are aligned with a much lower level of granularity than the corpus tested by Church and Gale. Scholars traditionally refer to classical texts using a standard system, such as line number for poetry or page/paragraph numbers of an early printed edition for prose. For example, the works of Plato are referenced by a pagination system from a three-volume collection of Plato's works published in 1578 by Henri Estienne. The three volumes were numbered consecutively and each page was divided into sections with the division marked by the letters a-e. Plato's dialogues are cited using the name of the dialogue, the page number from this edition, and the letter from the section containing the beginning of the citation. Other prose works are divided in similar ways based on other early printed antecedents. Our parallel corpora of prose are aligned at this level and the resulting blocks can range from a few hundred words to almost one thousand words. Poetry is even more complicated because line numbers offer a false sense of precision. In actuality, the number of lines in a translation can vary widely between the original and the translation and – even when this is accounted for – word order conventions are so different that words could appear on widely different lines. We have obtained good preliminary results by working with aligned segments of ten lines, but we need to determine if this lower level of granularity will work generally across our corpora or – alternately – if we need to explore methods for working with comparable corpora rather than parallel corpora.

Finally, this approach is similar to our query expansion routine in that it favors recall over precision. We will need a detailed study of our results to determine whether or not the information we are adding is useful to users translating their queries.

5 Visualizing Results

After users translate their queries with these tools, the search is passed to a monolingual search engine with several visualization front ends (described in more detail in [15, 16]). These front ends are alternatives to the traditional ranked list view of search results and are based on the on-the-fly calculation of keywords for the documents returned by the query. Keywords are calculated using the equation:

$$w_j = \frac{r_j}{d_j} \times r_j \log(|R|/r_j)$$

where $|R|$ is the total number of documents returned by the query, r_j is the number of documents in the returned set containing term j, and d_j is the number of documents in the entire collection containing term j. This factor is used in favor of *tf x idf* ranking because it favors salient words within the returned document set that are also discriminative. By calculating these scores at query time based on the query and the returned document set, we are able to improve our results as compared to a weight calculated for each term in the collection calculated in the indexing phase.

These interfaces group visually documents that our calculations have determined to be related, and label each group with the most appropriate keyword. They also offer users the opportunity to revisit some of the translation decisions that they made in the previous step, allowing them to eliminate certain keywords from the search results. A user may browse related documents or, alternately, refine searches by drilling down to sub-clusters. Our hope is that by placing related Greek or Latin passages in meaningful conceptual groups we will reduce the time the user spends sorting through a ranked list of search results.

The first visualization interface is a tree view that represents documents as the nodes of a binary tree flattened into a circular pattern. Due to constraints on size of display, the tree is only displayed at five levels, with the bottom level representing further sub-clusters where appropriate. The terminal nodes are distinguished by color cues, with red nodes representing documents and yellow nodes as further sub-clusters. Each node is also labeled with the highest-frequency keyword associated with that cluster.

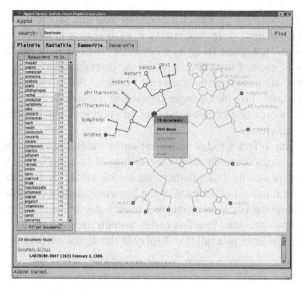

Fig. 3. Tree Visualization of Search Results

As the user mouses over the nodes, the selected nodes are highlighted, and the user is presented with a menu showing the number of documents and all of the keywords associated with that cluster. This menu also allows the user to drill down on any node and re-center the tree around the selected node. Further, within this visualization, the user is able to eliminate keywords from the search results, view fragments of every document in the collection, and follow a link to the complete document within the digital library.

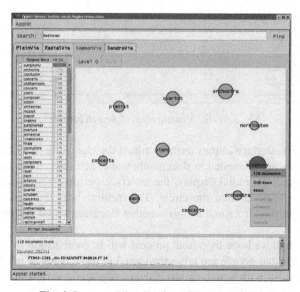

Fig. 4. Sammon Visualization of Search Results

The second visualization generates a Sammon map that provides users with a visual landscape for navigation. In this interface, each cluster is represented as a circle and is labeled with its highest frequency keyword. The radius of the circle indicates the relative size of each of the clusters, while the distance between the circles represents the relative similarity of the different clusters. As in the tree visualization, mousing over a cluster provides a menu containing the size of the cluster along with its associated keywords and offering the user an opportunity to re-center the display around the selected cluster.

The third display offers a radial visualization in which the twelve highest ranked keywords in the returned search results are displayed in a circle. Each document in the returned set is represented as a point in the middle of the circle with its placement determined by the relative pull of each of the keywords distributed around the circle. Users can determine the keywords contained in each document by mousing over each point. As in the two previous interfaces, this visualization allows users to eliminate keywords and follow links to a full text display in the digital library.

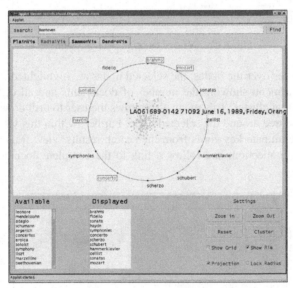

Fig. 5. Radial Visualization of Search Results

Further, this third interface allows users to adjust the clustering to suit their information needs. If they are interested in documents that contain keywords that are distributed widely around the radial display, the interface permits them to select keyword nodes and move them around the circle. This action shifts the position of related documents within the circle and brings together documents that are most useful for the end user.

Finally, although we hope the visual process will be more useful for our end users, we also are aware that people are not accustomed to these types of interfaces. Therefore, a traditional list with search results grouped together and ranked using the traditional $tf \times idf$ score is available as well.

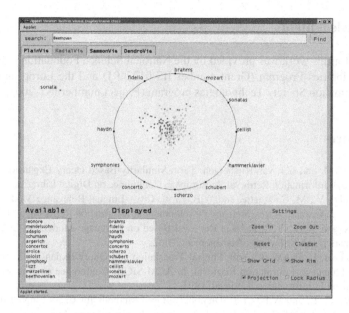

Fig. 6. Radial Visualization of Search Results with Dynamic Re-Clustering

6 Evaluation and Future Research

With these interfaces, we provide our users with a great deal of information that they can use to translate queries in a way that is most appropriate for their information-seeking interests. At the same time, we provide them with three innovative interfaces within which they can browse the resulting data. In addition to our work on automatically generated translation thesauri for Greek and Latin, our next phases will focus on user evaluation.

We have already done testing on the quality of the clusters and received user feedback on the visualization interfaces in English. We now need more controlled user studies of the clustering interface for Greek, Latin and Old Norse. The largest obstacle in this area is the lack of a standard set of documents, queries, and relevance judgments for the corpus of texts written in these languages that would allow us to generate standard precision and recall metrics for our work. As digital libraries expand from modern European languages to cultural heritage materials, the need for these sorts of evaluation corpora will become more urgent if we are going to be able to effectively evaluate these sorts of tools. Groups such as the Cross-Lingual Evaluation Forum (CLEF) and the Document Understanding Conference (DUC) provide a model; building a consortium to follow their lead in creating an evaluation corpus for cultural heritage materials must be one of the next priorities for our project.

Acknowledgments

Funding for this work was provided by the National Science Foundation International Digital Libraries Program (Grant number IIS-0122491) and the European Commission Information Society Technologies program (Project number IST-2001-32745).

References

1. Adriani, M. and C.J. van Rijsbergen. Term Similarity-Based Query Expansion for Cross-Language Information Retrieval. In European Conference on Digital Libraries, 1999.
2. Lavrenko, V., M. Choquette, and W.B. Croft. Cross-Lingual Relevance Models. In ACM SIGIR Conference on Research and Development in Information Retrieval, 2002.
3. Liu, X. and W.B. Croft. Passage Retrieval Based on Language Models. in Conference on Information and Knowledge Management, 2002.
4. Ballesteros, L. and W.B. Croft. Phrasal Translation and Query Expansion Techniques for Cross-Language Information Retrieval. In ACM SIGIR Conference on Research and Development in Information Retrieval, 1997.
5. Ballesteros, L. and W.B. Croft. Dictionary-Based Methods for Cross-Lingual Information Retrieval. In DEXA Conference on Database and Expert Systems Applications, 1997.
6. Hull, D.A. and G. Grefenstette. Querying Across Languages: A Dictionary-Based Approach to Multilingual Information Retrieval. In ACM SIGIR Conference on Research and Development in Information Retrieval, 1996.
7. Ballesteros, L. and W.B. Croft. Resolving Ambiguity for Cross-Language Retrieval. In ACM SIGIR Conference on Research and Development in Information Retrieval, 1998.
8. Sheridan, P. and J.P. Ballerini. Experiments in Multilingual Information Retrieval Using the SPIDER System. In ACM SIGIR Conference on Research and Development in Information Retrieval, 1996.
9. Sheridan, P., M. Braschler, and P. Schauble. Cross-Language Information Retrieval in a Multilingual Legal Domain. In European Conference on Research and Technology for Digital Libraries, 1997.
10. Berkowitz, L. and K. Squitier, Thesaurus Linguae Graecae Canon of Greek Authors and Works. 1990, Oxford: Oxford University Press.
11. Detienne, M. and J.P. Vernant, Cunning Intelligence in Greek Culture and Society. 1991, Chicago: University of Chicago Press.
12. Mueller, M., Electronic Homer. Ariadne, 2000. 25: p.
http://www.ariadne.ac.uk/issue25/mueller/.
13. Salton, G., Experiments in Multi-Lingual Information Retrieval. 1972, Computer Science Department, Cornell University: Ithaca.
14. Church, K. and P. Hanks. Concordances for Parallel Text. in Seventh Annual Conference of the UW Center for the New OED and Text Research, 1991. Oxford.
15. Carey, M., D. Heesch, and S. Rüger. Info Navigator: A Visualization Tool For Document Searching and Browsing. In Conference on Distributed Multimedia Systems, 2003.
16. Au, P., M. Carey, S. Sewraz, Y. Guo, and S. Rüger, New Paradigms in Information Visualization. In ACM SIGIR Conference on Research and Development in Information Retrieval, 2000.

Building Interoperability for United Kingdom Historic Environment Information Resources

Edmund Lee

English Heritage, National Monuments Record Centre,
Kemble Drive, Swindon, SN2 2GZ, UK
edmund.lee@english-heritage.org.uk

Abstract. The paper will present the work of the Forum on Information Standards in Heritage (FISH) – www.fish-forum.info – in the development of standards and protocols to support interoperability between historic environment sector information systems. The paper describes barriers to interoperability within the sector. These originate in the unique character of the historic environment as an information source. Progress in the development of relevant standards is reviewed and emphasis placed upon community building to support standardisation. Current work to develop an XML-based interoperability 'toolkit' of schema and protocols to support knowledge-sharing networks is described. This will be based on current FISH standards along with the CIDOC Conceptual Reference Model, an emerging ISO standard ontology for cultural heritage information.

1 The Historic Environment Information Landscape

The 'historic environment' is all around us. It consists of the totality of those aspects of the built heritage, archaeology and current and past landscapes that together form both the subject of study for academics, and a perceived 'sense of place' for those that live and work within such an environment. The holistic approach implicit in the phrase 'historic environment' presents particular challenges to the designers and managers of historic environment information resources (HEIRs). It is useful to introduce these challenges to provide a background to this presentation of the data standards that have emerged within the sector, the means by which they are developed, and the current work on interoperability to secure the benefits of that standardisation work.

1.1 Multiplicity of Interests

The historic environment is not 'owned' or curated by any one single organisation, and there are often many organisations interested in the same site. A contrast can be drawn between, for example, a museum object which will generally be documented by a single curating authority, and a Bronze Age burial mound. The latter may be recorded simultaneously by any or all of the following: a local authority for development control purposes, a national body for purposes of legal protection, the landowner for land management, a thematic national survey of sites of a particular type, a scientific or research group as the origin of a significant sample at the scale of microns and

R. Heery and L. Lyon (Eds.): ECDL 2004, LNCS 3232, pp. 179–185, 2004.

a landscape survey project working on a scale of kilometres. This contrast is reflected in the distinction between process-based standards current in the UK museums sector (SPECTRUM from mda) and object-based standards for the historic environment [1].

1.2 Separation of Data from Documented Object

Features of the historic environment do not usually provide their own documentation. This is in contrast to an item of archive, which may well convey enough information, either within itself or by virtue of its context within a collection, for it to be adequately described. In consequence the recorded information about a Bronze Age burial mound is arguably as significant as the original site. This issue becomes most acute in cases where the site no longer exists. In the jargon 'preservation by record' means that recorded information may well stand as surrogate for the actual site itself.

1.3 Unique Character

No two features of the historic environment are identical, and it is this diversity which is often the subject of interest. Two Bronze Age burial mounds, for all their similarities, cannot be treated in the same way as two copies of the same book. Often there is uncertainty over the correct interpretation of such a feature. Is it really a burial mound? Is it really Bronze Age? Maximising future retrieval of records suggests the requirement to index all the possible alternative interpretations that the available evidence supports. Opportunities for rigorous rules-based classification of features of the historic environment are very limited, and have received little attention in comparison to, for example the classification of archaeological artefacts.

2 Consequences for the HEIR User

Faced by these challenges, historic environment information resource managers have developed many different software platforms and database designs. Even within a single subset of the sector, the Historic Environment Records (formerly known as Sites and Monuments Records or SMRs) maintained by English local authorities, Newman has identified the need for extensive auditing to promote consistent quality [2]. The Historic Environment Information Resources Network has surveyed and reported on the variability and fragmentation of these diverse information systems [3].

To achieve a full picture of the existing knowledge of a site it is therefore necessary to draw upon information from a large number of different information systems, which will in most cases have different physical designs, and quite often different underlying logical models. They will support different types of search, and will not provide consistent output. The process of transmission of data between these incompatible data structures is therefore complex and costly. Each attempt to transfer data between systems requires individual design, so that to provide data to multiple partners quickly becomes prohibitively expensive. The routines developed are vulnerable to changes in technology in either partner in the exchange (Fig. 1).

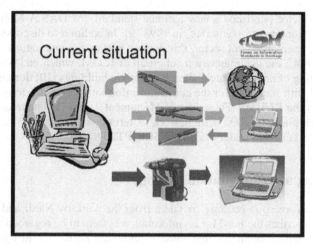

Fig. 1. A complexity of different information management 'tools' isrequired for an HEIR to provide data to a variety of external partners.

3   Data Standards for the Historic Environment

The growth of personal computing technology from the late 1970's onwards had a dramatic effect on the production and management of information relating to the historic environment, as in all other 'memory-based' sectors. A conference devoted to Computer Applications and Quantitative Methods in Archaeology has run annually since 1978: its first proceedings cover 84 pages. [4] The Royal Commission on Historical Monuments of England (RCHME) computerised the English National Archaeological Record, originally maintained by the Ordnance Survey, in 1985 [5].

The explosion of digital information was paralleled by development of standards and recommendations for the content of historic environment records. A data standard is taken to mean for this purpose an 'agreed definition of what is to be recorded, and how, to achieve a particular objective'. In 1981 the Department of the Environment issued an Advisory Note setting out the recommended fields of information to be recorded in an SMR [6]. In 1993 the RCHME and English Heritage published 'Recording England's Past' [7]. This recommended fields and specified terminology lists for the control of data entry to each field. A 'Standard Data Format' for the exchange of records of monuments, using 'tagged data' – text files using a form of mark-up language – was agreed by the RCHME and the representatives of the SMR community in 1994 [8].

These early standards were aimed at the professional sector. Increasing access to computing power and cheaper more user friendly database products stimulated the growth of the independent and voluntary sector inventories of the historic environment. The availability of National Lottery funding from the mid-1990's promoted this trend. The independent sector, exemplified by such groups as the Tiles and Architectural Ceramics Society, the British Sundial Society and The Letterbox Study Group, had a wider range of interest than the focused approach of the 1993 standard. They also needed more encouragement and assistance than a simple but inflexible standard could provide. In response, The RCHME, with partners from the English historic environment sector published a new national standard, 'MIDAS A Manual and Data Standard for Monument Inventories' in 1998 [9]. In addition to discussion within the English historic environment sector, this drew in part on the international work undertaken by CIDOC, the documentation subgroup of ICOM, which had issued guidance on the recording of archaeological sites and historic buildings [10] during the 1990s.

In parallel with standards for the content of information systems, terminology standards such as the RCHME Thesaurus of Monument Types [11] have developed rapidly, and multiplied. In 2000 a framework of terminology standards to complement MIDAS was established under the title INSCRIPTION [12].

4 Nuturing an 'Information Ecology'

The phrase 'information ecology' is taken from the work by Nardi and O'Day [11]. Their study describes the need for an information system to be regarded as one part in an interdependent community that must support the needs not just of the system builders, but also include the end users. The term ecology is deliberately chosen by Nardi and O'Day to evoke the sense of dynamism and fragility, inherent in a biological system. The same approach, I believe, can usefully be applied to the development of the standards that underpin information systems. This is particularly relevant in cases where interoperability is necessary, and a wide range of special interests need to be harmonised. It emphasises that information systems and data standards can only succeed where they also relate to the needs and experience of the creators and endusers of the information they relate to.

Two issues serve to illustrate this point: intellectual property rights, and access to confidential or sensitive data such as the exact location of sites that have yielded valuable artefacts. No system or data standard to support interoperability of data will succeed without attention to issues such as these that might otherwise prevent or constrain the movement of information between systems.

In the historic environment sector such an ecology evolved from the early 1990's work on 'Recording England's Past'. This established collaborative working between staff from the two major organisations in the English heritage sector. The decision to rework this standard into MIDAS, led to the creation of the Data Standards Working Party, with involvement from a wider, but still Anglo-centric, group. With publication of MIDAS complete the group remained in existence to foster its development and implementation. A new title, the Forum on Information Standards in Heritage, England (FISHEN) was adopted, and involvement of representatives from the Scottish, Welsh and Irish heritage organisations was sought. Eventually, the U.K. wide Forum on Information Standards in Heritage (FISH) was established (spawned?) in 2000. These then are the organisations (or organisms?) in the ecology. However the dynamism, the flow of energy round the ecology as it were, stems from the pattern of consultation and collaborative working which has emerged. At the heart of FISH is an email discussion list [14] with some 330 members from across the U.K. and from around the world. This is used to air ideas, share information, and seek advice and comment. The starting point for work on a new area of standards development is often a structured discussion or 'e-conference' held on the FISH list [15]. When a new standard is developed to a draft stage, the list can be used to contact potential reviewers to ensure that the new standard is relevant to the needs of the whole 'ecology' [16]. A formalised peer review then either supports the approval of the new standard by the steering committee of FISH or recommends further re-working. Additional structure and robustness is given to the process by the adoption for FISH projects of a formal project management methodology, PRINCE2 [17], a system widely used in UK public sector information technology projects.

Planned work for FISH includes the extension of the MIDAS standard to a broader range of historic environment resources, working towards publication of a second edition in 2005. The current focus of attention is, however, on the FISH Interoperability Toolkit.

5   The FISH Interoperability Toolkit

The work of FISH and its predecessors has done much to develop some commonality of content and terminology between HEIRs. However, the costs of export, manipulation and migration of data between systems are still prohibitive. To tackle this issue FISH has developed a vision of an interoperability 'toolkit', a range of protocols, formats, agreements and training materials necessary to provide HEIR developers and managers with the means to move data between systems. Subsidiary objectives include the development of a format that will be suitable for the long-term storage of archived data from project databases, and to assist in the migration of data from old systems to new systems. A contractor, Oxford ArchDigital, will undertake development of the toolkit, with funding supplied by English Heritage and the National Trust. The toolkit will initially have the following technical components:

5.1   The FISHXML Format and Data Validator

This will be an Extensible Markup Language (XML) schema, based upon the MIDAS data standard. It will be designed using the CIDOC Conceptual Reference Model to ensure that the basic schema can be extended to meet the wider range of information envisaged by the forthcoming second edition of MIDAS.

In addition, a separate tool will be developed to validate the content of FISHXML files. This will match terms used in the XML file exported from an HEIR with the terminology standards maintained within the INSCRIPTION framework, and report on possible problems.

Together these will ensure the creation of standardised information resources, which can be passed from organisation to organisation, or system to system or deposited in digital archives. (Fig. 2).

5.2   The FISH Historic Environment Protocol (HEEP)

This will be a protocol for the remote querying and retrieval of data from FISHXML compliant HEIRs. Protocol requests and results will be delivered in FISHXML.

This is the most exciting and innovative tool in the FISH Interoperability Toolkit. The protocol will support machine-to-machine exchange of 'live' information between HEIRs, as opposed to the manual approach of record copying, export and import of data. While the FISHXML schema dictates the structure used to exchange data between systems, the protocol provides complaint computers with the instructions for secure and structured transmission and data exchange.

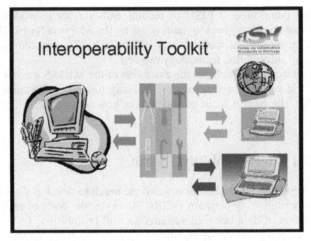

Fig. 2. The FISH Interoperability Toolkit sits between different HEIRs to assist with transfer of information.

6 Progress and Prospects

At the time of writing development work is underway on all these components, with a target date for completion of September 2004. Following on from that the Forum on Information Standards will maintain and develop the FISH Interoperability Toolkit on behalf of the historic environment sector. Future development may tackle other impediments to interoperability. One example is the problem of concordance between records derived from different HEIRs where it is important for one system not to include duplicate records for the same place. It is hoped that, using a standard format for the data such as the FISHXML format will support the development of software tools to automate the comparison of different datasets to identify sites recorded in both.

Further developments will be discussed via the FISH discussion list and promoted via the FISH website www.fish-forum.info. All are welcome to participate.

References

1. Lee, E.: MIDAS – Developing a Standard for the Objects that don't move. In Smith, L. (ed): MDA Information vol 3 no. 1- Papers from the Standards in Action Workshop, Churchill College Cambridge 1-3 October 1997. Mda, Cambridge (1998)
2. Newman, M.: Auditing Heritage Data – Ensuring Quality. In: Doerr, M, Sarris, A (eds): CAA 2002 The Digital Heritage of Archaeology. Hellenic Ministry of Culture (2003) 385-89
3. Chitty, G., Baker, D., Richards, J., Robinson, R.,: Mapping information resources: A report for HEIRNET. Council for British Archaeology (2000). Available from <http://www.britarch.ac.uk/HEIRNET/publications.html> [Accessed March 2004]
4. Laflon, S.,: Computer applications in archaeology 1978. University of Birmingham, Computer Centre, Birmingham (1978)

5. Leech, R., : Computerisation of the National Archaeological Record. In: Computer Applications in Archaeology: conference proceedings (1986). 29-37
6. Department of the Environment: Ancient Monuments Records Manual and county sites and monuments records Advisory Note 32. DoE London (1981)
7. Royal Commission on the Historical Monuments of England, Association of Local Government Archaeological Officers: Recording England's Past. Royal Commission on the Historic Monuments of England London (1993)
8. Lang, N.: ACAO/RCHME Data Exchange Agreement. Unpublished RCHME Internal Memorandum 11 September 1994.
9. Lee,E., (ed): MIDAS – A Manual and Data Standard for Monument Inventories. Royal Commission on Historical Monuments of England. Swindon (1998)
10. CIDOC: Draft international core data standard for archaeological sites and monuments. International Council of Museums International Committee for Documentation Paris (1995)
11. Royal Commission on the Historical Monuments of England: Thesaurus of monument types : a standard for use in archaeological and architectural recording. 2nd edn. Royal Commission on the Historical Monuments of England Swindon (1998)
12. Forum on Information Standards in Heritage INSCRIPTION Available from <http://www.fish-forum.info> [Accessed March 2004]
13. Nardi, B., O'Day, V.: Information ecologies – using technology with heart. Cambridge, Mass. MIT Press London (1999)
14. Forum on Information Standards in Heritage discussion list. Available from <http://www.jiscmail.ac.uk/lists/fish> [Accessed March 2004]
15. Lee, E.: HDM Information Sheet Is an e-conference right for you?. English Heritage Heritage Data Management Swindon (2001) Available from <http://www.english-heritage.org.uk/heritagedata> [Accessed April 2004]
16. Lee, E., Bell, A.: HDM Information Sheet How to do a Peer Review. English Heritage Heritage Data Management Swindon (2001) Available from <http://www.english-heritage.org.uk/heritagedata> [Accessed April 2004]
17. Managing Successful Projects with PRINCE 2. Office of Government Commerce 3rd edition The Stationery Office London (2002)

Prototyping Digital Libraries Handling Heterogeneous Data Sources – The ETANA-DL Case Study

Unni Ravindranathan[1], Rao Shen[1], Marcos André Gonçalves[1], Weiguo Fan[1],
Edward A. Fox[1], and James W. Flanagan[2]

[1] Digital Library Research Laboratory, Virginia Tech,
Blacksburg, VA, 24060, USA
{unni,rshen,mgoncalv,wfan,fox}@vt.edu
[2] Department of Religion, Case Western Reserve University,
Cleveland, OH, 44106, USA
jwf2@cwru.edu

Abstract. Information systems used in archaeology have several needs: interoperability among heterogeneous systems, making information available without significant delay, long-term preservation of data, and providing a suite of services to users. In this paper, we show how digital library techniques can be employed to provide solutions to three of these problems. We show this by describing a prototype for an archaeological Digital Library (ETANA-DL). First, ETANA-DL applies and extends the metadata harvesting approach to address some of the needs – interoperability, rapid access to data, and data preservation. Second, we show that availability of a pool of components that implement common DL services has helped in rapidly creating the prototype, which was subsequently used for requirements elicitation. However, understanding complex archaeological information systems is a difficult task. Third, therefore, we describe our efforts to model these systems using the 5S framework, and show how the partially developed model has been used to implement complex services helping users carry out key tasks with the integrated data.

1 Introduction

Archaeological research results in the production of vast quantities of heterogeneous information. Some of the kinds of digital objects include field records, GIS records, images, audio, video, 3D-models, and many more. Many projects in archaeology use custom information systems to store and process their information, generated both on the field, and inside laboratories. However, while these systems are of great utility, new problems arise because they are tailored to meet the needs of specific projects, are monolithic in nature, and more importantly use different schemes to store the information [5-7,15]. Thus, one of the three main problems we address in this paper is that achieving interoperability between these systems becomes very difficult. Archaeological research greatly depends on typologies, comparisons, and existence of relationships with information from other projects/sites, things that are possible to accomplish in a real-time fashion only if these various systems are highly interoperable.

R. Heery and L. Lyon (Eds.): ECDL 2004, LNCS 3232, pp. 186–197, 2004.
© Springer-Verlag Berlin Heidelberg 2004

A second problem is that primary data in archaeological research usually is available to researchers outside a project/site only after substantial delay. What is desirable to speed up the transfer of knowledge is a highly efficient information system that would make the primary data available as soon as it is produced, and which can be used both in the field and out. A third problem is that many of the tailor-made archaeological information systems do not provide a sustainable solution to long-term preservation and dissemination of information. Distributed and replicated existence of valuable information is necessary to ensure that the information is preserved for future use.

Archaeological information systems that, in addition to storing and retrieving information, provide services similar to those provided by modern Digital Libraries (DLs) would be highly desirable, affording solutions to the three problems described above. Having a single unifying system that is able to intelligently manage heterogeneous information from several sites along with providing a rich array of services, including those specific to archaeology – GIS visualization systems, object comparisons, complex workflow management, etc. – would greatly help archaeological research [8].

Our approach to dealing with the problems presented above is to create a Digital Library for archaeology – ETANA-DL[1]. ETANA-DL is a model-based, extensible, componentized DL that manages complex information sources using the client-server paradigm of the Open Archives Initiative Protocol for Metadata Harvesting (OAI-PMH) [14].

In this paper, we demonstrate how the development of information systems (e.g., digital libraries) that address key needs, as described above, can be efficiently and effectively accomplished by applying and extending the Open Archives approach to metadata harvesting, and by building upon componentized frameworks like Open Digital Libraries [3,12,16]. We note that requirements elicitation is critical to the success of our DL, because the services that ETANA-DL will support depend on the requirements of the archaeologists. Thus, we use a prototyping approach to elicit requirements and describe the design and implementation of our initial Digital Library as well as the various supported services. Our prototype is designed mainly from existing components, which saves development costs, if one has a good design based on an accurate model that reflects a deep understanding of the domain. However, understanding complex information systems is a difficult task. Hence, we use the very powerful 5S framework in our modeling of ETANA-DL. We show how our partially developed model for archaeological information systems has been used to integrate heterogeneous data from disparate sources, and implement complex services over the integrated data [10].

The rest of this paper is organized as follows. Section 2 describes our efforts to model ETANA-DL using the 5S theory. Section 3 describes the architecture of the prototype, and describes our approach to address some of the needs discussed above. Section 4 gives an overview of the various services supported by the current ETANA-DL prototype. We provide an analysis of our approach in Section 5. Conclusions and future work are presented in Section 6.

---

[1] ETANA-DL home page: http://feathers.dlib.vt.edu

2 Modeling ETANA-DL

Most archaeological projects approach the handling of data and information in diverse ways. In order to address the problems of managing such heterogeneous data and processing in archaeology, we apply 5S to model archaeological data and procedures. The 5S (Streams, Structures, Scenarios, Societies, Spaces) framework is a comprehensive modeling tool that allows a DL designer to describe most aspects of a DL. 5S has already been used to create meta-models for education-oriented digital libraries [11]. We are creating a unified (meta-)model for archaeological systems based on the 5S framework for information systems. Figure 1 represents our archaeological meta-model graphically, where relationships crossing sub-models show points where concepts are logically contained in one of the 'S' models, but are composed or work together with concepts in other Ss to define DL constructs.

In the archaeological setting, Streams represent the enormous amount of dynamic multimedia information gathered and created by specialists. Examples include photos and drawings of excavation sites, loci, or unearthed artifacts, audio and video recordings of excavation activities, textual reports, and 3D models which are used to measure, reconstruct, and visualize archaeological ruins.

Structures represent the ways archaeological information is organized along several dimensions. Examples include site organization, temporal organization, and taxonomies of specific unearthed artifacts like bones and seeds. Particularly important is the structure of sites, since it defines the core units of knowledge in the archaeological DL. Generally, specific regions of archaeological interest are subdivided into sites, normally administered and excavated by different groups. Each site is further subdivided into partitions, sub-partitions and loci, the latter being the nucleus of the excavation. Material or artifacts found in different loci are organized in containers for further reference and analysis.

Spaces model spatial and geographic distribution of found artifacts, as well as user interfaces, often employing metric or vector spaces, and are used to support retrieval operations, calculate distances, and constrain searches spatially. User classes defined in the Society model include archaeologists and the public who use DL services, the behavior of which is specified in the Scenario model. Besides Societies of users, service managers, which are electronic entities responsible for running services, also are specified in the Societies model. Scenarios and Societies act together to capture and model not only the services used by the public (search, browse, annotate, recommend), but also domain specific services for archaeological experts. More specifically, we have identified four main general classes of DL services [9]: repository building, value added, domain specific, and information satisfaction. Components in the Space and Structure models also interact with each other. For example, coordinate systems and different taxonomies are used in metadata records to describe different parts of the site.

This generic meta-model can be instantiated to create specific models of archaeological DLs. One example is the ETANA-DL model shown in Figure 2, which uses the metamodel to try to unify the models of several archaeological systems.

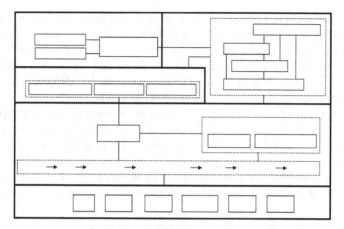

Fig. 1. Archaeological DL meta-model

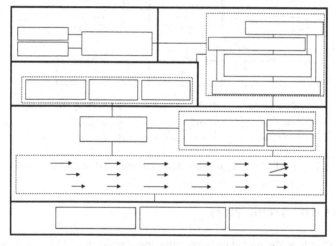

Fig. 2. ETANA-DL model

Current Streams of content that are present in ETANA-DL include figurine images, drawings and photos of (part of) the sites, and preliminary (final) reports. The core of ETANA-DL is its Union catalog which merges metadata harvested initially from three sites: Umayri [2], Nimrin [4], and Halif [1]. Each site has its own organization that can be mapped to portions of the meta-model. Partitions are large excavation units. The names of the partitions vary from project to project. They represent quadrants for Nimrin, but designate fields for Umayri and Halif. Sub-partitions are smaller units, which are typically a square, and within squares numerous loci are identified. A locus can be anything that is identifiable and distinguishable from its surroundings. They are typically the smallest excavation unit. Excavated materials and items (bones, seeds, and figurines) are collected in containers for preservation and analysis. Those containers can be bags (Nimrin), pails (Umayri), or baskets (Halif). Each site also has its own archaeological periods (chronology). The earliest occupation in Nimrin is represented by stone and mud-brick walls from the Middle Bronze I (MBI) period (c. 2000 B.C.E.); Halif has occupation history from chalcolithic through Modern Arab; and the chronology of Umayri is from Paleolithic through modern time. In ETANA-DL, each site mentioned above has its site-specific coordinate system, e.g., Nimrin used a Polar system. The ETANA-DL user interface is web-based. The ETANA-DL services are described in Section 5.

Figure 3 illustrates the modeling of the unifying schema for the prototype. In the current prototype, ETANA-DL handles three kinds of digital artifacts: bones, seeds, and figurines. The digital records of each of these kinds of artifacts have attributes that are specific for that artifact type. However, many of the artifacts share common attributes. For example, every digital object in the prototype has spatial attributes associated with it. Therefore, these attributes are associated with a base class object.

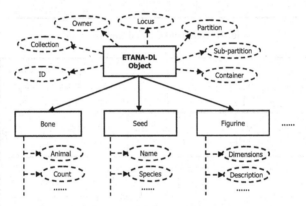

Fig. 3. ETANA-DL unifying XML schema – a design overview

3   ETANA-DL Architecture

We apply and extend the metadata harvesting approach of the OAI to address some of the needs of information systems in archaeology: heterogeneous data handling and interoperability, making primary data available, and long-term preservation. Figure 4 illustrates the architecture of the current prototype.

We convert partner archaeology sites into Open Archives by implementing data providers at the respective sites. We expose the metadata at each of these sites using a custom, unifying, metadata format that we have developed for the prototype, and one that will keep evolving as we ingest newer kinds of data from different sites [17]. This is a challenging task because of the custom schemas each of these sites use for storing their information.

As shown in Figure 4, we have implemented semi-automatic data-mapping components that convert the data from its local view known to the system at a local site, to a global view known to ETANA-DL, and described in Section 2. By doing this, we shift the complexity of data mapping the service provider to the data provider. If the schemas for representing the data change at a local site, the system remains unaffected, as only the data-mapping components at that local site need to be re-configured. Moreover, sites may not want to expose sensitive data. Such filtering is a part of the data-mapping layer, requiring the sites to customize only one layer of the system.

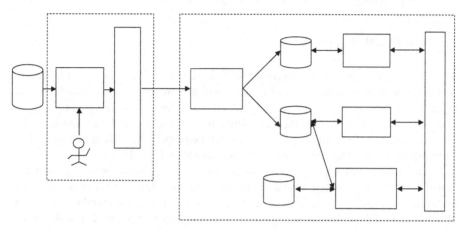

Fig. 4. ETANA-DL Prototype Architecture

Whenever a record is added or updated at the source, the time-stamp associated with the record changes. Service providers harvest all records from a data provider whose time-stamps have been updated since the archive was last harvested. Running the harvester at the service provider on a regular basis addresses the issue of the data changing at the source, and these changes being visible to the users of the DL. By implementing harvesters that can be configured to harvest data from the sites at fre-quencies proportional to the rate at which data changes at the respective sites, our approach make primary archaeological data available without significant delay.

The data exposed by each site in the common format is harvested into a Union Catalog at the service provider (ETANA-DL) on a regular basis. We index the har-vested data in two formats: as inverted files to provide IR-like services, and as rela-tional databases to provide DB-like services. The search engine component uses the inverted files to provide search services, and the browse engine uses the relational databases to provide browse services that allow a user to navigate the various kinds of data in ETANA-DL. Other ETANA-DL services rely on the relational databases containing indexed archaeological data or custom databases to provide their function-ality.

The web interface serves as the glue that binds the different services, some of them implemented as ODL components. All of the ODL components have been reused with little or no modification. These components communicate with each other, and the web interface using the XOAI protocol. XOAI is an extension to the OAI-PMH and provides the basis for developing inter-component communication protocols [16]. Other components are directly invoked by the web interface.

Replicating services providers (by creating mirror sites) that harvest data from the various Open Archives ensures replicated existence of data. Thus, by coupling our componentized approach to creating DLs with the metadata harvesting approach of the OAI, we provide a sustainable and easily maintainable approach that addresses long-term preservation of valuable archaeological information.

4 ETANA-DL Services

The ETANA-DL prototype supports several services. We describe the cross-collection browsing service in brief to demonstrate how the 5S model for ETANA-DL has been used to implement services over the integrated data. Table 1 provides an overview of the services, and their classification [9]. We also indicate which of the services have been implemented by re-using components in the current prototype. For more information on the current ETANA-DL services, refer to [13].

In the current prototype, there are three main dimensions for browsing the integrated data – by the structural organization of a site, by a time period taxonomy, and by taxonomies specific to the type of artifact. Browsing by the structural organization of a site is based on the 5S structural model described in Section 2. For the other dimensions, we have designed taxonomies for browsing, and map the harvested data to our generic taxonomies.

The dynamic nature of the browsing system allows a user to see only those categories for a dimension for which digital objects exist. The categories are chosen by querying the browse-index database at run-time, thereby allowing a user to freely move along any dimension, or a combination thereof. In addition, a user can search within a browsing context for information. This can be thought of as a way to restrict the search space using the information associated with a context. Figure 5 shows a sample interface for the browsing service. In this example, the user is browsing along all three dimensions. The interface shows the current context of the user, and allows the user to return to any of the previous contexts with a single click.

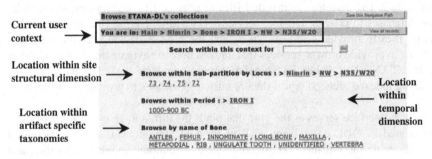

Fig. 5. Dynamic multi-dimensional browsing in ETANA-DL

Table 1. Overview of services supported by the current ETANA-DL prototype

Service	Description
Information satisfaction services	
Searching (Component-based)	Allows users to search for specific information in the DL. Users can use the advanced search option to formulate queries that are more complex.
Browsing	Allows users to discover new information in the DL. Users can browse along many dimensions, and categories for browsing are generated dynamically based on the DL content. Users also can search within a context, save browsing contexts, etc.
Recommendation (Component-based)	Recommends digital objects in the DL that the user is not aware of, based on similarity of interest with other users.
Domain-specific services	
Object Comparison	Allows users to perform comparisons between different digital objects and view the results. Users specify the various parameters that form the basis for comparison.
Marking items	Allows users to direct specific digital objects to other users of the system. Users can include annotations that are only visible to specific other users.
Value-added services	
Annotations (Component-based)	Allows users to discuss the various digital objects in the system. Users can post messages, and other users can respond to the posted messages.
Recent searches/discussions	Allows users to view their most recent searches and recent on-going discussions.
Items of Interest	Binding service that allows users to create personal collections out of items in the DL that interest them.
Miscellaneous services	
User management	User registration, system login, and other user management functions.
Collections description	Allows users to view detailed information about various collections in ETANA-DL.

5   Analysis

In this section, we provide an analysis for our approach to creating DLs that handle heterogeneous archaeological data. We demonstrate that, given a pool of components that implement common DL services, a prototype that supports useful services can be rapidly generated.

Heterogeneous Data Handling

The current ETANA-DL prototype harvests data from three different sites – Nimrin, Halif, and Umayri. We have converted these sites into Open Archives that partially expose their data, and have harvested records of different kinds of digital objects from these sites to prove the extensibility and scalability of our approach to handling heterogeneous archaeological data. Table 2 provides an overview of the data contained in the ETANA-DL Union Catalog.

Table 2. Heterogeneous data in ETANA-DL – an overview

Site	Artifact Type	Original data source	Attributes in original record	Attributes in harvested record	Records harvested
Halif	Figurine	Tab-delimited text file	15	18	564
Nimrin	Bone field record	Table in relational DB	21	24	7420
	Seed field record	Table in relational DB	12	15	430
Umayri	Bone field records	2 tables in relational DB	8	24	2123

In the current DL prototype, we have harvested bone records from two sites (Nimrin and Umayri) to show the heterogeneity of our approach (being able to handle data from disparate sources). More than 10,000 digital records have been harvested from the three sites. The increase in the number of attributes for each object type in its global view is due to attributes associated with information about the collection, object type, etc. being added to the metadata associated with each record.

Figure 6 shows a breakdown of the times required during various stages of converting an archaeological site into an Open Archive. It is evident that the majority of time required is in analyzing data (e.g., discovering relationships that exist in the schema at a local site) and mapping it to our unifying schema (more than 90%). Data and service provider implementation times include the time to implement the data provider, test the Open Archive, and harvest data into our Union Catalog, and are only a fraction of the time to analyze and map the data (less than 10%) due to the availability of easily configurable components.

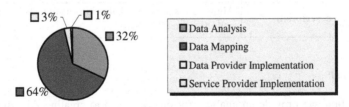

Fig. 6. Breakdown of times required during the various stages of conversion of a site into an Open Archive for the current prototype

Table 3. Analysis of prototype using the metric of Lines of Code

Type of Service	LOC for implementing service	LOC reused from component	Total LOC	Reuse Percentage
Componentized	350	3630	3980	91
Non-componentized	7950	-	7950	-
Total	**8300**	**3630**	**11930**	**30.4**

Rapid Prototyping

We used two software metrics to analyze the rapidity of our prototyping efforts: Lines of Code required for implementing services, and service development times.

Table 3 shows the **Lines of Code** (LOC) needed to implement componentized and non-componentized services. The final column in the table is the percentage savings in LOC gained from component re-use. It is clear that we can re-use a very significant percentage (approximately 30%) of DL code by designing common DL services as components. Moreover, for creating prototypes rapidly where quality of the service is as important as the speed with which services can be put together and modified, the approach to building DLs using pre-existing components is very useful. The components that we have developed for the prototype can be re-used in other DLs, thus resulting in an even higher re-use percentage value.

Prototyping services involve three stages: requirements analysis and design, implementation, and testing. Figure 7 shows a comparison of efforts (measured in **development time**) for the various stages of the prototyping cycle. Chart A shows the percentages of time required for the component-based services whereas Chart B shows the same for non-componentized services. It is clear from comparisons that more efforts can be spent on analysis, design, and testing for component-based services as compared to non-componentized services. Thus, a DL implementer can save a significant percentage of implementation time by re-using components that implement common DL services.

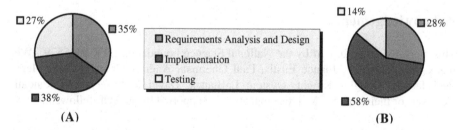

(A)   (B)

Fig. 7. Service development time percentages for various stages of prototyping: (A) componentized services, and (B) non-componentized services

User Analysis

Our prototype was evaluated by some members of the archaeology community, the results of which can only be summarized here because of space restrictions [13]. All the services provided in the current ETANA-DL prototype were found to be useful. Some of the services like advanced search and object comparisons, and some features of the multi-dimensional browsing service, were found to be less intuitive and difficult to use. Nevertheless, the organization of the browsing service around a generic site structure and common taxonomies (as described in Section 2) was seen as a plus. Moreover, we have been able to elicit many requirements for improving the current services using our rapidly generated prototype. When addressed, the utility of the system will increase. Our approach to handling heterogeneous archaeological data is further validated by the positive feedback for the cross-collection searching and browsing services supported by the current prototype.

6 Conclusions and Future Work

This paper has described our experiences in creating a prototype for a Digital Library for handling heterogeneous archaeological data. We have demonstrated that we can use digital library techniques to address some of the long-standing needs of archaeological information systems, and have demonstrated a scalable, and easily manageable approach for handling heterogeneous archaeological data from disparate sources. We have shown that given a pool of DL components that implement common DL services, a prototype for a DL providing useful services can be rapidly implemented, which can then be used to better understand requirements of users from the DL. The 5S framework has helped us in understanding complex archaeological information systems, and the resulting partially developed 5S archaeological model has been used to integrate heterogeneous data and guide useful services.

Future work on the prototype includes creating next generation DL services that address the requirements that we have gathered using the prototype, integrating richer content into the DL by extending the unifying metadata schema to cover more sites/artifact types, enhancing information access services (e.g., searching, browsing) to allow archaeologists to retrieve information easily, and extensive usability studies.

Acknowledgements

This work is funded in part by the National Science Foundation (ITR-0325579). We thank Douglas Clark, Joanne Eustis, Paul Gherman, Andrew Graham, Larry Herr, Paul Jacobs, Douglas Knight, Oystein LaBianca, David McCreery, and Randall Younker for their support. Marcos Gonçalves is supported by an AOL fellowship.

References

1. Lahav Research Project, 2004. http://www.cobb.msstate.edu/dig/lahav/ (as of April, 2004).
2. Madaba Plains Project – Tall al-'Umayri, 2004.
   http://www.wwc.edu/academics/departments/theology/mpp (as of April, 2004).

3. Open Archives Initiative, 2004. www.openarchives.org (as of April, 2004).
4. Tell Nimrin Project Report, 2004. http://www.cwru.edu/affil/nimrin/ (as of April, 2004).
5. Benenson, I. and Finkelstein, I.: The Megiddo Excavation Data Management System, 2000.
6. Clark, J. T., Slator, B. M., Bergstrom, A., Larson, F., Frovarp, R., Landrum, J. E., Perrizo, W., and Jockheck, W.: DANA (Digital Archive Network for Anthropology): A Model for Digital Archiving. Presented at 17th Association of Computing Machinery Symposium on Applied Computing, Madrid, Spain, March 10-14, 2002.
7. Condron, F., Richards, J., Robinson, D., and Wise, A.: Findings and recommendations from Digital Data in Archaeology: A Survey of User Needs, 1999. http://ads.ahds.ac.uk/project/strategies/index.html (as of April, 2004).
8. Crane, G., Wulfman, C. E., Cerrato, L. M., Mahoney, A., Milbank, T. L., Mimno, D., Rydberg-Cox, J. A., Smith, D. A., and York, C.: Towards a cultural heritage digital library. Presented at ACM/IEEE-CS Joint Conference on Digital Libraries (JCDL 2003), Houston, TX, June, 2003.
9. Goncalves, M. A.: Digital Libraries: formal theory, language, design, generation, quality, and evaluation. Ph.D. Dissertation Proposal. Department of Computer Science, Virginia Polytechnic Institute and State University, Blacksburg, VA, 2003.
10. Goncalves, M. A., Fox, E. A., Watson, L. T., and Kipp, N. A.: Streams, Structures, Spaces, Scenarios, Societies (5S): A Formal Model for Digital Libraries, in ACM Transactions on Information Systems (TOIS), vol. 22(2), pp. 270-312, 2004.
11. Kelapure, R., Goncalves, M. A., and Fox, E. A.: Scenario-Based Generation of Digital Library Services. Presented at European Conference on Digital Libraries (ECDL 2003), Trondheim, Norway, August 17-22, 2003.
12. Lagoze, C., Sompel, H. V. d., Nelson, M., and Warner, S.: The Open Archives Initiative Protocol for Metadata Harvesting - Version 2.0, Open Archives Initiative, 2002. http://www.openarchives.org/OAI/2.0/openarchivesprotocol.htm (as of April, 2004).
13. Ravindranathan, U.: Prototyping Digital Libraries Handling Heterogeneous Data Sources - An ETANA-DL Case Study. Masters Thesis. Department of Computer Science, Virginia Polytechnic Institute and State University, Blacksburg, VA, 2004.
14. Ravindranathan, U., Shen, R., Goncalves, M. A., Fan, W., Fox, E. A., and Flanagan, J. W.: ETANA-DL: A Digital Library For Integrated Handling Of Heterogeneous Archaeological Data. To be presented at Joint Conference on Digital Libraries (JCDL 2004), Tucson, AZ, June 7-11, 2004.
15. Ryan, N.: Managing Complexity: Archaeological Information Systems Past, Present and Future, http://www.cs.kent.ac.uk/people/staff/nsr/arch/baas.html (as of April, 2004).
16. Suleman, H.: Open Digital Libraries. Ph.D. Dissertation. Department of Computer Science, Virginia Polytechnic Institute and State University, Blacksburg, VA, 2002. http://scholar.lib.vt.edu/theses/available/etd-11222002-155624/.
17. Wise, A. and Miller, P.: Why metadata matters in archaeology, in Internet Archaeology, 1997. http://intarch.ac.uk/journal/issue2/wise_index.html.

zetoc SOAP: A Web Services Interface for a Digital Library Resource

Ann Apps

MIMAS, University of Manchester, M13 9PL, UK
ann.apps@man.ac.uk

Abstract. This paper describes the provision of a Web Services interface that will extend the possibility of machine-to-machine access to the **zetoc** current awareness service, within the JISC Information Environment and eScience applications. This bespoke interface includes open standard XML metadata for searches and responses where possible. Elements from the OpenURL XML metadata formats for journals and books are used to transmit the bibliographic citation information that is an integral part of a **zetoc** record for a journal article or conference paper.

Keywords: Web Services, bibliographic citation, metadata, OpenURL, Dublin Core, SRW.

1 Introduction

zetoc [1] [2] is a current awareness and document delivery service based on the British Library's [3] Electronic Table of Contents of journal articles and conference papers. Hosted at MIMAS [4], **zetoc** is available to researchers, teachers and learners in UK Higher and Further Education under a 'strategic alliance' [5], and to practitioners within the UK National Health Service. The **zetoc** database, updated daily, contains details of articles from approximately 20,000 current journals and 16,000 conference proceedings published per year. With over 20 million article and conference paper records from 1993 to date, the database covers every imaginable subject in science, technology, medicine, business, law, finance and the humanities. Human users can search **zetoc** through its Web interface to retrieve articles by one of the document delivery options. They may also use the popular email alert service to maintain current awareness of new articles of possible interest. Machine-to-machine searching is available by Z39.50 [6], the NISO (North American National Information Standards Organization) standard for information retrieval that provides a protocol for two computers to communicate and share information. It is also enabled by OpenURL [7], another standard way of passing information between machines, **zetoc** being enabled as an OpenURL 'link-to' resolver.

A new Web Services SOAP [8] (the World Wide Web Consortium's server-to-server protocol for object retrieval) interface to **zetoc** has been developed as part of the A2Z (Akenti acces to **zetoc**) project [9], the main purpose of which

R. Heery and L. Lyon (Eds.): ECDL 2004, LNCS 3232, pp. 198–208, 2004.
© Springer-Verlag Berlin Heidelberg 2004

was to investigate digital certificate authentication, in particular using Akenti [10], within eScience applications as well as within the Information Environment [11] under development by the JISC (the Joint Information Services Committee of the UK Higher and Further Education Funding Councils). Because eScience projects are generally outside the digital library domain, experimenting via the **zetoc** Z39.50 interface did not seem appropriate. Whereas a Web Services interface would be suitable for use in areas such as workflow modelling of composite services within eScience projects such as myGrid [12]. Within the digital library based JISC Information Environment portals and virtual learning development projects are beginning to use Web Services for machine-to-machine communication.

2 A SOAP Interface for zetoc

A Web Services interface deals with messages that are sets of XML elements wrapped within SOAP envelopes. The requesting and responding servers, both understanding the SOAP protocol, are able to extract the XML data from the messages sent to them and to package their responding XML results accordingly. SOAP messages are passed between machines by RPC (Remote Procedure Call). The **zetoc** SOAP interface is implemented by RPC over the Web Common Gateway Interface (CGI), and thus its address appears like a URL.

Provision of a Web Services interface is in two parts. Firstly a 'search request' is needed to submit search terms for discovery to the application. Secondly a 'search response' will return details of the results. To design the **zetoc** SOAP interface there appeared to be two options: use a standard or generally accepted schema; or develop a bespoke interface, that is an interface designed specifically for the particular service.

SRW (Search - Retrieve - Web) [13] is a specification for general search request and response developed under the auspices of the Z39.50 community, with the possibility of becoming a NISO standard for meta-searching [14]. SRW emulates Z39.50 by including various fields to return the number of search hits and to request the start position within the result set of the returned records. For the actual search SRW provides a Common Query Language (CQL) to enable Z39.50-like and interoperable search requests. The expected returned response for each record within the result set is simple Dublin Core [15].

In fact the **zetoc** SOAP interface developed as part of the A2Z project is bespoke, although based on open standard metadata schemes where possible. It seems that SRW is ideal for distributed searching within a wide domain such as the JISC Information Environment because it allows common search requests to be sent to a range of services. However SRW seems less appropriate for making a connection to a single service whose capability and specific domain is well understood. Similarly returning simple Dublin Core records provides clear interoperability for distributed searching. But a simple Dublin Core description for a result that is a bibliographic record would lose richness and significant detail, in particular the bibliographic citation information for a journal article or conference paper.

The XML elements that make up the various requests and responses of the **zetoc** SOAP interface are defined formally [16] as a Dublin Core Application Profile [17]. An application profile was a useful way to document all of these properties and their corresponding namespaces. However strictly a Dublin Core application profile is a flat structure, so some distortion of the application profile has been made to specify the hierarchical structure of the returned result set. This application profile effectively defines the **zetoc**-specific terms within a **zetoc** namespace.

3   Metadata for zetoc SOAP

Having decided to implement a bespoke SOAP interface for **zetoc**, it was desirable to use metadata properties from open standards wherever possible.

3.1   zetoc Search Request

The available **zetoc** SOAP search requests replicate the searches available on the **zetoc** Web interface. Thus three search requests are provided: general that searches over all the data; journal article; and conference paper. The search fields include the obvious possibilities such as 'all fields', article title, author, publication year, and ISSN, to specify a journal, or ISBN, a book identifier to specify a conference proceedings. The journal and conference searches include more specific fields related to those genre. To support the retrieval of large result sets in manageable chunks the **zetoc** SOAP search requests also need to indicate the position within the result set of the first record to be returned. Currently no Boolean operators are available. As in the **zetoc** Web interface, when several search terms are provided the implicit Boolean operator is 'and'.

There is an additional, fourth, 'identifier' request that returns a single **zetoc** full record corresponding to a specific **zetoc** identifier.

3.2   zetoc Response

The three search requests result in a search response that is a list of brief descriptions of **zetoc** records matching the search. The 'identifier' request results in a single, full **zetoc** record.

To avoid returning unmanageably large result sets, the **zetoc** search response is a list of a fixed number (25) of brief records. Thus the response must include the total number of hits and the number of the next record in the result set following those returned. Along with the 'first record position' requested, this data enables repeated requests to obtain the full result set. An indication of the search performed is also returned.

The brief records returned correspond to the **zetoc** brief records available from a Web search, including the position of the record within the entire result set, but with the addition of the **zetoc** identifier. Returning the **zetoc** identifier with the brief record enables a subsequent 'identifier' request to retrieve the full details of an item of particular interest.

An 'identifier' response results in a single, full **zetoc** record that corresponds to a full **zetoc** record available from the Web interface. It includes all details about the article or paper available from the database.

3.3 Dublin Core Properties

For maximum interoperability properties are taken from Dublin Core where possible. Thus from the simple Dublin Core namespace ('dc') the following terms represent: dc:title, the article or paper title; dc:creator, the authors; and dc:identifier, the identifier of the resource within the **zetoc** database, currently an identifier local to the **zetoc** service. In a search request 'title' and 'creator' could contain keywords from the field rather than the entire value. In addition dc:subject (for conference keywords), dc:contributor (for editors), dc:publisher, dc:language, dc:format and dc:type are used to return some detailed information in an 'identifier' full record response.

From the wider Dublin Core namespace ('dcterms') the following properties represent: dcterms:issued, the publication year of an article; and dcterms:bibliographicCitation, the citation details in a brief record of a search response.

3.4 SRW and Z39.50 Bath Profile Properties

The SRW namespace includes obvious properties to implement the retrieval of large result sets in manageable pieces. Thus from the SRW namespace ('srw') are taken: srw:numberOfRecords, the total number of search hits; srw:startRecord, the requested start position; srw:nextRecordPosition, the number of the record following those returned; and srw:recordPosition, the number within the result set of each brief record returned.

The Bath Profile [18] is a derivation of Z39.50 for digital library applications, defining search request attributes. From this namespace ('bath') these search request terms are taken: bath:any, an 'all fields' search; and bath:conferenceName, the conference details in a conference paper search.

3.5 OpenURL Properties

Because **zetoc** is a citation database providing bibliographic information to enable article requests, it is essential that the **zetoc** SOAP interface includes bibliographic details in its search requests and responses. It was preferred that this bibliographic information be passed using open standard properties where possible. Dublin Core provides 'dcterms:bibliographicCitation', which is used to return the information as a string value within a brief record response. But Dublin Core does not provide bibliographic properties at any finer granularity.

OpenURL was developed as a standard way of passing information about a resource between a source application and an OpenURL-aware resolver [19]. Its original and primary purpose is to enable a researcher to link from a referenced article to a full text copy of that article where the researcher's institution has a valid subscription to read the article. During the process of proposing the OpenURL Framework as a NISO standard, Z39.88-2004 [20], other possible uses of OpenURL were envisaged including server-to-server communication. Thus an XML schema for the OpenURL 'payload' (the ContextObect) was developed. The OpenURL Framework is extensible by means of a Registry [21]. The initial content of the OpenURL Registry, and hence the standard, includes metadata formats as XML schema for journals and books.

The OpenURL journal [22] ('oujnl') and book [23] ('oubook') metadata formats are used to capture the bibliographic citation properties within **zetoc** SOAP. Thus from the OpenURL journal metadata format are taken: oujnl:jtitle, the journal title; oujnl:issn, the journal ISSN; oujnl:volume, oujnl:issue and oujnl:spage, the volume and issue number and start page of an article within a journal search request; and oujnl:pages, the page range of an article or paper in a full record response. Similarly from the OpenURL book metadata format are taken: oubook:isbn, the ISBN of a conference proceedings; and oubook:spage, the start page within a conference paper search.

3.6   zetoc Properties

Although open standards are used as far as possible it was necessary to include several **zetoc**-specific properties within a **zetoc** namespace. This namespace includes all the containing XML elements of **zetoc** SOAP comprising the search and 'identifier' requests and responses, and the brief record and its containing array. The only **zetoc** term within the search requests is a field 'ISSN or ISBN' included in the general search. The only **zetoc** term in a search response holds a string value representing the search performed on the **zetoc** database.

Inevitably the full record 'identifier' response includes several **zetoc**-specific terms, for example the British Library's 'shelfmark' and 'location' information, and the frequency of publication for some journals. A 'zetoc:type' property indicates whether a returned record is for a journal article or a conference paper.

Subject terms are available in **zetoc** as Dewey and Library of Congress Classification. These are returned as properties 'dewey' and 'lccn' in the **zetoc** namespace. Ideally they would be returned as 'dc:subject' with an XML attribute 'xsi:type' of 'dcterms:DDC' or 'dcterms:LCC', something that may be implemented in future versions of **zetoc** SOAP.

Within the **zetoc** database journal volume and issue information is run together into a single field, reflecting the data supply from the British Library, thus necessitating another **zetoc**-specific property 'volissue'. A **zetoc**-specific term is used to return any journal issue title, for example the name of a special issue, recorded in **zetoc**, this being outside the scope of general journal metadata formats.

There did not appear to be an existing open standard metadata scheme to describe conference details. It would be possible to record the proceedings as a book title using the OpenURL book metadata format, but this would not necessarily capture all the data about the conference such as its venue and date. Thus a term within the **zetoc** namespace is used to return all the conference details concatenated into a string value. Another **zetoc** field returns the conference sponsors.

3.7 Examples

Journal Search. Some possible fields in a journal search request may be as in Table 1.

Table 1. Example journal search terms.

Property	Value
dc:creator	apps
oujnl:jtitle	materialia
oujnl:issn	1359-6462
oujnl:volume	48
oujnl:issue	5
oujnl:spage	475
dcterms:issued	2003

Search Response. A search response for the above example would return a list of brief records containing the single record shown in Table 2.

Table 2. Example brief record response.

Property	Value
srw:recordPosition	1
dc:title	Phase compositions in magnesium-rare earth alloys
dc:creator	Apps, P. J.; et-al
dcterms:bibliographicCitation	SCRIPTA MATERIALIA - 2003; VOL 48; NUMBER 5; Pages: 475-481
dc:identifier	RN125218404

'Identifier' Response. The 'identifier' full record response (omitting conference paper properties that are irrelevant to this article) would be as in Table 3.

3.8 An Alternative 'Identifier' Response

An alternative approach to implementing a full record 'identifier' response would be to return a simple Dublin Core record for the discovered article, including salient information such as its title and authors. This simple Dublin Core record would contain a 'by-reference' link, a pointer as the value of a 'dc:relation' property, to a full **zetoc** XML record. This pointer could be an OpenURL that

Table 3. Example full record response.

Property	Value
srw:numberOfRecords	1
dc:identifier	RN125218404
zetoc:type	J (ie. journal)
dc:title	Phase compositions in magnesium-rare earth alloys...
dc:creator	Apps, P. J.; Karimzadeh, H; King, J. F.; Lorimer, G. W.
zetoc:dewey	669
zetoc:lccn	TT273
oujnl:jtitle	SCRIPTA MATERIALIA
oujnl:issn	1359-6462
zetoc:volissue	VOL 48; NUMBER 5
oujnl:pages	475-481
dcterms:issued	2003
dc:publisher	Great Britain : Elsevier Science B.V., Amsterdam.
zetoc:frequency	Fortnightly: 15-30 issues per year
dc:language	English
zetoc:shelfmark	8212.970000

would return an XML record for the item in **zetoc** as in the following example. Note that in this example: a hypothetical resolver address is used, and an actual OpenURL would be 'URL escape encoded', with special characters in hexadecimal format for safe transmission, but this encoding has been omitted, and line-breaks have been added to the OpenURL, for readability.

```
http://zetoc.mimas.ac.uk/openurl/linkto?
    url_ver=Z39.88-2004
    &url_ctx_fmt=info:ofi/fmt:kev:mtx:ctx
    &rft_val_fmt=info:ofi/fmt:kev:mtx:dc
    &rft.identifier=RN125218404
    &svc_val_fmt=info:ofi/fmt:kev:mtx:dc
    &svc.format=text/xml
```

This OpenURL uses the Dublin Core metadata format to describe the **zetoc** record recquired, the referent, as a **zetoc** identifier. That identifier being local to **zetoc** makes an OpenURL 'referent-identifier' key inappropriate. The Dublin Core metadata format is also used to request a service type that returns an XML record.

An alternative OpenURL could use private data to pass the **zetoc** identifier, in which case the fourth and fifth lines of the above example would be replaced by:

```
    &rft_dat=RN125218404
```

If the **zetoc** identifier were to become a URI, possibly by registering it within the new 'info' URI scheme [24], then the fourth and fifth lines of the above example could be replaced by the preferable:

```
    &rft_id=info:zetoc/RN125218404
```

The returned record could possibly be an XML Dublin Core description with related metadata using the OpenURL journal or book metadata format as suggested in [25].

The advantage of this approach is that the 'identifier' response would return an interoperable simple Dublin Core record. The disadvantage is that any service retrieving this record would have to make a further retrieval to obtain the full **zetoc** reord, including its bibliographic citation information that could not be captured in the simple Dublin Core record. This approach would be suitable for returning a simple Dublin Core record from a **zetoc** SRW implementation.

4 Authentication

zetoc is available to members of institutions in UK Higher and Further Education and the UK National Health Service. It is also provided by modest subscription to various other bodies in UK academia, including the research councils, and to institutions in Ireland. Authentication is firstly by a machine domain name (DNS) or IP address check, and failing that by Athens [26], the access authorisation system used within UK Higher and Further Education. **zetoc** SOAP allows access using the same machine address checks. Access via Athens is not supported, human intervention not being possible. The same terms and conditions for the use of **zetoc** apply. This means that any portal must first check that a user has a right to use **zetoc** before providing a search through the **zetoc** SOAP interface.

The A2Z project has investigated and succcessfully demonstrated the use of Akenti digital certificate authenticated access to the **zetoc** Web interface, as reported elsewhere [9]. The original intention of the 'Web Services' part of the A2Z project was to investigate the use of digital certificate authenticated access to a **zetoc** SOAP interface within an eScience application such as myGrid. However it became apparent that this was not viable within the time frame of the project because digital certificates are not yet in use by the potential user base. Thus providing digital certificate authentication has not been taken forward. It would simply involve replacing the current machine address authentication module with the A2Z digital certificate 'black box' module and installing the access point to **zetoc** SOAP on the A2Z secure server.

5 Implementation

zetoc SOAP is implemented in C++ using gSOAP. gSOAP is a set of compiler tools that provide a SOAP/XML-to-C++ language binding to ease the development of SOAP/XML Web services and client applications in C++. Developed by Prof Robert van Engelen and his team in the Department of Computer Science and School of Computational Science and Information Technology at Florida State University, USA [27], it is available under a GNU licence from Source-Forge [28]. gSOAP is used to implement several major applications, including Adobe Version Cue, an innovative file-management feature of Adobe Creation Suite.

gSOAP takes care of all the details of the XML to support the SOAP protocol and also the serialisation of the XML elements of the **zetoc** requests and responses to and from the C++ public data of the **zetoc** SOAP server implementation. gSOAP also generates the requisite WSDL (Web Services Description Language) file that provides a machine readable definition of the interface. Requests are translated into searches in the format of the underlying Livelink Discovery Server (previously known as BRS/Search) [29] database, the searches being performed by existing C++ code modules. A **zetoc** SOAP client was implemented with gSOAP alongside the server for testing.

6   Conclusion

The use of Web Services is becoming increasingly important for machine-to-machine communication. It is already used within eScience Grid applications and projects. It is mandated for machine-to-machine applications within the UK government's interoperability framework (eGif) [30]. Within the JISC Information Environment portals are starting to use Web Services, the Resource Discovery network (RDN) [31] has a SOAP/SRW interface, and collections with Web Services access are recorded in the Information Environment Service Registry [32].

As discussed above, the **zetoc** SOAP interface is bespoke rather than using SRW. The short timescale available for the development of the **zetoc** SOAP interface within the funding of the A2Z project did not allow for any investigation into the provision of an SRW interface. A future SRW interface for **zetoc**, given the availability of funding, will be developed to allow its inclusion in Web Services distributed search requests within the JISC Information Environment, although distributed searching is already enabled via Z39.50. But it seems appropriate to provide an interface to an application that is specific to its data and purpose. The Common Query Language of SRW will provide interoperability but it seems to be too general when specific requests and results of an application are required. Also SRW will allow search requests inappropriate to an application resulting in null or distorted responses. For example a search for 'dc:description' in **zetoc** would return results from around 1994 only, later records not having abstracts.

Similarly the requirement of SRW to return simple Dublin Core records provides an interoperable result set for a distributed search but it does not cater for the return of richer application-specific details. **zetoc** SOAP provides a bespoke result format to include the important bibliographic citation details necessary to make use of any record from **zetoc**. There is no recommended way to include bibliographic citation information about a resource within a simple Dublin Core record. The alternative approach given above in section 3.8 would resolve this problem if **zetoc** were to provide an interoperable SRW impementation to support distributed searching. But it seems that a retrieval by a server that understands the **zetoc** application would be simpler using the bespoke interface.

Resembling the **zetoc** Web search interface, the **zetoc** SOAP interface does not allow the inclusion of Boolean operators in search requests, all search terms being implicitly 'anded'. Future developments to the **zetoc** SOAP interface would investigate the provision of Boolean operators between search terms when assembling searches on the underlying database. This functionality would be enabled if the Common Query Language of SRW were supported.

Developing **zetoc** SOAP has been a useful experience in exploring the design and specification of such an interface and the issues involved. Investigation into alternative implementations, such as SRW, was limited by the short timescale of this part of the A2Z project. But this development will provide a prototype for Web Services implementations for further information collections.

Acknowledgements

The A2Z project [33], including the **zetoc** SOAP interface development, was funded by the Joint Information Systems Committee (JISC) [34] of the UK Higher and Further Education Councils as part of the 'AAA' (Authentication, Authorisation, and Accounting) programme [35]. The **zetoc** data is provided by the British Library. The author wishes to acknowledge the assistance of colleagues in the development of **zetoc** SOAP, Ashley Sanders for the C++ search interface to **zetoc**, Ross MacIntyre the project manager and Mike Jones who implemented the Akenti authentication 'black box'.

References

1. Apps, A., MacIntyre, R.: Prototyping Digital Library Technologies in zetoc. Lecture Notes in Computer Science. **2458** (2002) 309-323
2. zetoc, Electronic Table of Contents from the British Library.
   http://zetoc.mimas.ac.uk
3. The British Library. http://www.bl.uk
4. MIMAS, a UK Higher and Further Education Data Centre.
   http://www.mimas.ac.uk
5. Strategic alliance emphasises British Library's central role in support of higher education. Press release, 19 March 2003.
   http://www.bl.uk/cgi-bin/press.cgi?story=1231
6. Z39.50, the North American National Information Standards Organisation (NISO) standard for information retrieval.
   http://www.niso.org/standards/resources/z3950.pdf
7. NISO Committee AX, Apps, A. Z39.88-2004: The Key/Encoded Value Format Implementation Guidelines. (2004).
   http://www.openurl.info/registry/docs/implementation_guidelines
8. W3C Web Services SOAP. http://www.w3.org/2000/xp/Group/
9. Jones, M.A.S., Apps, A., Hewitt, W.T., MacIntyre, R., Sanders, A., Weeks, A.: Akenti Access to zetoc. Paper and Poster at AHM2003 eScience 'All Hands' Meeting, Nottingham, 2-4 September 2003. (2003)
10. Akenti Distributed Access Control. http://www.itg.lbl.gov/akenti
11. JISC.: Investing in the Future: Developing an Online Information Environment. (2003). http://www.jisc.ac.uk/index.cfm?name=ie_home
12. myGrid project. http://www.ebi.ac.uk/mygrid/

13. SRW: Search - Retrieve - Web. http://www.loc.gov/z3950/agency/zing/srw/
14. NISO MetaSearch Initiative.
    http://www.niso.org/committees/MS_initiative.html
15. The Dublin Core Metadata Initiative. http://www.dublincore.org
16. Apps, A.: zetoc SOAP Interface Application Profile. (2004).
    http://zetoc.mimas.ac.uk/soap/
17. CEN/ISSS CWA 14855, Dublin Core Application Profile Guidelines. (2003). ftp:
    //ftp.cenorm.be/PUBLIC/CWAs/e-Europe/MMI-DC/cwa14855-00-2003-Nov.pdf
18. Z39.50 Bath Profile Indexes. http://www.loc.gov/z3950/agency/zing/cql/
    bath-indexes/v1.0/
19. Van de Sompel, H., Beit-Arie, O.: Open Linking in the Scholarly Information
    Environment Using the OpenURL Framework. D-Lib Magazine. **7**(3) (2001). doi:
    10.1045/march2001-vandesompel
20. ANSI/NISO.: Z39.88-2004, The OpenURL Framework for Context-Sensitive Ser-
    vices. Available via http://library.caltech.edu/openurl/Standard.htm
21. Registry for the OpenURL Framework. http://www.openurl.info/registry/
22. OpenURL Journal XML Metadata Format.
    http://www.openurl.info/registry/docs/info:ofi/fmt:xml:xsd:journal
23. OpenURL Book XML Metadata Format.
    http://www.openurl.info/registry/docs/info:ofi/fmt:xml:xsd:book
24. 'info' URI Scheme. http://info-uri.info
25. Apps, A., MacIntrye, R.: Using the OpenURL Framework to Locate Bibliographic
    Resources. In: Proceedings of the 2003 Dublin Core Conference (DC2003 - Support-
    ing Communities of Discourse and Practice - Metadata Research and Application),
    Seattle, Washington, USA, 28 September - 2 October 2003. ISBN 0-9745303-0-1.
    (2003) 143-152
26. Athens Access Management System. http://www.athens.ac.uk
27. Van Engelen, R.: gSOAP. http://www.cs.fsu.edu/~engelen/soap.html
28. gSOAP from SourceForge. http://sourceforge.net/projects/gsoap2
29. Livelink Discovery Server. http://www.opentext.com/brs/
30. The UK e-Government Interoperability Framework (eGif).
    http://www.govtalk.gov.uk/egif/contents.asp
31. RDN, the Resource Discovery Network. http://www.rdn.ac.uk
32. The JISC Information Environment Service Registry (IESR).
    http://www.mimas.ac.uk/iesr/
33. The A2Z Project. http://a2z.mimas.ac.uk
34. JISC, the Joint Information Systems Committee of the UK Higher and Further
    Education Funding Councils. http://www.jisc.ac.uk
35. The JISC 'AAA' (Authentication, Authorisation and Accounting) programme.
    http://www.jisc.ac.uk/index.cfm?name=aaa_docs

A Comparison of Text and Shape Matching
for Retrieval of Online 3D Models

Patrick Min[1], Michael Kazhdan[2], and Thomas Funkhouser[2]

[1] Utrecht University, Padualaan 14, 3584 CH, Utrecht, The Netherlands
[2] Princeton University, 35 Olden St., Princeton, NJ 08544, United States

Abstract. Because of recent advances in graphics hard- and software, both the production and use of 3D models are increasing at a rapid pace. As a result, a large number of 3D models have become available on the web, and new research is being done on 3D model retrieval methods. Query and retrieval can be done solely based on associated text, as in image retrieval, for example (e.g. Google Image Search [1] and [2,3]). Other research focuses on shape-based retrieval, based on methods that measure shape similarity between 3D models (e.g., [4]). The goal of our work is to take current text- and shape-based matching methods, see which ones perform best, and compare those. We compared four text matching methods and four shape matching methods, by running classification tests using a large database of 3D models downloaded from the web [5]. In addition, we investigated several methods to combine the results of text and shape matching. We found that shape matching outperforms text matching in all our experiments. The main reason is that publishers of online 3D models simply do not provide enough descriptive text of sufficient quality: 3D models generally appear in lists on web pages, annotated only with cryptic filenames or thumbnail images. Combining the results of text and shape matching further improved performance. The results of this paper provide added incentive to continue research in shape-based retrieval methods for 3D models, as well as retrieval based on other attributes.

1 Introduction

There has been a recent surge of interest in methods for retrieval of 3D models from large databases. Several 3D model search engines have become available within the last few years (e.g., [6–9]), and they cumulatively index tens of thousands of 3D polygonal surface models. Yet, still there have been few research studies investigating which types of query and matching methods are most effective for 3D data. Some 3D model search engines support only text queries [6], while others provide "content-based" queries based on shape [4]. But how do shape-based and text-based retrieval methods compare?

To investigate this question, we measured classification performance of the currently best-performing text-based and shape-based matching methods. We also evaluated several functions that combine text and shape matching scores. For the text matching, a 3D model is represented by a text document, created from several sources of text associated with the model, as well as synonyms and hypernyms (category descriptors) of the 3D model filename (added using WordNet, a lexical database [10]). For the shape matching, a 3D model is represented by a *shape descriptor*, computed from the polygons describing the model's surface.

R. Heery and L. Lyon (Eds.): ECDL 2004, LNCS 3232, pp. 209–220, 2004.

All classification tests were done using the "Princeton Shape Benchmark" (PSB) 3D model test database [5]. It contains 1814 3D models downloaded from the web, subdivided into a training set and a test set, containing 907 models each, manually classified into 90 and 92 comparable classes respectively. It is a subset of a larger database of about 33000 models downloaded from the web using an automatic crawler [11]. Retrieval results were evaluated using precision/recall curves [12].

We found that shape-based matching outperforms text-based matching in all our experiments. The main reason is that 3D models found on the Web are insufficiently annotated. They usually are presented in lists, annotated with at most a single name, which is often misspelled or a repeat of the filename. Of the available text sources, we found that the text inside the model file itself and the synonyms and hypernyms of the filename were the most discriminating. Additionally, we found that for combining the results of the shape and the text matching method a function returning the minimum of normalized scores showed the best performance.

The contribution of this paper is a comparison of text and shape matching methods for retrieval of online 3D models, and an evaluation of several different combination functions for combining text and shape matching scores. This paper shows that the relatively simple solution of using only associated text for retrieval of 3D models is not as effective as using their shape.

The rest of this paper is organized as follows. Text matching and our approach for maximizing text retrieval performance is described in the next section. Section 3 discusses shape matching and shows the performance of several recent shape matching methods. Text and shape matching are compared in Section 4 and combined in Section 5. Conclusions and suggestions for future work are in Section 6.

2   Text Matching

In this section we review related work on retrieval of non-textual data using associated text. Note that we do not discuss text retrieval itself. We refer the interested reader to [13–15]. We then describe the sources of text found with 3D models crawled from the web and investigate how well the text can be used to compute a similarity measure for the associated 3D models.

2.1   Related Work

There has been relatively little previous research on the problem of retrieving non-textual data using associated text. The web is an example of a large database for which such methods can be useful: (1) it contains many non-textual objects (e.g., images, sound files, applets) and (2) these objects are likely to be described on web pages using text. Examples of web search engines that take advantage of associated text are Google Image Search [1] (for images), FindSounds [16] (for sound files), and MeshNose [6] (for 3D models).

Probably the largest site for searching images using text keywords is Google's image search. Unfortunately there are no publications available about the method they use. A related FAQ page suggests that heuristics are used to determine potentially relevant text related to an image, for example, the image filename, link text, and web page title. Each source is probably assigned a different weight, depending on its importance, similar to how the main Google search site assigns weights to text terms depending on whether they are in the title, headers, and so on.

Sable and Hatzivassiloglou investigated the effectiveness of using associated text for classifying images from online news articles as indoor or outdoor [17]. They found that limiting the associated text to just the first sentence of the image caption produced the best results. In other work, Sable *et al.* use Natural Language Processing (e.g., identifying subjects and verbs) to improve classification performance of captioned images into four classes [18]. Our problem is slightly harder since our source text is less well-defined (i.e., there is not an obvious "caption"), and the number of classes is much higher. To our knowledge, there has never been a study investigating the effectiveness of text indexing for 3D models.

2.2 Text Sources

In our study, we focus on the common "bag of words" approach for text matching: all text that is deemed relevant to a particular 3D model is collected in a "representative document," which is then processed and indexed for later matching. This document is created using several potentially relevant text sources. Because we are indexing 3D model files linked from a web page, we are able to extract text from both the model file itself as well as the web page (note that because we convert all models to the VRML 2.0 format, we only refer to text sources of this format). The following list describes the text sources we can use:

From the model file:

1. **model filename:** The filename usually is the name of the object type. The extension determines the filetype. For example, `alsation.wrl` could be the filename of a VRML file of an Alsation dog
2. **model filename without digits:** From the filename we create a second text source by replacing all digits with spaces. Very often filenames contain sequence numbers (for example, `chair2.wrl`) that are useless for text keyword matching
3. **model file contents:** A 3D model file often contains labels, metadata, filenames of included files, and comments. In VRML, it is possible to assign a label to a scene-graph node (a part of the model) and then re-use that node elsewhere in the file. For example, in a model of a chair, a leg can be defined once, assigned the identifier `LEG`, and then re-used three times to create the remaining legs. As such, these identifiers typically describe names of parts of the model. To describe metadata, a VRML 2.0 file may contain a `WorldInfo` node, which is used to store additional information about the model, such as a detailed description, the author name, etc. Filenames of included files can be names of other model files, textures, or user-defined nodes. Finally, a model file may contain descriptive comments. The model file comments were left out from our experiments because we found that many files contain commented-out geometry, which, when included, would add many irrelevant keywords

From the web page:

4. **link text:** This is the descriptive text of the hyperlink to the model file, i.e., the text between the `<a>` and `</a>` HTML tags. For example: `<a href= "b747.wrl"> a VRML model of a Boeing 747</a>`

5. **URL path:** These are the directory names of the full URL to the model file. If multiple models are organized in a directory structure, the directory names could be category names helpful for classification. For example, as in the URL `http://3d.com/objects/chairs/chair4.wrl`

6. **web page context (text near the link):** We define the context to be all plain text after the `</a>` tag until the next `<a href>` tag (or until the next HTML tag if there is none). This text could for example read "1992 Boeing 747-400 passenger plane, 210K, created by John Doe". Context found *before* the link text was found to be mostly irrelevant

7. **web page title:** The title of the web page containing the link to the 3D model. It often describes the category of models found on the page, for example, "Models of Airplanes"

Additional text source:

8. **Wordnet synonyms and hypernyms:** We create an additional eighth text source by adding synonyms and hypernyms (category descriptors) of the filename using WordNet, a lexical database [10] (if no synonyms or hypernyms can be found for the filename, the link text is tried instead). In related work, Rodriguez *et al.* use WordNet synonyms [19], and Scott and Matwin use synonyms and hypernyms [20] to improve classification performance. Recently, Benitez and Chang showed how WordNet can be used to disambiguate text in captions for content-based image retrieval [21]. Adding synonyms and hypernyms enables queries like "vehicle" to return objects like trucks and cars, or "television" to return a TV. WordNet returns synonyms and hypernyms in usage frequency order, so we can limit the synonyms and hypernyms used to only the most common ones.

Following common practices from text retrieval, all collected text goes through a few processing steps. First, *stop words* are removed. These are common words that do not carry much discriminating information, such as "and," "or," and "my". We use the SMART system's stop list of 524 stop words [22], as well as stop words specific to our domain (e.g. "jpg," "www," "transform"). Next, the resulting text is *stemmed* (normalized by removing inflectional changes, for example "wheels" is changed to "wheel"), using the Porter stemming algorithm [23].

2.3   Text Matching Methods

Given a representative text document for each 3D model, we can define a textual similarity score for every pair of 3D models as the similarity of their representative text documents. To compute this score, we use a variety of text matching methods provided by `rainbow`, a program of the Bow toolkit, a freely available C library for statistical text analysis [24]. The tested methods were: three variations of TF/IDF [13], Kullback

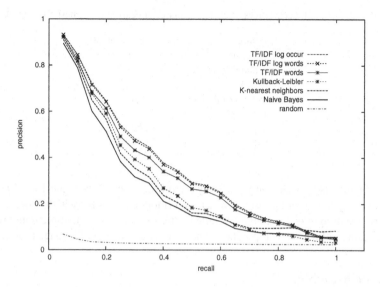

Fig. 1. Average precision/recall for four types of text matching methods, and random retrieval.

Leibler [25], K-nearest neighbors, and Naive Bayes [26]. A few methods supported by the `rainbow` program (e.g., Support Vector Machines) were also tested but failed to run to a finish.

Figure 1 shows the resulting precision/recall results obtained when the representative text document for each 3D model in the test set of the Princeton Shape Benchmark was matched against the representative text documents of all the other 3D models. The matches were ranked according to their text similarity scores, and precision-recall values were computed with respect to the base classification provided with the benchmark. From this graph, we see that the "TF/IDF log occur" method shows the best performance for our dataset, and thus we used this method for all subsequent tests.

To determine the most useful combinations of text sources, we ran a classification test using each combination of n out of the eight text sources for the representative text document, with $n \in \{1, ..., 8\}$ (so the total number of combinations tested was $\sum_{n=1}^{8} \binom{8}{n} = 255$). The performance of each combination was measured as the average precision over twenty recall values.

From these tests, we found that adding as many text sources as possible improves overall performance, in general. This may be explained by our observation that the addition of keywords helps classification performance if the keywords are relevant, but does not hurt performance if they are irrelevant, since they do not match many other models. We expect that as the database size increases, this property will no longer hold because irrelevant keywords would generate cross-class matches.

Looking more closely at how often each source occurs in the best combinations, we counted the number of times each source appears in the top 50 combinations (i.e., the 50 combinations out of 255 with the highest average precision). The results are shown as percentages in table 1. We see that the identifiers found inside the 3D model files themselves provided the most information for classification. The WordNet synonyms

Table 1. Percentage of all occurrences of each text source appearing in the best 50 combinations.

source	percentage in top 50
model file	100
synonyms and hypernyms	100
link	62
filename without digits	58
filename	58
path	56
page title	54
page context	50

and hypernyms also turned out to be very useful, despite the fact that for 279 models (31%) no synonym or hypernym was found (model names for which WordNet did not return a synonym or hypernym included names (e.g., "justin"), abbreviated words ("satellt"), misspelled words ("porche"), and words in a different language ("oiseau")).

3   Shape Matching

In this section, we briefly review previous work on shape-based retrieval of 3D models. Then, we present results comparing several standard shape matching methods to determine which works best on the Princeton Shape Benchmark.

3.1   Related Work

Retrieval of data based on shape has been studied in several fields, including computer vision, computational geometry, mechanical CAD, and molecular biology. For surveys of recent methods, see [27, 28]. For our purpose, we will only consider matching and retrieval of isolated 3D objects (so we do not consider recognition of objects in scenes, or partial matching, for example).

3D shape retrieval methods can be roughly subdivided into three categories: (1) methods that first attempt to derive a high-level description (e.g., a skeleton) and then match those, (2) methods that compute a feature vector based on local or global statistics, and (3) miscellaneous methods.

Examples of the first type are skeletons created by voxel thinning [29], and Reeb graphs [30]. However, these methods typically require the input model to be 2-manifold, and usually are sensitive to noise and small features. Unfortunately, many 3D models are created for visualization purposes only, and often contain only unorganized sets of polygons ("polygon soups"), possibly with missing, wrongly-oriented, intersecting, disjoint, and/or overlapping polygons, thus making them unsuitable for most methods that derive high-level descriptors.

Methods based on computing statistics of the 3D model are more suitable for our purpose, since they usually impose no strict requirements on the validity of the input model. Examples are shape histograms [31], feature vectors composed of global geometric properties such as circularity or eccentricity [32], and feature vectors (or *shape descriptors*) created using frequency decompositions of spherical functions [33]. The

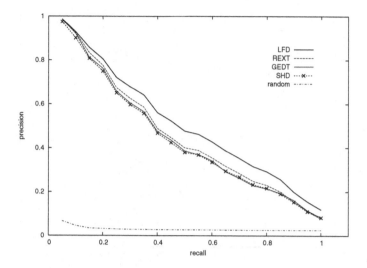

Fig. 2. Average precision/recall for four shape matching methods, and random retrieval. This figure is a partial reproduction of one in [5].

resulting histograms or feature vectors are then usually compared by computing their L_2 distance.

Some alternative approaches use 2D views (2D projections of a 3D model), justified by the heuristic that if two 3D shapes are similar, they should look similar from many different directions. Examples are the "prototypical views" of Cyr and Kimia [34], and the "Light Field Descriptor" of Chen *et al.* [35].

3.2 Shape Matching Methods

In our experiments, we considered four shape matching methods: (1) the *Light Field Descriptor* (LFD) [35], (2) the *Radialized Spherical Extent Function* (REXT) [36], (3) the *Gaussian Euclidian Distance Transform* (GEDT) [33], and (4) the *Spherical Harmonics Descriptor* (SHD) [33]. These four methods have been shown to be state-of-the-art in a recent paper [5].

We ran an experiment in which these four methods were used to compute a similarity score for every pair of 3D models in the test set of the Princeton Shape Benchmark. The similarity scores were used to rank the matches for each model and compute an average precision-recall curve for each matching method with respect to the benchmark's base classification. Results are shown in Figure 2 (see [5] for details). From these curves, we find that the Light Field Descriptor provides the best retrieval performance in this test, and thus we use it in all subsequent experiments.

4   Comparing Text Matching to Shape Matching

Next, we compare the classification performance of the best text matching method to the best shape matching method. Figure 3 shows the resulting average precision/recall plot.

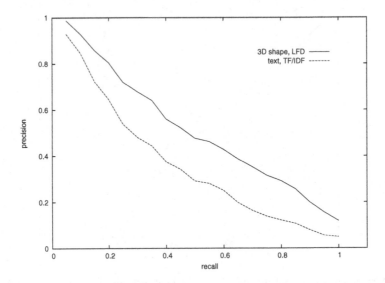

Fig. 3. Average precision/recall for text and 3D shape matching.

The shape matching method significantly outperforms text matching: average precision is 44% higher.

The main cause of the relatively poor performance of the text matching method is the low quality of text annotation of online 3D models. Upon examination of the actual text associated with each model, we found that many filenames were meaningless (e.g., "avstest" for a face), misspelled (e.g., "ferrar" for a ferrari), too specific (e.g., "camaro" for a car), or not specific enough (e.g., "model" for a car). Some models were annotated in a language other than English (e.g., "oiseau" for a bird). By running a spell checker on the filenames with the digits removed, we found that 36% of all model filenames were not English words.

Also, for several sources there is simply no useful text available. For example, many link texts were either a repeat of the filename, or contained no text at all: for 446 models in the training set (51%) no link text could be found (usually a thumbnail image is used instead). Furthermore, 4 (0.4%) models had no path information (i.e., no directories in their URL), 193 (21%) web page titles were missing, for 279 (31%) filenames or link texts no synonym could be found, for 692 (76%) models no web page context was found, and for 153 (17%) models no text inside the model file was found.

Even commercial 3D model databases are not necessarily well annotated. Of three commercial databases available to us (provided by CacheForce, De Espona, and Viewpoint, containing approximately 2000, 1000, and 1000 models respectively), only one was consistently well annotated.

In all text matching experiments, the representative document created for each 3D model was used as a query. However, because the size and quality of text annotation varies a lot from model to model, one may argue that this text is not representative of actual user queries. Users of a retrieval system are more likely to enter a few descriptive keywords or class names. To investigate classification performance given this kind of user queries, we ran an additional classification experiment in which the full category names of the Princeton Shape Benchmark were used as simulated user queries. Some obvious keywords were added manually (e.g., "blimp" and "zeppelin" for the "dirigible hot air balloon" category, or "house" for the "home" category). The average precision achieved when using these query keywords was 11% higher than when using the representative documents, but still 30% lower than the best shape matching method.

5   Combining Text and Shape Matching

In our final tests, we investigate how to combine the best text and shape matching methods to provide better retrieval results than can be achieved with either method alone.

5.1   Related Work

A considerable amount of research has been presented on the problem of how to best combine multiple classifiers [37]. Most work in this area has been done in content-based image retrieval. For example, Srihari presents a system ("Piction") that identifies faces in annotated news photographs using a face detection algorithm and Natural Language Processing of the captions [38]. Smith and Chang describe a system for the retrieval of arbitrary online images [3]. Relevant text for each image is extracted from the URL and the alt parameter of the HTML < img > tag, for example. However, searches based on low-level image features or on text can not be combined. This combination *has* been investigated in later retrieval systems. La Cascia *et al.* combine text and image features into a single feature vector, to improve search performance [39]. Text is extracted from the referring web page, with different weights assigned depending on the HTML tag that enclosed it (e.g., text in a <title> is more important than text in an <h4 > (small header) tag). Paek *et al.* present a method that combines a text- and image-based classifier for the classification of captioned images into two classes ("indoor" and "outdoor") [40], which improved classification accuracy to 86.2%, from 83.3% when using the text alone.

5.2   Multiclassifiers

In previous work we suggested that the results of text and shape matching can be combined to improve classification performance [4], and proposed a combination function that simply averaged mean-normalized matching scores. However, no evaluation was done to see which combination function works best. Here we consider the simple case of combining the scores of two classifiers, using a static combination function. We experimented with four types of functions: (1) linear weighted average, (2) minimum, (3) (minimum) rank, and (4) using confidence limits. The first two were also tested on mean-normalized scores.

1. **linear weighted average:** If s_1 and s_2 are the matching scores of a pair of models, then the combined score is $w \cdot s_1 + (1 - w) \cdot s_2$, with w the weight setting. We computed average precision/recall for $w \in \{0, 0.05, 0.1, ..., 1.0\}$, and picked the value of w which resulted in the highest overall precision. The optimal weight setting for the training set was $(0.1 \cdot text + 0.9 \cdot shape)$

Table 2. Average precision achieved when combining the matching scores of the text and shape matching methods using various static combiners, and the percentage improvement over shape matching alone.

method	average precision	% improvement over shape alone
shape (LFD)	0.507	-
minimum, normalized scores	0.536	5.8
confidence limits, normalized scores	0.533	5.1
weighted average, normalized scores	0.523	3.2
confidence limits	0.520	2.6
weighted average	0.519	2.4
minimum	0.508	0.2
minimum rank	0.495	-2.3
weighted average rank	0.487	-4

2. **minimum:** the lowest matching score (signifying highest similarity) is returned
3. **rank:** The matching scores are ordered, and the resulting rank of each query becomes its new matching score. We can then apply one of the first two functions (linear weighted average or minimum)
4. **confidence limits:** The "confidence limits" method is based on the idea that if a similarity score of a single classifier is sufficiently close to zero, then that classifier can be trusted completely. The output of other classifiers is then ignored. Sable uses a variant of this method when combining a text- and image-based classifier [2]: feature vectors from both are classified using a Support Vector Machine, and a confidence level is assigned to the classification, depending on the distance of the vector from the dividing hyperplane (the decision boundary). If the confidence level of the image-based classifier is high enough, then the text-based classifier is ignored. If not, then the text-based classifier is used and the image-based classifier is ignored. We used the training set to determine optimial limit settings of 0.09 and 0.22 for shape and text matching respectively (and -2.45 and -1.5 for mean-normalized scores). If both scores were above their limit, we reverted to the linear weighted average (other alternatives yielded worse results)

Table 2 shows the resulting average precision values achieved for each combiner, and the percentage improvement over using shape matching alone (computed using the test set). We achieve an additionol 5.8% improvement in average precision, using the function that returns the minimum of normalized scores. These results confirm that the text and shape representations of a 3D model are sufficiently independent, such that when they are combined, they become more discriminating. There may well be other representations (e.g. appearance-based) that capture a very different aspect of a 3D model, and as such could increase performance even further.

6   Conclusions and Future Work

This paper evaluates text and shape matching methods for retrieval of online 3D models, as well as their combination. Classification tests were done using the Princeton Shape Benchmark, a large benchmark database of 3D models downloaded from the web.

For text matching, we found that a variant of TF/IDF showed the best classification performance. Text found inside a 3D model file itself and synonyms and hypernyms (category descriptors) of the model filename were most useful for classification.

The currently best shape matching method (based on *Light Field Descriptors* [35]) significantly outperformed the best text matching method, yielding 44% higher average precision. The main reason is that the quality of text annotation of online 3D models is relatively poor, limiting the maximum achievable classification performance with a text-based method.

We investigated several simple multiclassifiers, and found that a function returning the minimum of normalized matching scores produced an additional performance improvement of about 6%. Studying other more sophisticated multiclassifiers is an interesting area for future work, considering there are many other attributes of 3D models (e.g., color, texture, structure) for which additional classifiers can be designed.

The main contribution of this paper is that it demonstrates the advantage of using shape-based matching methods over text-based methods for retrieval of 3D models. This should encourage designers of future 3D model retrieval systems to incorporate query methods based on shape, and other attributes that do not depend on annotation provided by humans, as they hold much potential for improving retrieval results.

Acknowledgements

Patrick Min was supported in part by the AIM@SHAPE Network of Excellence grant 506766 by the European Commission. The National Science Foundation provided partial funding for this project under grants CCR-0093343 and IIS-0121446.

References

1. Google: Image search. (http://www.google.com/images)
2. Sable, C.: Robust Statistical Techniques for the Categorization of Images Using Associated Text. PhD thesis, Columbia University (2003)
3. Smith, J.R., Chang, S.F.: Searching for images and videos on the world-wide web. Technical Report 459-96-25, Columbia University (1996)
4. Funkhouser, T., Min, P., Kazhdan, M., Chen, J., Halderman, A., Dobkin, D., Jacobs, D.: A search engine for 3D models. ACM Transactions on Graphics **22** (2003)
5. Shilane, P., Kazhdan, M., Min, P., Funkhouser, T.: The Princeton Shape Benchmark. In: Proc. Shape Modeling International, Genoa, Italy (2004)
6. MeshNose: 3D objects search engine. (http://www.deepfx.com/meshnose)
7. Suzuki, M.T.: A web-based retrieval system for 3D polygonal models. In: Proc. IFSA/NAFIPS, Vancouver, Canada (2001) 2271–2276
8. Chen, D.Y., Ouhyoung, M.: A 3D object retrieval system based on multi-resolution Reeb graph. In: Proc. Computer Graphics Workshop, Taiwan (2002) 16–20
9. Min, P.: A 3D Model Search Engine. PhD thesis, Princeton University (2004)
10. Miller, G.A.: WordNet: A lexical database for English. CACM **38** (1995) 39–41
11. Min, P., Halderman, A., Kazhdan, M., Funkhouser, T.: Early experiences with a 3D model search engine. In: Proc. Web3D Symposium, St. Malo, France, ACM (2003) 7–18
12. van Rijsbergen, C.J.: Information Retrieval. Butterworth (1979)

13. Salton, G.: Automatic text processing: the transformation, analysis, and retrieval of information by computer. Addison-Wesley, Reading, Massachusetts (1988)
14. Baeza-Yates, R., Ribeiro-Neto, B.: Modern Information Retrieval. Addison-Wesley (1999)
15. Sebastiani, F.: Machine learning in automated text categorization. ACM Computing Surveys **34** (2002) 1–47
16. FindSounds: Sound file search engine. (http://www.findsounds.com)
17. Sable, C.L., Hatzivassiloglou, V.: Text-based approaches for the categorization of images. In: Proc. Research and Advanced Technologies for Digital Libraries, Paris (1999)
18. Sable, C., McKeown, K., Church, K.W.: NLP found helpful (at least for one text categorization task). In: Proc. EMNLP, Philadelphia, PA (2002)
19. de Buenaga Rodríguez, M., Gómez-Hidalgo, J.M., Díaz-Agudo, B.: Using WordNet to complement training information in text categorization. In: Proc. RANLP, Stanford (1997)
20. Scott, S., Matwin, S.: Text classification using WordNet hypernyms. In: Proc. Workshop Usage of WordNet in Natural Language Processing Systems. (1998) 45–52
21. Benitez, A.B., Chang, S.F.: Semantic knowledge construction from annotated image collections. In: Proc. Int. Conf. on Multimedia and Expo ICME, Lausanne, Switzerland (2002)
22. Salton, G.: The SMART retrieval system. Prentice-Hall, Englewood Cliffs, NJ (1971)
23. Porter, M.: An algorithm for suffix stripping. Program **14** (1980) 130–137
24. McCallum, A.: Bow: A toolkit for statistical language modeling, text retrieval, classification and clustering. http://www.cs.cmu.edu/~mccallum/bow (1996)
25. Kullback, S., Leibler, R.: On information and sufficiency. Ann. Math. Stat. **22** (1951) 79–86
26. Mitchell, T.: Machine Learning. McGraw-Hill (1997)
27. Loncaric, S.: A survey of shape analysis techniques. Pattern Recognition **31** (1998)
28. Tangelder, J.W., Veltkamp, R.C.: A survey of content based 3D shape retrieval methods. In: Proc. Shape Modeling International, Genoa, Italy (2004)
29. Sundar, H., Silver, D., Gagvani, N., Dickinson, S.: Skeleton based shape matching and retrieval. In: Proc. SMI, Seoul, Korea (2003)
30. Hilaga, M., Shinagawa, Y., Kohmura, T., Kunii, T.L.: Topology matching for fully automatic similarity estimation of 3D shapes. In: Proc. SIGGRAPH. (2001) 203–212
31. A.P.Ashbrook, N.A.Thacker, P.I.Rockett, C.I.Brown: Robust recognition of scaled shapes using pairwise geometric histograms. In: Proc. BMVC, Birmingham, UK (1995) 503–512
32. Taubin, G., Cooper, D.: Object recognition based on moment (or algebraic) invariants. In: Geometric Invariance in Computer Vision. MIT Press (1992)
33. Kazhdan, M., Funkhouser, T., Rusinkiewicz, S.: Rotation invariant spherical harmonic representation of 3D shape descriptors. In: Proc. SGP, ACM (2003) 156–165
34. Cyr, C.M., Kimia, B.B.: 3D object recognition using shape similarity-based aspect graph. In: Proc. ICCV, IEEE (2001)
35. Chen, D.Y., Ouhyoung, M., Tian, X.P., Shen, Y.T., Ouhyoung, M.: On visual similarity based 3D model retrieval. In: Proc. Eurographics, Granada, Spain (2003)
36. Vranic, D.V.: An improvement of rotation invariant 3D shape descriptor based on functions on concentric spheres. In: Proc. ICIP. Volume 3. (2003) 757–760
37. Jain, A.K., Duin, R.P., Mao, J.: Statistical pattern recognition: A review. IEEE Transactions on Pattern Analysis and Machine Intelligence **22** (2000) 4–37
38. Srihari, R.K.: Automatic indexing and content-based retrieval of captioned images. IEEE Computer **28** (1995) 49–56
39. Sclaroff, S., Cascia, M.L., Sethi, S.: Unifying textual and visual cues for content-based image retrieval on the world wide web. CVIU **75** (1999) 86–98
40. Paek, S., et al.: Integration of visual and text-based approaches for the content labeling and classification of photographs. In: ACM Workshop on Multim. Indexing and Retr. (1999)

Corpus-Based Query Expansion
in Online Public Access Catalogs

Jeffry Komarjaya, Danny C.C. Poo, and Min-Yen Kan

School of Computing, National University of Singapore
3 Science Drive 2, Singapore 117543
jeffry.komarjaya@nus.edu.sg
{dpoo,kanmy}@comp.nus.edu.sg

Abstract. We propose a probabilistic method for query expansion in online public access catalogs that utilizes both historical query logs and the subject headings in the library catalog. Our method creates correlations between query and document terms, allowing relevant subject headings from the corpus to be retrieved and added to a query. Experiments demonstrate an average of 31.1% performance increase over currently fielded baselines.

1 Introduction

The problem of vocabulary mismatch is a deep-rooted problem in information retrieval as users often use different or too few words to describe the concepts in their queries as compared to the words that authors use to describe the concepts in their documents [1–3]. Despite this, many library online public access catalogs (OPACs), such as the INNOPAC system[1] used by *Library IN*tegrated *C*atalogue (LINC) at the National University of Singapore, still depend on keyword matching to determine the relevant documents for queries.

Short queries damage retrieval effectiveness in two ways: 1) they lead too many results and 2) the queries themselves are ambiguous. The first phenomenon, often called information overload, makes searching difficult as users are overwhelmed with information. In our case study of LINC, from March to September 2003, queries sent to LINC have a mean length of 2.815 words. For example, for the top query "java", LINC returned 32,000 books, of which 953 books had 100% relevance, leaving the user to select between 953 alternatives. Short queries are often polysemous (having multiple senses or meanings, as in "java": the computer language or the island in Indonesia). Such queries result in ambiguity as words that could disambiguate them are missing.

Query expansion, the process of expanding a user's query with additional related words and phrases, has been suggested to address the problem. However, finding and using appropriate related words remains an open problem. Research on query expansion has focused on intranet or internet web search. However, the typical digital library OPAC contains bibliographic records which are far more

---

[1] http://www.libdex.com/vendor/Innovative_Interfaces,_Inc.html

R. Heery and L. Lyon (Eds.): ECDL 2004, LNCS 3232, pp. 221–231, 2004.

structured than documents on the internet. On the other hand, traditional OPAC research has largely focused on rule-based systems that do not take advantage of corpora.

Our study melds the two approaches by analyzing library corpora for use in query expansion in the digital library OPAC. Our system combines both historical query logs and the library catalog to create a thesaurus-based query expansion that correlates query terms with document terms. Our process consists of three steps. First, historical query logs are analyzed to uncover frequent queries. These queries are sent to the OPAC to extract relevant subject headings from the top documents. In the last step, the system calculates probabilistic correlations between the retrieved subjects heading and users' queries. With these correlations, relevant subject headings can be selected from the corpus for new, unseen queries.

In Section 2, we discuss related work in query expansion. we detail the methods used to build the thesaurus (a matrix correlating query keywords and subject headings) by sending queries to the OPAC and analyzing the results, and describe how query expansion is done with the built thesaurus. Section 5 describes our case study in which we deployed our approach in our local OPAC. We conclude with a summary and directions of further work.

2   Query Expansion Techniques

In query expansion, there are two key aspects: the source of expansion terms and the method to weight and integrate expansion terms [4, 3, 5]. Existing techniques can be classified as global, local or external, based on the source of terms. Global techniques require corpus-wide statistics such as the occurrence of expansion terms in the corpus and the source of expansion terms is usually the whole corpus. Local techniques analyze a number of top-ranked documents retrieved by a query to expand it. In contrast, external techniques depend on external resources such as domain-independent thesauri for expansion terms.

2.1   Global Techniques

We define a global technique as one that analyzes the contents of a particular corpus to identify semantically similar terms. By gathering statistics of the co-occurrences of terms in the corpus, global techniques build statistical term relationships which can then be used to expand queries. Some global techniques are term clustering [6], global similarity thesauri [7], latent semantic indexing [8] and Phrasefinding [9]. Since global techniques focus only on the document and do not take into account the query, global techniques only offer a partial solution to the word mismatching problem [4]. Global techniques typically require co-occurrence information for every pair of terms. However, most global techniques compute this information offline, removing a potential computational bottleneck.

2.2   Local Techniques

As compared to global techniques, local techniques use only a subset of the documents retrieved by a query. Local techniques can be divided into two main categories: interactive (*i.e.*, relevance feedback) and automatic (*i.e.*, local feedback).

Relevance Feedback. In relevance feedback systems, related terms come from user-identified relevant documents. Relevance feedback was originally designed to be used with the vector space model [10]. However, relevance feedback has also been incorporated into Boolean retrieval models [11] and probabilistic retrieval models [12, 13]. Other methods such as incremental relevance feedback [14] have also been proposed, which analyzes previous queries and relevance judgments in the same session to improve search effectiveness. [15] proposed Adaptive Relevance Feedback (ARF) on top of incremental relevance feedback to detect changes in users' information goals. However, in a real search context, users are usually reluctant to provide any type of feedback [4, 16].

Local Feedback. Local feedback uses the top-ranked documents retrieved by a query as a viable source of information. The basic assumption is that the top-ranked documents retrieved are relevant, and thus the words in the top-ranked documents themselves can be used to expand the query. While the performance of local feedback can be erratic, it has shown good performance in Text REtrieval Conferences (TREC) experiments [17]. The TREC test collections are often used to evaluate query expansion techniques [1–3, 5].

Many improvements have been suggested to local feedback, such as using Boolean filters and proximity constraints to refine the set of top-ranked documents [16], exploiting potentially relevant documents from past similar queries [18] and using information theory in weighting and selecting expansion terms [1]. The idea of local context analysis was also proposed [3, 5] which combines the idea of global and local techniques to select expansion terms based on co-occurrences with the query terms within the top-ranked documents. More recently, historical user logs were also used to deduce likely user interactions [4].

2.3   External Techniques

External techniques make use of external resources, such as online thesauri which are not tailored for any particular collection, for query expansion. In past work, general reference resources such as Longman's Dictionary of Contemporary English (LDOCE) and WordNet [19] have been used. Because of the ambiguity of terms and the existence of specialized terms for certain collections, these thesauri might be difficult to use. Voorhees reported improvements of 1% for longer and less ambiguous queries but expanding shorter queries actually degraded performance. Based on these neutral results, we have decided not to pursue the use of general, external resources in our research.

3   Building a Learning Thesaurus

The Online Catalog Evaluation Projects reported that library patrons have problems matching their terms with those indexed in the online catalog and do not understand the printed LCSH (Library of Congress Subject Headings) [20]. To solve this vocabulary problem, one possible solution is to map query terms to the underlying vocabulary of the corpus by building a corpus-specific thesaurus.

To build such a thesaurus for an OPAC, frequently-occurring queries were first harvested from historical query log kept by the OPAC. Each of these queries were re-sent to the OPAC, generating a ranked list of relevant documents. We adopted local feedback to extract the top relevant documents, and extracted the subject headings for each document. We then mapped the query keywords to the frequency of the subject headings in the relevant documents.

There are two design details that are important in our system's architecture. First, we used local feedback rather than standard relevance feedback, as it requires no explicit relevance judgments or click-streams because it is fully automated and requires no user effort [15]. Second, we used frequently-occurring queries in our historical query logs to build our thesaurus for the initial queries. Subsequent new queries submitted by users need to also be analyzed and the thesaurus updated to reflect the change in query patterns.

3.1   Subject Headings

Subject headings are usually assigned by expert cataloguers. These headings are used to index the documents in OPACs. Standardized, controlled vocabulary terms or subject headings are usually employed, such as the Library of Congress Subject Headings (LCSH), the Library of Medicine's Medical Science Subject Headings (MeSH), or the Dewey Decimal Classification (DDC).

Compared to book titles, subject headings are more objective and precise. For example, subject headings "Genetics", "Evolution (Biology)" and "Behavior genetics" are clearer than the title "The Selfish Gene". Thus we feel that it would be less ambiguous to use the subject headings as expansion terms in comparison to book titles. Using subject headings also provides us with knowledge from experts, which are less prone to errors, and eliminates the need to use automatic term weighting algorithms, such as Term Frequency × Inverse Document Frequency (TF×IDF), to extract terms from the corpus.

3.2   Correlating Query Terms and Document Terms

In this study, we attempt to create links between keyword query terms and the subject headings documented in OPACs by the librarians and cataloguers. Our key observation is that if queries containing a certain term often lead to the selection of documents containing another term, then we consider that there is a strong relationship between these two terms [4].

We assumed that subject headings from the top documents retrieved using queries containing a particular keyword were related to that keyword. For example, the terms, "macromedia" and "flash", in the query "macromedia flash" are

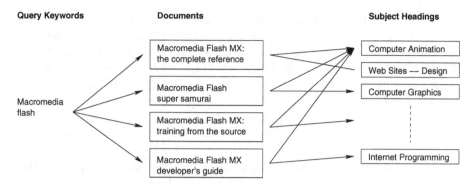

Fig. 1. Correlations between query keywords and subject headings.

regarded as relevant to the documents that the query retrieved, *e.g.*, "Macromedia Flash MX developer's guide", and the subject headings of these documents, "Computer animation". By acquiring and analyzing a large pool of queries and collecting their top-ranked documents, we are able to form associations between the queries and documents. These associations allow us to create a thesaurus that will aid in query augmentation by mapping keywords in the queries to the subject headings. Figure 1 shows how the subject headings are related to the query keywords.

4   A Corpus-Based Query Expansion Model

4.1   Relation of a Document Term to the Entire Query

Xu and Croft [5] and Qiu and Frei [7] hypothesized that relevant terms tend to co-occur with all query terms in the top-ranked documents. A similar idea is applied in this study; subject headings that occur with all or most of the query keywords in the thesaurus are considered more relevant than subject headings that only occur with a few keywords. In other words, we should consider a term that is similar to the query concept rather than one that is only similar to a single term in the query.

Consider the queries Q1: "Java" and Q2: "Java Indonesia". While Q1 is ambiguous and could mean the programming language developed by Sun Microsystems, the Indonesian capital island or the coffee bean, Q2 is much less ambiguous and more likely to refer to the Indonesian capital island than to the other meanings. Subject headings that co-occur with both "Java" and "Indonesia" are likely to be relevant to Q2 and should be given a higher weight than terms that only occur with "Java" or "Indonesia". Terms should be selected based on their similarity to the entire query instead of just a few query terms. In contrast, many query expansion techniques add a term even when the term is only strongly related to just one of the query terms [7], resulting in suboptimal performance. As a result, our approach prefers subject headings that co-occur with more query terms over those co-occurring with fewer query terms.

To determine the correlation between a query term w_q and a subject heading w_d, we calculate the degree of co-occurrence of w_d and w_q. That is, we need to calculate $co\_degree(w_d, w_q)$ [5]. We estimate $co\_degree(w_d, w_q)$ as the likelihood that w_d and w_q co-occurs non-randomly in the top-retrieved documents retrieved by queries containing w_q by using an adapted equation from the normalized TF*IDF weighting scheme [21]:

$$co\_degree(w_d, w_q) \equiv f(w_d) \times ln\frac{m}{df(w_d)} \qquad (1)$$

where $f(w_d)$ is the frequency which the subject heading w_d co-occurs with the query keyword w_q in the thesaurus, m is the total number of distinct query keywords and $df(w_d)$ is the total number of distinct query keywords that co-occur with w_d in the thesaurus. A higher $f(w_d)$ will indicate that the subject heading w_d is more important over another subject heading with a lower $f(w_d)$. On the other hand, the higher $df(w_d)$ is, the more likely that w_d co-occurs with the query keyword w_q by chance or that w_d might be ambiguous because it is related to many different keywords.

The above calculates the relevance of the subject headings with individual query terms. We also need to measure the relationship of the subject heading with regards to the entire query. Many researchers [4, 7, 5] have proposed methods to measure the degree of co-occurrence with all query terms. We measure the relationship of a term to the entire query using the following cohesion weight calculation [5]:

$$g(w_d, w_q) \equiv \prod_{all\ query\ terms} (\delta + co\_degree(w_d, w_q)) \qquad (2)$$

where, δ is a smoothing factor to assign a small, non-zero probability to subjects that only co-occur with only one query term that would otherwise receive a weight of zero. With a small δ, subject headings that co-occur with all query terms are ranked higher and with a large δ, subject headings having significant co-occurrences with individual query terms are ranked higher [5]. As we prefer subject headings that co-occur with more query terms over those co-occurring with fewer, we set the smoothing factor δ to a small value of 0.001.

After the cohesion weights of the subject headings related to the query have been calculated and the weights normalized, subject headings for query expansion have to be selected. We select subject headings which have weights above the threshold β. The default value of is 0.03. The new query Q' will be reformulated by adding these subject terms into the original query. Q' will then be used to retrieve documents.

5   Experimental Evaluations

In this section, we describe the methodology and data collection of the experiment before illustrating our experimental findings.

5.1   Evaluation Methodology

The objective of the experiments reported in this section is to test whether query expansion using the thesaurus we have constructed can be used to improve the retrieval effectiveness compared to the original (unexpanded) queries. Our local OPAC, an INNOPAC-based system, allows the user to select the method for sorting the results. The two most common methods are to sort by relevance or date; i.e. either the most relevant documents or the most recent documents are ranked higher. Thus, we compare our query expansion results using both date and relevance sorting methods.

IR performance are usually assessed using standard metrics of precision and recall. However, boolean retrieval (used in many OPACs) with or without query expansion retrieves the same set of documents and thus query expansion changes only the ranking of the documents within the ranked list. As such, absolute precision and recall are not as suitable metrics. Instead, we use precision of the top k documents or precision-at-k [1, 2, 22] as our performance metric.

We measured the precision over first k documents for both our system and the baseline method, sorted by date and relevance, where $k = 12, 24, 36, 48$ or 60, as our INNOPAC shows twelve documents per screen. The objective of this experiment is to determine which solution will retrieve more relevant documents in the first k retrieved documents. The user model for this experiment is that the user typically reads only the first k documents and not all the documents [22]. In addition, users are usually more interested in the precision of the results displayed in the first page of the list of retrieved documents [23]. The default threshold β-value is set to 0.03 and the δ-value is set to 0.001 in this experiment.

To determine the optimal threshold β-value, we also tested the effect of using different thresholds, β-values, for query expansion. We experimented with β-values of 0.01, 0.03, 0.05 and 0.1, and we measured the precision over first k documents, where $k = 12, 24, 36, 48$ or 60. The δ-value is set to 0.001 for this experiment. In addition, we also tested the effect of using different δ-values in the cohesion weight Equation 2 to find out the optimal δ-value in our cohesion weight equation. For the δ-values of 0.001, 0.01, 0.05 and 0.1, we measured the precision over first k documents for query expansion, where $k = 12, 24, 36, 48$ or 60. We used the default β-value of 0.03 for this experiment.

5.2   Data Collection

For our experiments, we collected queries from real OPAC users in the School of Computing at National University of Singapore (NUS) and at various discipline specific libraries. We conducted short interviews with the users to document their information needs. A total of 39 queries and their descriptions were collected. The users were requested to provide the query keywords they used, describe what they were searching for in detail, and identify topics that are likely to be relevant as well as topics that are likely to be irrelevant. Based on the descriptions given, we were able to judge the relevance of the documents.

These queries had an average length of 2.05 words and cover various topics from computer science to medicine. The experiments were conducted on the

Table 1. Comparison of baseline and query expansion results.

k	Baseline (Date)	Baseline (Relevance)	Query Expansion
12	0.4209	0.4209	0.5747 (+36.55%, +36.55%)
24	0.3536	0.3856	0.5128 (+45.02%, +32.96%)
36	0.3169	0.3589	0.4686 (+47.87%, +30.56%)
48	0.2932	0.3440	0.4375 (+49.18%, +27.17%)
60	0.2743	0.3192	0.4038 (+47.20%, +26.51%)
Average	0.3318	0.3657	0.4795 (+44.51%, +31.10%)

heterogeneous NUS LINC corpus, which consisted of 1,209,509 unique titles as at June 2003[2].

5.3 Experimental Results

We now present the experimental results of query expansion on LINC, using the metric discussed earlier, precision-at-k. The original (unexpanded) queries, sorted by date and relevance, were used as the baseline in the experiments. The results are presented in Table 1.

Our thesaurus-based query expansion performed very well as compared to using LINC without query expansion, with an improvement of 44.51% and 31.10% performance improvement over the average precision-at-k, for date and relevance sorting, respectively. This suggests that our version of query expansion is indeed useful in improving the retrieval effectiveness of the search. The reason for the improved performance is that some relevant documents which are ranked low by the original queries are propelled to the top of the ranked output because they contain many subject headings. In addition, query expansion was able to improve the retrieval performance of ambiguous queries. An example is the query "erp", in which the user's intention was to find books related to Enterprise Resource Planning (ERP) but some of the documents retrieved by the unexpanded query included terms such as expressway robbery permit and Event-Related Potentials, which were irrelevant to the user's information needs.

Determining the Threshold, β-Value. In Table 2, we list the retrieval performance of query expansion using different β-values of 0.01, 0.03, 0.05 and 0.1.

Table 2 shows the effect of β-value on the performance of query expansion. We can see that the average precision-at-k tends to be slightly higher for β-values of 0.03 and 0.05. This is because when β-value gets too large, potentially relevant subject headings lower than the threshold are sometimes not selected, for example, for the query "statistics", the relevant subject heading "Mathematical Statistics" was omitted. Thus, setting β-value too high will degrade retrieval performance by omitting potentially relevant subject headings. On the other hand, when β-value is too small, irrelevant subject headings are selected, for example for the query "culture shock", irrelevant subject heading "Cell Culture" was added. A small β-value will allow irrelevant subject headings to be added, which also decreases retrieval performance.

---

[2] http://www.lib.nus.edu.sg/about/stats02-03.html

Table 2. Effect of threshold β-value on performance of query expansion.

k	$\beta = 0.01$	$\beta = 0.03$	$\beta = 0.05$	$\beta = 0.1$
12	0.5512	0.5747	0.5534	0.5427
24	0.4882	0.5138	0.4967	0.4679
36	0.4487	0.4707	0.4537	0.4301
48	0.4209	0.4380	0.4262	0.4059
60	0.3863	0.4038	0.3910	0.3756
Average	0.4591	0.4802	0.4642	0.4445

δ-Value. To find out the optimal value for δ in the cohesion weight equation, we measured the precision over the first k documents retrieved by our system. We use different values for δ in the cohesion weight Equation 2 and compare the results below.

Table 3. Effect of δ-value on performance of query expansion.

k	$\delta = 0.001$	$\delta = 0.01$	$\delta = 0.05$	$\delta = 0.1$
12	0.5747	0.5384	0.5128	0.4914
24	0.5128	0.4850	0.4529	0.4423
36	0.4686	0.4423	0.4166	0.4002
48	0.4375	0.4145	0.3931	0.3755
60	0.4038	0.3833	0.3662	0.3504
Average	0.4795	0.4527	0.4283	0.4120

Table 3 shows the effect of δ-value on the performance of query expansion. We can see that the average precision-at-k tends to decrease as δ-value increases. Using a δ-value of 0.001 as the baseline, average precision-at-k fell by 5.59%, 10.67% and 14.08% when the δ-value increases to 0.01, 0.05 and 0.1 respectively. This is because when δ-value gets too large, it dominates the cohesion weight equation that we discussed earlier, making the more crucial factor co_weight less important. The cohesion weights of the subject headings then become inaccurate, which often causes relevant subject headings to be omitted. To illustrate, the relevant subject heading "Evolution (Biology)" was omitted for the query "evolution" and for the query "C", the relevant subject heading "C (Computer Program Language)" was omitted. If a small δ-value is used, subject headings co-occurring with more terms are given heavier weights. Xu and Croft [5] mentioned "concepts co-occurring with all query terms are good for precision". Our experimental results also imply that δ-value should not be too large, as it is only a smoothing factor and should not dominate the cohesion weight equation.

6   Conclusion

We proposed a method for automatic query expansion in OPACs based on the domain knowledge contained in an automatically constructed thesaurus which maps query keywords to document subject headings. To build this thesaurus, historical query logs were analyzed to find out the most frequently-occurring queries and keywords library patrons use. Document terms were then extracted from the top-ranked documents retrieved by these queries and statistical correlations between query keywords and document subject headings were created to support query expansion. The experimental results show that our solution is practical and offers significantly better performance than the unexpanded baseline. Precision on the first screen of ranked documents improved by over 30% in our experiments.

Although we have successfully incorporated our query expansion technique into a widely-used OPAC and demonstrated its effectiveness, there is still much room for improvment. In our future work, we plan to investigate how phrase structure can refine the terms collected in our OPAC-specific thesaurus. In addition, we are exploring how document metadata such as MARC metadata, can be harnessed for further query expansion.

Acknowledgments

We wish to thank our colleagues over at NUS Libraries for their generous contribution of the LINC query logs for our research use and their continued support of our on-going work to improve OPAC usability. We also would like to thank the anonymous reviewers for their helpful suggestions.

References

1. Carpineto, C., De Mori, R., Romano, G., Bigi, B.: An information-theoretic approach to automatic query expansion. ACM Transactions on Information Systems **19** (2001) 1–27
2. Carpineto, C., Romano, G., Giannini, V.: Improving retrieval feedback with multiple term-ranking function combination. ACM Transactions on Information Systems **20** (2001) 259–290
3. Xu, J., Croft, W.: Query expansion using local and global document analysis. In: Proceedings of the 19th Annual International ACM SIGIR Conference on Research and Development in Information Retrieval, (SIGIR '96), Zurich, Switzerland, ACM Press (1996) 4–11
4. Cui, H., J.-R., W., Nie, J.Y., Ma, W.Y.: Query expansion by mining user logs. IEEE Transactions on Knowledge and Data Engineering **15** (2003) 829–839
5. Xu, J., Croft, W.: Improving the effectiveness of information retrieval with local context analysis. ACM Transactions on Information Systems **18** (2000) 79–112
6. Sparck Jones, K.: Automatic Keyword Classification for Information Retrieval. Butterworths, London, UK (1971)
7. Qiu, Y., Frei, H.: Concept based query expansion. In: Proceedings of the 16th Annual International ACM SIGIR Conference on Research and Development in Information Retrieval, (SIGIR '93), Pittsburgh, USA, ACM Press (1993) 160–169
8. Sebastiani, F.: Machine learning in automated text categorization. ACM Computing Surveys **34** (2002) 1–47

9. Jing, Y., Croft, W.: An association thesaurus for information retrieval. In: Proceedings of the Intelligent Multimedia Information Retrieval Systems. (RIAO '94), New York, USA (1994) 146–160
10. Salton, G., C., B.: Improving retrieval performance by relevance feedback. Journal of the American Society for Information Science and Technology **41** (1990) 288–296
11. Radecki, T.: Incorporation of relevance feedback into boolean retrieval systems. In: Proceedings of the 5th Annual ACM Conference on Research and Development in Information Retrieval, West Berlin, Germany, ACM Press (1982) 133–150
12. Robertson, S.E., Sparck Jones, K.: Relevance weighting of search terms. Journal of the American Society for Information Science **27** (1976) 129–146
13. Sparck Jones, K.: Search term relevance weighting given little relevance information. Journal of Documentation **35** (1979) 30–48
14. Aalbersberg, I.: Incremental relevance feedback. In: Proceedings of the 15th Annual International ACM SIGIR Conference on Research and Development in Information Retrieval, Copenhagen, Denmark (1992) 11–22
15. Eguchi, K., Ito, H., A., K., Y., K.: Adaptive and incremental query expansion for cluster-based browsing. In: Proceedings of the 6th International Conference on Database Systems for Advanced Applications, (DASFAA '99,, Hsinchu, Taiwan, IEEE Computer Society (1999) 25–34
16. Mitra, M., Singhal, A., C., B.: Improving automatic query expansion. In: Proceedings of the 21st Annual International ACM SIGIR Conference on Research and Development in Information Retrieval, (SIGIR '98), Melbourne, Australia, ACM Press (1998) 275–281
17. Voorhees, E.M., Harman, D.: Overview of the 6th text retrieval conference (trec-6). In: Proceedings of the 6th Text Retrieval Conference (TREC-6). Number 500-240 in NIST Special Publication (1998)
18. Fitzpatrick, L., Dent, M.: Automatic feedback using past queries: Social searching? In: Proceedings of the 20th Annual International ACM SIGIR Conference on Research and Development in Information Retrieval, (SIGIR 1997), Philadelphia, USA, ACM Press (1997) 306–313
19. Voorhees, E.M.: Query expansion using lexical-semantic relations. In: Proceedings of the 17th Annual International ACM SIGIR Conference on Research and Development in Information Retrieval, (SIGIR '94), Dublin, Ireland, ACM Press (1994) 61–69
20. Markey, K.: Subject searching in library catalogs: Before and after the introduction of online catalogs. Number 4 in OCLC Library, Information and Computer Science Series. OCLC Online Computer Library Center, Dublin, Ohio (1984)
21. Wu, H., Salton, G.: A comparison of search term weighting: term relevance vs. inverse document frequency. In: Proceedings of the 4th Annual International ACM SIGIR Conference on Information storage and retrieval: theoretical issues in information retrieval, Oakland, California, ACM Press (1981) 30–39
22. Davis, E.: Web search engines: Retrieval. http://www.cs.nyu.edu/courses/fall02/G22.3033-008/lec5.html (2002)
23. Kobayashi, M., Takeda, K.: Information retrieval on the web. ACM Computing Surveys **32** (2000) 144–173

Automated Indexing with Restricted Random Walks on Large Document Sets

Markus Franke and Andreas Geyer-Schulz

Institut für Informationswirtschaft und -management
Universität Karlsruhe (TH), 76128 Karlsruhe, Germany
{maf,ags}@em.uni-karlsruhe.de

Abstract. We propose a method based on restricted random walk clustering as a (semi-)automated complement for the tedious, error-prone and expensive task of manual indexing in a scientific library. The first stage of our method is to cluster a set of (partially) indexed documents using restricted random walks on usage histories in order to find groups of similar documents. In the second stage, we derive possible keywords for documents without indexing information from the frequencies of keywords assigned to other documents in their respective cluster.

Due to the specific clustering algorithm, the proposed algorithm is still efficient with millions of documents and can be deployed on standard PC hardware.

1 Motivation and Introduction

As of today, the index quality of catalogues in scientific libraries is deplorable: Large parts of the inventory are not indexed and will probably never be, since manual indexing is a time-consuming and thus expensive task. For instance, in a sample of 38720 documents drawn at random from the Online Public Access Catalogue (OPAC) of the Universitätsbibliothek at Karlsruhe University (TH), 11594 (approximately 30%) had no keyword, although the library has the reputation for having the best catalogue in Germany. This problem has to be faced by most libraries today, whether they are conventional or digital.

Given the dimensions of the network catalogue of the Südwestdeutsche Bibliotheksverbund (SWB) hosted at Karlsruhe with approximately 15 million documents, a manual post-editing of the missing classifications cannot be financed. On the other hand, proper index information is a crucial condition for scientific work with the library's literature. However, for the use in our scenario, the methods sketched in section 2 that perform a classification based on the content of the library's documents cannot be applied since no digital representation exists for the major part of the documents in a conventional and even a hybrid library like the one at Karlsruhe. We therefore had to resort to the only data available, which means in this case three years' worth of usage histories of the documents, gathered from the log file of the library's web interface. These usage histories describe the course of user sessions with the interface and contain identifiers for all documents viewed.

R. Heery and L. Lyon (Eds.): ECDL 2004, LNCS 3232, pp. 232–243, 2004.

On the basis of the usage histories, a recommender system based on Ehrenberg's repeat buying theory [1] is already operative at Karlsruhe [2] that returns, for a given document, documents that are similar to this one. The recommender system is based on the assumption that, if two documents have been inspected by a user in one session with the OPAC, there is a high probability that they are complementary. The user acceptance of this recommendation service has been consistently high, details on the evaluation can be found in [3]. For scientific libraries, complementarity of documents frequently follows from the highly specialized structure of research enquiries. In addition, research enquiries usually aim at getting a survey of the state of the art in a very limited field. This property supports the assumption that cross-occurrences may serve as a good predictor of similarity. Commercial recommender systems as e.g. amazon.com's are usually hybrids which allow product managers to introduce biases into recommendations. The exact information on the frequency of bias is not available for the general public.

Departing from this idea, we perform a clustering of the documents based on usage histories so as to determine the distribution of keywords in document clusters. From these distributions we derive recommendations for further associations between documents and keywords that can be used by the library's personnel as a suggestion for indexing or even generate these associations automatically.

This paper comprises the following sections: After the introduction, section two will briefly present common approaches to automated document classification. Section three describes the basic restricted random walk clustering algorithm that enables us to cluster such large document sets efficiently while section four presents the derivation of keywords from the clusters. In section five, we will discuss the results, especially the quality of the generated keyword suggestions before concluding the paper with section six.

2   Existing Approaches

Presently the mainstream methods for automated indexing or classification of documents are based on some kind of content analysis of a digital full text or abstract. Yang [4] gives an overview and a comparison of statistical approaches of text classification. Among these, the idea of kNN indexing (k nearest neighbors) is quite close to our approach in some aspects: While we use restricted random walk clustering on usage histories in order to determine similar documents, kNN is based on a search for the k nearest neighbors in terms of a textual similarity measure. The common aspect is the actual generation of indexing information: Potential classifications are derived from the neighboring documents' classifications, possibly weighted with their respective similarity to the first document in the case of kNN. The kNN approach has been tested as a specific sample of memory based reasoning (MBR) by Creecy et al. [5] on answers to the questionnaire of the 1990 Decennial Census in the United States. However, for this specific application setting, only a relatively low precision of 60% could be achieved.

Sebastiani [6] gives a survey on variants of the currently predominant approach, namely machine learning (ML) that has replaced the knowledge engineering paradigm of the 1980s. While the latter relies on the encoding of expert knowledge in a set of rules, machine learning algorithms acquire their knowledge from a training data set and generalize the insights thus gained to the "real" data. In this context, Neural Network [7] and Support Vector Machines [8] should be mentioned.

Among the ML-based solutions, there exist some that take into account not only the textual information, but also the (graphical) context of the text and its layout [9].

However, the basic principle of all these techniques is to use intrinsic information from the documents themselves. This aspect differentiates our idea from the ones cited above in that we cannot resort to digital full texts in a hybrid library like Karlsruhe. We use external data on documents instead, namely usage histories, and derive similarity information from them. Consequently, we are not dependent on a digital representation of the documents to be classified, simple usage statistics that can be gathered from the IT systems present at most of today's libraries at little cost are sufficient for generating indices of at least comparable quality. In a digital library, it is even easier to gather the usage histories, since the whole process of information search, purchase and delivery is embedded in a digital process. Of course, nothing precludes a treatment of the digital documents with sophisticated content-analysis methods in a second stage.

3   The Cluster Method

A comprehensive survey of commonly used cluster algorithms is given in [10–12].

The library of the Karlsruhe University (TH) offers access to bibliographic data of about 15 million documents available in the SWB. Clearly conventional cluster algorithms cannot be applied to a data set of this size since these methods have a superlinear time complexity so that clustering of very large data sets becomes computationally intractable. For the single linkage clustering algorithm, this has been described exemplarily by Viegener [13]. The method that we propose in this article is based on the work of Schöll and Paschinger [14] and has been adapted for the specific environment of library usage histories [15]. It has the advantage of a linear time complexity while producing results of a high precision.

The actual clustering algorithm can be divided into two stages, the walk stage and the cluster construction stage. These are followed by the evaluation of the clusters in order to gain keyword information.

The Walk Stage

The fundamental principle of clustering with restricted random walks (RRW) as proposed in [14] is to execute a series of random walks on a set of objects given a complete distance measure between them in such a way that, with growing length of the walk, only closer and closer objects are chosen. The walk terminates when there is no object closer to the current one than the previous one.

In the context of library usage data, we change the perspective: Instead of distances, we consider similarity measures, which is the more natural approach for our application. Of course, this transformation does not imply any substantial changes; a strictly monotonous transformation suffices. As a similarity measure, we use the co-usage or cross-occurrence frequency that is defined as follows:

Definition 1. *When a user browses the detail page of a document in the library's WWW OPAC interface, this is a purchase occasion for this document. If, in the course of the session, the user browses the detail page of another document, this is a cross-occurrence between the two.*

In order to obtain a similarity measure, we extract the cross-occurrence frequencies from the WWW server's log files and store them in so-called raw baskets. A raw basket exists for every document that has been viewed at least once together with another document. It contains all its cross-occurrences with other documents as well as the respective frequencies. The similarity measure $s(i, j)$ for two documents i and j having usage histories is defined as the absolute frequency of their cross-occurrence. The self-similarity $s(i, i)$ can be defined arbitrarily, it is not used by the algorithm.

This interpretation of cross-occurrences is justified by the intuition that products – documents in this case – that are frequently bought together will in general have a high complementarity. In the context of scientific research, complementarity of information products often relates to similarity with respect to topic. This fact is used for example by market basket analysis in the marketing.

We construct a weighted similarity graph $G = (V, E, \omega)$ as input for the algorithm. Since we work on a document set, the set of vertices V is naturally given as the set of documents available in the SWB that have a usage history.

For the edges and the weights, we used the implied similarity information contained in the usage histories of the documents: E, the set of edges contains an edge between each pair of documents with a positive similarity. The weights ω_{ij} on the edges are set to the respective similarity $s(i, j)$ between the vertices they connect. Formally, the similarity graph thus constructed can be written as $G = (V, E, \omega)$: $E = \{(i, j) \in V \times V | s(i, j) > 0, i \neq j\}$, $\omega_{ij} = s(i, j)$.

We begin the walk by picking a start node i_0 from V. For this node, we define a set of possible successors as the neighbors of i_0:

$$T_0 = \{j \in V | (i_0, j) \in E\} \tag{1}$$

The second node i_1 is chosen with equal probability from T_0. We store the similarity between these nodes as the step width $s_1 = s(i_0, i_1)$. For each further step, the following restriction is added, based on the step width of the last step. This last step width is used as a minimum requirement for the similarity of the documents participating in the following steps. Generally, in the m-th step, $m \geq 1$, the node i_{m+1} is picked from the set

$$T_m = \{j \in V | (i_m, j) \in E, s(i_m, j) > s_m\} \tag{2}$$

with equal probability. The step length is updated accordingly: $s_{m+1} = s(i_m, i_{m+1})$. These iterations are repeated until T_m is empty.

The walks are very short compared to the size n of the object set, Schöll and Paschinger give an estimation of $O(\log n)$. Since this is not sufficient to cover the whole document set, several walks must be started. We followed the approach in [14] to start a walk from each node. Results from random graph theory [16] however suggest that walks comprising a total number of $\frac{1}{2}n \log n + 10\,n$ randomly chosen edges, that is $O(\frac{1}{2}n + \frac{10\,n}{\log n})$ walks, are sufficient to cover the object set with a 99.995% probability.

The Cluster Construction Stage

Clustering with restricted random walks generates a (quasi-)hierarchical clustering of the documents. Graphically, the result can be represented by a dendrogram. In order to obtain a grouping of the data, it is sufficient to choose a cutoff parameter l, that is a height at which we make a "cut" through the dendrogram. Two possible methods exist for the construction of clusters from the data of the walk stage: Component clusters and the walk context.

1. The original method developed by Schöll and Paschinger [14] is that of component clusters. From the step data of the walk, a series of graphs $G_k = (V, E_k)$ is constructed, with V the set of objects having a usage history. For every pair of objects that has formed the k-th step of any walk, E_k contains an edge between these two vertices. For each cutoff l, the union

$$H_l = \cup_{k=l}^{\infty} G_k \tag{3}$$

   is constructed. On this structure, Schöll and Paschinger define clusters as components (connected subgraphs) of H_l. Thus, at level l, two documents are in the same cluster if and only if there is a path in H_l between them.

   Unfortunately, this variant of the cluster construction stage has proven to return results that are much too large with respect to the aim of our application [15]. This is due to so-called bridge elements, i.e. documents that are frequently viewed together with documents from different domains. For example, a book on statistics might be viewed by economists and sociologists alike, thus building a "bridge" in the data that allows the restricted random walk to still change between clusters at a late stage of the walk. If this happens, the two clusters are merged by the concept of component clusters, even though they only share one single link. The effect is known in clustering literature as chaining, and while it is much weaker with restricted random walks than with single linkage clustering [13], it is still too pronounced for the results to be usable for indexing.

2. Therefore, we developed the concept of the walk context. The intuition is that if the histories of the walks are taken into account, the probability of merging clusters completely is much weaker. If a walk crosses cluster boundaries, the effect is much more limited.

   Furthermore, we introduced the step level: Since the discriminatory power of the step numbering as used in the component cluster variant is blurred

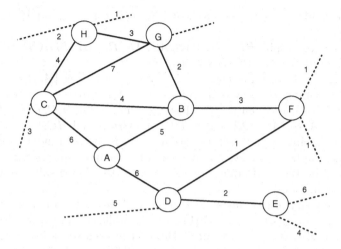

Fig. 1. An example section of a similarity graph.

when walks of strongly differing lengths are present in the data, we added a normalization and defined the level of a step as the ratio $\frac{\text{step number}}{\text{walk length}}$. With this, we stress the relative position of a step in a walk rather than its absolute value. For instance, step number two in a two-step walk is important, whereas it would be quite insignificant in a walk comprising 25 steps which is reflected in the respective levels of 1 and 0.08.

For the walk context of a document i at a given level l, we consider all walks containing i in a step with a level greater or equal to l. The walk context is composed of all documents contained in steps of these walks also at a level greater or equal to l. The cluster is the union of the walk context with i.

The walk context variant has proven to produce clusters with a considerably better precision for our specific setting than the component cluster variant [15].

For an example, consider Fig. 1 depicting a section of a similarity graph. We will construct clusters for the node A of the graph. Edges contained in a set will always be alphabetically ordered. The dotted lines depict edges to nodes that belong to the graph, but do not participate in the example.

We start our first walk at node $i_0 = A$. The set $T_0 = \{B, C, D\}$ contains the possible successors, from which we pick one at random, say $i_1 = C$. The step width is set to $s_1 = s(A, C) = 6$. The set T_1 is composed of all nodes neighboring to C and having a similarity greater than 6, so $T_1 = \{G\}$. Since only G is left as successor, we pick it and update $s_2 = s(C, G) = 7$. Now T_2 is empty, so the walk ACG ends. We assign the step levels of 0.5 and 1 to the steps AC and CG. Similarly, we might get the walks $BGHCA$, $CBAD$, DA, EDA, $FBCA$, $GHCA$ and HCA.

Using the component cluster approach, we obtain the series $G_k = (V, E_k)$ with $E_1 = \{AC, AD, BC, BF, BG, CH, DE, GH\}$ for the nodes participating in the first step and $E_2 = \{AB, AC, AD, BC, BG, CH, GH\}$, $E_3 = \{AC, AD, CH\}$, $E_4 = \{AC\}$.

This leads to graphs $H_1 = (V, \{AB, AC, AD, BC, BF, BG, CH, DE, GH\})$, $H_2 = (V, \{AB, AC, AD, BC, BG, CH, GH\})$, $H_3 = (V, \{AC, AD, CH\})$ and $H_4 = (V, \{AC\})$. A cluster at level $l = 2$ for node A is the set $\{A, B, C, D, G, H\}$.

With our approach, the walk context for A at level $l = 0.6$ is the set $\{B, C, D, H\}$, so consequently, the cluster is the set $\{A, B, C, D, H\}$ from the walks $BGHCA$, $CBAD$, DA, EDA, $FBCA$, $GHCA$ and HCA.

There exists an alternative formulation for the restricted random walk on the edges of the graph that allows an analysis of the random process with the tools of Markov chain theory. Details can be found in [15]. The results are the same for both formulations.

The complexity of the cluster generation with restricted random walks normally is in the order of $O(n \log n)$ [14], since a walk has an expected length of $O(\log n)$ and $O(n)$ walks are executed. However, for our scenario, we conjecture that the neighborhood size is bounded by a constant [15] so that the algorithm has a linear complexity which allows for an efficient execution on large data sets.

4   Indexing with RRW Clusters

Our goal is to develop a system that is able to complement the indexing information of documents in a scientific library. It should work with both libraries that are on the transition to a digital library and completely digital libraries. For our example application, we consider the hybrid library at Karlsruhe that offers a mix between conventional and digital services, for instance access to electronic journals, electronic publications or a digital document delivery service. The indexing system at this library is based on the classification scheme of the SWD Sachgruppen devised by the Deutsche Bibliothek [17]. This scheme offers four levels of classification, of which we only considered the first two due to the sparse classification mentioned in the introduction. Each of the categories has a numerical classifier like 13.5, and a textual one, the keyword, like "PHOTOGRAPHY". In total, the two-level classification scheme comprises 213 classes.

Classification methods for documents can be categorized by several criteria used in literature, for an example consider Sebastiani [6] with the categories single- vs. multilabel, category- vs. document-pivoted and hard vs. ranking.

Our system can assign multiple keywords per document, it is document-pivoted (this means that we try to find all keywords that match a given document) and gives a "hard" categorization, i.e. a binary decision whether a keyword should be assigned to a document or not. A ranking of keywords and a degree or probability of fit could be generated by our application, however, this is not supported by the indexing system of the library and thus will not be considered.

With the clusters derived from clustering the usage histories, we proceed to use their inherent similarity information for automated indexing. The general idea is that clustering based on usage histories reveals semantic similarity between documents without the need for any analysis of the documents' content.

This is quite contrary to conventional approaches that have their foundations in information retrieval and try to gain insights in possible classifications by analyzing the text itself, for example by evaluating the distribution of word frequencies. Clearly, this approach is not feasible in a library where no digital full-text information exists for many documents and it calls for very sophisticated and efficient methods when categorizing large sets of digital full texts.

Thus, analogously to ideas from recommender systems, the textual analysis is substituted by an analysis of usage histories. We conclude that, if a document j is contained in a cluster for a document i, the two have a high similarity. In a second step, when we consider the keyword frequencies assigned to j and the other documents in i's cluster, these should also fit for i due to the similarity of the documents in the cluster to i. Consequently, if the cluster for a given document contains only documents having a certain keyword, the probability is very high that the keyword also fits the first document.

As an example, consider the keywords derived from an example cluster belonging to the book "UNIX system administration handbook" by Evi Nemeth at level 0.5: Of the 14 documents in this cluster, all 14 were associated with the index 30: "Computer Science and Data Processing" (There are no more specific sub-topics under this one), one had the index 31.9: "Electrical Engineering" and another one 10.11: "Business Administration".

In an earlier work [15] we scrutinized the performance of the clustering algorithm on large data sets. General information about the quality of the RRW method can be found in [14]. In this paper, we concentrate on the quality of keyword recommendations obtained from the clusters.

We start by gathering indexing information about the documents having a usage history. Since the library does not offer direct access to their catalogue data, we query the WWW interface that returns an HTML page with embedded MAB (an electronic data exchange format devised by the Deutsche Bibliothek [18]) information. We extract the keywords as well as the document name and author and store them in a relational database.

In the next step all documents are selected from this database that do not have any keywords associated as potential candidates for automated indexing. We then generate a set of clusters at different levels l for each of these documents. Within each cluster, we query the database for the keywords assigned to the documents in the respective cluster and count their frequencies. As a result, we obtain $t_l(i)$, the total number of documents in the cluster for document i at level l that have any keyword and, for a keyword k, the number of documents in the cluster it has been assigned to that is denoted by $f_l(k, i)$.

We cannot use all keywords suggested by the algorithm since not all of them really fit. Instead, we use a minimum significance threshold for the judgement of the fit of a keyword-document combination. Three possible basic measures $\mathrm{sig}_l(k, i)$ for the significance of a keyword k with respect to a given document i and its cluster at level l are conceivable: First, the absolute frequency

$$\mathrm{sig}_l^{\mathrm{abs}}(k, i) = f_l(k, i) \; , \tag{4}$$

second, its relative frequency

$$\text{sig}_l^{\text{rel}}(k, i) = \frac{f_l(k, i)}{t_l(i)} \tag{5}$$

or an adjusted measure,

$$\text{sig}_l^{\text{adj}}(k, i) = \frac{f_l(k, i) - 1}{t_l(i)} . \tag{6}$$

The first two have a major drawback concerning the scale dependency. The absolute frequency (4) does not take into account the relative importance of the result. While the event of three documents out of four having one keyword in common is quite significant, three documents out of 30 do not imply a very good fit between keyword and document. On the other hand, if only one document with assigned keywords is found at all, the relative frequency (5) reaches a maximum while this event could still be pure coincidence without any significance.

5 Results

For the evaluation, we first generated a database of random walks based on five walks starting from every document with a raw basket (total number of documents: 562 295). Empirically, five walks suffice to give the algorithm enough stability. However, further investigations will have to aim at theoretically supporting these results. More than 40% of the documents having usage histories have no keywords which is an even higher proportion than in the random sample drawn from the OPAC (approximately 30%). This implies that in the context of our study, index information currently does not increase the probability that a document is actually used.

The evaluation was carried out in two steps: First, for determining acceptable parameters for the algorithm (cutoff level for the clusters, choice of a significance measure and a significance threshold) for a random sample of 200 documents without keywords (sample A), clusters were generated by the algorithm, the keywords were extracted and manually evaluated by one of the authors. Second, based on these parameters, we extracted the keyword recommendations for a random sample of 15 000 documents with keywords (sample B) and compared the results of the algorithm with the keywords assigned by the librarians.

For sample A, a grid of the cutoff levels for the clusters of 0.5, 0.61, 0.75 and 1 was constructed (0.61 was the optimal level found in [15]). For these levels, we extracted the possible keywords as described in section 4 as well as their frequencies. These keywords were then screened by one of the authors – without any clue as to the ranking the algorithm gave those words so that a bias could be avoided – together with the bibliographic data of the corresponding book and had to be classified into the categories "fit" and "no fit". (While evaluation by one of the authors is always problematic, a comparison of the results of sample A with sample B shows that the results of both samples are in line.) In total, for the level of 0.5 a total of 1160 keywords proposals for the 200 documents was found by the system, out of which 458 were found to be appropriate for the document in question and 702 were not. The results of the other levels were

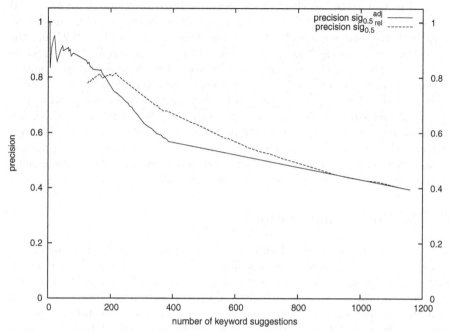

Fig. 2. Keyword suggestion precisions for $\text{sig}_{0.5}^{\text{rel}}$ and $\text{sig}_{0.5}^{\text{adj}}$ (interpolated).

either too small or of lower quality than those at level 0.5. Consequently, we set the cutoff level for the second stage to 0.5.

The choice of the significance measure $\text{sig}_l \in \{\text{sig}_l^{\text{abs}}, \text{sig}_l^{\text{rel}}, \text{sig}_l^{\text{adj}}\}$ proposed in equations (4) – (6) and the significance threshold is based on a complete grid search over all levels. With regard to precision, $\text{sig}_l^{\text{adj}}$ dominates $\text{sig}_l^{\text{rel}}$. Because of its different domain, $\text{sig}_l^{\text{abs}}$ is incomparable. However, when we consider the number of suggested keywords at an acceptable precision level, Fig. 2 shows no dominant significance measure. $\text{sig}_l^{\text{abs}}$ is ruled out and not drawn in Fig. 2 because except for around 30 (not enough keyword suggestions) and above 390 keyword suggestions (equals $\text{sig}_l^{\text{adj}}$), it is inferior in precision. Depending on the number of keyword suggestions, a choice must be made between $\text{sig}_l^{\text{rel}}$ and $\text{sig}_l^{\text{adj}}$.

We consider a precision of about 80% with at least 170 keyword suggestions as an acceptable compromise. Table 1 shows the results for the relevant parameters. Based on this, we chose $\text{sig}_{0.5}^{\text{adj}}$ at a significance threshold of 0.27 for the evaluation of sample B. For sample A this means that 114 documents out of 200 would have received one or more keyword assignments.

Table 1. Error table for more than 170 suggestions at level 0.5.

measure	found ok	found not ok	precision	significance threshold
$\text{sig}_l^{\text{abs}}$	138	74	0.6509	3
$\text{sig}_l^{\text{rel}}$	137	35	0.7965	0.69
$\text{sig}_l^{\text{adj}}$	145	36	0.8011	0.27

In a second stage, we checked the keyword recommendations for sample B – of course without using the keywords manually assigned to the documents by librarians. We used the cutoff level 0.5, the significance threshold 0.27 and the significance measure sig_l^{adj} as suggested by the analysis of sample A. The recommendations the algorithm returned were compared to the indexing information of these documents. We could show that the precision is slightly smaller (77.0%) when only direct hits (a document has the keyword 9.2 and the algorithm proposes 9.2) are counted. In that case, a recall of 66.8% could be reached. We attribute the slightly higher precision of sample A (0.8011, as evaluated by one of the authors) to higher small sample variance and a variance in the evaluations done by different librarians. In addition to this automated test, the manual evaluation of a larger sample by librarians is planned.

6   Conclusion and Outlook

In this paper, we proposed a (semi-)automated complement for the manual indexing of large document sets in a library. The advantage of the method is that – even though it uses data that are easier obtainable in a digital library – its principal functioning is independent of the representation of the documents. Furthermore, it does not require costly analyses of document content, but uses relatively light-weight usage data, which enables our method to handle large document sets in the order of some million documents with modest hardware requirements, for example a standard PC with a 1.5 GHz CPU and 1 GB RAM.

Even for a document collection without keywords clusters can be generated, assigned keywords, and used to reduce the amount of manual indexing necessary. Furthermore, repeated application of the algorithm – although not studied in detail – will help in completing the covering of the whole set of unclassified documents, when interleaved with manual acceptance of certain keywords.

Further research is still needed for some aspects of the underlying clustering algorithm that is the key component in the good performance of the overall method. For instance, questions of convergence and stability of the results need some further considerations. Equally, many possibilities for fine-tuning the algorithm exist that have not yet been investigated. A more thorough evaluation of the quality of the results of this algorithm by reference librarians needs to be done.

As for the aspect of keyword assignment, the use of semantic information in the keywords could yield further improvements of the results: If, for example, a book has high recommendations for the classifications 4.1 (philosophy, general subjects) and 4.4 (metaphysics), these two classifications support each other.

Acknowledgement

We gratefully acknowledge the funding of the project "Scientific Libraries in Information Markets" by the Deutsche Forschungsgemeinschaft within the scope of the research initiative "V^3D^2".

References

1. Ehrenberg, A.S.: Repeat-Buying: Facts, Theory and Applications. 2 edn. Charles Griffin & Company Ltd, London (1988)
2. Geyer-Schulz, A., Neumann, A., Thede, A.: Others also use: a robust recommender system for scientific libraries. In Koch, T., Solvberg, I.T., eds.: Research and Advanced Technology for Digital Libraries : ECDL 2003. Volume 2769 of LNCS., Berlin, Springer (2003) 113–125
3. Geyer-Schulz, A., Neumann, A., Thede, A.: An architecture for behavior-based library recommender systems – integration and first experiences. Information Technology and Libraries **22** (2003)
4. Yang, Y.: An evaluation of statistical approaches to text categorization. Information Retrieval **1** (1999) 69–90
5. Creecy, R.H., Masand, B.M., Smith, S.J., Waltz, D.L.: Trading mips and memory for knowledge engineering. Communications of the ACM **35** (1992) 48–64
6. Sebastiani, F.: Machine learning in automated text categorization. ACM Computing Surveys **34** (2002) 1–47
7. Chung, Y.M., Pottenger, W.M., Schatz, B.R.: Automatic subject indexing using an associative neural network. In: Proceedings of the 3rd ACM International Conference on Digital Libraries, ACM Press (1998) 59–68
8. Lauser, B., Hotho, A.: Automatic multi-label subject indexing in a multilingual environment. In Koch, T., Solvberg, I.T., eds.: Research and Advanced Technology for Digital Libraries : Proceedings of the ECDL 2003, Trondheim, Norway, August 2003. Volume 2769 of LNCS., Berlin, Springer (2003) 140–151
9. Semeraro, G., Ferilli, S., Fanizzi, N., Esposito, F.: Document classification and interpretation through the inference of logic-based models. In P. Constantopoulos, I.S., ed.: Proceedings of the ECDL 2001. Volume 2163 of LNCS., Darmstadt, Springer Verlag, Berlin (2001) 59–70
10. Bock, H.: Automatische Klassifikation. Vandenhoeck&Ruprecht, Göttingen (1974)
11. Duda, R.O., Hart, P.E., Stork, D.G.: Pattern Classification. 2 edn. Wiley-Interscience, New York (2001)
12. Hartigan, J.A.: Clustering Algorithms. John Wiley and Sons, New York (1975)
13. Viegener, J.: Inkrementelle, domänenunabhängige Thesauruserstellung in dokumentbasierten Informationssystemen durch Kombination von Konstruktionsverfahren. 1 edn. infix, Sankt Augustin (1997)
14. Schöll, J., Paschinger, E.: Cluster Analysis with Restricted Random Walks. In Jajuga, K., Sokolowski, A., Bock, H.H., eds.: Classification, Clustering, and Data Analysis, Heidelberg, Springer-Verlag (2002) 113–120
15. Franke, M.: Clustering of very large document sets using random walks. Master's thesis, Universität Karlsruhe (TH), Karlsruhe (2003)
16. Erdös, P., Renyi, A.: On random graphs I. Publ. Mathematicae **6** (1957) 290–297
17. Kunz, M., et al.: SWD Sachgruppen. Technical report, Deutsche Bibliothek (2003)
18. Die Deutsche Bibliothek: MAB2 : Maschinelles Austauschformat für Bibliotheken. Dt. Bibliothek, Leipzig (1999)

Annotations in Digital Libraries
and Collaboratories – Facets, Models and Usage

Maristella Agosti[1], Nicola Ferro[1], Ingo Frommholz[2], and Ulrich Thiel[2]

[1] Department of Information Engineering, University of Padua, Italy
{maristella.agosti,nicola.ferro}@unipd.it
[2] Fraunhofer IPSI, Darmstadt, Germany
{frommholz,thiel}@ipsi.fraunhofer.de

Abstract. This paper presents the results of our study regarding the different facets and ways of using annotations in both digital libraries and collaboratories. This study represents an innovative attempt at gathering methodological tools and synergies from both fields in order to effectively define a comprehensive model for annotations. Thus we propose a conceptual model for annotations in order to develop an annotation service that can be plugged into digital libraries and collaboratories. Finally, starting from our model, we introduce a search strategy for exploiting annotations in order to search and retrieve relevant documents for a user query.

1 Introduction

The research field regarding the design and development of software systems, that are able to provide annotation capabilities on the content that they manage, e.g. digital libraries and collaboratories, is very active and productive. On the other hand the problem of how to incorporate annotations is usually faced separately in the field of digital libraries and collaboratories without exploiting the synergies that can be common to both fields. Our research work represents a first effort to face these issues together in both fields. This way we can benefit by the methodological tools coming from both fields in order to define a comprehensive model for annotations and to design an annotation service that can be seamlessly plugged into different digital libraries and collaboratories.

The paper is organised as follows: the remainder of this section presents digital libraries and collaboratories and the beneficial usage of annotations in those fields. Section 2 discusses different angles about annotations, Section 3 introduces our conceptual model for annotations and some access and retrieval strategies that exploit annotations; finally, Section 4 draws some conclusions and presents the future work.

1.1 Digital Libraries and Collaboratories

Digital libraries are not only the digital versions of traditional libraries, but offer means going beyond mere presentation of the content stored in a digital repository. Two definitions of digital libraries, coming from two different directions

R. Heery and L. Lyon (Eds.): ECDL 2004, LNCS 3232, pp. 244–255, 2004.

and thus focusing on different aspects, point to this fact. The more computer science oriented view is expressed in the introduction to the first issue of the *International Journal on Digital Libraries* (cited in [8]):

> Digital Libraries are concerned with the creation and management of information resources, the movement of information across global networks and the effective use of this information by a wide range of users.

Librarians have a different definition of Digital Libraries:

> Digital Libraries are organisations that provide the resources, including the specialised stuff, to select, structure, offer intellectual access to, interpret, distribute, preserve the integrity of, and ensure the persistence over time of collections of digital works so that they are readily and economically available for use by a defined community or set of communities. (Digital Library Federation (DLF), 1998, cited in [8])

Both these definitions highlight some distinguishing features of digital libraries: firstly the central point of both definitions is that information resources should be *accessed* and *used*; then they further couple this concept with the one of *community of users*. In this way a digital library is jointly characterised by its collection of information resources and by the community of users for whom the collection is *managed* and made available. Other aspects addressed by the above definitions are the *creation* and *interpretation* of resources. The two definitions share the common view that information resources have to be accessed with the last point addressed in the definition of a *collaboratory* formulated by William Wulf, who sees such a collaboratory as

> ...center without walls, in which nation's researchers can perform their research without regard to geographical location – interacting with colleagues, accessing instrumentation, sharing data and computation resource, and accessing information in digital libraries. [14]

Collaboratories focus on facilitating scientific *interaction* within a team. Besides this, they should support the *sharing* of data and resources. Figure 1 summarises the aspects of digital libraries and collaboratories. As we will discuss in the following, all these aspects are particularly relevant for annotations and they can greatly benefit from having annotations available as an additional tool.

1.2 Annotations Within Digital Libraries

Annotations can be exploited in order to realise the distinguishing features of digital libraries highlighted above. The *creation* of new information resources is supported by annotations in two ways. First, when users add annotations to existing information resources, these are new information resources themselves. Second, annotations can also assist in the creation of new information resources. Through annotations, new ideas and concepts can be discussed and the results of such a discussion can then be integrated into the newly created

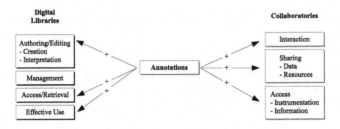

Fig. 1. Digital Libraries, Collaboratories and Annotations

object. Annotations might increase and expand the information resources managed by the digital library. In this way, they may provide *interpretations* of information resources. User communities benefit from such interpretations in that they help understanding the annotated resource and contain additional information about it. In the Humanities, for instance, interpretation is one of the basic tasks scholars perform. Systems like COLLATE or IPSA support this task through annotations [1, 7]. Annotations support user communities in *accessing* the information resources provided by the digital library in a personalised and customisable way: indeed users can create annotations that link different documents, enabling alternative paths for browsing digital contents and thus structuring them in alternative ways, like virtual books [19]. Different layers of annotations can coexist in the same document: a private layer of annotations accessible only by the annotations author himself, a collective layer of annotations, shared by a team of people, and finally a public layer of annotations, accessible to all the users of the digital library; in this way user communities can benefit from different views of the information resources managed by the digital library [16, 15]. Annotations can contain interpretations, reviews and additional information about the resources they belong to. They reflect what others say about a resource, which establishes an interesting context exploitable for information retrieval [7]. Furthermore the access and retrieval of information resources can be aided by means of automatic annotations. Employing topic detection techniques, a document can be segmented into topics of desired granularity and automatic annotations represent a summary of these topics. Then, exploiting automatic hypertext construction techniques [3], automatic annotations can be linked to the original document. Finally, the content of annotations can support the *effective use* of the digital resources. Automatic annotations, interpretations, alternative paths, and all other information contained in annotations help the user in approaching a document.

1.3   Annotations Within Collaboratories

As we pointed out above, the main characteristics of collaboratories are interaction, sharing and access. Annotations can be beneficial for all of them. Indeed, many systems use annotations to establish collaboration. Wilensky sees annotations as an example for spontaneous collaboration [23]. *Interaction* within a community can be supported by means of shared or public annotations. In COL-LATE, annotations are used to model a scientific discourse between film scientists. The system supports *strong collaboration* through nested annotations; users can directly react to other users' contributions and do not have to rely on traditional means like e-mail or telephone [7]. Annotations are an important way to *share* one's results with others. Shared or public annotations are visible to more persons than the author who created them. Systems supporting data sharing through annotations are, among others, those reported in [1, 7, 9, 19]. Sharing data triggers at least *weak collaboration* - users can view others' results, without necessarily directly reacting to them. The *access* aspect in collaboratories can be supported by annotations the same way as discussed in the last subsection.

2   Annotations

Since annotations intrinsically entail an active involvement of the users with information resources, they naturally bring digital libraries and collaboratories closer, so that it is advisable to investigate how to exploit methods and techniques coming from both fields in order to effectively employ annotations. Over the past years a lot of research work regarding annotations has been done [18, 20], which led to different viewpoints about what an annotation is. The following sections describe the different angles about annotations that we consider.

2.1   Annotations as Metadata

Annotations are considered as additional data about an existing content, that is annotations are metadata [18]. This reflects a *data specific* view on annotations. From a syntactic point of view one of the main characteristics of metadata is that it is connected to the object it refers to; annotations have a similar connection to what they are annotating. This way, they are indeed data about data.

The World Wide Web Consortium (W3C) considers annotations as metadata and interprets them as the first step in creating an infrastructure that will handle and associate metadata with content towards the Semantic Web [11]; examples are the Annotea Project[1] and the Extensible MultiModal Annotation (EMMA)[2] markup language. Also systems that employ annotations as an extension of bookmarks can fall within this definition. Indeed the additional data provided by annotations are exploited to describe, organise, categorise and search the bookmarks [13]. As a further example, MPEG-7, named "Multimedia Content Description Interface" and developed by the International Organization for Standardization (ISO)[3], is a standard for describing the multimedia content data to be processed by a device or a computer code. Finally also automatic annotations can be considered metadata, since they extract summary sentences or significant phrases from the document they annotate, thus providing additional data for highlighting the key-points of the document.

---

[1] http://www.w3.org/2001/Annotea/

[2] http://www.w3.org/TR/2003/WD-emma-20031218/

[3] http://www.iso.ch/iso/en/prods-services/popstds/mpeg.html

2.2   Annotations as Content

Another view on annotations is seeing them as content, reflecting an *information specific view*. Annotations can be regarded as content in two ways: they can be content about content and they can be considered as additional content [18]. Both ways do not mutually exclude each other: interpretations, for example, are content about content, but they might also contain additional content. Reviews and judgements, as another example, are basically content about content.

Annotations being additional content augment existing content and allow the creation of new relationships among existing contents, by means of links that connect annotations together and with existing content. In this sense we can consider that existing content and annotations constitute a hypertext, according to the definition of hypertext provided in [5]. For example, [17] considers annotations as a natural way of enhancing hypertexts by actively engaging users with existing content in a digital library [16].

Normally digital libraries do not have a hypertext connecting documents with each other; thus annotations can represent a means for associating an hypertext to a digital library. In this way it is then possible to exploit the associated hypertext in order to enjoy alternative browsing paths and to perform advanced document searches, employing hypertext information retrieval techniques [4].

2.3   Annotations as Dialogue Acts

Another viewpoint on annotations, regarding them as dialogue acts, covers a *communication specific view*. This view is concerned with the question of the *pragmatics* conveyed in annotations, i.e. the intention behind a user's statement. Gaining information about pragmatics is an important means to distinguish between the different kinds of content we have discussed in the last subsection. We may find out about the semantics of utterances in annotations, but this does not mean that we can distinguish whether we can see the annotation as content about content or an extension of existing content, or even something completely different. This distinction might be important when applying appropriate retrieval functions, as we will see in Section 3.3.

Each annotation implicitly consists of certain *communicative acts*, which, according to Searle can be classified as (among others) *assertives*, *directives* (e.g., requests), and *commissives* (e.g., promises) [22]. Communicative acts both allow for communication on the content and on the meta level. On the content level, assertives connected with a certain *discourse structure relation* are the units with which a coherent interpretation of the material can be created [6]. On the other hand, directives and commissives can trigger further collaborative acts on the meta level. Directives can be used to attempt to get some other person to do something; an example would be if a user asks the author of a comment if he could further elaborate on it. The author, in turn, can answer the request with a promise to provide the needed information (and actually provide it later on). Certain communicative acts can thus enable strong collaboration, and they can be realised as annotations.

3   Comprehensive Model of Annotations

We aim to design and develop a comprehensive model for annotations able to address all the previously described facets and to define an appropriate strategy for exploiting annotations in searching and retrieving documents or other annotations.

3.1   Design Choices

Considering the complexity of the annotation and the need for a proper conceptual model of annotation, as explained above, we have decided to make the effort of modelling the annotation using a conceptual modelling tool of general use as the Entity-Relationship (ER) model is. As introduced in our previous work [2], in order to capture the complex semantics of the annotation, which emerged also from the discussion of Section 2, we can distinguish between the meaning and sign of annotations. The *meaning of annotation* is a main aspect concerning the concept of annotation, which identifies conceptual differences within the semantics of the annotation. For example the different angles about annotations introduced in Section 2 can be considered as different meanings of annotation. Furthermore, within a given angle, we can identify different meanings of annotation; for example, within the "annotation as content" viewpoint we can point out three different meanings of annotation: comprehension and study, interpretation and divulgation, and revision and cooperation. The *sign of annotation* is a way of representing a meaning of annotation. For example we can identify a textual or a graphic sign of annotation. These basic signs can be combined together in order to create a more complex sign of annotation, capable to express complex meanings of annotation, such as those explained above. Thus an annotation is expressed by one or more signs of annotation, that in turn are characterised by one or more meanings of annotation, defining the overall semantics of the annotation.

Before discussing the proposed conceptual schema, our reference architecture introduced in [2] has to be borne in mind: we aim to design and develop an annotation service that can be easily plugged into different digital libraries or collaboratories, allowing these systems to seamlessly extend their functionalities. As an important consequence of this architectural choice, we assume that *the annotation service knows everything about annotations but it has no knowledge about documents managed by the system it is plugged into*. This is due to the fact that the annotation service directly manages annotations while documents and information pertaining to them are provided by the system the annotation service is plugged into. Thus the annotation service deals with handles to document, that allow it to connect annotations to documents, without the need to actually manage them.

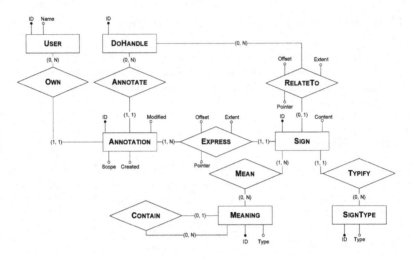

Fig. 2. Entity-Relationship schema for modelling annotations

3.2 Annotation Conceptual Schema

The proposed conceptual schema is shown in Figure 2. It is centred around two main issues: how to model annotations and how to connect them to information resources. The next sections describe these two issues in detail.

How to Model Annotations. The ANNOTATION entity represents the abstraction of the annotation, i.e. it expresses the existence of an object capable of annotating another object, without further specifying its characteristic. This is the pivot entity, which provides the basis for modelling annotations. The ANNOTATION entity owns the following attributes: ID is a unique identifier for the annotation, e.g. an Uniform Resource Identifier (URI); Created and Modified represent, respectively, the creation date and the last modified date of the annotation; and Scope specifies if the annotation is private, shared by a team or public.

The discussion carried out in the previous sections showed that the ANNOTATION entity alone is not sufficient for covering the semantics of the general concept of annotation, so it needs to be partnered with two other entities MEANING and SIGN, representing respectively the meaning of annotation and the sign of annotation. The MEANING entity is characterised by a unique identifier, ID, and by a Type, which describes the meaning of annotations. On the MEANING entity there is a recursive relationship, CONTAIN, that expresses the existence of broader meanings and narrower meanings; thus the meanings of annotation can be organised in a simple hierarchy and some navigation facilities within this hierarchy can provided to the user. The CONTAIN relationship expresses the fact that a meaning may be contained only in one other meaning and that it may contain one or more other meanings. The SIGN entity owns an unique identifier, ID, and a Content attribute, which represent the actual content of the sign of annotation, e.g. a piece of text. The SIGNTYPE entity describes the kind of a sign of annotation, e.g. a textual sign or a graphic sign, and makes it possible to correctly interpret the Content attribute of a SIGN. The SIGNTYPE entity is connected to the SIGN entity by means of the TYPIFY relationship, which expresses the fact that a SIGN must have exactly one SIGNTYPE, while a SIGNTYPE may specify one or more SIGN entities.

Two relationships, EXPRESS and MEAN, allow the three entities ANNOTATION, MEANING and SIGN to cooperate together for defining the semantics and the materialisation of an annotation. The EXPRESS relationship denotes that an ANNOTATION entity have to be expressed at least by one SIGN entity, and eventually more, and that a given SIGN entity has to be employed in order to express one and only one ANNOTATION entity. The attributes of EXPRESS allow us to physically identify which part of the information resource has to be annotated. In particular the Pointer attribute identifies a portion of a digital object, e.g. it could be an XPath expression in case of an eXtensible Markup Language (XML) document; the Offset attribute selects a starting offset with respect to the portion identified by Pointer, e.g. the initial character within an XML element; finally the Extent attribute specifies the size of the sign of annotation, e.g. the number of characters that are annotated within the portion identified by Pointer starting from Offset.

The MEAN relationship expresses the fact that a SIGN entity has to be related at least to one MEANING entity, and eventually more, and that a MEANING entity may characterise one or more SIGN entities.

How to Connect Annotations to Information Resources. As explained in the previous section, the ANNOTATION entity represents the abstraction of an object capable of annotating another object. In order to connect annotations to information resources we need also an entity that represents the abstraction of an object that can be annotated; this entity is called DOHANDLE, which represents a digital object by means of an handle to it. Thus the cornerstones for connecting annotations to information resources are the ANNOTATION and DOHANDLE entities which represents the fact that there are two kinds of related objects: digital objects that can be annotated and annotations that annotate those digital objects.

The relationship between annotations and annotated digital objects is represented by the ANNOTATE relationship, which links an ANNOTATION entity to the DOHANDLE entity it annotates. This relationship expresses the fact that an annotation must annotate one and only one digital object and that a digital object may be annotated by one or more annotations. Once we have annotated a digital object, the annotation itself can be considered as a digital object eligible to be annotated. Thus the conceptual schema has the additional constraint that, after that the annotation has been created, also an occurrence of the DOHANDLE entity corresponding to the annotation have to be added, in order to allow the newly created annotation to be annotated too. Users can therefore create not only sets of annotations concerning a digital object, but also threads of annotations – i.e. annotations in reply one to another – which are the basis for actively engaging users with the system and for enabling collaboration.

The RELATETO relationship is used for the purpose of relating to other digital object and it associates a sign of an annotation with the digital object it refers to. This relationship holds between DOHANDLE and SIGN and not between DOHANDLE and ANNOTATION, because the ANNOTATION, perceived as abstraction, does not have to be related to a digital object, since its main purpose is to contribute to modelling the fact that there exist annotating objects and annotated object. On the contrary, the sign of annotation takes charge of relating to a digital object and the explanation of this relation is given by the meanings of annotation associated with that sign. The RELATETO relationship allows a SIGN entity to refer or not to a digital object, while a digital object may be referred to by one or more signs of annotation. The attributes of RELATETO have the same meaning of the attributes of EXPRESS. On the whole the EXPRESS relationship specifies the origin of the link and the RELATETO relationship identifies the destination of the link.

Finally the USER entity represents a user, granted by the system. The OWN relationship relates an annotation with its author; a user may create one or more annotations, while an annotation must belong to one and only one user.

The proposed conceptual schema provides us a great flexibility, because we can express the different aspects of an annotation, couple them together and it does not constrain us to fixed types of annotations for fixed tasks. So our proposal represents an enhancement and a generalisation with respect to [11, 21]; in fact being a conceptual schema, our model can be easily mapped to different models, such as a relational schema, a Resource Description Framework (RDF) schema or a XML schema; this way it provides us great flexibility with respect to different architectural choices.

3.3   Search and Retrieval Issues

Although annotations are quite a useful and common concept in digital libraries and collaboratories, there do not exist many retrieval approaches taking annotations into account. As one of the few examples, Golovchinsky et al. use annotations to construct full-text queries out of them [10]. What is missing so far are retrieval functions which are potentially able to take the different facets of annotations, which constitute a valuable context for document retrieval, into account.

As we have seen in Section 2.2, annotations and the referenced resources constitute a hypertext. This makes hypertext information retrieval approaches [4] potential candidates to be adapted to annotation-based retrieval. On the other hand, annotations might also be content about content such as reviews containing judgements about documents and thus cannot be seen as an extention of the document content. Nevertheless, such annotations contain information which are appropriate to take relevance criteria other than just topicality into account. Consider an example of a digital library where students could give judgements about documents, like "this book is a very good introduction", by annotating them. Another student might search for books which introduce her to the field of digital libraries. In this scenario we can see that the actual information need can be mapped onto two queries: One made to the set of documents for topicality (e.g., q_{doc} = "digital libraries"), and one made to the set of annotations (e.g., q_{ann} = "good introduction"). This results into a composed query $q = (q_{doc}, q_{ann})$. When seeing retrieval as uncertain inference, the retrieval weight of a document d w.r.t the query q is determined by the probability that d implies q. A retrieval function calculating $P(d \rightarrow q)$ considering the annotation context of d could roughly be outlined as, for example,

$$P(d \rightarrow q) = (P_{doc}(d \rightarrow q_{doc}) + P_{ann}(d \rightarrow q_{ann}) - \Theta) \cdot (1 - P_{ann}(d \nrightarrow q_{ann}))$$

$\Theta = P_{doc}(d \rightarrow q_{doc}) \cdot P_{ann}(d \rightarrow q_{ann})$ reflects the possible jointness of events. The value for P_{doc} is determined by the weight of d w.r.t. q_{doc} whereas the computation of P_{ann} is based on the annotations made on d. Negative annotations made on the document increase the probability $P_{ann}(d \nrightarrow q_{ann})$ that the document does not imply the query and thus decrease $P(d \rightarrow q)$. The calculation of P_{ann} might need an in-depth analysis of the annotation thread as discussed in [7][4]. When seeing annotations as additional content rather than judgements, we do not need a composed query; in this case, it is $q = q_{doc} = q_{ann}$.

4   Conclusions

In this paper we have discussed the several ways in which digital libraries and collaboratories can benefit from annotations. We have shown different viewpoints on annotations, which can be seen as metadata, content, and dialogue acts. These realise a data, information and communication specific view on annotations. All our thoughts led to the presentation of annotation models covering a conceptual model and search and retrieval issues.

The proposed conceptual model for annotations is capable to represent the different viewpoints concerning annotations and enables the design and development of advanced retrieval functions. Furthermore it can be easily mapped to different models, such as a relational schema, an RDF schema or an XML schema, and it is suitable for developing an annotation service that can be seamlessly plugged into different digital libraries and collaboratories. Our considerations will be borne in mind for the specification and realisation of an annotation service within the BRICKS project[5] which aims at establishing the organisational and technological foundations of a Digital Library at the level of a European Digital Memory.

With respect to annotations supporting access and retrieval in both digital libraries and collaboratories we have shown that there do not exist many retrieval models for annotation-based document retrieval. Our discussion of this resulted in an outline of a potential retrieval function based on the view of retrieval as uncertain inference. This function incorporates positive and negative evidence

---

[4] The proposed retrieval function can be seen as a generalisation of the one presented in [7].

[5] http://www.bricksfactory.org

found both in the document content and in the according annotation thread. By applying such a retrieval function, relevance criteria other than topicality can be considered to satisfy users' information needs. Future research will discuss this issue more thoroughly and introduce suitable retrieval functions more precisely.

Acknowledgements

M. Agosti and N. Ferro were partially funded by ECD (Enhanced Contents Delivery), a joined program between the Italian National Research Council (CNR) and the Ministry of Education (MIUR), under the law 449/97-99. I. Frommholz and U. Thiel were partly funded by the 6th Framework IP BRICKS (IST-2002-2.3.1.12).

References

1. M. Agosti, L. Benfante, and N. Orio. IPSA: A Digital Archive of Herbals to Support Scientific Research. In T. M. T. Sembok, H. B. Zaman, H. Chen, S. R. Urs, and S. H. Myaeng, editors, *Proc. 6th Int. Conf. on Asian Digital Libraries. Digital Libraries – Digital Libraries: Technology and Management of Indigenous Knowledge (ICADL 2003)*, pages 253–264. LNCS 2911, Springer, Heidelberg, Germany, 2003.
2. M. Agosti and N. Ferro. Annotations: Enriching a Digital Library. In Koch and Sølvberg [12], pages 88–100.
3. M. Agosti and M. Melucci. Information Retrieval Techniques for the Automatic Construction of Hypertext. In A. Kent and C.M. Hall, editors, *Encyclopedia of Library and Information Science*, volume 66, pages 139–172. Marcel Dekker, New York, USA, 2000.
4. M. Agosti and A. Smeaton, editors. *Information Retrieval and Hypertext*. Kluwer Academic Publishers, Norwell (MA), USA, 1996.
5. M. Agosti. An Overview of Hypertext. In Agosti and Smeaton [4], pages 27–47.
6. H. Brocks, A. Stein, U. Thiel, I. Frommholz, and A. Dirsch-Weigand. How to incorporate collaborative discourse in cultural digital libraries. In *Proc. of the ECAI 2002 Workshop on Semantic Authoring, Annotation & Knowledge Markup (SAAKM02)*, Lyon, France, July 2002.
7. I. Frommholz, H. Brocks, U. Thiel, E. Neuhold, L. Iannone, G. Semeraro, M. Berardi, and M. Ceci. Document-centered collaboration for scholars in the humanities - the COLLATE system. In Koch and Sølvberg [12], pages 434–445.
8. N. Fuhr, P. Hansen, M. Mabe, A. Micsik, and I. Sølvberg. Digital libraries: A generic classification and evaluation scheme. In *Proc. of the 5th European Conf. on Research and Advanced Technology for Digital Libraries (ECDL2001)*, pages 187–199, Heidelberg et al., 2001. Springer.
9. M. Gertz, K.-U. Sattler, F. Gorin, M. Hogarth, and J. Stone. Annotating scientific images: A concept-based approach. In *Proc. of the 14th Int. Conf. on Scientific and Statistical Database Management*, pages 59–68. IEEE Computer Society, 2002.
10. G. Golovchinsky, M. N. Price, and B. N. Schilit. From reading to retrieval: Freeform ink annotations as queries. In F. Gey, M. Hearst, and R. Tong, editors, *Proc. of the 22nd Annual Int. ACM SIGIR Conf. on Research and Development in Information Retrieval*, pages 19–25, New York, 1999. ACM Press.

11. J. Kahan and M.-R. Koivunen. Annotea: an open RDF infrastructure for shared Web annotations. In V. Y. Shen, N. Saito, M. R. Lyu, and M. E. Zurko, editors, *Proc. 10th Int. Conf. on World Wide Web (WWW 2001)*, pages 623–632. ACM Press, New York, USA, 2001.

12. T. Koch and I. T. Sølvberg, editors. *Proc. 7th European Conf. on Research and Advanced Technology for Digital Libraries (ECDL 2003)*. LNCS 2769, Springer, Heidelberg, Germany, 2003.

13. M.-R. Koivunen and E. Swick, R. Prud'hommeaux. Annotea Shared Bookmarks. http://www.w3.org/2001/Annotea/Papers/KCAP03/annoteabm.html, last visited 2004, March 18.

14. R.T. Kouzes, J.D. Myers, and W.A. Wulf. Collaboratories: Doing science on the Internet. *IEEE Computer*, 29(8), 1996.

15. C. C. Marshall and A. J. B. Brush. From Personal to Shared Annotations. In L. Terveen and D. Wixon, editors, *Proc. Conf. on Human Factors and Computing Systems (CHI 2002) – Extended Abstracts*, pages 812–813. ACM Press, New York, USA, 2002.

16. C. C. Marshall. Annotation: from Paper Books to the Digital Library. In R. B. Allen and E. Rasmussen, editors, *Proc. 2nd ACM Int. Conf. on Digital Libraries (DL 1997)*, pages 233–240. ACM Press, New York, USA, 1997.

17. C. C. Marshall. Toward an Ecology of Hypertext Annotation. In R. Akscyn, editor, *Proc. 9th ACM Conf. on Hypertext and Hypermedia (HT 1998): links, objects, time and space-structure in hypermedia systems*, pages 40–49. ACM Press, New York, USA, 1998.

18. K. Nagao. *Digital Content Annotation and Transcoding*. Artech House, Norwood (MA), USA, 2003.

19. D. M. Nichols, D. Pemberton, S. Dalhoumi, O. Larouk, C. Belisle, and M. B. Twindale. DEBORA: Developing an interface to support collaboration in a digital library. In J.L. Borbinha and T. Baker, editors, *Proc. of the 4th European Conf. on Research and Advanced Technology for Digital Libraries (ECDL2000)*, pages 239–248. Springer: Berlin, 2000.

20. I. A. Ovsiannikov, M. A. Arbib, and T. H. McNeill. Annotation technology. *Int. J. Hum.-Comput. Stud.*, 50(4):329–362, 1999.

21. T. Sannomiya, T. Amagasa, M. Yoshikawa, and S. Uemura. A framework for sharing personal annotations on web resources using XML. In M. E. Orlowska and M. Yoshikawa, editors, *Proc. Workshop on Information Technology for Virtual Enterprises*, pages 40–48. IEEE Computer Society Press, 2001.

22. J.R. Searle. A taxonomy of illocutionary acts. In J.R. Searle, editor, *Expression and Meaning. Studies in the Theory of Speech Acts*, pages 1–29. Cambridge University Press, Cambridge, 1979.

23. R. Wilensky. Digital library resources as a basis for collaborative work. *J. Am. Soc. Inf. Sci.*, 51(3):228–245, 2000.

P-News: Deeply Personalized News Dissemination for MPEG-7 Based Digital Libraries

Qiuyue Wang[1], Wolf-Tilo Balke[2], Werner Kießling[1], and Alfons Huhn[1]

[1] Institut für Informatik, Universität Augsburg,
89165 Augsburg, Germany
{wang,kiessling,huhn}@informatik.uni-augsburg.de
[2] Computer Science Department, University of California
Berkeley, CA 94720, USA
balke@eecs.berkeley.edu

Abstract. Advanced personalization techniques are required to cope with novel challenges posed by attribute-rich MPEG-7 based digital libraries. At the heart of our deeply personalized news dissemination system P-News is one extensible preference model that serves all purposes, preventing impedance mismatches between the various stages: User modeling by structured preference patterns, automatic query expansion including ontologies, preference query evaluation by Preference XPath including nested preferences on categorical data, quality assessment of query results, personalized notification and news syndication.

1 Introduction

The amount of information available in digital libraries via the Internet is overwhelming and the task of extracting all valuable knowledge increasingly time-consuming. Especially in areas with short innovation cycles like IT not only new documents arrive in large bulks every day, but also what is considered to be relevant will strongly differ among various user groups like business-oriented consultants, technology-oriented developers or highly specialized researchers. Users find themselves confronted with a well-known dilemma: spending too much time on going through new, but probably irrelevant information will cost valuable research or working time, whereas spending less time may result in missing some vital information. Many users of digital libraries or subscribers of news services have suffered the troublesome problem of getting 'properly' notified about latest publications. Definitively this should happen in a personalized manner as much as possible. The acquisition and maintenance of user preferences about topics of interest and preferred content characteristics are prerequisites for better solutions than current ad hoc approaches. The P-News[1] project tackles this challenge by applying a highly flexible preference method-

---

[1] P-News is funded within the German Research Foundation's strategic research initiative
'

R. Heery and L. Lyon (Eds.): ECDL 2004, LNCS 3232, pp. 256–268, 2004.

ology with powerful query capabilities and managed usage stereotypes throughout the process of dissemination.

Previous approaches for news dissemination are mainly focusing on IR-techniques matching a set of (weighted) keywords against the document collection. The introduction of structured documents in XML and related meta-data lead to applying IR techniques on well defined parts of the document like its title or annotations. However, recent work in personalized information systems shows that not only the document is structured, but already the user's query, sets of keywords, notions of relevance, preferences for notification, etc. The contribution of this paper therefore is twofold; first we present an intuitive way for users to express a structure on their information needs and preferences accompanying the entire process of dissemination way beyond Boolean combinations. Secondly we focus on different roles for interaction and providing predefined structures of the information to express common knowledge and thus ease the usage of the system. Unlike common dissemination engines, notifications in P-News are supposed not only to involve matching content-based preferences, but also closely adapting to particular users and situations. Consider a sample scenario:

Example: Cathy is a professor at university and besides research projects also manages a spin-off business. She uses fast Internet access with a PC, but also uses a mobile phone to keep track of current events. Cathy of course wants to know about news related to her research and is interested in specific business news. Assume a suitable document arrives at P-News, e.g. a new research article. The dissemination process first has to recognize from the representation of Cathy's topical preferences that the new article is *relevant*, from her quality preferences that its *degree* of relevance justifies a notification and from her notification preference, how to *syndicate* the document and where to deliver it to. For instance research-related items could always be sent as emails containing the full document. Her preferences as a business woman could also consider current business events as interesting enough triggering notification to the WAP cell-phone. Due to its limited capabilities, the syndication will automatically put up only the headline and a short abstract for delivery.

Please note that Cathy can interact with the system in different roles having different (even contradictory) topical preferences, can have different notions of relevance, i.e. what degree of quality she is willing to accept within these different roles, and can have different preferences on how to be notified in each role. Moreover, in each role there will generally be certain stereotypical preference patterns for user groups. To cater for such deep personalization scenarios we need more powerful techniques than today's publish/subscribe technologies or IR-based keyword searches in XML documents. In this paper we will address all relevant topics towards building such a deeply personalized dissemination engine using a single consistent preference model for all types of preferences. We will show step by step how to tackle each necessary task and present innovative techniques for the application in news dissemination. We will in detail discuss its impact on specialized digital libraries with a focus on the use of categorical metadata and attribute-based searches in an intuitive and cooperative fashion.

The paper is organized as follows: section 2 will revisit related work and MPEG-7 metadata. In section 3 we present the technological innovations for our news dissemination task. Section 4 finally will show how to build these techniques into a running system, and will present a use case interaction lifecycle.

2 News Dissemination

2.1 Related Work in News Dissemination

As a first approach to overcome the problem of having to sift through vast amounts of information, publishing companies have introduced customizable news letters. Users can subscribe to a variety of general terms describing areas of interest, and are periodically informed which new books might be of specific interest (e.g. 'Springer-Alerts' [1]). However, subscription services have still a long way towards personalization, because users might not be offered a specifically interesting category they need, might find that the publisher has chosen too broad/narrow terms as categories, or may have an entirely different understanding of some categories altogether.

The area of news dissemination therefore has moved to employing advanced techniques for keyword matching in the texts of documents. Engines like SIFT [2] show already good results for full-text retrieval featuring IR techniques and prove that the task of finding relevant documents for notification can be efficiently performed even for large numbers of concurrent users. With the advent of XML engines for the search in XML documents like XIRQL [3] or XXL [4] applied the probability-based keyword retrieval to structured XML documents. However, none of these techniques focused on retrieval over structured categorical attributes that is needed for deep personalization, i.e. not only the document structure should be taken into account, but also the structure of query terms (keywords, attributes,...) with respect to each other.

In terms of advanced usability of digital libraries and ease of querying user profile modeling has been proposed, see e.g. [5], and already proved its usefulness through advanced personalization in the field of news dissemination [6]. User models can be automatically expanded and profit from already existing similar user profiles. In this respect also the mining of related information to adapt recommendations more closely to the individual user has been applied [7]. Our work is a direct continuation of these advances; however, we smoothly embed these advances in a powerful preference framework and thus do not have the overhead of managing user profiles, mined data or query terms of different structure. Moreover, we enhance the benefits by using an ontology-based approach to incorporate common domain knowledge into the retrieval process respecting the role of each individual user.

In today's digital libraries compound documents containing text, images, audio or even video files together with adequate annotations or comments are quite common. Acknowledging its necessity, within standardized multimedia description frameworks like MPEG-7 already a simple set of description tools for describing user preferences (*UserPreferences*) [8] has been provided. It enables users to select their preferred multimedia content in terms of attributes related to the creation, classification, and source of the content. Multiple preference components can then be organized into a hierarchical structure, each one carrying a numerical value indicating the relative importance of this preference. The expressiveness of *UserPreferences* descriptions, however, is far more limited than our approach, since only exact matching is supported, even for simple numerical attributes (e.g. media duration time).

```
<CreationInformation>                    <CreationInformation>
  <Creation>                               <Creation>
    <Creator>                                <Creator>
      <Role>                                   <Role>
        <Name>Producer</Name>                    <Name>Producer</Name>
      </Role>                                   </Role>
      <Agent>                                  <Agent>
        <Name>IBLabs</Name>                      <Name>Microsoft</Name>
      </Agent>                                 </Agent>
    </Creator>                               </Creator>
  </Creation>                                <Creator>
</CreationInformation>                        <Role>
                                                <Name>Editor</Name>
                                              </Role>
                                              <Agent>
                                                <Name>IBLabs</Name>
                                              </Agent>
                                            </Creator>
                                          </Creation>
                                        </CreationInformation>
```

        (a)   (b)

Fig. 1. Example MPEG-7 descriptions

2.2 MPEG-7 Annotations and Use in Digital Libraries

The introduction of standardized metadata descriptions facilitates search and retrieval of multimedia content in digital libraries. Currently MPEG-7 [8] is the most complete description standard for multimedia data providing a comprehensive set of standardized tools to describe multimedia data. For example, a video segment can be described in many different aspects, like *MediaInformation* (e.g. storage format, visual coding), *CreationInformation* (e.g. title, creator, classification), *UsageInformation* (e.g. access rights, distributor), structural aspects (e.g. subsegments) and conceptual aspects (e.g. text annotation, semantics). The description tools are specified in the Description Definition Language based on XML schema. Thus MPEG-7 descriptions are complex XML documents. For instance (a) and (b) in Fig. 1 are excerpts from MPEG-7 descriptions of the creation information for two video segments.

With this standard the focus in searching digital libraries or evaluating a document's relevance shifts to attribute-rich search on *categorical data*. Consider for example the information in Fig. 1. A query on all documents that have been created and preferably produced by 'IBLabs' will need more than today's capability of searching the creator tag in e.g. XQuery for the existence of the keywords 'IBLabs' and 'Producer'. Here the evaluation of a nested preference is needed where the keyword 'Producer' has to be the role within the *same* creator tag that also contains the keyword 'IBLabs'. Thus document (a) in figure 1 would be a better match than document (b). However, document (b) should nevertheless still be considered more relevant than other documents because of the keyword 'IBLabs' as 'Editor', which is another role of a creator. So the creator attribute has certain *categories* ('producer', 'author', 'editor') as domain on which users might express preferences. Traditional IR techniques or the MPEG-7 description tools, however, can handle such preferences only up to a certain extent yet, and provide no intuitive (i.e. declarative) way of expressing them. In the following we will show how our system can deal even with such complex preferences.

3   Basic Concepts of Deep Personalization for Dissemination

3.1   A Model for Structured User Preferences in XML Libraries

MPEG-7 descriptions are basically XML data. In searching or filtering XML data, traditional IR approaches, keyword sets or vectors, are often unable to refer to the data structure and incorporate semantic relations between the query terms. Query languages for XML, such as XPath or XQuery, can be used to formulate precise queries over data. But they can only express Boolean (or hard) conditions; no ranking or soft conditions are possible. Many efforts are spent on combining the structure and ranking-based search, e.g. XXL [4] and XIRQL [3]. They mainly use vague predicates and probability-based combination function to score structurally matched document fragments. However, numerical ranking approaches are generally less expressive than qualitative ones [21].

In [9], an approach for preference modeling is proposed utilizing strict partial orders featuring an intuitive "I like A better than B" semantics. User preferences are generally considered soft conditions that are evaluated as strict partial orders over the data set. Thus all *best matching* objects, not necessarily exact matches, will be returned. As an essential feature of the approach in [9], a set of predefined *preference constructors* are used to construct arbitrary preferences. For example, *AROUND(x)* is a base preference constructor on numerical attribute values preferring values closest to the stated value x. *Pareto* and *Prioritized* are complex constructors for combining preferences of equal importance or with priorities. This set of constructors is extensible and users are enabled to define their own constructors if needed. For P-News we will add a novel preference constructor, called *nested* preference, extending the model to handle complex XML data. Formally let *<path>* be an XML path expression and let *dom(<path>)* denote the domain of objects reachable by *<path>*. Then a preference P is defined as P = (*<path>*, $<_p$), where $<_p$ is a strict partial order over dom(*<path>*).

Definition 3.1   Strict partial order relation between sets
Given P = (*<path>*, $<_p$) we define a strict partial order $<<_p$ over the set of all finite subsets of dom(*<path>*) as follows. For all finite subsets X, Y of dom(*<path>*):

$$X <<_p Y \quad iff \quad (\forall\, x \in X, \exists\, y \in Y: x <_p y) \wedge Y \neq \varnothing$$

It can be proved that $<<_p$ is a strict partial order.

Definition 3.2 Nested preference

Given a preference P = ($<path>$, $<_p$) and objects O_j, $O_k \in$ dom($<path^*>$), let $\{O_j.<path>\}$ and $\{O_k.<path>\}$ denote the sets of selected objects by navigating $<path>$ from O_j and O_k, respectively. Then a *nested* preference $P^* = (<path^*>, <_{p^*})$ is defined as: $\forall$ O_j, $O_k \in$ dom($<path^*>$): $O_j <_{p^*} O_k$ iff $\{O_j.<path>\} <<_p \{O_k.<path>\}$

Preference XPath [10] has been developed to evaluate preference queries. It extends standard XPath by soft filtering conditions bracketed in '#[' and ']# ' in contrast to hard conditions in brackets ' [' and '] '. A soft condition defines a strict partial order over the set of elements to be filtered and returns only the best matches. Extending the preference model by nested preferences, we extend Preference XPath as follows:

```
LocationStep : axis nodetest (predicate | pref_pred)*
```

pref_pred is the extension part to the standard XPath, i.e. soft filtering conditions.

```
pref_pred : '#[' preference ']#'
preference : base_preference
           | xpath '{' preference '}'
           | preference 'and' preference
           | preference 'prior to' preference
```

base_preference is defined on atomic attribute values, e.g. strings or numbers. The second case, *xpath '{' preference '}'*, is the extension for nested preferences. The *'and'* and *'prior to'* are for Pareto and Prioritized combinations respectively.

Example (cont.): Assume Cathy prefers videos produced by 'IBLabs'. Using the schema of MPEG-7, such a preference can only be expressed in a nested way:

```
/Mpeg7/Description/MultimediaContent//*
#[CreationInformation/Creation/Creator
{Role/Name is 'Producer' and Agent/Name is 'IBLabs'}]#
```

Here 'Role/Name is 'Producer'' and 'Agent/Name is 'IBLabs'' are base preferences combined by the Pareto constructor 'and', which means both preferences are equally important. The combined preference induces a strict partial order on objects of CreationInformation/Creation/Creator, which in turn gives a strict partial order on higher level elements, i.e. multimedia segments accessed by /Mpeg7/Description/MultimediaContent//*; thus a nested preference. Evaluating the query on the documents in Fig. 1, for each Creator in (b), there is a better Creator in (a). So video segment (a) is considered better than (b) and the intuitively expected result set {(a)} will be returned.

It is important to note that keyword search on full-text attributes using standard IR methods can be orthogonally embedded in our preference model. For instance, keyword search using the vector space model can be implemented as a basic $rank_F$ constructor [9] on the full-text attribute, possibly combined with preferences on other attributes [11]. Thus, P-News caters for arbitrary queries on XML data.

3.2 Structured Preference Patterns of User Groups

For meta-data-based document retrieval in digital libraries users will always assume a certain amount of common knowledge within the system. In recent years ontologies as a way of representing common knowledge or shared vocabulary within a domain have spread widely [13]. With ontologies we can model complex semantic relationships and exploit them for subsequent structured querying. As shown in [12] expanding queries along certain ontology-based patterns will result in improved querying, because the choice of useful preferences for relaxation can be limited down to a sensible applicable set. While an ontology can be as complicated as arbitrary semantic graphs including various relationships and inference rules, P-News does not attempt entirely ontology-driven querying, but instead uses ontologies in their most basic incarnation: concept hierarchies. Such ontological information poses a partial order on the string-valued domain set, e.g. the specified term is preferred to its synonyms and hyponyms, which in turn are preferred to its hypernyms, while the hypernyms are still considered better than other values. When a preference query is evaluated, the partial order induced by the ontology structure is respected. The basic technique is to use the EXPLICIT [9] or a user-defined preference constructor to expand the original query.

Since different interest groups often show different but within the group sufficiently similar interests, useful default values can be assumed for all preferences not explicitly provided by a user. We refer to what is typically considered relevant in different user groups as default preference patterns. These patterns are predefined and can evolve over the usage cycle of group members by the feedback given. As in dissemination frameworks unnecessary notifications have to be avoided, integrating this common knowledge into user queries in an unstructured way would often confront users with lots of useless results. With the preference query model, we can use the "prior to" preference combination to integrate the user group's preference pattern into user's query, however in a lower level of priority. Figure 2 shows the structure of query terms induced by query expansion with ontologies and preference patterns.

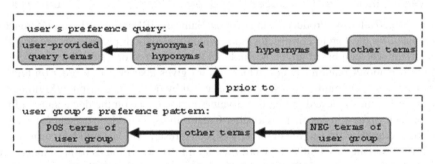

Fig. 2. Query expansion with ontologies and preference patterns

Example (cont.): Consider that our sample user Cathy might research concepts of object-oriented programming in Java. Our system has a simple ontology as concept hierarchy in IT domain that models the terms 'Java', 'C++', 'Smalltalk' as subtypes of 'object-oriented languages', which in turn is a subtype of 'programming languages'. Note that 'C++' and 'Smalltalk' are not synonyms for 'Java', but unlike systems developers focusing on Java programming, researchers, who are interested in the basic concepts of Java might with high probability also be interested in C++ concepts. Thus, if Cathy has a POS preference on 'Java', and a video talk on 'C++' arrives, we might consider a notification based on the specific group or pattern Cathy belongs to. However, we can always ensure by not relaxing above the 'object-oriented languages' node in our ontology that query results have still enough in common with Cathy's query. Moreover, individual preferences always override preferences of the group. Now assume that a significant number of Cathy's group members have stated to be no longer interested in 'Smalltalk'. After query expansion with ontologies and group preferences, Cathy's original query (represented in the compact algebra notation of [9] due to the limited space), P = POS(keyword, {'Java'}), is expanded into P' = EXPLICIT(keyword, {'C++' < 'object-oriented languages', 'Smalltalk' < 'object-oriented languages', 'object-oriented languages' < 'Java'}) prior to NEG(keyword, {'Smalltalk'}). Hence, we get a new single preference query that can simply be evaluated like before, but now takes common interests of a user group into account.

3.3 Selecting Best Matches by Assessing Result Quality

The knowledge maintained in the structure of preferences can also be used to assess the quality of retrieved results. To distinguish relevant from non-relevant objects declarative query languages offer capabilities that will stop the relaxation at a certain degree of generalization or will only relax within a certain range of objects, e.g. in the previous example Cathy's constraints were only relaxed to languages that are object-oriented. P-News takes quality assessment beyond mere numerical thresholds to a relaxation directed by the needs of each individual user even for categorical data. To assess the quality of each object returned by a query, the preference structure of the query is compared with the actual matches of attributes/keywords like shown in [18]. Our model uses different linguistic quality levels to express the relevance of an object ranging from 'sufficient', 'acceptable', 'good', 'very good' to 'perfect match'. The user can individually assign his/her perception of these levels for each base preference, e.g. in the case of keyword matching using standard IR distance measures or in the case of categorical data using the tolerated discrepancy for relaxation. Within complex preferences these basic measures are then aggregated again according to the specifications of the user, e.g. *median*, *maximum* or *minimum* (see [22] for details).

Example (cont.): Assume Cathy prefers videos produced by 'IBLabs', but would also rather prefer files with a size of about 250 MB. She only wants to be notified of results having 'very good' quality or better. Evaluating the nested keyword matching Cathy can easily define acceptable quality thresholds. For the numerical attribute, file size, Cathy may state a tolerable deviation of 10%. For each 10% more or less the quality level drops one step. Assume that P-News has to compare documents (a) and (b) from Fig. 1 for possible notification with file sizes {(a), 310 MB} and {(b), 240 MB}. In terms of quality on two base preferences this leads to {(a), perfect, good} and {(b), very good, very good}. Now Cathy again can express her exact needs in terms of overall quality. She might e.g. define a *maximum* of 'very good' as sufficient and gets notified about both documents or she might only be willing to accept documents with a *minimum* of 'very good' and gets notified about document (b) only. In any case she is enabled to intuitively specify her notion of relevance.

4   The P-News System for Personalized Dissemination

Having presented the underlying technologies to build a running system let us now take a closer look on the prototype system's architecture and a lifecycle of interaction.

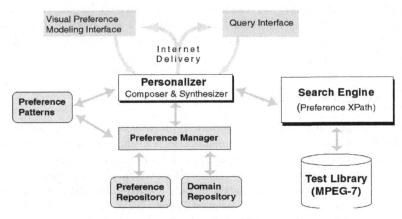

Fig. 3. General architecture of the P-News system

4.1   P-News MPEG-7 Library and System Architecture

In P-News MPEG-7 annotations for multimedia content are stored in XML repositories, associated with a query engine for evaluating Preference XPath queries [10]. As in our running example, we set our use case in the domain of IT technology. The test library consists of about 90 videos (ca. 24 GB) from Computer Chronicles [14] and colloquium series of computer science department in the University of Washington. All videos have been manually annotated using MovieTool [15]. The annotations focus on a set of *controlled-term* attributes provided by the MPEG-7 standard, whose values are from a predefined vocabulary. This use of controlled vocabulary leads to a standardized annotation and subsequent querying with categorical data that shows a strictly typed structure and thus makes user queries comparable within user groups.

Fig.3. sketches the general architecture of the P-News system. The central component of our architecture is called *personalizer*. It composes the user query by integrating a user's preferences. Then it expands the query using the preference pattern of the user's group (respecting his/her current role) and poses it to the retrieval engine. The result is evaluated and all data whose quality assessment allows for notification are syndicated into the preferred format, layout, etc. and delivered to the appropriate client device. To adapt his/her stored preferences or enter new preferences our architecture also provides a visual preference modeling interface for users to graphically construct structured preferences. These components are built on top of a *preference manager* that manages the different kinds of preferences. For the query composition and expansion the *user provided preferences* and d*omain-specific knowledge* grouped into *preference patterns* are used. Furthermore, each user's notion of relevance (i.e. the expected quality of the results) is represented within the patterns stating individually how much relaxation is still acceptable. Notification preferences of each user are specified for content syndication. Please note, though all these different preferences are used for specific tasks, their basic structure is always defined by our underlying preference model. Arbitrarily complex preferences thus can be stored in the same repository individually characterized by the user they belong to, and the group, in which they are applicable. We store all the preferences in XML format; our repository [16], however, distinguishes between user preferences, the group specific preference patterns, and the ontologies stored in the domain repository. Using Preference XPath, the preference manager chooses all applicable preferences for the personalizer.

4.2   The User Interaction Lifecycle

User Registration and Preference Modeling. Our use case focuses on a digital library of IT-related content annotated in MPEG-7. The system maintains a set of predefined preference patterns for different user groups. Each new user registering with the system is provided a default preference pattern from the user group that he/she has been assigned to. The user now can view, edit, construct or remove his/her individual preferences using a visual interface, before they are stored in a preference repository.

Query Composition. As discussed in section 3.1, complex preference queries can include keyword search, attribute matching etc. In MPEG-7, there is a predefined vocabulary associated with each *controlled-term* attribute, which can be viewed as a simple ontology specifying all the valid terms and subsume relationship between terms for the attribute. For each user group there is an ontology representing their view of the world, i.e. a taxonomy of all the categories, topics and keywords in IT domain, which is applied to the full-text attributes. When scheduling user queries P-News expands them with the predefined vocabularies or ontologies and group-specific preference patterns as discussed in section 3.2.

Query Evaluation. According to timing information specified for each query, i.e. StartTime, Interval and ExpireTime, queries are activated periodically and evaluated over the set of new data, i.e. the data that come into the system between the last processing time of the query and the current time. To improve the efficiency and/or scalability, the common parts of the activated queries, e.g. common data sets, common XPath expressions, are identified and the computation is shared among them. Existing work on multiple XML query evaluation have been adapted for this purpose [17].

Quality Assessment. Before making a decision on notifying a user, P-News analyzes the returned results in terms of quality as discussed in section 3.3, and filters objects, for which soft constraints have been too far relaxed. The preference structure of the query is constructed and compared with respective structure of the matches in the result set. P-News enables users to specify the acceptable distances for relaxation on each base preference and computes quality values for complex preferences again according to user preferences. Thus an overall quality value for the object in terms of the query can be computed inductively and all irrelevant objects discarded.

Notification and News Delivery. When P-News decides for notification, the system sends a message summarizing new media data that might be of interest. This message is syndicated according to the user-specified form and sent to the preferred device (see [19] for details on personalized multimedia content delivery). By default P-News notifications are simple e-mails listing the interesting documents and containing links to the full multimedia content. When the user follows a link, the P-News server will automatically adapt the content to user's technical device characteristics. Currently we use SMIL (Synchronized Multimedia Integration Language [20]) files to deliver video data. SMIL also offers a set of attributes facilitating limited adaptations.

Relevance Feedback. Our current implementation features only a limited approach to exploit relevance feedback. For example, P-News assumes a user to be interested in a particular video (and related keywords/topics), when he/she follows the link to open a video after reading the respective abstract. This behavior is recorded on the server and can be used for modifying the user's preference as well as his group's preference pattern. Deriving good patterns from feedback will be part of P-News ongoing work.

5   Summary and Outlook

In this paper we addressed the problem of deep personalization in news dissemination systems. The key technology in implementing the P-News system is one coherent extensible preference model that serves all purposes, preventing an impedance mismatch between various stages. Enabling the user to apply individual preferences in every single step throughout the dissemination process, P-News facilitates a tailored notification about relevant documents in a digital library. We focused on multimedia documents described by MPEG-7 metadata to allow users to express their preferred content, notion of relevance and delivery preferences in an intuitive way. We presented an extension by nested preferences that are essential in structured querying of XML documents, using our unique Preference XPath. Moreover, in addition to exploit the document structure to gain better result sets, we also allowed for expressing preference structures on users' preferred keywords or categorical attribute values. Since users should not be burdened with all the extensive modeling of preferences within stereotypical interest groups, an ontology-based approach for automatic query expansion with typical preference patterns has been realized. Finally, we enabled users also to specify their individual quality preferences to avoid unnecessary notifications as far as possible. Merging these techniques into the workflow of dissemination the P-News system essentially extends the expressiveness of dissemination in digital libraries catering for both textual information and categorical metadata descriptions.

Our future work will concentrate on the experimental evaluation of the system, user case studies and the relevance feedback used to reflect current changes of interest within the user groups. Also managing users changing between different groups needs some deeper research. A detailed analysis of each individual user's interaction with the delivered results can be expected to allow for monitoring dynamic changes in each group's profile. Finally, to keep up with standards, we will migrate from Preference XPath to Preference XQuery.

Acknowledgements

Part of this work was funded by the German Research Foundation DFG within an Emmy-Noether Grant. The authors would like to thank José Maria González Pinto and Timotheus Preisinger for their helpful comments and work on the P-News system.

References

1. SpringerAlerts, http://www.springer.de/alert
2. Yan T.W., Garcia-Molina H.: The SIFT information dissemination system. ACM TODS, Vol. 24, Issue 4 (1999) 529–565
3. Fuhr N., Großjohann K.: XIRQL: A Query Language for Information Retrieval in XML Documents. Proc. Int. ACM SIGIR Conf. (SIGIR 2001) 172–180
4. Theobald A., Weikum G.: The Index-based XXL Search Engine for Querying XML Data with Relevance Ranking. In Proc. Int. Conf. on Extending Database Technology (EDBT 2002) 477–495
5. Amato G., Straccia U.: User Profile Modeling and Applications to Digital Libraries. In Proc. Europ. Conf. on Digital Libraries (ECDL 1999) 184–197
6. Esteban A.D., Gómez-Navarro P.G., Jiménez A.G.: Evaluating a User-Model Based Personalisation Architecture for Digital News Services. In Proc. Europ. Conf. on Digital Libraries (ECDL 2000) 259–268
7. Hwang S.-Y., Lim E.-P.: A Data Mining Approach to New Library Book Recommendations. In Proc. Int. Conference on Asian Digital Libraries (ICADL 2002) 229–240
8. MPEG-7 Overview, http://mpeg.telecomitalialab.com/standards/mpeg-7/mpeg-7.htm
9. Kießling W.: Foundations of Preferences in Database Systems. In Proc. Int. Conf. on Very Large Databases (VLDB 2002) 311–322
10. Kießling W., Hafenrichter B., Fischer S., Holland S.: Preference XPATH, A Query Language for E-Commerce. In: Buhl H.U., Huther A. Reitwiesner, B. (eds.): Information Age Economy. Physika-Verlag, Heidelberg (2001) 427–440
11. Leubner A., Kießling W.: Personalized Keyword Search with Partial-Order Preferences. Proc. Brazilian Symposium on Database Systems (SBBD 2002). 181-193
12. Balke W.-T., Wagner M.: Cooperative Discovery for User-Centered Web Service Provisioning. In Proc. Int. Conf. on Web Services (ICWS 2003) 191–197
13. Fensel D.: Ontologies: Dynamics Networks of Meaning, In Proc. of the Semantic Web Working Symposium (2001), Stanford, CA, USA
14. Computer Chronicles, http://www.archive.org/movies/computerchronicles.php

15. MovieTool, http://www.ricoh.co.jp/src/multimedia/MovieTool/
16. Holland S., Ester M., Kießling W.: Preference Mining: A Novel Approach on Mining User Preferences for Personalized Applications. Proc. Conf. on Principles and Practice of Knowledge Discovery in Databases (PKDD 2003) 204-216
17. Chen J., DeWitt D.J., Feng T, Wang Y.: NiagaraCQ: A scalable Continous Query System for Internet Databases. In Proc. Int ACM SIGMOD Conf. (SIGMOD 2000) 379–390
18. Balke W.-T., Wagner M.: Through Different Eyes – Assessing Multiple Conceptual Views for Querying Web Services. Proc. Int. World Wide Web Conf. (WWW 2004)
19. Wagner M., Balke W.-T., Kießling W.: An XML-Based Multimedia Middleware for Mobile Online Auctions. Proc. Int. Conf. on Enterprise Information Systems (ICEIS 2001), 934–944
20. SMIL, http://www.w3.org/AudioVideo/
21. Chomicki J.: Preference Formulas in Relational Queries. ACM Transactions on Database Systems, 28(4), December 2003, pp.427–466.
22. Kießling W., Fischer S., Döring S.: COSIMA B2B - Sales Automation for E-Procurement. 6th IEEE Conference on E-Commerce Technology (CEC04), San Diego, USA, July 2004

Laws of Attraction:
In Search of Document Value-ness for Recommendation

Tiffany Y. Tang[1,2] and Gordon McCalla[2]

[1] Department of Computing, Hong Kong Polytechnic University
Hung Hom, Kowloon, Hong Kong
cstiffany@comp.polyu.edu.hk
[2] Department of Computer Science, University of Saskatchewan
Saskatoon, Saskatchewan, Canada
mccalla@cs.usask.ca

Abstract. In this paper we explore the uniqueness of paper recommendation for e-learning systems through a human-subject study. Experiment results showed that the majority of learners have struggled to reach a '*harmony*' between their interest and educational goal: they admit that in order to acquire new knowledge, they are willing to read not-interesting-yet-pedagogically-useful papers. In other words, learners seem to be more tolerant than users in commercial recommender systems. Nevertheless, as educators, we should still maintain a balance of recommending *interesting* papers and *pedagogically helpful* ones in order to retain learners and continuously engage them throughout the learning process.

1 Introduction

One of the criteria used in recommendation systems is consumers' interest toward the item being recommended. For instance, a recommendation system in an e-shop will recommend a new jazz CD to a customer who likes jazz music; or in the case of digital library, the system recommends a journal article to a scholar whose research interest matches the topic of the article. In e-business, recommending items according to the customers' interest has been proven to be effective for cross-selling, up-selling, and mass marketing [9]. In e-learning, however, the effectiveness of recommendation based solely on learners' interest has not been studied extensively yet. In our previous survey, it is shown that most learners are willing to read not-interested-but-useful paper [10]. The result supports our conjecture that learner interest may not be the only factor that affects the effectiveness of recommendation in e-learning. We believe that learners' knowledge of domain concepts and learning goals might be more important. Therefore, the system should not recommend highly technical papers to a first-year-undergraduate student or popular-magazine articles to a senior-graduate student. To illustrate the uniqueness of making recommendation for e-learning systems, let us first look at a motivational example.

A Motivational Example

User A and B are to receive recommendations on research articles and news stories respectively as shown in Table 1. For user A, s/he is expecting an item which is not

R. Heery and L. Lyon (Eds.): ECDL 2004, LNCS 3232, pp. 269–280, 2004.
© Springer-Verlag Berlin Heidelberg 2004

only interesting, but also understandable and useful. Even if an article is interesting, we cannot recommend it if user A is not yet pedagogically ready (without enough prerequisite knowledge) to consume it. Hence, we should recommend user A some other article(s) before an interesting but pedagogically not suitable item is given. For user B, however, we can simply recommend items of interest to her/him. Therefore, it is obvious that in order to make recommendation for educational system, we should consider a very important feature, i.e. pedagogically-oriented data, which can directly *affect* as well as *inform* recommendation process, thus, enhancing the quality of recommendations.

Table 1. A comparison of User A and B in e-learning and news story recommendation

	User A	User B
Items to be recommended	Research articles	news
Item value-ness (the most important from user's perspective)	Interesting, understandable, useful	interesting
Prerequisite knowledge	Yes	No
Item presentation order	Yes	No

Therefore, it is obvious that making recommendations in our system is different from that in other domains where users' interests were the most important in order to retain them by way of delivering personalized recommendations. Moreover, depends on the syllabus, items contained in a recommendation list might not be entirely interesting to learners, but sometimes all learners must read some of the items regardless of their interest (e.g. required reading materials). However, if the system continues to recommend something that cannot stimulate learners' interest in one way or another, it may reduce learners' learning performance which is also undesirable. Finally, for e-learning, customization should also be made not only of learning content, but also of the presentation style [3, 5]. This paper extends our previous work [11, 12], but mainly focuses on the value-ness of reading items for recommendation in an e-learning system through a human-subject experiment.

The rest of this paper is arranged as follows. In the next section, we will discuss some related work. In Section 3, we will present the technical aspects of our approach. Then we will report in detail the experiment we conducted as a way of assessing and comparing our proposed recommendation techniques. Finally, we conclude this paper by pointing out our future work.

2   Related Work

Paper Recommendations
There are several related works concerning tracking and recommending technical papers. Basu *et al.* [1] define the paper recommendation problem as: *"Given a representation of my interests, find me relevant papers."* They study this issue in the context of assigning conference paper submissions to reviewing committee members. Bollacker *et al.* [2] refine CiteSeer, NEC's digital library for scientific literature, through an automatic personalized paper-tracking module which retrieves user interests from well-maintained heterogeneous user profiles. Woodruff *et al.* [13] discuss an enhanced digital book with a spreading-activation-geared mechanism to make customized recommendations for readers with different type

of background and knowledge. McNee *et al.* [6] investigate the adoption of collaborative filtering techniques to recommend papers for researchers; however, the paper did not address the issue of how to recommend a research paper, rather, how to recommend *additional* references for a target research paper. In the context of an e-learning system, additional readings cannot be recommended purely through an analysis of the citation matrix of a target paper. Recker *et al.* [8] study the pedagogical characteristics of a web-based resource through Altered Vista, where teachers and learners can submit and review comments provided by learners. However, although they emphasize the importance of the pedagogical features of these educational resources, they did not consider the pedagogical features in making recommendation.

These works are different from ours in that we not only recommend papers according to learners' interests, but also pick up those *not-so-interesting-yet-pedagogically-suitable* papers for them. In some cases pedagogically valuable papers might not be interesting and papers with significant influence on the research community might not be pedagogically suitable for learners.

Document Value-ness
The majority of scientific literature as well as other document retrieval systems (and many other systems) has been focusing on finding document relative to users' interests, to name a few [2, 6]. Recently, there have been approaches that augment the mostly commonly adopted similarity-based retrieving. Among them, Paepcke *et al.* [7] propose a *context-aware content-based filtering*. In particular, *context-aware* content-based filtering attempts to determine the contextual information about a document, e.g. the publisher of the documents, the time when the document was published etc. For instance, they argued that '*documents from the New York Times might be valued higher than other documents that appear in an unknown publication context*'. This contextual information provides additional rich information for users, thus, constitutes a very important aspect of the value-ness of the item.

Our proposed approach takes into account of one type of contextual information: the *pedagogical* feature of learners. In particular, we argue that users' pedagogical goal and interest should be regarded as two of the most critical considerations when we are making recommendations in e-learning systems.

3 Pedagogically-Oriented Paper Recommendation

Specifically, our goal can be stated as follows:

Given a collection of papers and a learner's profile, recommend and deliver a set of materials in a pedagogically appropriate sequence, so as to meet both the learner's pedagogical needs and the learner's interests.

Ideally, the system will maximize a learner's utility such that the learner gains a maximum amount of useful knowledge and is well motivated in the end. Fig. 1 shows the flow diagram of the proposed recommendation system in our previous and current experiment. The uniqueness of our system is in the incorporation of artificial learners in order to solve the cold-start problem in collaborative filtering (CF). The following steps are the recommendation processes:

① A tutor manually assigns the properties of each paper (paper model).

② We create artificial learners (group A) with specific learner model.

③ *Model-based RS* recommends a paper to the learners in group A by comparing learner model and paper model.

④ Learners in group A rate the paper.

⑤ We elicit human learners' (group B) learner model.

⑥ *Hybrid-CF module* recommends a paper to each learner in group B by comparing his/her learner model with those from group A (artificial learners) and searching paper with the highest rating.

⑦ After learners in group B read the paper, they rate the paper, which will be used in our analysis.

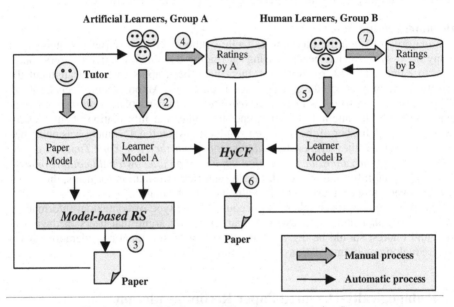

Fig. 1. Process of the Proposed Paper Recommendation System

Pedagogical Model-Based Recommendation Technique

The model-based recommendation is achieved through a careful assessment and comparison of both learner and paper characteristics. There will be two layers of filtering. More specifically, each individual learner models will first be analyzed, in terms of not only their interest, but their pedagogical features, such as their background knowledge in specific topics. Paper models will also be analyzed based on the topic, technical level, material covered and presentation. The recommendation is carried out by matching the learner interest with the paper topics where the technical level of the paper should not impede the learner in understanding it. Therefore, the suitability of a paper toward a learner is calculated as the summation of the fitness of learner interest toward the paper and the easiness to understand the paper.

Pedagogical Hybrid Collaborative Filtering Technique
However, the layered model-based recommendation, which is achieved through a careful assessment of learner characteristics and then matches them against papers is very costly due to the following reasons:

- when a new paper is introduced into the system, a detailed identification is required, which cannot be done automatically;
- when a learner gains some new knowledge after reading a paper, a new matching process is required in order to find the next suitable paper for him/her, resulting in the updating of his/her learner model;
- the matching between learner model and paper model may not be a one-to-one mapping, which increases the complexity of the computation.

Alternatively, we can use a collaborative filtering technique (CF) to reduce the complexity of the recommendation process. The idea of CF is to pass on the 'burden' of 'learning' the features of a paper to learners by allowing peer learners (nearest neighbors) to filter out unsuitable papers. Therefore, the matching process is not performed from learner models to paper models, but from one learner model to other learner models, i.e. by comparing the closeness of both learners' interest and background knowledge in order to find nearest neighbors of a target learner. Therefore, papers are actually annotated by fellow learners themselves, while the system does not need to modify the features of papers, which greatly improve system performance and efficiency. Moreover, this type of the *social filtering* technique utilizes the *network value* of learners with similar interest (like those traditional recommender systems do) and pedagogical characteristics.

4   Experimental Results and Discussions

In our experiments, we intend to answer some specific questions: when recommending articles to learners, what are the most important criteria for recommendation? Are a student's learning interests more important than other aspects? Or their learning goal? Should we also recommend something which will aid their learning based on their pedagogical characteristics?

4.1 Experiment Background and Setup

The human subject study is conducted in a university in Hong Kong. The course is a senior level undergraduate course in software engineering, where the first author is the instructor of the course. There are altogether 48 students, and there are 23 candidate papers in English related to software engineering and internet computing. Those 23 papers are well selected from a pool of more than 40 papers originally selected for the course. Those papers are selected as part of the required reading materials for the group project in this course. The length of the papers varies from 2 pages to 15 pages. However, most of them are popular articles with low technical level that are suitable for those students.

For the purpose of testing, we first generate 50000 artificial learners (ArLs) (Group A in Fig. 1). Each ArL then rate those 23 papers according to their individual learner model (pure model-based). The rating mechanism was the same as what we reported in [12]. After that, we used *human subjects* as the target learners (Group B in Fig.1). Then, two cold-start recommendation techniques were applied for these target learners. The first technique used a hybrid-CF approach (as shown in Fig. 1), while the second used random assignment as the control [11].

Learner Interest		Learner Background Knowledge	
Software development	5 4 3 2 1	Network security	5 4 3 2 1
Web design and application	5 4 3 2 1	Statistics	5 4 3 2 1
User interface design	5 4 3 2 1	Algorithm complexity analysis	5 4 3 2 1
Recommender system	5 4 3 2 1	Discrete Mathematics	5 4 3 2 1
Search engine	5 4 3 2 1	Marketing and management	5 4 3 2 1
Security and privacy on the web	5 4 3 2 1		
Trust on the Internet	5 4 3 2 1		
Reputation system in e-comm	5 4 3 2 1		Find It
Social network	5 4 3 2 1		
Data mining	5 4 3 2 1	Recommended Paper Title:	
E-commerce	5 4 3 2 1		
E-banking	5 4 3 2 1	recommeded paper title here	
Case study in software dev	5 4 3 2 1		
Software testing	5 4 3 2 1		
Project management	5 4 3 2 1		Generate ArtLearner

Fig. 2. Survey questions for target learner

We first distributed 48 surveys asking about students' interest, and their knowledge background (Fig. 2). The background knowledge consists of knowledge items students have learned in other courses, items which are also needed to understand the papers. After we received 41 feedbacks, we used the ratings by artificial learners and hybrid-CF to find the most suitable paper for each of them. Furthermore, we also select another paper randomly. Thus, each student was assigned to read two papers within five days and was required to give a pair of feedback forms, one for each paper (Fig. 3). The feedback form basically collected their subjective evaluation after reading the papers. In addition, we also asked them to write some critical comments about the papers, and this became an indicator of their seriousness in reading the papers. They were informed that adequately filling in their feedback from would give them a bonus mark. None of the learners knew that one of the papers was selected randomly, but they did know that they will receive personalized articles which can be used in their group projects (for this course).

4.2   Experiment Results and Discussion

In all, 24 pairs of valid feedback forms were received on time. 6 pairs of feedback form were received more than a week later, and 3 feedback forms were not valid, e.g. containing multiple answers, blanks, etc. 8 students did not return their feedback forms. In this paper, we only show the result of the 24 pairs of valid feedbacks. Fig. 4

shows partial result of them. The vertical axis of the diagram denotes the number of subjects who answer the respective question. The horizontal axis denotes the option of the answer given by the subject on a 4-point scale, e.g. 4 for "very", 3 for "relatively", 2 for "not really", and 1 for "not at all" as shown in Fig. 3. Moreover, the left bar contains the result for the recommended paper, while the right bar is for the randomly assigned paper.

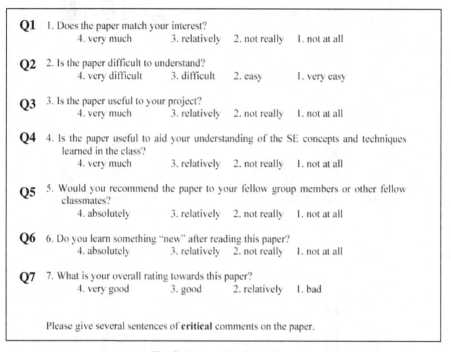

Fig. 3. Learner Feedback Form

Fig. 4(a) shows that learners were more interested in the recommended paper (left bars) than a randomly selected paper (right bars). For example, 6 subjects felt that the recommended papers are very interesting, while only 1 subject felt that the random paper was very interesting. Fig. 4(b) shows that learners felt that recommended papers were easier to understand than a randomly assigned one. This result conforms to our prediction, since the rating mechanism used by ArLs incorporates both learner interest and knowledge background in understanding a paper. Thus, a recommended paper generated by ArLs will also fit human interest and knowledge backgrounds.

Fig. 4(c) shows the answer for the question whether the papers are useful to their class project or not. It can be seen from the result that most subjects admitted that the recommended papers were more useful than random papers. Fig. 4(d) shows that recommended papers were more likely to be recommended by learners to others. However, when we asked them whether they learned something new or not after reading the paper, it is not clear whether or not a recommended paper really gave them more new knowledge compared to a randomly-assigned paper does (see Fig. 4(e)). The result is not surprising: since all the candidate papers are well-selected for this

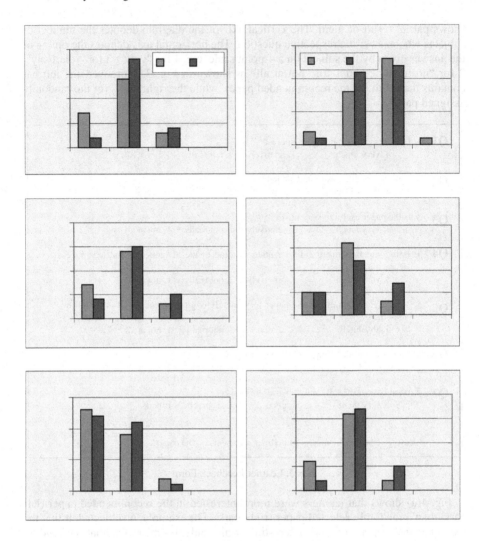

Fig. 4. Results of learner feedback

course, where the value-added for learners is high (most subjects felt that they learned a lot after reading those papers). Finally, Fig. 4(f) shows that recommended papers got higher ratings in terms of overall rating.

From Fig. 4, it is ambiguous whether the overall ratings depend on learner interest or usefulness of the paper. It is also not clear how individual difference (orientation in giving the rating) affects the results, because the data only show the total number of subjects for each option. To overcome this problem, we analyze the ratings given by each subject on both recommended and randomly assigned papers. Specifically, we assign a numerical value to represent the difference between the ratings of both papers. For instance, if a subject rates the recommended paper as "very interesting" (4) and the randomly assigned one as "relatively interesting" (3), then the difference is +1

(4 − 3 = 1). However, if the subject rates the recommended paper as "not really useful" (2) and the randomly assigned one as "very useful" (4), then the difference is -2 (2 − 4 = -2). Fig. 5 shows the distribution of these numerical differences. Except for the category "difficult to understand", a positive value on the horizontal axis represents that the recommended paper outperforms the randomly assigned one. Compared to Fig. 4, two results are worthwhile to be discussed here. First, in Fig. 5, the pattern of "overall rating" is similar to those of "useful to project" and "recommend to others"; while in Fig. 4, the pattern of "overall rating" is closer to those of "interesting article" and "useful to project". Second, in Fig. 4, it is difficult to tell whether learners gain more new knowledge from recommended paper or not. But from Fig. 5, it appears that on average, learners gain the same amount of new knowledge from both papers.

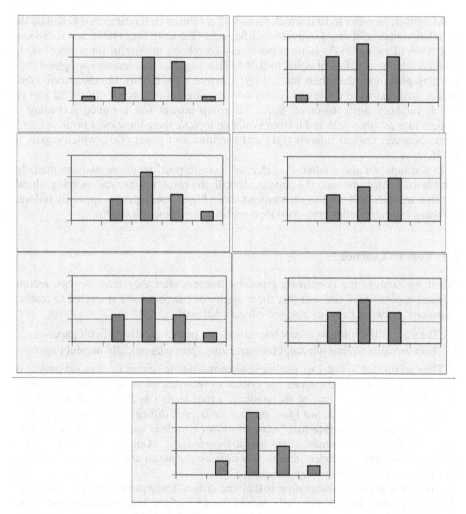

Fig. 5. The frequency of responses in terms of the differences between rating given to recommended and assigned papers

Table 2. The correlation matrix of the differences between recommended and randomly assigned paper (for 7 different Questions in Fig. 3)

	Q1	Q2	Q3	Q4	Q5	Q6	Q7
Q1	1						
Q2	-0.578	1					
Q3	0.535	-0.312	1				
Q4	0.475	-0.343	0.552	1			
Q5	0.635	-0.305	0.653	0.658	1		
Q6	0.373	-0.127	0.189	0.205	0.486	1	
Q7	0.616	-0.332	**0.765**	0.517	0.696	0.346	1

Moreover, in order to find which factors affect the overall ratings, we calculate the correlation matrix of those individual differences (Table 2). From table 2, it is obvious that "overall rating" (Q7) is most positively correlated to "useful for project" (Q3), with correlation coefficient equal to 0.765. This suggests that learners weighted their learning goal more than their interest (Q1, correlation = 0.616). In other words, they appreciated and were willing to read not-interesting-yet-pedagogically-useful papers, which validates our conjecture. Since the group project was assigned according to student interest (they selected it from available topics), there must exist positive correlation between student interest (Q1) and usefulness of paper (Q3), which equals to 0.535.

In addition, we also studied the effect of 'peer-to-peer' recommendations made by each learner after s/he read the papers. Overall, the result is quite encouraging, showing that learners will tend to recommend those highly rated papers specially tailored for them to other similar learners (Q5, correlation coefficient = 0.696).

4.3 Lessons Learned

When we analyze the comments given by learners after they read the two recommended papers, we found out that the majority of learners have struggled to reach a '*harmony*' between their interest and educational goal:

- They are still willing to accept interesting, yet pedagogically difficult paper
- They are also willing to accept un-interesting, yet pedagogically helpful paper

They admit that in order to acquire new knowledge for either their group project or long-term goal, they will tolerate the system to recommend those '*unsuitable*' papers to them. For example, one of the students wrote in the feedback form as follows: '*..interesting article on..., but I find this article is quite difficult to me, too many technical terms*'. Another wrote that "*to be frank, the article is not likely to be what I am interested in, but, it contains some useful knowledge...*'. One similar comment was also made by another student that ' *..it is difficult for me to understand, yet the topic that the paper discussed is very interesting.*'

Another interesting observation is that one critical features of the papers lies in its 'interestingness'. This is especially true in the case of the higher education in Hong Kong, since most of the students are 'application-oriented'. Hence, one big challenge for the RS is to retain learners and continuously engage them in the track of learning through the recommendation of 'interesting' papers.

As specified in [4] that the bottom-line measure of recommender system success is user satisfaction. One possible way of measuring user satisfaction is not just to collect the information on the degree of how much they like the recommended items, but to ask users whether or not they will recommend the items received to other fellow users (Fig. 3).

In general, conform to our hypothesis about the uniqueness of paper recommendations for educational purpose, users' pedagogical goal and interest have remained to be two of the most important features. How to balance between these two features will be one of the biggest challenges for research in the area.

5 Conclusion

In this paper, we explore the uniqueness of paper recommendation for e-learning systems through a human-subject study. Experiment results showed that the majority of learners have struggled to reach a '*harmony*' between their interest and educational goal: they are willing to read non-interesting-yet-pedagogically-useful papers in order to acquire new knowledge for either their group project or their long-term goal. Hence, from this perspective, learners seem to be more tolerant than users in commercial RSs. Nevertheless, as educators, we should still maintain a balance of recommending *interesting* papers and *pedagogically helpful* ones in order to retain learners and continuously engage them throughout the learning process. This is especially true in our case, since most of the students in Hong Kong are more 'application-oriented'.

In the future, we plan to conduct a larger scale of experiments to explore the issue of '*cross-recommendation*' where users will receive recommendation from both artificial and human learners.

References

1. Basu, C., Hirsh, H., Cohen, W. and Nevill-Manning, C. 2001. Technical paper recommendations: a study in combining multiple information sources. *JAIR*, 1, 231-252.
2. Bollacker, K., Lawrence, S. and C. Lee Giles, C. L. 1999. A system for automatic personalized tracking of scientific literature on the web. *ACM DL*, 105-113.
3. Brusilovsky, P. and Rizzo, R. 2002. Map-based horizontal navigation in educational hypertext. *Journal of Digital Information*, 3(1).
4. Herlocker, J., Konstan, J., Terveen, L. and Riedl, J. 2004. Evaluating collaborative filtering recommender systems. *ACM Transactions on Information Systems*, 22(1): 5-53. January 2004.
5. Kobsa, A., Koenemann, J. and Pohl, W. 2001. Personalized hypermedia presentation techniques for improving online customer relationships. *The Knowledge Engineering Review* 16(2):111-155.
6. McNee, S, Albert, I., Cosley, D., Gopalkrishnan, P., Lam, S., Rashid, A., Konstan, J. and Riedl, J. 2002. On the Recommending of Citations for Research Papers. *ACM CSCW'02*. 116-125.

7. Paepcke, A., Garcia-Molina, H., Rodriguez-Mula, G. and Cho, J. 2000. Beyond document similarity: understanding value-based search and browsing technologies. *SIGMOD Records*, 29(1): 80-92, March 2000.
8. Recker, M., Walker, A. and Lawless K. 2003. What do you recommend? Implementation and analyses of collaborative information filtering of web resources for education. *Instructional Science* 31:299-316, 2003.
9. Schafer, J., Konstan, J. and Riedl, J. 2001. Electronic Commerce Recommender Applications. *Data Mining and Knowledge Discovery*, 5, (1/2, 2001), 115-152.
10. Tang, T.Y. and McCalla, G. 2004. On the pedagogically guided paper recommendation for an evolving web-based learning system. *FLAIRS Conference 2004*. AAAI Press.
11. Tang, T.Y. and McCalla, G. 2004. Utilizing artificial learners to help overcome the cold-start problem in a pedagogically-oriented paper recommendation system. To appear, AH 2004.
12. Tang, T.Y. and McCalla, G. 2004. Evaluating a smart recommender for an evolving e-learning system: a simulation-based study. *Canadian AI 2004*.
13. Woodruff, A., Gossweiler, R., Pitkow, J., Chi, E. and Card, S. 2000. Enhancing a digital book with a reading recommender. *ACM CHI 2000*.153-160.

Sound Footings:
Building a National Digital Library of Australian Music

Marie-Louise Ayres[1], Toby Burrows[2], and Robyn Holmes[1]

[1] National Library of Australia, Canberra ACT 2600 Australia
{mayres,rholmes}@nla.gov.au
[2] University of Western Australia Library,
35 Stirling Highway, Crawley WA 6009 Australia
tburrows@library.uwa.edu.au

Abstract. MusicAustralia is a Web portal for anyone interested in Australian music. A joint development of the National Library of Australia and Screen-Sound Australia: National Screen and Sound Archive, it provides users with access to a federated resource discovery service for Australian music in notated and audio representations and in digital and non-digital formats, as well as a directory service providing information on people, organisations and services associated with Australian music. This paper outlines the architecture of the MusicAustralia service, focusing particularly on its federated service model and the infrastructure elements and business processes developed to support this architecture. It also looks at the way in which another major component of the federated digital library of Australian music – the Peter Burgis Performing Arts Archive – is using the MusicAustralia service model and architecture to shape its own strategies and structures.

1 Introduction

Ensuring access to music resources in the digital environment is a challenging task. Rapid developments in digital music technology, Web delivery of sound, score, image and multimedia, rights management and interactive technology systems are all changing the face of music. This means that the 'documents' of musical culture are becoming more complex to capture, preserve, manage and deliver and necessitates stronger linkages between the musical world and the collecting institutions.

The National Library of Australia is responsible for ensuring that documentary resources of national significance relating to Australia and the Australian people are collected, preserved and made accessible. Music resources have always been a major component of this mission. But in such a rapidly changing environment, how can long-term sustainable policy and planning for music resources best be developed at a national level?

In a federated national, state and local government system, and with music documented in different and complex formats, no single organisation can address these issues independently. Indeed, even the national music collection is primarily shared across two institutions. The National Library collects and preserves printed and manuscript music and personal papers, pictorial and ephemeral documentation, and oral history and archival sound recordings, mainly of folklore and vernacular mu-

R. Heery and L. Lyon (Eds.): ECDL 2004, LNCS 3232, pp. 281–291, 2004.
© Springer-Verlag Berlin Heidelberg 2004

sic. ScreenSound Australia: the National Screen and Sound Archive collects and preserves all commercially recorded music and its associated documentation.

The National Library and ScreenSound Australia identified a strong case for developing a national service for music which applied new technologies in an integrated
and holistic way and embodied a national digital strategy for music. Such a strategy
needed to address convergence of technologies and methodologies as well as interoperability. The service would have to be cost-efficient, in order to encourage participation and to generate content. It also needed to be built on collaboration and partner-
ships across cultural institutions, the research and education sectors, and the music
industry and communities.

This vision of a national music service has now become reality in the form of
MusicAustralia. [1] MusicAustralia is a new federated service developed jointly by
the National Library and ScreenSound Australia, together with a range of content
partners. Through a single Web interface, users can find comprehensive information
about Australian contemporary and heritage music and music-related resources, including printed scores, sound recordings, manuscripts, texts, images, moving images,
and Web sites. Users can also have access to digital musical materials in a variety of
formats and from a range of institutions and sectors, though the Australian digital
music collection is in its infancy and only a portion of the resources discoverable
through MusicAustralia are available online. MusicAustralia also enables users to
locate information about people, organisations, collections, activities and services.

2   Federated Service Model

The service model for MusicAustralia builds, in part, on the National Library's previous experience and success in developing PictureAustralia. [2,3] This federated service supports access to multiple collections of digitised images – more than 1,000,000
in all. In PictureAustralia users 'discover' digitised images from 30 different institutions through a single Web interface, and then navigate via image thumbnails back to
the home institution's server, where viewing copies and further information are located. Aggregation of metadata for PictureAustralia is highly automated. The National Library uses the Open Archives Initiative Protocol for Metadata Harvesting
(OAI-PMH) [4] to harvest descriptive metadata from contributing institutions, either
from Web pages generated by local collection management systems or via a local
OAI repository. Each institution must map and convert its own metadata schema to
the simple Dublin Core [5] schema deployed in PictureAustralia. This architecture
suits the Australian pictorial 'scene', in which a variety of descriptive record formats
are deployed to describe image collections.

The same basic approach has been applied in the design of MusicAustralia. Descriptive metadata are harvested and aggregated at a national level, with links back to
digital objects stored on the servers of contributing institutions. But a significantly
greater level of complexity is imposed by the nature of music resources, both in terms
of their description and in terms of their digital representations. Cooperative delivery,
at a national level, of digital music objects and their associated metadata is a significant challenge.

The MusicAustralia model builds on and aggregates existing processes, adapted to
a Web environment. The key aim is to maximise the quantity of bibliographic cover-

age while supporting the creation and delivery of digital music objects. These objects – digitised and 'born digital' – are retrieved from multiple and disparate databases, which the user is able to interrogate and navigate. The service model aims to facilitate participation by smaller, specialist organisations and independent artists, as well as by large national institutions.

3 Service Architecture – Resource Discovery

MusicAustralia has adopted a service architecture for resource discovery based on Australia's National Bibliographic Database (NBD). [6] The NBD is a national union catalogue with more than 14 million bibliographic records and 36 million holdings records. In 2003, the NBD held records in MARC format [7] for more than 55,000 Australian printed music items, almost 30,000 Australian music sound recordings, and several hundred Australian manuscript music items.

Nevertheless, significant portions of the Australian music corpus, especially commercially recorded music, were not represented in the NBD. These included the substantial holdings of ScreenSound Australia, the Australian Music Centre, the National Archives of Australia and the Australian Broadcasting Corporation (ABC). Many of these organisations create rich and detailed records to describe their music holdings. ScreenSound Australia's MAVIS [8] system, for instance, supports inclusion of both descriptive and collection management data.

The business model of the NBD has been changing in recent years, in response to a growing need to harvest metadata in formats other than MARC and to integrate them into the NBD. Placing the NBD at the centre of resource metadata aggregation for MusicAustralia has benefited both the NBD and MusicAustralia. The coverage of music resources in the NBD has grown dramatically with the addition of records destined for MusicAustralia, and MusicAustralia has been able to import the large number of existing records from the NBD.

In addition to resource metadata, MusicAustralia also aggregates metadata about people and organisations ('party metadata') for single point access. The initial content for the party data within MusicAustralia was derived from the NBD's Name Authority File, but this is being augmented with richer information from other sources. Institutions contribute party metadata as a separate process. Party metadata are stored in a local schema which has been developed in the international context of MAPS and EAC [9], and is seen as the first stage of a generic Australian party schema.

4 Business Processes for Resource Metadata

In 2003 the National Library implemented a Harvester service as a generic framework for updating repositories with data gathered from various sources. This includes support for the acquisition of 'batch' data as well as support for online data contribution. The Harvester batch system uses OAI or FTP to gather non-MARC data in standard formats and convert it for input to the NBD or another 'downstream' repository. The combination of the Harvester and the NBD in the MusicAustralia service model means that contributors can provide metadata in two different ways: as MARC records directly to the NBD, or as non-MARC records via the Harvester.

Current MARC record contributors to the NBD can continue to add their music records to the NBD by using the Kinetica cataloguing client or by using Kinetica Batch*Link from their local cataloguing system. [10] In both cases, MARC records are extracted from the NBD for the MusicAustralia database. Contributors of MARC records do not need to establish additional methods of presenting their data for inclusion in the MusicAustralia service.

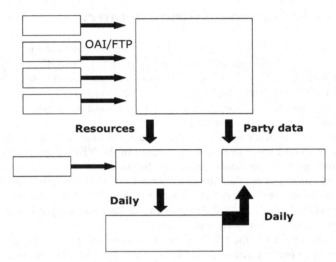

Fig. 1. MusicAustralia: Service Architecture and Business Processes for Resource Discovery

4.1   Contributing Non-MARC Resource Records and Party Records

Contributors of non-MARC records must present records extracted from their collection management system to the Harvester, which performs the following processing stages.

Harvest the Data. In many cases, contributors are establishing an organisational OAI repository to present their records for OAI harvesting. In some cases, contributors are choosing to FTP their records to the Harvester instead. The great advantage of the OAI method is that only new and/or updated records are presented, which significantly reduces processing loads.

Format and Analyse the Data. In most cases, data are presented in the Metadata Object Description Schema (MODS), which the National Library has adopted as its exchange XML schema for Harvester purposes. MODS is richer than Dublin Core and more adaptable than MARC, and was developed with digital objects firmly in mind. The Library of Congress offers a number of stylesheet tools for converting data between Dublin Core, MODS and MARC. [11]

MODS meets all identified MusicAustralia resource metadata needs, and offers significant advantages over Dublin Core, especially in its capacity to represent 'constituent parts'. In some cases, however, data are harvested in Dublin Core or institution-specific formats. The Harvester must therefore recognise and invoke any contribution-based rules, including rules specifying automated conversion from one of these formats to MODS.

Submit the Data for Further Processing. The Harvester separates new, updated and deleted resource records into different processing streams, converts them from MODS to MARC, and submits them to the NBD. This involves three steps:

Using an XSLT [12] stylesheet (provided by the Library of Congress but amended to meet local conditions) to convert the MODS data to the MARCXML [13] schema;

Using a MARCXML to MARC converter (provided by the Library of Congress but amended to overcome some difficulties with character encoding schemes) to convert the MARCXML data to the MARC binary format; and

Passing the MARC data via FTP to the Kinetica Batch*Link service, which undertakes additional match and merge and data processing actions before loading the data into the NBD.

In the case of party records, new, updated and deleted records are received by the Harvester (already converted via stylesheet processes to the MusicAustralia party schema) and passed directly to the MusicAustralia party database, which must directly manage functions such as match, merge and error identification. It is possible that a more generalised, intermediate party database may be developed in the future, or that batch updating of the NBD Name Authority File will eventually be supported.

The processes described above relate to batch contribution of data via the Harvester. An online update and review component for the Harvester is currently being developed. This will allow data to be input or edited via a Web form, reviewed by repository administrators (or not, depending on business needs) and approved for passing to the NBD or another 'downstream' repository.

It should be noted that the decision to pass resource data through the NBD does not impose any additional requirements on non-MARC MusicAustralia contributors. To contribute to MusicAustralia, contributors must be able to extract data from their own collection management systems, convert that data to an agreed exchange format (in this case, MODS) and present the data for harvesting. Each MusicAustralia contributor is free to make its own decisions about what and how much of its data it wishes to expose. This includes the freedom to decide to expose all Australian music records, or only those that are associated with digital content.

4.2 Extracting and Storing Resource Metadata

MARC records are extracted from the NBD to MusicAustralia based on a combination of criteria: material type, 'Australian content' flags, music-related classification numbers, physical description, and subject headings. Following the initial extraction of records from the NBD, MusicAustralia regularly polls the NBD for new and changed records. The MARC records extracted from the NBD are converted to MARCXML using a Library of Congress XSLT stylesheet and stored in the MusicAustralia resource database on the National Library's TeraText [14] platform. MARCXML was chosen as the storage format for the resource database because it is consistent with the work being done in the Kinetica redevelopment and is likely to simplify the extraction process from the NBD once this redevelopment is completed.

While the Library of Congress had done considerable work on conversion from MARC to MODS, the National Library was the first institution to use MODS as an exchange format to incorporate non-MARC data into a MARC database. Various modifications to the MODS schema and to the MODS to MARCXML stylesheet were identified during the development of MusicAustralia. This process required a considerable investment of time and intellectual resources, but the lessons learned – and the opportunity to contribute to MODS schema and stylesheet development – outweighed the costs. The National Library now has a sound understanding of MODS, is confident that it is an appropriate schema for data exchange and storage, and has the skills to assist contributors to convert and present their data in this schema.

5   Service Architecture: Digital Objects

While the initial focus of the development of the MusicAustralia service has been on resource discovery, a framework for the delivery of digital objects has also been established. As with the PictureAustralia service, the key principle is that the digital objects themselves are stored on the home institution's server, with a link from the MusicAustralia metadata record. But music poses a series of different challenges. In the first place, PictureAustralia delivers a single object type – the image. MusicAustralia delivers digitised sheet music and larger scores, sound recordings, born digital scores and MIDI files, pictorial images, manuscripts, multimedia and text (books and theses). The single images in PictureAustralia are relatively simple to deliver, but MusicAustralia's digital objects are not so simple. Digitised scores and manuscripts contain multiple images which must connect to form a whole. Born-digital scores pose significant challenges arising from the different forms of proprietary software used to create them. Sound recordings also raise a number of significant delivery issues, including whether to stream or not, how to integrate digital audio with meaningful bibliographic information, and how to deliver the files at resolutions which make for good listening but can still be available to the majority of Australians who do not have access to broadband services.

Digitisation of music has proceeded slowly in Australia to date. By mid-2004, about 7,500 Australian scores were available online. More than 6,000 of these come from the National Library's collections. The remainder come from five State libraries, and were digitized as part of a cooperative project supported by the National Library. Several thousand sound recordings have been digitized by ScreenSound Australia, the National Library, and some Australian universities. But only a fraction of these are currently available online, as a result of the complexities of clearing copyright and delivering derivatives of preservation masters for public access. Negotiations are in progress with rights management organizations to permit the delivery of in-copyright materials under a blanket licence.

Links to digital audio files are invoked from icons appearing in the MusicAustralia metadata record. MusicAustralia does not prescribe how digital objects are stored, managed and delivered on participants' servers, nor the metadata schema used to record information about the digital objects locally. But it does provide advice and guidelines for digitising audio files, both for preservation purposes and for online delivery. These cover such issues as file types, connection and access methods, and quality. The guidelines for online delivery are aimed especially at enabling optimum access by a wide range of users across different types of network connections. They suggest that contributing institutions consider delivering audio files in two different formats, so that users can choose whichever is more appropriate for them. These may be of mid-range quality (for broadband connections) or low quality (for modem connections), depending on bit rates. Whether to provide downloading MP3 files or streaming files is largely a matter of local I.T. resources, since the latter require streaming server software. The National Library itself provides two streaming formats: RealAudio and QuickTime (at a minimum bit rate of 24kbps).

Digitised scores are delivered initially as thumbnail images retrieved from the participant's server and embedded in the MusicAustralia metadata record. MusicAustralia prescribes the size and format of these thumbnail images, but not of the full image which is displayed by clicking on the thumbnail. Thumbnail images should be 150 pixels in their longest dimension, with the other dimension set to 150 pixels or less in order to maintain the aspect ratio of the image. The preferred format for these thumbnails is JPEG. MusicAustralia recommends the creation of a 'view copy' and a larger 'examination copy' of image files, as well as a PDF file containing a collated version of the entire item, for printing purposes. Satisfactorily delivering multi-page image files has been a major issue for the participants, with a variety of solutions being tried. New delivery software is likely to make this easier in the future.

For text files, contributing organisations are encouraged to use a standardized format such as XML for the preservation copy, encoded using a schema such as EAD or TEI. A less satisfactory, but less resource-intensive alternative would be PDF. For online delivery, XML files should be converted to HTML for Web viewing, or transformed to PDF for printing or downloading the entire file. For 'born digital' scores, the preference is for online delivery in HTML format, created from within the original software package (such as Finale or Sibelius). These files will still require the installation of an appropriate browser plug-in. A PDF version is recommended where the original software does not offer the facility for HTML conversion.

6   Using MusicAustralia

Users of MusicAustralia can search at two different levels: a simple search across all creator, title, subject and date fields, and an advanced search of specific fields. The simple search resembles a Google-type search, and is designed to provide an easy entry into the service. The advanced search is designed for more sophisticated users and more complex queries. It can be limited to specific item types or to the collections ofspecific institutions, and can also be restricted to records with digital objects attached. Standard Boolean operators can be used to combine searches of different fields. Browsing of works by title, creator or date is also possible, as is browsing people by name.

Search results are presented as a brief summary of each item, together with a link to more detailed information and related items, a link to information about the holding institution, and a thumbnail or icon representing a digital object (if available). Related items will include links to audio recordings related to sheet music (and vice versa), different versions of a piece of sheet music, and different audio recordings of the same piece of music. Thumbnail images link to digitised sheet music, while appropriate icons link to audio files, digital scores, multimedia and digital texts. Audio files from a results set can be selected to form a playlist and played in sequence.

A particular feature of MusicAustralia is its ability to enable simultaneous viewing of scores (or texts) and listening to audio files. Each item selected from the results summary will open a separate browser window. The user can choose a digitised score or text from the results summary, open a separate window for it, and then go back and choose an audio recording, which will appear in a third window. The audio file can then be played while viewing the score. Digital scores can also be combined into this process.

7   MusicAustralia and the PASH Project

In parallel with the development of MusicAustralia, a major project is underway to catalogue and digitise the contents of the Peter Burgis Performing Arts Archive, the most significant private collection of music and music-related resources in Australia, recently acquired by the University of Western Australia. [15] The Burgis Archive covers the work of Australian musicians and composers in all musical fields over the last hundred years. It encompasses Western art music, blues, jazz, country and western, folk, pop and rock, ethnic music, indigenous music, music theatre, radio shows and advertisements, recordings of historic events and oral history. In all, it contains almost 200,000 individual items: 112,000 sound carriers and 72,000 print documents. The sound recordings include rare cylinder recordings (3,000), Edison discs (2,200) and 78s (64,000). The print library includes posters, photographs, concert programmes, sheet music and biographical files. The value of the Archive for research into the history of musical composition and performance and the history of entertainment is immense. Cataloguing and digitising the Burgis Archive is the major component in Preserving Australia's Sound Heritage (PASH), a national project which also covers the Australian Archive of Jewish Music held at Monash University.

The Burgis Archive will form a major component of the national digital library of Australian music. It is essential that the service model and architecture developed for this collection are closely integrated with the overarching approach of MusicAustralia. The PASH project is uniquely placed to take advantage of the framework laid down by MusicAustralia, since no retrospective conversion of metadata is required and the resource discovery architecture for PASH is being developed from scratch.

The PASH project is developing strategies in two main areas: resource discovery, and digital content management. As far as resource discovery is concerned, the overriding strategic aim is to ensure that resource metadata from PASH can be integrated into MusicAustralia. The project is currently carrying out a comparative evaluation of MARC cataloguing and resource description based on metadata schemas like MODS. A major consideration is the level and nature of training and expertise required. MARC-based music cataloguing is particularly specialised and time-consuming, on the one hand, but MODS-based resource description is a new field with little in the way of precedents or expertise.

If the MODS approach is followed, PASH will need to establish its own method for exposing its metadata to the National Library's Harvester service for inclusion in MusicAustralia. If MARC is used, records can either be created directly in the NBD using the Kinetica Cataloguing Client or created locally and uploaded using Kinetica's Batch*Link service. One advantage of direct cataloguing would be the ability to reuse existing catalogue records from the NBD for items also held in other collections, but the proportion of unique material in the Burgis Archive is relatively high.

The extent to which the PASH project will create, contribute and use 'party metadata' for composers' and performers' names is also being analysed. In large part, this is dependent on the decisions made about local creation and direct Web availability of resource metadata.

Compatibility with MusicAustralia in digital content management is also an important consideration for the PASH project, though direct integration is not a requirement here. PASH intends to establish its own digital repository, initially to hold digitised versions of selected sound recordings, with priority in the digitisation process is being given to the most rare and fragile items in the Burgis Archive. The different delivery and management systems being used by MusicAustralia contributors for their digital objects are being evaluated by the PASH project to ensure that, as far as possible, it identifies and adopts national best practice in this field. MusicAustralia also specifies its own preferred formats for image and audio files, and the PASH project will aim to comply with these.

One area of particular interest is the possible applicability of software solutions for institutional research repositories, such as DSpace and Fedora. These are currently the subject of national investigation by two projects funded by the Australian Research Information Infrastructure Committee (ARIIC): Australian Research Repositories Online to the World (Project ARROW) [16] and the Australian Partnership for Sustainable Repositories. [17] The National Library is a partner in both these projects. The PASH project is investigating the use of this kind of repository to store and deliver digitised music files.

8 Related Work

As part of its planning for the MusicAustralia service, the National Library has monitored a range of international digital music initiatives. These have included digitisation projects, Web gateways, and technical investigations. [18]

Several significant music digitisation projects have been undertaken in North America. These have generally focused on sheet music, notably the Lester Levy and Duke University digital sheet-music collections, with their impressive descriptive analysis and depth of functionality. Canada's Virtual Gramophone service is a major audio digitization project, focusing on 78s, while Jukebox was a European pilot project for access to distributed collections of archival audio files.

Various music gateway services have also been developed in Europe and North America. They include collection-level descriptions (e.g. Cecilia), union catalogues (e.g. Ensemble and Music Libraries Online) and information about musical activities (e.g. European Musical Navigator). Other projects, such as Variations2 and WEDELMUSIC, have addressed the technical requirements for Web-based delivery of digital music objects, and associated issues in music information retrieval.

MusicAustralia is unique in the way it combines various current strands of international digital initiatives in music. It combines a national framework, a union catalogue, and innovative approaches to metadata harvesting and aggregation. It also provides a Web gateway to distributed collections of digital objects, representing various different musical formats – sheet music, audio files, multimedia, and digital scores.

9 Conclusion

MusicAustralia has laid the foundations for a national digital library of Australian music and has provided the basis for future infrastructure development in this key subject area. For closely related national initiatives like the PASH project, it is crucial to ensure that their strategies and outcomes are compatible with MusicAustralia, at the very least, and are integrated with it wherever possible.

As with the national pictorial collection, the national music collection has traditionally been split between sectors which have not shared information. Users have therefore been unable to use a single service to discover the location of music materials – even such closely related materials as a score and an associated recorded performance of an Australian work. In addressing this need, MusicAustralia has not only created an innovative resource discovery service; it is concurrently encouraging and supporting the creation of the national digital music collection.

Its specific benefits and achievements already include:

- Using the existing infrastructure of the NBD to handle contributor business processes, both offline and online, as well as record de-duplication processes;
- Reducing costs to MARC-based MusicAustralia contributors, by avoiding the need to support two separate processes for generating resource metadata;
- Increasing the representation of Australian music records in the NBD by incorporating records from organisations and sectors not currently contributing to it;
- Testing and developing large-scale processes for harvesting, gathering and converting data in a range of non-MARC formats.

A key challenge is to broaden data contribution options and therefore the data contributor profile, while retaining data quality and consistency. Including records from organisations which may not have as much expertise as the MARC community in creating and managing descriptive metadata may mean some compromises on data quality. But such data quality issues are probably of more concern to libraries than they are to end users. End users, especially those who 'discover' materials through a specialist service such as MusicAustralia, tend to use simple search terms and their discovery needs can largely be met through relatively simple records.

Several key goals for the further development of MusicAustralia in the medium term have been identified. They include:

- Encouraging the creation and contribution of a greater level of digital content, especially through the selective digitization of score- and sound-based music resources. The PASH project will serve as an exemplar for this process.
- Developing infrastructure to accept, manage and deliver knowledge annotations contributed by users of the service, and using these annotations to improve resource descriptions.
- Developing an authoritative directory of biographical and organizational information about Australian composers, performers and music organizations.

- Providing seamless integration between the resource description, biographical and annotation components of the service.
- Positioning the service to take advantage of likely developments in music information retrieval systems and the online delivery of commercial recordings.

The launch of MusicAustralia in 2004 is a major cooperative achievement, and has provided a firm foundation for the continuing development of a national digital library of Australian music.

References

1. http://www.musicaustralia.org
2. http://www.pictureaustralia.org
3. Holmes, R., Ayres, M.-L. : Federating access to Australian culture: PictureAustralia, Australia Dancing and MusicAustralia. http://www.nla.gov.au/nla/staffpaper/2003/ayres2.html (2003)
4. http://www.openarchives.org/
5. http://dublincore.org/
6. Missingham, R. Electronic Resources: New Issues for Library Systems with New Solutions. (2001) : http://www.nla.gov.au/nla/staffpaper/2001/missingham2.html
7. http://lcweb.loc.gov/marc/bibliographic/ecbdhome.html
8. http://www.wizardis.com.au/ie4/products/mavis/introducingmavis.html
9. http://www.loc.gov/standards/mads/   http://www.library.yale.edu/eac/
10. http://www.nla.gov.au/kinetica   [Kinetica is the National Library's national cataloguing and resource sharing service, currently undergoing a major redevelopment.]
11. http://www.loc.gov/standards/mods/MODS
12. http://www.w3.org/TR/xsltXSLT
13. http://www.loc.gov/standards/marcxml/MARCXML
14. http://www.teratext.com/home.html
15. UWA News 22 (16) (20 Oct. 2003) 6:
    http://www.publishing.uwa.edu.au/uwanews/2003/uwanews20031020.pdf
16. http://www.arrow.edu.au
17. http://sts.anu.edu.au/downloads/APSR.pdf
18. http://www.musicaustralia.org/info/internationalprojects.html

Content-Based Retrieval
in Digital Music Libraries

Michael Clausen, Frank Kurth, Meinard Müller, and Andreas Ribbrock

Department of Computer Science III, University of Bonn
Römerstraße 164, 53117 Bonn, Germany
{clausen,frank,meinard,ribbrock}@iai.uni-bonn.de
http://www-mmdb.iai.uni-bonn.de

Abstract. MiDiLiB is a six year research project on digital music libraries funded by the German Research Foundation (DFG) as a part
of the *Distributed Processing and Delivery of Digital Documents* (V^3D^2)
research initiative. MiDiLiB's main focus is the development of content-
based retrieval algorithms for both score- and waveform-based music. In
this paper we give an overview of our research results, describe several
prototypical systems for content-based music retrieval which have been
developed during the project, and discuss applications of the presented
techniques in the context of today's and future digital music libraries.

1 Introduction

During the course of the development of digital libraries for non-textual or *non-
standard* document types, the last five years have seen increasing efforts in the
field of music libraries[1]. Problems arising from the task of handling non-standard
document types in digital libraries are manifold. A rough and non-exhaustive life-
cycle of a non-standard document within a digital library may include the stages
of digitization, choice of a suitable data format, transfer to and registration with
the library. Furthermore, one has to deal with the issues of content-analysis
(and annotation) as well as the generation of classical and content-based index-
structures for efficient document access and retrieval. Finally, the creation of
(multimodal) user interfaces, usage of system independent mechanisms for long-
term document storage, and development of novel services for end-users to access
the documents are of fundamental importance within a library scenario.

Among those tasks, content-based document analysis and retrieval is one
of the most challenging problems. In *content-based* document processing, raw
data contained in a document are processed directly, rather than relying on
secondary document descriptions such as annotated metadata related to the
document. With regard to the huge existing collections of digital documents,
efficient mechanisms for content-based document analysis are of fundamental

---

[1] To avoid confusion, in this paper we shall use *music* as a general term comprising
score- and digital waveform-based data. The term *audio* denotes digital waveform-
based data like CD-audio or radio broadcast signals.

R. Heery and L. Lyon (Eds.): ECDL 2004, LNCS 3232, pp. 292–303, 2004.

importance, in particular as generally the manual creation of secondary document descriptions is unfeasible. In content-based retrieval, queries to document collections are processed based on suitable index structures derived from an automatic content analysis.

One of the earliest and most intuitive tasks in content-based music retrieval is the *name-that-tune* application, where a user is interested in finding the title of a tune or a song which has been broadcast on the radio. Frequently, a listener is familiar with parts of the main theme or the hook line of the song although he might not remember the composer or interpreter. In order to find out about such kind of information (metadata), one could call the radio station or, provided availability, investigate the station's playlist on the internet. In case none of these alternatives is available, a comfortable solution could be to hum or whistle the tune in question into a microphone and let a computer do the work of finding the desired information. For this purpose, the whistled tune is converted into a suitable sequence q of notes and then compared to a collection $m_1, \ldots, m_N$ of melodies which are used as a reference database. All melodies which are close to q with respect to a suitable distance measure are returned as query results. Music search based on note-representations is commonly refered to as *score-based retrieval*. One of the pioneering works in this field [1] is based on transforming query and database melodies into so called down-up-repeat (DUR, also known as *Parson's code*) sequences, for roughly representing pitch intervals between subsequent notes. Such sequences provide a certain robustness against query errors with respect to musical intervals and absolute pitches of queried notes. The book of Barlow and Morgenstern [2] is one of the first content-based music dictionaries for manual search. It contains key-normalized pitch sequences representing the introductory parts of a large number of classical pieces.

Although the previous example as well as the sketched solution sound intuitive, real score-based retrieval scenarios impose several fundamental problems such as developing methods and user interfaces for query formulation, facilitating fault-tolerant queries, or devising index structures for efficient query processing. While the scenario of melody-based search allows us to use well-known data structures and algorithms form the field of text retrieval, the search in collections of complex, polyphonic musical scores requires data models and retrieval algorithms which are better adapted to music data. When the underlying music documents consist of audio signals as, e.g., CD-audio, content-based retrieval requires methods from digital signal processing. Important research topics in the field of content-based audio retrieval are audio identification, genre classification, and recommendation ("customers who bought song a also bought song b").

By now, the community of researchers specializing in music information retrieval (MIR) has grown to a considerable size, which is documented by the success of the the annual *International Conferences on Music Information Retrieval (ISMIR)* bringing together music researchers, audio engineers, computer scientists, librarians, and music industry [3]. The recently finished MiDiLiB-project, which has been funded by the German Research Foundation (DFG) as a part of the *Distributed Processing and Delivery of Digital Documents* (V^3D^2) research initiative, has contributed to several of the recent advances in content-based music retrieval. In this paper, we outline the technical concepts on music retrieval developed by the MiDiLiB-project. Besides developing techniques for content-based indexing and search of music documents this includes concepts for the important tasks of audio monitoring and synchronization of musical documents in different formats. We present several of our prototypical systems for efficient music retrieval and give an overview on our test results. Taking into account related work, we outline current issues in music retrieval and discuss future trends in the area of digital music libraries.

Concerning content-based music retrieval, MiDiLiB's main contributions are the development of data structures and efficient, fault tolerant techniques for polyphonic search in collections of polyphonic scores [4]. Besides for the first time allowing efficient search in polyphonic scores, a particular strength of the proposed techniques is a natural mechanism for finding and precisely localizing partial matches, the latter accounting for possibly incomplete user knowledge. Extensions of our technique have been successfully applied to the problems of fast audio identification [5]. As a generalization, we developed a technique for content-based search in large classes of multimedia documents including digital 2D-images, shapes, and 3D-models [6].

The paper is organized as follows. In Sections 2–4, we give an overview on our techniques for content-based music retrieval on different types of music documents. Section 2 deals with the task of searching in scores of polyphonic music. As a second task, in Section 3 we discuss melody-based retrieval, which may be considered as the monophonic version of the latter (general) score-based retrieval. However, when allowing vague user queries such as melodies whistled into a microphone, special care has to be taken to develop suitable mechanisms for incorporating fault tolerance. Sections 4 sketches how the developed techniques may be extended to search in large collections of audio signals. In particular, we describe a technique for identifying short excerpts of audio signals and present some recent applications. Finally, Section 5 discusses techniques for synchronizing music documents given in different data formats (like, e.g., score- or signal-based formats) and outlines the importance of such algorithms in digital library scenarios. Concluding, Section 6 discusses possible applications of the retrieval techniques in the context of future digital music libraries.

2   Score-Based Retrieval

One of the key problems in searching scores of polyphonic music by content is to find appropriate models for representing the score data. In a classical approach, which has already been sketched in the introduction, a sequence of notes is simply modeled as a string of symbols representing the notes' pitches. For example, the melody *Twinkle twinkle little star* would be represented by the string ccggaagffeedc. In a score-based retrieval scenario, a collection of N melodies would be modeled by a database of strings $m_1, \ldots, m_N$. Likewise, a user's query is represented by a string q. For query processing, q would be compared to all melody strings m_i using a suitable similarity measure d. A simple similarity measure is given by the *edit distance* $d(A, B)$ between two strings A and B, i.e., the minimum number of *edit operations* required to transform string A into string B. The three classical edit operations are insertion, deletion, and replacement of individual symbols.

It turns out that when considering polyphonic music, the classical string-based approach is no longer feasible. One of the main reasons is that simultaneous notes cannot be modeled appropriately. Also note durations and rhythmic behaviour are not modeled by the above string-based representation. A main problem with the string-based approach is the treatment of the notes' onset positions which are represented only implicitly, i.e., by their respective position within the melody string. In [4] we present a framework for modelling polyphonic music where note onset positions are made *explicit*. In this, a note is a pair $[t, p]$ consisting of a pitch p and an onset position t. Then, a score-based music document may be easily modelled as a *set* of notes. For example $D_1 := \{[10, c^1], [10, e^1], [14, c^2]\}$ is a music document consisting of three notes, two simultaneous notes of pitches c^1 and e^1 played at time position 10 and one note of pitch c^2 played at time 14. The set of all possible notes will hence be denoted by $U := \mathbb{Z} \times \{c^1, d^1, e^1, \ldots\}$, i.e., each note has an integer time-component ($\mathbb{Z}$) and a certain pitch ($c^1, d^1, e^1, \ldots$). We consider a database $D_1, \ldots, D_N$ where each document D_i is simply a set of notes, i.e., $D_i \subseteq U$. *Exact matches* for a query $Q \subseteq U$ may then be easily defined by requiring that a time-shifted version $Q + \tau$ of Q occurs in a document D_i. As a toy example, consider the query $Q := \{[5, c^1], [9, c^2]\}$. As $Q + 5 := \{[5 + 5, c^1], [9 + 5, c^2]\} = \{[10, c^1], [14, c^2]\}$ is contained in the above document D_1, the pair $(5, 1)$ will be called a match, the number 1 specifying the matching document and the number 5 representing the time-lag required to shift the query to the matching position.

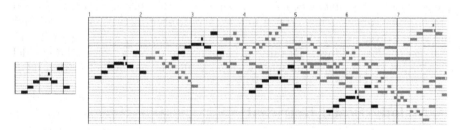

Fig. 1. Query to a database in the piano roll notation (left) and excerpt J.S. Bach's Fugue in C major, BWV 846, where all occurrences of the query are highlighted (right).

The proposed idea may be easily extended to other types of matches. As an example, assume that instead of using symbols $c^1, d^1, e^1, \ldots$, pitches are modelled using integers $0, 1, 2, \ldots$. Then we could define a match to be a triple (τ, ρ, i) satistfying $Q + (\tau, \pi) \subseteq D_i$, i.e., the query Q time-shifted by τ *and* pitch-shifted by π semitones occurs in document D_i. Score-based music is typically visualized using the so called *piano-roll* notation, where each note is represented by a rectangle located at position $[t, p]$ corresponding to its pitch p and onset-time t. The width of a rectangle is proportional to the corresponding note's duration. As an example, Fig. 1 (left) shows the piano-roll representation of a small query document. To the right, all pitch- and time-shifted occurrences of the query within an excerpt of J.S. Bach's Fugue in C major, BWV 846, are highlighted. Further types of matches are necessary when considering fault-tolerant search. An important example is that a few, say k, notes of a query Q do not match a target position $Q + t$ within document D_i. To account for this, we say that (t, i) is a hit with k *mismatches*. Further types of fault tolerance including a concept of *fuzzy notes* as well as a mechanism for incorporating a user's prior knowledge on certain aspects of the desired document are discussed in [4].

Efficient index-based algorithms for the proposed types of matches have been devised and successfully tested on a database of 12,000 pieces of music containing about 33 million notes. The algorithms are based on a modified version of inverted files, which are well-known from classical full-text retrieval. Intuitively, for a given database $\mathcal{D} = (D_1, \ldots, D_N)$, one inverted file $H_{\mathcal{D}}(p)$ is created for each pitch p. If a note $[t, p]$ occurs in piece D_i, an object (t, i) is included in the inverted file $H_{\mathcal{D}}(p)$. Together, the inverted files form an *inverted index*. In our PROMS system [4], exact queries consisting of some 10–100 notes can be answered in about 50 milliseconds on a Pentium II, 300 MHz PC. The underlying database consists of music given in the popular score-like MIDI format [7]. Queries may be specified, e.g., by using an integrated piano-roll editor or by recording a piece of music using a MIDI-piano connected to the system.

We summarize some related work in the field of polyphonic score retrieval. Lemström et al. recently considered several retrieval tasks using a data model which is very similar to our approach [8]. Doraisamy et al. [9] model polyphonic scores based on n-grams and use standard database techniques for query processing. Pickens et al. [10] consider polyphonic score-based retrieval where the query consists of an *audio signal*. For this purpose, the query is first transformed into an approximate score version and then processed further. A very difficult and yet unsolved aspect of score-based retrieval is *similarity-based* search. Typke et al. use the Earth Movers Distance in combination with a set-based data model to incorporate a similarity measure within an efficient retrieval algorithm [11].

3   Melody-Based Retrieval

In a melody-based retrieval scenario we assume that a melody, i.e., a monophonic sequence of notes, is used for querying a database of melodies. Typically, a melody-based retrieval system allows queries to be formulated by humming, singing, or whistling a tune into a microphone. Hence such a system is targeted to a much broader class of users than a system for polyphonic retrieval.

The above set-based approach may be naturally extended to handle melody queries. However, due to the differences in the general query scenario, much more fault-tolerance is needed to successfully process a query. First, the hummed or whistled query is is transformed into a sequence of notes using a suitable ex-

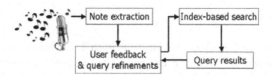

Fig. 2. Overview of the NWO system architecture.

traction algorithm. Besides note extraction being an error-prone task in itself, the users's input may contain wrong notes, missing notes, deviations in rhythm and tempo, or the query may be formulated in the wrong key. Taking into account such sources of errors, our set-based approach to score-retrieval has been extended by a tempo-tracking mechanism as well as a technique to account for missing notes. The tempo-tracker is used to account for the typical tempo variations occurring in many hummed or whistled queries. For this purpose, during query processing each match candidate is assigned a tempo-tracking parameter. In each step of the retrieval algorithm, a limited variation of this parameter (w.r.t. the queries' tempo curve) is allowed, otherwise a match candidate is excluded from further processing. In [12], we present the NWO-system (notify!-by-whistling online) for recognizing tunes whistled into a microphone. Fig. 2 shows an overview of the NWO system's architecture. Following the extraction step, the extracted notes are presented to the user in a piano-roll representation. The user then may verify his query by acoustic playback and make corrections to the extracted notes. Before actually issuing a query, the user is allowed to incorporate his prior knowledge about the desired query result by specifying parameters like rhythm tolerance or the maximum number of missing notes. After querying the user is allowed to copy melody fragments of particular query results for reusing them as new queries. Hence a special type of relevance-feedback is possible. An online version of NWO working on a manually compiled (and hence limited) database of about 2,000 melodies is currently made available.

It turns out [12] that our set-based approach for tempo-tracking shows significant advantages when users are able to remember rythmic and harmonic details of the query item. In such a case our search algorithms, in contrast to the classical edit-distance based approaches, only retrieve the few relevant database items as query results. This holds even if a query consist of only a few, say 4–6, notes. If, on the other hand, queries are of low quality, an edit distance- (or generally string-) based retrieval approach usually yields better results. However, this comes at the expense of longer result lists and longer required query lengths.

In the field of melody-based retrieval, a significant amount of research has been done during the last decade. Besides the pioneering work carried out in the New Zealand Digital Library project [1] we only mention two recent contributions. First, the Cuby-Hum system incorporates many of the essential technical aspects of a state-of-the-art query-by-humming system. The paper [13] is thus a good starting point for further reading. As a second aspect, a robust extraction of note events from user queries is crucial for obtaining high quality queries. In connection with the musicline.de database project, a query-by-humming technique has been developed which uses a physiological model for pitch extraction [14].

4 Audio Retrieval

In audio retrieval, rather than working on high level musical features such as notes, retrieval is performed based on the digital waveform signals of the underlying music. An early approach for classifying sounds according to characteristic acoustic and perceptual features has been proposed by Wold et al. [15]. In this approach, short acoustic fragments constituting similar sounds are grouped to clusters, examples being clusters for laughter, scratchy sounds, or barking dogs.

An important problem in audio retrieval is the *identification* of audio signals. Given a large database of known audio signals, the latter may be regarded as a retrieval problem. Typically, a query signal will be a short and probably very noisy excerpt of an original signal. A recently very popular application scenario consists of recording a part of an unknown song using a mobile phone. Such a scenario could take place in a car, a restaurant, or some other noisy environment. The recorded song is then transmitted to an identification agency. After successful identification, the user is provided with the song's title, composer, interpreter, and possibly ordering information for the corresponding CD.

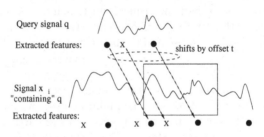

Fig. 3. Waveforms and feature representations extracted from a query signal q (top) and a database signal x_i (bottom). A t-shifted version of the query signals' feature representation $F[q]$ occurs in $F[x_i]$.

A main problem in audio retrieval are the large volumes of data which have to be handled. However, it turns out that the set-based approach to score-retrieval presented in Section 2 may also be used to obtain efficient algorithms for audio identification. Fig. 3 gives an overview on the underlying concepts, where the basic idea consists of converting the huge number of sample values constituting an audio signal to a so-called *feature representation*. Indexing and searching is then performed based on those feature representations. Feature representations are obtained using a so-called *feature extractor* F, which assigns class labels c from a set $\mathcal{X}$ of available feature classes to signal positions t within an audio signal. A *feature* $f = [t, c] \in \mathbb{Z} \times \mathcal{X}$ is a pair consisting of a time position t and a class label c assigned to this position. Fig. 3, shows a feature extractor F extracting significant local maxima and minima from an input signal. In this case, $\mathcal{X} = \{\text{x}, \bullet\}$, where feature class $\bullet$ denotes essential local maxima and class x denotes essential local minima. The figure shows a query signal q and a database signal x_i which are processed by F. The upper part shows the waveform signal q and the feature representation $F[q]$. Note that the the extracted features are plotted at their respective sample positions. Hence, for the given signal q, the feature representation $F[q]$ contains three elements. The lower part of Fig. 3 shows the corresponding data for the signal x_i. To illustrate our concept of feature-based identification, we note that a t-shifted version of the query signal q occurs in the database signal x_i. This in turn is reflected by the t-shifted feature representation $F[q]$ matching a subset of the feature representation $F[x_i]$. As compared to the above technique for score-based search, the notes $[t, p]$ are just replaced by features $[t, c]$, hence making the full index-based retrieval technique available. Thus for audio indexing, instead of creating inverted files for each pitch, the search index consists of one inverted file for each feature class.

To give an impression of resulting index sizes, we mention one of our test collections consisting of 15 GB of uncompressed audio which has been indexed using several different feature extractors. The resulting index sizes range from 33 to 128 MB amounting to averages of 85–420 features per second. For more test results and detailed information on the various feature- and application-settings as well as our prototypical *audentify!*-system, we refer to [16, 17].

As a second retrieval task we briefly discuss *audio monitoring*. Monitoring applications generally deal with the detection or inference of certain events from particular real-time data streams and have recently gained a great deal of attention, particularly in the fields of databases and information retrieval. When monitoring real time audio streams such as broadcast channels (e.g., radio or TV), one is interested in detecting occurrences of known audio fragments or, more generally, particular acoustic events within those streams. To illustrate how audio monitoring may be performed using our retrieval technique, we assume that a collection of radio commercials is given as a database. In a preprocessing step, a search index is built from this collection as described above. During the process of monitoring, a computer receives a radio program via cable or network connection. Subsequently, the incoming audio signal is transformed into a feature representation. After a fixed number of features have been extracted, we use this so-called *feature segment* as a query to the search index. By storing the query results of each feature segment in an appropriate data structure, it is possible to precisely transcribe which commercial of the database has been broadcast at what time. Applications of such a scenario include automatical creation of advertising statistics, or, using a search index built from a large collection of music signals, automatic generation of playlists. For a description of our prototypical monitoring systems *audentify!-live* and Sentinel we refer to [5, 18].

We briefly summarize related work on audio retrieval. An early approach to recognize distorted musical recordings was proposed in [19]. In the context of large data collections, algorithms for robust audio identification include audio hashing [20], geometric hashing-based approaches as proposed by Wang et al. [21], hidden markov models (HMMs) [22], or clustering-based approaches [23]. An overview on the proposed techniques may be found in [24]. Only recently, audio identification services for the above mobile phone scenario have been launched in several parts of Europe as, e.g., the service offered by Shazam Entertainment. Future work will also be concerned with using compact feature representations of audio signals for exchanging content-based information [25].

5 Music Synchronization

Modern digital music libraries contain textual, visual, and audio data. Among this multi-media based information, musical data poses many problems, for musical information is represented in many different data formats which, depending upon the application, fundamentally differ in their respective structure and content. So far we have encountered two such data formats: the score data format and the digital waveform-based data format which we simply referred to as audio. Score data roughly describes music in a formal language depicted in a graphical-textual form, whereas audio data encodes all information needed to reproduce an acoustic realization of a specific musical interpretation. Other data formats such as MIDI may be thought of as a hybrid of the score and audio data format. In MIDI, relevant content-based information such as the notes of a score as well as agogic and dynamic niceties of a specific interpretation can be encoded.

Hence, a musical work in the digital context is far from being unique since it can have several different realizations in several different formats. This heterogeneity makes content-based browsing and retrieval in digital musical libraries a challenging tasks. For example, one may think of a user who tries to find a specific passage in some audio CD but only roughly knows the melody or only remembers some score-based information such as a configuration of certain notes.

One important step towards a solution is the synchronization of multiple information sets related to a single piece of music. In the audio framework, by *synchronization* we denote a procedure which, for a given position in one representation of a piece of music, determines the corresponding position within another representation (e.g., the coordination of score symbols with audio data). Such linking structures could extend score-based music-retrieval to facilitate access to a suitable audio CD and could assist content-based retrieval in heterogenous digital music libraries – for example, allowing melody-based retrieval in the audio scenario and vice versa. Furthermore, linking of score and audio data could be useful for automatic tracking of the score position in a performance or for the investigation of tempo studies.

Within the MiDiLiB-project, we designed and implemented algorithms for the automatic synchronization of score-, MIDI- and audio-data streams representing the same piece of music [26]. To align, for example, an audio data stream with a score data stream, we first extract score-like parameters such as onset times and pitches from the audio data stream. Then the actual alignment is computed based on the score-parameters by a technique similar to the classical dynamic time warping (DTW) approach. Only recently, two similar DTW-based synchronization algorithms have been proposed: Turetsky et al. [27] first convert the score-data stream into an audio-data stream using a suitable synthesizer and perform the alignment in the audio domain. Soulez et al. [28] use the score data to design a sequence of suitable filter models which can then be compared with the audio data stream. In contrast to these two approaches, we perform the synchronization purely in the score-like domain which has advantages in view of both efficiency and accuracy.

However, due to the complexity and diversity of music data the problem of automatic music alignment is still far from being solved – not only concerning the data format but also concerning the genre (e.g., pop music, classical music, jazz), the instrumentation (e.g., orchestra, piano, drums, voice), and many other parameters (e.g., dynamics, tempo, or timbre). For the future it seems promising to devise a system incorporating multiple competing strategies (instead of relying on one single strategy) in combination with statistical methods as well as explicit instrument models in order to cope with the richness and variety of music.

6   Conclusions and Future Work

In this paper, we discussed recent advances in the field of digital music libraries. We focused on the important aspect of content-based retrieval and gave an overview on some of the techniques which have been developed in our MiDiLiB-project. More precisely, we described a set-based technique for searching scores of polyphonic music by content. Subsequently, we showed how this technique may be exploited in melody-based retrieval, e.g., name-that-tune applications, as well as efficient audio identification and monitoring. The underlying general technique is not restricted to the field of music retrieval, but may be used for searching in general collections of multimedia documents by content [6] Another important aspect of the MiDiLiB-project are algorithms for synchronizing music given in different formats. We sketched an underlying technique and pointed to several applications in the context of digital music libraries.

The last years have seen significant technological progress in content-based music retrieval, where several retrieval tasks such as polyphonic score search and audio identification for the first time became manageable on large scale document collections. Whereas complex score-based search by now is mostly restricted to music experts, existing prototypes for melody search offer a sufficient degree of fault tolerance to make them suitable for a broader class of users.

Based on the technological advances and the large existing collections of music data, the next years will probably see an increasing number of publicly available (online-) music services. To conclude our paper we briefly sketch such a scenario of a client-server based service for real-time exchange of music-related information. In our scenario, a modified audio player (serving as a client application) during acoustic playback of an audio track receives the track's lyrics from a server application, possibly located within some library. The lyrics may then be displayed synchronously to the actual acoustic playback. Such a service may be realized using techniques for audio indexing, identification and audio-to-text snychronization. For this, an index of audio fingerprints is generated in a proprocessing step. The audio fingerprints (consisting of suitable feature sets) of a certain track are then suitably linked to the corresponding lyrics. During playback of an audio track, fingerprints are extracted from that track. Those are transmitted to the server and then used to determine the actual song and playback position. Subsequently, the corresponding lyrics are transmitted to the client application. Note that in the proposed approach one is not required to make the actual audio tracks publicly available, but works on extracted finger-prints only. Besides efficiency issues this has significant advantages concerning legal issues such as copyright- and content-protection.

Future work will be more and more concerned with developing the latter type of applications. However, in spite of the significant recent advances in the underlying technologies for content-based document processing, there is still much fundamental research work to be done in the field of semantic content analysis.

References

1. Rodger J. McNab et al.: The New Zealand Digital Library MELody inDEX. D-Lib Magazine (1997)
2. Barlow, H., Morgenstern, S.: A Dictionary of Musical Themes. Faber and Faber, London (1991)
3. ISMIR: International Conference on Music Information Retrieval (2001) http://www.ismir.net/.
4. Clausen, M., Engelbrecht, R., Meyer, D., Schmitz, J.: PROMS: A Web-based Tool for Searching in Polyphonic Music. In: Proceedings Intl. Symp. on Music Information Retrieval 2000, Plymouth, M.A., USA. (2000)
5. Clausen, M., Kurth, F.: A Unified Approach to Content-Based and Fault Tolerant Music Recognition (2003) IEEE Transactions on Multimedia, Accepted for Publication.
6. Clausen, M., Körner, H., Kurth, F.: An Efficient Indexing and Search Technique for Multimedia Databases. In: SIGIR Workshop on Multimedia Retrieval, Toronto, Canada. (2003)
7. Selfridge-Field, E., ed.: Beyond MIDI: The Handbook of Musical Codes. MIT Press (1997)
8. Ukkonen, E., Lemström, K., Mäkinen, V.: Geometric Algorithms for Transposition Invariant Content-Based Music Retrieval. In: International Conference on Music Information Retrieval, Baltimore. (2003)
9. Doraisamy, S., Rüger, S.: Robust Polyphonic Music Retrieval with N-grams. Journal of Intelligent Information Systems **21** (2003) 53–70
10. Pickens, J., Bello, J.P., Monti, G., Crawford, T., Dovey, M., Sandler, M., Byrd, D.: Polyphonic Score Retrieval Using Polyphonic Audio. In: International Conference on Music Information Retrieval, Paris. (2002)
11. Typke, R., Giannopoulos, P., Veltkamp, R.C., Wiering, F., van Oostrum, R.: Using transportation distances for measuring melodic similarity. In: International Conference on Music Information Retrieval, Baltimore. (2003)
12. Kurth, F., Clausen, M., Ribbrock, A.: Efficient Fault Tolerant Search Techniques for Full-Text Audio Retrieval. In: Proc. 112th AES Convention, Munich, Germany. (2002)
13. Pauws, S.: CubyHum: a fully operational query by humming system. In: International Conference on Music Information Retrieval, Paris. (2002)
14. Heinz, T., Brückmann, A.: Using a Physiological Ear Model for Automatic Melody Transcription and Sound Source Recognition. In: Proc. 114th AES Convention, Amsterdam, Netherlands. (2003)
15. Wold, E., Blum, T., Kreislar, D., Wheaton, J.: Content-based classification, search, and retrieval of audio. IEEE Multimedia **3** (1996) 27–36

16. Ribbrock, A., Kurth, F.: A Full-Text Retrieval Approach to Content-Based Audio Identification. In: Proc. 5. IEEE Workshop on MMSP, St. Thomas, Virgin Islands, USA. (2002)
17. Kurth, F., Clausen, M., Ribbrock, A.: Identification of Highly Distorted Audio Material for Querying Large Scale Data Bases. In: Proc. 112th AES Convention, Munich, Germany. (2002)
18. Kurth, F., Scherzer, R.: Robust Real-Time Identification of PCM Audio Sources. In: Proc. 114th AES Convention, Amsterdam, Netherlands. (2003)
19. Fragoulis, D., Roussopoulos, G., Panagopoulos, T., Alexiou, C., Papaodysseus, C.: On the automated recognition of seriously distorted musical recordings. IEEE Trans. SP **49** (2001) 898–908
20. Haitsma, J., Kalker, T.: A Highly Robust Audio Fingerprinting System. In: Proc. ISMIR 2002. (2002)
21. Wang, A.: An Industrial Strength Audio Search Algorithm. In: International Conference on Music Information Retrieval, Baltimore. (2003)
22. Cano, P., Battle, E., Mayer, H., Neuschmied, H.: Robust Sound Modeling for Sound Identification in Broadcast Audio. In: Proc. 112th AES Convention, Munich, Germany. (2002)
23. Allamanche, E., Herre, J., Fröba, B., Cremer, M.: AudioID: Towards Content-Based Identification of Audio Material. In: Proc. 110th AES Convention, Amsterdam, NL. (2001)
24. Cano, P., Battle, E., Kalker, T., Haitsma, J.: A Review of Audio Fingerprinting. In: Proc. 5. IEEE Workshop on MMSP, St. Thomas, Virgin Islands, USA. (2002)
25. Tzanetakis, G., Gao, J., Steenkiste, P.: A Scalable Peer-to-Peer System for Music Content and Information Retrieval. In: International Conference on Music Information Retrieval, Baltimore. (2003)
26. Arifi, V., Clausen, M., Kurth, F., Müller, M.: Synchronization of Music Data in Score-, MIDI- and PCM-Format. In Hewlett, W.B., Selfridge-Fields, E., eds.: Computing in Musicology. MIT Press, accepted for publication (2003)
27. Turetsky, R.J., Ellis, D.P.: Force-Aligning MIDI Syntheses for Polyphonic Music Transcription Generation. In: International Conference on Music Information Retrieval, Baltimore, USA. (2003)
28. Soulez, F., Rodet, X., Schwarz, D.: Improving polyphonic and poly-instrumental music to score alignment. In: International Conference on Music Information Retrieval, Baltimore. (2003)

Knowledge-Based Scribe Recognition
in Historical Music Archives

Ilvio Bruder, Temenushka Ignatova, and Lars Milewski

Database Research Group, Computer Science Department
University of Rostock, Germany
{ilr,temi,mile}@informatik.uni-rostock.de

Abstract. For the content-based management and access to domain-specific data in digital libraries, special domain-knowledge and knowledge processing functionality are required. However, the integration of knowledge components has not yet become an integral part of existing digital library systems. The current paper represents the realization of a digital archive of historical music scores, integrating special domain-specific data and functionality for writer identification in historical music scores. We introduce the basic formalisms and heuristics for the representation of handwriting characteristics. To compare two handwritings we propose the usage of a normalized, weighted Hamming distance function to calculate the degree of similarity between their handwriting characteristics. For the identification of writers we employ the k-nearest neighbor method to build clusters of similar writers, based on the calculated distance. And finally, we represent and evaluate the test results from the prototype implementation of the system.

1   Introduction

A necessary step towards improving the usability of digital libraries and archives is to provide specialized services, to users with special needs in management and representation of documents and knowledge. Examples for special users' needs can be found in numerous domains. In our work we elaborate the requirements of a special-users group, of music scientists, towards a specialized digital archive of music scores. Historical music scores are valuable sources of information about the circulation and practicing of music in the past. Musicologists are concerned with the extensive analysis of numerous copies of scores made by professional scribes at different geographical locations. At the University of Rostock there exist about 5000 handwritten music sheets from the 17th and 18th century. The manual management and analysis of such amount of sheets and facts about them is a tedious work. Digital libraries provide the organization of the data in a way allowing easier access and enhanced research possibilities for the historical documents of this interesting collection.

Few existing digital libraries foster the integration of domain-knowledge and user-specific management of information. The digital library project "Perseus" [1], for example, aims at providing specialized services for the needs of users of cultural heritage digital libraries. One of the biggest digital libraries projects for

R. Heery and L. Lyon (Eds.): ECDL 2004, LNCS 3232, pp. 304–316, 2004.

cultural heritage ECHO (http://echo.mpiwg-berlin.mpg.de) as well as the New Zealand digital library project - Greenstone rely on specialized mechanisms for content-based text annotation and retrieval supported by the integrated GATE software for human language processing system (gate.ac.uk). Multimedia digital libraries for video, audio, and images such as the Informedia Digital Library (http://www.informedia.cs.cmu.edu) focus on annotating, indexing, and retrieval of multimedia content for the extraction of "digested" data. However, specialized services for domain-specific data have not yet become an integral part of digital library systems.

In this paper we represent some achieved results in the ongoing project "eNoteHistory". The project has the aim to build a digital archive, integrating knowledge components and specialized functions for writer identification in historical music scores. We have realized the modeling, storing and retrieval of the digital documents and their metadata, using existing methods from document management systems [2]. In this communication we focus on the integration of special domain-specific data and methods for the scenario described in section 2. Section 3 contains a formal concept of the knowledge data structure and methods. Implementation details and an example are provided in section 4. Section 5 and 6 conclude with extensive evaluations and a general assessment of the system.

2   A Writer Identification Scenario

We accomplished several steps, in the process towards developing a specialized archive for the identification of scribes in music scores. After digitalizing documents and bibliographical metadata, we defined a data model for structuring and linking the digital information. The mapping of the unstructured information onto the data model was realized with an adequate preprocessing and import procedure. Having accomplished this step we could provide a couple of simple search and browsing possibilities in the digital collection of music scores. The next step was gathering and representing domain-specific knowledge to be used for the analysis of handwriting characteristics in the music scores. And finally we formalized and implemented methods for the comparison and classification of the handwriting features, to make special queries for the identification of scribes possible.

Identifying and gathering relevant and accurate knowledge is a task, which we undertook in cooperation with domain-experts, who are best aware of what features are necessary for recognizing a handwriting. They also know well which relations and coherences exist between these features. Thus we created a *Knowledge Base* consisting of two groups of data. On the one hand, we have the descriptions and data structures for representing the domain of handwriting features. And on the other hand, we have measures and evaluations to iterate and interpret the data structure, as well as relations and coherences between the elements of the data structure. These data are our abstract knowledge about the collection of music documents. We need to represent each document in terms of this abstract knowledge in the form of handwriting feature descriptions.

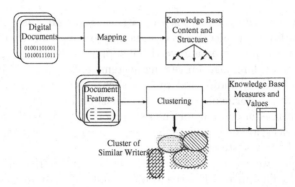

Fig. 1. Creation of Document Features.

Figure 1 illustrates the extraction and clustering of features from the digitalized documents. From an abstract point of view the extraction process represents the mapping of documents into the feature space, thus allowing us to search in the knowledge base for documents, based on their handwriting features. Using the features extracted from the music scores and the distance information in the knowledge base we could classify the scores according to their handwriting characteristics. The result is a set of clusters of handwriting characteristics, where each cluster in the best case represents exactly one scribe. It should be also possible to classify new handwritten music sheets by trying to find a cluster containing similar scores or by creating a new cluster if similar scores cannot be found.

To determine appropriate classification methods we analyzed different classification and clustering techniques [3–5]. Inductive methods, such as 1-rule, ID3, C4.5, and SVM could not be applied for the classification of music handwriting features due to several reasons: the similarity values between the features don't have a conventional metric (a special similarity measure is needed); the feature values are nominal scaled so that, e.g., no spanning of a space for SVMs is possible; integration of external knowledge is required, e.g., feature priorities; overfitting and one-shot-learning. To cope with these restrictions, we use the instance-based method, k-nearest neighbor [6], which classifies all existing feature instances and learns with each new instance. Any similarity measure can be used in the k-nearest neighbor method to calculate the similarity between features. The k-nearest neighbor method has already been used in other writer recognition projects, e.g.: a project from the State University of New York [7] for writer identification based on 62 symbols subdivided in so called micro and macro features; and an information retrieval-based writer identification from the University of Rouen (France) [8] for handwriting recognition using patterns (writer's invariants) for recognizing handwritten graphemes.

3 Feature Base: The Knowledge

About 80 handwriting features in historical music scores have been defined as relevant for the writer identification, by the cooperating group of music scientists.

These features are categorized in 13 feature groups: clefs, slant, note stems, note flags, note beams, accidentals, note heads, time signatures, bar lines, note beams offset, rests, writing habits, staves. Each feature group represents a hierarchy of detailed characteristics, which build up the concrete features. In this way the different kinds of note flags, for example, eighth and sixteenth note flags are grouped together as shown in Figure 2. Each of these two features are further on particularized in note flags of notes with ascending and descending stems. The node enumeration in the tree hierarchy, represented as a *dot-separated notation*, e.g., "4.1.1.", is used for the identification of the features. We refer to the set of all feature hierarchies as the *Feature Base*. The Feature Base contains not only the features themselves, but also the possible values for each feature. The set of possible values is organized also hierarchically, and represents an extension of the feature hierarchy as shown in Figure 2. The feature values are also identified with the dot-separated notation. This organization has the aim to facilitate the manual handwriting feature analysis. To determine the feature values for an analyzed music score, one has to navigate through the tree-like structure. The deeper in the hierarchy the feature value is determined the more precise is the feature description. However it is not always necessary to choose a value from the leaves of the tree. The analysis may stop on a higher level.

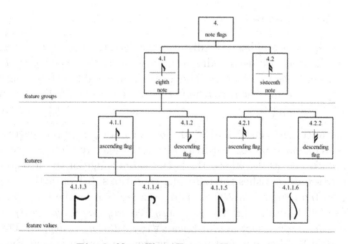

Fig. 2. Note Flags Feature Hierarchy.

3.1   Feature Base – Hierarchical Model

A set of feature values representing the characteristics of a handwriting is a feature vector γ. The feature vector contains values for the features $f_1 \ldots f_n$ and has the form $\gamma = (v_1, \ldots, v_n)^T$ where v_i is a value from the value range W_i of the feature f_i. The set of all feature vectors is $\Gamma = \{\gamma \mid \gamma = (v_1, ..., v_n)^T, \forall i : v_i \in W_i\}$. The set of all features is $F = \{f \mid f \text{ is a feature}\}$.

The structure of the *Feature Base* is realized as an acyclic, directed graph (tree): $FB = (V, E, \mu, \nu, \tau)$, where $V(v_1, \ldots, v_n)$ is a set of nodes and $E \subseteq V \times V$ a set of directed edges, which connect the nodes. All feature groups are represented in the same tree, thus a common root for the *Feature Base* is defined. Each node has a description μ. Furthermore, each node has a sequential number, which distinguishes it from its neighbor nodes from the same level $\nu : V \to \mathbb{N}$. The function τ is defined as $\tau : V \to Type$. This function assigns each node from the tree a value from the set $Type = \{\text{'prefix', 'value', 'feature'}\}$ where: $\forall x \in V :$ $\tau(x) = \text{'feature'} \Rightarrow \forall y \in \Lambda_x : \tau(y) = \text{'value'}$; and $\forall x \in V : \exists y \in \Lambda_x : \tau(y) = $ 'feature' $\Rightarrow \tau(x) = $ 'prefix'. A node x with $\tau(x) = $ 'feature' is called a feature. The underlying partial tree is the value range of this feature. Each node in the underlying tree has the type 'value'. Thereafter, we can refine the definitions for the set of Features F and the set of values W_i: $F = \{f \mid f \in V \wedge \tau(f) = $ 'feature'$\}$ and $W_i = \Lambda_{f_i}$ for all $f_i \in F$.

The path in a tree represents a unique identifier for a node: $PATH : V \to P$. P is a set of paths which are built in the following way. A path $PATH(x)$ for a node x is calculated by following the nodes from the root node to the node x. $PATH(x)$ is a sequence of the numbers of each of these nodes in the order from root to the specified node with a separating point between each number.

3.2   Distance Measure

Two handwritings are similar if the distance between their feature vectors γ_a and γ_b is small. Therefore we need a distance measure of the type $d_\Gamma : \Gamma \times \Gamma \to [0 \ldots 1]$ to compare the two vectors. The normalized weighted Hamming distance function proved to return the best results (see tests in section 5.2). Thereafter, for $\gamma_a = (v_1^a, \ldots, v_n^a)^T$ and $\gamma_b = (v_1^b, \ldots, v_n^b)^T$ we use: $d_\Gamma = \frac{w_1 d_{f_1} + \cdots + w_n d_{f_n}}{\sum_{j=1}^n w_i}$, where d_{f_i} is the distance between v_i^a and v_i^b and w_i is the weight of the feature f_i. The distance between each pair of features f_i from the feature vectors is represented by $d_{f_i} : W_i \times W_i \to [0..1]$, where W_i is the value range of the feature f_i. The distance function d_{f_i} satisfies the following conditions: (a) $\forall x, y \epsilon W_i : d(x, y) \geq 0$ with $d(x, y) = 0$ only if $x = y$; (b) $\forall x, y \epsilon W_i \wedge$ x and y have the same path length from the root: $\forall x' \epsilon \Lambda_x : d_{f_i}(x', y) > d_{f_i}(x, y) \; \forall y' \epsilon \Lambda_y : d_{f_i}(x, y') > d_{f_i}(x, y)$; (c) The distance function is not symmetrical: $\forall x, y : d(x, y) \neq d(y, x)$. This means that if a typical handwriting feature of a writer is to put a curl at the end of a music element line, it would be more probable that the same writer omits the curl in some cases than if a writer who usually does not use curls decides to put a curl at the end of a clef line; and (d) The triangular inequality rule is also not valid, because the categorical values do not have a continuous order: $\forall x, y, z \epsilon W_i : d(x, y) \not\geq d(x, z) + d(z, y)$.

We distinguish three possibilities to measure, represent and interpret the distance between single features. (1) Comparison of values: The simplest solution is to employ boolean logic: $d_{f_i}^{Bool}(x, y) = \begin{cases} 0, \, if \; x = y \\ 1 \end{cases}$. This distance metric is however for most features inappropriate because even very small changes in the handwriting of the same scribe will be treated in the same way as significant differences between the handwritings of different scribes. Thereafter, a measure is needed which maps the similarities in the whole value range between 0 and 1. (2) Comparison of values based on value analysis: If the features are represented as digit sequences (derived from the dot-separated notation), they can be split into digits and thus compared. We can extract the digits of two feature values $x_P = PATH(x)$ and $y_P = PATH(y)$ in $(x_P^1, \ldots, x_P^n)$ and $(y_P^1, \ldots, y_P^n)$ respectively and compare each pair from the same hierarchy level: $d_{f_i}^{Ana}(x, y) = \frac{\sum_{j=1}^n d_{f_i}^{Bool}(x_P^j, y_P^j)}{n}$. This distance function has an accuracy of $\frac{1}{n}$ where n is the depth of the value range tree. The fact that the function is still based on boolean logic does not allow similarities between values from the same level to be found. (3) Comparison of values based on value analysis and additional information: The similarity between the feature values, was defined heuristically by the music scientist for each feature tree. For most of the features the similarities between the feature values are known not only for a level but also for whole value range. We use a distance matrix to represent the similarities as scalar values, between each pair of feature values:

$$dis_{f(i)} = \begin{pmatrix} d_{x_1,y_1} & \cdots & d_{x_n,y_1} \\ \cdots & \cdots & \cdots \\ d_{x_1,y_n} & \cdots & d_{x_n,y_n} \end{pmatrix}, \forall j : x_j, y_j \epsilon W_i.$$ Therefore, the distance function

can be represented in the following way: $d_{f_i}^{Inf}(x, y) = d_{x,y}$ with $d_{x,y}$ from $dis_{f(i)}$ on position (x, y).

We use (3) to represent the distances between most of the feature groups. However, there are some exceptions, which make use of the (1) and a combination of the (2) and (3) metric.

3.3   Special Feature Values

Null Values. We distinguish two types of null values, which can appear in the handwriting feature vectors:
(1) Non-Information-Null (?) – there exists no information about a certain feature value; e.g., in a particular music score the C-clef is not used, thus no value can be defined for the writer. In this case a distance between two features can be calculated only if both values are not equal to (?). In the calculation of the Hamming distance participate only those pairs of features, for which the distance can be calculated. We named the distance between two features, where none of the values is equal to (?) a *usable* distance function. $d_{f_i}(v_1, v_2)$ is usable $\Leftrightarrow v_1, v_2 \epsilon W_i \wedge v_1 \neq ? \wedge v_2 \neq ?$. Then the normalized, weighted Hamming distance will look like this: $d_\Gamma = \frac{\sum_{\forall i : d_{f_i} \text{ usable}} w_i * d_{f_i}}{\sum_{\forall i : d_{f_i} \text{ usable}} w_i}$.
(2) No-Applicable-Null ($\top$) – a value for this feature will never exist for a writer. This null value is regarded as an additional value in the feature value range, and the distance between the no-applicable-null and all the other values of a feature is the maximum distance between features.

Complex Values. Until now we have considered only the case when for each feature in a feature vector exactly one value can be assigned. However, in a more general scenario we have to consider that there could be more than one value for a feature assigned: $\gamma_C = (V_i, ..., V_n)^T$, $\forall i \in \{0..n\} : V_i \subseteq W_i$. Therefore, we defined a distance function for complex features: $d_{f_i}^C : \mathfrak{P}(W_i) \times \mathfrak{P}(W_i) \to [0...1]$. $\mathfrak{P}(W_i)$ is a power set of (W_i), which satisfies the condition: $min_{\forall v^1 \in V_1, v^2 \in V_2}(d_{f_i}(v^1, v^2)) \leq d_{f_i}^C(V_1, V_2) \leq \frac{\sum_{\forall v^1 \in V_1, v^2 \in V_2} d_{f_i}(v^1,v^2)}{|V_1| \times |V_2|}$. We tested different possible distances (see section 5.2). It turns out that the best value comparison results are achieved when the distance function value tends to minimum. The conditions concerning the non-information-null values have also an effect on the calculation of the distance function for complex values. A complex feature distance function we name *usable* when none of its arguments is equal to (?). $d_{f_i}^K(V_1, V_2)$ is usable $\Leftrightarrow V_1, V_2 \subseteq W_i \wedge V_1 \neq \emptyset \wedge V_2 \neq \emptyset$. The final form of the Hamming distance is: $d_\Gamma^K = \frac{\sum_{\forall i : d_{f_i}^K usable} w_i * d_{f_i}^K}{\sum_{\forall i : d_{f_i}^K usable} w_i}$.

4   The Implemented Prototype

The implemented prototype[1] is based on an object-relational database management system (IBM DB2). The database consists of schemas for metadata and images of music scores, for the Feature Base, and for the handwriting feature vectors of writers. It also integrates functions and methods for distance determination and clustering/classification of handwritings. The current version of the prototype has web interfaces for searching and navigating metadata and images and an interface for recognizing similar writers, using a describing tool for handwriting features.

4.1   Existing Tools

We set the following requirements for the implementation of the prototype application: (1) Support for instance-based classification, (2) Unlimited choice of distance functions, (3) Unlimited adaptation of distance parameters, (4) Choice of a distance matrix for each attribute, and (5) Support for null values and multiple values. We could identify only three data mining tools, which satisfy our first criteria: Darwin, MLC++, and Weka.

Darwin [9] uses an instance-based classification method 'Match Model' which is based on the k-nearest neighbor method. The value of k and the weights can be modified. Null values are supported, using the data preselection possibilities. However, multiple values and user-defined distance matrices are not supported. *Weka* [4] has two classes IB1 ((I)nstance (B)ased with k=1) and IBk also based on the k-nearest neighbor method. The value of k is modifiable, but the distance function is not. Weights can only be determined by a training set. It is though possible to specify a distance matrix. The source code is free and could be

---

[1] The prototype is available at http://www.enotehistory.de

used for a modified implementation. *MLC++* [10] provides an abstract class for classification. A subclass IB is an implementation of Aha [11]. The feature weights for the classification are modifiable. Both MLC++ and Weka can be used. But, we need significant modifications in order to adapt the standard methods to our needs. Furthermore, considering the need of integration of the methods in the database management system, we decided to reimplement the methods taking account of each requirement that we have.

4.2 Implementation in a Database Environment

The *Feature Base* was implemented as a database schema in the IBM DB2 Database Management System (in principle the use of any other object-relational database system is possible). The integration of the classification functionality into the database environment was planned, in order to provide a transparent interface with short communication ways for the clients.

IBM DB2 supports the integration of methods by so called user-defined functions (UDF) or stored procedures. UDFs are usable within SQL statements, where stored procedures are only accessible by a special call mostly from an application.

We implemented two user-defined functions A_{FV} and A_S. A_{FV} returns the k-nearest feature vectors for a given query vector γ_q: $A_{FV} = \{\gamma \epsilon \Gamma | d_\Gamma(\gamma, \gamma_q) \leq t\}$ using the distance function d_Γ. The threshold t influences the number of relevant results. A list of relevant scribes is returned by the A_S function based on A_{FV}. Both functions use a couple of interfaces to features and distance matrices in the database. The result table includes a feature vector or a scribe name with a similarity measure.

4.3 Example

The procedure from the recognition of features to the scribe identification is shown by the example in Figure 3.

First, the music scientist has to recognize a characteristic notation of the g-clef in the original music score. Then, he/she has to navigate through the g-clef feature tree to find the most similar notation in the tree (in Fig. 3 it's a g-clef with a closed and descending loop left of the g-point). This notation is a possible value of the g-clef. The numerical value (...1.2.2.1.7) is needed for the similarity determination, which follows. To determine the similarity between two different notations, we need the similarity matrices. If we compare the g-clef of this example handwriting with another one with g-clef value ...1.2.2.1, we can find the similarity of 0.6 in the g-clef matrix. For a convincing similarity between both handwritings at least 40 % of the features have to be determined. Using only the g-clef would lead to a low similarity value, because the g-clef is only one of 80 possible features. The following table 1 shows a result set of a query. The result set includes the similarity, a quality measure, and the scribes name. Scribe names are often fictitious, because the name is not known.

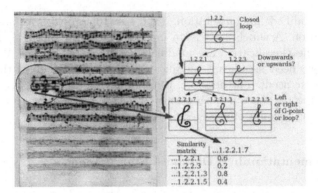

Fig. 3. Example of a Semi-Automatic Feature Extraction and Writer-Identification Procedure.

Table 1. A result set including similarity, quality measure (N_D see following evaluation measures), and the writers name (_a and _b specify different periods of a writer).

No	Similarity	Quality	Scribe
1.	0,018	0,534	AN305_a
2.	0,091	0,564	AN305_b
3.	0,126	0,548	Reichardt I_a
4.	0,192	0,394	J.M. Baldauff_a
5.	0,214	0,434	Büchler IV_a

5   Evaluations

To test our approach, we defined measures for evaluating the distance function, its parameters, the feature weights, and the query results. The objective was to achieve an optimal configuration of the current system which meets the requirements of the music historical experts.

5.1   Evaluation Measures

Scoring Function: We use a scoring function (SF) for instance-based clustering methods to evaluate the distance function and its parameters. SF is a measure of the tightness of a cluster [3]. The distance between instances of the same cluster has to be as small as possible, compared with distances between instances of different clusters, in order to reach an optimal scoring function value:

$$SF = \frac{\sum_{\forall (\gamma_1, \gamma_2) \in \Gamma^2_{\neq}} d_\Gamma(\gamma_1, \gamma_2)/|\Gamma^2_{\neq}|}{\sum_{\forall (\gamma_1, \gamma_2) \in \Gamma^2_{=}} d_\Gamma(\gamma_1, \gamma_2)/|\Gamma^2_{=}|}, \text{ with}$$

$\Gamma^2_{=} = \{(\gamma_1, \gamma_2)|\gamma_1 \neq \gamma_2, \gamma_1 \text{ and } \gamma_2 \text{ are instances of the same cluster}\}$, and
$\Gamma^2_{\neq} = \{(\gamma_1, \gamma_2)|\gamma_1 \neq \gamma_2, \gamma_1 \text{ and } \gamma_2 \text{ are instances of different clusters}\}$. The aim is to maximize the SF measure.

In the current case we do not need to perform the clustering step because we already have a set of predefined clusters of writers. Therefore, we can use this measure to evaluate directly the distance function and the parameters. A maximum value for the SF measure indicates a good choice of the distance function and its parameters.

Precision/Recall: The evaluation measures, precision and recall [12], are broadly used for evaluating information retrieval systems. We adopt these measures to evaluate the developed system for writer identification queries. For each query Precision $= \frac{|A \cap B|}{B}$ and Recall $= \frac{|A \cap B|}{A}$, where A is a set of all relevant features of the query, and B is the set of features in the result set. Precision is a measure of quality and recall is a measure of quantity regarding query results.

$K = kind\ of\ average\ precision$: K is used to evaluate the result sets after their interpretation of the best result feature. The result of a query for identifying a writer should contain the correct writer class. Precision/recall evaluates the system based on information retrieval aspects: whether the best results have the highest relevance and the last results the lowest relevance. Contrary to that measure, K evaluates the system based on classification aspects: either the right class is recognized or not. $K = \frac{X}{N}$, where X is the number of all result sets with correct identified writers and N is the number of all result sets.

Impact of Null Values (N_F, N_D): We defined two measures to evaluate the impact of null values. The first measure represents the relationship in a feature vector between the weights of null values and the weights of all values: $N_F(\gamma) = \frac{\sum_{\forall i: v_i = null} w_i}{\sum_{\forall i} w_i}$. The second measure defines the proportion of features which are not used for the distance calculation due to a null value in one or both of the vectors: $N_D(d(\gamma_a, \gamma_b)) = \frac{\sum_{\forall i: v_i^a = null \vee v_i^b = null} w_i}{\sum_{\forall i} w_i}$.

5.2 Evaluation Interpretations

We applied the evaluation measures in order to prove the reliability of the methods and query results. Apart from the particular tests, some of them (distance function, distribution of feature weights, and distribution of feature values) were combined to consider possible interferences between the tests.

Distance Function. Different distance functions, including Hamming Distance, Euclidean Distance, and one higher order distance metrics were tested. The higher order distance measures increased the influence of bigger differences between single features on the overall feature vector distance. The Hamming distance led to the best results according to the SF and the K measure and proved to be significantly better than the Euclidean distance and the higher order distance.

Feature Relevance and Weights. Every feature participates with a certain weight in the calculation of the overall distance between feature vectors. The feature weights can be used to increase or decrease the impact of a feature on the result of the distance function. We determined the weight of features by calculating the distance between two feature vectors omitting the feature for which we want to determine the weight. If the result of the distance function improved, the omitted feature received a lower weight and vice versa. The next step was to estimate the distribution of weights for each feature. We tested (1) a constant, (2) a linear grouped, (3) a linear, (4) a quadratic grouped, and (5) a quadratic distribution. The test results show that the SF improves after each test from (1) to (5) and K improves in the opposite direction from (5) to (1). Therefore, we chose to use the linear distribution as a compromise for a good SF and a good K. This distribution corresponds also best with the expert knowledge of the music scientists.

Optimization of Distance Matrices. The similarity values in the distance matrices were heuristically determined by music scientists, without considering the classification/clustering algorithms. For example, a value of 0.95 is very close to a 1.0 and this distance could be overvalued. Therefore, we needed to check the range of all values in a matrix by altering them with the following functions: translation with $x - 0.2$, $x - 0.1$, $x + 0.1$, $x + 0.2$; scaling with $x/4$, $x/2$, $x * 2$; exponentiation with x^2, x^3, $\sqrt{x}$, $\sqrt[3]{x}$. The results indicated that the preliminary determined values were slightly too high. Functions which decreased the values led to a better evaluation. But, the improvement is not significant. Thus, we can use the original values further on.

Null Values and Multiple Values. The presumption that incorrect or false distances between feature vectors are based on too many null values (low N_D) could be validated. Correctly recognized writers have less null values in their feature vector (high N_F). In the case of multiple values for a feature another problem is detected. Which one of the possible values should be taken for the distance calculation? The presumption is that the resulting distance should be between the minimum and the average of the possible distances. We tested: (1) the minimum $min_{\forall v^1 \in V_1, v^2 \in V_2}(d_{f_i}(v^1, v^2))$, (2) the maximum $max_{\forall v^1 \in V_1, v^2 \in V_2}(d_{f_i}(v^1, v^2))$, (3) the arithmetic average $\frac{\sum_{\forall v^1 \in V_1, v^2 \in V_2} d_{f_i}(v^1, v^2)}{|V_1| \times |V_2|}$, (4) the maximum in direction $\sqrt[k]{\frac{\sum_{\forall v^1 \in V_1, v^2 \in V_2} d_{f_i}(v^1, v^2)^k}{|V_1| \times |V_2|}}$, (5) the minimum in direction $(\frac{\sum_{\forall v^1 \in V_1, v^2 \in V_2} \sqrt[k]{d_{f_i}(v^1, v^2)}}{|V_1| \times |V_2|})^k$. The minimum method (1) results in best SF values, the minimum in direction (5) results in best K values.

Precision/Recall. We measured precision and recall for a set of queries with a threshold between 0.5 and 0.01 (see table 2). Each time we chose one feature set from 150 test feature sets and made a query with the chosen feature set to the remaining sets of features. The precision and recall values are the average of the precision and recall for all the queries. The best precision/recall for a writer identification query is about 85% precision and 75% recall.

6 Conclusions

The aim of the project "eNoteHistory" is the development of a system to support music scientists in the study and the analysis of historical music documents. A

Table 2. Test results (abridgment): Precision, Recall, K, and Null Values using a fixed threshold value.

Threshold Value t	Precision PR	Recall RE	K K	N_D reg. right class. instances	N_D reg. false class. instances
0,50	0,201	0,918	0,382	0,392	0,357
0,40	0,256	0,918	0,382	0,392	0,357
0,30	0,335	0,911	0,427	0,388	0,349
0,20	0,668	0,766	0,674	0,403	0,332
0,10	0,883	0,550	0,787	0,403	
0,01	0,898	0,093	0,461	0,481	

simple management of metadata and digital documents, e.g., in a digital catalog system, however, was not enough, to satisfy their requirements. The need to integrate special methods into the catalog system to enhance the possibilities for data usage and retrieval, led us to the definition of a specialized archive system. We integrated methods and domain-knowledge components to enable the semi-automatic handwriting recognition for writers of music scores. The recognition accuracy of this early prototype of the system is about 90%. The confidence of this evaluation, however, is still not strong enough, because we have performed our tests using only about 150 feature sets. Another project partner works on an automatic procedure for the recognition of features which can improve the tedious manual work of feature analysis. That implies the future integration of the automatic feature extraction in the system. Thereafter, we hope to receive more feature sets to give a better evaluation of the system. Nevertheless, until now we have defined an extensive test environment and we have learned much about adapting and improving the performance of the system, using different parameters.

References

1. Crane, G., Wulfman, C., Cerrato, L., Mahoney, A., Milbank, T., Mimno, D., Rydberg-Cox, A., Smith, D., York, C.: Towards a cultural heritage digital library. In: 2003 Joint Conference on Digital Libraries. (2003)
2. Bruder, I., Finger, A., Heuer, A., Ignatova, T.: Towards a digital document archive for historical handwritten music scores. In: 6th International Conference of Asian Digital Libraries ICADL, Kuala Lampur, Malaysia (2003)
3. Hand, D., Mannila, H., Smyth, P.: Principles of Data Mining. MIT Press, Cambridge, MA (2001)
4. Witten, I.H., Frank, E.: Data Mining - Practical Machine Learning Tools and Techniques with Java Implementations. Morgan Kaufmann, San Francisco (2000)
5. Berkhin, P.: Survey of clustering data mining techniques. Technical report, Accrue Software, San Jose, CA (2002)
6. Aha, D., Kibler, D.: Instance-based learning algorithms. Machine Learning, vol.6 (1991)
7. Zhang, B., Srihari, S.N., Lee, S.: Individuality of handwritten characters. 7th International Conference on Document Analysis and Recognition (2003)

8. Bensefia, A., Paquet, T., Heutte, L.: Information retrieval based writer identification. 5th International Conference on Enterprise Information Systems (2003)
9. Oracle: Darwin Installation and Administration. Release 3.7. (2000)
10. Kohavi, R., Sommerfield, D.: MLC++ Machine Lerning Library in C++. (1996)
11. Aha, D.: Tolerating noisy, irrelevant and novel attributes in instance-based learning algorithms. International Journal of Man-Machine Studies 36(1) (1992)
12. van Rijsbergen, C.J.: Information Retrieval. (1979)

Enhancing Kepler Usability and Performance

Kurt Maly[1], Michael Nelson[1], Mohammad Zubair[1], Ashraf Amrou[1],
Sathish Kothamasa[1], Lan Wang[1], and Rick Luce[2]

[1] Old Dominion University Computer Science Department, Norfolk VA 23529 USA
{maly,mln,zubair,aamr,kumar_s,wang_l}@cs.odu.edu
[2] Los Alamos National Laboratory, Research Library, Los Alamos NM 87544 USA
rick.luce@lanl.gov

Abstract. Kepler is an attempt to bridge the gap between established, organiza-
tion-backed digital libraries and groups of researchers that wish to publish their
findings under their control, anytime, anywhere yet have the advantages of an
OAI-compliant digital library. We describe an architecture and implementation
of the Kepler system that allows an archivelet to be installed in the order of
minutes by an author on a personal machine and a group server in less than an
hour. The group server will harvest from all archivelets and make the union of
all published papers available for search to a community. We describe how a
group administrator can provide an XML schema for the metadata and how the
Kepler engine will validate against them when an author publishes a paper and
completes the metadata. We have demonstrated that we can surmount the technical difficulties for authors to publish as easy as to a website yet produce OAI-
compliant digital libraries.

1 Introduction

One of the largest obstacles for information dissemination to a user community is that
many digital libraries use different, proprietary technologies that inhibit interoperability. The Open Archives Initiative (OAI) addresses interoperability by using a framework to facilitate the discovery of content stored in distributed archives through the
use of the Open Archives Initiative Protocol for Metadata Harvesting (OAI-PMH) [1].
Realizing the benefits of OAI, a number of communities are interested in an out-of-
the-box solution that will help them deploy OAI-based digital libraries. However,
building a communal digital library is currently severely hampered by the lack of easy
to use tools that address the diverse requirements of different communities. In particular, metadata, as the codification of the worldviews that define a community, needs to
accommodate varying formats, uses, encodings and pedigrees. Creating a system for
communal digital libraries poses a number of challenging research questions:

One of our initial efforts in this direction is Kepler [2], which gives publication
control to individual publishers, supports rapid dissemination, and addresses interoperability. In Kepler, OAI-PMH is used to support "personal data providers" or "archivelets". Archivelets are meant to be "personal pocket libraries" that are on the one
hand OAI-PMH compliant data providers, and on the other hand overcome the reluc-
tance of authors to publish into a digital library (instead of putting their work on their
website) through user-friendly publishing tools and total control through having all
files and metadata reside on the author's personal machine. This latter characteristic
has some serious implication on the reliability issue since these machines are not

R. Heery and L. Lyon (Eds.): ECDL 2004, LNCS 3232, pp. 317–328, 2004.
© Springer-Verlag Berlin Heidelberg 2004

necessarily always up or connected to the Internet (e.g. the author might keep the archivelet on a laptop and be on travel or on a field trip). In our vision, individual publishers can be integrated with an institutional repository like DSpace [3] via a Kepler Group Digital Library (GDL). The GDL aggregates metadata and full text from archivelets and can act as an OAI compliant data provider for institutional repositories. As a demonstration, we provided an initial registration service and a service provider at Old Dominion University. Once an archivelet registered with our registration service, the service provider could harvest metadata from it. We faced a number of issues during the initial deployment of Kepler: the software did not have the flexibility of customizing and deploying it for a community, and archivelets were often installed behind NATs (Network Address Translator) making it difficult for the service provider to harvest them. In this paper, we build upon our experiences with the initial Kepler distribution and describe tools and software for groups within communities to deploy digital libraries that are customized for their needs, easily populated, managed, and "open" for development of future services. The main contributions of this paper are: (a) a modular framework for defining, describing and supporting the publication/dissemination requirements for different communities; (b) enhanced packaged tools and software to create an out-of-the-box solution for deploying communal digital libraries for diverse groups; (c) for use behind firewalls, we have developed a server-based publication tool that mirrors the archivelets in terms of functionality. The architecture of just the archivelet is summarized in [4]. At this point we do not have the implementation of hierarchically aggregating groups into communities. There are a number of issues we are currently addressing and will report on in future reports. For the test deployment, we are working with the US Geological Survey (USGS), Los Alamos National Laboratory (LANL), and the Open Language Archives Community (OLAC). The rest of this paper is organized as follows: section 2 presents the Kepler architecture as it has been released in open source. Server-side archivelet is presented in Section 3. In section 4, we present the new features we have added to the Kepler system and section 5 presents related work. We present future work in section 6.

2   Enhanced Archivelet

The original archivelet implementation [2] only supported Dublin Core (DC) format. We remedied this problem by allowing an arbitrary number of formats to be realized by one or more communities. We have re-engineered the architecture to be extensible with regard to formats and functions (See Figure 2). The new design has a well-defined API specification defining the various functions that are implemented by every module that in turn are available for other modules. Support for new metadata formats requires just the implementation of a metadata driver module. In the Kepler software documentation, we provide developer guidelines for fast and easy implementation of a metadata driver. The metadata manager module is responsible for instantiating the various metadata drivers the system is configured to use. It also implements the OAI-PMH API that provides a method for each of the six OAI-PMH requests. OAI-PMH requests received by the Webserver module are forwarded to the Driver Manager that decides what metadata drivers are involved and invokes these drivers to get partial responses from each. The Driver Manager then constructs the whole response from these partial responses. The Driver Manager also implements a User Interface API. This API contains methods that are invoked in response to user interactions with the main interface. For example, when the user clicks "publish", the Driver Manager brings a simple GUI that allows the user to select which metadata format she wants to use and then the Driver Manager invokes the appropriate Driver to display the appropriate Publishing tool (Figure 1). We refer to this tool as a publishing tool rather than a metadata editor because it does involve the infusion of the full text document into a repository in the local archivelet.

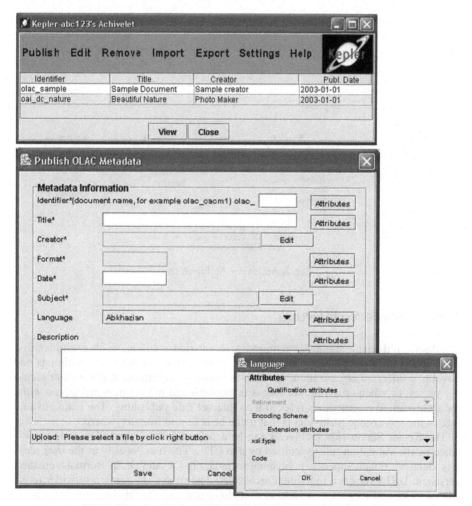

Fig. 1. Main Interface and OLAC Publishing Tool for Archivelets

The metadata driver module implements the OAI-PMH processing and the user interface functions such as publishing tools for the specific metadata format that the Driver handles. The publishing interface (bottom left of Figure 1) has dynamic field types (mandatory or optional), which are determined by a configuration file, based on

XML schema, managed by the group server administrator. The Driver invokes the Validation module whenever new metadata is published to validate the metadata against the constraints specified in the configuration file and uses the repository API to store metadata and files.

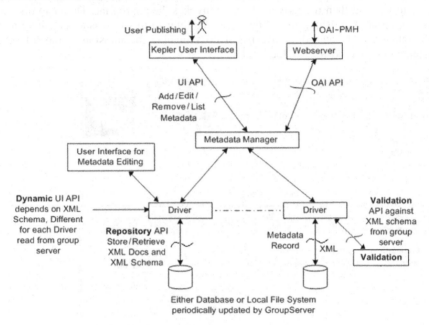

Fig. 2. Archivelet Architecture

3 Server-Side Architecture

We discovered many situations required a server-side solution. Such examples include when the firewall is not controllable by the author, or when the author is on travel to a different organization, or when the author's organization has a strict security policy, or when only Internet access is available but not the personal laptop with the archivelet. We sometimes refer to it as Internet café publishing. The main advantage of the server-side archivelet is that it can be accessed from anywhere.

The Kepler Server-side archivelet can be accessed from Kepler GDL and is governed by the validation rules specified by that GDL. The functionality as the user sees it is identical, thus it supports publishing metadata in DC and OLAC formats, creates persistent URLs for each individual archivelet, and allows any service provider (e.g. GDLs) to harvest metadata and allows users to import/export metadata.

The server-side archivelet system can be logically divided into 3 layers as shown in Figure 4: View (User Interface), Controller, and Model. Comparing to Figure 2, it can be seen that the basic, extensible driver architecture is the same, though not the implementation; the difference lies in the user interaction modules and the interaction with the GDL. In the server-side architecture, the archivelet resides on the GDL. The user interface layer provides various user interfaces for authors to create an archivelet,

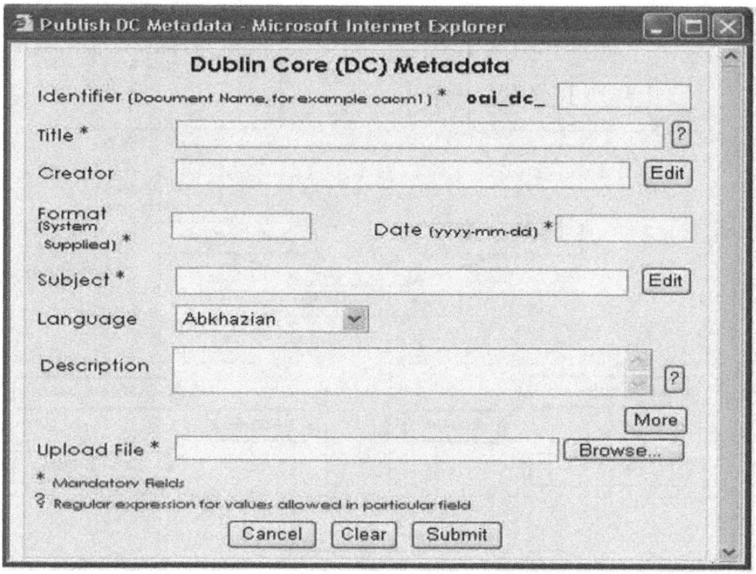

Fig. 3. DC Publishing Tool for Server-side Archivelet

publish metadata and perform the other activities defined in the main archivelet interface (Figure 3). Compared to the archivelet interface we needed to make some adjustments as we wanted to keep it strictly within html to make it as widely operable as
possible. The controller layer has several components (servlets and metadata drivers)
that control the sequence of transitions between user interfaces, flow of data between
user interfaces and the database, as well as handle OAI-PMH requests. The repository
layer performs the actual database operations. The key component of this layer is the
DB Repository. It has the capability to handle metadata regardless of its native format. It provides database operations that are required for archivelet registration, configuration, saving and extracting metadata.

4 New Features

Persistent URLs: Archivelets are roamers; they can be at different locations with different IP addresses at different times. One of the metadata items in each published
record in the archivelet is the URL of the document associated with the metadata. The
document is stored on the machine the archivelet resides. Clearly we have a problem
with using an archivelet's current IP addresses as part of the URL. We use instead
persistent URLs for archivelets and their metadata records and their documents. In
prior implementations every archivelet had a base URL of the format:

   http://machinename.or.ip[:port]/OAIRequestHandlerScript

This base URL was distributed to service providers (e.g. Kepler group servers), so
they could issue OAI-PMH requests to harvest metadata from the Archivelet. It is
possible that an archivelet can be installed on a machine whose IP address changes
every time it connects to a network. In this scenario, if the change in an archivelet's

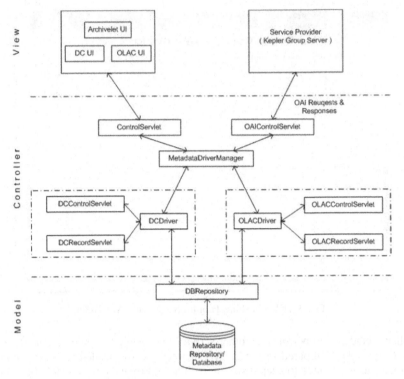

Fig. 4. Server-side Archivelet Architecture

base URL is not updated at the service providers, they cannot contact the archivelet to harvest metadata. A persistent URL for an archivelet is a base URL that is independent of archivelet's IP address. The archivelet distributes this persistent URL to service providers instead of its actual base URL.

To use an archivelet for publishing metadata, it has to be registered with a Kepler GDL. While registering, the archivelet sends its actual base URL, along with other information, to the group server. On successful registration, the group server creates a persistent URL of the format

```
http://group.server.url[:port]/path-to-
OAIControlServlet/tr/archivelet-name
```

```
http://kepler.cs.odu.edu/testgroup/servlet/OAIControlSe
rvlet/tr/maly
```

The group server stores a mapping between an archivelet's actual base URL and its persistent URL. Also, it sends this persistent URL to the archivelet as a response to the registration request. To ensure that the persistent URL always maps to the most current base URL, the archivelet sends its current base URL to the group server at a predefined interval (e.g. on every startup) and the group server updates the persistent URL mapping for that archivelet.

When an OAI-PMH request is issued to this persistent URL, the OAIControlServlet on the appropriate Kepler GDL gets the request. The OAIControlServlet parses this request into two parts: the persistent URL and the OAI-PMH request (verb and parameters). Using the persistent URL it looks up its mapping table to resolve the actual base URL of the archivelet. Once it obtains the actual base URL, it appends the OAI-PMH request and directs the request to the archivelet. The archivelet responds to the OAI-PMH request and the OAIControlServlet redirects it to the actual requestor. Thus the persistent URL masks the dynamic nature of an archivelet's base URL.

Validation Tool: One defining feature of a group within a community is its publication process and the level of associated control. The minimal requirement that Kepler institutes is the use of DC metadata. However, DC in itself has no mandatory fields and its is up to a community to define the rules on how exactly a field should be filled and how it is to be used. This motivates us to adopt a process that can be described, and more importantly, enforced. The Validation module serves two purposes: (1) it provides declarations and implementations of a set of Validation APIs(figures 2 and 4), that can be called by drivers (or any other Kepler modules) for metadata validation; (2) it provides a set of tools to facilitate the driver developer to generate an administration GUI for a new metadata set. The motivation of such an administration GUI is to give the group administrator some flexibility to tailor a general metadata set to an enforceable set of guidelines. For example, some groups may require that the creator field of an OLAC metadata record published in this group is mandatory and must begin with a capitalized letter. Such constraints are not documented in the published OLAC XML schemas. By using the administration GUI, a group administrator can impose these constraints conveniently in her group without directly editing the OLAC schema files. Figure 5 shows the administration GUI while tailoring an OLAC

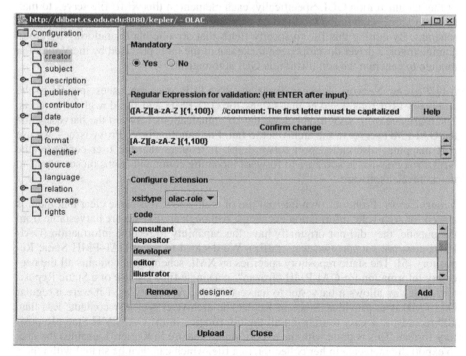

Fig. 5. An example administration GUI for OLAC

metadata set. The general concept is to allow for entities at lower levels to impose more rules than are defined at higher levels. As long as they can be easily mapped into a specification at say the OLAC level to adhere to OLAC's schema.

The current implementation of the Validation module allows a group administrator to: (1) specify whether a field is mandatory or optional; (2) specify regular expressions for a field (for example, the date field must be in the format yyyy-mm-dd); (3) add/delete items in the option list for some specific fields (for example, the value of language field can only be chosen from "dz", "el", "en", "eo", "es"). The validation module is designed to work from an XML schema describing a metadata set. In this implementation we assume that the XML Schemas for any new metadata set always will follow the authoring style of DC and OLAC schemas in defining and qualifying elements by means of Element Refinement and Encoding Schemes. The Validation module depends on these authoring styles as useful heuristics when extracting initial configuration from the original metadata XML Schemas. The initial configuration is extracted, then stored in an intermediate configuration file, which maps an XML namespace and element/type/attribute pair to its mandatory/option setting, regular expression and option list documented in the original schemas. The subsequent changes on the configuration that a group administrator makes through the administration GUI are written into this intermediate configuration file, without polluting the original metadata schemas.

As part of a new metadata driver, the administration GUI needs to be implemented by the driver developer. To facilitate this process, the Validation module introduces an additional layer of indirection – GUI configuration file. A GUI configuration file is actually an XML instance file controlling the tree structure displayed on the left panel of the administration GUI. Specifically, each element in this XML file serves to map between a tree node in the GUI and an element/type/attribute defined in the metadata schemas. By editing this file to specify fields that are eligible for tailoring by group administrator, a driver developer can make use of the tools provided by the Validation module to generate the administration GUI automatically.

NAT/Proxies: Network Address Translator (NAT) Proxies are issues specific to the archivelet as it runs a server that listens for OAI-PMH and file download requests. The existence of a NAT might cause the communications between the harvester and the OAI-PMH server in the archivelet to fail. For handling NAT/Proxy issues, we use port mapping (also called port forwarding). It requires that the user configure the NAT/Proxy device or software to forward incoming communications on some port to the archivelet software.

Import/Export: From our own internal use of archivelets, it became clear that there is a need for archivelet information exchange. Although archivelets are harvestable from the outside, they did not originally have the capability to receive information (OAI-PMH does not support two-way traffic). We decided to adopt OAI–PMH Static Repository [5]. The static repository specifies an XML schema that contains all the necessary information for OAI-PMH "frozen" in a single file. The use of a Static Repository Gateway allows a harvester to harvest a static repository as if it were a regular OAI-PMH data provider. Since in Kepler the archivelet typically contains less than 100 records, it is easy to transmit all the information in the OAI-PMH Static Repository format. This is done with the export/import feature in Kepler. It enables the user to export the metadata in her collection to a file, which can then be shared with others directly to avoid re-entry of metadata again and again. A typical scenario is when an author has several co-authors and can share the metadata with them, having them avoid entering the information into their archivelets. This does raise though the issue of duplication at the group server. In this implementation we have not addressed the duplication issue; duplicate records will simply be listed multiple times as coming from different archivelets.

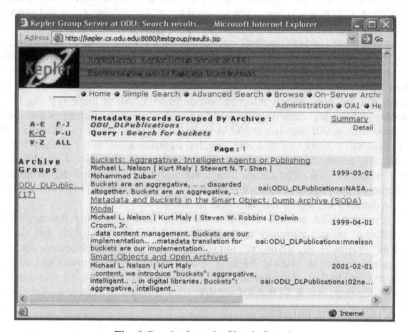

Fig. 6. Results from the Simple Search

Search Service and Caching: The group server offers a search service on the metadata harvested from the Kepler archivelets (and other OAI-PMH data providers). The search service is based on the Arc search engine [6, 7]. The group server offers a simple search interface that searches all metadata fields, an advanced search interface that allows fielded searching, and a browsing interface (any of the archivelets that the group server harvests can be browsed) for extemporaneous resource discovery. Using the demonstrator group server in use at the Old Dominion University Computer Science Department, Figure 6 shows the metadata records resulting from a query. The group server performs caching by default. Clicking on the title in a record (Figure 6) displays all the metadata fields of that record in a separate window. The original resource is available in the DC.Identifier field, for example: http://128.82.7.77:2048/EDICTfinal0913.doc

However, the URL of the original resource may not always be available. Although the original URL is always presented, the GDL will also preemptively cache the resource at the GDL. Preemptively caching the resources increases the availability of the resources and insulates the GDL from the varying accessibility of the archivelets. For example, the URL of the above source is also available at: http://kepler.cs.odu.edu:8080/testgroup/cache/oai.ODU_DLPublications.EDICTfinal0913.doc.

5 Related Work

The version of Kepler described in this paper draws from a significant base of existing OAI-PMH projects, developed both at Old Dominion and throughout the community. In addition to the original Kepler project [2], some of the features draw from the Arc [6, 7] and Archon [8, 9] projects. As mentioned above, the OAI-PMH Static Repository format [5] was adopted when the need for archivelet importing and exporting was addressed.

In the emerging field of "institutional repository software", many open source entries have emerged. The eprints.org software [10] from the University of Southampton has been widely adopted. CDSWare [11] was created at CERN and has been adopted in other locations as well. DSpace [3] is created by Hewlett Packard and the MIT Libraries, but has been widely adopted outside of MIT. All of these systems feature significant features and capability for building large-scale digital libraries and institutional repositories. All also use the OAI-PMH as a core technology. However, they are in contrast to Kepler in that they require significant resources to establish and maintain; the installation of these systems falls significantly beyond the 10-minute target of a Kepler GDL. The choice of a community of institutional digital library is an extremely important one, and we recommend surveys such as [12], [13] or [14] as guides in determining which DL suits your needs.

The persistent URL work is similar to the Extensible Repository Resource Locators (ERRoLs) project currently underway at OCLC [15], and which was first described as "Partial PURL Redirects" in [16]. ERRoLs, and its predecessor, describe a way to attach persistent, "human-friendly" URLs to OAI-PMH repositories and metadata objects inside those repositories. Our approach differs in that we focus only on repository naming, and is CDL/GDL-centric – as opposed to centric to a registry at OCLC or UIUC.

6 Conclusions and Future Work

We have done extensive use testing of both the installation process and the publishing tasks. The testing was done by project participants and a few persons within the participating institutions: LANL, CERN, UPenn (now University of Melbourne), USGS, and ODU. The original user interfaces (both publication and resource discovery) are surprisingly similar to current interfaces. Most of the changes are behind the scene or are new features. All of the new features such as server-side archivelet, export/import, persistent URLs, and validation are the result of perceived needs by the project participants. Installation packages for group server (including archivelet server-side implementation) and archivelet are available in the project website shown in [17]. At the site a test group server can be found that can be used by anyone to experiment with creating archivelets of their own and seeing them harvested by the test group server (as long as the owner registers with the test group server). Most importantly, we have tested repeatedly with both experts (developers) and novices (faculty and students not related to the project and system people for the group server) that the installation is indeed within the target of 10 minutes and 1 hour respectively for the archivelt and the group server.

In the near term future we are set to field test Kepler version 1.2 in four testbeds. USGS has developed a public warehouse of publications (http://infotrek.er.usgs.gov/docs/usgs_pubs/publication_warehouse_contents.html) and wants to develop a harvesting and data provider interface using the Kepler concept. The data provider end will connect to a new Journal on Natural Organic Materials that will use directly the Kepler software. The harvester interface will be a Kepler Group server that will connect to the USGS' other offices. OLAC is considering using a Kepler group server to harvest from its current collection and vice versa. Also they will experiment with the archivelets to publish field work and use the export/import feature to deliver delayed results from field studies where authors are away for prolonged periods. LANL is discussing to give researchers access to archivelets and to have "MyLibrary" [18] harvest from a Kepler groupserver that aggregates the individual archivelets.

Acknowledgements

Our thanks to Herbert Van de Sompel, who suggested the idea of persistent URLs and S. Zunjarwad, who worked on the implementation of version 1.2. We wish to acknowledge our partners: Bob Wershaw and Greg Allory from the USGS, and Steven Bird from the University of Melbourne. This work is supported by NSF grant 0205486.

References

1. Lagoze, C., Van de Sompel, H., Nelson, M., Warner, S.: The Open Archives Initiative Protocol for Metadata Harvesting. January 2002 Available at

2. Maly, K., Zubair, M., Liu, X.: Kepler - An OAI Data/Service Provider for the Individual. D-Lib Magazine 7(4), (April 2001) Available at

3. Smith, M., Barton, M., Bass, M., Branschofsky, M., McClellan, G., Stuve, D., Tansley, R., Harford W. J.: DSpace - an open source dynamic digital repository. D-Lib Magazine, 9(1), (January 2003) Available at http://www.dlib.org/dlib/january03/smith/01smith.html.

4. Maly, K., Nelson, M., Zubair, M., Amrou, A., Kothamasa S., Wang L., Luce, R.: Light-Weight Communal Digital Libraries. Proc. of the fourth ACM/IEEE Joint Conference on Digital Libraries, Tucson AZ (2003) 237-238

5. Hochstenbach, P., Jerez, H., Van de Sompel, H.: The OAI-PMH Static Repository and Static Repository Gateway. Proc. of the third ACM/IEEE Joint Conference on Digital Libraries, Houston TX (2003) 210-217

6. The Arc Cross Archive Searching Service,

7. Liu, X., Maly, K., Zubair, M., Nelson, M.: Arc: An OAI Service Provider for Cross Archive Searching. Proc. of the First ACM/IEEE Joint Conference on Digital Libraries, Roanoke VA (2001) 65-66

8. A Digital Library that federates Physics collections with varying degrees of metadata richness, http://archon.cs.odu.edu.

9. Anan, H., Maly, K., Nelson, M., Zubair, M., Liu, X., Gao, J., Tang, J., Yang, Z. ARCHON: Building and Learning Environments Through Extended Digital Library Services. Proc. of the fifth International Conference on New Educational Environments, Lucerne Switzerland (2003)

10. Self-Archiving and Open Archives,

11. Gold, A. K., Baker, K. S., LeMeur, J., Baldridge, K.: Building FLOW: federating libraries on the web. Proc. of the second ACM/IEEE-CS joint conference on Digital libraries, Portland, OR (2002) 287-288 Available at http://doi.acm.org/10.1145/544220.544286

12. Brogan, M.L.: A Survey of Digital Library Aggregation Services. The Digital Library Federation Council on Library and Information Resources, Washington, DC. (2003) Available at

13. Crow, R.: The Case for Institutional Repositories: A SPARC Position Paper. The Scholarly Publishing and Academic Resources Coalition, Washington DC (2002) Available at

14. Crow, R.: Open Society Institute - A Guide to Institutional Repository Software. Open Society Institute, New York, NY (2004) Available at
http://www.soros.org/openaccess/software/

15. Young, J.A.: Extensible Repository Resource Locators (ERRoLs) for OAI Identifiers. Available at http://www.oclc.org/research/projects/oairesolver/default.htm

16. Van de Sompel, H., Young, J.A., Hickey, T.B.: Using the OAI-PMH ... Differently. D-Lib Magazine (July/August 2003) Available at
http://www.dlib.org/dlib/july03/young/07young.html

17. Kepler, http://dlib.cs.odu.edu/#kepler

18. Di Giacomo, M., Mahoney, D., Bollen, J., Monroy-Hernandez, A., Ruiz Meraz, C.M.: MyLibrary, A personalization service for digital library environments. Joint DELOS-NSF Workshop on Personalisation and Recommender Systems in Digital Libraries, Dublin, Ireland, (18-20 June 2001) Available at http://lib-www.lanl.gov/lww/MyLibrary.pdf

Media Matrix: Creating Secondary Repositories

Mark Kornbluh, Michael Fegan, and Dean Rehberger

310 Auditorium MATRIX Michigan State University East Lansing, MI 48824-1120 USA
{kornbluh,mfegan,rehberge}@msu.edu

Abstract. This paper argues for the necessity of digital libraries to increase access to their holdings and have greater impact on e-learning and education by facilitating the creation of secondary repositories. These repositories will provide discipline/community specific metadata and applications and will allow users to find, use, manipulate and analyze digital objects more easily. To this end, MATRIX has developed Media Matrix 1.0 – an online, easy to use server-side suite of tools that allows users to locate specific media and streaming media files found in digital repositories and segment, annotate and organize this media online. This application provides users with an environment both to work with and personalize digital media, and also to share and discuss their findings with a community of users. Through creating a secondary repository of usage statistics and user-generated materials/metadata to supplement both traditional cataloging records and discipline-specific online indexes, tools like Media Matrix can help extend the usefulness of digital libraries without increasing costs to the libraries

1 Introduction

For the purposes of preservation and increased use of their holdings, libraries, archives and cultural organizations have been researching and developing best practices for digitizing their analog collections. These efforts have given users unprecedented access to information. Scholars have long realized, however, that "access" to information must mean more than the ability for a user to link to computer networks. Underlying the meaning of access in relation to digital equity and universal service is the need for a community of users to have the ability to retrieve information "in some form in which it can be read, viewed, or otherwise employed constructively" [2][4][5]. Access thus implies four related conditions that go beyond the ability to link to a network: **equity**, the ability of "every citizen" and not simply technical specialists to use the resources; **usability**, the ability of users to easily locate, retrieve, use, and navigate resources; **context**, the conveyance of meaning from stored information to users, so that it makes sense to them; and **interactivity**, the capacity for users to be both consumers and producers of information. While access to online resources has steadily improved in the last decade, online archives and digital libraries still remain difficult to use, particularly for students and novice users [1].

While access to digital resources has had positive affects on both scholarly research and teaching and learning at all levels of instruction, digital libraries must take the next step and redefine access in ways that help users to **use** digital objects. To this end, MATRIX has developed Media Matrix 1.0 – an online, easy to use server side suite of tools that allows users to find, segment, annotate, organize, and publish digital

R. Heery and L. Lyon (Eds.): ECDL 2004, LNCS 3232, pp. 329–340, 2004.
© Springer-Verlag Berlin Heidelberg 2004

media found on the Internet and in digital repositories. This application provides users with an environment not only to work with and personalize digital media, but to share and discuss their findings with a community of users. Because Media Matrix stores a significant amount of information about the digital objects selected by users and user generated annotations per digital object, it both provides a corpus of data on how digital repositories are being used and creates materials that augment traditional cataloguing records. In so doing, it forms a secondary repository that holds metadata generated by its users, additional resources for its users, specialized searches and galleries, extended materials, and pointers to digital objects in primary repositories. Thus the value of the application is that it can enhance the usability, access, and interactivity of digital libraries by facilitating the creation of secondary repositories on top of their collections without significantly increasing costs and time needed to prepare and maintain additional resources. Digital libraries can also utilize, if desired, usage statistics and user generated materials/metadata to supplement traditional cataloging records and applications.

1.1 Spoken Words, Digital Libraries and Users

Even though access to digital objects has grown at an exponential rate, tangible factors have prevented users from fully taking advantage of these resources. We have a long history of working with texts and are comfortable moving through texts, making annotations, summaries, and quotations. Beyond a host of traditional methods, we have at our disposal sets of tools, both freeware and commercial, which help us to cite, catalogue, and annotate texts (*e.g.*, Endnote, Procite, Biblioscape). Streaming media, however, is another matter. Scholars and students, beyond some specialized areas, rarely have worked in the past with media and have often preferred the transcript over the original. While contemporary bibliographic tools have expanded to allow users to catalogue and keep notes about media, they do not allow users to mark specific passages and moments in multimedia, segment it, and return to specific places at a later time. While several initiatives and products (e.g., Annotea, SHOE Knowledge Annotator, NetSnippets) allow users to point to specific online materials or portions of online materials and add their annotations to those pointers, it does not allow users to work with the non-textual, digital media present on those pages. Multimedia thus remains underutilized in education because the tools to manipulate the various formats often "frustrate would be users" and take too much cognitive effort and time to learn [3].

Over the past decade, the digital library community has tried to reduce the labor and expense of creating, cataloging, storing, and disseminating digital objects through the research and development of specific practices to facilitate each of these stages. Although these processes have become easier, better documented, and more automated, creating and working with digital objects is still a very specialized endeavor that requires specialized hardware, software and expertise – often outside the realm and resources of the general user. Even with the resources to work with digital media, copyright restrictions and streaming technologies make it difficult for users to download, manipulate, and use digital objects in their own practices.

To compound this, traditional cataloging and dissemination practices often make it difficult for users to locate and utilize digital objects within the framework and practices of their discipline [10]. Digital objects are typically cataloged to describe their content (bibliographic information), composition (technical metadata), maintenance (administrative metadata) and dissemination (rights metadata and any information for delivering the object via online applications). While these practices are essential for preserving the digital object and making it available to users, the practices also make it available to users in a language and guise that is often difficult to understand within the context of use [10].

While the author's name, the title of the work, and keywords are essential for describing and locating a digital object, this kind of information is not always the most utilized information when users are looking for and ascertaining the relevance of a digital object. K – 12 teachers, for instance, often do not have specific authors or titles in mind when searching for materials for their classes. They more frequently search in terms of grade level, the state and national standards that form the basis of their teaching, or broad, overarching topics (*e.g.*, core democratic values or textbook topics) that tend to retrieve too many search returns to make the information of value. Although the addition of more discipline specific information at the object level would open up the digital libraries to larger constituency and enhance the impact and usability of digital libraries, it would be a huge and unrealistic endeavor for digital libraries given the multitude of disciplines that would benefit from the addition of discipline specific information attached to each object.

The keys to making better use of multimedia in education and to enhancing the use of multimedia for specific contexts and disciplines, are to build secondary repositories with resources and tools that allow users to enhance and augment materials [11], share their work with a community of users [14], and easily manipulate the media with simple and intuitive tools (or at least build interfaces that match existing, well-known and heavily-used applications). Users will also need portal spaces that escape the genre of links gateways and become flexible work environments that allow users to become interactive producers [8]. In short, secondary repositories are the result of users integrating digital objects into their research and work in ways that make sense to them given their backgrounds and tasks.

Herbert Van de Sompel has proposed a successful system (OpenURL/SFX framework for context sensitive reference linking) for disaggregating reference linking services from e-publishing [15]. In his framework, the service of providing links between references and across e-publishers' digital repositories is separated from the services provided by the e-publishers. In so doing, the service provides "seamless interconnectivity between ever-increasing collection of heterogeneous resources," freeing primary repositories from the difficult and expensive task of ensuring links to references while giving users greater access to resources and increasing the value of the digital object [16]. Similarly, we propose the creation of secondary repositories that would be responsible for handling secondary metadata, extended materials and resources, and interactive tools and application services. Generated by interactive, online tools, these resources would work to contexutalize, add meaning, and provide new ways of discovering the original digital object. Primary repositories would continue to be responsible for preservation, management, and long-term access but would be freed from creating time-consuming and expensive materials, resources, services, and extended metadata for particular user groups.

2 Media Matrix

MATRIX – The Center for Humane Arts, Letters, and Social Sciences Online is a humanities computing research center based at Michigan State University. Over the last five years, MATRIX has participated in the ongoing discussion and development of digital library practices and has built a large-scale digital repository. This digital repository holds over fifteen collections that contain a diverse range of materials from different disciplines – from images of quilts to nineteenth-century renderings of tumors, to recordings of indigenous practices of West African tribes-people, to the interviews of the oral historian, Studs Terkel. The variety of these materials has drawn a diverse crowd of users who come to the sites from different disciplines and with vastly different agendas. MATRIX's research agenda – initially under a five-year National Science Foundation Digital Libraries II grant (1998) to develop a National Gallery of the Spoken Word – has focused on how best to build the infrastructure of a spoken word repository and the best practices for digitizing and disseminating the objects within repositories. While this research has been very successful and rewarding, the focus of MATRIX's research agenda has shifted – under the Spoken Word Project funded by Digital Libraries Initiative II: Digital Libraries in the Classroom Program, National Science Foundation in conjunction with UK's Joint Information Systems Committee – in part, toward how to best make digital objects useful to digital library users, especially for education and e-learning.

The Spoken Word project focuses on helping to transform undergraduate learning and teaching through integrating the media resources of digital repositories into undergraduate courses in history, political science and cognate disciplines in the U.S. and Britain. The project takes advantage of the flexibility inherent in digital repositories to build processes for learning that will expand how students and teachers understand knowledge, knowledge resources, and their own complementary roles in higher education. The project is a collaboration of Michigan State University, Northwestern University, the National Archives and Records Administration (NARA), Glasgow Caledonian University, and the BBC – Information & Archives. Project researchers are testing whether and with what effect the integration of digital audio resources into university courses achieves four major project outcomes: (1) improving student learning and retention, (2) developing aural literacy in our students, (3) augmenting student competence to write on – and for – the Internet, and, (4) enhancing digital libraries through a focus on learning.

Research on these areas has led to the development of an application called Media Matrix (version 1.0) – an online, server side tool that helps users to find, segment, annotate, organize, and publish streaming media found on the Internet.

2.1 Media Matrix Tool Set and Operation

A user begins using Media Matrix 1.0 by registering for a user account at the Media Matrix web site. In the process, users complete a short profile that describes generally their teaching and scholarly backgrounds. Users are then issued an account that gives them access to the Media Matrix tools and a personal portal page for gathering, organizing, and publishing the materials they create and gather. Users are also given the ability to create groups to which they can invite other users to join. The group function is a key element of the tool set because it allows users to share resources and collaborate on the development of resources and projects with other members of the group. Teachers can thus create a group for each of their classes and invite students to join that group. This allows both the teacher and students to preview the work of and collaborate with other members of the class easily.

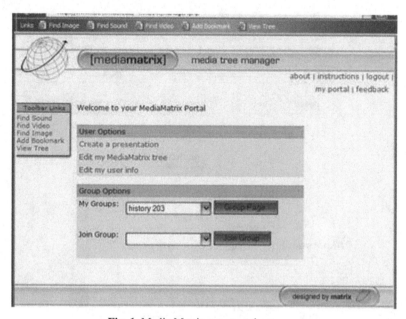

Fig. 1. Media Matrix user portal page.

Media Matrix does not require any special downloads or plug-ins, a feature that makes the tool more accessible to teachers, students and researchers, who may be working in computer labs and at library work stations that often do not easily allow for the downloading of additional software. Focusing on maintaining a familiar work environment, Media Matrix works within the browser of the user, and works with the same media players normally used to play digital objects. Users continue to use Media Matrix by dragging five links (favlets) provided on their portal page to the bookmark bar of their browser (see Figure 1). Users can then search for objects on the internet using their own methods and preferred tools or go directly to sites where they want to work with digital media. When users find a digital object that they would like to use or work with, they simply click the appropriate link and Media Matrix is launched. In the case of audio, the user would, for instance, find an audio clip on any site on the internet (e.g., American Memory, CNN, BBC, or ESPN). They would then press the "Find Audio" link saved on their bookmark bar. Media Matrix then uses regular expressions and string matching to isolate any audio files referenced on the page and loads the sound into the editor. If multiple sounds are on the page, Media Matrix has been designed to allow users to preview and select the sound they want to load into the editor. Because there are virtually any number of ways a digital object can be embedded and described on a web page,

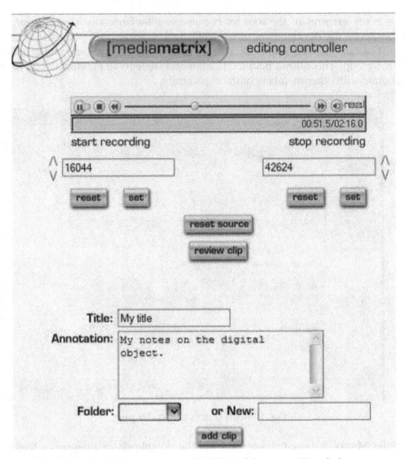

Fig. 2. Media Matrix segmenting in online editing controller window.

Media Matrix can only reliably identify the URIs of media found on a specific web page. The streaming media is then loaded into the appropriate media player (Real Player, QuickTime, Windows Media) and embedded into the Media Matrix online editor (see figure 2). Taking advantage of existing resources on users' computers and working with formats supplied by repositories, Media Matrix allows users to employ common players to control the playback of the audio. While the audio is playing, Media Matrix permits users to "record" portions of the streamed clip. When the user finds a portion he/she believes is important, he/she simply clicks the "Start Recording" button and then the "End Recording" button to capture a segment of the sound. Media Matrix does not actually record the audio, but instead stores the URI of the clip and the time offsets for that portion of the clip selected by the user. When the user replays the clip those offsets and the URI of the clip are then passed back to the player and thus only the selected portion of the streamed audio is replayed.

After segmenting the sound file and isolating the portion(s) of the streaming clip users want, users can then add their own thoughts or analysis to the clip in the form of annotations. The user then titles the clip/annotation and submits it to his/her personal portal page. The annotations can then be easily saved, accessed, combined, exported organized, edited, shared, and published.

Using the same basic steps, Media Matrix works with other media types. Users can work with video in much the same way as audio, allowing students and researchers to isolate portions of the video and add an annotation to the sections of the clip that they have selected. Media Matrix also allows users to bookmark whole web pages or pages of text or copy portions of the text into their portal as well as describe that text through the use of a title, annotation, and keywords. Similarly images can be cropped and resized by the user as well as annotated. This can be particularly effective for students and researchers who need to fit images into a presentation or would like to demonstrate specific nuances and details about portions of images or artwork.

In the case of each media type, Media Matrix works much like standard note-taking and bibliographic tools but gives users greater control over manipulating the media and maintains users' work in an online (and optionally collaborative environment). Once users find, segment, and annotate streaming media, they can then organize those entries on their personal portal page. The portal page allows users to create trees of meaning and organization through the use of nested folders. Users have the ability to display the contents of each of their folders to particular groups they have joined, to the general public by removing any access restrictions, or maintain the resources for personal use only. Once they have organized the media that they have collected, they can integrate that media into multimedia publications.

2.2 Media Matrix Delivery Presentation Layer

Users can choose from a number of presentation templates that allow them to select digital objects from their portal page (audio and video segments, images and image selections, text, and annotations) add text and analysis, and submit for publication. This creates a web page presentation with a persistent URI that features the writing of the user and the digital clips he/she has selected. This is an especially important feature requested by instructors because it allows teachers and students both to make presentations in the classroom and to create multi-media essays for submission.

The suite of tools developed for Media Matrix not only allows users to work with and analyze digital objects, but also affords users the ability to locate new digital objects. Media Matrix uses the information users submit when creating their profiles and groups to create browse-able and searchable access points to portal pages created by other users. Historians, for example, can browse the portals of other historians working specifically in their research areas or K-12 teachers can browse grade appropriate sections defined by specific grade levels and subjects to see what digital objects other teachers are using or, more important, for time challenged teachers, they can find specific presentations created around standard topics and curriculum frameworks.

Users can also perform keyword searches over the annotations created by all users or specific groups of users. A teacher, for instance, can choose to search through only the information in eleventh-grade Civics groups in hopes of finding information that speaks directly to his/her needs. Because users have gathered content from across the Internet and from a variety of digital repositories, searching Media Matrix is equivalent to searching multiple repositories at once. Once users find an object from a particular digital library, they can jump to that repository to find what other objects are available.

2.3 Media Matrix and Metadata Augmentation

One way to alleviate the high costs of augmenting metadata is to create a distributed model of augmentation. Not unlike the model for the development of open source software, digital libraries can rely on communities of users to develop the accessibility and usability of their collections in a secondary repository. Along these lines, Media Matrix allows users to create rich sets of discipline specific user generated metadata. The segments, presentations, and annotations created for each digital object can serve to augment the original finding aid for the digital object. It also supplies information not only about the popularity and relevancy of specific resources, but also about most used segments and the content of files.

Collections can also benefit by defining communities of users. For example, with the recent release of secret White House tapes [7], the sheer number of tapes and hours make it impossible for adequate cataloging of content as well as the difficulty of determining the context and people involved (or even what is said given the poor quality of many tapes). Those historians and scholars (a more regulated and highly defined set of experts) allowed access to the collections could use Media Matrix to supply information about content and context as well as set terms for debates over more questionable areas of interpretation (e.g., when sound quality makes passages inaudible). While metadata gathered in these ways would need to be qualified (maintained in a secondary repository) because of lack of quality control, the processes could make large quantities of sound more available and usable (as well as searchable since annotations will be keyed to particular time offsets).

Because users can search directly using the Media Matrix environment, MATRIX also plans to give any digital library and online sound collection open access to its logs (those logs that apply to the specific collection). A digital library can export from Media Matrix any usage statistics and information about the specific digital objects users are accessing in their collections. This information can provide digital libraries with information, i.e., who is accessing their holdings, which objects are being accessed and in what portions of those objects are users most interested. MATRIX is planning on using this information to build for users dynamic recommendation lists based on other users' preferences (e.g., Amazon). In doing so, we can search Media Matrix and find users who have annotated specific objects and then suggest other segments and objects in that content folder of their portal page, a service that would greatly enhance the usability while helping to augment context for digital objects.

2.4 Media Matrix Programming Environment

Media Matrix is a PHP based server side application that stores information in a MYSQL database and exports that information into XML for display. The development of the tool and programming environment have been designed to keep it library and archive independent so that it can work with almost any site on the internet. It can also work easily with any of the standard courseware packages. The tool is also search independent because it relies on traditional internet search tools and a site's discovery tools to find an object. Once objects are found, Media Matrix is deployed by the user. Because Media Matrix does not actually copy the digital object from the site (it only stores a pointer to the object in the form of a URI and whatever time offsets are created by the user), it avoids some of the copyright and fair use pitfalls that often keep users from working with digital objects (although there are issues of deep linking to be addressed).

The continued development of Media Matrix faces several challenges. Media players and browsers are central to the development of the application. Media Matrix, as noted, uses both browsers as its native environment and media players to stream media because users are comfortable with these environments and it does not necessitate further software installation. The most popular media players – Real Player, Quick-Time, and Windows Media Player – all have API's that allow information to be passed between the player and the browser. Because of this, clip information such as time parameters can be grabbed from the player to record time offsets or passed back to the player to play only the portion of a clip. The most common method of doing this is with JavaScript. Although this is an adequate development platform given some OS environments and browsers, it is highly problematic in others.

Players have a troubled history of playing clips formatted for other players (although several claim to allow trouble-free playing of a number of formats). Real Audio does not play QuickTime files, for instance. Because of this, code must be written to identify and interpret the kinds of files that are being edited by Media Matrix and then separate code must be written for each player to pass information back and forth to the browser. Although JavaScript is a popular, standardized scripting language, not all browsers interpret it in the same manner, particularly event functions. Because of this, the full functionality of Media Matrix remains limited to Internet Explorer 6.0 and PCs. It remains functional in Netscape and other browser environments but currently has limited functionality on Mac OS X. Further research and development should allow us to expand its use and functionality in terms of players, browsers and platforms. MATRIX has considered employing Macromedia's Flash as an environment for Media Matrix and will continue to do so, but Flash also has limitations in working with particular players and browsers, especially Real Audio in its native environment.

2.5   Media Matrix Beta Testing

Steve Cohen of Tufts University completed an initial assessment of using digital libraries and Media Matrix in a classroom setting. For the assessment, a survey history course of 150 students at Michigan State University, History 203, which covered twentieth-century American history, was chosen. A sample of 40 students in three different sections of the course was given written surveys to complete and of these, 10 students were interviewed in more detail. No controls or quasi experimental protocols were used, so results can only be considered as trends and will be used to design more comprehensive assessments for the Fall Semester of 2004 and to do initial usability revisions of Media Matrix.

In sum, students were positive about their experience with both digital libraries and Media Matrix. Most students visited between 2 and 5 digital libraries to review and acquire sources for their essay assignment and spent totals of 4-8 hours on task (low=2, high=20). Most reported that, based on their experience in History 203, they would be more motivated to enroll in a course that used digital libraries and Media Matrix, and. most reported that the images and audio helped to improve their work, the material "came alive."

2.5.1   Digital Libraries Usability. Overall students would like more digital library resources given to them that work for the assignment and work with Media Matrix. They would like the search capabilities of digital libraries improved with more advanced features, annotations, thumbnails, topic searches, and easier access. Often students were not clear about what they meant by easier access and better navigation and searches, but they found digital libraries hard to use because it was difficult for them to sort through the resources or find resources that fit their topics. Often they noted that they would like materials to be better annotated and organized by topics. As Cohen noted, the problems with digital library interfaces were "not an issue of technical skill but rather design and informatics. During the group interview students suggested that the DLs did not have good interfaces for browsing, but seemed to be designed for users who already knew what they were looking for."

2.5.2   Media Matrix. The suggestions for Media Matrix fell into three main categories:

1) Improved instructions: the instructions need to be written for those not familiar with technology, step by step, and placed at point of need.
2) Improved presentation layer: students would like to be able to have more format controls over text ("to work like a word processor") and do in-text citations; they wanted to create a more professional looking essay.
3) Easier to use: what was meant by easier to use was more difficult to define but for the most part, students wanted Media Matrix to work with more kinds of file formats, digital library sites, and operating systems; and they wanted more information on the pop-up window that listed resources found on a web page (if more than one source was found on the page) to identify the resource.

Other significant comments focused on creating a FAQ; starting with a smaller assignment (students were asked to write a 2500 word essay using text, images, and sound) or shorter sequenced assignments; students would also like to add resources to their resource tree without leaving the presentation layer.

Based on the surveys and interviews, in addition to improving the usability of digital libraries and Media Matrix, Cohen has initially concluded that students need more help with understanding the value and use of sources that they do find. One way we will attempt to do this will be to increase the number of fields that students will be required to complete for an annotation, allowing students, for example, to note who, when, where and the motives of the creator(s)/participant(s). Students should also be given space and prompts to evaluate the source and its context. These and several of the other above suggested improvements are being incorporated into the tool set.

3   Conclusions

Digitizing collections and putting them online provides new and unprecedented access to information, but to have an impact on e-learning and education, it is no longer enough for digital libraries to stop at search and browse. Digital libraries must take the next step and help users employ those digital objects in ways that make sense to specific user communities and academic disciplines. Whether it is the addition of GIS information and the creation of GIS aware applications that let historians view objects in time and space, or search interfaces that take into account the pedagogical environment of educators and help them find resources to utilize within specific assignments, or applications that bring content alive for students through 3D rendering and role play, digital libraries must work closely with users to discover the unique perspectives they bring to the site and build applications that bring digital object alive within those worlds.

Given the present budget crises and the costs and time associated with digitizing materials and managing digital repositories, it is often not feasible for digital libraries to offer extended services. Creating secondary repositories that can make use of a number of collections and focus on the needs of particular user groups (especially for e-learning) makes more sense for users and digital librarians. Correctly deployed secondary repositories, created from user generated data with specific applications, can increase visibility and accessibility of existing collections and thereby help digital libraries and archives to cultivate the full meaning of access: equity, usability, context, and interactivity.

Although development of applications to work with more browsers and players is necessary, Media Matrix 1.0 has proven highly successful in its first run. It has been a marriage that has proven fruitful for both users and digital libraries. Users have a way to utilize and personalize digital objects and digital libraries have access to a wealth of information that can be tied to the digital object. Creating Media Matrix has helped us to redefine the term access and to imagine a more flexible and interactive work space for scholars and students. This is particularly crucial when it comes to sound archives: if we do not enhance the value of sound for users and increase the demand, then our sound archives will continue to languish in neglect and decay.

Acknowledgements

Support for the project comes in large part due to the JISC/NSF Digital Libraries Initiative II: Digital Libraries in the Classroom Program – National Science Foundation, award no. IIS-0229808

References

1. Arms, W.: Digital Libraries. MIT Press: Cambridge, MA, 2001.
2. Borgman,C.: From Gutenberg to the Global Information Infrastructure: Access to Information in the Networked World. MIT Press: Cambridge, MA, 2000.
3. Cooperstock, J.R.: "Classroom of the Future: Enhancing Education through Augmented Reality." HCI International, Conference on Human-Computer Interaction, New Orleans, pp.688-692 (2001). <http://www.cim.mcgill.ca/ ~jer/pub/hcii01.pdf>.
4. Kahin, B and Keller, J.: Public Access to the Internet. "Introduction." MIT Press: Cambridge, MA 1995.
5. Lynch, C.: Interoperability: the Standards Challenge for the 90s in Wilson Library Bulletin, March: 38-42 (1995).
6. Marshall, C.: Annotation: from Paper Books to the Digital Library in Proceedings of the ACM Digital Libraries '97 Conference, Philadelphia, PA (July 23-26, 1997) <http://www.csdl.tamu.edu/~marshall/dl97.pdf>.
7. Miller Center of Public Affairs, Charlottesville, Virginia <http://millercenter.virginia.edu/>.

8. Miller, P. The Concept of the Portal Ariadne Issue 30 (20-December-2001) <http://www.ariadne.ac.uk /issue30/portal/intro.html>.
9. Page, K. R., Cruickshank, D. and Roure, D. D.:   Its About Time: Link Streams as Continuous Metadata. in Proceedings of The Twelfth ACM Conference on Hypertext and Hypermedia (Hypertext '01), pages pp.93-102 (2001).
10. Callan, J., et al.: Personalization and Recommender Systems in Digital Libraries Joint NSF-EU DELOS Working Group Report. May 2003. <http://www.dli2.nsf.gov/internationalprojects/working_group_reports/ personalisation.html>.
11. Shabjee, P.: Primary Multimedia Objects and Educational Metadata': a Fundamental Dilemma for Developers of Multimedia Archives. D-Lib Magazine, March 2000 <http://www..dlib.org/dlib/june02/shabajee/06shabajee.html>.
12. Rydberg-Cox, J.: Cultural heritage language technologies: building an infrastructure for collaborative digital libraries in the humanities, Ariadne Issue 34 (14-Jan-2003) <http://www.ariadne.ac.uk /issue34/rydberg-cox/intro.html>
13. Walker, P.: Audio collections in the archives report from Sound Savings: Preserving Audio Collections conference held July 24-26, 2003.
14. Walker, R.: Functionality of digital annotation: imitating and supporting real-world annotation in Ariadne Issue 35 (30-April-2003) <http://www.ariadne.ac.uk/issue35/waller/>.
15. Van de Somple,: H., Beit-Arie, O., Open linking in the scholarly Information Environment Using the open URL framework. D-Lib Magazine, March 2001, <http://www.dlib.org/dlib/ march01/vandesompel/03vandesompel.html>.
16. Van de Sompel,: H., The SFX framework for context-sensitive reference linking. Project briefing at CNI 2000 Spring Task Force Meeting. CNI Spring 2000 Task Force Meeting, March 27-28, 2000. <http://www.cni.org/tfms/2000a.spring/handout/Sompel-SFX2000Stf.pdf>.

Incorporating Physical and Digital Artifacts into Growing Personal Collections

Pratik Dave, Luis Francisco-Revilla, Unmil P. Karadkar, Richard Furuta, Frank M. Shipman, and Paul Logasa Bogen II

Center for the Study of Digital Libraries and Department of Computer Science Harvey R. Bright Building, TAMU 3112, College Station, TX 77843-3112, USA
walden@csdl.tamu.edu

Abstract. We have produced a system that automatically incorporates syndicated materials from sources including library acquisition records and online news sites to form growing hypertextual structures. This system enables users to create personal and shared collections built atop a growing substrate. It also seeks to empower users through the use of information filters to create dynamic personal collections that can themselves grow over time to include materials as they appear within the underlying collection. In addition, we are investigating particular benefits of intersecting hypertextual paths as a useful structure for representing such sub-collections and the resources extracted from the feeds themselves. We present our prototype system, the emerging standards for syndicating online content, and a discussion of the importance of supporting growth within digital libraries generally.

1 Introduction

Although often useful, the tendency to view digital collections as static is seldom true to the model of physical collections. Libraries, for instance, continuously acquire new materials and such growth over time provides a better model for both digital and physical collections [18]. Users and maintainers of digital collections require tools built to anticipate and accommodate patterns of continuous growth. As users increasingly rely upon expanding collections of electronic resources they require advanced filtering techniques to easily locate materials suited to their needs. We have created a prototype system to investigate methods of assisting users to select, manage, and share materials gathered from growing collections.

Studies of patrons work practices in libraries have emphasized the tendency of users of physical libraries to create personal sub-collections that are often shared. Examples include students' annotated texts or a knowledge worker's notes becoming reference materials for her colleagues [2, 19, 20]. Furthermore, individuals benefit when their personal collections are interrelated, tying together resources (e.g., memos and email messages) that are generally separated in today's computing environments [9]. Motivated by these observations, our system enables users to create dynamic personal collections that intersect with other users' collections into a richly associative linked lattice of meta-documents. We have previously investigated its use with networked news feeds from the Web [8] and in this paper concentrate upon its use with bibliographic information produced by a physical library.

R. Heery and L. Lyon (Eds.): ECDL 2004, LNCS 3232, pp. 341–352, 2004.

Our prototype system relies upon the recent emergence of standardized digital formats for the syndication of materials commonly referred to as RSS feeds ("Really Simple Syndication" or "RDF Site Summary" [32, 33]). These formats provide an XML-based mechanism for encapsulating metadata in a standardized and harvestable manner. The prototype builds upon our earlier work with the Walden's Paths system [25] to enable users to create, maintain, and share Web-based materials. We have adapted our Walden's Paths tools to automatically harvest information from syndicated data feeds and to support building personal collections atop this growing set of resources. In cooperation with the Texas A&M University System's libraries we are incorporating metadata about all new library acquisitions into this system. We have also been harvesting news feeds from 30 different news-related Web sites and lexically analyzing the articles appearing within them.

This paper proceeds as follows: in the next section we discuss related work, the evolution of the RSS standard for syndicating information online, and our Walden's Paths system. The subsequent section provides a high-level discussion of our approach to supporting personal collections built atop growing information substrates and scenarios of use. Section 4 describes the architecture of our prototype and is followed by a discussion of our work to date with the system. We conclude in section 6 with the directions in which we aim to extend this work in the future.

2   Related Work

Many researchers have explored how individuals seek, organize, and share information from physical collections. While the environments of digital and physical collections differ, this work has largely sought to identify processes intrinsic to information seeking. Across the various studies users were found to employ idiosyncratic and individual methods but also to demonstrate a basic propensity for using personal notes and reference lists in information seeking. Such lists were useful not only to their authors but provided a vantage into an individual's needs, activity, or interests.

O'Hara, et al., [20] studied the work practices of graduate students performing research in libraries. The students relied upon hand-written notes, primarily bibliographic references, to assist them in returning to found information and for future reference. Bishop's study [2] of researchers' work and communication practices examined their use of structured documents, particularly scientific journal articles. Most interviewees depended upon personal procedures in their work practice, but all shared a tendency to craft transitional documents and to use annotation to filter documents. Crabtree, et al., [5] performed an ethnographic study of library help desks. Library patrons were found to often be incapable of expressing their needs clearly. When the patrons brought lists of materials with them, staffers could use those lists to establish the patrons' context of investigation. Kracker and Pollio [17] apply content analysis and phenomenological interpretation to undergraduate students' rhetorical descriptions of their experience of libraries. They find that library patrons are often overwhelmed by the sheer scope of available materials in their first encounter with research libraries. Patrons often adapted by locating and subsequently centering themselves within specific locales that had been previously perceived as containing relevant materials.

Marshall [19] provides an ethnographic study of a university library's use of metadata to describe a collection of physical artifacts and digital materials. Her research helps outline the dimensions of the problem space that collection maintainers face in creating metadata for collections comprised of heterogeneous materials. In her analysis of a study of the cataloging codes and conventions used in U.S. libraries, Tillett [28] establishes 7 classes of linkage appearing between bibliographic items. The spectrum of categorizations she uses encompasses all possible relationships between similar materials in a collection. She explores the current practice, at the time, of librarians in recording relationships between materials and her findings emphasize the importance of accommodating variable linkages between catalogued materials.

2.1 Personal and Shared Digital Libraries

The Berkeley Digital Library's Personal Libraries system [30] enables users to create collections built from materials extracted from a document collection. UpLib [16] provides a thumbnail visualization interface for searching and browsing the documents and images that comprise one's daily life, such as receipts, articles, and photos. Salticus [3] develops a predictive model of a user's interests during her navigation of the Web based upon structural features of pages and the user's actions.

Geisler, et al., [13] propose bringing the concept of special collections from physical libraries into digital libraries. They discuss the benefits accruing to both users and collections from enabling "virtual collections". MiBiblio [10, 23] provides users with personal spaces in which to store information found while navigating digital library collections. Materials can be placed into public categories for inclusion into others' spaces according to personal characteristics – thus enabling professors, for instance, to place items onto a virtual reserve for students in their classes. Their system also seeks to provide transparent access to multiple digital collections through standardized information federation protocols. Robertson, et al., describe [24] a Web-based interface for a corporate research library system. Reference librarians shared the results of their information gathering sessions and questioners could view their earlier interactions. Patrons and librarians were able to comment upon, upload, download, and email the results of their earlier activity.

2.2 Information Filtering

In contrast, Foltz and Dumais mention how, in their examination of systems for information filtering, information filtering is hardly a novel concept [12]. People perform filtering when subscribing to particular magazines or watching certain television channels. Belkin and Croft explain the difference between information filtering and information retrieval [1]. Distinguishing characteristics of filtering systems are: that they deal with unstructured or semi-structured data; particularly data that appears in continuous streams; and that they tend to focus upon users' long-term or repeated interests.

Personal collection systems of the sorts described in the preceding section have generally been oriented toward the extraction of materials from within static collections. The systems generally classified as information filtering systems work upon streams of information, an approach better suited for use within continuously growing collections. Several researchers have applied filtering techniques in seeking to help users to manage various computer-based information forms that generally undergo continuous growth or change.

Gifford's Semantic File System (SFS) [14] and Gopal and Manber's HAC ("Hierarchy and Content") systems [15] provide dynamic access to file system objects based upon "virtual" files and folders encapsulating specific selection criteria. Other systems have applied filtering techniques to computer mediated communication such as Usenet and electronic mail, including INFOSCOPE [11], Phoaks [27], and Information Lens and GroupLens [22]. Largely as a result of the dearth of widely adopted standards for describing Web-based materials, such as Fedora [31], few systems have applied filtering techniques to the Web.

2.3 Syndicated Feeds and the RSS Standard

In 1999 the Netscape Corporation created a portal site providing customized news feeds to its users. To facilitate extracting and presenting news from different sources they used an XML-based format called RSS (RDF Site Summary) [33] designed to encapsulate resource description framework (RDF) metadata [32]. The format was kept intentionally simple and lightweight, initially containing little more than a headline and URL to some Web-based material. This ease-of-use gradually led to its adoption by other sites as a method for summarizing newly available materials.

Netscape ultimately lost interest in both their portal endeavor and the RSS format, but work upon the format continued. In subsequent years the initial (version 0.9) format would evolve into a set of related standards for presenting syndicated metadata online. Although the majority of these standards retain the name RSS (versions span from the initial 0.9 through 2.0) a newer variant is called ATOM [34]. The authors of these later standards retained the inclusion of RDF metadata and subsequently incorporated the Dublin Core Metadata Initiative's elements [35]. Although originally developed to encapsulate news articles, with the emergence of the Web log (or blog) phenomenon syndicated feeds have begun to gain far more widespread popularity and usage.

2.4 Hypertextual Paths and Walden's Paths

Hypertextual paths find their first mention in the well known paper by Vannevar Bush, "As We May Think." [4] Bush proposed hypertext paths as a means for associating conceptually related but physically separated items within an information space. The Walden's Paths system [25] is a suite of tools that supports the creation, presentation, and maintenance of hypertextual paths inspired by such associative trails of found knowledge. Our work has largely focused upon the use of paths built from Web-based materials in educational environments [26]. In our system individual paths contain pages from the Web that all share some common topic, supplemented by author-provided annotations, to form coherent narrative presentations.

Paths provide readers with both local and global contexts of their constituent information elements. Each item in a path is implicitly related to every other item by merit of inclusion within the path and the ordering of elements may be used to express some narrative purpose. Web syndication feeds similarly present ordered lists of materials and are themselves a form of hypertextual path structure. Paths derived from these Web feeds provide an ideal mechanism for describing hypertextual paths that continuously grow over time.

The items selected by human path authors are chosen for their explicit relevance to some context. With Web feeds the common context derives from their common point of origin, although more complex associations can also exist. Pages appearing in the syndicated feed for the computer news site Slashdot.com generally deal with computers, and those appearing in the feeds from ABCNews.com's entertainment and politics sites will deal with those respective topics. The elements of syndication feeds are ordered chronologically, meaning that individual items are unlikely to be directly related to their immediate neighbors other than by happenstance.

Elements of hypertextual paths can also provide points of intersection between the different paths containing them, providing jumping off points from one narrative or contextual thread to another [7]. Recently we have begun investigating whether implied intersections between materials within paths can assist with knowledge management and information seeking. We are harvesting RSS feeds from thirty Web sites and applying semantic similarity techniques to the linked pages to deduce the general topic of individual pages and automatically generate implicit virtual paths between related pages [8]. In this way, hypertextual paths evolve the information space from one comprised of individual, isolated, collections to one that embodies an information collective.

3 Approach

In addition to harvesting articles from online news feeds we are investigating uses of library bibliographic records. We have begun to import a syndicated feed containing materials newly acquired by the Texas A&M University Libraries every day. These libraries, along with over 250 other libraries in 7 countries, currently use Michael Doran's New Books software [38] to provide an OPAC interface to new acquisitions. We adapted the data files used with the New Books software to generate a daily RSS feed; we are investigating the use of interconnected paths as a flexible interface to such information. While the number varied daily, our libraries acquire, on average, over a thousand new items every week; consequently the RSS feed represents a resource that is both quite sizable (perhaps *too* sizable for consumption via available RSS browsers) but also one that is of immediate value to scholars on our campus.

We have modified our Walden's Paths system to automatically retrieve and incorporate materials from online syndicated feeds. For Web-based feeds, including those from news feeds, we perform semantic analysis and key phrase extraction over the full resource as a means of supplementing the metadata provided by the feed itself [8]. The metadata associated with library records is richer than that provided with Web feeds, but the content linked to library records is not as informative as that associated with Web feeds. Consequently, for the library feeds, we focus our processing on ingesting the metadata of interest. Once processed, library records are collected into a path that is otherwise treated identically to any other path. We are interested in the potential for such a system to allow users to select elements from among the various feeds, particularly through the specification of dynamic information filters. Such an approach would enable materials not yet available at the time of collection creation to be automatically included into personal collections as they arrive, for long-term collection growth.

Consider a researcher looking for materials from her local research library. She begins by applying filters to the feed of library acquisitions, requesting only materials with the Library of Congress classification for Computer Science (QA76) and the subject heading "Wireless Communications." She further limits the selection to include only materials that arrived after a specific date or within a date range. To ensure that she does not retrieve the same materials over and over, she might also constrain the display to include items never previously viewed. This set of criteria can be saved as a dynamic path which might, for instance, stay empty until some relevant resources are acquired by the library or a pertinent event appears in the news feeds.

Consider next a professor who might select individual elements from the library path, or even the previously described researcher's path, for inclusion into one of her personal paths. She can then insert items from the ACM digital library [36] perhaps along with documents such as a Web page describing her course's grading requirements or assignments. In this fashion, her path forms the reading list or syllabus for a seminar she teaches. Her students might create sub-paths interconnected to their class' path to point to their individual summaries or assignments for each reading.

In this fashion we hope to exploit the attractive combination of interconnected hypertextual paths and information filtering to facilitate sharing and organizing information within growing collections. Personal, dynamic paths can be used to passively collect information over time as with filtered news feeds that grow to include only articles meeting some criteria. The intermixing of references between physical materials and purely digital information may also produce an opportunity to study the differences in individuals' uses of each.

4 Architecture

Our Walden's Paths system has been modified to automatically incorporate syndication feeds and to allow filtered navigation of paths. The prototype interface works within most recent Web browsers and operates in two modes: the Path Server and the Path Publisher. The former provides a browsing interface for paths: users may view lists of publicly available paths, including those shared by other users in the system, and specify filters to their browsing. Users can, optionally, log into the system to enable additional functions, such as filtering based upon whether materials have previously been seen, saving elements into personal paths, and saving filter criteria into personal dynamic paths. In the Path Publisher perspective logged-in users see an overview of all of their personal paths, can create new paths, add new syndicated feeds to the system, edit their paths, and publish their private paths to enable others to view them.

The system currently distinguishes between two types of feeds: Web-syndication feeds such as news sites, and bibliographic library feeds. In the Path Publisher interface a user can provide the location of an available feed in one of these two formats via an URL. The system attempts to retrieve a feed from that location to ensure that it exists and is in an understood format. Because generating feeds requires processing on the part of their originating servers the user must specify the interval between successive attempts to update a feed. For library materials this value is currently once daily (due to the frequency of updates from our library), for Web feeds values between hourly and monthly are allowed. All syndicated feeds are explicitly public (and not owned by any particular user) and the system ensures that different users do not request the same feed to avoid duplication. Every hour feeds due to be harvested are retrieved and compared with their previous contents. New items are identified and appended to the path corresponding to that feed.

In a single month fifteen feeds from online news sites provided roughly 15,000 items. As new Web pages are identified, the system adds them to a queue of pages pending textual processing. A distributed set of systems periodically selects pages from this list to be downloaded and processed for identifying key phrases and the extraction of similarity metrics. We use an approach akin to that described by Phelps and Wilensky to extract key phrases to characterize the contents of these pages [21]. The pages are tagged to identify parts-of-speech and we use one, two, or three term phrases in a manner informed by Turney's approach, modified to use available hyper-text markup cues [29]. Our work in extracting key phrases was initially developed as part of our work in locating replacement pages for Web pages that have disappeared, and is described in more detail elsewhere (see [6] and [8]).

In the same month, the campus library feed added 4,656 items to the collection. The feed contains several elements in addition to the title, abstract, and link appearing in most Web sites' RSS feeds. Each item in the feed possesses an URL to the library OPAC's Web page for that item, which provides up-to-date status information such as whether that item is currently checked out. The feed also provides any available Library of Congress subject headings and the call number assigned to the materials, from which we extract Library of Congress classifications [37]. Additional information provided by the library includes location, a description field providing media-specific information such as physical dimensions, number of pages (for printed materials), and information about copyright and publisher. All of the information provided by the library is concatenated into a textual annotation block although a subset of this metadata currently is used as criterion for filtering.

Figure 1 shows the path selection mode of the Path Server interface to our prototype. In the figure the user is in the process of specifying filters that will define a membership function for a dynamically generated path. In the upper left portion of the figure a new window has opened within which the user is in the process of specifying that matching entities must belong to a particular Library of Congress classification. In addition, in the upper portion of the main window, the user had previously specified that all matching items must have been added after the 15th of March, must not have been previously seen, and should be associated with the key term "wireless". Key phrases are matched against both items originating from Web-feeds and library materials, with Library of Congress subject headings used for the latter. In this instance, however, because items must also have a specific Library of Congress classification code only bibliographic material will be included. Having specified constraints, the user can next either apply them to one of the available paths (two are listed in the lower portion of the figure), apply them to all available paths (via the link to generate a dynamic path), or, because she had previously logged in, save the constraints to create a new dynamic path.

Figure 2 shows the browsing interface after the user has generated a path using the constraints shown in the previous figure. The Web browser window has been split into two panels with the lower one displaying the linked materials, in this case an overview page from the campus library, and the upper providing navigation and control options. To the right of the upper panel is an annotation, in this case it lists all of

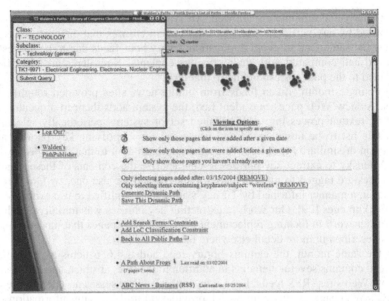

Fig. 1. The Path Selection Interface: Specifying Constraints and Creating a Dynamic Path

the metadata provided by the feed with this item. To the right a set of icons provides the user with the ability to scroll between the available items, moving the mouse over each numbered icon displays the title of that element. The number of items contained in this path is listed to the right of the right-scroll icon, in this case eight items matched. There are also back and next buttons to linearly traverse the included items, alternatively the user can scroll to a particular item, or enable a "table of contents" perspective to see all items by title and navigate to specific items. In this figure, the user has opened the configuration menu (shows in the upper left) by clicking on an icon seen at the extreme left of the upper panel. This menu provides her with the ability to save the current page to one of her personal paths, to switch to the "table of contents" view, list other paths including this item, and to make change to the information filtering criteria currently in use. This interface is discussed in greater detail in ([8] and [25]).

5   Discussion

The additions to Walden's Paths provide two services that are imperative for digital libraries that gracefully accommodate the growth of their collections over time. It helps users to identify relevant new materials from amidst the greater set of all available items, much like the "new titles" shelves in a video store. It also helps users to create and, importantly, share personal collections. As the literature of information seeking in libraries and amongst knowledge workers demonstrates, individuals rely upon personal and idiosyncratic techniques for keeping track of and returning to found information. By allowing users to flexibly organize information, to readily locate new relevant materials, and to unify formerly separated classes of information streams, our system seeks to empower users in their use of digital collections.

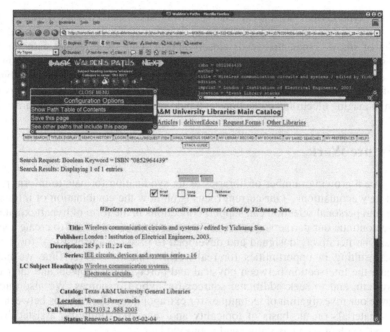

Fig. 2. The Path Browsing Interface: Configuration Menu Displayed

Through the use of information filtering techniques upon Web-based and biblio-graphic materials, our system emphasizes the necessity of adapting technology to accept the inevitable growth of collections over time. Users of our system can save their requirements as a set of constraints which will resolve upon access to contain relevant materials from within a collection. Rather than requiring users to perform complex search and subsequent filtering operations, these dynamic paths are treated as formal, first-class objects in our system. Beyond providing basic awareness possi-bilities ("tell me when such and such a book is published") our system lets a user create a growing personal collection of information to be referred to and used as a perusable and harvestable resource on its own ("show me every article the New York Times has published about 'Haiti' and 'Aristide' since March 2004 that I have not previously read.")

Our work in cooperation with the campus library is partially motivated by their de-sire for better tools for gauging patron's wants and interests and for sharing informa-tion with their patrons. Subject specialist librarians often lack for a powerful tool with which to notify their audience of newly acquired materials, one of their most basic work duties. With our system for publishing syndicated content and for sharing paths built atop library bibliographic records we provide them with one possible approach for doing so. Furthermore, as a technology that enables users to build knowledge structures and narratives that contain references to both online resources and proxies to physical and library materials, patrons can use our system to create library wish-lists and reading lists. Through this process a library may gain a better understanding of what resources are most desired by their patrons and make more user-focused pur-chasing decisions as a result of this feed back.

While hypertextual paths are a relatively well established concept within academic circles, the development and evolution of syndicated feeds is a new phenomenon worthy of study. Syndicated feeds closely approximate hypertextual paths but raise interesting questions as a result of their intrinsic tendency to change and grow over time. As with blogs, which are increasingly related to syndicated feed technology, the use of these emerging technologies within digital libraries and as mechanisms to assist in managing electronic collections is a field with much promise for future work.

6 Future Work

There are a growing number of libraries using syndication formats to inform patrons about new acquisitions. Our current focus is on how the combination of information filters and personal selection can support collections in the form of hypertextual paths. As we continue our partnership with our campus library, we intend to create a system that can be iteratively designed and developed to produce a useful tool for their patrons, resulting in opportunities for real-world evaluation. Over time we hope to evaluate the intersection between physical and purely digital objects and their use in our system, and to seek additional sources for hybrid resources. We also intend to continue our investigation of techniques for extrapolating relationships between Web-based materials on the basis of topicality and semantic similarity, assisted by user input and explicit path navigation and authoring behavior.

Acknowledgements

This material is based upon work supported by the National Science Foundation under grant numbers DUE-0121527 and IIS-0219540. We acknowledge the support of the Humanities Informatics Initiative, Telecommunications and Informatics Task Force and of the Texas A&M University Libraries.

References

1. Belkin, N., Croft, W. B. Information Filtering and Information Retrieval: Two Sides of the Same Coin? In Communications of the ACM, 35(12) (December 1992) 29-38.
2. Bishop, A.P.: Digital Libraries and Knowledge Disaggregation: The Use of Journal Article Components. In Proceedings of DL '98 (Pittsburgh, PA USA, June 1998), ACM Press, 29-39.
3. Burke, R.: Salticus: Guided Crawling for Personal Digital Libraries. In Proceedings of JCDL 2001 (Roanoke, VA USA, June 2001), ACM Press, 88-89.
4. Bush, V.: As We May Think. In The Atlantic Monthly, 176(1) (July 1945), 101-108.
5. Crabtree, A., Twidale, M.B., O'Brien, J., Nichols, D.M.: Talking in the Library: Implications for the Design of Digital Libraries. In Procedings of DL '97 (Philadelphia, PA USA, July 1997), ACM Press, 221-228.
6. Dalal, Z., Dash, S., Dave, P., Francisco-Revilla, L., Furuta, R., Karadkar, U., Shipman, F.: Managing Distrubuted Collections: Evaluating Page Changes, Movement, and Replacement. Accepted to Proceedings of JCDL 2004 (Tucson, AZ USA, June 2004), ACM Press.

7. Dave, P., Karadkar, U.P., Furuta, R., Francisco-Revilla, L., Shipman, F., Dash, S., Dalal, Z.: Browsing Intricately Interconnected Paths. In Proceedings of Hypertext 2003 (Nottingham, England, August 2003), ACM Press, 95-103.
8. Dave, P., Bogen, P., Karadkar, U.P., Francisco-Revilla, L., Furuta, R., Shipman, F.: Dynamically Growing Hypertext Collections. Accepted to Proceedings of Hypertext 2004 (Santa Cruz, CA USA, August 2004), ACM Press.
9. Dumais, S., Cutrell, E., Cadiz, J.J., Jancke, G., Sarin, R., Robbins, D.C.: Stuff I've Seen: A System for Personal Information Retrieval and Re-Use. In Proceedings of SIGIR 2003 (Toronto, Canada, August 2003), ACM Press, 72-79.
10. Fernández, L., Sánchez, J.A., García, A.: MiBiblio: Personal Spaces in a Digital Library Universe. In Proceedings of JCDL 2000 (San Antonio, TX USA, June 2000), ACM Press, 232-233.
11. Fischer, G., Stevens, C.: Information Access in Complex, Poorly Structured Information Spaces. In Proceedings of CHI 1991 (New Orleans LA, April 1991), ACM Press, 63-70.
12. Foltz, P., Dumais, S.: Personalized Information Delivery: An Analysis of Information Filtering Methods. In Communications of the ACM, 35(12) (December 1992), 51-60.
13. Geisler, G., Giersch, S., McArthur, D., McClelland, M.: Creating Virtual Collections in Digital Libraries: Benefits and Implementation Issues. In Proceedings of JCDL 2002 (Portland, OR USA, June 2002), ACM Press, 210-218.
14. Gifford, D., Jovelot, P., Sheldon, P., O'Toole, J.: Semantic File Systems. In Proceedings of the Third Symposium on Operating Systems Design and Implementation 1999 (New Orleans LA, February 1999), USENIX Press, 16-25.
15. Gopal, B., Manber, U.: Integrating Content-based Access Mechanisms with Hierarchical File Systems. In Proceedings of the Third Symposium on Operating Systems Design and Implementation 1999 (New Orleans LA, February 1999), USENIX Press, 265-278.
16. Janssen, W.C., Popat, K.: UpLib: A Universal Personal Digital Library System. In Proceedings of DocEng 2003 (Grenoble, France, November 2003), ACM Press, 234-242.
17. Kracker, J., Pollio, H.R.: The experience of libraries across time: Thematic analysis of undergraduate recollections of library experiences. In Journal of the American Society for Information Science and Technology (JASIST), 54(12), 2003, 1104-1116.
18. Levy, D, Marshall, C.: Going Digital: A Look at Assumptions Underlying Digital Libraries. In Communications of the ACM, Vol. 38 (4), April 1995, ACM Press, 77-84.
19. Marshall, C.C.: Making Metadata: A Study of Metadata Creation for a Mixed Physical-Digital Collection. In Proceedings of DL '98 (Pittsburgh, PA USA, June 1998), ACM Press, 162-171.
20. O'Hara, K., Smith, F., Newman, W., Sellen, A.: Student Readers' Use of Library Documents: Implications for Library Technologies. In Proceedings of CHI '98 (Los Angeles, CA USA, April 1998), ACM Press, 233-240.
21. Phelps, T. & Wilensky, R.: Robust Hyperlinks: Cheap, Everywhere, Now. In Proceedings of Digital Documents and Electronic Publishing 2000 (DDEP00) (Munich Germany, September 2000), 13-15.
22. Resnick, P., Iacovou, N.: Suchak, M., Bergstrom, P., Riedl, J.: GroupLens: An Open Architecture for Collaborative Filtering of Netnews, In Proceedings of CSCW 1994 (Chapel Hill NC, October 1994), ACM Press, 175-186.
23. Reyes-Farfán, N., Sánchez, J.A.: Personal Spaces in the Context of OAI. In Proceedings of JCDL 2003 (Houston, TX USA, June 2003), ACM Press, 182-183.
24. Robertson, S., Jitan, S., Reese, K.: Web-Based Collaborative Library Research. In Proceedings of DL '97 (Philadelphia, PA USA, July 1997), ACM Press, 152-160.
25. Shipman, F., Furuta, R., Brenner, D., Chung, C., Hsieh, H.: Guided Paths through Web-Based Collections: Design, Experiences, and Adaptations. In Journal of the American Society of Information Sciences (JASIS), 51(3), March 2000, 260-272.
26. Shipman III, F.M., Furuta, R., Brenner, D., Chung, C., and Hsieh, H.: Using Paths in the Classroom: Experiences and Adaptations. In Proceedings of Hypertext '98 (Pittsburgh, PA USA, June 1998), ACM Press, 267-276.

27. Terveen, L., Hill, W., Amento, B., McDonald, D., Creter J.: Building Task-Specific Interfaces to High Volume Conversational Data. In Proceedings of CHI 1997 (Atlanta GA, March 1997), ACM Press, 226-233.
28. Tillett, B.: A Summary of the Treatment of Bibliographic Relationships in Cataloging Rules. In Library Resources and Technical Services (LRTS), 35(4), 393-405.
29. Turney, P.: Learning Algorithms for Keyphrase Extraction. In Information Retrieval 2(4), 303-336.
30. Wilensky, R.: Personal libraries: Collection Management as a Tool for Lightweight Personal and Group Document Management. Technical Report SDSC TR-2001-9, 2001.
31. The Flexible Extensible Digital Object and Repository Architecture (Fedora), *http://www. fedora.info*, visited April 2004.
32. The Resource Description Framework (RDF), *http://www.w3.org/RDF/*, visited April 2004.
33. The RSS Schema, *http://blogs.law.harvard.edu/tech/rss*, visited April 2004.
34. The ATOM Syndication Format, *http://www.atomenabled.org/developers/syndication/ atom-format-spec.php*, visited April 2004.
35. The Dublin Core Metadata Initiative, *http://dublincore.org/*, visited April 2004.
36. The ACM Digital Library, *http://portal.acm.org/dl.cfm*, visited April 2004.
37. The Library of Congress Classification Outline, *http://www.loc.gov/catdir/cpso/lcco/ lcco.html*, visited April 2004.
38. New Books List Software, *http://rocky.uta.edu/doran/autolist/*, visited April 2004.

Enhancing the OpenDLib Search Service

Leonardo Candela, Donatella Castelli, and Pasquale Pagano

Istituto di Scienza e Tecnologie dell'Informazione "Alessandro Faedo" – CNR
Via G. Moruzzi, 1 - 56124 PISA - Italy
{candela,castelli,pagano}@isti.cnr.it

Abstract. This paper presents a new technique for supporting query formulation and processing experimentally integrated in the OpenDLib search service. This technique provides a better support for unified search by enhancing the capability of the digital library to satisfy the user needs. The paper presents the theory underlying the proposed technique and describes how it has been exploited in the OpenDLib system.

1 Introduction

Digital libraries (DLs) are often built by re-using and integrating information sources, originally created by single institutions to serve their own purposes. Each institution describes its documents using specific cataloguing rules. Even when a standard metadata format is used, the semantic interpretation of the metadata fields and the cataloguing terms used are strongly influenced by the assumptions and terminology of the application context in which the institution operates. The content acquired by a DL from different heterogeneous sources can be used to serve a multitude of users coming from institutions that have not necessarily contributed to provide this content. The different cataloguing rules used at the source level are completely transparent to the DL users, who formulate queries that express their information needs in terms of the metadata format and controlled vocabularies supported by the DL search service.

This dichotomy between the information source cataloguing environment and the search environment complicates both the formulation and the processing of user queries. As in the DL framework the users neither know how documents have been originally described nor have access to the original description format, they are not always able to formulate precisely the conditions required to retrieve documents that satisfy their needs. Most DL search services attempt to minimize this problem by automatically expanding the user query with the help of stemming and query expansion algorithms.

In order to process the user queries the system must be able to map the query conditions against the descriptive metadata of the documents provided by the different information sources. The most common solution implemented today to carry out this task is to enforce interoperability by requiring to every DL information source provider to expose the descriptions of their documents in at least a shared common metadata format. This format is usually also the one accepted by the DL search service language. In order to fulfill this requirement, the source provider establishes a mapping between its internally used metadata format(s) and the mandatory metadata format and then it applies this mapping to all the metadata records of its resources. The DL search service

R. Heery and L. Lyon (Eds.): ECDL 2004, LNCS 3232, pp. 353–365, 2004.

thus operates in a context where the metadata descriptions and the query language are homogeneous and can process the query with traditional techniques.

Current DL systems support both query formulation and processing using techniques based on syntactic manipulations, without exploiting any semantic information about the metadata schemas and controlled vocabularies. One of the reasons for this choice is the lack of techniques for exploiting it successfully.

This paper presents a new technique for supporting query formulation and processing that uses such semantic information. This technique, which has been experimentally integrated in the OpenDLib search service, takes advantage of the specialization relationships among the metadata fields and among the terms of the controlled vocabularies used. This information is obtained by exploiting the translation relationships that are produced by the information source providers when they transform the local description formats into the common format. This information, usually discarded, is semantically richer than the final common format and can be used for building more powerful search services. The OpenDLib search service is thus able to offer the choice among a range of possible different interpretations for the same query and the users can select the one that better satisfy their needs. Note that this technique does not require any explicit generation of the metadata records in a pre-defined shared format.

This paper presents also the model that formally justifies the proposed technique. This model modifies the work on ontologies presented in [13] in order to apply it to the DL framework that is characterized by both metadata schemas and controlled vocabularies.

The outline of the paper is as follows: next section discusses the limitations of the current search services that exploit only syntactic relations; Section 4 and 5 justify the proposed technique formally; Section 6 describes the application of this model in the OpenDLib framework; finally, Section 7 concludes.

2   Motivation

In experimenting DLs built by re-using content from heterogeneous sources, we have often encountered situations in which the users could not formulate queries that express their needs and the system was not able to process them properly. These observations have motivated this work. This section gives examples illustrating some of problems we faced.

Let us consider a simple DL in which the provider of the information source IS_1 publishes the following metadata records:

	Subject	Subject.ACM
doc1	text processing	unspecified
doc2	unspecified	I.7.1 Document and Text Editing

According to the internal rules of the DL institution, the authors can describe their documents by assigning either a code extracted from the ACM Computing Classification System to the field *Subject.ACM* or a free term to the more generic field *Subject*. The records produced are processed by the system in order to extracts the information required to process the user queries.

Imagine now that the user John Smith wants to retrieve exactly those documents that have been described with *Subject* equal to "text processing". The trivial solution is to formulate the following query: *"Subject = text processing"*. The search service has only to match the query condition against the information extracted from the metadata records and it usually replies including *doc1* and excluding *doc2*.

Consider now another user of the same DL, Henry Stamp, who is interested in retrieving all the documents about the topic that his community of interest refers as "text processing". Using a traditional search service, this user cannot do anything better than formulate the same query as that expressed by John Smith. However, the result expected in this case is different. It should include: *i*) the documents retrieved under the previous more strict interpretation; *ii*) the documents whose *Subject* contains values morphologically and syntactically close to the query term, e.g. "textual processing" and "documents and text processing", and *iii*) the documents whose more specific subject, i.e. *Subject.ACM*, contains values that are semantically close to the query term. Under this interpretation the system should, therefore, return not only *doc1*, but also *doc2* since its more specific subject field, Subject.ACM, contains I.7.1 "Documents and Text Editing" which is an ACM subcategory of I.7 "Documents and Text Processing".

While the majority of DL search services that support an interpretation of the query based on automatically extracted morphological and syntactic relationships, e.g. stemming and query expansion, are able to return the documents described in *i*) and *ii*) above, they are not capable to exploit the semantic relationships that exists among the different concepts represented by the metadata fields. This means that the current search services do not usually return documents, like *doc2*, which are indexed under metadata fields that are specializations of those indicated in the query, i.e. *subject.ACM*.

Despite this example may seem very trivial, it must be remembered that in order to satisfy the requirements of the second user, the query must find *doc2* which has been classified using *a narrower subject field but a broader classification term*. When manipulating complex metadata formats and sophisticated categorization schemas this kind of document identification is not a simple task.

The limitation described above becomes more incisive in DLs composed by multiple information sources, each describing its documents with different metadata formats. In order to achieve search interoperability over a set of information sources, DLs often require them to publish their metadata in a shared format, e.g. Dublin Core (DC) [1]. To adhere to the rules of the DL, each information source provider maps its local format into the shared format. This mapping is done locally by people that have a clear understanding of the semantics associated with the original metadata fields. This information is never transmitted to the DL system that only receives the metadata records in the shared format. The query interpretation made by the system is thus defined *without taking into account the local descriptive interpretations*. This behavior negatively influences the quality of the DL search service.

To exemplify this point, let us add another information source, IS_2, to our example. It maintains a set of audio-video (A/V) documents of university courses described as in the following example:

	CourseArea	CourseTopic	AudioVideoSubject
doc3	Computing Methodologies	Text processing	Document Management

where *AudioVideoSubject* is the subject of the A/V document, i.e. the subject of a specific course lecture, *CourseTopic* is the topic of the course, and *CourseArea* is the course research area. Following this semantics, the A/V document, being a course element, which belongs to a specific area, is also implicitly classified under the subject of the course and the subject of the area.

Suppose now that DC is the common metadata format. The institution that maintains IS_1 maps both *Subject* and *Subject.ACM* into *dc:subject*, whereas the institution that maintains IS_2 maps only *AudioVideoSubject* to this field. Under this hypothesis, any query interpretation provided by the search service is unable to return *doc3* as a result of the query presented at the beginning of this section even if the query term exactly matches the subject of the course whose the video is a part of.

The situations exemplified above, and many others, convinced us that the search functionality implemented so far by DLs are too strict. Search services that better satisfy the user needs must be provided. We propose an approach, which can be implemented with reasonable costs, able to exploit, as far as possible, the existing semantic mapping about the document description terminologies.

3   The Architectural Framework

Figure 1 shows the logical DL architectural framework that we assume. The content of the DL is given by a number of independent heterogeneous Information Sources $IS_1, \ldots, IS_n$ that disseminate metadata records in one or more formats. These records are indexed by Index services. Moreover records of different ISs in different formats are indexed by separate Index services[1]. An Index thus processes queries formulated according to the same terminology, i.e. metadata format and controlled vocabularies, used for the indexed records.

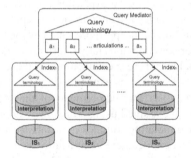

Fig. 1. The architectural framework.

This terminology and the corresponding semantic descriptions are known to the Index, i.e. it has access to the schema that specify the metadata format and the controlled vocabularies associated with the metadata fields. Moreover, we assume that all the Index services accepts the same query structure and relational operators.

An Index service supports different interpretations of the same query condition. Each interpretation is characterized by a different level of precision given to the condition. For example, the different intended semantics given by John Smith and Henry Stamp to the query "*subject = text processing*" are two different interpretations of this condition.

The DL user queries are actually not directly evaluated by the Index services but are first processed by the Query Mediator (QM) service. This service hides the heterogeneity of the underlying information space serving search operations in terms of the query

---

[1] This assumption is only given for simplicity of exposition, it does not compromise the generality of the solution.

terminology shown to the user[2]. It first maps the user's queries into queries formulated in the terminology of the underlying information sources, then it dispatches them to the Index services and, finally merges the results received. The mapping is done by exploiting the knowledge of specific semantic relationships between the handled terminology and the local indexed terminologies. These relationships, defined by the IS providers, are stored by the corresponding Index services[3]. The QM, similarly to the Index, can support different mapping modalities, the user choose that to use.

The next two sections introduce the theory that justifies our approach. Following [13], we propose a formalization that applies to the DL framework which has to do with metadata schemas and controlled vocabularies. In particular, we specify the different query interpretations that can be supported by the Index and QM services and how they are obtained by the existing terminology mappings. More details can be found in [5].

4   The Index

Each information source uses a metadata schema to describe its own documents. This metadata schema is a pair $(\mathcal{F}, \leq_{\mathcal{F}})$, where $\mathcal{F}$ is a set of schema fields and $\leq_{\mathcal{F}}$ is a *subsumption* relation over $\mathcal{F}$[4] that models the existing specialization relationship among these fields. For example in Figure 2, *Subject. ACM* $\leq_{\mathcal{F}}$ *Subject* means that *Subject. ACM* is a more specialized

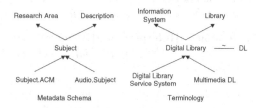

Fig. 2. A metadata schema and a terminology.

property than *Subject*. Each field *f* of the schema is populated via an appropriate *terminology* defined as a pair $(\mathcal{V}_f, \leq_{\mathcal{V}_f})$ where $\mathcal{V}_f$ is a set of terms and $\leq_{\mathcal{V}_f}$ is a subsumption relation over $\mathcal{V}_f$ that models the existing specialization relationship among these terms. For example, in Figure 2 *Multimedia DL* $\leq_{\mathcal{V}_f}$ *DL* means that *Multimedia DL* is a more specialized term than *DL*. In certain cases the latter assumption is too *strong*. A field is often populated via free terms or free text. In these cases, the terminology can easily and automatically be obtained considering that each term is in relation only with itself or, if we are going to use stemming, we can assume that the term is subsumed by the stemmed term.

---

[2] A DL can also offer search operations defined on more than one terminology. This situation can be handled by introducing a QM for each of these terminologies.

[3] Protocols, like OAI-PMH, require that any IS provides at least a common DC metadata description of its items. In order to adhere to this protocol, each IS provider must first define the mapping between its local metadata format and DC, and then generate the DC records. Our approach is less demanding, it only requires the mapping and does not need any explicit record generation.

[4] Each subsumption relation $\leq$ is a *reflexive* and *transitive* relation over the reference universe. We write $o_1 \sim o_2$ meaning that the two objects are *equivalent* w.r.t. $\leq$ if both $o_1 \leq o_2$ and $o_2 \leq o_1$.

Combining the metadata schema with the set of terminologies $\mathcal{V}_f{}^5$ that the Index uses, one for each field of the schema, we can define the *query terminology* that the Index "speaks" as a pair $(\mathcal{C}, \leq_C)$, where $\mathcal{C}$ is a set of *conditions* (f, v) such that $f \in \mathcal{F}$, $v \in \mathcal{V}_f$. This models the boolean condition "field f equals term v". For example, a valid condition for the Index in Figure 2 is *(Subject, Digital Library)* representing the information need "the documents whose *Subject* is *Digital Library*".

The subsumption relation $\leq_C$ models the specializations among conditions and is formally defined as follows:

Definition 1. [Subsumption relation] *Let* $(\mathcal{F}, \leq_{\mathcal{F}})$ *be a metadata schema,* $(\mathcal{V}_f, \leq_{\mathcal{V}_f})$ *be the terminology for the schema field* f. *Given* $c_1, c_2 \in \mathcal{C}$ *where* $c_i = (f_i, v_i)$, $f_i \in \mathcal{F}$ *and* $v_i \in \mathcal{V}_{f_i}$ *we define* $c_1 \leq_C c_2 \iff f_1 \leq_{\mathcal{F}} f_2 \wedge v_1 = v_2$.

Figure 2, for example, says that *(Audio.Subject, Library)* $\leq_C$ *(Research Area, Library)* and that *(subject.ACM, DLSS)* $\leq_C$ *(Subject, DLSS)* meaning that the first condition is a specialization of the second one.

A query for the Index is either a simple condition or a combination of conditions using the boolean connectives $\wedge, \vee, \neg$. For example, a simple query can be *(subject, Digital Library)* $\vee$ *(Description, Library)*.

Definition 2. [Interpretation] *An interpretation* I *of a query terminology* $\mathcal{C}$ *is a function* $I : \mathcal{C} \to 2^{Obj}$ *that associates each condition of* $\mathcal{C}$ *with a set of objects of the domain.*

Each Index has an *interpretation* I that is the result of the indexing phase. Table 1 in columns I presents an interpretation of the Index presented in Figure 2[6].

The interpretation that an Index uses for query evaluation must comply with the structure of the query terminology (i.e. $\leq_C$). This requirement is expressed by introducing the notion of *model*.

Definition 3. [Model] *An interpretation* I *is a model of a query terminology* $(\mathcal{C}, \leq_C)$ *if* $\forall c, c' \in \mathcal{C}, c \leq_C c' \Rightarrow I(c) \subseteq I(c')$.

For example, suppose that an Index has indexed a set of documents under the condition c_1 and another set of documents under the condition c_2 and no documents under the condition c that subsumes the previous two conditions. This interpretation is acceptable as we can "respect" the structure of $\leq_C$ by defining the interpretation of c as the union of the set of documents indexed under c_1 and those indexed under c_2.

As there may be several models of $\mathcal{C}$, we assume that each Index is able to process queries from one or more models of its interpretation. In this paper, as suggested in [13], we will consider two families of models for query processing, the *sure evaluation models* and the *possible evaluation models*. In order to define these models formally we need two preliminary definitions that allow us to follow the subsumption relation, respectively, over the fields of the metadata schema and over the controlled vocabularies.

Definition 4. [Tail and Head] *Given a condition* $c \in \mathcal{C}$, $c = (f, v)$, *we define*
$$tail(c) = \{c' \in \mathcal{C} | c' \leq_C c\} \qquad head(c) = \{c' \in \mathcal{C} | c \leq_C c'\}$$

---

[5] We will use $\mathcal{V}_f$ instead of $(\mathcal{V}_f, \leq_{\mathcal{V}_f})$ when no confusion arises.

[6] For simplicity, we will use the same terminology to populate all the schema fields.

Intuitively, $tail(c)$ and $head(c)$ contains c and, respectively, all the conditions that are stricter than c and wider than c according to the query terminology and, in particular, to the subsumption relations over the schema fields. For example, considering Figure 2, $tail(subject, DL)=\{(subject, DL), (subject.ACM, DL), (Audio.subject, DL)\}$ while $head(subject, DL)=\{(subject, DL), (Research\ Area, DL), (Description, DL)\}$.

Definition 5. [Value models] *Given an interpretation I of C and a condition $c \in C$, $c = (f, v)$, we define three kinds of value models for c generated by I as follows:*
$$I_{\sim}^{\mathcal{V}}(c) = \bigcup \{I(c') | f = f' \wedge v' \sim_{v_f} v\} \qquad I_{\leq}^{\mathcal{V}}(c) = \bigcup \{I(c') | f = f' \wedge v' \leq_{v_f} v\}$$
$$I_{\geq}^{\mathcal{V}}(c) = \bigcap \{I_{\leq}^{\mathcal{V}}(c') | f = f' \wedge v \leq_{v_f} v' \wedge v \not\sim_{v_f} v'\}$$

The above interpretations correspond to three different ways in which the Index can evaluate a condition that involves the field f using the stored interpretations and the semantic information on the controlled vocabularies. These interpretations correspond to the set of documents indexed under conditions involving the field f and, respectively, the value v or values equivalent to v ($I_{\sim}^{\mathcal{V}}$), the value v or values subsumed by v ($I_{\leq}^{\mathcal{V}}$), and all the values that subsume v ($I_{\geq}^{\mathcal{V}}$).

We can now define the *sure evaluation model* and the *possible evaluation model* of the stored interpretation I. These are obtained by taking into account both the subsumption relations among the schema fields and the subsumption relations among terminologies.

Definition 6. [Sure and Possible models] *Given an interpretation I of C we define three types of sure evaluation models (I_*^-) and three types of possible evaluation models (I_*^+) of C (where "$*$" stands for $\sim | \leq | \geq$) generated by I as follows:*
$$I_*^-(c) = \bigcup \{I^{\mathcal{V}}(c') | c' \in tail(c)\} \qquad I_*^+(c) = \bigcap \{I_*^-(c') | c' \in head(c) \wedge c' \not\approx_c c\}$$

Table 1[7] shows the sure evaluation models of our Index that use the terminology in Figure 2, based on the stored interpretation I.

Table 1. Interpretations of an information source index.

Condition	I	$I_{\sim}^-$	$I_{\leq}^-$	$I_{\geq}^-$
(Subject,Digital Library)	{1}	{1,2}	{1,2,3}	{1,2,3,4}
(Subject,DL)	{2}	{1,2}	{1,2,3}	{1,2,3,4}
(Subject,Info. Sys.)	{5}	{4,5}	{1,2,3,4,5}	{1,2,3,4,5,6}
(Subject,Library)	{6}	{4,6}	{1,2,3,4,6}	{1,2,3,4,5,6}
(Subject.ACM,DLSS)	{3}	{3}	{3}	{3}
(Audio.Subject,Info. Sys.)	{4}	{4}	{4}	{4}
(Audio.Subject,Library)	{4}	{4}	{4}	{4}
(Research Area,DL)	{7}	{1,2,7,10}	{1,2,3,7,8,10}	{1,2,3,7,8,9,10}
(Research Area,DLSS)	{8}	{3,8}	{3,8}	{3,8}
(Research Area,Info. Sys.)	{9}	{4,5,9}	{1,2,3,4,5,7,8,9,10}	{1,2,3,4,5,6,7,8,9,10}
(Research Area,Library)	{9}	{4,6,9}	{1,2,3,4,6,7,8,9,10}	{1,2,3,4,5,6,7,8,9,10}
(Research Area,Dig. Lib.)	{10}	{1,2,7,10}	{1,2,3,7,8,10}	{1,2,3,4,7,8,9,10}
(Description,Multimedia DL)	{8}	{8}	{8}	{1,2,3,7,8,11}
(Description,DL)	{7,11}	{1,2,7,11}	{1,2,3,7,8,11}	{1,2,3,4,7,8,9,11}
(Description,Info. Sys.)	{9}	{4,5,9}	{1,2,3,4,5,7,8,9,11}	{1,2,3,4,5,6,7,8,9,11}
(Description,Library)	{9}	{4,6,9}	{1,2,3,4,6,7,8,9,11}	{1,2,3,4,5,6,7,8,9,11}

---

[7] In this table we have used i referring to d_i.

Even if the indexing phase is correct, certain documents may not have been indexed under all the conditions that could apply to them. So, given a simple query c, we may want the source to be able to answer including either all the documents that are known to be indexed under c or all the documents that are possible indexed under c. In the first case we want the sure evaluation model while in the latter case we ask for the possible evaluation model.

Definition 7. [Sure and Possible Query answering] *Let q be a query over C and let I be an interpretation of C. The sure answer $I_{\leq}^{-}(q)$ and the possible answer $I_{\leq}^{+}(q)$ are defined as follows:*

$$I_{\leq}^{-}(c) = \bigcup \{I_{\leq}^{\nu}(c')|c' \in tail(c)\} \qquad I_{\leq}^{+}(c) = \bigcap \{I_{\leq}^{-}(c')|c' \in head(c) \wedge c' \approx_C c\}$$

$$I_{\leq}^{-}(q \wedge q') = I_{\leq}^{-}(q) \cap I_{\leq}^{-}(q') \qquad I_{\leq}^{+}(q \wedge q') = I_{\leq}^{+}(q) \cap I_{\leq}^{+}(q')$$

$$I_{\leq}^{-}(q \vee q') = I_{\leq}^{-}(q) \cup I_{\leq}^{-}(q') \qquad I_{\leq}^{+}(q \vee q') = I_{\leq}^{+}(q) \cup I_{\leq}^{+}(q')$$

$$I_{\leq}^{-}(\neg q) = \overline{I_{\leq}^{-}(q)} \qquad\qquad I_{\leq}^{+}(\neg q) = \overline{I_{\leq}^{+}(q)}$$

All the other sure and possible answers for the other models, i.e. $I_{\sim}^{-}$, $I_{\geq}^{-}$, $I_{\sim}^{+}$ and $I_{\geq}^{+}$, are defined in a similar way.

Each of the above query answering modes represent a modality of query processing. Note that the sure answer is appropriate for users that focus on *precision* while the possible answer is for users that focus on *recall*. Moreover, in both the family of sure and possible answers, we can distinguish more precision-oriented responses, i.e. $I_{\sim}^{-}$, versus more recall-oriented responses, i.e. $I_{\geq}^{-}$. An Index that stores an interpretation, like the one given in Table 1, and that has access to the semantics of the metadata schema and its controlled vocabularies, can thus potentially offer a range of other interpretations, like the ones given in the same table, to any of its clients to express their information needs more precisely.

For example, expressing the query (*Subject*, *DL*) user could be interested in documents that have been described using the field *Subject*, or a more specialized one, and the term *DL* or an equivalent term, so this user is asking for $I_{\sim}^{-}$. Another user expressing the same query could be interested, instead, in those documents that have been described using the field *Subject*, or a more generic field, and the term *DL* or an equivalent term, so this user is asking for $I_{\sim}^{+}$. In the case of Table 1, the Index returns the set of documents $\{d_1, d_2\}$ to the first user and the set of documents $\{d_1, d_2, d_7\}$ to the second user. Note that while d_1 and d_2 are indexed under the condition (*subject*, *DL*) and (*subject*, *Digital Library*) respectively, the document d_7 is indexed under a pair of conditions, (*Research Area*, *DL*) and (*description*, *DL*), more general but still pertinent to the one expressed by the user.

5   The Query Mediator

The previous section has described which are the potential query evaluation choices of an Index service that exploits semantic information. We can now examine the more general problem of understanding which query evaluation choices can be supported by a Query Mediator service. In what follows we will assume that such kind of mediator dispatches queries to Index services that behaves as described in the previous section.

Abstractly a QM service can be considered as an Index service that *virtually stores all the objects* of the underlying sources and supplies a query language that satisfies the needs of its users community. However, there is an important difference between a QM and an Index: the QM does not store explicitly any interpretation of the information space. Such interpretations are maintained by the Index services. The QM only stores an *articulation* for each source, i.e. a set of relationships among the Mediator terminology and the Index terminology. A QM is formally defined as follows:

Definition 8. [Query Mediator] *A QM over n Index services $I_1, \ldots, I_n$, such that $I_i = (\mathcal{C}_i, \leq_{\mathcal{C}_i})$, consists of:*

1. *a query terminology $(\mathcal{C}_M, \leq_{\mathcal{C}_M})$ and*
2. *a set of articulations a_i, one for each Index I_i; each articulation a_i is a subsumption relation over $\mathcal{C}_M \cup \mathcal{C}_i$ which contains:*
   - *a subsumption relation, $\preceq^i_{\mathcal{F}}$, over $\mathcal{F}^M \cup \mathcal{F}^i$, i.e. a set of relationships among the Mediator metadata schema and the Index metadata schema,*
   - *a set of subsumption relations, $\preceq^i_{\mathcal{V}_f}$, over $\mathcal{V}^M_f \cup \mathcal{V}^i_{f'}$, i.e. a set of relations among each field terminology of the Mediator and the corresponding ones in the Index. There exists one of such relation for each pair of (Mediator field terminology, Index field terminology).*

We introduce a special subsumption relation between Mediator and Index field terminologies, Π_f, to indicate that every term of the first terminology is mapped into the *same* term of the second terminology. In such case we impose that $\mathcal{V}^i_{f'} = \mathcal{V}^M_f$, i.e. the terminology of the Index is the *same* as that of the Mediator, and $\preceq^i_{\mathcal{F}}$ is defined such that for each $v \in \mathcal{V}^i_{f'}$ and $v' \in \mathcal{V}^M_f$, $v \sim^i_{\mathcal{V}_f} v'$ if and only if $v = v'$, i.e. the term on the Mediator is *equivalent* to the same term of the Index w.r.t. the articulation.

The Mediator query terminology is defined similarly to the Index one, i.e. $\mathcal{C}_M$ is a set of pairs (f, v) such that $f \in \mathcal{F}^M$, $v \in \mathcal{V}^M_f$, and $\leq_{\mathcal{C}_M}$ is a subsumption relation over $\mathcal{C}_M$. Moreover each $\mathcal{V}^M_f$ is a terminology, i.e. a pair $(\mathcal{V}^M_f, \leq_{\mathcal{V}_f})$ where $\leq_{\mathcal{V}_f}$ is a subsumption relation over $\mathcal{V}^M_f$.

Figure 3 shows an example of a QM that operates over two Indexes. This mediator uses the DC metadata schema and the ACM Computing Classification System as controlled vocabulary for the field *subject*[8].

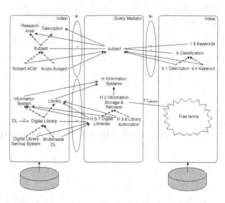

Fig. 3. A Query Mediator over two Indexes.

The Index services in Figure 3 are $Index_1$, that has been introduced in the previous section, and $Index_2$, an Index service that uses the LOM metadata schema [2] and free terms to populate the fields shown in the figure. The query interpretations supported

---

[8] For brevity, the example shows only a partial view of the Query Mediator.

by the QM are defined in terms of both the interpretations stored by the Index services and the existing articulations. In order to identify these interpretations we show how the mediator proceeds in order to reply to a query:

1. define a query c^i for I_i as a translation of each $c \in C_M$ obtained using a_i, $i = 1, \ldots, n$;
2. evaluate c^i at I_i, $i = 1, \ldots, n$; and finally
3. define $I(c)$ as the union of the answers to c^i returned by the Index services.

Several possible translations, considering the semantic relationships among QM and Index terminologies, can be identified. We define (for details see [5]) *precise*, *lower* and *upper approximations* of a conditions $c_i \in C_M$. Roughly speaking, the first one, $c_{p_*}^i$, is the disjunction of all the conditions in C_j that are *equivalent* to c_i in a_j; the second one, $c_{l_*}^i$, is the disjunction of all the conditions in C_j that c_i subsume in a_j; while the last one, $c_{u_*}^i$, is the conjunction of all the conditions that subsume c_i in a_j.

Examples of approximations for the QM shown in Figure 3[9] are:
$$(DC.subject, H.3.7)_{p_\sim}^1 = (subject, Digital\ Library) \vee (subject, DL)$$
$$(DC.subject, H.3.7)_{l_\sim}^2 = (1.5, H.3.7) \vee (9, H.3.7) \vee (9.1, H.3.7) \vee (9.2, H.3.7)$$

The approximations are just queries to the information source S_i and can have sure or possible answers as shown in Section 4. For this reason we can define at least 54 possible interpretations I for the QM[10], denoted with $I_{a,b}$ where a is the type of QM approximation and b is the answer type from the source, e.g. $I_{u_\leq, +_\leq}$ means that the mediator uses the upper approximation with $\leq$, while the sources reply following the possible model $I_\leq^+$. These approximations are defined as the set union over the source interpretations w.r.t. the mediator approximation, e.g. $I_{u_\leq, +_\leq}(c) = \bigcup_{i=1}^n I_{i\leq}^+(c_{u_\leq}^i)$.

As the QM is an IS it can give either one of the three sure answers or one of the three possible answers for each of the above interpretations, i.e. we can have 324 possible modes under which the mediator can operate. These operation modes are denoted with $I_{a,b}^c$ where a is the type of mediator approximation, b is source answer-type and c is the mediator answer-type, e.g. $I_{u_\leq, +_\leq}^{+\geq}$ means that the mediator use the upper approximation with $\leq$ and reply following the possible model with $\geq$ while the sources reply following the possible model $I_\leq^+$.

6   The Enhanced OpenDLib Search Service

The approach described theoretically above has been exploited for building a more advanced search service for the OpenDLib Service System [7].

The OpenDLib architecture is very similar to the logical one described in Section 3. Its search service does not support any subsumption between attributes of the metadata format and assumes the standard subsumption relation between terms and their stems. Moreover, the search functionality over heterogenous metadata formats is supported thanks to a common metadata format.

---

[9] We used the code of the fields/terminology terms instead of the value when no confusion arise.

[10] For simplicity we assume that all the Indexes respond using the same type of answer.

One of the on-line DLs powered by the OpenDLib software is called *tLibrary*. It manages documents harvested from different ISs. Some of these sources represent their content using DC, others use the qualified version of this format, others apply proprietary metadata descriptions. The different semantic interpretations of the same metadata fields and the presence of a variety of field qualifiers reduce the quality of the search functionality when heterogeneous information sources are selected by the user, even when all the different metadata descriptions of the content are indexed.

To overcome this problem we decided to design an experimental search service fully based on the illustrated techniques. We needed to *i*) easily drive users in querying both homogeneous and heterogenous information sources; *ii*) simply present how to ask for a more precision-oriented, or recall-oriented, query evaluation; and *iii*) hide the complexity of the proposed approach.

Taking into account that our harvested information sources have not used controlled vocabularies, and therefore was not possible to identify subsumption relations between values, we decide to maintain the support of the standard subsumption relation between terms and their stems. Moreover, we decide to only support the Π_f approximation, i.e. we chose to simplify the approach of the users with the system loosing the exploitation of the relation among different controlled vocabularies, e.g. the Dewey Decimal Classification (DDC), the Library of Congress Classification, etc.

The resulting search service is based on two relation operators[11], *literal* and *contain*, and two search functionalities, *simple* and *cross-schema*.

The *simple* search functionality supports query requests on homogeneous information sources. It allows to choose between two possible query interpretation models, *sure* and *possible*. This means that, for each query, users can now specify the personalized recall that they think is needed to satisfy their needs. For example, the user John Smith, who is confident that he is interested only in documents that are classified exactly with token "text processing", can specify the query as "subject *literal* text processing". The second user, Henry Stamp, who searches for documents about the same token but does not know how they have been classified, can ask for an interpretation of the query that also takes into account documents that are classified under the semantically specialized "subject" field, i.e. he can select the *sure* interpretation that will return also *doc2*. Finally, we can consider a third user, who want to retrieve documents about "digital libraries", clearly focusing his interest on recall, can specify the query as "subject *contain* digital libraries" and select the *possible* interpretation, implicitly asking for a $I_{\geq}^+$ query answering. In order to implement this functionality the Index service has been enhanced to support the *sure*, $I_{\sim}^-(c)$ and $I_{\geq}^-(c)$, and *possible*, $I_{\sim}^+(c)$ and $I_{\geq}^+(c)$, evaluation models described in Section 4. Preliminary tests demonstrate that we can best manage field qualifiers using the *sure evaluation model* if the query has been expressed on a field that supports qualifiers, and the *possible evaluation model* if the query has been expressed on a qualifier of a field.

The *cross-schema* search functionality supports query requests on heterogenous information sources. It allows to choose between three possible query interpretation models, *precise*, *lower*, and *upper*, that indicate the type of approximation the system apply to navigate heterogenous metadata schemas. This means that, for each search request,

---

[11] Using relation operators, the user specifies how the system must interpret the query tokens.

users can now specify how the system, using the relation among the different metadata schemas, must reformulate the user query. Clearly, the *lower* is more precision-oriented while the *upper* is more recall-oriented. In order to implement this functionality we enhance the QM service to ingest the mapping schema, which contains the definition of the non-trivial articulations between metadata schemas, and to support the *precise, lower,* and *upper* approximations as defined in Section 5. In particular, we verify the benefits in query processing where the QM applies *lower approximations* asking the Indexes to use the *sure evaluation models*, and where the the QM applies *upper approximations* and Indexes use *possible evaluation models.*

These restrictions on the set of possible combinations mean that a user of tLibrary can only ask for six possible interpretations of the query on heterogenous information sources and four possible interpretations of the query on information sources that use the same metadata schema. Nevertheless, from the user's point of view, the appropriate use of these personalized search evaluations makes it possible to improve recall without losing search precision.

We are now working to identify other combinations between approximations and query evaluation models that could help users to satisfy their needs without increasing too much the complexity of the interaction between users and system. We also plan to support the articulation between terminologies to offer a second generation search service over metadata schema and ontologies.

7   Conclusion

We present a new approach to query formulation and processing experimented in the OpenDLib. This approach exploits subsumption links among metadata fields of different metadata formats, and among the terms of controlled voacabularies.

Much work, especially in the area of information retrieval, has been done in order to better satisfy the search requirements of the user. Our technique is not intended as an alternative to the current well consolidated search processing techniques, but as a complementary one. Its implementation can be embedded in a conventional framework.

One objective was to come out with a low-cost solution. Our solution requires information source providers to specify only the mapping between their local document description metadata fields and the metadata fields of the QM service. Unlike other approaches does not require the generation of descriptive records in a shared format. Moreover, we expect that in a next future its cost can be further decreased with the advent of new techniques for ontologies (semi-)automatic mappings.

The complexity of our Index and QM services partly depends on the number of query processing options that are supported. Certainly, some of them are intuitively useful, while others have only a theoretic value. We have exploited only few of them.

The fuller exploitation of semantic information in query processing is not only useful to enhance the quality of the search service, but also to improve the quality of any other service that queries the DL. For example, it can be useful for a service that provides a virtual view of the DL collections or for a recommender service. One of our next steps will be certainly to study the impact that the proposed approach may have on the quality of these other DL services. We are firmly convinced that the exploitation of semantic information can have a very positive effect on these "user-centered" services.

References

1. Dublin Core Metadata Initiative. http://dublincore.org.
2. IEEE Standard for Learning Object Metadata. http://ltsc.ieee.org/wg12.
3. R. Baeza-Yates and B. Ribeiro-Neto. *Modern Information Retrieval*. Addison-Wesley, 1999.
4. J. P. Callan, F. Crestani, and M. Sanderson, editors. *Distributed Multimedia Information Retrieval*, volume 2924 of *Lecture Notes in Computer Science*. Springer, 2004.
5. L. Candela, D. Castelli, and P. Pagano. A Theory for a Semantic-based Search Service. Technical Report 2004-TR-18, Istituto di Scienza e Tecnologie dell'Informazione, CNR, 2004.
6. D. Castelli and P. Pagano. A flexible Repository Service: the OpenDLib solution. In *Proc. of the 6th International ICCC/IFIP Conference on Electronic Publishing*, pages 194–202, 2002.
7. D. Castelli and P. Pagano. OpenDLib: A Digital Library Service System. In *Proceedings of the 6th European Conference on Digital Libraries (ECDL2002)*. Springer-Verlag, 2002.
8. C.-C. K. Chang and H. García-Molina. Mind your vocabulary: Query mapping across heterogeneous information sources. pages 335–346, 1999.
9. S. Chawathe, H. Garcia-Molina, J. Hammer, K. Ireland, Y. Papakonstantinou, J. D. Ullman, and J. Widom. The TSIMMIS project: Integration of heterogeneous information sources. In 16th *Meeting of the Information Processing Society of Japan*, pages 7–18, Tokyo, Japan, 1994.
10. C. Lagoze and H. Van de Sompel. The open archives initiative: building a low-barrier interoperability framework. In *Proceedings of the first ACM/IEEE-CS Joint Conference on Digital Libraries*, pages 54–62. ACM Press, 2001.
11. E. Rahm and P. A. Bernstein. A survey of approaches to automatic schema matching. *VLDB Journal: Very Large Data Bases*, 10(4):334–350, 2001.
12. Y. Tzitzikas. *Collaborative Ontology-based Information Indexing and Retrieval*. PhD thesis, Department of Computer Science, University of Crete, September 2002.
13. Y. Tzitzikas, P. Constantopoulos, and N. Spyratos. Mediators over ontology-based information sources. In *WISE (1)*, pages 31–40, 2001.
14. G. Wiederhold. Mediators in the architecture of future information systems. *Computer*, 25(3):38–49, 1992.

Multi-level Exploration of Citation Graphs

François Boutin and Mountaz Hascoët

LIRMM – UMR 5506 – CNRS – University Montpellier II
34000 Montpellier, France
francois.boutin@univ-montpl.fr, mountaz@lirmm.fr

Abstract. In previous work, we proposed a focus-based multi-level clustering technique. It consists in computing a particular clustered graph from a given graph and a focus. The resulting clustered graph is called multi-level outline tree. It is a tree whose meta-nodes are sub-sets of nodes. A meta-node is itself hierarchically clustered depending on its connectivity. In this paper we introduce a cluster cohesiveness measure to enhance the results of the previously proposed algorithm. We further propose an optimization of this algorithm to support fluid interaction when focus changes. Finally, we report the results of a case study that consists in applying the enhanced algorithm to citation graphs where documents are considered as vertices and citation links as edges.

1 Introduction

In a digital library, scientific papers are linked together by citation relations. The resulting graph, called citation graph, is easy to explore but usually not so easy to organize. Indeed, when users can simply browse papers using citation links, they usually feel lost after a long navigation. Keeping a synthetic view of navigation is challenging. Users need efficient tools to explore and organize papers [7].

Various approaches have been proposed to organize documents. Supervised classification methods use training examples to sort out documents according to text similarities. Whereas unsupervised classification techniques (called clustering) try to discover natural clusters of documents without any prior knowledge. The aim is to provide an automatic organization of documents into cohesive groups (clusters) according to some measure of similarity.

In this paper, after rapidly reviewing related work, we recall the principles underlying our multi-level clustering method 34. Then we propose a new similarity measure that extends co-citation and bibliographic coupling. Indeed, we consider not only direct citations (in links or out links) but also "paths" of citations between nodes in a k-neighborhood. K-articulation nodes are defined as nodes at distance k that disconnect these paths. K-articulation nodes are used to introduce cluster cohesiveness. We further propose an optimization of our algorithm to support fluid interaction when focus changes. To end with, we apply our technique to a digital library of computer science literature: ResearchIndex [12]. We think that multi-level outline trees are well suited to organize citation graphs according to user focus.

R. Heery and L. Lyon (Eds.): ECDL 2004, LNCS 3232, pp. 366–377, 2004.

2 Related Work

Many clustering techniques can be used to cluster documents. We rapidly review existing work by presenting techniques with their main characteristics. Since most approaches are based on similarity measures, we begin with addressing this measures.

Text-Based or Link-Based Similarity Measures

The most popular content-based similarity measure is cosine similarity 9. It takes into account the angle between two documents represented as vectors in a term space (see Vector Space Model 1517). Unfortunately computing this measure for each possible pair of documents in a given set of documents can be time-consuming. So it is usually devoted to only small sets of documents. Considering that documents belong to a citation graph, we can also use similarity measures based on co-citation or bibliographic coupling 17. Co-citation between document p and p' is a similarity measure defined as the number of papers that co-cite p and p'. Bibliographic coupling is the number of papers that are both cited by p and p'. These measures are easy to compute with adjacency matrix 5. Some hybrid similarity measures exploit both content and link similarity 16. If the citation graph is viewed as an undirected graph we can define distance between documents as the length of the shortest path between them. Then, simple, average and complete linkages define distances between clusters.

Clustering Techniques

A partitioning method like K-means provides iteratively k clusters in linear time. However, clustering is highly dependent on k-value and initial position 15. A hierarchical clustering technique usually proceeds iteratively with merging or splitting the most fitting clusters according to similarities (using either cosine or linkage measure). It provides a tree called dendrogram in quadratic time 15. Hybrid methods exploit K-means efficiency and hierarchical clustering quality (see Chameleon in 15). Min-cut techniques propose to minimize inter-cluster connectivity (the number of links between clusters) and maximize intra-cluster connectivity 14. Fuzzy clustering is used when a document can belong to overlapping clusters. Self-Organizing Map (SOM) is a neural network based clustering technique 11.

Hierarchical Clustered Graph

A hierarchical clustered graph is defined by a graph G=(V,E) and a rooted tree T 8. Leaves of T are vertices of G. Each node of T is a set of nodes of G called cluster. T is an inclusion tree since it describes an inclusion relation between clusters 6.

Applying recursively a one-level clustering technique (K-means or Min cut) on each cluster provides a hierarchical clustered graph. In another hand, cutting a dendrogram for different levels of similarity also provides a hierarchical clustered graph.

Multi-level Outline Tree

We proposed in 3 a focus-based multi-level clustering technique that provides a particular hierarchical clustered graph, called *multi-level outline tree*. It is a new structure easily displayed without edge-crossing. The next section describe the main principle underlying this technique and illustrates it with an example.

3   Multilevel Outline Tree – Principles

We presented formally in 4 a focus-based clustering algorithm that transforms an undirected connected graph in a new structure called *outline tree*. It is a tree whose meta-nodes are sets of nodes. We extended our algorithm in 3 to provide a *multi-level outline tree*. It is an *outline tree* where each meta-node is itself hierarchically clustered. We recall the main definitions and illustrate the technique with an example:

$G = (V,E)$ is an undirected graph with a set of vertices (or nodes) $V=\{v_i, 1 \leq i \leq N\}$ and a set of edges $E=\{(v_i,v_j), 1 \leq i < j \leq N\}$. v_1 is a specific vertex called focus.

$d(v_i)$ is defined as the distance of the shortest path between v_1 and v_i.

L_m (m-layer) is the set of vertices at distance m from v_1: $L_m = \{v_i \in V, d(v_i) = m\}$.

G^k_m is defined by $G^k_m=\{v_i \in V, m \leq d(v_i) \leq m+k\} =\{v_i \in L_r, m \leq r \leq m+k\}$.

Nodes v_i and v_j on L_m are said k-relatives if there is a path between them in G^k_m.

L_m is partitioned into sets of k-relatives nodes called k-clusters and denoted $V^k_{m,j}$.

Two clusters on L_i are said k-relatives or k-linked if they contain k-relatives nodes.

We apply our method on graph G displayed in five layers from focus a (**Fig. 1**).

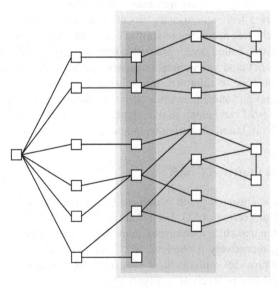

Fig. 1. Graph G from focus a

Clustering technique is presented on layer L_3. We proceed similarly with other layers:

0-clusters: Nodes h and i are 0-relatives since there is a path from h to i that belongs to G^0_3 (**Fig. 1**). So, they are grouped in a 0-cluster denoted by $V^0_{3,1}$ (**Fig. 2**). The other nodes (i, k, l, m) are called singleton 0-clusters.

1-clusters: Nodes j and k are 1-relatives since there is a path from j to k that belongs to G^1_3 (**Fig. 1**). They are grouped in a 1-cluster $V^1_{3,1}$ (**Fig. 2**).

2-clusters: Nodes j, k and l are 2-relatives since there is (at least) one path between them in G^2_3 (**Fig. 1**). So they are grouped in a 2-cluster $V^2_{3,1}$ (**Fig. 2**).

The algorithm described in 3 is computed in linear time and provides a particular clustered graph. We simplify the resulting view considering only links between meta-nodes. We get a tree of meta-nodes called *multi-level outline tree* where each meta-node is itself the root of an inclusion tree of clusters (Fig. 3).

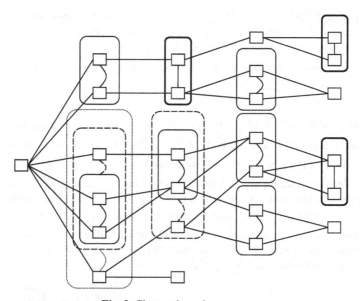

Fig. 2. Clustered graph

4   Cluster Cohesiveness

4.1   k-Articulation Node – Definition

Let consider clusters V_m and V'_m on L_m that are k-relatives and belong to k-cluster $V^k_{m,n}$. We define $S^k(V_m,V'_m)$ as a minimal set of nodes on L_{m+k} that connect V_m and V'_m. Nodes in $S^k(V_m,V'_m)$ are called *k-articulation nodes* between V_m and V'_m. They are also said *k-articulation nodes* of $V^k_{m,n}$. Indeed, removing them disconnect V_m and V'_m, and split up $V^k_{m,n}$. Note that $S^k(V_m, V'_m)$ labels k-relation between V_m and V'_m.

For instance, $V^2_{2,1}$ and g are 3-relatives and belong to $V^3_{2,1}$ (**Fig. 2**). $S^3(V^2_{2,1}, g) = \{x, z\}$. x and z are 3-articulation nodes of $V^3_{2,1}$. Their removal disconnect $V^2_{2,1}$ and g and so split up $V^3_{2,1}$. x and z label the 3-relation (curved arrow) between $V^2_{2,1}$ and g.

Now, since a k-articulation node is obviously a (k-1)-articulation node, we can easily define k-articulation nodes using (k-1)-articulation nodes.

For instance, z is a 1-articulation node that connect s and t. It is also a 2-articulation node that connect $V^1_{3,1}$ and l. Moreover, z is a 3-articulation node between $V^2_{2,1}$ and g.

4.2 k-Cluster Cohesiveness

We define cohesiveness of a k-cluster using the set of its k-articulation nodes. Indeed, removing these nodes split up the cluster. For instance (see **Fig. 2**, Fig. 3) cohesiveness of cluster $V^3_{2,1}$ depends on its 3-articulation nodes: x and z.

We propose to define k-articulation node density. It is an index computed by:

$$= \frac{\quad}{\quad}$$

where N is the size of $V^k_{m,n}$ and A is the number of k-articulation nodes (if k>0) or the number of links between nodes (if k=0). For instance, cohesiveness($V^3_{2,1}$) = 2/3, cohesiveness($V^2_{2,1}$) = 1/2 and cohesiveness($V^1_{2,2}$) = 1/1. Note that $V^1_{2,1}$ contains two possible 1-articulation nodes h and i. So the shortest path between b and c is longer than the shortest path between o and p. We consider that (h-i) is a double articulation node. Its weight is 0.5 and consequently cohesiveness($V^1_{2,1}$) = 0.5/1.

Many cluster validity indices may be applied 2. Cohesiveness index can be added as visual tips in *multi-level outline tree* layout: the more cohesive is a cluster the darker its background is (see Fig. 3).

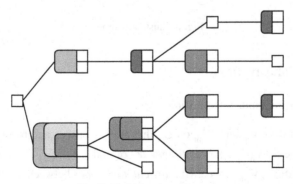

Fig. 3. Multi-level outline tree

5 Optimization Issues

5.1 Changing Focus – Invariant Sets

We get various multi-level outline trees depending on the focus we take. We propose an efficient method to recompute *multi-level outline tree* when user changes focus:
First of all, we recall two definitions:

> v is a *cut-vertex* if G is connected and the graph $G - \{v\}$ is disconnected.
> A *biconnected component* is a maximal subgraph with no cut-vertex. In fact, we need to remove at least two vertices to disconnect a biconnected component.

Removing cut-vertices split up a connected graph G in biconnected components denoted S_k (Fig. 4). Cut-vertices belong to two or more biconnected components.

Adjacency tree of biconnected components: Biconnected components of an undirected connected graph G belong to an adjacency tree T.

For instance, S_1, S_2, S_3, S_4, S_5, S_6 belong to an adjacency tree T (see Fig. 4).

Path of biconnected components: Considering foci v_i and v_j, we denote $\Pi(v_i, v_j)$ the shortest path of biconnected components in tree T that connect v_i and v_j.

For instance, considering foci a and p, $\Pi(a, p) = \{S_2, S_3\}$ (see Fig. 4).

Invariant sets: Multi-level outline trees $M(v_i)$ and $M(v_j)$ share *sub-outline trees* (invariant sets) corresponding to biconnected components that do not belong to $\Pi(v_i, v_j)$.

For instance $M(a)$ and $M(p)$ share invariant sets S_1, S_4, S_5, S_6 (see Fig. 5, Fig. 6).

Corollary: If v_i and v_j belong to a same biconnected component S_k then all biconnected component layout are the same in $M(v_i)$ and $M(v_j)$ excepted S_k layout.

5.2 Merging Multi-level Outline Tree of Biconnected Components

We propose an algorithm to improve multi-level outline tree computing:

> We first compute adjacency tree T that nodes are biconnected components S_i.
> Let v_1 be user-focus that belongs to biconnected component S_k. We compute multi-level outline tree of S_k based on v_1.
> For each biconnected component S_i (with i≠k), we consider the closest articulation node from v_1. We compute multi-level outline tree of S_i based on this node.
> Merging multi-level outline trees for all biconnected components provides a global multi-level outline tree of graph G.

For instance, considering user-focus p (see Fig. 6), we merge multi-level outline trees of biconnected components S_1, S_2, S_3, S_4, S_5, S_6 based on nodes a, i, p, h, n, g.

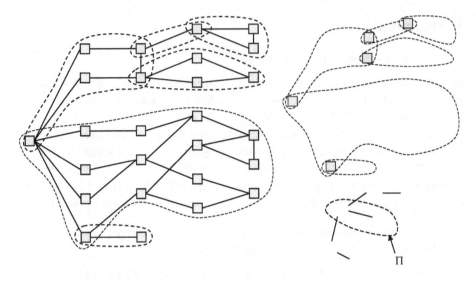

Fig. 4. Graph decomposition in biconnected components – tree T

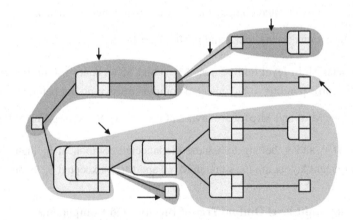

Fig. 5. Multi-level outline tree M(a)

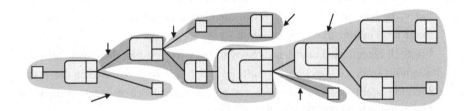

Fig. 6. Multi-level outline tree M(p)

5.3   Overview Versus Local View

When the number of documents increases it may be difficult to visualize information like title in the overview (see Fig. 8). In this case we can apply a tree layout algorithm 13 to expand or collapse a meta-node and its sub-tree. We can also use a filtering technique. For instance we display only clusters with high connectivity.

Fisheye techniques provide also focus + content views. We presented in a previous work our main visualization and interaction paradigms 10.

6   Citation Graph Exploration

We apply our multi-level clustering algorithm to organize and explore citation graphs collected on *ResearchIndex (Citeseer)*, a scientific literature digital library 12. We used a robot to explore *ResearchIndex* database based on links between documents. Note that *Citeseer* proposes different types of links: "related documents", "similar documents", "citations" or "co-citations". Our method is based on links between documents whatever their type. Note that we consider only undirected graphs.

A study of citation graph structure was presented in 1 based on three hundred thousand papers collected on *ResearchIndex*. Authors observed that 90% of the nodes form a giant connected component which in turn contains a biconnected nucleus with 58% of all nodes. They also found that the connectivity of citation graph is extremely resilient and is not due to the existence of hubs and authorities.

In the first citation graph described below, 29 nodes (48%) belong to non trivial biconnected components (see dark areas in Fig. 7). Note that we do not get a real biconnected nucleus since the graph is too small (only 61 nodes).

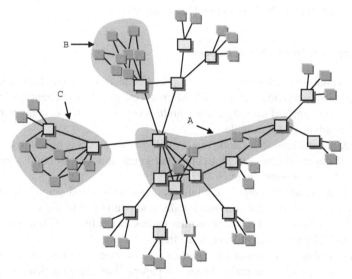

Fig. 7. Graph G – a spring view – invariant sets

6.1 Exploration from a Focus Paper

In this section, we propose an automatic organization of articles in the k-neighborhood of a focus paper which title is "*Navigation and Interaction in Graphical Bookmarks*". In practice we consider that k = 4. We explore iteratively most "related articles" at distance 1, 2, 3 and 4 from the focus. Then we build a citation graph with 61 papers.

In a classical spring layout (Fig. 7) we do not display titles not to overload the view. On the other hand, we easily display them in *multi-level outline tree* (Fig. 8).

Additional visual tips have been added to the *multi-level outline tree*: the more a node has connections, the darker its background is. Similarly, the stronger a k-cluster is connected the darker its background is (see cohesiveness – section 4).

6.2 Interaction

Interaction is used to display information dynamically. Node's relations become visible, when a user pointer comes over the node. At the same time, connected nodes are also highlighted and a tool-tip displays the entire title of the associated paper.

User can change focus by simply clicking on a node. The *multi-level outline tree* is then recomputed. We present (Fig. 9) different *multi-level outline trees* based on three different foci: 1, 9 and 25. Titles are not displayed in order to simplify the view.

We consider the three largest biconnected components denoted A, B and C (Fig. 7, Fig. 9). Foci 1 and 9 belong to the same biconnected set A. Consequently sets B, C and all sets excepted A are displayed identically in resulting multi-level outline trees. Now, foci 1 and 25 belong to biconnected components A and C. Moreover B do not belong to the path between A and C. So B is display in the same way in multi-level outline trees M(1) and M(25) based on foci 1 and 25.

6.3 Exploration from a Set of Papers

Exploring a citation graph from a set of papers (for instance, a search results set or a bibliography) may provide a graph with different connected components. So the algorithm can not be applied directly since a *multi-level outline tree* is computed from a connected graph and a focus node.

If we add an artificial focus node that we call query node, it is linked to every node in the set of papers. Thus, we get a connected graph and we can build a *multi-level outline tree* based on *query node*.

Let suppose we are looking for documents about "compound graph". We compute a *multi-level outline tree* based on *query node* "compound graph" for k = 3.

We collect recursively 3 levels of similar papers (according to *Citeseer*). We build a graph with 221 papers and links between them.

We present (Fig. 10) a *multi-level outline tree* overview without displaying titles. At level 2, we observe two main clusters of papers. The other singleton-clusters (at level 2) and resulting sub-outline trees may be removed to simplify the view.

7 Conclusion

Multi-level outline tree seems well suited to browse and organize citation graphs. Its double tree structure provides rich overviews of the graph that are easy to explore. User focus is either a specific document or a set of documents resulting from a query. In both cases, user focus is the root of an adjacency tree of meta-nodes that user can further explore. Each meta-node is itself the root of an inclusion tree of k-clusters. This makes multi-level outline trees very useful not only to explore citation graphs but also to organize search results or bibliographies from different perspectives.

In this paper, we introduced k-articulation nodes that participate to k-cluster cohesiveness. For that, we extended co-citation and bibliographic coupling, considering undirected citation paths between two nodes. We also used graph decomposition in biconnected components to optimize multi-level outline tree recomputing when changing focus.

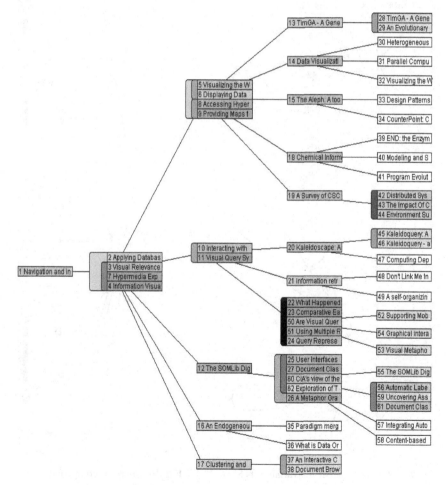

Fig. 8. Multi-level outline tree with titles

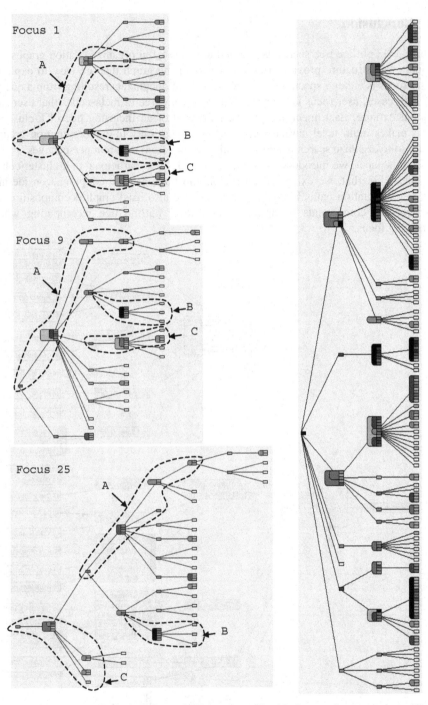

Fig. 9. Different foci – invariant sets Si   **Fig. 10.** Query = "compound graph"

References

1. An Y., Janssen J.C.M., Milios E.E., Characterizing the Citation Graph as a Self-Organizing Networked Information Space. IICS 2002: 97-107
2. Boutin F. and Hascoët M., Cluster Validity Indices for Graph Partitioning, Proceedings of the Conference on Information Visualization IV'2004
3. Boutin F. and Hascoët M., Focus Dependent Multi-level Graph Clustering. Proceedings of the Conference on Advanced Visual Interfaces, AVI 2004, ACM.
4. Boutin F. and Hascoët M., Focus-Based Clustering for Multi-Scale Visualization. Proceedings of the Conference on Information Visualization, IV'2003, IEEE, pp 53-59.
5. Brandes U. and Willhalm T., Visualization of bibliographic networks with a reshaped landscape metaphor, Proceedings of the symposium on Data Visualisation 2002, pp. 159-
6. Brockenauer R. and Cornelsen S., Drawing Clusters and Hierarchies. In Michael Vaufmann and Dorothea Wagner (Eds.): Drawing Graphs: Methods and Models, LNCS 2025, pp. 194 - 228. © Springer-Verlag, 2001.
7. Chen C., Visualizing Semantic Spaces and Author Co-Citation Networks in Digital Libraries. Information Processing & Management 35: 401-420, 1999.
8. Eades P., Multilevel Visualization of Clustered Graphs, Proceedings of Graph Drawing'96, Berkeley, California, September,1996.
9. Han E.-H, and Karypis G., Centroid-Based Document Classification: Analysis and Experimental Results, in Proc. of the 4th European Conference on Principles and Practice of Knowledge Discovery in Databases (PKDD), September 2000.
10. Hascoët M., Interaction and visualisation supporting web browsing patterns, Information Visualization, IV'2001, London, IEEE, p 413-419, 2001.
11. Kohonen, T., Self-Organizing Maps, New York : Springer-Verlag, 1997
12. Lawrence S., Bollacker K., and Giles C. L., *ResearchIndex*. NEC Research Institute, IST Information Sciences and Technology, http://citeseer.ist.psu.edu/
13. Plaisant C., Grosjean J., and Bederson B.B., SpaceTree: Supporting Exploration in Large Node Link Tree, Design Evolution and Empirical Evaluation INFOVIS 2002. IEEE Page(s): 57 -64, Boston, October 2002
14. Roxborough T. and Sen A., Graph clustering using multiway ratio cut, Proceedings of Graph Drawing Symposium, GD'97 Rome, September 1997. Lecture Notes in Computer Science, Berlin: Springer-Verlag, 1353, pp. 291-296, 1998.
15. Steinbach M., Karypis G. and Kumar V., A Comparison of Document Clustering Techniques, Proc. TextMining Workshop, KDD 2000.
16. Weiss R., Velez B., Sheldon M. A., Nemprempre C., Szilagyi P., Duda A., and Gi ord D. K., Hypursuit: A hierarchical network search engine that exploits content-link hypertext clustering. In Proc. of the 7th ACM Conf. on Hypertext, 1996
17. Yitong Wang and Masaru Kitsuregawa, Link based clustering of web search results, in 2nd International Conference on Advances in Web-Age Information Management (WAIM 2001). vol. 2118 of Lecture Notes in Computer Science, pp. 225-236, Springer.

Collaborative Querying
for Enhanced Information Retrieval

Lin Fu, Dion Hoe-Lian Goh, Schubert Shou-Boon Foo, and Yohan Supangat

Division of Information Studies
School of Communication and Information
Nanyang Technological University
Singapore 637718
{p148934363,ashlgoh,assfoo}@ntu.edu.sg
fyohans@pmail.ntu.edu.sg

Abstract. Communication and collaboration with other people is a major theme in the information seeking process. Collaborative querying addresses this issue by sharing other users' search experiences to help users formulate appropriate queries to a search engine. This paper describes a collaborative querying system that helps users with query formulation by finding previously submitted similar queries through mining web logs. The system operates by clustering and recommending related queries to users using a hybrid query similarity identification approach. The system employs a graph-based approach to visualize the query recommendations.

1 Introduction

Information seeking is a broad term encompassing the ways individuals articulate their information needs, seek, evaluate, select and use information. In the course of a search, the individual may interact with people, manual information systems (such as libraries) or with digital libraries. A major theme in the various information seeking models is that interaction and collaboration with other people is an important part in the process of information seeking and use (e.g. [13] [14]).

Given this idea, collaborative querying aims to assist users in formulating queries to meet their information needs by harnessing other users' expert knowledge or search experience [6] [17]. A common approach in collaborative querying is known as query clustering, which is to group similar queries automatically without using predetermined class descriptions. Such queries are typically stored in user logs, which are then extracted and clustered to obtain recommended queries to users. A query clustering algorithm could provide a list of suggestions by offering, in response to a query Q, the other members of the cluster containing Q. In this way, there is an opportunity for a user to take advantage of previous queries and use the appropriate ones to meet his/her information need.

Since similarity is fundamental to the definition of a cluster, measures of similarity between two queries are essential to the query clustering procedure. We propose a hybrid query similarity measure that exploits both the query terms and query results URLs. Experiments reveal that using the hybrid approach, more balanced query clusters can be generated than using other techniques. Further we describe a prototype

R. Heery and L. Lyon (Eds.): ECDL 2004, LNCS 3232, pp. 378–388, 2004.
© Springer-Verlag Berlin Heidelberg 2004

collaborative querying system which exploits the hybrid similarity measure to cluster queries and a graph visualization approach to represent the query clusters. The system gives users the opportunity to rephrase their queries by suggesting alternate queries.

The rest of this paper is organized as follows. In Section 2, we review the literature related to this work. We then present the design and implementation of the collaborative querying system. A scenario is given to highlight the usefulness of this system. Finally, we discuss the implications of our findings for collaborative querying systems and outline areas for further improvement.

2 Related Work

There are several useful strands of literature that bear some relevance to this work. This section reviews literature from these fields. Firstly, a survey of interactive query reformulation is provided as the background for this research. Next, a review of different query clustering approaches is presented.

2.1 Interactive Query Reformulation Systems

With the proliferation of online search engines, more attention has been paid to assist the user in formulating an accurate query to express his/her information needs. A number of approaches have been proposed. One approach is to use interactive query reformulation systems which aim to detect a user's "interests" through his/her submitted queries and give users opportunities to rephrase their queries by suggesting alternate queries. Several techniques have been used to incorporate aspects of interactive query reformulation systems into the information retrieval process.

One approach to obtain the recommended queries is to use terms extracted from the search result documents. Examples include HiB [5], Paraphrase [1] and Altavista Prisma [2], which parse the list of result documents and use the most frequently occurring terms as recommendations. Some popular commercial search engines, such as Altavista [3], Askjeeves [4], Eurekster [9], etc, incorporate term recommendation functions in the hope that it can help users reformulate an accurate query and then locate relevant content.

Another approach is collaborative querying. Related queries (the query clusters) may be calculated based on the similarities of the queries in the query logs [12] which provide a wealth of information about past search experiences. The system can then either recommend the similar queries to users [12] or use them as expansion term candidates to the original query to augment the quality of the search results [7]. Here, calculating the similarity between different queries and clustering them automatically are crucial steps. This will be discussed in the next section.

2.2 Query Clustering Approaches

Traditional information retrieval research suggests an approach to query clustering by comparing query term vectors (content-based approach). Various similarity functions are available including cosine-similarity, Jaccard-similarity, and Dice-similarity [16]. Using these functions have provided good results in document clustering due to the large number of terms contained in documents. However, the content-based method might not be appropriate for query clustering since most queries submitted to search engines are quite short [21]. A recent study on a billion-entry set of queries to Alta-Vista has shown that more than 85% queries contain less than three terms and the average length of queries is 2.35 [18]. Thus query terms can neither convey much information nor help to detect the semantics behind them since the same term might represent different semantic meanings, while on the other hand, different terms might refer to the same semantic meaning.

Raghavan and Sever [15] determine similarity between queries by calculating the overlap in documents returned by the queries. This is done by converting the query result documents into term frequency vectors. The similarity between two queries is then decided by comparing these vectors. Fitzpatrick and Dent [10] further developed this method by weighting the query results according to their position in the result list. They argue that the beginning of a result list is more likely to include a relevant document to the original query. Using the corresponding query results is useful in boosting the performance of query clustering in terms of precision and recall [10, 15]. However this method is time consuming to execute [15]. Glance [12] thus uses the overlap of result URLs as the similarity measure instead of the document content. Queries are posted to a reference search engine and the similarity between two queries is measured using the number of common URLs in the top 50 results list returned from the reference search engine.

3   A Collaborative Querying System

We have designed a collaborative querying system based on the query clusters generated using the hybrid query similarity measure. In our system, the query clusters can be explored using a graph visualization scheme.

3.1   System Architecture

Figure 1 sketches the architecture of the collaborative querying system. After capturing a new query, the system will search for matching documents, which is similar in function to traditional information retrieval systems. However, beyond the search results, the system will identify related queries and use them as recommended queries to users. The recommended queries are displayed together with the search results, similar to [1, 2, 5]. Users may further explore the recommended queries by visualizing the query clusters which contains the initial query and recommended queries. Our query graph visualizer is designed to be an independent agent and can be incorporated into different information retrieval systems. Put differently, our collaborative querying system can provide additional information that a user is originally unaware of so that the user can use it to formulate a better query to express his/her information needs.

It can be seen from the architecture that there are three essential processes to accomplish collaborative querying. The first is the query repository construction procedure which involves query cluster generation. The second process is the query recommendation phase that includes related query detection and query graph visualization. The third process the maintenance of the query repository.

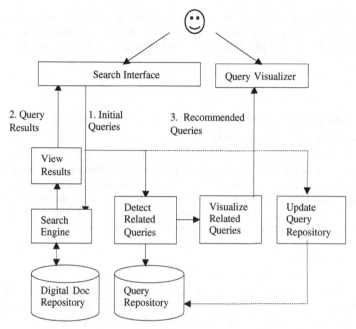

Fig. 1. Architecture of the collaborative querying system

3.2   Query Repository Construction

In this phase, we need to cluster related queries and save the query clusters into the query repository. As discussed, our approach to query clustering uses a hybrid method based on the analysis of query terms and query results. Here, two queries are similar when (1) they contain one or more terms in common (content-based approach); or (2) they have results that contain one or more items in common (result-based approach). The remainder of this section provides definitions of different query similarity measures used in our experiments. Our method of constructing query clusters based on different query similarity measures is also presented.

The content-based approach clusters queries by calculating the overlap of identical terms between queries. Taking the term weights into consideration, we can use any of the standard similarity measures [16]. Here we only present cosine similarity measure since it is most frequently used in information retrieval.

$$= \frac{= \qquad \times}{\sqrt{ =} \quad \sqrt{ =}} \tag{1}$$

where cw_{iQi} refers to the weight of ith common term between Q_i and Q_j in query Q_i and cw_{iQi} is calculated by TFIDF.

The results-based approach uses the overlap of result URLs as the similarity measure instead of the query content as shown in formula (2). The results returned by search engines usually contain a variety of information such as the title, abstract, topic, etc. This information can be used to compare the similarity between queries. In our work, taking the cost of processing query results into consideration, we consider the query results' unique identifiers (e.g. URLs) in determining the similarity between queries.

$$= \overline{\hspace{6cm}} \tag{2}$$

where the $|U(Q_i)|$ is the number of result URLs for Q_i, and $|R_{ij}|$ is the number of common result URLs between Q_i and Q_j.

For the content-based approach, a single query term can represent different information needs. For the result URLs-based approach, the same document in the search results listings might contain several topics, and thus queries with different semantic meanings might lead to the same search results. Thus, we hypothesize that using both query terms and the corresponding results may compensate for the drawbacks inherent in each method. Hence, the hybrid approach is expressed as:

$$= \tag{3}$$
$$\alpha \qquad\qquad\qquad + \beta$$

where α and β are parameters assigned to each similarity measure, with $\alpha+\beta=1$.

Two queries are in one cluster whenever their similarity is above a certain threshold. We construct a query cluster G for each query in the query set using the definition in (4).

$$= \qquad\qquad\qquad \geq \tag{4}$$

where $1 < j < n$; n is the total number of query.

Note that there are alternative clustering algorithms besides the one used in our experiments [8]. Compared with these approaches, our method is relatively less time consuming.

In order to test the usefulness of the hybrid query clustering approach, we collected 20000 queries from the digital library at Nanyang Technological University (Singapore). After preprocessing the original queries, including stop word removal, misspelled term checking, etc, there were 16000 queries for our experiments.

We generated different sets of query clusters based on different approaches. Computation for the similarity between two queries based on query content (sim_cosine) was straightforward using function (1). For sim_result, we posted each query to a reference search engine (Google) and retrieved the corresponding result URLs, similar to [11]. Since search engines rank highly relevant results higher, we only considered the top 10 result URLs returned to each query. The result URLs were then be used to compute the similarity between queries according to function (2). For the hybrid approach (sim_hybrid), the issue was to determine the values for the parameters α and β. We used pairs of α and β with the following values respectively: (0.25, 0.75), (0.5, 0.5) and (0.75, 0.25). Due to space constraints, we only report results for $\alpha=0.25$ and $\beta=0.75$ since this pair of values generates the best quality query clusters.

Recall that the threshold is the minimum value, obtained from a given similarity measure, that determines whether two queries should be clustered into to the same group. Here, thresholds were set to 0.25, 0.5, 0.7 and 0.9.

In our experiments, the quality of query clusters is measured using the F-measure [21]. The F-measure used here examines the overall quality of query clusters by combining precision and recall, with the value varying from 0 to 1. The larger the F-measure value, the better the quality of query cluster. Figure 2 shows the F-measure values of the three approaches.

Along with the change of threshold from 0.25 to 0.9, the F-measure value of sim_hybrid increases from 56% to 77%, sim_cosine increases from 49% to 52% and sim_result decreases from 21% to 20%. We see that sim_hybrid generates the best results comparing with sim_cosine and sim_result. This confirms our hypothesis that a combination of both query terms and result URLs provide a better quality of query clusters than using each separately. More experimental results can be found in [11]

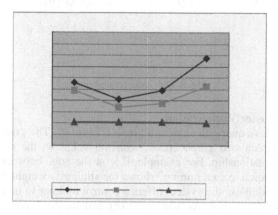

Fig. 2. F-measure for different approaches

3.3 Query Recommendation

This process involves identifying related queries in the query repository constructed in the previous step and visualizing the related queries.

3.3.1 Detecting Related Queries

Given a query submitted by a user, we first search the query repository for related queries. These queries are then recommended to the user. Here a recursive algorithm was implemented to search the query clusters in the query repository and the initial query will regarded as root node. First, the system will detect the query cluster $G(Qi)$ containing the initial query Qi. Given the definition of a query cluster (Section 3.2), all its members are directly related to Qi. Therefore $G(Qi)$ can be regarded as the first level in the graph structure of all queries related to Qi, as shown in Figure 3. Besides the query cluster $G(Qi)$, the system will further find query clusters containing the members of $G(Qi)$. For example since $Q1$ is a member in the cluster $G(Qi)$, therefore the system will compute the query cluster $G(Q1)$, which forms the second level as shown in Figure 3. This process is iterative and will stop at the user-specified maximum level to be searched. In our algorithm, the default maximum value is 5 which means the algorithm will only detect the top five levels of query clusters related to the root node. Thus the final related queries to Qi might go beyond the members within $G(Qi)$, giving a range of recommended queries directly or indirectly related to Qi.

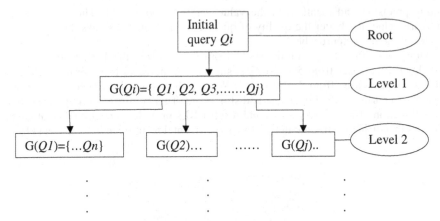

Fig. 3. Detecting related queries

3.3.2 Query Cluster Visualization

Our system displays query clusters in a graph (Figure 4). The graph edges show the relationship between two graph nodes, with the value on the edge indicating the strength of the relationship. For example, 0.1 on the edge between the nodes "data mining" and "predictive data mining" shows the similarity weight between these two nodes is 0.1. In addition, the system offers a control tool bar to manipulate the graph visualization area including zooming, rotating and locality zooming. The zooming function allows users to shrink or enlarge the graph visualization area. The rotating function allows users to view the visualization area from different directions. Finally, locality zooming refers to levels of the related queries to be displayed.

By right clicking on an individual node, a popup menu appears offering a variety of options. Firstly, users can use the selected query node and post it to a search engine (e.g. digital library at Nanyang Technological University). Recall that the query graph visualizer is running as an independent agent and can be incorporated into various search engines. Secondly, users may use this query to carry out another round of searches across the query repository and detect queries related to the selected one. Further, users can expand and collapse each query node on the graph. Note the number beside each node that denotes how many child nodes that have not been expanded yet.

The query graph visualizer was implemented using "Touchgraph" which is an open source component to visualize information in graph formats [20].

3.4 Updating Query Repository

When new queries arrive at the system, there is a need to update the query repository so that the system can harness and recommend the latest useful queries. This process can be done periodically offline. Figure 5 shows the steps of updating the query repository. Most of the steps are similar to the query repository construction process except the first one – capturing the new queries. This means the newly submitted queries will be captured and compared with existing queries and incorporated into the query database only if they are unique. For the rest of the steps, refer to Section 3.2.

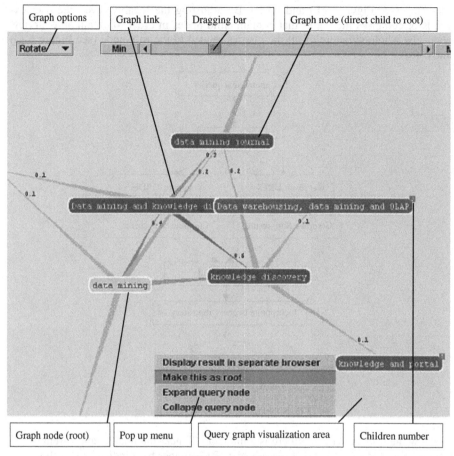

Fig. 4. Query graph visualizer

4 A Scenario of Use

The following scenario illustrates one of the potential users of the system and high-lights the operation of the system.

Suppose that a user is interested in the field of data mining and he is a novice in this area. When he uses the collaborative querying system, the user first submits a query "data mining" to search for information. A moment later, a list of queries related to "data mining" is displayed as the query recommendations in addition to the search results. After looking through the result list and the recommended queries, he wants to generate a query graph using "data mining" as the root node. Thus the user triggers the query cluster visualizer. A query graph will appear on the visualization area (see Figure 4 for an example). While browsing the graph, he is interested in the node "knowledge discovery". It is a new phrase to him but seems related to his search topic. Wanting to peruse the queries related to "knowledge discovery", he zooms in the visualization area by dragging the bar next to the option box from left to right (see Figure 6-(a) and 6-(b)). He may also rotate the visualization area to facilitate his browsing (see Figure 6-(b) and 6-(d)). By adjusting the locality level, the user expands or collapses the nodes that contain child nodes in order to obtain an overview about the whole structure of all the queries related to the root node (see Figure 6-(a) and 6-(c)).

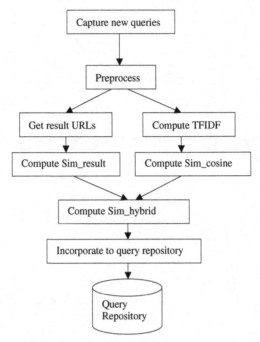

Fig. 5. Updating Query Repository

Now the user notices that there is a number "3" near the node "data warehousing, data mining and OLAP" (see Figure 6-(d)). The number here indicates that this node has two child nodes which have not been expanded. He right clicks on the node and chooses 'expand this node' on the popup menu. Note this action will only affect the selected node while the locality zooming option discussed previously take effect across the whole visualization area. After examining the graph carefully, the user is prepared to carry out another around of information retrieval by using the node "knowledge discovery". He thus right clicks on the node and chooses "display result in a separate browser". The query "knowledge discovery" will be posted to the search engine automatically and the results will be displayed in a separate browser. He may repeat this process until he finds the desired information.

5   Conclusions and Future Work

In this paper, we first compared different query similarity measures. Our experiments show that by using a hybrid content-based and results-based approach, considering both query terms and query result URLs, better query clusters can be generated than using either of them alone. We then introduced a collaborative querying system which utilizes the hybrid query similarity measure to generate query clusters for each query.

We described the design and implementation of a collaborative querying system based on the query clusters. Our work can contribute to research in collaborative querying systems that mine query logs to harness the domain knowledge and search experiences of other information seekers found in them. Firstly we propose a hybrid query clustering approach which differs from [10, 12, 15] since all them do not use the query content itself. Secondly, we employ a graph-based approach to visualize the recommended queries which differs from [1, 3, 4, 12] since all them only adopt text or HTML to display the recommended queries.

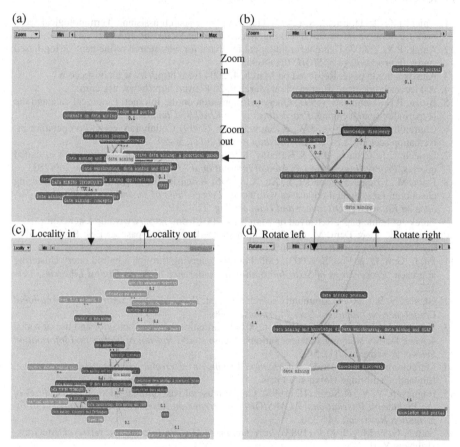

Fig. 6. Query cluster visualization

In addition to the initial experiments performed in this research, alternative approaches to identifying the similarity between queries will also be attempted. Adaptive elements will be introduced to reflect the growing and changing nature of the collection of documents to ensure the quality of query clusters when using the results-based approach. In addition, word relationships like hypernyms can be used to replace query terms before computing the similarity between queries. Finally, a user evaluation to test the usefulness and usability of the collaborative querying system will be conducted.

Acknowledgements

This project is partially supported by NTU with the research grant number: RCC2/2003/SCI. Further we would like to express our thanks to the NTU library and the Centre for Information Technology Services at NTU for providing access to the queries.

References

1. Anick, P.G. & Tipirneni, S. (1999) The paraphrase search assistant: Terminological feedback for iterative information seeking. *Proceedings of SIGIR 99*, 153-161.
2. Anick, P. G. (2003) Using terminological feedback for web search refinement: A log-based study. *In proceedings of SIGIR'03*, 88-95.
3. Altavista home page. Retrieved on March, 4, 2004 from http://www.altavista.com
4. Askjeeves home page. Retrieved on March 9, 2004 from http://www.ask.com
5. Bruza, P.D., Dennis, S. (1997) Query reformulation on the Internet: Empirical data and the Hyperindex search engine. *Proceedings of the RIAO 97 Conference*, 488-499.
6. Churchill, E.F., Sullivan, J.W. & Snowdon, D. (1999) Collaborative and co-operative information seeking, *CSCW'98 Workshop Report* 20(1), 56-59.
7. Crouch, C.J., Crouch, D.B. & Kareddy, K.R. (1990) The automatic generation of extended queries, *Proceedings of the 13th Annual International ACM SIGIR Conference*, 269-283.
8. Ester, M., Kriegel, H., Sander, J., Xu, X., (1996) A density-based algorithm for discovering clusters in large spatial databases with noise. *Proceedings of second International Conference on Knowledge Discovery and Data Mining*, 226-231.
9. Eurekster home pape. Retrieved on March 15, 2004 from http://www.eurekster.com
10. Fitzpatrick, L. & Dent, M. (1997). Automatic feedback using past queries: Social searching? *Proceedings of SIGIR'97*, 306-313.
11. Fu, L. Goh, D. & Foo, S. (2003). Collaborative querying through a hybrid query clustering approach. *Proceedings of Sixth International Conference of Asian Digital Libraries*, 111-122.
12. Glance, N. S. (2001). Community search assistant. *Proceedings of Sixth ACM International Conference on Intelligent User Interfaces*, 91-96.
13. Lokman, I. M., & Stephanie, W. H. (2001) Information–seeking behavior and use of social science faculty studying stateless nations: A case study. *Journal of library and Information Science Research*, 23(1), 5-25.
14. Marchionini, G. N. (1995). *Information seeking in electronic environments*. Cambridge, England: Cambridge University Press.
15. Raghavan, V. V., & Sever, H. (1995). On the reuse of past optimal queries. *Proceedings of the Eighteenth International ACM SIGIR Conference on Research and Development in Information Retrieval*, 344-350.
16. Salton, G. & Mcgill, M.J. (1983). *Introduction to Modern Information retrieval*. McGraw-Hill New York, NY.
17. Setten, M.V & Hadidiy, F.M. Collaborative Search and Retrieval: Finding Information Together. Available at: https://doc.telin.nl/dscgi/ds.py/Get/File-8269/GigaCE-Collaborative _Search_and_Retrieval__Finding_Information_Together.pdf
18. Silverstein, C., Henzinger, M., Marais, H., & Moricz, M. (1998) Analysis of a very large Altavista query log. *DEC SRC Technical Note 1998-14*.
19. Taylor, R. (1968). Question-negotiation and information seeking in libraries. *College and Research Libraries*, 29(3), 178-194.
20. Touchgraph website. Retrieved on January, 1, 2004 from http://toughgraph.sourceforge.net
21. Wen, J.R., Nie, J.Y., & Zhang, H.J. (2002) Query clustering using user logs. *ACM Transactions on Information Systems*, 20(1), 59-81.

Servicing the Federation:
The Case for Metadata Harvesting

Fabio Simeoni

Centre for Digital Library Research (CDLR)
Strathclyde University
Livingstone Tower, 26 Richmond Street
Glasgow G1 1XH, UK
fabio.simeoni@cis.strath.ac.uk

Abstract. The paper presents a comparative analysis of data harvesting and distributed computing as complementary models of service delivery within large-scale federated digital libraries.
Informed by requirements of flexibility and scalability of federated services, the analysis focuses on the identification and assessment of model *invariants*. In particular, it abstracts over application domains, services, and protocol implementations.
The analytical evidence produced shows that the harvesting model offers stronger guarantees of satisfying the identified requirements. In addition, it suggests a first characterisation of services based on their suitability to either model and thus indicates how they could be integrated in the context of a single federated digital library.

1 Introduction

As digital libraries grow to accommodate more resources and users, their architectures embrace distribution and, in the process, discover the observables of the *federation*: a widely dispersed and loosely coupled system of cooperating but otherwise mutually autonomous parties.

1.1 Federated Digital Libraries

Federated digital libraries, or *FDLs*, are the subject of increasing development efforts across the globe: from subject-based and sector-based international initiatives – such as the Open Language Archive Community initiative [1] – to grand, cross-sectoral, and nationally-scoped initiatives which account for a large part of the current development and research efforts within the field – including the JISC's Information Environment in the UK [2], the SURF's Digital Academic Repository in Netherlands (DARE) [3], the ARIIC's Information Infrastructure in Australia [4], the NSF's National Digital Library for Science Education (NSDL) [5,6] and the Networked Computer Science Technical Research Library (NCSTRL) [7] in the US, and the Deutsche Initiative für Netzwerkinformation (DINI) [9] in Germany.

R. Heery and L. Lyon (Eds.): ECDL 2004, LNCS 3232, pp. 389–399, 2004.

Admittedly, distribution is not a necessary implication of scope, and large-scale resource sharing may still rely on a centralised design. This is, for example, the approach adopted by the learning object community in UK for the in-progress development of the nation-wide JORUM repository [10]. Exceptions to the federated approach, however, are best interpreted as interim and exploratory solutions intended to mitigate the challenges of interoperability whilst fostering the formation of large communities of users. It is then anticipated that the cost of adequately serving such communities requires the organisational and technical support of a distributed infrastructure of local administrative domains.

In the absence of centralised content, the identity and raison d'etre of a FDL lie exclusively in its service provision layer. It is through their services that FDLs hope to improve over the ubiquitously deployed and extremely popular services of another, globally distributed, and yet largely unmanaged federation, namely the World Wide Web. The goal is clear: by reflecting the needs and leveraging the means of comparatively smaller and more cohesive communities, FDLs set out to challenge the scope and accuracy of existing Web services, primarily search engines. The strategy is also clear: to build federated services against structured descriptions of resources, that is *metadata*, rather than the resources themselves. The underlying assumption – to date unqualified and largely untested – is that a structured approach will fare better than content-based or link-based analysis. Given the predominant implementation strategy, it is indeed suggestive to think of FDLs as 'mini-webs', more focused, homogeneous, and thus potentially functional subsets of the HTTP-based Web on top which they are conceptually and technically layered.

Service provision is also where FDLs meet most directly the challenges of interoperability. A federated service faces the heterogeneity of tools, policies, means, and largely purpose which derives from the foundational assumption of autonomy across participating parties. From a technical perspective, it must be able to accommodate significant variations in metadata syntax, semantics and exchange protocols. From an organisational perspective, it must also account for often dramatic variations in resource allocation, technical know-how, and local and community-wide agendas. Further, a federated service is expected to meet the qualitative requirements which its users normally associate with the provision of Web services, and to do so as the parties, resources, and users in the FDL scale up towards largely unknown bounds.

1.2   Distributed Computing and Data Harvesting

Informed by the core requirements of *flexibility* and *scalability*, this paper looks into technical models for the provision of federated services. To limit an otherwise prohibitive scope, it ignores issues related to metadata quality and metadata semantics and focuses instead on models of service delivery in the presence of distribution.

In its most generic form, the problem of service delivery is one of computing over widely distributed data and, as such, it admits either one of two complementary solutions. In *distributed computing*, the computation (i.e. the service) is distributed along with the remote data (i.e. the resource metadata), while in *data harvesting* the data is first gathered and then computed over locally.

Until recently, the distributed computing model has received most of the theoretical and practical attention, both within and outside the field. Its use for resource discovery, in particular, has been standardised and widely tested within the library community through, respectively, specifications and implementations of the Z39.50 protocol [11]. More modern, lightweight, and web-oriented interpretations of the model – most noticeably the SDLIP [14], SRW/SRU [13], and SQI [15] protocols – are also becoming increasingly popular.

At least in principle, the harvesting model is also familiar within the field. In diverse, domain-specific, and often implicit guises, it can be recognised as the approach underlying many physical union catalogues and all web-based search engines. First proposed and indeed named in the context of scalable architectures for Web-wide search services [21], harvesting can now count on an application-independent specification which has become the standard de-facto for a rapidly increasing number of implementations, namely the OAI-PMH protocol of the Open Archive Initiatives [16].

While both models are well represented in the field, early experimental evidence (e.g. [19],[20]) suggests that the harvesting model offers stronger guarantees to meet the service requirements of flexibility and scalability. The FDL initiatives mentioned in Section 1.1 vary substantially in terms of scope, architectural detail, and ultimately design philosophy; nonetheless, they have all chosen harvesting as the preferred model for the delivery of their services. One, the NC-STRL initiative, has recently undergone a phase of redeployment to replace its mechanisms for distributed computing with mechanisms for data harvesting [8].

1.3 Motivations and Outline

In the light of such extensive support, it is perhaps surprising that a high-level, comprehensive, and principled case for metadata harvesting within FDLs has not yet found, to the best of the author's knowledge, a dedicated place in the literature. Granted, terse references to the 'simplicity' and sometimes 'efficiency' of metadata harvesting are nearly ubiquitous in publications related to the OAI-PMH protocol (e.g. [17],[18]). Similarly, complementary problems of 'complexity', 'poor performance', and 'limited interoperability' of Z39.50 have been repeatedly flagged some time before the advent of harvesting, most noticeably in relation to virtual and physical union catalogues (e.g. [22],[23]). Finally, some design considerations on the applicability of the two models, again predating the OAI specifications, may be discovered in service-specific consultancy reports (e.g. [24]).

Partly, the goal of this paper is to collect, expand, contextualise, and instantiate the arguments that have been produced so far. Even when the sparse analytical evidence is collated, however, it is unclear whether the identified properties are accidents of specific protocol implementations and services, or whether they can be considered as *invariants* of the models underlying those protocols. Subsequently, it remains difficult to characterise the application domains and services which suit one model rather than the other and thus support decision makers in their choice of service delivery protocols.

In an attempt to fill this gap, the paper presents a comparative analysis of the two models which is independent of the application domains in which they are used, the services which adopt them, and the protocols which implement them. In particular, the paper seeks answers to questions like 'if the OAI-PMH is to be preferred over Z39.50 for a given federated service, is it also more indicated than SRW/SRU for the same service?' and 'what services are better accommodated by the OAI-PMH and which ones suit instead a Z39.50-based or a SRW/SRU-based approach?', and again 'how can the two models coexist in the context of a single FDL?'.

Presented in Section 2, the analysis is carried out in five steps. Section 2.1 contextualises the general requirement of flexibility to the case of service delivery and shows how it can be approximated by the simplicity of delivery models. Section 2.2 discusses the degrees of complexity of the two models under examinations, Section 2.3 illustrates the manifestations of such complexity within an FDL, and Section 2.4 outlines the potential for scalability associated with the models. Section 2.5 considers their limitations in terms of functionality and how these limitations may inform a characterisation of services in relation to their suitability to either model. Finally, Section 3 draws some conclusions and relates service delivery models to other aspects of interoperability.

2   Analysis

One way of capturing the complementary nature of data harvesting and distributed computing is by noticing that while the former localises service provision within the FDL, the latter spreads it across all the federated parties. This Section shows how this simple observation bears profound consequences in terms of both flexibility and scalability of federated services.

2.1   Flexibility as Simplicity

In any deployment scenario, the technical and organisational costs associated with the complexity of a given solution – whether a metadata model, a service delivery model, or a service delivery protocol – must be carefully measured against the gain in functionality that justify them and the heterogeneity of the community that must absorb them [28]. The price of misjudgements is a partitioning of the community intended for that solution.

In principle, any given degree of complexity identifies a sub-community of the initially intended one, potentially excluding: (i) members who cannot sustain the solution or do not want to in response to functionality deemed unnecessary (*the solution is too complex*), or (ii) members who desired and could have sustained a higher degree of functionality (*the solution is too simple*). If the *community of adoption* does not have or assume significance with respect to the one initially targeted, the solution fails and tends to be progressively abandoned. At best, the solution is re-purposed within a narrower scope, and the problem for which it was originally conceived remains an open one. This is, for example, the case of the Dublin Core metadata model, which was originally intended for resource description over the unmanaged Web and it is now re-purposed within more disciplined FDLs.

Undoubtedly, the diversity of organisational structures remains a primary observable within FDLs and thus the simplicity of solutions intended for FDLs is to be treasured above the functionality they can offer. When it comes to service delivery, in particular, the simplicity of a model translates into a measure of its flexibility. Simply put, a flexible model for the delivery of federated service should present a 'low barrier' to the interoperability of federated parties.

2.2 The Causes of Complexity

Notice now that distributed computing requires that *each* federated party participate of the implementation, deployment, and maintenance of *all* the federated services its metadata contributes to. In contrast, harvesting requires only that federated parties be able to disclose the metadata they hold, a task which is in general much simpler than service provision and, most importantly, one which offer more *resilience* across different federated services.

Consider, for example, a federated service for resource discovery. In a distributed computing interpretation of the service, federated parties must be able, at the very least, to parse, translate, and execute all the queries submitted to the service by its users. In addition, the service requires that the parties return query results in a format the service is willing to accept, and thus that parties be potentially engaged in data transformation tasks. Depending on the service functionality, the service may also require that parties perform additional functions, such as management of the result set (e.g. filtering, ordering, browsing, providing statistics, etc).

Different are the demands parties must satisfy with a harvesting interpretation of the same service. Besides the potential data transformation tasks which are necessary in any data exchange scenario, federated parties are required at most to recognise and execute a small and fixed number of simple queries to scope the disclosure of their metadata. In particular, they are *not* expected to parse and interpret the expression of a full-fledged and potentially complex query language.

The simplicity of disclosure over full service provision should not be considered in the limited context of single service, as it is normally done. Rather, it should be viewed in the common assumption that federated parties will contribute to more than one service within the FDL, where different services may offer: (i) different functions (e.g. resource discovery, citation linking, metadata enhancement, current awareness, etc.), or (ii) specialise similar functions to the needs of different sub-communities within a single FDL (e.g. cross-community resource discovery versus learning object or eprints discovery), or (iii) simply compete on the basis of additional added value services (e.g. user interfaces, service customisation, etc).

In a 'multi-service' scenario, the additional complexity of the distributed computing approach leaves more room for variations across services and thus place higher costs on the 'mobility' of federated parties across different services. When moving across different resource discovery services, for example, a federated party may need to process different query languages and perform different result management functions as well as carry out different data transformation tasks. In contrast, only the costs associated with the latter may be faced by a federated party which simply discloses its metadata. For example, a party that discloses simple Dublin Core metadata for resource discovery will face no additional costs when 'moving' to another DC-based discovery service and in fact to any other service which relies on the same metadata format. Even when the party does have to translate its own metadata into other formats than DC (e.g. IEEE LOM), the availability of a FDL-wide syntactic interoperability solution – normally one based on the XML standard – implies that the costs are incremental rather than *ex novo*.

2.3   The Costs of Complexity

Once the complexity of the distributed model has been ascertained, one may consider the effects of that complexity within the FDL. Obviously, complexity raises implementation costs and thus tends to limit the number of available implementations to those produced by resourceful parties and commercial vendors. Even when free implementations are made available, the tight coupling between the functions of any delivery model and the metadata back-end of individual parties makes off-the-shelf reuse an elusive goal and does not eliminate the need of installation, customisation, and maintenance tasks.

Another way in which complexity undermines interoperability is by increasing the possibility of incomplete or erroneous specifications whilst reducing their understandability. In particular, complex protocol specifications are prone to unstable releases, problems of backward compatibility, and mutually inconsistent implementations.

Most importantly, complexity amplifies almost invariably problems of *semantic interoperability* within the model [25]. Full service provision, in particular, multiplies the requirements of semantic alignment between federated parties and thus is more prone to breaking interoperability through inconsistent implementations of the model. For example, the lack of interoperability between z39.50 targets caused by differences in mappings of search attributes onto local database indexes, extraction and normalisation algorithms for search keys, and stopwords handling is well documented in the literature (e.g.[22]).

To avoid the problem, services may make a degenerate, almost 'syntactic' use of the model [12], which is suitable only for high-level meta-services not oriented to the end-user (e.g. server implementation browsing). Alternatively, they may restrict their scope to all the federated parties which comply with some community-specific instantiation of the model. Instantiations may concern the query language, the format of the metadata, or the support for optional functionality, and may be approached in a number of ways, including profiling [29] and MOP-based expansion and refinement [14]. Normal practice is then to mandate support for a minimal instantiation to support the implementation of federated services against the greatest common denominator of the implementations deployed at the federated parties (e.g. [26],[33],[27]).

Clearly, the harvesting model is not immune to the interference of semantics with service deliver and thus does not obviate the need for a 'spectrum of interoperability' solutions within the FDL [6]. By limiting such interference to a profiling of metadata formats , however, harvesting simplifies the organisational aspects of the profiling process whilst maximising the scope of the community which adopts the profile within the FDL.

2.4 Scalability

Section 2.2 and Section 2.3 have shown that an approach to interoperability based on the harvesting model promises to contain service deployment costs within FDLs. The model, however, is also beneficial for service implementation, for it delivers all the good properties which are normally associated with local computations.

With harvesting, in particular, the diverse capabilities of federated parties and the observables of the network may be factored out real-time interactions with the end-users and be faced instead off-line, possibly through flexibly configurable processes [16]. Latency-inducing factors associated with slow, congested, or simply unavailable connections have virtually no impact on the *reliability* and *responsiveness* with which a service interfaces its users.

In contrast, a service distributed across the FDL is intimately dependent on the federated parties and the underlying network, and thus tends to be constrained by the performance of the 'weakest' party and the fluctuations of the available bandwidth. The fact that parties and network are in principle required to sustain the full service load (e.g. all the user queries submitted to a discovery service) cannot but worsen the situation. Experimental evidence indicates that the performance of basic implementations of distributed discovery services tend to rapidly decrease as the number of participating parties grows beyond 10-15 [30].

Admittedly, manual or automated clustering techniques [31], proxy-based solutions [14], and replication strategies [7] may help to more equally distribute the service load across the FDL. However, the pragmatic and intellectual costs of scaling these approaches against the number and capabilities of participating parties are largely unclear but promise to raise significantly the overall costs of the FDL infrastructure. Significantly, advanced implementations of distributed services have been so far confined to the prototypal domain.

If reliability is largely related to distribution, performance may be also influenced by network-independent requirements. With distributed computing, the costs of pre-processing the metadata received from participating parties before presenting it to the users must also be accommodated in real-time. The resulting penalties discourage or severely limit the possibilities of metadata translation, de-duplication, versioning, and enhancement which are so important in the diverse environment of the FDL. It is hard, for example, to imagine distributed services with consolidation capabilities which go beyond straightforward identifier-based de-duplication [22]. Again, the harvesting model allows to hide these inherently difficult and computationally intensive processes away from the users and, by doing so, paves the way for a family of middleware services which remain instead elusive in the distributed computing scenario.

Of course, the harvesting model raises its own scalability issues. A federated service based on harvesting operates on a centralised copy of the remotely distributed metadata and thus may rapidly become large in response to the number and growth of participating collections. However, the costs associated with local scalability are relatively lower when compared with those raised by network-based solutions. Equally important, the technical processes required for local scalability are well understood and require opportunistic intervention on variables which are entirely under the control of service implementors (e.g. memory, disks, processors, local networks) [22].

Clearly, more experience is needed to identify the limits of the harvesting approach beyond the positive results of early experimental services [19]. However, it may be argued that no realistic degree of scalability can be predicated on soaring costs. In this sense, the very existence of comprehensive and long-established physical union catalogues (e.g. [24], [32]) and Web search engines suggests that, whatever may be the precise limits of harvesting, these may be approached at relatively contained costs.

2.5   Functionality

In the light of the principles presented in Section 2.1 and the advantages attributed to harvesting over distributed computing in Section 2.2 and Section 2.3, it is interesting to observe that neither model enables more functionality than the other within the FDL.

At first, this statement may appear controversial for – by exposing the functionality of specific services – even the most streamlined server-side implementations of the distributed computing model (e.g SRW/SRU) are more expressive than any server-side implementation of the harvesting model. Indeed, the advantages associated with the simplicity of harvesting are ultimately predicated on this argument. However, from a broader, service-oriented perspective – and thus from a client-side perspective – the situation is quite different.

In a strict computational sense, the harvesting model enables more expressive federated services than are possible under the distributed computing model. The reasons for this are largely those discussed in Section 2.4, and relate to the limited possibilities of metadata pre-processing which are allowed under the distributed computing model. Not only does this apply to processes which are theoretically possible but pragmatically unfeasible under that model (e.g. format translation). It also applies to processes – such as advanced consolidation and standard ranking algorithms [22]– which require the totality of the remotely distributed metadata and cannot rely solely on the responses of participating parties to individual service transactions (e.g. queries). Put another way, not all computations can be distributed across the disjoint union of participating metadata collections.

The harvesting model, on the other hand, relies on a mono-directional information flow from data providers to service providers and is thus bound to the
subclass of service architectures which can be gracefully accommodated within
this assumption. Whenever the intended functionality requires information to
flow in the opposite direction or in both directions – and thus relies on a different distribution of roles between communicating parties – harvesting looses
much of its appeal.

One case which defeats the harvesting approach is when data exhibits an
extremely dynamic nature. As an example in the classic library domain, consider
the needs of union catalogues which whish to offer circulation data along with
bibliographic data. Here, harvesting is not an effective solution for the harvesting
rates required by the dynamicity of circulation data would prove so intensive to
essentially reintroduce the network as a real-time observable of service provision.

Similarly, harvesting has little to offer for the implementation of a local interface to a remote service (e.g. a local Z39.50 interface to an existing discovery
service), even if the latter had facilities in place to offer its data for third-party
harvesting. Here, the local interface is best viewed as an extension of the remote
service and no clear distinction between data and service provision can be made.
In particular, local harvesting of the remote data would simply reintroduce deployment costs which have been already absorbed within the FDL. In contrast, a
two-party dialog is an ideal and indeed prototypical application scenario for the
distributed computing model [12] and one in which the problems of inter-party
interoperability discussed in Section 2.2 simply do not arise.

There are services, accordingly, which are – in any practical sense – outside the scope of the harvesting model and yet may play an important role
within the FDL. It should be noted, however, that such services rely on strong
agreements between communicating parties which can only be expected within
tightly-coupled subsets of the FDL. Put another way, these services operate
within the FDL but do not belong to the category of truly federated services.

3   Conclusions

Data harvesting and distributed computing may both serve as models of service
delivery in the context of large-scale federated digital libraries.

Harvesting clearly separates the concerns and responsibilities of data providers from those of service providers, while distributed computing views data
provision and service provision as inherently overlapping processes. In particular, harvesting induces a 2-phase view of service delivery which distinguishes
the aspects related to communication – which involve both service and data
providers – from those that relate to service-specific implementation – which instead concern only service providers. In contrast, distributed computing collapses
communication and service-specific implementation within a single protocol of
interaction.

That communication between service and data providers may take place in
conceptual isolation from service-specific implementation is beneficial to data

providers, for it shifts the costs of their participation where they are expected to be affordable, at the service providers. Vice versa, service implementation benefits from abstracting over communication, for it can deliver all the good properties normally associated with local and off-line computations.

For these reasons, the harvesting model offers stronger guarantees to meet requirements of flexibility and scalability of federated services. In contrast, the distributed computing model offers complementary support for services that operate within more cohesive subsets of the federated library.

To conclude, it is worth noticing that the harvesting model offers little help with semantic issues of metadata interoperability: successfully exchanged metadata must still be uniformly understood. In particular, the model alone cannot guarantee a uniform implementation of federated services against metadata modelled according to different models, formats, profiles, and standards. The model abstracts over the complexity of the metadata which may be harvested within sub-communities of the federated library and thus reflects a bipartite conceptual model which helps to more clearly separate, and thus tackle, different pieces of the interoperability jigsaw.

References

1. Simmons, G., Bird, S.: The Open Language Archives Community: An Infrastructure for Distributed Archiving of Language Resources. *Literary and Linguistic Computing*, 18(2) 117–128 (2003)
2. Joint Information Systems Committee (JISC): Investing in the Future: Developing an Online Information Environment. http://www.jisc.ac.uk/ie (2004)
3. Stichting SURF: DARE: Specifications for a Networked Repository for Dutch University. http://www.surf.nl/download/ReportSpecs3.0.pdf (2003)
4. Australian Government, Department of Education, Science, and Training: Information Infrastructure – Outcomes of http://www.dest.gov.au/highered/research/outcomes2003.htm (2003)
5. Lagoze, C., Hoehn, W., Arms, W., Allan, J. et al.: Core Services in the Architecture of the National Digital Library for Science Education (NDSL). Cornell University, Ithaca, arXiv Report, cs.DL/0201025, http://arxiv.org/abs/cs.DL/0201025 (2002)
6. Arms, W., Hillmann, D., Lagoze, C. et al.: A Spectrum of Interoperability: The Site for Science Prototype for the NDSL. *D-Lib Magazine*, 8(2) (2002)
7. Davis, J.R., Lagoze,C.: NCSTRL: Design and Deployment of a Globally Distributed Digital Library. *Journal of the American Society for Information Science (JASIS)* 51(3) 273–280 (2000)
8. Anan, H., Liu, X., Maly, K. et al.: Preservation and Transition of NCSTRL Using an OAI-Based Architecture. *Proceedings of the second ACM/IEEE-CS joint conference on Digital libraries* 181–182 (2002)
9. Deutsche Initiative für Netzwerkinformation (DINI). http://www.dini.de. (2003)
10. The JISC Learning Materials Repository Service: JORUM Scoping and Technical Appraisal Study. http://www.jorum.ac.uk (2003)
11. Z39.50 Maintenance Agency: Information Retrieval (Z39.50): Application Service Definition and Protocol Specification. http://www.niso.org/standards/resources/Z39-50-2003.pdf (2003)

12. Lynch, C.: The Z39.50 Information Retrieval Standard: Part I: A Strategic View of Its Past, Present, and Future. *D-Lib Magazine* (1997)
13. Z39.50 International: Next Generation: SRW - Search/Retrieval Web Service. http://www.loc.gov/z3950/agency/zing/srw/spec-index.html (2003)
14. Paepcke, A., Brandriff, R., Janee, G. et al.: Search Middleware and the Simple Digital Library Interoperability Protocol. *D-Lib Magazine*, 6(3) (2000)
15. CEN/ISSS: The Simple Query Interface (SQI) specification. http://nm.wu-wien. ac.at/e-learning/inter/sqi/sqi.pdf (2003)
16. The Open Archives Initiative: The Open Archives Initiative Protocol for Metadata Harvesting (2.0). http://www.openarchives.org/OAI/openarchivesprotocol.html (2003)
17. Lagoze, C., Van de Sompel, H.: The Open Archives Initiative: Building a low-barrier interoperability framework. *Proceedings of the First ACM/IEEE-CS Joint Conference on Digital Libraries (JCDL'01)* (2001)
18. Lynch, C.: Metadata Harvesting and the Open Archives Initiative. *Bi-monthly Report of the Association of Research Libraries (ARL 217* (2001)
19. Van de Sompel, H., Krichel, T., Nelson, M.J.: The UPS Prototype: An Experimental End-User Service across E-Print Archives *D-Lib Magazine*, 6(2) (2000)
20. Halbert, M., Kaczmarek, J., Hagedorn, K.: Finding from the Mellon Metadata Harvesting Initiative.*Proceedings of the 7th European Conference on Digital Libraries (ECDL)*, (2003)
21. Bowman, C.M., Danzig, P.B., Hardy, D.R. et al.: Harvest: A Scalable, Customizable, Discovery and Access System). Technical Report TR CU-CS-732-94, Department of Computer Science, University of Colorado-Boulder (1994)
22. Lynch, C.: Building the Infrastructure of Resource Sharing: Union Catalogues, Distributed Search, and Cross-Database Linkage. *Library Trends*, 45(3) 448-461 (1997)
23. Husby, O.: Real and Virtual Union Catalogue. *6th International Seminar of the Check and Slovak Library Information Network (CASLIN)*, http://www.caslin. cz:7777/caslin99/a2.htm (1999)
24. Crossnet Systems Ltd.: SCURL Feasability Study To Investigate Potential Applications Strategic Implications of Z39.50 Technology on the COPAC Service. http://www.curl.ac.uk/projects/z3950.pdf (1998)
25. Paepcke, A. et al.: Interoperability for Digital Libraries Worldwide. *Communications of the ACM*, 41(4) 33-42 (1998)
26. Z39.50 International: Next Generation: CQL - Common Query Language (1.1). http://www.loc.gov/z3950/agency/zing/cql/, (2004)
27. Nilsson, M., Sibersky, W.: RDF Query Exchange Language (QEL) - Concepts, Semantics, and RDF Syntax. (2003)
28. Arms, W.: Digital Libraries. *Digital Libraries and Electronic Publishing*. Cambridge, Ma.:MIT Press (2000)
29. Z39.50 Maintenance Agency: Z39.50 Profiles. http://www.loc.gov/z3950/agency/profiles/profiles.html (2004)
30. Davenby, J.: Aiming at quality and coverage combined: blending physical and virtual union catalogues. *Online Information Review*, 26(5) 326-334 (2002)
31. Nicholson, D.: Clumping towards a UK National Catalogue? *Ariadne*, 22 (1999)
32. Online Computer Library Centre (OCLC), http://www.oclc.org/ (2004)
33. Reddy, S., Lowry, D., Reddy, S. et al.: DAV Searching and Locating, Internet Draft. *IETF* (1999)

Developing a Technical Registry of OAI Data Providers

Thomas G. Habing, Timothy W. Cole, and William H. Mischo

University of Illinois at Urbana-Champaign
Grainger Engineering Library Information Center
1301 W. Springfield Ave., Urbana, Illinois 61801, USA
{thabing,t-cole3,w-mischo}@uiuc.edu

Abstract. With the continued growth of the Open Archives Initiative Protocol for Metadata Harvesting (OAI-PMH) [1] it has become increasingly difficult for OAI service providers to discover new and keep up-to-date with existing data providers. There are currently several registries of OAI data providers. Most of these registries are incomplete. Most contain minimal information about registered providers – typically a base URL and little if anything else – providing service providers no clue as to repository scope, content, or size. These deficiencies mean significant extra overhead for service providers. This paper describes a more comprehensive registry of OAI data providers (available at http://oai.grainger.uiuc.edu/registry), developed to address some of these issues. While our registry as it presently exists facilitates discovery of data providers, utility is limited by lack of consistent practice for collection-level metadata. To realize the full potential of a better registry, the OAI community needs to develop better practices for collection-level description.

1 Why Another OAI Registry?

We developed our own OAI metadata provider registry to better support a range of OAI-based projects at the University of Illinois Libraries. These projects have included the Mellon funded UIUC Digital Gateway to Cultural Heritage Materials[1], the Grainger Engineering Library's OAI Search Portal for Engineering, Computer Science, and Physics[2], the IMLS Digital Collections and Content project[3], the NSDL Second Generation Digital Mathematic Resources project[4], and most recently the CIC-OAI Metadata Harvesting Service project[5]. Especially for those projects which are building focused OAI-based services, it has became clear that a significant amount of effort is required to discover relevant data providers and/or relevant sets within a single data provider. This has usually involved manually browsing data providers whose base URLs are listed in one of several existing registries such as that maintained at the Open Archives Initiative web site[6] or at the OAI Repository Explorer

---

[1] http://oai.grainger.uiuc.edu/

[2] http://g118.grainger.uiuc.edu/engroai/

[3] http://imlsdcc.grainger.uiuc.edu/

[4] http://nsdl.grainger.uiuc.edu/

[5] http://cicharvest.grainger.uiuc.edu/

[6] http://www.openarchives.org/Register/BrowseSites.pl

R. Heery and L. Lyon (Eds.): ECDL 2004, LNCS 3232, pp. 400–410, 2004.
© Springer-Verlag Berlin Heidelberg 2004

web site at Virginia Tech.[7] As we employed other discovery methods such as 'Googling,' it became clear that the existing registries were not complete, even taken together. For various reasons there seemed to be a large number of OAI data providers that were not registered with any of the existing lists.

At the same time, various other OAI researchers were reporting similar problems discovering and characterizing OAI repositories. At the JCDL 2003 conference, Kat Hagedorn, manager of the OAIster project[8], suggested an OAI service that "classifies and tracks repositories." [2] In the conclusions of her report for The Digital Library Federation, Martha Brogan also comments on the lack of any comprehensive registry of data or service providers. [3] To address the issue, the Open Archives Forum (OA-Forum)[9] project developed a very useful registry of OAI resources, including data providers. However, because their registry was purposefully focused on European repositories and required self-registration its coverage was not as comprehensive as would have been desired. In addition, it lacked some of the functionality that we felt would be useful for a technical registry designed to support service providers in a more automated fashion.

Also, once our registry began to take shape and after the feedback we received following its announcement[10] in the OAI-implementers mailing list we realized that there was potential for many features beyond just discovery that a technical registry could address. This functionality will be described in the next section of this paper.

2 Features and Functionality

This section describes the key features and functions of the technical registry.

2.1 Comprehensive

First, we wanted the registry to be as complete as possible. This meant that we could not be limited to only the repositories listed in existing registries; we could not rely on self-registration, and we wanted the registry maintenance to be as automated as possible. Towards this end we developed several techniques for discovering and processing OAI data providers.

First, we identified all existing registries or lists of OAI data providers that were available. These included the Open Archives Initiative lists (including their list of rejected sites)[11], the list maintained by the Virginia Tech Repository Explorer, and several others[12]. These lists were presented in different formats from XML, to flat ASCII text files, to HTML pages. We developed automated means for processing all of these various lists.

Second, we utilized various optional features of the OAI protocol itself. These include the friends description container, [4] which can be part of the OAI Identify

---

[7] http://jingluo.dlib.vt.edu/~oai/cgi-bin/Explorer/2.0-1.45/testoai

[8] http://www.oaister.org/o/oaister/

[9] http://www.oaforum.org/index.php

[10] http://www.openarchives.org/pipermail/oai-implementers/2003-October/001017.html

[11] http://www.openarchives.org/OAI/RejectedSites

[12] See the http://oai.grainger.uiuc.edu/registry/#repoLists for a complete list

response. The friends container lists other OAI data providers that may be confederates of the current data provider. We also utilized the provenance about container, [5] which can be part of an OAI record. The provenance container describes the origin OAI data provider for records that have been aggregated by another OAI data provider. Our processing scripts will automatically identify repositories from these sources and recursively process any newly identified data providers.

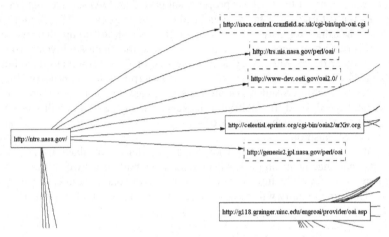

Fig. 1. This is a fragment of a graphic showing the relationships between various repositories which have been established either via the friends or provenance containers. The complete graphic is available from http://gita.grainger.uiuc.edu/registry/FriendsGraph.png.

Third, using the Google SOAP APIs, [6] we developed scripts to periodically search the Google web indexes to discover new OAI data providers. We are able to use various search strategies, from looking for web pages containing OAI related terms and then testing each URL contained in those web pages to determine whether the URL can respond to an OAI Identify request, to using advanced Google queries such as 'allinurl:verb=Identify' which only lists pages whose URLs contain the string 'verb=Identify.' Running these scripts approximately every month has identified numerous new data providers. All of the above techniques are executed on a periodic (currently irregular) basis to keep the registry as current as possible.

Finally, new repositories can be easily added one-at-time as they are identified manually. Numerous repositories have been added at the request of their administrators, and monitoring various mailing lists and web pages that focus on the Open Archives Initiative has identified other providers.

2.2 Searchable and Discoverable

The ability for service providers to discover relevant OAI data providers was another primary goal. However, we wanted to achieve this goal with as little manual cataloging of data providers as possible. To accomplish this we developed processes to automatically harvest and index various data from each data provider.

First for each repository we collect all responses from the Identify, ListSets, and ListMetadataFormats requests. These data are parsed and placed into a relational database (described later). In addition, the complete XML responses are indexed for full-text searching.

Second, for each combination of setSpec and metadataPrefix a minimal record harvest is performed to collect one or more sample records and, if possible, a record count. These data are also parsed into the relational database, and the sample XML records indexed for full-text search.

A key observation resulting from our search system is that repositories that include rich collection level metadata either in the optional Identify description containers or the optional ListSets setDescription containers will fare better in terms of discoverability. This suggests the desirability of broader use of collection-level metadata by the OAI community (discussed further below).

Once these data were all indexed, several methods of search and discovery were enabled. First, the full-text of all the OAI protocol responses, including the sample records, can be searched. Second, repositories can be browsed according to various different parameters, such as all repositories which support a specific metadata schema, all repositories which support a specific setSpec, all repositories originating from a particular top-level internet domain (such as a country domain), all repositories which support persistent deleted records, all repositories which are friends of a given repository, and so forth[13].

In addition to searching and browsing, the registry also provides a detailed HTML view of each individual repository. This view includes, in a human readable format inspired by Jeff Young's work at OCLC with XSLT and OAI, [7] all of the collected responses from the data provider. Plus, the detailed view includes various other summarizations of the repository, such as the number of records that occur in each combination of setSpec and metadataPrefix and a link to a sample record for each combination. The view also lists other repositories that are related to this repository via the friends or provenance containers. The registry also tracks different protocol versions of the same repository and provides links between the newer and older versions.

2.3 Amenable to Machine Processing

In addition to making the registry accessible to human users, we wanted to expose its data in ways that were useful for machine processing.

The most obvious way to do this was to make the registry harvestable using the OAI-PMH itself[14]. The details of the implementation, especially the mapping of registry records to Dublin Core (DC) and the choice of OAI and DC Identifiers, was in large part driven by conversations with Jeff Young who needed an OAI registry data provider for his ERRoL system. [8] Essentially, the registry data provider exposes simple DC records (title and identifier) about each registered OAI data provider from one of two sets: ID or URL. The primary difference between these two sets is how the OAI Identifier for the registry record is derived. For the ID set, the OAI Identifier scheme of the repository, if any, is used to derive the OAI Identifier used for the registry record, for example: oai:id-registry.uiuc.edu:lcoa1.loc.gov. The OAI Identifier for the repository is either derived from the optional oai-identifier description container, [9] or it can be explicitly set by request in the registry. For the URL set, the

---

[13] See the http://oai.grainger.uiuc.edu/registry/ for a complete list
[14] http://oai.grainger.uiuc.edu/registry/px/oai.asp

repository baseURL is used to derive the OAI Identifier used for the registry record, for example: oai:url-registry.uiuc.edu:http://memory.loc.gov/cgi-bin/oai2_0.

The base URLs of all the repositories in the registry are also exposed using the standard friends description container, [4] or optionally in the same XML format as used by the Open Archives Initiative ListFriends.pl script[15]. Users also have the option of exporting any repository list that was generated from a search or browse operation in one of these two standard XML formats, either the friends description container or the ListFriends.pl format.

An RDF Site Summary (RSS) [10] feed of the most recently added or modified registry records is also available[16]. This feed can be used by various RSS news readers to automatically keep service providers notified when a repository is added or modified in the registry.

The most recent addition to the registry is an SRU (Search and Retrieve URL)[17] Service. [11] SRW/SRU builds on the Z39.50 protocol along with various web protocols, such as SOAP, HTTP, and XML, to define a service for searching databases across the web. Implementing this service for the OAI registry allows standard SRU clients to perform basic searches against the registry, returning the results as XML records. The service currently supports a subset of the CQL (Common Query Language),[18] allowing either the repository name, repository base URL, repository identifier, or the full text of various OAI responses to be searched. Records are returned using either Dublin Core or ZeeRex (The Explainable "Explain" Service)[19].

Finally, we are exploring methods for service providers to export a list of repositories that they would like to harvest, including information on the sets and metadata formats to harvest from each repository. We are currently calling this feature the Harvest Bag (analogous to the "book bag" feature of many online digital library services). It would allow a user to accumulate a list of base URLs, sets, and metadata formats that they would like to harvest. Once the list is complete they could export it in a new standard XML format which is being developed for the project. The ultimate goal being that they could then import the XML file into their OAI harvest software so as to initiate or schedule harvests against the selected repositories.

3   Implementation Details

The registry was built on a Windows 2000 Server platform. The web server is Internet Information Server (IIS) using Active Server Pages (ASP). The database is Microsoft SQL Server. The registry maintenance programs were written in VBScript using a harvesting API that was developed for previous OAI projects at the UIUC Library. This API was implemented as an ActiveX dynamic link library (OAIHarvester.dll), which is freely available[20] from the SourceForge[21] open source repository.

---

[15] http://www.openarchives.org/Register/ListFriends.pl

[16] http://oai.grainger.uiuc.edu/registry/rss.asp

[17] http://oai.grainger.uiuc.edu/registry/sru/sru.asp

[18] http://www.loc.gov/z3950/agency/zing/cql/

[19] http://explain.z3950.org/

[20] http://sourceforge.net/project/showfiles.php?group_id=47963&package_id=46165

[21] http://sourceforge.net/

3.1 Registry Maintenance Programs

There are two primary programs used for maintaining the registry. The first program is called RegistryPop. The main input for this program is either the base URL to a single repository to be added to the registry or the base URL of a list of repositories all of which are to be added. RegistryPop supports various different formats for these lists. As previously described, RegistryPop performs a minimal harvest of each repository, parsing the various XML responses, and inserting appropriate values into a relational database. RegistryPop is also responsible for recursively harvesting any other data providers that are identified from the friends or provenance containers. The script can also accept a number of optional parameters used for controlling its behavior, such as userid and password for harvesting password protected repositories, flags to indicate whether it should only add new repositories or whether it should only refresh the metadata of previously harvested repositories, or a flag to indicate whether it should ignore invalid repositories.

The second major program is called gOAIglePop. This program uses the Google SOAP API [6] to programmatically query the Google system to find potential OAI data providers. The main input for this program is one or more query phrases that are submitted to the Google search engine. Typical queries would be phrases that would be indicative of an OAI related web site, such as 'OAI', 'OAI-PMH', or 'Open Archives Initiative'. The most successful search has been to look for the string 'verb = Identify' directly in the URL using the Google 'allinurl': special query term. The results of the Google queries are then parsed, and each URL is tested to determine whether it can respond to an OAI Identify request. URLs that lead to an OAI data provider are added to the output list. This output list can then be used as the input for the RegistryPop program.

In addition to the two main programs, there are a number of smaller programs and scripts, some implemented as SQL stored procedures, to perform various other maintenance tasks such as to identify only new repositories given a list of base URLs, extract namespace URIs or xml:lang attributes from XML files, or to add a list of repositories to a virtual collection. All of these scripts are intended to be run from the command line and can be scheduled to run in an automated fashion using the system task scheduler. Most of the programs and scripts also output an activity log using a uniform XML format.

3.2 Registry Database

Data about repositories is stored in a relational database, Figure 2. This database consists of the primary Repositories table along with several tables that are related to this table via primary-foreign key relations. The Repositories table contains data about the OAI data providers, such when they were last harvested, links to previous versions of the same provider, HTTP headers returned by the provider web server, and the full-text of the Identify response.

The MetadataFormats and Sets tables contain the parsed responses to the List-MetadataFormats and ListSets requests to a repository. The Sets table will also contain the full-text of any optional setDescription containers.

The RecordCounts table contains the results of a minimal harvest of the repository. Using every combination of set and metadataPrefix a small harvest is performed, and

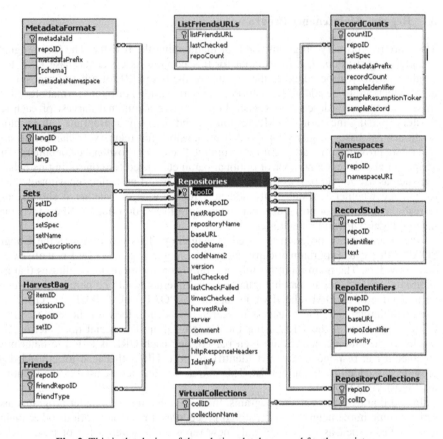

Fig. 2. This is the design of the relation database used for the registry.

the results stored in this table, including a count of records, a sample OAI identifier, a sample resumptionToken, and the full-text of a sample record. We are calling this a minimal harvest because only the first resumptionToken's worth of data is retrieved for processing. This means that a record count is only obtained if the repository supports the optional completeListSize attribute on the resumptionToken element or if there is only one resumptionToken's worth of data for the given request.

The Friends table identifies all the repositories that are related to a given repository. The type of the relation is either via the friends container [4] or the provenance container. [5]

There are a number of other tables that contain derived data to support specific queries. The Namespaces table contains a list of every namespace URI that is used by a given repository. The XMLLangs table lists all the xml:lang attribute values that are associated with a given repository. The RepoIdentifiers table lists possible OAI Identifiers that are being used by the repository, either pulled from the optional oai-identifier container [9] or by parsing sample OAI item identifiers.

The HarvestBag table allows a user to develop a custom list of OAI repositories that she would like to harvest, including which sets. This list can then be exported as an XML file.

The VirtualCollections and RepositoryCollections tables provide a means for creating virtual collections of related repositories. Currently, the only data that are maintained are the names of the virtual collections, such as 'DSpace Collections' or 'Eprints.org Collections'. These data are currently maintained manually, and are mostly a convenience for harvesters who would like to identify all the repositories that fall into a certain category. However, these tables will allow us to attach more diverse collection level metadata to OAI repositories or collections of repositories in the future.

As already mentioned, various OAI protocol responses are indexed for full-text search. These include the Identify response, the ListSets response, and the sample records for every combination of set and metadataPrefix. The full-text search is implemented using the full-text capabilities of Microsoft SQL Server. [12] The search algorithm currently used is that all words or phrases (strings enclosed in quotes) must be found in the records full-text index to generate a hit. Right-hand truncation of search terms is also enabled by default. We may implement more advanced search capabilities in the future – for example, limiting a search to a particular index, such as sample records or setDescriptions.

3.3 Registry Web Interface

The web interface used for the registry is implemented as an Active Server Page (ASP) written in VBScript running on the Microsoft IIS web server. This includes the pages intended for use by humans, plus the Registry OAI data provider and RSS feeds intended for machine consumption. The top-level page and all of the various reports are implemented as separate ASP scripts (currently 51 separate scripts). However, there are multiple common functions which are implemented in common include files. Extensive use is made of XSLT for transforming the OAI XML responses into HTML for display. Cascading Style Sheets (CSS) are also used extensively for customizing the display output.

4 Future Plans and Collection-Level Description

4.1 Registry Enhancements

While the registry is now fully operational, there remain a number of improvements we would like to make to increase its usefulness. Most of these are derived from our own internal use of the registry and the desire to decrease the manual workload associated with its maintenance. Other enhancements have been derived from conversations with the registry's users, such as Kat Hagedorn at Michigan who is using the registry to discover new repositories for her OAIster service or Jeff Young at OCLC who is using the registry for his ERRoL service. [8] Following, in no order, are some plans for future enhancements to the registry:

- We would like to provide more automated maintenance of the registry, including the ability of OAI data providers to securely add or modify their repository's records in the registry, including collection-level descriptive data.

- We would also like to improve the automated discovery of new repositories, such as automatically running the gOAIglePop script.
- We would like the ability to delegate the creation and maintenance of virtual collections of repositories, including collection-level metadata.
- We would like to improve the view of search results, especially the context of the search hit. The current system does not identify the context of a search hit, which could be the Identify or ListSets responses or the sample records.
- We would like to improve the ability of service providers to generate custom lists of repositories that can be added to their HarvestBag, exported, and then used to create harvesting schedules.

We are eager to make this registry a valuable resource to the OAI community, and we are very open to new ideas, suggestions, or collaborations. If you are interested please contact the authors.

4.2   Collection-Level Description in OAI

Our registry is intended especially to facilitate discovery and exploitation of OAI-compliant metadata providers. In this regard the utility of the registry is dependent in large part on the quality and extent of information about repositories and sets made available by providers. Beyond the largely technical enhancements described above, the usefulness of the registry could be further enhanced through the inclusion of richer collection-level description of provider repositories and sets. Current practice varies, but in general implementers provide at most sparse descriptive information about the topic and scope of content described by their OAI metadata sets. Early on, when the number of metadata providers was small, machine-accessible collection-level description was not emphasized and arguably not needed. More recently however, with over 400 OAI metadata providers up and active, with many more in development, with larger providers becoming more common and making available increasingly diverse content, there is evidence of a renewed interest in collection-level description within the OAI community..

The need for collection-level description was considered by the OAI Technical Committee in developing the 2.0 version of the protocol. This led to the addition in the 2.0 version of the protocol of the optional setDescription container within the ListSets response. [1] The use of setDescription (and also the already existing description element within the Identify response) for collection-level description is explicitly encouraged in section 4.2 of the Implementation Guidelines for Repository Implementers. [13] The interest in collection-level description within the OAI community corresponds to a period of significant progress and interest in collection-level description within the digital library community as a whole. The initial work described here on a more sophisticated OAI metadata provider registry service suggests an opportunity for the OAI community to exploit emerging collection-level description best practices, both to facilitate the discovery and use of data providers and to provide context for item-level metadata records delivered.

Much of the current work in collection-level description has roots in Michael Heaney's "An Analytical Model of Collections and Their Catalogues"[22]. This model

---

[22] http://www.ukoln.ac.uk/metadata/rslp/model/amcc-v31.pdf

was used as a foundation for the RSLP collection description schema[23], indirectly for work now being done by the DC Collection Description Working Group[24], and by other projects, such as our own project to create a registry for collections developed by or associated with National Leadership Grant projects funded by the U.S. Institute of Museum and Library Services[25]. In the Heaney model, and in associated schemas derived in large part from this model, core collection description is distinguished from description of related entities and agents, such as the 'collector' who assembled the collection, the 'owner' who holds rights over collection content, the 'location' of the collection, and the 'administrator' of the collection who administers it in its location.

A few of these collection-related entities, for instance the repository administrator, are already explicitly mentioned within the OAI protocol. Not specifically defined in OAI, however, are the core collection-level descriptive attributes identified in Heaney's model, and in other emerging models of digital content description. While there remain important issues with these models, and several of the formal XML schemas for expressing collection-level descriptive properties are still under development, there does seem to be an emerging consensus within the broader community about the identity and meaning of the most important, core collection-level description properties and attributes. This work is of a maturity suitable for broader use and experimentation.

In our opinion it is time for the OAI community to develop initial consensus as to best practices for collection-level description in the context of OAI. This implies also a reconsideration of best practices for how OAI sets are implemented. Note, better collection-level descriptive practices and better use of OAI sets can be implemented effectively without changes to the base OAI protocols. Sufficient flexibility and capacity was included in the protocols by design. Arguably the future work that will lead to the greatest improvements in the utility of ours or any other OAI metadata provider registry will be work that addresses the need for richer collection-level descriptive information about OAI repositories and sets.

References

1. Lagoze, Carl, Van de Sompel, Herbert, Nelson, Michael, and Warner, Simeon: The Open Archives Initiative Protocol for Metadata Harvesting - Version 2.0. (2002)
   http://www.openarchives.org/OAI/openarchivesprotocol.html
2. Warner, Simeon and Nelson, Michael: Report on the Metadata Harvesting Workshop at JCDL 2003. SIGIR Forum, 37 (2), (Fall 2003)
   http://www.acm.org/sigir/forum/2003F/jcdl03_warner.pdf
3. Brogan, Martha L.: A Survey of Digital Library Aggregation Services. The Digital Library Federation Council on Library and Information Resources, Washington, DC (2003)
   http://www.diglib.org/pubs/brogan/brogan2003.htm
4. Lagoze, Carl, Van de Sompel, Herbert, Nelson, Michael, and Warner, Simeon: Implementation Guidelines for the Open Archives Initiative Protocol for Metadata Harvesting - XML Schema for repositories to list confederate repositories. (2002)
   http://www.openarchives.org/OAI/2.0/guidelines-friends.htm

---

[23] http://www.ukoln.ac.uk/metadata/rslp/schema/

[24] http://dublincore.org/groups/collections/

[25] http://imlsdcc.grainger.uiuc.edu/CDschema_overview.htm

5. Lagoze, Carl, Van de Sompel, Herbert, Nelson, Michael, and Warner, Simeon: Implementation Guidelines for the Open Archives Initiative Protocol for Metadata Harvesting - XML schema to hold provenance information in the "about" part of a record. (2002) http://www.openarchives.org/OAI/2.0/guidelines-provenance.htm
6. Google Web APIs. Google (2003) http://www.google.com/apis/index.html
7. Van de Sompel, Herbert, Young, Jeffery, A., and Hickey, Thomas, B.: Using the OAI-PMH ... Differently. D-Lib Magazine, 9, (7/8), (July/August 2003) http://www.dlib.org/dlib/july03/young/07young.html
8. Young, Jeffery, A.: Extensible Repository Resource Locators (ERRoLs) for OAI Identifiers. OCLC Online Computer Library Center (2004) http://www.oclc.org/research/projects/oairesolver/default.htm
9. Lagoze, Carl, Van de Sompel, Herbert, Nelson, Michael, and Warner, Simeon: Implementation Guidelines for the Open Archives Initiative Protocol for Metadata Harvesting - Specification and XML Schema for the OAI Identifier Format. (2002) http://www.openarchives.org/OAI/2.0/guidelines-oai-identifier.htm
10. RSS-DEV Working Group: RDF Site Summary (RSS) 1.0. http://web.resource.org/rss/1.0/spec
11. Denenberg, Ray (ed.): SRW/SRU Version 1.1. The Library of Congress, Washington, DC (2004) http://www.loc.gov/z3950/agency/zing/srw/
12. Cencini, Andrew B.: Building Search Applications for the Web Using Microsoft SQL Server 2000 Full-Text Search. Microsoft Corporation. (2002) http://msdn.microsoft.com/library/default.asp?url=/library/en-us/dnsql2k/html/sql_fulltextsearch.asp
13. Lagoze, Carl, Van de Sompel, Herbert, Nelson, Michael, and Warner, Simeon: Implementation Guidelines for the Open Archives Initiative Protocol for Metadata Harvesting – Guidelines for Repository Implementers. (2002) http://www.openarchives.org/OAI/2.0/guidelines-repository.htm

Applying SOAP to OAI-PMH

Sergio Congia, Michael Gaylord, Bhavik Merchant, and Hussein Suleman

Department of Computer Science, University of Cape Town
Private Bag, Rondebosch, 7701, South Africa
{scongia,mgaylord,bmerchan,hussein}@cs.uct.ac.za

Abstract. The Web Services paradigm for distributed computing promises to provide a breakthrough in interoperability by defining standardised mechanisms for inter-process communication. The SOAP standard, in particular, is widely discussed but not as widely adopted by standards bodies. The OAI is one such organisation that has been criticised for not adopting SOAP. Since the OAI-PMH is driven by semantics and SOAP describes syntax, a merger of the two technologies seems natural and inevitable. This paper discusses an attempt to remodel and repackage the OAI-PMH as a layer over SOAP and implement an end-to-end solution based on this experimental protocol. The project highlighted important concerns, such as the relative efficiency of layering in structured textual data and the problem of moving standards. The results show that few compromises are needed for a move to SOAP provided that protocol design is appropriately abstracted, and this has far reaching implications for the adoption of SOAP and Web Services within the DL community and OAI in particular.

1 Preamble

It must be noted at the very outset that the OAI protocol (OAI-PMH v2.0 [12]) is a fixed standard that is implemented in a consistent manner in a growing community of users. This work was simply an experiment, in consultation with members of the OAI, rather than an attempt to suggest a new alternative standard. Based on the results of this experimental work, it is hoped that the OAI and other organisations will more seriously consider an informed adoption of Web Services standards as an underlying layer for future interoperability efforts.

2 Background

2.1 OAI-PMH

The Open Archives Initiative (OAI) was formed to drive the process of developing low-barrier solutions to the problem of interoperability among digital library systems [11]. The primary product of experimentation and standards development was the Protocol for Metadata Harvesting (PMH) [12], a high level application layer network protocol that defines how to synchronise a source of

R. Heery and L. Lyon (Eds.): ECDL 2004, LNCS 3232, pp. 411–420, 2004.

metadata with a remote copy, or user of the data. From the early stages of development in 1999, it was agreed that the protocol would adopt current standards such as XML Schema [4] and Dublin Core so that it would additionally serve as an implicit testbed and reinforcement for those standardisation activities. The OAI-PMH has since established itself as an important standard for information exchange among a large and varied group of digital archives [3].

Technically, OAI-PMH is a client-server protocol layered over HTTP, with requests specified using URL-encoded parameters and responses delivered in strictly validifiable XML. Specifically, there are 6 request/response pairs: Identify, ListMetadataFormats and ListSets return administrative information about the archive; ListIdentifiers, GetRecord and ListRecords facilitate the transfer of metadata from a source archive on demand. Some of these requests have optional and/or mandatory parameters to restrict the list of results to a subset of the full set, for example, the response for ListIdentifiers can be restricted by specifying a particular set of the archive to list identifiers for, as opposed to the full contents of the archive.

A typical request and response is shown in Fig 1.

Request

```
http://abc.org/OAI?verb=Identify
```

Response

```
<OAI-PMH>
    <responseDate>2004-02-02T12:00:00Z</responseDate>
    <request verb="Identify"/>http://abc.org/OAI</request>
    <Identify>
        <repositoryName>Somewhere</repositoryName>
        <baseURL>http://abc.org/OAI</baseURL>
        <protocolVersion>2.0</protocolVersion>
        <earliestDatestamp>2001-01-01T01:00:00Z</earliestDatestamp>
        <deletedRecord>no</deletedRecord>
        <granularity>YYYY-MM-DD</granularity>
    </Identify>
</OAI-PMH>
```

Fig. 1. Typical OAI-PMH v2.0 request and response (namespace and schema attributes are not depicted).

2.2 SOAP

SOAP [8] is a standard for encoding messages in a distributed computing environment. It originated from industrial efforts to leverage XML technology for standardised messaging and has tracked best practices as they emerged. SOAP is part of a larger framework to specify external interfaces to network-accessible services: SOAP specifies the syntactic encoding of messages, the Web Services Description Language (WSDL) [2] is a formal specification of a network-accessible API to a service and the Universal Description, Discovery and Integration of Web Services (UDDI) registries list public interfaces. Together these specifications are at the core of the Web Services paradigm of computing, where applications are sequences and aggregations of independent service-oriented components [17].

The current status of Web Services can be confusing to adopters as there is much talk about how it will revolutionise computing, but there are few actual case studies illustrating its use in large-scale interoperable scenarios. This is partly because of the divergence of standards - Microsoft adopted v1.1 of the SOAP specification [1] for its Web Services work, while the W3C only recognises v1.2 [8] as a "recommendation". Between the release of these two versions, the XML Schema standard was formalised - thus, while the earlier SOAP specification allowed the use of XML Schema but supported its own type system, the newer v1.2 SOAP specification does not define its own type system to avoid overlapping with XML Schema functionality. In spite of these issues, some well-known services, such as Google [7], have been publicly exposed using a version of the SOAP protocol.

A typical request and response is shown in Fig 2.

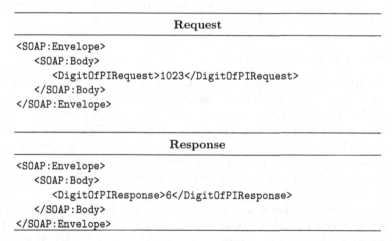

Fig. 2. Typical SOAP v1.2 request and response (namespace and schema attributes are not depicted).

3   Context for OAI-PMH + SOAP

The earliest version of the OAI-PMH (v1.0) was disseminated through many avenues, including a paper presented at JCDL 2001 [12]. One of the first questions posed to the presenter of that paper asked why SOAP was not used. This has led to much discussion in the OAI community, but it was felt that as long as SOAP was not a formal standard, it should be avoided. This was largely motivated by prior experiences with the change in status of the XML Schema specification, an event that necessitated the release of OAI-PMH v1.1.

In mid-2003, SOAP v1.2 was finally released by the W3C as a "recommendation", their equivalent of a standard. At around this point in time, it was decided to try to use the SOAP specification as the basis of an updated experimental OAI protocol, to investigate its applicability and tease out any implementation issues that could inform future standards efforts.

4   Experimental Systems

This investigation involved 4 parts:

- Analysis and design of a new protocol using SOAP as an underlying layer instead of HTTP, hereafter referred to as SOAP-PMH
- Implementation of a SOAP-PMH-based data provider
- Implementation of a SOAP-PMH-based service provider
- Implementation of a SOAP-PMH-based testing and validation tool

Each of the latter 3 parts was implemented to support both the former experimental protocol as well as the original OAI-PMH, to determine the feasibility of supporting multiple transports or bindings in a single implementation.

4.1   Protocol Specification

Since SOAP defines only a syntactic framework, the encoding of OAI-PMH requests and responses needed to be modified, keeping the core semantics unchanged. Unlike standards such as the IMS Metadata Set [10], the protocol specification for OAI-PMH does not define an abstract information model and concrete bindings. As a result, it was not possible to define a new binding as a layer over the abstract semantics. To overcome this, in the context of this experimental work, a parallel specification was defined by editing a copy of the original specification.

Requests were encoded in a manner similar to the SOAP Request/Response use case [9]. Schema for these requests were defined to match the existing OAI-PMH responses. During the development of OAI-PMH v2.0, XML Schema data types were explicitly defined for each PMH parameter in preparation for a possible migration to SOAP. Thus, in SOAP-PMH these data types are imported directly from the original OAI-PMH schema [16] to maintain a high degree of data type consistency.

In order to maintain independence from the underlying transport, the responses were embedded within SOAP envelopes. To some degree, this design choice goes against SOAP recommendations for error handling, which state that semantic errors are handled by special cases defined in the SOAP protocol. It was felt that this yet again mixed syntax and semantics at different layers of

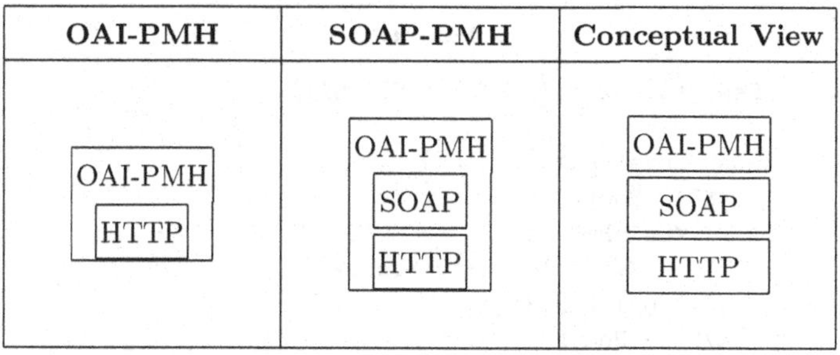

OAI-PMH	SOAP-PMH	Conceptual View
OAI-PMH HTTP	OAI-PMH SOAP HTTP	OAI-PMH SOAP HTTP

Fig. 3. Different conceptual views of OAI-PMH as a transport-independent protocol.

a structured model. Instead, OAI-PMH errors were retained at the OAI-PMH level, while only SOAP errors were handled at the SOAP protocol level. A typical example of a SOAP error is a message with non-SOAP tags at the top level of its body. HTTP errors were yet another case to consider and had to be handled at the layer below SOAP. In the existing OAI-PMH, errors are specified at the semantic, encoding and transport levels, thus HTTP errors that should already have been handled at a SOAP layer still exist at the upper semantic layer. This was not dealt with in this study, but is an important consideration for future protocol design activities.

Fig 3 depicts the current onion-peel design of OAI-PMH, an onion-peel version of SOAP-PMH and an ideal conceptual view of the layers. In this model, OAI-PMH is built around HTTP, implying that they are not separable. The SOAP-PMH version is built over SOAP, layered over HTTP – implying that neither the SOAP nor HTTP encodings are essentially separable from the core protocol, but that SOAP and HTTP are not necessarily bound together. Conceptually, in the ideal case, the semantics of the protocol should be specified independently of the encoding mechanism and transport layer. Thus, if the protocol was written with this in mind, it would have been simpler to retarget it from the combination of URL encoding and XML responses to SOAP messages. Similarly, since SOAP does not intrinsically depend on HTTP, upper level protocols ought not to do so – so that if HTTP was replaced by, say, SMTP, no changes in the core semantics would be necessary.

A typical request and response pair from this experimental SOAP-PMH is shown in Fig 4. The regular OAI-PMH response is cleanly encapsulated within the Body of a SOAP Envelope. The SOAP Header is not used since its definition suggests it is intended for intermediate or non-payload processing and the OAI-PMH essentially requires end-to-end payload delivery.

4.2   Data Provider

A database-driven data provider was built to conform to the SOAP-PMH. For a reasonable level of completeness, this module supported the following optional features of the OAI-PMH:

Request

(Sent to: http://abc.org/SOAPOAI)

```
<SOAP:Envelope>
  <SOAP:Body>
    <OAI-PMH-Req>
      <verb>Identify</verb>
    </OAI-PMH-Req>
  </SOAP:Body>
</SOAP:Envelope>
```

Response

```
<SOAP:Envelope>
  <SOAP:Body>
    <OAI-PMH>
      <responseDate>2004-02-02T12:00:00Z</responseDate>
      <request verb="Identify"/>http://abc.org/SOAPOAI</request>
      <Identify>
        <repositoryName>Somewhere</repositoryName>
        <baseURL>http://abc.org/SOAPOAI</baseURL>
        <protocolVersion>SOAP2.0</protocolVersion>
        <earliestDatestamp>2001-01-01T01:00:00Z</earliestDatestamp>
        <deletedRecord>no</deletedRecord>
        <granularity>YYYY-MM-DD</granularity>
      </Identify>
    </OAI-PMH>
  <SOAP:Body>
</SOAP:Envelope>
```

Fig. 4. Typical SOAP-PMH request and response (namespaces and schema attributes are not depicted).

- multiple metadata formats
- flow control using resumption tokens
- sets for selective harvesting

The implementation was done in Java, using JDBC for database connectivity to a MySQL source of data. The Web interfacing was accomplished using Java servlets. Processing of requests and responses was performed in layers to avoid duplication of code in supporting different bindings of the core OAI-PMH semantics.

4.3 Testing Tool

An intemediate-level testing tool was developed to test data provider implementations of both OAI-PMH and SOAP-PMH. This tool built on typical tests carried out by the Repository Explorer [15] and OAI Data Provider Registry [14] by including the following capabilities:

- Users may choose which tests to conduct in a batch, as a subset of the full suite.
- The testing tool was implemented as a portable Java application, thus enabling efficient testing of local data providers, even those behind firewalls or those that are domain-restricted.
- Exploiting its nature as an application, the human interface was designed for greater usability e.g., tabbed dialogs where used where this seemed most natural and progress indicators were used during batch testing.

4.4   Service Provider

From a service provider perspective, a simple search engine was built, based on the Lucene [6] open source package. A Web-based interface was developed using Java servlets, both for searching through harvested data and for management of the harvesting operations. Once again, the harvester was developed such that it would work with either the regular OAI-PMH or the experimental SOAP-PMH.

5   Evaluation

Evaluation of the software was conducted on multiple levels, to confirm that the testbed was realistic and then to deduce emergent properties that were a result of using SOAP.

In the first instance, usability testing was conducted on the testing tool and the service provider. These tests confirmed that non-expert users were able to successfully harvest data, conduct searches and test data providers.

All three components were then tested for OAI protocol compliance, by interconnection and by connection with external components. For example, the testing tool was used to validate existing OAI data providers and the data provider was validated by the Repository Explorer.

Finally, performance testing was conducted on the data provider to determine the effect of the intermediate layer on network traffic and necessary processing. For this purpose, the data provider was primed with a copy of approximately 77000 ETD records, themselves obtained from an OAI data provider. Measurements for a typical **ListRecords** request formulated to disseminate a subset of records specified by *set*, *metadataPrefix*, *from* and *until* parameters are shown in Table 1. The first column confirms that there is a large increase in the size of the request, and this is due to the switch from URL encoding to XML. The response, on the other hand, has a size differential that is due only to the additional layering and therefore does not have a sizable impact on bytes transferred. The processing time, similarly, is only minimally affected by SOAP layering.

Table 1. Performance measurements for SOAP-PMH vs. OAI-PMH for a typical request/response pair.

Protocol	Request(bytes)	Response (bytes)	Processing Time (ms)
SOAP	645	167037	1609.22
HTTP	140	166616	1594.87
Diff	505	421	14.4

6   Analysis and Conclusions

The process of developing a protocol and development and testing of initial implementations conforming to it have revealed a number of issues that could assist with future protocol design efforts.

Firstly, and most importantly, the migration to SOAP was deemed to be relatively straight-forward by the developers. The implication of this is that there need be no additional complexity in software development because of the use of SOAP. Further, it was possible in all instances to create tools that could understand multiple bindings of the core protocol.

In most cases, the use of SOAP also resulted in only marginal increases in bytes transferred and processing time required. During the course of performing these tests, it was discovered that XML indentation for human-readability caused a major increase in bytes tranferred (typically 6 bytes per line of XML embedded in a SOAP Body). This reinforces the notion that XML should be optimised for data transfer by removing indentation and linefeeds, and introducing compression where possible. Such techniques will further reduce the effects of adding SOAP layers.

While SOAP supports the use of alternative lower layers, the tight integration of OAI-PMH and HTTP prevents a clean separation at the SOAP layer. In contrast, the Blox project successfully used SMTP as a SOAP transport because of less overhead than HTTP [13]. This is not possible in SOAP-PMH because of, for example, the requirement for a *baseURL* in the *request* header tags of all responses. There is understandably tension between the usefulness of abstractions and the utilitarian benefit of complete specifications. However, unless a new complete specification is to be released for every underlying transport, abstracting the semantics of OAI-PMH should be considered.

The SOAP standard is itself not cleanly separated from the semantics it encapsulates. By specifying that semantic errors are to be returned as SOAP Faults, it makes tight integration a requirement and this once again introduces complications, albeit minor, into the protocol design/layering process.

All these issues notwithstanding, the benefits of Web Services as a standard framework, with integrated support in many modern development tools, coupled with the verified ease of a migration of OAI-PMH to SOAP, makes it imperative that this is pursued by the OAI.

7   Future Work

It is hoped that the results of this experimental work will lead to the formation of a new working group to investigate the migration of OAI-PMH towards a SOAP-based standard.

This study was initially intended to include investigations into WSDL specifications for the OAI protocol. This was abandoned largely because of the state of flux of the WSDL protocol, with differences in encoding between the existing WS-I version and the draft W3C standard (as at mid-2003). By the completion of the project, WSDL was not yet standardised by W3C - when this happens, a formal description of the existing and SOAP protocols can be created.

New formalisms such as REST (REpresentational State Transfer) [5] also need to be taken into account. Where SOAP's request/response message pattern suggests that requests be encoded as XML messages, REST recommends that if no state is changing, requests should be encoded as HTTP GETs. These sometimes conflicting notions must be reconciled so that Web Service interfaces are indeed standardised. XML messages have the advantage of standardised data encoding while services such as ERRoLs have the advantage that they can be completely referred to by a simple URL. More work is needed to investigate how to bridge the gap from RESTful URLs to possibly RESTful SOAP communications.

References

1. Box, Don, David Ehnebuske, Gopal Kakivaya, Andrew Layman, Noah Mendelsohn, Henrik Frystyk Nielsen, Satish Thatte and Dave Winer (2000), Simple Object Access Protocol (SOAP) v1.1, W3C, 8 May 2000. Available http://www.w3.org/TR/SOAP/
2. Christensen, E., F. Curbera, G. Meredith and S. Weerawarana (2001), Web Services Description Language (WSDL) 1.1, W3C. Available http://www.w3.org/TR/wsdl
3. Dobratz, Susanne, and Birgit Matthaei (2003), "Open Archives Activities and Experiences in Europe: An Overview by the Open Archives Forum", in D-Lib Magazine, Vol. 9, No. 1, January 2003. Available http://www.dlib.org/dlib/january03/dobratz/01dobratz.html
4. Fallside, David C. (editor) (2001), XML Schema Part 1: Structures and Part 2: Datatypes, W3C, 2 May 2001. Available http://www.w3.org/TR/xmlschema-1/ and http://www.w3.org/TR/xmlschema-1/
5. Fielding, Roy, T. and Richard N. Taylor (2002), "Principled design of the modern Web architecture", in Transactions on Internet Technology, Vol. 2, No. 2, ACM Press, pp. 115-150.
6. Goetz, Brian (2000), The Lucene search engine: Powerful, flexible and free, in JavaWorld. Available http://www.javaworld.com/javaworld/jw-09-2000/jw-0915-lucene.html
7. Google (2004), Google Web APIs. Website http://www.google.com/apis/
8. Gudgin, M., M. Hadley, N. Mendelsohn, J. Moreau and H. F. Nielson (2003), SOAP Version 1.2 Part 1: Messaging Framework and Part 2: Adjuncts, W3C, 24 June 2003. Available http://www.w3.org/TR/2003/REC-soap12-part1-2003-0624/ and http://www.w3.org/TR/2003/REC-soap12-part2-2003-0624/

9. Ibbotson, J. (2002), SOAP Version 1.2 Usage Scenarios, W3C, 26 June 2003. Available http://www.w3.org/TR/2002/WD-xmlp-scenarios-20020626/

10. IMS Global Learning Consortium, Inc. (2001), IMS Learning Resource Meta-data Information Model, IMS, 28 September 2001. Available http://www.imsglobal.org/metadata/imsmdv1p2p1/imsmd_infov1p2p1.html

11. Lagoze, Carl and Herbert Van de Sompel (2001), "The Open Archives Initiative: Building a low-barrier interoperability framework", in Proceedings of JCDL 2001, Roanoke, VA, USA, June 2001, ACM Press, pp. 54-62.

12. Lagoze, Carl, Herbert Van de Sompel, Michael Nelson, and Simeon Warner (2002), The Open Archives Initiative Protocol for Metadata Harvesting – Version 2.0, Open Archives Initiative, June 2002. Available http://www.openarchives.org/OAI/2.0/openarchivesprotocol.htm

13. Moore, David, Stephen Emslie and Hussein Suleman (2003). BLOX: Visual Digital Library Building, Technical Report CS03-20-00, Department of Computer Science, University of Cape Town. Available http://pubs.cs.uct.ac.za/

14. Open Archives Initiative (2004), Open Archives Initiative Data Provider Registry. Website http://www.openarchives.org/data/registerasprovider.html

15. Suleman, Hussein (2001), "Enforcing Interoperability with the Open Archives Initiative Repository Explorer", in Proceedings of the ACM-IEEE Joint Conference on Digital Libraries, Roanoke, VA, USA, 24-28 June 2001, pp. 63-64.

16. Van de Sompel, H. and S. Warner (2004), XML Schema which can be used to validate replies to all OAI-PMH v2.0 requests, 29 March 2004. Available http://www.openarchives.org/OAI/2.0/OAI-PMH.xsd

17. Yang, J. (2003), "Web Service Componentization", in Communications of the ACM, Vol. 46, No. 10, October 2003, ACM Press, pp. 35-40.

Connexions: An Alternative Approach to Publishing

Geneva Henry

Rice University, P.O. Box 1892, Houston, Texas 77251-1892
ghenry@rice.edu

Abstract. Web technologies offer new methods for quickly sharing and disseminating knowledge. Digital libraries of scholarly assets are proliferating
online, with materials being openly licensed and shared. Sharing knowledge
provides learners, instructors and researchers with access to the most recent
findings, encouraging more rapid breakthroughs that lead to positive impacts to
society. These new publication processes pose challenges to traditional publishers by redefining methods for providing quality information in a timely manner.
The Connexions project at Rice University is a collaborative, community-
driven approach to authoring, teaching, and learning. By collaborating both
within and across disciplines, communities of authors work together to pool
their expertise in the form of knowledge modules. These modules form the basis for building courses that are authored by many, with each author receiving
attribution for his or her contributions. Information can be modified under an
open license to tailor the material for the audiences of learners.

1 Introduction

Scientists and engineers working in disciplines where new discoveries impact the
well-being of society and result in transformational products increasingly demand fast
paced communications that will accommodate their rapid knowledge discovery needs.
Traditional peer reviewed publications are bottlenecks for researchers seeking to understand the latest discoveries that will aid them in identify the most fertile areas for
new breakthroughs in their respective fields. To close this gap in timely communications, researchers increasingly rely on informal exchanges of knowledge with their
colleagues around the globe using Internet technologies. This exchange of information electronically is leading to new cultural norms. Communications are becoming
less formal since they can occur much more frequently with e-mail. Written electronic
communications are beginning to approximate dialog. Jointly authored papers can
quickly evolve as authors pass "the token" to each other during revision cycles. Geographic location is no longer a barrier to participating in research and publishing the
results. Sharing knowledge is valued rather than keeping it hidden until research results are published in peer-reviewed journals. The result is increased collaboration,
more rapid dissemination of research results, and breakthroughs occurring more rapidly [1].

In addition to facilitating more rapid advances in research, electronically available
information can benefit educational institutions by enabling the inclusion of new
knowledge in the curriculum to ensure that students graduate with the most current
knowledge available in their field of study. A greater challenge, however, lies in providing an infrastructure that researchers, authors, instructors and students need to

R. Heery and L. Lyon (Eds.): ECDL 2004, LNCS 3232, pp. 421–431, 2004.

easily facilitate shared communications. Traditionally published textbooks, whether in print or electronic format, have generally continued to be the means adopted for teaching and learning, even as collaboration has increased with the availability of the Internet. This paper describes an alternative framework to enable rapid knowledge exchanges and collaboration without relying on traditional peer reviewed publications to mediate between members of these knowledge communities.

1.1 Quality Control and Easy Sharing of Knowledge

Quality control of information has relied on the peer review process to ensure that published works are verified as legitimate by the most knowledgeable professionals in a given field. Publishers have been the honest brokers of knowledge, arranging for articles and books to be peer reviewed by an author's disciplinary colleagues prior to publication. While the peer review process helps to ensure high quality and integrity, the process is long, resulting in delayed publication of new findings. Thus, the rapid sharing of knowledge is compromised. With the Web, however, authors can publish their findings immediately, with their peers weighing in just as immediately on the legitimacy of the new knowledge. The widespread dissemination afforded by the Internet subjects this knowledge to the scrutiny of many more experts who can confirm or deny the claims of the author. Web publications, however, are perceived as lacking the quality assurances that non-experts and third party institutions need in order to recognize the work as legitimate [6,7].

Despite the rapid information updates enabled by the Web, traditional publishers have maintained all the aspects of traditional print publications in their e-publications. Articles and books are peer reviewed before they are published on the Web with the publisher's stamp of approval. Just as with the print publications, sharing of knowledge continues to be delayed. Textbooks, the mainstay of teaching for many science and engineering disciplines, discourage collaborative authoring due to the detailed interactions required between the author and publisher. This causes authors to write about specialties in which they are not experts so that the textbook is comprehensive. Once published, the works cannot be quickly updated because changes would compromise the "approved" text that has been through the peer review process. Thus, electronic publications become frozen, just like their paper counterparts. Students cannot realize the benefits of electronic publications such as a decrease in the costs of textbooks and a genuinely current understanding of their field.

Online counterparts to print publications are beginning to receive new challenges from new models of publication. Consumers and authors alike have much to gain from the free exchange of knowledge, especially with regard to rapidly impacting both intellectual and technological growth. [5,6,8,9] Higher education institutions will, in time, find the legitimacy they require for published works through other means, such as increased use and citation of online books and articles; in time, this will likely factor more meaningfully into the measure by which the faculty and researchers are judged.

1.2 Motivation for Collaboration and Sharing Knowledge

The traditional publication process, with its revision cycles, copyright assignments and delayed publication due to pre-publication peer review all present barriers to co-authoring books and articles as a community. Today it is common for researchers to work with each other across institutions and geographic boundaries. In online environments, colleagues can share knowledge freely, allowing works to be annotated, discussed, reworked and rapidly republished. [19] Shared knowledge results in new ideas, hypotheses, discoveries: the advancement of knowledge [1,15].

As authors take advantage of the way they can communicate online, they are finding it is possible to communicate much more effectively by incorporating simulations, images, audio and video in their works. This promotes further collaboration as knowledge creation becomes a team effort, with programmers, artists, and multimedia specialists working with the author, who is trying to find the best way of delivering his or her message to interested parties.

Interactive content not only conveys knowledge in new and exciting ways, it *requires* electronic publication rather than static presentation. Traditional publications are limited in how they can accommodate these new expressions of knowledge. To address the interactive nature of an online publication, some publishers issue CDs with their print publications, enabling interactive elements to be captured for the consumer. Self contained multimedia objects are limited in their ability to deliver the desired information as authors work more and more in the "web" of collaboration, linking to other resources that help to better illustrate their communications. New forms of dynamic publication come much closer to approximating a dialog, engaging colleagues and students in the work by inviting feedback and allowing them to derive new works from ideas expressed online [7].

The spectrum of shared online content traverses the publishing continuum, with some projects simply collecting existing Web resources and providing services to help users explore relevant sites for their use in education (e.g., the National Science Digital Library (NSDL) [13]), while others provide free access to full courses an institution has developed (e.g., Open CourseWare (OCW) [12]). [18] Sharing knowledge, however, requires an environment that invites participation by the community rather than the *push* models these dissemination sites currently provide. The Connexions project at Rice University [4] seeks to fill this need by providing a repository and environment to facilitate shared authoring and publication, course composition, knowledge exploration and personal customization of knowledge resources to meet the needs of students, instructors, authors and researchers.

2   Connexions: A New Model for Freely Sharing Knowledge

The Connexions project began in the fall of 1999 as an idea, building into a vision, for moving teaching and learning from a static, linear progression through a set of topics to a dynamic "ecosystem" of shared knowledge. Figure 1, below, shows the process of creating and using knowledge with Connexions. In Connexions, communities of instructors, authors and learners share knowledge, continually updating it and weaving together a variety of concepts to provide a more comprehensive perspective on how topics across disciplines interrelate. Today, Connexions hosts a repository of openly licensed knowledge modules, with over 2,000 unique modules available at no charge. The goal of Connexions is to provide and maintain a commons where individuals and communities worldwide can create and freely share knowledge. This is accomplished through the following 5 objectives that guide the projects activities: 1)

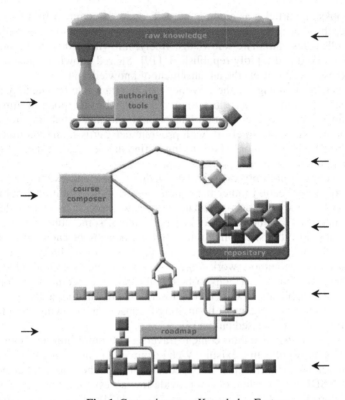

Fig. 1. Connexions as a Knowledge Factory

Provide a *content commons* of free, interconnected educational materials; 2) Facilitate *access* to the commons and foster its *growth*; 3) Facilitate content *reuse*; 4) Foster *community participation* in the commons; and 5) Ensure *sustainability* of this resource into the future [4].Achieving these goals requires a solid core of enabling technologies that provide a foundation for supporting the needs of Connexions participants. Connexions has been available to anyone to use since the project's inception, but in February 2004 the project announced Release 1 of the system, signaling a maturity and level of functionality available in the software to ensure its robustness and scalability. The Connexions roadmap, course composer/instructor interface, and authoring interface tools, along with a powerful knowledge repository provide an environment to encourage knowledge sharing and reuse, supporting collaboration and building of communities across geographic, cultural and disciplinary boundaries.

By collaborating both within and across disciplines, communities of authors work together to pool their expertise in creating courses composed of knowledge chunks that are authored by many, with each author receiving attribution for his or her contributions. Information can be modified under an open license to tailor the material for the audiences of learners. This approach invites contributions by authors, whether they are senior or novice, recognizing that each may have valuable insights that will advance overall knowledge and learning. In this environment, the peer review communities collaborate directly with each other, modifying contributions as they go and keeping the knowledge current. Authoring becomes a much simpler task. Rather than write an entire book or article, individuals can write on a single topic in which they are expert. Reuse of knowledge is encouraged and new ideas can readily evolve without waiting for the long pre-publication peer review process to take place. While initially focused on creating customizable courses, the Connexions concept works just as well for the publication of research articles. As new findings are published, the relevant concepts can be picked up by multiple disciplines that may be affected and can be quickly integrated into the curriculum or used in further research activities to promote new discoveries at an increasing pace.

2.1 Overall Software Platform

Connexions has prioritized its software development efforts by identifying the capabilities needed to provide a robust, stable platform for continued growth of the content commons. All software for Connexions is freely available, licensed under open source software licenses. In open source software development, one of the keys to ensuring sustainability of a project is ensuring that there is a community of developers who are interested and active in maintaining the code base. [16,17] The approach Connexions has consistently taken towards software development is to find existing open source software projects that most closely fulfill Connexions requirements and build on top of those existing tools. This helps to provide a stronger base of support, with established communities of open source programmers who support and enhance the existing toolsets. This has proven to be a very effective path for Connexions to follow.

2.1.1 Course Roadmap Software

The Connexions course roadmap provides a persistent guide to instructors and learners using Connexions. Through the roadmap, a course can be opened with a listing of all the modules that are used in that course, ordered and grouped according to the instructor's needs for teaching the material. The course roadmap is a software plug-in to the web browser and is downloaded from the Connexions web site.

The roadmap allows learners to navigate through a course, following links both internal to the knowledge module and external links, such as recommended links the instructor has added, without getting lost. The roadmap provides an "anchor" to show them where they were in the course when they began exploring links.

Learners can add their own annotations to the materials, which are kept private to them. These annotations behave like browser bookmarks, following the student wherever they go. This is a useful feature for students who access their Connexions courses from multiple computers throughout the campus. The Connexions team developed the annotation software from the Annozilla project code base, an open source software project. The enhancements developed to support Connexions were contributed back to the Annozilla project so others needing similar capabilities would not have to recreate them.

Additional functionality of the course roadmap includes an ability to display a course in a different presentation style, view the revision history of the module, print a module as a pdf file, and view metadata related to the module. In addition, users can use the Connexions toolbar that is added to the browser to search for other modules, consult an on-line dictionary, seek help with using the system, and hide/show the roadmap if desired.

At present, Connexions supports all features of the course roadmap in the Mozilla browser and most features in other browsers such as Internet Explorer and Safari on the Macintosh platform. Mozilla is the initial browser for deployment of all software tools, since it is open source and allows us to easily understand how the Connexions software will interface with the browser.

2.1.2 Authoring Interface Software

The authoring interface provides a sophisticated environment to support authors in creating modules to contribute to the Connexions repository. Within the authoring interface, authors can work in their own individual workspace to create drafts of modules prior to submitting them to the repository. They can also work in work-groups with colleagues to collaborate on modules they are developing jointly. Within the authoring interface, the repository can be searched for other modules the author wishes to work with, either to modify them or create a derivative module. Files can be uploaded to an author's workspace or workgroup. A template is provided to collect the metadata associated with the module. Authors can also assign roles to members of a workgroup, indicating whether or not they are the author, maintainer, copyright holder or some combination of these roles. Members of a workgroup can e-mail each other, or add or remove workgroup members. The authoring interface is intended to support the creation, modification, derivation and patching of knowledge modules in the content commons. Prior to finalizing a module, authors can preview how it will look both on the Web and in print. When ready to publish to the content commons, the author can submit the module through the authoring interface.

At the time an author decides to create a new module, they are presented with a Creative Commons attribution license that they must agree to. At present, this is the only license accepted by Connexions. It was chosen because it is the most open license and provides a means for continuing to give attribution to the author(s) throughout the derivation process. In the future, other licenses will also be supported.

Authors and instructors are required to have accounts on Connexions. This provides information necessary to associate the author or instructor with materials they are creating, as well as ensures they have agreed to the licensing for the system. In addition to the Creative Commons attribution license that is agreed to at the time a module or course is created, authors and instructors must agree to the site license for Connexions when they log into the system for the first time.

All of the Connexions content is marked in xml, using the cnxML mark-up specification; until recently, this has been a barrier to widespread utilization of the Connexions platform since authors have been required to understand the nitty-gritty details of inserting xml tag information in the document. Fortunately, more user-friendly editors designed specifically for editing xml documents are now coming onto the market. Their biggest limitations are that they are more suited to forms than to text documents. Connexions is currently in development on an open source WYSIWYG xml editor with Disruptive Innovations (http://www.disruptive-innovations.com/) In the interim, Connexions has tailored a commercial editor, called xmlspy, to work with the Connexions platform. Xmlspy provides a robust and easy to use editing environment for xml, allowing users to add the necessary tags to their data without necessarily viewing the details behind the various tags. Additionally, the xmlspy vendor (Altova, http://www.xmlspy.com/) provides a free (but not open) version of the editor, called "authentic," that provides an excellent basic level of editing capability, and will be adequate for many users.

2.1.3 Course Composer/Instructor Interface Software

The Course Composer/Instructor Interface allows instructors to work individually as well as collaboratively in workgroups to create courses using modules in the Connexions repository. Working with a course composer template, instructors search through the repository for relevant modules to include in a course. These are then placed in a roadmap for the course that will be the basis for students to navigate through the system.

As with individual modules, courses are licensed using the Creative Commons attribution license. Since the attribution license currently is associated with all the modules in the content commons, this is a very straightforward application of the license across a combination of modules that make up a course. Future copyright licensing of courses will need to consider multiple license types that are associated with the course's collection of modules, since incompatibilities between the licenses must be considered when assigning a license to a course.

Through the instructor interface, the particular notation to be applied across all modules of information is selected, if appropriate. For example, modules that reference the logic operators "AND" and "OR" do not dictate how those symbols will look when presented. Instructors choose a common notation that will apply across all the logic symbol references that appear in modules that have been collected for the course. Some prefer that these be presented simply as "and,or", others always want them to look like "& , |," still others prefer to have them be shown as " • , + ," and others insist on "∧ ,∨ ." The actual content of the module simply tags the appropriate element as a logic symbol in xml mark-up, leaving the choice of rendering on the display or print up to the instructor.

Courses can be annotated using the annotation tool. This is one way in which the modules to a course can be customized to meet a specific instructor's goals if he or she does not wish to create a derivative module. Course level annotations are available for viewing to anyone who is using a Connexions course. This promotes reuse of modules within differing contexts, where the instructor may want to point out the relevance of the concept to the overall course.

2.1.4 Repository Software

The Connexions repository software supports searching and management of the content in the Connexions content commons. One of the features of the Connexions repository is that all of the content is available to the popular Web search engines. It is not only the metadata for the knowledge modules that can be searched by Google, Excite, Yahoo and others, but the modules themselves. This has been an additional benefit for Connexions authors and instructors as they receive much more visibility throughout the world when their modules are returned from the general Web searches. Many Connexions modules appear in the top set of search results for a topic. Authors who did not previously know each other have formed new, international collaborations with colleagues working in the same areas as them. These colleagues are providing an additional level of peer review for the authors as they detect mistakes or typos in the content. Many more people have found out about Connexions as a result of modules being returned in Google search results, leading to positive visibility for the project. Connexions modules have also been linked to "best practices" pages, or examples of high quality materials as a result of returns by Web search engines.

2.2 Connexions Content Commons

As new participants in Connexions discover Connexions' ability to provide a powerful suite of technologies that facilitate authoring, teaching and learning in an open, collaborative environment, their excitement becomes contagious. They tell their colleagues and soon there are new communities involved, growing the overall knowledge base available for use and modification.

The key to sharing knowledge is agreeing to a set of protocols by which it can be shared. In Connexions, this is the use of xml to mark-up the content so that the elements in the materials are easily identified. Xml has begun to emerge as the universally accepted method for identifying meaningful information in content so that it may be effectively searched, used, reused, and displayed with great flexibility.

2.3 Legal Issues

"Open" is not always easily achieved. Current copyright laws automatically "protect" content at the time it is presented for anyone to see. [3,10,11] Connexions has addressed licensing issues in 3 areas: 1) Open Source license of software tools; 2) Open Content Licensing; and 3) Site License for Connexions. The team has worked closely with leaders in open source and open content licensing to address the licensing needs for the project.

2.3.1 Open Source License of Software Tools

As discussed earlier, all software for the Connexions project is released under open source licenses either through existing open source projects or through Connexions for newly developed Connexions software tools. Through the porting of Connexions to the Plone content management system, the Connexions software development team has contributed significant functionality to this existing open source project and all contributions have been incorporated into Plone's existing open source license [14].

The annotations capability developed for Connexions was released as an update to the open source Annozilla project. As the open source development community continues work on annotation capabilities, Connexions will benefit from the improved annotation capabilities.

The Connexions Roadmap component is an example of software developed specifically for the project. It has an explicit open source license associated with it as part of Release 1 of Connexions.

2.3.2 Open Content Licensing

The project team has proactively addressed licensing issues associated with providing content that is free, modifiable, reusable and easily distributed so that sharing knowledge is easy and desirable. Through our collaboration with Creative Commons, we have provided a framework to allow authors and instructors to associate their materials with a Creative Commons open license that clarifies the rights associated with content. At the time Creative Commons launched in 2002, Connexions was the largest contributor of openly licensed content using the Creative Commons licenses.

Connexions has taken on a roll of educating faculty about what openly licensed content means and why it is beneficial. An initial workshop on the subject was held at Rice in the fall of 2002. A larger, more highly visible workshop on fair use and open content was recently held in June 2004.

At present, the content commons only supports material licensed with the Creative Commons attribution license, which allows full use, including for commercial purposes, provided adequate attribution is made. Various other Creative Commons licenses are available for authors to specify whether they want attribution for the work when it is used, whether the work can be used for commercial purposes, and on what terms the work may be modified. Depending on the choices an author makes in each of these 3 categories, one of 11 machine readable licenses is offered to the author to attach to a work so others will know what they are or are not allowed to do with it. Additionally, Creative Commons provides a means for authors to contribute their works to the public domain. When the copyright is donated to the public, no license is involved. Connexions plans to support multiple content licenses in the future. [2]

2.3.3 Site License for Connexions

As with most Web sites, users of Connexions are bound by the project's site license. The project team worked closely with Lawrence "Larry" Rosen, a renown open source attorney who is the general counsel and secretary of the Open Source Initiative (OSI), and served as its executive director. OSI manages and promotes the Open Source Definition for the good of the community, specifically through the OSI Certified open source software certification mark and program. Larry and Rice's general counsel worked to develop a Connexions site license that would be acceptable to users and maintain the spirit of the open source community. Whenever a user requests an account on the system (authors and instructors), they must agree to the site license. The license is available for review to all users of the system, whether or not they have an account.

2.4 Assessment

Assessment has been incorporated throughout various parts of Connexions. Many of the knowledge modules in the content commons include elements of assessment that allow learners to test their comprehension of the concepts the module is addressing. This approach of embedded assessment enables students to study a subject until they can be certain of understanding if fully. There is immediate feedback, which helps them correct any misunderstandings quickly and within the context of their studying.

Throughout the software development process, the project has employed Human Computer Interface (HCI) experts to test the usability of the system. Using proven methodologies for conducting usability testing, these tests have identified areas within the interface in need of change and confirmed those that have been well designed. The feedback from the test groups has been used to make modifications to the system.

New, experimental approaches for assessing student learning with Connexions have been used. Concept mapping techniques have been employed whereby students create concept maps that represent the knowledge they are gaining throughout a course. These are compared to the "expert" concept maps of the professor teaching the course. Preliminary use of concept maps as an assessment tool for Connexions-based courses has been very limited in scope, thus it is not yet possible to conclude their effectiveness in measuring student learning. One of the challenges the project has faced is getting instructors to think in term of the concepts they are teaching rather than the traditional course outlines they are used to following.

2.5 Post-publication Peer Review

With a view to incorporating "lenses" that will filter the content according to a preferred view (e.g., recommendations of a professional organization or recognized authority), Connexions challenges traditional publishing models by relying on post-publication peer review. While this approach is not new to the software development community where it has proven to be successful in open source software development [16,17], it is new to content. How will someone be able to confirm the validity of the content if anyone can contribute? For peers in a scholarly discipline, it is easy to collaborate and judge materials in their field. After all, they are the peer review process that has already been in place for traditional publishing. For the public at large, however, the availability of trusted lenses for looking at materials in the repository will be important.

3 Conclusion

The continued growth of the Connexions Content Commons, with global participation by instructors, learners and authors alike demonstrates the need for providing knowledge in a way that does not lock it up and restrict its dissemination. Connexions has not grown by top down declarations of institutions dictating to their faculty that they will use this technology. Rather, it has been a grass roots movement, starting with the shared knowledge that comprised the first two courses in Connexions in the fall of 2000. As people discover the knowledge, they discover the technology that enables its sharing and collaboration. The excitement of Connexions users is contagious; when someone in a discipline discovers its power, their colleagues come on board and spread the excitement while building the knowledge base. These people find their rewards not in hoping for royalties they'll receive from a textbook that took them years to write, but in being able to openly share their knowledge for free, while continuing to receive credit when their original works are modified and even more widely disseminated.

The Connexions content commons is in its fourth year as an available open repository of shared knowledge. Connexions has been "real" at a time when many others simply espoused a desire to achieve the same goals. Now with over 2,000 original knowledge modules, more than 40 full courses, and a fully supported set of tools available in Release 1, the enabling technology of Connexions is poised for even more significant growth. The content commons is regularly searched by all of the popular web search engines, exposing knowledge and the authors of that knowledge to a wide variety of communities.

Additional enhancements to further lower barriers to adoption of Connexions will support even wider dissemination of the technology. New domains of knowledge are planned for inclusion in the content commons, including knowledge modules and courses in art history. There will be increased participation internationally as Connexions establishes a center of excellence in Europe at the International University of Bremen.

References

1. Anonymous: An open-source shot in the arm? The Economist Newspaper Limited, London, UK (10 June 2004) Available from:
   http://www.economist.com/displaystory.cfm?story_id=2724420
2. Berlin Declaration on Open Access to Knowledge in the Sciences and Humanities. Berlin (2003). Available from: http://www.zim.mpg.de/openaccess-berlin/berlindeclaration.html
3. Boyle, J.: The Second Enclosure Movement and the Construction of the Public Domain in Law & Contemporary Problems. (2003) 63(33), 33-74. Available from:
   http://www.law.duke.edu/pd/papers/boyle.pdf
4. The Connexions Project http://cnx.rice.edu/
5. Davis, R.: The digital dilemma. Communications of the ACM (2001) 44(2), 77-83, (ACM Press). Available from: http://doi.acm.org/10.1145/359205.359234
6. Harnad S.: Open Access to Peer-Reviewed Research through Author/Institution Self-Archiving: Maximizing Research Impact by Maximizing Online Access. J Postgrad Med (2003);49:337-342. Available from: http://www.jpgmonline.com/article.asp?issn=0022-3859;year=2003;volume=49;issue=4;spage=337;epage=342;aulast=Harnad
7. Henry, G.: On-line Publishing in the 21st Century. D-Lib Magazine (2003) 9(10), Available from: http://www.dlib.org/dlib/october03/henry/10henry.html
8. Houghton, J., Steele, C., Henty, M. 2003 "Changing Research Practices in the Digital Information and Communication Environment," Department of Education, Science and Training, Commonwealth of Australia (2003). Available from:
   http://www.dest.gov.au/highered/respubs/changing_res_prac/exec_summary.htm
9. Krowne, A.: Building a Digital Library the Commons-based Peer Production Way. D-Lib Magazine (2003) 9(10). Available from:
   http://www.dlib.org/dlib/october03/krowne/10krowne.html
10. Library of Congress, Copyright Office: Copyright Law of the United States of America and Related Laws Contained in Title 17 of the United States Code. (2000). Available from: http://www.copyright.gov/title17/circ92.pdf.
11. Loren, L. P.: The Purpose of Copyright. [Electronic Version] in Open Spaces Quarterly (2000) 2(1). Available from: http://www.open-spaces.com/article-v2n1-loren.php.
12. MIT OpenCourseWare http://ocw.mit.edu/index.html
13. National Science Digital Library (NSDL) http://nsdl.org/
14. Plone http://plone.org/
15. PloS http://www.plos.org/index.html
16. Raymond, E. 1998 "The Cathedral and the Bazaar"   . Volume 3 Number 3. 1998. http://www.firstmonday.dk/issues/issue3_3/raymond/index.html.
17. Raymond, E. 1998 "Homesteading the Noosphere.   Volume 3 Number 10. 1998. http://www.firstmonday.dk/issues/issue3_10/raymond/index.html.
18. Suber, P.: Timeline of the Open Access Movement. (2004)
    http://www.earlham.edu/~peters/fos/timeline.htm
19. Wikipedia: The Free Encyclopedia. http://www.wikipedia.org/wiki/Main_Page

<teiPublisher>: Bridging the Gap Between a Simple Set of Structured Documents and a Functional Digital Library

Amit Kumar[1], Alejandro Bia[2], Martin Holmes[3], Susan Schreibman[1],
Ray Siemens[4], and John Walsh[5]

[1] Maryland Institute for Technology in the Humanities (MITH), University of Maryland, USA
[2] Miguel de Cervantes DL & DLSI, University of Alicante, Spain
[3] University of Victoria Humanities Computing and Media Centre, Canada
[4] Department of English, Malaspina University College
[5] Digital Library Program / University Information Technology Services, University of Indiana

Abstract. Digital Libraries are complex systems that take a long time to create and tailor to specific requirements [1]. Their implementation requires specialized computer skills, which are not usually found within humanities text encoding projects. Many encoders working on text encoding projects find they cannot take their work to the next level by transforming their collections of structured XML [2] texts into a publishable web searchable and browsable service. Most often these teams find the way to encode their texts with a high degree of sophistication, but unless they have funds to hire computer programmers their collections remain on local disk storage away from public access. *<teiPublisher>* is a novel tool designed with the aim of bridging the gap between simply having a collection of structured documents and having a functional digital library for public access via the web. The goal of this project is to build the tools to manage an extensible, modular and configurable XML-based repository which will house, search/browse on, and display documents encoded in TEI-Lite [3] on the World Wide Web. *<teiPublisher>* provides an administrative interface that allows DL administrators to upload and delete documents from a web accessible repository, analyze XML documents to determine elements for searching/browsing, refine ontology development, decide on inter and intra document links, partition the repository into collections, create backups of the entire repository, generate search/browse and display pages for users of the website, change the look of the interface, and associate XSL transformation scripts and CSS stylesheets to obtain different target outputs (HTML [4], PDF, etc.)[*].

1 Background

Administrators of TEI[1] repositories working in SGML were limited to few databases, such as Dynaweb, to deliver their documents over the World Wide Web. While Dy-

---

[*] This is an open source initiative which is being made available through SourceForge
(   )

[1] There are only three widely-used general-purpose markup vocabularies: HTML, DOCBOOK and TEI. HTML is more focused on presentational than on structural issues, while the other two are meant exclusively for structural markup. DOCBOOK is more adequate for manuals while TEI is mostly used to structure humanities contents. TEI stands for Text Encoding Initiative, and is run by the TEI-Consortium:

R. Heery and L. Lyon (Eds.): ECDL 2004, LNCS 3232, pp. 432–441, 2004.
© Springer-Verlag Berlin Heidelberg 2004

naweb was revolutionary in its day, throughout the late 1990s, advances in web technology and plugins for HTML rendered the Dynaweb look old fashioned.

With the release of the XML standard in 1998, industry experts predicted that there would be a proliferation of XML-aware software as programmers would find it easier to program applications to deliver XML over the Web. This has indeed come to pass. Over the past few years, a number of open source XML or native XML databases have been developed utilizing the XML:DB API[2], such as eXist[3] and Xindice to name only two.

Programmers in the humanities computing community have begun using these databases for individual projects with great success. However, for projects that cannot afford programming support, the bar is still extremely high. Thus, a group of programmers and content developers teamed to create an extensible, modular and configurable XML-based repository entitled *<teiPublisher>*, that can house, search on, browse on, and display documents encoded in TEI-Lite. This is an open source initiative which is being made available to the digital library community to allow projects with limited programming support to mount their TEI-Lite encoded texts in a web-deliverable database. The date for the beta release of *<teiPublisher>* is June 2004.

2 Functionality and Features

<teiPublisher> utilizes the native XML database eXist and upon it, it generates a public interface for browsing and searching. Equally as important, it provides an administrative interface that will help repository administrators with limited technical knowledge to:

- establish an XML repository for TEI-Lite documents;
- upload and delete documents;
- analyze XML documents to determine elements for searching;
- develop ontology consistency and refine ontology development;
- index and store XML documents for efficient search and retrieval;
- generate search/browse, results and metadata display pages for users of the site;
- provide an extensible framework with plugin architecture;
- decide on inter and intra document links;
- partition the repository into collections;
- create backups of the entire repository;
- change the look of the interface;
- associate XSL transformation scripts to transform documents or metadata to different output formats;
- associate CSS stylesheets to control rendering.

Some of the features mentioned above, particularly ontology development, cannot be met by the software alone. Rather, *<teiPublisher>* provides a helper application to allow content creators to view the content of elements and attributes used in controlled vocabularies, and highlight semantic inconsistencies. It also assists in selecting elements and attributes which will ultimately be searched on.

---

[2] Application programming interface for XML Databases:
[3] eXist: an Open Source Native XML database:

The following UML Use-Case diagrams serve to clarify the tasks of the Administrator:

Fig. 1. The *teiWizard* helps the administrator of the repository with XML Analysis.

The helper application *teiWizard* provides a rich user interface to the administrator of the repository for XML Analysis (figure 1) which allows for the selection of nodes for browse and search purposes. The generated information or sets of rules are serialized to XML configuration files that are then read by a set of XSL style sheets to render the browse/search and index pages.

The administrator customizes the looks of the repository (figure 2), by modifying the header/footer and CSS stylesheet of the project. The dynamic repository, search and browse pages can be further customized by selecting an appropriate HTML form element like a select box or an anchor.

The administrator performs a number of repository management tasks (figure 3) such as building the search and browse queries, and modifying XPath expressions. A coarse grain rights management system is built into the application using the filter component of Java Servlets specification 2.3 [5]. It provides the administrator the ability to allow only certain Internet Protocol addresses, for example, from a particular University, to access the repository. The administrator is responsible for adding new TEI encoded texts into the repository, taking backups of the data, and configuring the XSL stylesheets for display.

Fig. 2. Presentation tasks.

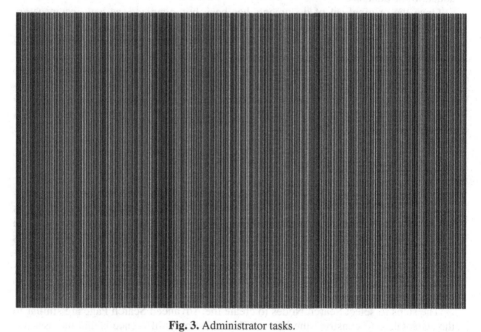

Fig. 3. Administrator tasks.

The rest of this paper will describe various components of *<teiPublisher>* in detail.

3 Structure and Operational Issues

The application can be divided into two broad parts: an **XML Analysis Tool** and a **Repository Management System**.

Analysis of Document Instances

A majority of elements typically searched on via a search page are contained in the *teiHeader*[4]. The *teiHeader* provides declarative and descriptive information about the text (metadata) which is composed of four distinct parts: the *fileDesc*, *encodingDesc*, *profileDesc* and *revisionDesc*. These elements, along with their associated child elements, can be selected as areas of interest in an XML document and be checked for uniformity across the entire repository. This check can be as broad as confirming the existence of a particular element or elements, or an element set, or confirming that a predefined set of values developed for an ontology has been adhered to.

When administrators first load documents into the repository, *<teiPublisher>*'s XML analyzer will take them through a series of steps that will highlight information regarding elements in the *teiHeader* present across the document set. It will then point out elements missing from particular instances, and will act as a visualizer so that the administrators can decide if missing elements need to be added before the instance is added to the database.

Once the original set of documents has been homogenized, as new instances are added, *<teiPublisher>* will process the XML document confirming whether particular elements from the *teiHeader* are present, and that elements which contain controlled vocabulary information are not only present, but conform to a pre-existing scheme.

For the first release of the software, the customization tools of *<teiPublisher>* are predicated on a project using TEI-Lite. By developing *<teiPublisher>* for the TEI-Lite DTD, certain assumptions can be made which are built into the logic of the application. These rules can be overridden or customized by an administrator to match a particular repository's requirements.

Repository Management

Search and browse facilities are a key aspect of DLs. Thus, a key feature of *<teiPublisher>* is the ability to allow administrators to construct search or browse pages based on TEI elements or attributes. The selection of a node or attribute creates an XPath[5] expression that is used for search purposes. This mechanism also allows scholars with knowledge of XPath to further refine searches. For example, the application may automatically generate an XPath expression to search for the *<author>* element, but to search both for *<author>* and *<editor>*, the administrator will have to modify the XPath. An example of this feature can be seen in figure 4.

The steps to select Search Nodes to create the Advanced Search Page are similar to the steps taken to construct the Browse Page. The only difference is that the user has the option of creating a text search within a particular node. The search node is dis-

---

[4] *teiHeader* is the element used by TEI to mark the beginning of the metadata section of a TEI document.

[5] XML Path Language (XPath):

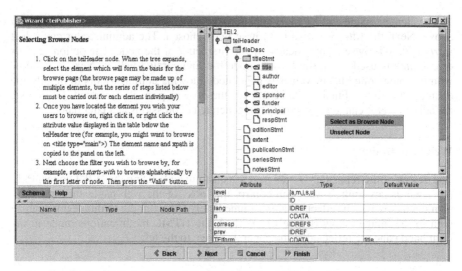

Fig. 4. Selecting browse nodes.

played as a textbox for full text search. Given this similarity, and for the sake of brevity, we will focus on how the browse page is implemented to demonstrate how easy and user friendly this procedure is.

First, administrators select a node from the *teiHeader* via the DTD tree structure shown by the application (see the right window of figure 4). When the tree expands, the administrator then selects the elements which will form the basis for the browse/search page (the browse page may be made up of multiple elements). Once the element to be browsed on is selected, a right click allows the administrator to choose an attribute to further refine the browse parameter (for example, you might want to browse on *<title type="main">*).

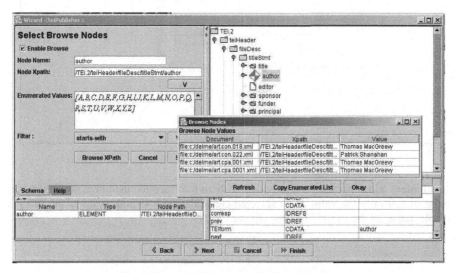

Fig. 5. The node XPath, and the filter selection.

The element name and XPath is copied to the panel on the left, as in the illustration above. Next, the filter we wish to browse by is chosen. The administrator can select *starts-with* to browse alphabetically by the first letter of the node. The options *equals* or *contains* is used when the browse node has enumerated values. Next, a window with the enumerated list of values is generated, allowing administrators to modify the enumerated values. Finally, the XPath for the browse page is generated. Of course, the administrator can always modify the generated expressions at a later date.

Web Page Design

The design of the repository's web pages is customizable using the WIKI concept[6]. In other words, an administrator can control the looks of the web pages through a dynamic window which reflects changes immediately. An example of this feature can be seen in the image below (figure 6) in which the HTML modifications made in the right hand pane are reflected in the generated page to the left.

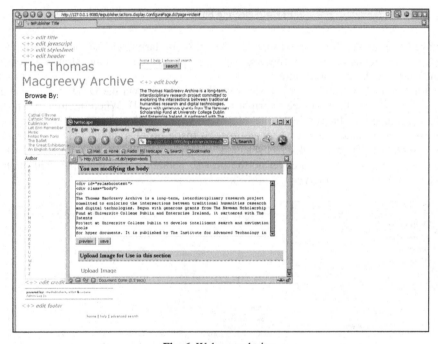

Fig. 6. Web page design.

In addition, administrators are provided with an interface to customize the first result page so that only the value from selected elements (such as author, date, and title) is displayed, as in the example below (figure 7):

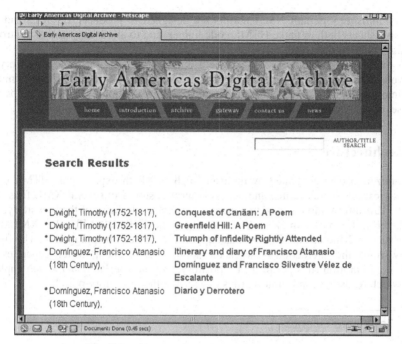

Fig. 7. Interface to customize the first result page.

By the same token, the browse page will allow the contents of repositories categorized by collection, such as primary and secondary texts, or another sorting mechanism, such as alphabetical or date order, to be displayed by category. The repository will also allow administrators to control access to the collection by allowing only certain IP addresses or a range of IP addresses to access content.

4 Publishing Documents

<teiPublisher> allows a broad range of customizations. Since we are employing XSLT scripts to produce display documents, these scripts can be customized according to project needs.

Usually XSL transformations produce fairly static output, in the form of nicely formatted HTML with tables of contents and hyperlinks. In exceptional cases we can find examples of more sophisticated interaction like data from one part of the document (such as biographical or bibliographical information) being retrieved and popped up in response to mouseover events. This high level of flexible interactivity is the real payoff from the XML-XSLT-browser chain. This sort of functionality is usually programmed specifically for individual projects, given that it's highly dependent on the nature of the markup in any given document. By using XSLT, we are able to provide this ability within *<teiPublisher>* as part of the user customization capabilities. XSLT transformations with some Java scripting embedded can automatically produce HTML with sophisticated functionality based on structural markup information, providing added-values to collections.

<teiPublisher> default XSLT scripts are designed to produce XHTML, and use CSS stylesheets both to make HTML code lighter, and to allow easy global control of certain rendering properties.

As the application includes an Apache Tomcat server to publish the repository on the web, very little technical knowledge is assumed of administrators. The administrative interface is thus designed to guide administrators through a series of steps that will set up and publish the repository.

5 Architecture

Customization data generated by the user, such as XPath expressions, HTML code, CSS stylesheet, search terms, and access control is stored in several XML files (figure 8). This information is used to generate the public interfaces of the repository.

The project is based on eXist. Since it utilizes the XML:DB API, other XML databases such as Xindice and Tamino that support the API can be plugged in. The figure below shows the interaction between the administrative client, which generates the XML configuration files per project repository, and the *<teiPublisher>* web application which reads the configuration files to generate the repository portal:

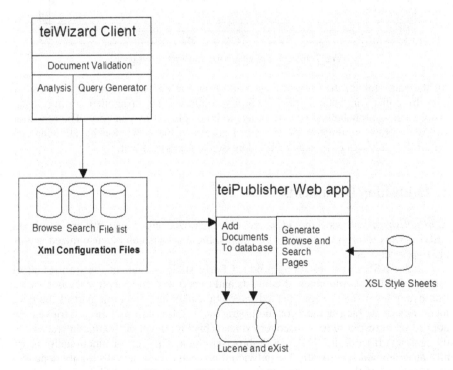

Fig. 8. *<teiPublisher>* architecture.

The user interface elements are represented as stateful objects on the server, separating rendering and event management. The use of Model View Controller Architecture along with XSLT helps to decouple the binding between data, logic and view. The customization data for logic is largely based upon XPath expressions which are generated by administrators' interaction with the XML analyzer. Data customization, such as the development of a controlled vocabulary, is made possible through XPath expressions which, in turn, create the search and browse facility.

6 Conclusion

The process of making a customizable repository is much more challenging than developing a repository for specific content. Even a restricted tagset, such as TEI-Lite, allows users great flexibility. For example, an administrator of a repository based on letters might want to create a browse page which is date based. An administrator of repository based on poems might want her browse page to be searched in alphabetical order by poem title and author. Thus the approach we have taken in configuring *<teiPublisher>* is to allow the administrator to make the widest variety of choices. Thus the problems or unsatisfactory results created by a one size fits all solution are mitigated by the customization modules which provide administrators with choices, from how to store the data, to what elements will be searched on, to display modes. In addition, the more an administrator knows about the XML publishing environment, the more she will be able to work with*<teiPublisher>* to customize her site. For example, knowing CSS and HTML will allow her to customize the looks even further, by adding a background image, or an image-based logo. Knowing XPath will allow administrators to go into the code and create search possibilities, for example, searching on two nodes at one time, which are currently not possible using teiWizard alone. Not only is the *<teiPublisher>* team committed to improving the software based on feedback from the beta and subsequent releases, in the spirit of open source software in which this product was created, we plan on incorporating the contributions of others into the product, which will further refine and improve it, making it a truly community-based tool.

References

1. Qinwey Zhu, Marcos-André Gonçalves, Rao Shen, Lillian Casell, and Edward Fox.Visual Semantic Modeling of Digital Libraries. In T. Koch and I.T. Solvberg, editors, *Research and Advanced Technology for Digital Libraries: 7th European Conference, proceedings/ECDL 2003*, volume 2769 of Lecture Notes in Computer Science, pages 325-337, Trondheim, Norway, 17-22 August 2003. (c) Springer-Verlag.
2. Tim Bray, Jean Paoli, C. M. Sperberg-McQueen. Extensible Markup Language (XML) 1.0 W3C Recommendation, World Wide Web Consortium, 10th February 1998, ttp://www.w3.org/XML/
3. Sperberg-McQueen, C.M.. and Burnard, L. (eds.) (2002). TEI P4: Guidelines for Electronic Text Encoding and Interchange. Text Encoding Initiative Consortium. XML Version: Oxford, Providence, Charlottesville, Bergen.
4. Dave Raggett, Arnaud Le-Hors and Ian Jacobs, HTML 4.0 Specification (W3C Recommendation), World Wide Web Consortium, 24th April 1998, http://www.w3.org/HTML/
5. Sun Microsystems The Essentials of Filters http://java.sun.com/products/servlet/Filters.html

Managing a Paradigm Shift – Aligning Management, Privacy Policy, Technology and Standards

Jonas Holmström

Department of Management and Organisation, Swedish School of Economics and Business
Administration, PB 479, FIN 00101 Helsinki, Finland
jonas.holmstrom@hanken.fi

Abstract. It is argued that we are experiencing a paradigm shift from a user perspective to a client perspective in library and information science. The paradigm shift is brought about by recent changes in scholarly publishing, which have enabled end-users to search for and retrieve information by themselves. Libraries are increasingly providing services that are more and more personalized. The implications of the paradigm shift for management, privacy policy, integration of services, and standards are discussed. It is suggested that libraries are increasingly considering customer relationship management and that privacy policy should be split up in to personal and professional privacy. Current systems should be developed to support successive searching behaviour. Finally the need for an Open Services Initiative to solve the appropriate service problem is discussed.

1 Introduction

University and research libraries are experiencing a rapid transition to a digital environment. In this article it is argued that current events in reference services and digital libraries are significant enough to constitute a paradigm shift replacing the user-view paradigm with a client paradigm. The article begins with a review of these current events and synthesises them into the proposed paradigm shift. Then follows a discussion of customer relationship management, privacy policy, technologies and standards needed for a successful transition to the new paradigm.

2 Background

2.1 The Evolution of Scholarly Publishing

Scholarly publishing is in the midst of one of its greatest transformations ever. Publishers, secondary publishers (producers of abstracting and indexing databases), libraries and end-users are all affected in one way or the other. The publishing market is characterized by rapid consolidation through mergers and acquisitions both vertically and horizontally. This blurs the lines between publishers, secondary publishers, and all other service providers in the market. The largest companies keep getting larger in both scale and scope, but smaller players, both commercial and non-

R. Heery and L. Lyon (Eds.): ECDL 2004, LNCS 3232, pp. 442–451, 2004.

commercial, still proliferate as they strive to take advantage of the Internet and experiment with new publishing and service models.

Publishers are transferring their journals from print to electronic format and implementing value added services such as inter-linking via DOI and OpenURL, which directly benefit end-users. Additionally, publishers are merging their journal collections with other services and developing their sites into full-fledged portals. The secondary publishers are also participating in inter-linking initiatives and implementing emerging standards [1]. Non-commercial publishers such as university presses and professional associations are working together with libraries to make their resources as accessible as possible. Universities and individual researchers are also increasingly making many of their publications available on institutional repositories and e-print archives that are compatible with the Open Archives Initiative Protocol for Metadata Harvesting (OAI-PMH). In turn, the OAI-PMH enables service providers to create versatile services.

The ever-increasing amount of information available in digital form and the proliferation of computerised search tools have moved the emphasis from the size of collections to the ability to access collections. As will be shown below, libraries have modified their old systems and work methods, and are now developing new digital collections and services. The end-users have benefited greatly from the transformation from print to electronic format. They can now perform searches in a previously unimaginable number of abstracting and indexing databases and access the full-text of millions of journal articles from their desktops. The main drawback from this development is information overload.

2.2   Changes in the Behaviour of End-Users

As previously mentioned, the changes in scholarly publishing have brought about radical changes in the behaviour of end-users. This part summarises the most important trends related to end-users.

Self-sufficient End-Users. Outsell, Inc., an information industry research and advisory firm, reports that more than two thirds of corporate end-users prefer to obtain external information by seeking it out themselves. The research surveyed the habits of 6,300 corporate end-users [2]. This trend is also reflected in reference statistics presented by the Association of Research Libraries. The statistics show that reference transactions have declined 12 percent 1991-2000 [3]. Librarians will have to work hard to promote their expensively licensed resources to their users who are increasingly used to searching for information using free information sources such as Google.

Perceived Skills vs. Observed Skills. In the study by Outsell, Inc. [2] most knowledge workers rated themselves as very skilled using online or web-based information products, although they had received little or no formal instruction on information skills. However, studies of end-user behavior tell a different story. Chowdhry [4] reviewed some recent studies involving end-users' search behavior. The review shows that very few queries incorporated advanced search features, and when they did, half of them were mistakes. In fact, in most cases users formulated very short and simple queries, with one or two search terms and very few search operators. Users also spend very little time looking at and deciding the usefulness or relevance of the retrieved items.

Ke *et al.* [5] analyzed transaction logs of the Taiwan ScienceDirect OnSite E-journal system. At the time it hosted more than 1,300 journals published by Elsevier Science. All major Taiwanese universities and research institutes could access the system. The analysis found that users seldom read online help documentation, and that more than 90 percent of the queries were of the simple type. They also reported that use of query operators beyond the most common was low. Worlock [6] reported on a study among four scientific disciplines in the UK. More than half of all respondents worked in the academic sector, with the rest divided between the public and corporate sectors. The study found that customized alerting services were utilized by less than 25 percent of the respondents.

Librarians Do It Better, Faster and Cheaper. The literature abounds with evidence of how valuable libraries and their services are. Griffiths and King [7] present extensive evidence that documents provided by the library generate on average 44 percent larger savings than documents obtained from other sources. Ellis *et al.* [8] analyzed the information-searching behaviour of academic researchers during a mediated interaction with an information retrieval system. The interaction process aided the users to obtain very useful results with help from the intermediary. This research shows that end-users benefit from interaction with a librarian. The benefits are both short-term and long-term. In the short-term, end-users receive immediate assistance on specific research questions. In the long-term, interaction with a librarian make end-users more information literate.

2.3 Libraries React

Moving Up the Value Ladder: Librarians Get Personal. Librarians have not been standing idle by, watching their customers disappear one by one. Nowadays, librarians have to work hard to attract and retain customers. Increased competition for end-users attention has librarians speaking about concepts such as customer loyalty and service quality. These concepts are well known in the business world and are now receiving increased attention from the library community.

Libraries have traditionally offered instructional classes on how to use different library services and systems such as the OPAC. Additionally, libraries have offered groups of students, researchers and faculty discipline specific education. The library has seen itself not only as a provider of information sources and services, but also as an institution providing significant educational services. Librarians are now moving away from tool-based, library-centred instruction to the teaching of information literacy skills [3]. For example, Cardwella *et al.* [9] describe what they call personalized research clinics (PRCs). PRCs are highly individualized, scheduled consultations with a librarian that focus on a specific research need. PRCs are also a way to place student learning and research firmly in the forefront of library service. Frank *et al.* [10] take this one step further and propose that librarians should start information consulting. The concept of information consulting denotes a dynamic, interactive process in which librarians are active, full partners with faculty and students. The trend is towards providing personalized information literacy skills and recognising that it is a value added service.

My Library: Personalizing the Library. Chowdhury [4] reviewed 20 digital libraries and found that they hardly put emphasis on the service aspects. However, this is changing as libraries shift their attention from developing digital collections to developing personalized services for their end-users. But this development is far from unproblematic. While discussing personalization and recommender systems Lynch [11] notes that today personalization is something that occurs separately within each system or digital library. This means that an end-user has to maintain several different disparate and unconnected profiles requiring duplicate work and leading to loss of synergy effects. Some efforts, here labelled *My Library*[1], are currently addressing these problems. The term My Library is used here to refer to an end-user customizable library. The primary reason for developing My Library services is to help end-users deal with the information overload by enabling end-users to bring together only the services they find useful [12]. A My Library allows end-users to make their own classifications and arrangements of library resources. Librarians used to applying the Universal Decimal Classification might have to get used to the subjective classification, importance, and context principles as proposed by Bergman *et al.* [13]. During the NSF post-digital library futures workshop Borgman [14] considered the next research front in digital libraries to be personal digital libraries. JISC has also issued an invitation to tender[2] to undertake a study on the role personalization might play in ongoing developments within the JISC Information Environment.

Reference Services: The Librarian Left the Building. Jackson [3] reports that reference services are responding to the challenges they face by offering tiered reference structures and also by going out to their customers. Tiered reference services involve having a general reference or information desk, staffed by paraprofessionals or students, who answer general and directional questions. Questions they have been trained not to answer are referred to librarians, usually in a separate office. Reference librarians have also segmented themselves and become subject specialists [10]. Going out to customers can be as easy as moving out from behind the reference desk into the library and taking a proactive role asking users if they need help. But, it can also involve going as far as to the users' workplace [3].

Additionally, libraries have started offering e-reference or virtual reference services (VRS). Frank *et al.* [10] note that the concept of a library as a place is changing and, as a result, libraries need to be actively involved with end-users, who are at increasing numbers accessing the libraries' collection from other locations. Reference services have a central place in libraries and they have been regarded as personal services [4]. This is why an increasing number of libraries are planning VRS. Most VRS are intended to address short inquiries such as brief factual and ready reference questions (addresses, phone numbers, etc.), general questions about the library, ques-

---

[1]   The most well known My Library systems are My Library @ LANL
<http://lib-www.lanl.gov/lww/mylibweb.htm>, MyLibrary at University of Notre Dame,
<http://dewey.library.nd.edu/mylibrary/>, and ELIN@LUND
<http://pluto.lub.lu.se/about/one.html>

[2]   http://www.jisc.ac.uk/index.cfm?name=funding_personalisation

tions about the online catalogue and database searching, and provide help in locating information found on databases and websites. Other, more time consuming and otherwise complex questions are not yet suitable to be handled by a VRS. VRS also differ from traditional reference services in significant ways - particularly concerning the extent to which the users are involved in finding the information they seek [15].

3 What It All Adds up to

3.1 From a User Paradigm to a Client Paradigm

This chapter analyzes the previous chapter and suggests that we are moving from a user paradigm to a client paradigm. Implications of this shift are then discussed.

The System, User, and Client Paradigms. According to Kuhn [16] a paradigm is a theory or a group of theories that a) are sufficiently unprecedented to attract an enduring group of adherents away from competing modes of scientific activity, and b) are sufficiently open-ended to leave all sorts of problems for the redefined group of practitioners to resolve. When Dervin and Nilan [17] reviewed the post-1978 literature on information needs and uses they concluded that a paradigm shift was well under way within library and information science and the user-view has ever since the 1980s guided a lot of the research within the field. Dervin and Nilan defined the old paradigm as the *system-view paradigm*, and the new paradigm as the *user-view paradigm*. The system-view focuses on the observable interaction between the user and the system (a system can e.g. be an OPAC or an entire library). The user-view focuses on how users perceive the system. The user-view has brought both cognitive and psychological aspects into library and information science research. However, the user-view still *assumes the context of a system and a user*. This assumption is now changing. The author argues that *we are now in a transition from a user paradigm to a client paradigm*.

Libraries have viewed students, researchers, and faculty as users, patrons, customers, or clients and given different reasons for doing so. Hernon [18] has proposed that customers should be turned into clients, indicating the long-term relationship between the library and its customers. Reference services are adapting a client perspective with the introduction of tiered reference services and information consulting. The reasoning behind My Library services also indicates that libraries view the end-user relationship as a long-term commitment. Additionally, the development of My Library services such as the ability to add links to web resources found anywhere on the Internet (not limited to the library's collections) indicates that libraries now acknowledge the importance of assisting clients in their information seeking, regardless of which services they use.

When a client is considered a customer, there is an implicit assumption that the customer is *the library's customer and therefore uses its products and services*. On the other hand, *a client relationship assumes that the library works together with the client and resolves the client's problem with whatever products and services are needed, regardless of who provides them*. The client paradigm assumes the context-of-client, rather than context-of-library. A shift to a client paradigm has major implications for how libraries function as service organizations. Libraries are re-tooling their systems around clients and are re-focusing on client relationships as long-term relationships rather than single non-related events. In order to do this efficiently libraries are creating new processes for client management. These processes require new management thinking, policies, and tools. New tools in turn will be built upon new standards.

The remainder of the article deals with some of the most important implications of taking a client perspective to libraries. First, libraries must start thinking about their business in new ways. This is discussed using the concepts of enterprise resource management (ERM) and customer relationship management (CRM). Second, since the CRM approach requires collection of vast amounts of information about clients, privacy policy will require reconsideration. Third, libraries must connect the short-term with the long-term in order to serve their clients in the most personal way possible. It is argued that integrating My Library services and VRSs is one way to achieve this. Finally, all automated library services require some sort of standards and there are currently none used in libraries that are suitable for a client-perspective.

3.2 New Management Thinking: From ERM to CRM

This part describes the concepts of enterprise resource management (ERM) and customer relationship management (CRM) and discusses how they apply to libraries. ERM is the acronym used in the business world to describe processes and tools used to manage all resources a business needs to go about its business. It is possible to transfer ERM concepts onto libraries and look at the library's activities through ERM-glasses. Libraries have their own set of ERM processes and tools. These are e.g. collection policies, the OPAC, and all other standards and procedures for handling books, journals, databases etc. Libraries have an excellent track record of ERM and they have very actively used information technology to streamline all ERM-processes.

CRM is the acronym used in the business world to describe processes and tools used to manage all aspects of the relationship between a company and its customers. Looking at libraries through CRM-glasses reveals that libraries have spent far less effort implementing CRM than ERM. In general, libraries know quite a lot about their clients, but only on an aggregated or average scale. Libraries can report how many times a day the reference desk is visited and they can also tell how many times, on average, a client uses a service. However, libraries hardly know anything about individual clients. As will be discussed, concern over privacy has played an important role in limiting CRM-activities. The information libraries happen to have about clients they have only in an ad-hoc manner. The OPAC is used to keep track of the library's books and therefore keeps track of who has which book. Increasingly, software for context-sensitive linking such as SFX[3] has been used to match clients with appropriate resources and services via the OpenURL standard. Nevertheless, context-sensitive linking software is still more of an ERM-application than a CRM-application.

Smaller department libraries generally employ one or two librarians and they serve a relatively small, stable, and homogenous client base. When this is the case, librarians are able to learn the different information needs of students, researches, and faculty. But this system is like a corner shop where the shopkeeper knows his customers

---

[3] http://www.sfxit.com

personally and keeps the information he needs in his head. This system does not scale well, and when the librarian leaves the, CRM-system walks right out the door with the librarian because all CRM-data is in the librarian's head.

Fletcher [19] views CRM from the perspective of a large journal publisher when he states that the totality of customer information may be spread among several different databases on different platforms and in different formats, perhaps even in different geographical locations. When looking at libraries the same way the situation is even worse. For example, the members of the FinELib consortia do get aggregated user statistics, but no real CRM data. The data about a client's use of products and services provided by FinELib is scattered among all primary and secondary publishers. FinELib or any of the participating libraries have no way of keeping track of their individual client's use of services such as keyword alerts from abstracting and indexing databases, table of contents alerts, cited author alerts etc. Finally, current VRS and My Library services might each separately support some CRM-activities, but as will be shown, they are not integrated, far from comprehensive, and they do not span over the lifetime of the client-library relationship.

3.3 New Policy: Personal and Professional Privacy

A client relationship assumes great knowledge of the client, thereby affecting privacy issues. Ketchell [12] and Peters [20] note that libraries traditionally have guarded their clients' data very carefully. Indeed, most client data is rapidly deleted with respect to privacy. However, the development of systems such as My Library and VRS, which are built to support a client relationship, require preservation of large amounts of client data.

Morgan [21] is also concerned about privacy, but argues that librarians should develop a relationship with their clients similar to the doctor-patient relationship in medicine and the lawyer-client relationship in law. How can libraries provide excellent personalized services while still respecting a client's privacy? There are three things to consider. First, libraries need to realise that clients use the library for both personal and for professional reasons. This reasoning leads to the introduction of the two concepts of *personal privacy* and *professional privacy*. Second, libraries must become aware of the differences between the two concepts and clearly separate them. The personal privacy sphere includes the client's interests in health, hobbies, personal finance, politics, sports, religion, sex, etc. The client most likely wishes to be as anonymous as possible when enquiring about these matters. On the other hand, professional privacy may actually prescribe just the opposite. Lynch [22] notes that people are sometimes not just willing, but eager to be identified. A client may wish that the library knows as much as possible about his or her information need and may also wish that others should know about his or her preferences. Finally, libraries must develop privacy policies, which consider both personal and professional privacy. Then libraries can begin to implement services, which are capable of supporting both policies. Several of the My Library projects consider giving clients the possibility of multiple profiles. One possible solution would be to have two profiles, one personal, and one professional. Whatever the solution, libraries cannot use the respect for privacy as an excuse for providing inferior services.

3.4 Divided They Stand: The Short-Run and the Long-Run

Cohen *et al.* [23] note that if librarians know of student or faculty research interests, they have traditionally attempted to keep those researchers informed of potentially useful sources. However, due to the size of the research population, it is not possible to know everyone's research topics. Recent research by Spink *et al.* [24] into information seeking behaviour shows that information-seekers with a broad problem (as distinct from the search for a specific fact) often seek information in stages (they labelled this search episodes) over extended periods and use a variety of information resources. This is called *successive searching behaviour*. They also found that information retrieval systems generally are built according to a single search paradigm, i.e. one search episode is unrelated to any subsequent search episodes.

VRSs and My Library services have emerged as solutions for providing large amounts of clients with personalized services. But VRS and My Library services have been developed *separately*. A comparison between the two services reveals several interesting facts. Both VRS and My Library are highly *personalized* services. VRS and reference services in general start from scratch. Each interaction with a client starts as if the client appeared out of the blue. Chowdhury [4] notes that the reference interview is an important part of the reference service. Furthermore, Chowdhury describes the extensive information about the client's need, situation, and previous knowledge etc. that the librarian has to collect during the interview. This process has the characteristics of a single search paradigm as described above. Most reference service interactions are *very brief*, lasting for only a few minutes. Indeed, most VRS are built to answer only brief factual questions. My Library services assume a *long-term* client-library relationship. Clients are encouraged to create their own lists of resources etc. Clients do so by themselves and without the ongoing assistance of a librarian. Over time, a My Library service becomes a detailed description of a client's preferences and much of the information collected during the reference interview may actually already be stored in the client's My Library, but the librarian has no way of accessing this information. The comparison shows that in order for libraries to support successive searching behaviour, VRS and My Library services must be *integrated*.

3.5 New Standards Needed: An Open Services Initiative

Libraries rely heavily on standards. Librarians know the benefit of standards like MARC, Z39.50, OpenURL, and OAI-PMH. Indeed, a working day of a librarian is filled with adhering to standards of one kind or another. But, not surprisingly, most standards relate to ERM not CRM. For example, while discussing further development of My Library services Ghaphery and Ream [25] noted that systems such as borrowing records and alerts do not have an open architecture or room to integrate with other services. Therefore, in order to integrate client data there is a need for CRM standards related to services and clients.

Standards related to services must consider that *services* provided by primary and secondary publishers as well as others will increasingly a) support personalization, and b) be scattered all over the Internet. Van de Sompel [26] speculates along these lines and when he writes about distributed service provisioning.

Suitable standards describing *clients* will have to take into account that clients will a) seek information in stages over extended periods, b) move from place to place and want to take their profiles with them, c) play an active role in searching for the information they need, d) still need specialized assistance from the library, e) access freely available services as well as services paid for by entities other than the library. Additionally, clients will not mind that some information about them is stored or made public. A client paradigm might very well require an "Open Services Initiative". When talking about the emerging infrastructure of scholarly communication, Hitchcock[4] comes close to this when he mentions the Web services standards[5] as a possible future path for digital libraries.

4   Conclusion: If We Supply the Tools, Will They Build It?

In this article it has been argued that libraries increasingly consider their customers as clients and that this transformation is so fundamental that it can be seen as a paradigm shift. Increasingly, libraries no longer address the information needs of their client in the context-of-library, but rather in the context-of-client.

The library has also been looked at through ERM- and CRM-glasses, and while libraries have been found to be good at ERM, they are bad at CRM. One of the reasons for this is the library's respect for the client's privacy. Privacy the clients may not need or want. The application of CRM-technologies in libraries is only just beginning and further research into innovative uses is needed. An already sorely missing CRM-technology is the integration of virtual reference services (VRS) and personal digital libraries (My Library).

Technologies are built on standards and CRM-technologies require standards that relate to clients. At the third workshop on the Open Archives Initiative requests for guidance were issued on how to use standards to describe resources such as "people" who are not like the classic "document-like" objects[6]. The OpenURL standard might have solved the *appropriate copy problem* but we are now in need of a solution to the *appropriate service problem*, so that clients and librarians can cooperate in building personal digital libraries. Adopting already existing CRM-standards from other fields as well as extending and developing new library and information science specific standards is bound to occupy both practitioners and researches for a long time. Libraries will be increasingly stressed between maintaining their traditional services and participating in client paradigm type of collaborations [27].

References

1. Kaser, R.T.: Getting it! The Added Value of Helping Users Find Information. Learned Publishing 15 (2002) 33–42
2. Outsell, Inc.: Outsell, Inc. Releases Findings Analyzing Content Habits, Preferences and Budgets of More Than 6,300 Information End Users. Press release, 2001.
3. Jackson, R.: Revolution or Evolution: Reference Planning in ARL Libraries. Reference Services Review 30 (2002) 212-228
4. Chowdhury, G.G.: Digital Libraries and Reference Services: Present and Future. Journal of Documentation 58 (2002) 258-283

---

[4] http://opcit.eprints.org/talks/nottingham/emerging-framework.ppt
[5] http://www.w3.org/2002/ws/
[6] http://info.web.cern.ch/info/OAIP/Breakout.html#group2

5. Ke, H.-R., Kwakkelaar, R., Tai, Y.-M., Chen, L.-C.: Exploring Behavior of E-journal Users in Science and Technology: Transaction Log Analysis of Elsevier's ScienceDirect OnSite in Taiwan. Library & Information Science Research 24 (2002) 265–291
6. Worlock, K.: Electronic Journals: User Realities – the Truth About Content Usage Among the STM Community. Learned Publishing 15 (2002) 223-226
7. Griffiths, J.-M., King, D.W.: Special Libraries: Increasing the Information Edge. Special Libraries Association, Washington (D.C.) (1993)
8. Ellis, D., Wilson, T.D., Ford, N., Foster, A., Lam, H.M., Burton, R., Spink, A.: Information Seeking and Mediated Searching. Part 5. User–Intermediary Interaction. Journal of the American Society for Information Science and Technology 53 (2002) 883–893
9. Cardwell, C., Furlong, K., O'Keeffe, J.: My Librarian: Personalized Research Clinics and the Academic Library. Research Strategies 18, (2001) 97–111
10. Frank, D.G., Raschke, G.K., Wood, J., Yang, J.Z.: Information Consulting: the Key to Success in Academic Libraries. The Journal of Academic Librarianship 27 (2001) 90–96
11. Lynch, C.: Personalization and Recommender Systems in the Larger Context: New Directions and Research Questions. Second DELOS Network of Excellence Workshop on Personalisation and Recommender Systems in Digital Libraries (2001)
12. Ketchell, D.S.: Too Many Channels: Making Sense out of Portals and Personalization. ITAL 19 (2000)
13. Bergman, O., Beyth-Marom, R., Nachmias, R.: The User-Subjective Approach to Personal Information Management Systems. Journal of the American Society for Information Science and Technology 54 (2003) 872–878
14. Borgman, C.: Personal Digital Libraries: Creating Individual Spaces for Innovation. NSF Workshop on Post-Digital Libraries Initiative Directions (2003)
15. Kibbee, J., Ward, D., Ma, W.: Virtual Service, Real Data: Results of a Pilot Study. Reference Services Review 30 (2002) 25-36
16. Kuhn, T.S.: The Structure of Scientific Revolutions 2nd edn. The University of Chicago Press, Chicago (1970)
17. Dervin, B. and Nilan, M.: Information Needs and Uses. In: Williams, M.E. (ed.) Annual Review of Information Science and Technology. White Plains, NY: Knowledge Industry Publications, Inc., Vol. 21 (1986) 2-33
18. Hernon, P.: Editorial: First, Embracing Customer Service and, Second, Moving Beyond It: A Client Relationship. The Journal of Academic Librarianship 28 (2002) 189–190
19. Fletcher, L.A.: Going Beyond the Buzzword: What Exactly is CRM? Learned Publishing 14 (2001) 213–222
20. Peters, T.A.: E-Reference: How Consortia Add Value. The Journal of Academic Librarianship 28 (2002) 248–250
21. Morgan, E.L.: The Challenges of User-Centered, Customizable Interfaces to Library Resources. ITAL 19 (2000)
22. Lynch, C.: Digital Library Opportunities. The Journal of Academic Librarianship 29 (2003) 286-289
23. Cohen, S., Fereira, J., Horne, A., Kibbee, B., Mistlebauer, H., Smith, A.: My Library Personalized Electronic Services in the Cornell University Library. D-Lib Magazine 6 (2000)
24. Spink, A., Wilson, T.D., Ford, N., Foster, A., Ellis, D.: Information-Seeking and Mediated Searching. Part 1. Theoretical Framework and Research Design. Journal of the American Society for Information Science and Technology 53 (2002) 695–703
25. Ghaphery, J., Ream, D.: VCU's My Library: Librarians Love It. . . . Users? Well, Maybe. ITAL 19 (2000)
26. Van de Sompel, H.: Roadblocks. NSF Workshop on Post-Digital Libraries Initiative Directions, (2003)
27. Lynch, C.: Colliding with the Real World: Heresies and Unexplored Questions About Audience, Economics, and Control of Digital Libraries. In: Bishop, A., Butterfield, B., Van House, N. (eds.): Digital Library Use: Social Practice in Design and Evaluation. MIT Press, Cambridge, Massachusetts (2003) 191-216

Towards an Integrated Digital Library: Exploration of User Responses to a 'Joined-Up' Service

Ken Eason[1], Susan Harker[2], Ann Apps[3], and Ross MacIntyre[3]

[1] The Bayswater Institute, 9 Orme Court, London, W2 4RL, UK
K.D.Eason@lboro.ac.uk
[2] Department of Human Sciences, Loughborough University, LE11 3TU, UK
S.D.Harker@lboro.ac.uk
[3] MIMAS, Manchester Computing, The University of Manchester, M13 9PL, UK
{ann.apps,ross.macintyre}@man.ac.uk

Abstract. Digital library users have to deal with many separate services. This paper describes efforts in the United Kingdom to use OpenURL technology to provide 'joined-up' services. The focus is on **zetoc**, a national electronic service, which enables users to find references in a British Library bibliographic database. **zetoc** now uses OpenURL technology to provide routes to services, which might give users access to electronic full text versions of references they have found. Data is provided from two questionnaire surveys and an interview programme conducted to explore user responses to these services. These evaluation studies show that users want these integrated services and are extremely positive about them when they work. However, 'joined-up' services depend for their success on the access rights that each user has to full text sources in their institution. As a result, the success level in obtaining full text varies considerably between institutions. Users in disadvantageous positions have expressed disappointment and frustration; the service may be regarded as a promise not fulfilled. The paper describes the development of 'joined-up services' as a partnership at national and local levels.

Keywords: integrated services, electronic full text, user evaluation, usage analysis, OpenURL, resolver.

1   Towards a 'Joined-Up' Service

A positive view of the rapid expansion of digital services is that many users now have access to a powerful array of services. A negative view is that they are faced with a bewildering array of overlapping services that are in a constant state of growth and change. How are users responding to these developments? Are they delighted by the new possibilities and grabbing every opportunity as it emerges? Or are they dazed and confused by the acronyms, the passwords, the procedures? Do they cling to the simpler world of shelves of books and journals? One finding that is emerging strongly from early studies of user responses to the digital library [1] [2] is that users value the convenience of being able to access

R. Heery and L. Lyon (Eds.): ECDL 2004, LNCS 3232, pp. 452–463, 2004.

digital resources from their workstations. However, they are concerned about the fragmentation of services and the different rules and procedures associated with them. They would really like to see more integration of the services available to them. They want to be able to move material found in one service to another and, in particular, to get from a reference they have found in one service to a full electronic text version that is available in another service.

The JISC (Joint Information Systems Committee) [3], which funds digital library developments for the education and research communities in the United Kingdom, has been supporting service suppliers and universities in attempts to provide users with a 'joined up' digital service. MIMAS [4], a JISC-supported national data centre at the University of Manchester, provides a number of national digital services and has been at the forefront of these developments. It has been part of a community of service providers and universities who have been exploring the potential of searching and linking technologies, specifically Z39.50 [5] and OpenURL (Z39.88-2004) [6], as a means of providing users with seamless movement from one service to another. The focus of this paper is the **zetoc** service, a national bibliographic reference service hosted by MIMAS [7]. **zetoc** is at the centre of attempts to provide joined up services and, since 2000, there have been several stages of technical development that have strengthened links with other services. User evaluations have been conducted throughout the development of this service to determine the impact on end users. This paper provides two perspectives on these developments; the technical and service provider viewpoint as the service has been developed, and the user viewpoint as the service becomes available to them. The service has evolved steadily since 2000 but for convenience it is described below in two phases September 2000 – June 2002 and July 2002 – December 2003.

2   The Technical Development of zetoc Mark One

In September 2000, the British Library [8], in partnership with the University of Manchester, made available to UK Higher and Further Education institutions its Electronic Table of Contents data, which lists journal articles and conference papers in all subjects and currently includes more than 20 million records from 1993 to date. This service, **zetoc**, which was developed and is hosted by MIMAS [9], provides a Web interface for searching by end users, and also a Z39.50 interface. The NISO Z39.50 standard [5] for information retrieval defines a protocol for two computers to communicate and share information. **zetoc**'s Z39.50 interface enables data interchange with other Z39.50 services, including meta-search discovery requests. The **zetoc** service is free to UK institutions (supported by the JISC) and by subscription to UK Research Councils, Irish higher education institutions and, since 2001, to National Health Service staff.

Since its inception **zetoc** has been part of initiatives to provide an integrated, 'joined-up', digital service [10], a 'discover – locate – request – deliver' [11] sequence that would provide a seamless route to the full electronic text of an article. The initial **zetoc** service provided users with the opportunity to 'discover' the bibliographic citation details of research articles of potential interest within its large database in a timely fashion. Early enhancements to the service provided electronic 'request' opportunities primarily for non- electronic 'delivery' by, for example, document supply directly from the British Library and indirectly through traditional inter-library loan (ILL) routes, tailorable for each institution. With customized Z39.50 connections users can transfer references 'discovered' in **zetoc** to their personal bibliographic databases using software such as EndNote or Reference Manager.

An orthogonal purpose of **zetoc** since its introduction is as a current awareness service. Users may request alerts when new journal issues of interest, or articles that match saved searches on keywords in an article title or author's name, appear in the nightly **zetoc** data load. The **zetoc** alert function emails details of each article within the requested journal issue or that matches a saved search, including a URL that provides direct entry into the **zetoc** web service, enabling the alerted user to take advantage of the document delivery, and more recent linking, functionality.

The service rapidly became popular in UK higher education institutions with over 13,000 users registered for email alerts in May 2002 setting 20,000 journal alerts that typically resulted in 8,000 emails being sent out per night. On the same date **zetoc** database use was around 20,000 sessions and 40,000 searches per month via the web interface. **zetoc** has received many very positive reviews including the accolade of '800lb Gorilla of UK email alerts' [12] because of its breadth of service.

3   User Responses to zetoc Mark One

In 2001 an evaluation of user responses to **zetoc** was conducted by Loughborough University. This took the form of an electronic questionnaire announced on the Website and on email alerts sent to users. The questionnaire asked users to report the usage they were making of **zetoc** and what they regarded as its strengths and weaknesses. A full account of the evaluation is available on the Website [7] and is reported in Eason et al [13]. A summary of the main conclusions is presented below.

The questionnaire generated 655 responses from users in over 100 different institutions. The overwhelming view of **zetoc** was that it provided a very valuable service as a broad-based means of keeping up-to-date with developments. It was regarded as a simple service to use and the great majority of comments were positive.

The questionnaire asked users to report what aspects of **zetoc** they made use of. It identified 8 specific services, e.g. alerts, searching the database, ordering articles etc, 11 support and adaptation features, e.g. the helpline, website demonstrations, revising alerts that had been set, saving searches etc, and 3 linking services, e.g. to bibliographic services such as EndNote. This gave a total of 22 possible features that could be used. The analysis showed that 75% of the users had set journal alerts (an average of 13 journals per user) and that 50%

had made a search using the database. Only 10% of the users had made use of the Z39.50 capabilities to link with other services. Many of the features were hardly used at all and very few users made use of the document ordering features in the system.

What was striking about the results was that there was a group of active users who made wide use of the functionality of the service and another group who made very limited use of it. The average use across the sample was 4.1 features but 108 users (17%) were in the range 6 to 18 and 543 (83%) used between 1 and 5 features. For the purposes of further analysis we called these two groups the 'active integrators' and the 'passive majority' and explored further who they were.

The active integrators were spread across many institutions and were primarily librarians (41%) and research staff and doctoral students (37%). The average score for the librarians in the sample was 5.2. From their reports this group were knowledgeable about the electronic services available to them and keen to exploit the resources of the digital library from their workstation. They made use of many other services and, for example, often used **zetoc** as a secondary resource, i.e. they used a domain specific service to reach the main journals they used (and could often get full electronic text) and they used **zetoc** to keep abreast of developments in a broader array of journals. It was this group that were making use of the Z39.50 facilities and they indicated that developing a seamless electronic service that enabled them to move from an interesting reference to full electronic text was a major priority for them.

The passive majority primarily used **zetoc** as an alerting service. As one user put it "I set up some alerts and just let the service do its job". To most of these users **zetoc** was the stream of emails they got giving them the table of contents of recent issues of journals. Some but by no means all also made occasional use of the database. They were largely unaware of the other features of the service and made little or no use of the linking services. These users reported that, when they found some references of interest, they often went to the library to check them out. These users also expressed a desire for a seamless route to electronic full text but were much more concerned by the plethora of services that existed and the knowledge they needed to make use of them. They wanted better services but they already felt overloaded and did not want anything that would further complicate their lives. There was representation of all categories of user in this group but it was noticeable that it contained nearly all of the faculty users (the average score for faculty staff was 3.2).

The conclusions drawn from the first evaluation were that **zetoc** was providing a valued service for a large number of users by providing them with a simple way of keeping abreast of developments in their field. For most users, however, this was all it did. When they wanted to follow up references they left **zetoc** and either went to other systems or visited the library. However, there was a strong desire to achieve seamless integration from 'discovery' through to 'delivery'. It was clear that there was, in the active users, a group of people who would be watching for developments and would be the likely early adopters of any enhancements to the service. These were likely to be librarians, who had a professional interest in developments to the 'tools of their trade' and researchers and doctoral students who had reasons (and the time) to keep up-to-date with the technical resources available to them. Getting adoption by the passive majority, even if they wanted the enhancements, might be more difficult to achieve.

4   The Technical Development of zetoc Mark Two

During 2002, a series of enhancements were made to the **zetoc** service, the major change being the enabling of **zetoc** as an OpenURL [14] 'source'. Alongside this service-specific activity, MIMAS was part of the NISO OpenURL Committee and was proactively supporting institutions in their exploitation of OpenURL technology. This included hosting instances of Ex Libris' SFX software [15] for a number of institutions and holding a series of 'Talking Shops' [16] with early implementers, both actual and potential.

An obvious enhancement to the **zetoc** web service was to provide access to the full text of an article when it is available electronically, and maybe also article abstracts and further relevant information. The problem of providing a link to the full text of an article is twofold if the user is to be given a link that is not a dead end. Firstly the bibliographic citation information must be translated into a URL that will link to an article, preferably using a standard, interoperable syntax. Secondly this link must, if possible, be to a version of an article that the user may access freely, maybe by a valid institution subscription.

The 'OpenURL Framework for Context-Sensitive Services' is a proposed ANSI/NISO standard, Z39.88-2004 [17] that provides a standard way to describe a referenced resource, bundled together with the associated resources that comprise the context of the reference. Before the publication of the OpenURL Framework standard applications were based on the draft, 'de facto' standard, OpenURL version 0.1 [18], which transports as its 'payload' a description of the scholarly resource, such as a journal article, inline as the 'query string' of a URL.

Typically, in a digital library context, a user will click on an OpenURL link in an HTML page, for example beside a citation within a reference list of an electronic article, or alongside a record in a service such as **zetoc**. The OpenURL for the reference is passed to a linking server, or 'resolver', which will return to the user a selection of resources pertinent to the cited article, preferably including a link to a copy of the full text of the article that the user is entitled to access. Typically an organisation's OpenURL resolver includes a knowledge base that records holdings, subscription and preference information specific to that organization.

zetoc, now being an OpenURL source, provides the users with the potential to link from a full record of an article to 'more information' about the article. This functionality is implemented using OpenURL, currently version 0.1, to provide a consistent linking syntax 'from' **zetoc**. For **zetoc** users whose institution has an OpenURL resolver the OpenURL query is passed to that resolver. When a user activates the 'more information' link they immediately see the menu of their appropriate resolver, as defined by their institution, which will include a link to the full text of the article if the institution has a valid subscription.

The problem when implementing OpenURL linking from an information service is that of knowing to which resolver to send the OpenURL query. An institution wishing to use **zetoc** as an OpenURL source can register their resolver address via the **zetoc** helpline. A user's institution can be determined from their login to **zetoc**. Several institutions had enhanced their electronic services available to their users by the introduction of OpenURL resolvers at the time **zetoc** was enabled as an OpenURL source, and more have acquired OpenURL resolvers since then.

For the benefit of users at institutions without OpenURL resolver software, a default 'more information' facility is provided by **zetoc** – an online article search using MDL's 'LitLink' resolver [19], which provides links to places where an electronic version of the article is available. This cannot determine whether or not the user has rights of access, but where access is allowed the user will be able to obtain the full text of the article. Even where full text is not accessible, the user may still perhaps retrieve an abstract. In order to manage user expectations, this facility is deliberately undersold and announced as "worth a try".

Enabling **zetoc** as an OpenURL source has proved to be popular since it was introduced in November 2002 and Table 1 provides a summary of the logged usage statistics. Usage has grown considerably during the course of the first year of service. This is particularly true for the institution resolver service, an increase partly the result of more universities having a resolver accessible from **zetoc** (from 4 to 16 universities), and partly the result of more users using the facility.

Table 1. Usage Statistics for OpenURL Enhancements.

Facility	Usage Nov 2002	Usage Nov 2003	% Increase
Institution Resolver	152	1,755	948
Default LitLink Resolver	3,328	5,557	67

A parallel development, though independent from **zetoc**, was the introduction by some institutions of software to provide integration of their electronic services using meta-searching portals that propagate a user's search request across several resource collections, generally implemented using Z39.50. As a result, many users were able to access the **zetoc** database from other services, for example from portals, from bibliographic software, and from links 'to' **zetoc** via OpenURL resolvers. The introduction of these enhancements had a dramatic effect on the usage of **zetoc** In September 2002 there were 2,317 Z39.50 target sessions across UK academic institutions. By October 2003 it had risen to over 38,000. In March 2003 two of the institutions with meta-searching portals had achieved over 20,000 **zetoc** sessions in the first quarter of 2003.

A recent JISC-funded case study on the implementation of library portal software (Ex Libris' MetaLib) [20] revealed a significant increase in network database usage once the portal was launched to users. Included were databases that could be cross-searched and top of the list was **zetoc**, searches on which rose by 1385%.

The **zetoc** service has then become a technical mechanism by which users can, on many occasions, achieve a seamless link between discovering a reference and obtaining a full text electronic copy. The statistics show that these features are gaining popularity. But what view do the users take of these developments?

5 Evaluation of the Enhanced zetoc Service

In 2003 a user evaluation was undertaken by Loughborough University and the Bayswater Institute with the specific intention of examining the impact of the enhanced services. An electronic questionnaire was made accessible from the **zetoc** Website in order to collect quantitative information. A small number of interviews were undertaken to provide in-depth qualitative evidence of the way users were integrating **zetoc** with other services they used.

5.1 User Views of the Enhanced Service

There were 167 responses to the questionnaire and 26 interviews were conducted. Both data collection methods asked the same questions about usage of **zetoc** and reactions to the enhancements and the initial analysis was of the total of 193 users. The users were given a list of properties of digital libraries that they were asked to rate. Asked what was the most important service they were now receiving they chose 'keeping up to date with current developments'. This is the primary role that **zetoc** fulfils. Asked what was the most important service they wanted to see they chose 'getting from a reference to electronic full text'. This confirms the view that 'joined-up services' are a priority for users.

Users were likely to receive different levels of service in different institutions and in Tables 2 and 3 below findings are reported for four types of institution:

Resolver Universities – are those that have implemented their own OpenURL resolver service and have given **zetoc** access to it. These universities tend to have rich electronic journal subscriptions. As a consequence users in these universities using the 'more information' facilities will be told whether their university has access to a full text version of the article they are pursuing.

Established universities – in the UK there are many established universities that have rich electronic journal subscriptions but do not have their own resolver. Under these circumstances the **zetoc** 'more information' facilities will tell them whether an electronic full text version of an article is available but not whether their university has access to the service that provides it.

New universities – in the UK there are many institutions that have recently achieved university status but do not have access to a comprehensive electronic journal resource and do not have their own resolver.

Others – This includes colleges, research centres and National Health Service Trusts. They tend to be in a similar position to the new universities in terms of resolvers and of subscriptions to electronic journal services.

Table 2 reports the number of users responding from each category of institution and the percentage within each category who were librarians. This is significant because the first **zetoc** survey demonstrated that librarians were more active users than the general population of users. For three categories of institution in the sample, for example, librarians are in the majority in the sample. It is worthy of note that the sample from the resolver universities has the lowest percentage of librarians. It appears that this sample is dominated by the 'active integrators' amongst the user population perhaps because it was a specific request to report on the enhancements.

Table 2. User Evaluations of the **zetoc** Enhancements.

Institutions	Users			zetoc Score	
	No.	% Libs	Overall Score		Integration
Resolver Universities	34	35	8.2		1.6
Established Universities	48	70	8.9		1.0
New Universities	40	60	7.8		0.8
Others, e.g.Colleges	71	69	7.2		0.6
Total / Average	193	62	7.8		1.0

Table 3. User Evaluations of the **zetoc** Enhancements (continued).

Institutions	zetoc Enhancements					
	Total	Better		Same		Worse
	No.	No. %		No. %		No. %
Resolver Universities	28	26	93	1	4	1	3
Established Universities	31	25	81	5	16	1	3
New Universities	25	14	56	10	40	1	4
Others, e.g.Colleges	34	14	41	18	53	2	6
Total / Average	118	79	67	34	29	5	4

A **zetoc** usage score was again calculated, this time out of a total of 29 because the enhancements introduced more functionality. The overall **zetoc** usage score in Table 2 is 7.8. This is higher than expected from the pro rata increase in the functionality and is probably correlated with the high percentage of librarians in the sample. Table 2 shows the part of the usage score that is the result of using the integration facilities, including 'more information', seeking an article on-line, exporting results to other services, e.g. EndNote etc. The highest scores for integration are in the resolver and established universities where these opportunities are likely to be most effective.

There were a total of 118 comments about the enhanced facilities and the results are reported in Table 3. The columns 'better', 'same' and 'worse' record the results of asking users to evaluate the enhancements. 67% of the responses were that the enhancements had led to a better service. However, much higher results were obtained for the resolver and established universities (93% and 81% of responses reporting the service had improved). The percentage of 'better' is lower for the other categories and nearly half report that the service is the 'same'. The numbers reported in some categories are too small for these results to be statistically significant but there is some evidence that, whilst users with rich electronic resources are benefiting from the 'join-up' features, others do not find them helpful.

5.2   User Strategies from 'Discovery' to 'Delivery'

To explore the reactions of users to the new services in greater depth, 26 interviews were undertaken at six universities: three with and three without local resolvers. This sample is too small to yield statistically valid results; the study was undertaken to provide rich qualitative data about user strategies and the reasons for them. The users were recruited from respondents to the first questionnaire who had expressed a willingness to help with further research. The sample consisted of 12 faculty members, 6 researchers, 4 doctoral students and 4 librarians. The method of recruitment is again likely to have created a bias towards more active users. The **zetoc** scores of the users was assessed using the scale developed for the second interview and the users were asked to describe how they discovered references of interest to them and how they obtained full copies when they needed them. The average **zetoc** score for the 16 users at universities with resolvers (RU) was 7.6; the average for the 10 users at non-resolver universities (NRU) was 5.9.

From the descriptions of their usage strategies, the users were placed in four categories:-

- **Ad hoc uses.** Five users (2RU;3NRU) used **zetoc** primarily to provide them with regular alerts but struggled to make good use of the alerts. They were unaware of the new services that were available and found it difficult to find the time to follow up interesting alerts but, when they did, they were most likely to visit the library. They were busy members of faculty who found it difficult to find the time to keep up-to-date:
  "I've started to hate the service. The alerts flood into my inbox when I am busy and just make me feel guilty". (a senior member of faculty)
- **Traditional users.** Another four users (1RU:3NRU) were quite well organised in their use of **zetoc** alerts and searching the database for new articles but consciously stuck to traditional methods to obtain printed documents. They showed little interest in, or knowledge of, ways of obtaining articles electronically. These two groups had an average **zetoc** score of 4.2 and may be considered to represent the large number of passive users found in the first survey.
- **DIY electronic users.** Eleven users (7RU:4NRU) were committed to electronic means of getting from discovery to delivery of full text (average **zetoc** score 6.5) but were not making successful use of the OpenURL facilities.

However, different reasons for this were given by those who were in resolver universities and those who were not. The seven users at universities that had a local resolver knew how to get to full text articles in their favoured journals by using specialist services that were available to them, e.g. publisher sites and other services available in their university. They felt no particular need to try other services. The four users in universities without resolvers wanted an electronic service but had limited service in their institutions. They had tried the 'more information' route in **zetoc** and they had encountered problems. Using the 'more information' facility in **zetoc** they received details of all available sources of electronic full text for the article they were seeking but with no guarantee they would have access to any of them. They found they could spend quite a lot of time following the leads, often with little success because their universities did not have the relevant subscriptions.

"It can be very frustrating to keep clicking on the links to get full text electronically only to find that the university does not have a subscription". (a member of faculty)
- **Integrated electronic users.** Six users, all in the universities with their own resolvers, were using the OpenURL facilities as a strategy of first choice (either through **zetoc** or other services in their university) and they were excited by the outcome. The average **zetoc** score for this group of users was 10. As a member of faculty expressed it:

"When it gets you directly to a full text electronic publication it is magic. It saves all those trips to the library, photocopying, filling out ILLs etc".

The numbers of users in these categories is too small to draw more than the following tentative conclusions. First, that awareness of the OpenURL services is not high. The problem is that the passive users are not, by definition, listening to news about new services and, often overset by current systems, are unwilling to try new ones. Of those interested in electronic services, there is a group who have found an acceptable strategy and see no reason to experiment further. But there is a group in the universities with resolvers who are using the OpenURL services, are meeting with success, are excited by the new possibilities and are extending the range of their use of services like **zetoc**. Perhaps the group to have most concern about are those in non-resolver universities who discover that electronic full text is available but find they are refused access. These users mirror those in the second survey who reported the new services to be 'no better' or 'worse' than before. Frustration and disappointment could well turn these users away from electronic services.

6   Discussion

There can be little doubt from this research that users want to see digital libraries develop in a way which provides a 'seamless' route from reference details to full electronic texts. **zetoc** has an established position as a leading national service that provides users with a current awareness service and it has now demonstrated that OpenURL technology can be used as a basis for offering users this seamless route. The users' response to the delivery of what they have been requesting has shown a lot of variability and this has many lessons for the evolutionary path by which the digital library is being built. There is clearly a section of the user population that is making use of these new facilities and is excited by the 'reality' of a seamless digital library service. However, these users are a small part of the total population and there are a number of barriers to overcome before all users are taking advantage of these innovations.

One significant barrier is the provision of electronic resources in each university and the use of resolver services. A service like **zetoc** can only create a means of discovery and links to possible sources of full text; the local institution has to provide the rest. Widespread adoption of seamless link-up depends on a partnership at national and local levels. One specific need is to help users appreciate at an early stage what permissions they do have in order that they can avoid time wasting and frustrating hunts that only lead to denials of access.

Another barrier is the existence of a large number of passive users. We suspect that this is a property not just of **zetoc** but of all complex information services. This research has identified a passive majority who use a limited range of facilities and are not willing or able to spend time understanding new services. Many of them want a seamless, electronic service but not if it involves spending time learning new systems and experimenting with new facilities. We have noted elsewhere [21] that users of computer systems work out for themselves an implicit 'cost-benefit' strategy that seeks to maximise success and minimise failure and time wasting. Many of the users in this study (especially librarians) are prepared to accept considerable effort for what may be limited return because of the great promise of a seamless route to electronic full text. Many other users, especially members of faculty, expect to get new benefits from relatively little effort and will continue to use the facilities which are familiar to them if the effort to change is considered too great or the benefit problematic. One advantage of OpenURL technology is that the effort of following a few links is quite limited and straightforward and, if it works and provides electronic full text, the effect on users is dramatic. On the basis of the interviews it seems that once they taste the 'magic' of seamless delivery they will want to continue. This problem, however, is that, as passive users, they may never discover the new facilities. It could be that the local librarians could play a pivotal role in bringing them to the attention of passive users. This cannot be done by traditional mechanisms; by definition passive users do not respond to invitations to training events. But suppose there is a major service improvement, for example, registering a local resolver with **zetoc**. A message to end users saying 'try this' with step-by-step instructions may be sufficiently well targeted, easy to do and likely to be successful to encourage many passive users into action.

Acknowledgements

We are pleased to acknowledge the funding from the British Library and the Joint Information Systems Committee that has supported the provision of the **zetoc** service, the 'join-up' work and the evaluation studies that have been reported. We wish to thank two colleagues for their contribution to the evaluation studies; Martin Ashby, for work on the two questionnaires, and Sue Richardson, for help with the interview programme.

References

1. Eason, K. D., Yu, L., Harker, S. D.: The use and usefulness of functions in electronic journals: the experience of the SuperJournal Project. Program. **34**, 1 (2000) 1-28
2. Pullinger, D., Baldwin, C.: Electronic Journals and User Behaviour. Deedot Press, Cambridge. (2002)
3. JISC. http://www.jisc.ac.uk
4. MIMAS. http://www.mimas.ac.uk
5. Z39.50. http://www.niso.org/standards/resources/z3950.pdf
6. Apps, A., MacIntyre, R:. Using the OpenURL Framework to Locate Bibliographic Resources. In: The 2003 Dublin Core Conference. 0-9745303-0-1. (2003) 143-152.
7. zetoc. http://zetoc.mimas.ac.uk
8. The British Library. http://www.bl.uk
9. MacIntyre, R., Apps, A.: Working with the British Library - the zetoc experience. In: Libraries Without Walls 4. Facet Publishing, London. (2002) 261-272.
10. The Join-Up Programme. http://edina.ac.uk/projects/joinup/
11. Moving to Distributed Environments for Library Services. http://www.ukoln.ac.uk/dlis/models/
12. Carnall, D. Website of the week: Email alerting services. BMJ **324** (2002) 56
13. Eason, K. D., MacIntyre, R., Apps, A., Ashby, M. A.: Early integrators and the Passive Majority: An evaluation study of a large web-based bibliographic reference database. In: Digilib Conference. (2003).
14. Van de Sompel, H., Beit-Arie, O.: Open Linking in the Scholarly Information Environment Using the OpenURL Framework. D-Lib Magazine **7**, 3 (March 2001).
15. Ex Libris.: SFX Context-Sensitive Reference Linking. http://www.sfxit.com/
16. ITAM SFX Talking Shops. http://www.mimas.ac.uk/metadata/ITAM/sfx.html
17. Z39.88-2004. http://www.niso.org/committees/committee-ax.html
18. Van de Sompel, H., et-al: OpenURL Syntax Description (0.1). (2000). http://www.openurl.info/registry/docs/pdf/openurl-01.pdf
19. MDL Information Systems.: LitLink. http://www.litlink.com
20. Institution-wide and Library Portal Case Studies. Loughborough University. http://www.jisc.ac.uk/project_portal_casestudies.html
21. Eason, K. D.: Ergonomic considerations in the design of products and services. Chapter 17 in Oodan A., Ward K., Savolaine C., Daneshman M. and Hoath P.(eds): Telecommunications Quality of Service Management. Institution of Electrical Engineers, London. (2003) 323-338

Supporting Information Structuring in a Digital Library

George R. Buchanan[1], Ann Blandford[2], Harold Thimbleby[2], and Matt Jones[1]

[1] University of Waikato, Hamilton, N.Z.
{g.buchanan,mattj}@mdx.ac.uk
[2] UCL Interaction Centre, London, U.K.
{a.blandford,h.thimbleby}@ucl.ac.uk

Abstract. In this paper we present Garnet, a spatial hypertext interface to a digital library. Spatial hypertext systems support information structuring – the organisation of documents performed by a user to complement their information seeking. In the past, spatial hypertext systems have suffered from poor connectivity with information sources such as digital libraries. Conversely, digital libraries have provided strong support for document retrieval whilst offering little support for information structuring over the retrieved documents. Garnet provides an integrated environment for both seeking and organising information. We report on the results of a user study that elicits the response of users to a combined seeking and structuring environment. The feasibility of exploiting the information structuring of users to identify the interests of users is also investigated.

1 Introduction

The information seeking behaviour of library users has been studied for many years. This research has influenced the development of digital libraries and the facilities they provide. The focus of most digital libraries is upon supporting the discovery and retrieval of documents. Researchers such as David Ellis [7] and Carole Kuhlthau [12] have observed patterns within information seeking that are not simply about retrieving documents. For instance, Kuhlthau identifies the practice of *Collecting*, where documents are grouped together and organised. 'Collecting' supports a variety of tasks, ranging from the identification of topical themes to discerning 'missing' information. Researchers from a human-computer interaction background such as Malone [13] and Kidd [11] have observed patterns of document use in physical environments that coordinate and support tasks such as the identification of outstanding information needs and emerging topical strands. Examples of such patterns of use include positioning documents in such ways that they act as reminders of outstanding work, or piling together documents needed for the same task. Together, these different activities are known as information structuring.

Spatial hypertext systems support information structuring in an electronic environment. They provide a freeform visual workspace within which each document is represented by a shape. Examples of spatial hypertext workspaces will appear later in this paper. Implemented spatial hypertext systems include Pad++ [2] and VIKI [14]. Studies of VIKI have demonstrated that users employ similar patterns of document positioning in spatial hypertexts to those seen in physical environments by Kidd and Malone [15, 17].

R. Heery and L. Lyon (Eds.): ECDL 2004, LNCS 3232, pp. 464–475, 2004.
© Springer-Verlag Berlin Heidelberg 2004

We know that visual patterns of organisation carry between physical and digital workspaces. On the other hand, it is not clear whether information structuring's relationship with wider information seeking, and particularly with document retrieval, applies in digital libraries. Spatial hypertexts have seldom been connected to information sources such as digital libraries, and there is no reported work observing the relationship of information structuring and information seeking in an integrated environment.

Garnet, our spatial hypertext interface to a digital library, was created to allow us to observe the behaviour of users in a combined, digital, information and structuring environment. In [3] we introduced Garnet, describing its architecture and operation, an initial informal evaluation and a brief comparison of visual DL interfaces.

In this paper we undertake a more detailed formal user evaluation of our refined implementation, identifying work flows and information structuring behaviour, and update our review of Garnet's comparison to visual DL interfaces. This paper proceeds in four parts: first, the operation of Garnet is demonstrated in a simple example; second, we compare Garnet with existing visual interfaces to digital libraries; thirdly, the user study that we performed with Garnet is reported; the paper then concludes with a summary of our findings.

2 Garnet in Use

A pilot version of Garnet has been created, which is integrated with the New Zealand Digital Library Project's Greenstone software [20]. Greenstone is a comprehensive open-source Digital Library software system, supporting common actions such as full-text and index searching, and browsing in category hierarchies. Access to the digital library system is via a remote digital library protocol. As demonstrated in our earlier work [1], the Greenstone protocol can be trivially mapped to the three other common DL protocols – Dienst, Z39.50 and SDLIP – so Garnet could readily be integrated with alternative digital library systems that employ these other protocols.

We will now demonstrate the system in use.

2.1 Overview

In Fig. 1, we see a typical Garnet user session in progress; a window appears inside the main browser window. This window is a collection of materials that the user has recorded in the current, or a previous, session. Each document is represented by a rectangle containing some text that we term a 'label' for simplicity.

Within a collection, the user is free to place, size and colour each document label as they see fit – the space is entirely freeform. Labels can be moved and/or copied between collections in the usual way for similar direct manipulation environments. Document labels can be added explicitly by the user or through interaction with the digital library's search facilities.

Therefore, the user is free to use the document labels both in freeform structures of their own making inside collections, and in a more formal organisation by using the explicit hierarchical forms of a set of document collections. In Fig. 1 above, we have a collection called "Cattle", which has a column of three documents on the left-hand side and a pile of three documents near the bottom. The column and pile are structures

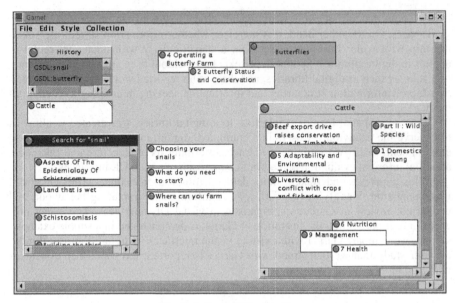

Fig. 1. A Garnet Client in Use

created by the user's exploitation of space – not features enforced by the system. The column idiom can also be seen in the root collection – on the left-hand side. Some use of colour can also be seen – e.g "Butterflies" – but the creator's intention in grouping and colouring is not clear to us as readers of the hypertext.

A search history appears on the top left-hand corner, and the current search for "Snail" is seen on the left-hand side of the main window. It appears like a normal collection, though its contents are selected and ordered by the digital library. As with most web and digital library searches, the search is ordered by relevance. Documents can be dragged from the search to the main workspace or a collection. Also, the user can delete items from the search list by clicking on the small red 'blob' on the top left of a document label. To read a document, the user double-clicks on its label. Garnet then displays the document in a separate window.

2.2 Demonstration of "Scatter"

Garnet can exploit the organisation done by the user in a novel manner. We can "scatter" a set of documents (including search results) from a selected window over the existing layout of documents in the workspace. A "Scatter" places the search documents near groups of existing documents which they have a strong similarity to.

In Fig. 2 we have selected a few useful-looking documents on the subject of snail farming on the main workspace, but let us suppose that a couple of questions remain unanswered. We have a plentiful supply of bananas which we would like to use, but we are not sure whether this food would be appropriate. If we did a naïve search, on "banana", the initial results do not match our particular interest well (Fig. 2, left).

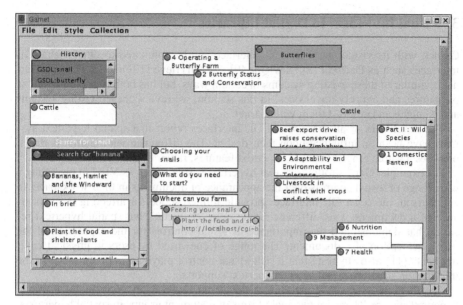

Fig. 2. An example "scatter". Note the shaded document labels in the centre of the display

In fact, documents that relate to our interest can be found in both the "snail" and "banana" searches. However, these documents of interest may not appear at the very top of either list. Normally, we would have to try and re-work our query manually to make it more targeted. With Garnet, we can use the 'scatter' feature to discover any material similar to documents we have already selected. Or, in other words, Garnet can generate existing search terms or filtering to represent our user's interests, based on the workspace layout they have already created.

Viewing Fig. 2, note the third item from the top of the "Search for 'banana'" list: "Plant the food and shelter plants". This item is related to the three documents on the main workspace (for clarity we've chosen something that is visible in this example). A "scattered" subset of the "banana" search results appears on the workspace in light grey. These documents closely matched the existing set of documents, which appear in white. Suggestions are displayed in this grey colour, and below and to the right of the group of documents that they are believed to be similar to.

We can now investigate the two suggested documents that are similar to the previously selected pair. As it happens, these documents would confirm that ripe bananas can indeed be used to feed snails. If we wanted to permanently add one or other suggestion to the workspace, we can click on the 'blob' which appears on the top right corner of each of the suggestions.

If we no longer wish to see the existing suggestions, or when another set of documents is scattered, the current suggestions are cleared.

In this section, the basic functions of Garnet have been briefly introduced. We will now compare Garnet to other visual DL interfaces, and follow that with a report of a user study of Garnet in use.

3   Visual Interfaces to Digital Libraries

Garnet, with its visual, graphical DL interface can be compared to other visual DL interfaces such as Daffodil [8], NaviQue [9], SketchTrieve [10] and DLITE [5]. Garnet is similar to these existing systems in certain ways, but has both new combinations of features and entirely novel ones. In this section, we review these existing systems and compare and contrast them with Garnet.

The developers of all these visual DL interfaces report that spatial hypertext systems have been an influence upon their design. The difference with Garnet is that it provides a whole range of spatial hypertext features, rather than a subset.

For example, Garnet follows spatial hypertext systems such as VIKI in providing a wide range of visual controls over the appearance of documents in their workspace. In comparison, the other DL interfaces provide limited scope for affecting the appearance of a document. This difference may seem 'cosmetic', but spatial hypertext research has demonstrated the importance of visual controls for the expression of the user's perception of a document. The range of cues used by users in physical environments [11] also suggests that a rich visual control plays an important role in the information structuring that spatial hypertext supports.

The tools that support structuring of document sets are key elements of a spatial hypertext system. There are two main forms of document groups in spatial hypertexts: *explicit groups* where the group and its membership are directly and precisely defined; and *implicit groups* where the existence of the group and its membership are uncertain. Explicit groups can be found in many organisational systems – the folders of a filing system and the documents that they contain, or the subject hierarchies in a library. Implicit groups, on the other hand, are common when structure is transitory or provisional. Implicit groups are more a key feature of spatial hypertexts than explicit groups, given their role in supporting the task of structuring and organising a set of documents.

Garnet supports the identification of implicit groups of documents – e.g. documents placed close together in a pile or column. A spatial parser [17] identifies separate groups of documents in a single window or 'collection'. No published information about the existing visual DL interfaces suggests that any of them have a spatial parser or other means of identifying implicit groups. In NaviQue [9], the user can manually identify a group of documents by selecting an area of the workspace. The group created is transitory, but the explicit selection that creates it means that it is in fact an explicit group.

Turning to explicit groups, NaviQue has only the transitory groups just mentioned. In DLITE [5] document groups only exist as the product of searches and other retrieval operations – explicit sets produced indirectly by the user's action. Groups cannot have documents added or removed; neither can they be used as the target of a search. SketchTrieve [10] has a similar approach.

The information structuring support of existing visual digital libraries is thus weak when compared to spatial hypertexts: visual cues are restricted, implicit structuring is absent and explicit structures are often system- rather than user-controlled.

However, the representation of DL facilities such as search and browsing access are relevant to developing a spatial hypertext workspace for a digital library. Spatial hypertext systems have had little or no connection to information repositories such as DLs [18], and have not needed to represent the features of such a system in their workspace. Garnet needs to do just that, and so we were influenced by these existing visual DL interfaces.

The Daffodil system [8] provides another novel visual interface to digital libraries. Users are presented with a number of strategies and tools which they can choose from to recover material from the digital library. An example strategy would be citation linking – which is delivered through the transparent (to the user) use of underlying search technologies. Browsing nodes and search result sets are presented in individual windows that contain vertical, textual lists of documents or child nodes – i.e. somewhat similar to a traditional web-based interface. Documents, as in DLITE for example, do not appear as individual objects that can be manipulated independently. It is unsurprising, therefore, that Daffodil does not support information structuring. How information structuring support, as provided by Garnet could be integrated with Daffodil's strategy-centred interface is a matter worthy of further investigation.

Daffodil also allows users to order search result sets in unorthodox ways – e.g. by similarity to a single selected document. This provides some common ground with Garnet's 'scatter' and 'find similar' features. NaviQue's 'Similarity Engine' provides a feature that will highlight documents that are similar to a selected set of documents. Again, this bears some similarity to Garnet's 'scatter' facility. However, Garnet matches documents in external libraries, not only in its own workspace, and also will either bring similar documents to a selected group, or conversely scatter the individual documents in the selected group to other groups that they match. Garnet also includes a spatial parser that can identify visual groups automatically.

Garnet therefore provides a much stronger set of information structuring tools, and a richer set of similarity tools than found in existing visual interfaces to digital libraries. We wished to discover the benefits that users perceived in having the facilities of a spatial hypertext interface to a digital library, and their response to the related textual similarity tools we provided. The next section will discuss the user study that we undertook to explore these issues.

4 User Study

Garnet provides a novel interface for a digital library, providing facilities for both information structuring and traditional information seeking. Though earlier studies in physical environments noted the frequent interleaving of these activities, we are not aware of any similar study in an integrated digital environment. In our earlier paper on Garnet [3] we reported the findings of informal, formative evaluations.

We present a new, formal study that we undertook to identify salient issues in integrating Garnet's digital library and spatial hypertext elements. This was a qualitative study to elicit design considerations and identify problems for further investigation. We followed a pattern of similar probing studies established in our previous DL work, e.g. [4]. A panel of ten participants was recruited, each studying a degree in psychology or computer science at final year honours level or above. Our participants were frequent users of digital documents. As information structuring has only been closely studied in skilled information workers, we believed that participants with casual information seeking skills and needs would be less realistic. The participants also had no prior exposure to spatial hypertext systems, which permitted us to capture the initial expectations of how they could benefit from an information structuring tool.

Participants were initially screened in a pre-study questionnaire to capture their information seeking and structuring skills. Then, they were introduced to Garnet in a ten-minute tutorial, followed by an open-ended period of self-directed exploration. The main study was then undertaken, with the participant and their activity on the computer being recorded on videotape. At the conclusion of the main study, a post-experimental interview and questionnaire captured the participants' impressions, views and experiences. Where users were asked to express an opinion, scoring was on a seven-point Likert scale.

Each participant was given the same task for the main study – a simple information-seeking task (to find papers that would be good source material for a literature review on digital libraries). They were given a brief description of digital libraries and a list of related topics to assist the selection of their initial queries. After completing the initial digital library topic task, a further requirement for documents upon human-computer interaction as a theme in digital libraries was introduced, and participants asked to obtain specific information on that. They first used the "scatter" tool described above to support this task, before embarking upon an independent search for this material. For this task, participants used a digital library collection of over ten thousand computer science technical reports.

4.1 Results

Participants were asked to compare their experiences of working with Garnet with a number of familiar systems that support information structuring or information seeking. We also observed their pattern of work and their organisation of documents during the study. We will first report the effectiveness of Garnet as a DL interface, before moving on to the patterns that we observed in the participants' use of Garnet and concluding with an examination of the participants' response to the information structuring support of Garnet.

Accessing Digital Library Features

In [4] we reported some potential problems when digital library functions were provided within a spatial hypertext interface. Anticipated problems included difficulties such as metaphor dissonance and the effectiveness of the presentation of suggestions from the 'scatter' facility. Our first goal was to identify the actual degree of problems encountered in real use.

We started by evaluating particular features of a digital library. Participants reported that basic digital library tasks such as searching and reading documents were comparable in ease-of-use with the same features in a web-based digital library. No participant reported, or was observed, experiencing problems with these features. This strongly suggests that the spatial hypertext interface of Garnet does not impede access to digital library features.

Participants were also asked whether they had problems distinguishing parts of the system that they could manipulate – e.g. documents in their own workspace – with parts where they could not – e.g. in browsing structures of the library. Given the known problems of different modes of operation in human-computer interaction, we were concerned that this could prove a major problem. However, all participants denied having a problem with this. There are some contributory factors that may have influenced this. Firstly, all parts of the workspace which included a view upon a digital library component – e.g. a search result set or a browsing node – were very regular in appearance, containing a column of documents or other items, and had a different colour background. Compared with the more freeform organisation preferred by our participants, the contrasting regularity of system items in the workspace provided a subtle distinction to the users' own creation. The distinction between system-owned and user-owned items may also have been generally assisted by the fact that many operations could be achieved on both system- and user-owned objects of the same type, minimising the scope for unexpected behaviour.

Participants were also asked to rate the particular visual representation of documents, search lists and other items individually. All items were rated positively: however some useful and interesting ideas were suggested, as follows:

Firstly, six of the ten participants independently expressed their wish to be able to alter the title of documents. We had not allowed for this, as it is at odds with the nature of a digital library where documents are not normally editable. It is, however, very much within the nature of spatial hypertexts. Explanations included opaque titles of documents, and that titles often did not fit the immediate task of the user. This suggests that even for users who, like our subjects, have not been exposed to spatial hypertexts before, some spatial hypertext features that disrupt digital library expectations may be an important contribution of integration. Such a feature may, on the other hand, raise issues concerning copyright and authorship.

Secondly, five participants requested a more visual access to digital library features that were obtained from outside the workspace – e.g. the launch of new queries. Here, the preference could be explained both from the persistent appearance of such elements in web interfaces to digital libraries and the visual interactive style of spatial hypertext. In addition, two existing visual DL interfaces – DLITE [5] and SketchTrieve [10] – have used such a representation. For example, in DLITE each service of a library is represented by its own object in the workspace. Whether a 'toolbar' item – directly suggested by two users – or an object in the workspace – not actually suggested – is the appropriate design remains to be seen.

We also elicited the user response to our "scatter" facility, which matches the documents in a search result- or browsing- set against the workspace organised by the user. Seven participants rated the matches it found as "useful" or "very useful". Two of the dissenting three participants had used a large, miscellaneous list for most of their documents. Given the text-matching approach we used to implement "scatter", such heterogeneous groups would not result in any matches being found [21]. Our participants also approved of the search history provided by Garnet – corroborating the expectations of the designers of both SketchTrieve [10] and NaviQue [9].

To summarise, our participants found no difficulties using Garnet to access DL facilities. They were able to distinguish between system- and user- owned areas with apparent ease, quickly recognising the different behaviours of each. Our users identified areas for improvement, such as being more consistently focussed on the workspace presentation of tools, and permitting more editing of items than our digital library origins led us to anticipate. Our novel features, that exploit the user's own organisation of documents, were positively received, and we were able to corroborate the claims made by the designers of other visual DL systems.

Patterns of Behaviour

We were also interested in how users followed their information seeking and information structuring tasks throughout the study. This was captured through both the video recording and post-experimental interview.

A first point of interest is that subjects closely interleaved information seeking and information structuring. Once a user decided to keep a document, even provisionally, it was immediately moved onto the spatial hypertext workspace. Organisation of the document was performed at the same time. This simple pattern was observed in every participant.

A document on a new subject or of uncertain role would often be placed in a particular group in the workspace before being reorganised to another position later in the user's work. This behaviour mirrors the patterns of work previously observed in physical environments [11]. However, two participants (8 and 10) focused on a single miscellaneous column, minimising their organisation work within the task. In interview, one reported that they would organise their documents more precisely at the end of their detailed reading, and before doing any final searching. The other participant stated that they would probably not organise documents within a task, though they would organise documents between separate tasks.

When the remaining eight participants identified a theme in two or more documents, this would result in the creation of new group. However, the consequences did not stop there. In half of all cases, the creation of a new group would result in the user doing a new query to the digital library to attempt to obtain similar documents to add to that group.

Given these behaviours, the organisational activity of information structuring was certainly interlinked in a manner that resonates with previous information seeking and spatial hypertext research [7, 12, 15].

Information Structuring and Spatial Hypertext

In the pre- and post-experimental questionnaires, we screened the participants for their use of information structuring features in existing digital libraries and their rating of these features in comparison to those in Garnet. Though six participants regularly used digital libraries (monthly or weekly), none used any information structuring tools provided by them. For example, the ACM Digital Library (used by all six of these subjects) provides a means of organising documents into 'binders'. Only two participants had attempted to use this feature, and neither found it useful.

Participants were also probed as to their use of bookmarks (or favourites) in their web browser. Nine participants used the bookmark facility, but only three organised their bookmarks each month or more frequently. Nine participants rated Garnet as being superior to the bookmark facility – the exception being the one who did not use bookmarks. Our participants reported that the purely visual interface of Garnet was better suited to organising work than a browser's bookmarks – the latter often being invisible, and organisation is done separately to adding a new bookmark. E.g. User 2 said: "it is nice to have it all in one area". More comments on using Garnet's workspace appear later in this section. The only advantage of bookmarks that was reported was the advantage of being able to change the title used – see Section 4.1.1.

We asked the participants to compare the informal structuring tools that they used in the experiment with the formal, explicit organisation that they could perform in other environments – e.g. the folders in a filing system. Garnet contains support for both explicit and implicit structures, and we wished to elicit the perceived advantages of implicit structures. Seven users rated implicit structuring as being superior to explicit structures, and three rated it equally. Implicit structuring was noted as being particularly beneficial in the middle of searching for documents, and explicit structuring superior for long-term storage towards the end of a searching cycle.

Participants embraced the ability to organise documents on their workspaces. When asked what benefits they perceived in this, answers included: User 4, "I can see a document on the desktop without having to go back"; User 7, "being able to store stuff and organise them is good…this way you can have stuff that relates between a couple of areas". Seven participants specifically mentioned the advantages of having an overview of what they collected, and eight reported storing documents as being an important benefit over traditional Web-based DL interfaces.

Participants also commented positively on the tangible, drag-and-drop interaction of the interface: e.g. User 9, "I really like the ability to manipulate here and move them around and take them off"; User 6, "You just drop stuff where you want it".

Other advantages reported included supporting deciding which search to do next, remembering which searches had already been done and prioritising documents in perceived order of importance. All these are activities previously reported in physical environments, and claimed as potential advantages of spatial hypertext.

A DL/Spatial hypertext system similar to Garnet, is evaluated in [19]. However, the experiment uses a fixed set of documents and subjects do no queries or searches. In contrast, our study reveals the connection between seeking and structuring.

Discussion

Our study clearly suggests that spatial hypertext's information structuring facilities are supportive of traditional information seeking in a digital library. Participants' observed patterns of workflow matched the interleaved patterns observed in [7, 11, 12, 13, 16] and they reported the same patterns in post-experimental interviews.

Our participants also demonstrated known patterns in spatial hypertext, despite none having used any similar system before (the closest analogy was that two had used 'MindMap' software). This corroborates existing hypertext research and suggests that our subjects demonstrated typical rather than exceptional behaviour.

The visual, gestural interaction of spatial hypertext was particularly noted as an advantage by the participants, and suggested changes such as editing document titles and presentation of search facilities on the workspace are consistent with both spatial hypertexts and other visual DL interfaces like DLITE [5].

5 Conclusion

In evaluating Garnet, we have discovered that information structuring occurs in electronic as well as in physical environments. Given the evidence from observations such as Ellis and Kuhlthau, it is clear that users of digital libraries, as information seekers, benefit from information structuring during their searches. Support for information structuring in digital libraries is currently poor, and even for systems with traditional web-based interfaces there is a strong case for providing good information structuring support. However, the fluid organisation of documents seen in information structuring is, we feel, more readily supported by a drag-and-drop visual interface than a dialog-centred web one. The response of our participants to web-based tools for information structuring that they had used was notably negative.

Previous systems have used existing classifications or automatically generated ones [6, 20] to organise the results of searches. From our user study, we have obtained evidence that the topical structures implicitly created during information structuring may be a further kind of classification that can be used for this purpose.

Information structuring is, however, at odds with some expectations of libraries. For instance, the ability to re-title documents was regularly requested by our subjects. Support for information structuring in the digital library is clearly worthy of much more research.

Acknowledgements

This work was supported by: Middlesex University, London; University College, London; and University of Waikato, New Zealand.

References

1. Bainbridge, D., Buchanan, G., McPherson, J.R., Jones, S., Mahoui, A., Witten, I. H.: "Greenstone: A Platform for Distributed Digital Library Applications". Proceedings of the European Conference on Digital Libraries, Springer-Verlag, pp. 137-148, 2001.
2. Bederson, B. and Hollan, J. "Pad++: A zooming graphical interface for exploring alternate interface physics." In Proceedings of the ACM Symposium on User Interface Software and Technology (UIST '94, Marina del Rey, CA,) ACM Press, New York, 1994, pp. 17-26.
3. Buchanan, G., Blandford, A., Jones, M., Thimbleby, H.: "Spatial Hypertext as a Reader Tool in Digital Libraries", K. Börner, C. Chen (Eds.), Lecture Notes in Computer Science, Volume 2539, Springer-Verlag, ISSN: 0302-9743, pp. 13 – 24, 2002
4. Buchanan, G., Jones, M., Marsden, G.: "Exploring Small Screen Digital Library Access with the Greenstone Digital Library". Proceedings of the European Conference on Digital Libraries, Springer-Verlag: pp. 583-596, 2002.
5. Cousins, S.B., Paepcke, A., Winograd, T., Bier, E.A., Pier, K.A.: "The Digital Library Integrated Task Environment (DLITE)". Procs. ACM DL Conference, pp.142-151, 1997.
6. Cutting D., Karger D., Pedersen J., Tukey, J. W.: "Scatter/Gather: A Cluster-based Approach to Browsing Large Document Collections", Proceedings of the 15th Annual International ACM/SIGIR Conference, Copenhagen,. pp. 318-329, 1992.
7. Ellis, D., "Modelling the information seeking patterns of engineers and research scientists in an industrial environment", Journal of Documentation 53(4):pp.384-403, 1997.
8. Fuhr, N., Klas, C.P., Shaefer, A., Mutschke,: "Daffodil: An Integrated Desktop for Supporting High-Level Search Activities in Federated Digital Libraries", Proceedings of European Conference on Digital Libraries 2002, Springer, pp. 597-612, 2002.
9. Furnas, G. W., and Rauch, S.: "Considerations for information environments and the NaviQue workspace". Proceedings of the Third ACM Conference on Digital Libraries (DL '98), ACM Press, New York, pp. 79-88, 1998.
10. Hendry, D. G. and Harper, D. J.: "An informal information-seeking environment". Journal of the American Society for Information Science, 48(11), pp. 1036-1048, 1997.
11. Kidd, A.: "The Marks are on the Knowledge Worker", Proceedings of the ACM CHI Conference, Boston, MA, pp. 186-191, 1994.
12. Kuhlthau, C. C.: "Seeking Meaning: a process approach to library and information services" Ablex Publishing, Norwood, New Jersey, 1992.

13. Malone, T. W.: "How do People Organise their Desks? Implications for the Design of Office Information Systems", ACM Transactions on Information Systems, v. 1 (1), pp. 99-112, January 1983.
14. Marshall, C., Shipman, F. and Coombs, J.: "VIKI: Spatial Hypertext supporting emergent structure". Procs. of the ACM European Conference on Hypermedia Technology ACM Press, pp. 13-23, 1994.
15. Marshall, C. and Shipman, F.: "Spatial Hypertext and the practice of information triage". Proceedings of the Eighth ACM Conference on Hypertext, ACM Press, pp. 124-133, 1997.
16. O'Day, V and Jeffries, R.: "Orienteering in an Information Landscape: How Information Seekers Get From Here to There", Proceedings of INTERCHI, ACM, pp. 438-445, 1993.
17. Shipman, F., Marshall, C., and Moran T.: "Finding and Using Implicit Structure in Human-Organized Spatial Layouts of Information", Proceedings of Human Factors in Computing Systems (CHI '95), pp. 346-353, 1995.
18. Shipman, F.: "Seven Directions for Spatial Hypertext Research", First International Workshop on Spatial Hypertext, ACM Hypertext Conference 2001, Aarhus, Denmark, 2001. Online at: http://www.csdl.tamu.edu/~shipman/SpatialHypertext/SH1/shipman.pdf
19. Shipman, F., Hsieh, H., Moore, M.J., Zacchi, A. "Supporting Personal Collections across Digital Libraries in Spatial Hypertext", Procs. JCDL 2004, in press.
20. Witten, I., McNab, R., Boddie, S., Bainbridge, D.: "Greenstone: A Comprehensive Open-Source Digital Library Software System". Proceedings of the Fifth ACM Conference on Digital Libraries, ACM Press, pp.113-121, June 2000.
21. Zamir, O., Etzioni, O., Mandani, O. and Karp, R. M.: "Fast and Intuitive Clustering of Web Documents". Third International Conference on Knowledge Discovery and Data Mining, AAAI Press, Menlo Park, California. pp. 287-290, 1997.

Evaluating Strategic Support for Information Access in the DAFFODIL System*

Claus-Peter Klas, Norbert Fuhr, and André Schaefer

University of Duisburg-Essen
{klas,fuhr,schaefer}@uni-duisburg.de

Abstract. The digital library system DAFFODIL is targeted at strategic support of users during the information search process. For searching, exploring and managing digital library objects it provides user-customisable information seeking patterns over a federation of heterogeneous digital libraries. In this paper evaluation results with respect to retrieval effectiveness, efficiency and user satisfaction are presented. The analysis focuses on *strategic support* for the *scientific work-flow*. DAFFODIL supports the whole work-flow, from data source selection over information seeking to the representation, organisation and reuse of information. By embedding high level search functionality into the scientific work-flow, the user experiences better strategic system support due to a more systematic work process. These ideas have been implemented in DAFFODIL followed by a qualitative evaluation. The evaluation has been conducted with 28 participants, ranging from information seeking novices to experts. The results are promising, as they support the chosen model.

1 Introduction

The ongoing process of the acquisition of information is a major part of scientific work. A broad spectrum of tasks, like the preparation of seminars or the creation of scientific papers and writings is preceded by a time intensive literature search phase. Then the retrieved information has to be perceived by the user. Furthermore it needs to be organised and analysed before it can be reused.

Working with many different digital library interfaces has known problems. For example the user often experiences ongoing uncertainty whether the revealed information is complete and if it really covers the information need. This leads to increased uncertainty and doubt over time. The user may feel the ongoing need to discover and search through further digital libraries. As this leads to increasing time consumption, many users tend to switch to general purpose web retrieval engines, well knowing, that they may miss high quality information hidden in scientific databases.

The digital library system DAFFODIL is targeted at strategic support of users during the information search process, in order to overcome these problems.

---

* The project DAFFODIL is funded by the German Science Foundation (DFG) as part of the research program "Distributed Processing and Delivery of Digital Documents".

R. Heery and L. Lyon (Eds.): ECDL 2004, LNCS 3232, pp. 476–487, 2004.

For searching, exploring and managing digital library objects it provides user-customisable information search patterns and access to a federation of heterogeneous digital libraries.

The integration of syntactically and semantically heterogeneous information and functionality yields synergies and a much broader information access. This leads to more confidence and user *satisfaction*. Efficient and effective information access through *strategic support* places the user in a position to reduce the workload.

As pointed out e. g. by Bates [1], the realisation of *strategic support* is crucial for the acceptance of digital libraries. Steinerova [2] shows that users underestimate the *strategic aspect* in their information search. It turns out that this strategic aspect consumes much more time than users expect. Thus, information integration and seeking strategies are key issues for effective information searching. Furthermore, users initially overestimate quality and usefulness of the results in data sources. This leads to a recursive process where users try to discover new sources and redefine their problem or their information need.

In the following the evaluation of DAFFODIL regarding efficiency and effectiveness of the informational process will be presented. We will show that our model of strategic support improves the retrieval process and user satisfaction. For the evaluation questionnaires and video controlled usability tests were utilised.

2   Strategic Support in Daffodil

In this section we describe the virtual digital library (DL) DAFFODIL, along with the underlying concepts focused on *strategic support*.

2.1   The Idea of Strategic Support

Strategic support and *proactive support* have been proposed by Bates [1,3] as important concepts for usable information systems. The description of the concepts *scientific work-flow* and *personalisation* follow below. For a deeper discussion see [4–6].

Based on empirical studies on the information seeking behaviour of experienced library users, Bates distinguishes four levels of search activities. Where typical information systems only support low-level search functions (so-called moves), Bates distinguishes three additional levels of search functionality called tactics, stratagems and strategies.

The DAFFODIL architecture is structured according to these levels. Each service fulfils a function at a certain level and can invoke functions on its own or lower levels. On the *move* level, *wrapper services* connect to various DLs or services like thesauri or spell-checkers. The *tactic* level provides simple strategic actions by combining appropriate moves, e. g. a coauthor search performs a search for all publications of an author and extracts the coauthors. *Stratagems* provide domain specific depth-search-functionality by applying tactics to a set of similar items, like e. g. journals (browsing table of contents) or citation databases (following references in both directions). Finally *strategies* are chains of actions on the lower levels following a plan or goal. These are not yet automatically supported by DAFFODIL, as suggested by Bates. Instead the user is enabled to work much more strategy-oriented, by applying the high level functions of the *stratagems* and *tactics*.

To open the complex level of *strategies* for the user, we divided the information retrieval task into phases, called the *Digital Library Life Cycle* [7] (see also [8]). This whole work-flow, from data source selection over information seeking to the representation, organisation, analysis and reuse of information should be supported by a DL.

Additionally Bates defined five *levels of system support*, where we focus on the highest level called *proactive support*. Here the system should automate certain search services as much as possible if required. For this purpose, proactive services permanently observe the user and the system for the occurrence of specific situations (e. g. misspelled terms, empty query results, frequent occurrence of an author, a journal or a conference in a query result). In such a situation, the system offers appropriate tactics to further the search.

As a first step towards *personalisation*, a personal library has been integrated, which supports individuals as well as groups. Retrieved objects, like documents, authors, key terms, URLs, journals and conferences as well as query formulations can be stored persistently in a personal folder hierarchy. For any of these objects, alerting (awareness) can be activated; in this case, the user will be informed if the system has new information concerning this object (e. g. new publications by an author, a new issue of a journal, new references to a document, new answers to a query). For group folders, awareness will highlight objects which have been added, modified or annotated by other users.

2.2   Visualisation

DAFFODIL's high-level search activities, as outlined above, have been designed in close accordance with the *WOB* model [9]. WOB is a german acronym and stands for "strictly object oriented graphical user interfaces based on the tool metaphor".

On the desktop (see Figure 1) the user finds a set of tools, representing search or browsing access to the data-sources, or higher level functions, representing stratagems to exploit more complex domains. The goal of DAFFODIL's graphical user interface is to provide an extensible environment for retrieval, searching, and browsing tasks, as well as collation, organisation and re-usage of the retrieved information in a user-friendly way. This covers a wide range of functionality up to visualisation of complex structures, like coauthor networks. Furthermore, the tools are tightly integrated, e.g. by Drag&Drop mechanisms or links to external information sources. In [5] we discuss the user interface of DAFFODIL in depth. The desktop comprises the search-tool for searching in over ten computer science digital libraries in parallel, the personal library, a subject-specific thesaurus, a conference and journal browser, a classification browser (ACM CC) and two

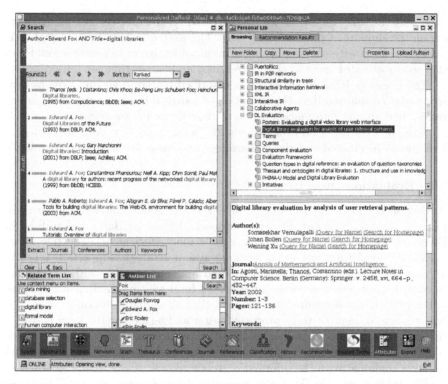

Fig. 1. Desktop: Search-Tool; Personal Library, Related Terms, Author-Name Completion.

tools to search for coauthors, one tree-based and one showing an animated view of the coauthor network graph. The proactive tools for spell checking, author name completion and related terms complete the tool set.

3   Evaluation

Based on a reliable (stable) DAFFODIL system, the main theme of this paper is the question, if strategic support will improve the information seeking process for the user. We decided to answer this question adequately through a three-phase evaluation. However, there is no general conceptual framework for the evaluation of digital libraries as a whole today, since the task is highly complex and difficult to handle.

In [10], three central questions for DL evaluation are discussed: *Why to evaluate?*, *What to evaluate?*, and *How to evaluate?*. The *context of evaluation* is characterised by the question *Why to evaluate?* and describes the overall goal of the DAFFODIL project in our case. It is essential to achieve high effectiveness and efficiency during the information retrieval process with federated data sources and to overcome the inadequate user-orientation and missing integration of different services. Saracevic and Covi distinguished thereby different levels for validating. In this evaluation, we concentrated on the user-centred view, focusing on the support of the *individual user*. The *user interface* itself (though it is strongly related with the user) is not a major objective in this evaluation. From the *system-oriented point of view* correctness and access-time are major issues.

The question *What to evaluate?*, is described by Saracevic and Covi as *constructs for evaluation*. Here the definition of a digital library range from preservation, persistence, information access to security and economics.

To answer the question *How to evaluate?*, a catalogue of *criteria* for each goal level has to be created and the *methodology* and *measures* have to be defined.

3.1   Evaluation Objectives

As described above, the overall goal of DAFFODIL is differentiated by the main focus on strategic support. Strategic support, defined by Bates and realised in DAFFODIL as higher search services, enable more efficient and effective information retrieval than any other system without strategic support. DAFFODIL is more efficient since users would need to invest more time without support through higher search services, in order to fulfil the information need. DAFFODIL's effectiveness results from the fact, that all available information is carefully visualised, in order to be processed faster and be interpreted more easily by the user. Through the tight integration of all services according to the strategic support, the retrieval task becomes easier. Consequently, the user is satisfied and becomes confident with the information retrieval task.

Proactive support in DAFFODIL raises the *level of system support*. The workload should be reduced while the cognitive task should not be disrupted; thus, we reach further efficiency and effectiveness gains.

3.2   Evaluation Objects

Following the constructs of evaluation, our major focus is on *information access*, especially search and browse in combination with the user-interface and higher search services, realised by a range of tools [5]. The search-tool and the personal library as central objects played an important role. Since DAFFODIL is not an information provider, criteria like preservation, persistence and economics are not under evaluation.

3.3   Evaluation Processing

This section describes how the evaluation has been accomplished, by clarifying methods, objectives and measures. The evaluation is processed in three phases and for each phase the setup is presented.

The criteria efficiency and effectiveness can be further classified. For efficiency we distinguish between real-time, how long the user needed for a task and the subjective time, the time the user felt finishing the task.

For effectiveness, we differentiate between relevance, quality and satisfaction, where relevance is based on the stored information objects in the personal library.

Quality is described by the graphical view and the content of an information object. User satisfaction is affected by relevance, quality, the subjective time and the level of trust in the DAFFODIL system.

The methodology for gathering the criteria uses two instruments, a *free search* based on some example tasks and a *questionnaire*. The free search was performed by search experts only (librarians and professors). This group could choose an arbitrary task of current interest, in order to evaluate the different DAFFODIL services. All other test persons, composed of computer science students and research staff, had to use the questionnaire.

To measure the criteria efficiency and effectiveness, different techniques are used:

Video recording. All test persons are video recorded during the questionnaire tasks and the free search. Two video streams are created, one view on the monitor, the other a side view of the user. We aimed at recording all statements, attitudes and gestures. The user's comments and attitudes indicate the user satisfaction. Finally, the video gives us the real time needed for each task – in contrast to the subjective user time.

Protocol. All test persons are also observed by the tester and a protocol of the session is created.

System logs. The test person's interaction with the user interface leaves a trail of individual events. All events are persistently stored in a database and therefore a complete reconstruction of the search path is possible. The system-time from the log can complement the video analysis.

Relevance. The manual relevance assessment is the last technique used. All information objects stored in the personal library are judged with regard to their relevance. Furthermore, the objects filed by different users can be compared.

For the documentation of the user satisfaction, we developed a questionnaire, where the tasks are comparable to information searches of daily scientific work. The tasks differ according to a complexity scale from one to four. Starting from complexity level one, the user also learns about DAFFODIL services and their handling along the way.

The complexity classification of tasks is based upon the "information need typology matrix" by Ingwersen [11], where he separated *work task* as one axis and the *information need* on the other.

In our case the knowledge of the user about the object or theme (work task) ranges from unknown to complete knowledge. The information need is characterised by the kind of searched objects which vary between a single object and a set of heterogeneous objects. We define levels of complexity based on these two dimensions. On the first level (full knowledge – one object) the user has complete knowledge about an object, also called *known-item instantiation*. On the second level (partial knowledge – one object) the complexity is rising, since the user has incomplete knowledge. At the third level (partial knowledge – heterogeneous objects), a set of objects is searched, which may also be heterogeneous in type; however, all objects are the result of a similar work task. Level number four (no

482 Claus-Peter Klas, Norbert Fuhr, and André Schaefer

knowledge – heterogeneous objects) presents the most complex task. Here the user has only a vague idea about the work task, and the need for orientation in the search domain is high. The more complex a situation or work task is, the higher are uncertainty and the knowledge gap.

The order of tasks on the questionnaire follow the described complexity classification, starting from the first level.

Task 1: Known Item. The test person gets the assignment to find a known article based upon a complete title. Since the title[1] is precise, Google will find it directly. This task is on complexity level one.

Task 2: Known Item. The test person gets again the assignment to find a known article based upon a complete title. But this time the title[2] is not precise, we have incomplete knowledge, so complexity level is two.

Task 3: All Articles. The task is to find all articles of "Norbert Fuhr" in the area of "digital libraries" of the last four years, so we have level three here.

Task 4: Author. The test person searches for the main research area of an author. The level of complexity is three.

Task 5: New Area. The most complex task (level four) is to let the test person find literature about a specific subject[3]. The subject was chosen such that no test persons had any knowledge about it.

The evaluation is performed in three phases. In all phases, test persons first were given an introduction (about half an hour) in order to present the functionality and usage of DAFFODIL, so all test persons were able to work on the given tasks.

In the first phase, we had 14 computer science students as test persons. Here we investigated two aspects of DAFFODIL with the questionnaire. The first aspect was to find critical (from the user's point of view) program or system errors. The second aspect was the comparison with another search engine. For reasons of comparable functionality and parameter control, only the search-tool and the personal library are available to the test persons in this phase. The phase is documented by protocols.

In phase two, eight computer science research assistants served as test persons. In this phase we still evaluated the baseline, along with the verification of the corrected system errors from phase one and the proactive services. The test persons could use all tools on the DAFFODIL desktop, also the proactive "related-terms" service. This phase is documented by protocols and video recordings.

The test persons on phase three were three librarians and three professors, seen as experts in information seeking. The test persons choose a free subject as work task, could apply all DAFFODIL tools and used also the WWW as additional service. The major evaluation focus is first on comments and critics, second to verify the results from phase one and two. Third, the experts should compare

---

[1] "Search strategies in content-based image retrieval".

[2] "Methods of Automated Reasoning".

[3] Subject described by terms: interactive information retrieval; information searching; information seeking.

the tools of DAFFODIL to their daily work tactics. This phase is documented by video recordings.

3.4   Expectations

In this section first the expectations according the tasks are specified and justified. After these the overall expectations on efficiency and effectiveness are presented.

Task 1: Known Item. The user should accomplish task one (search for a known document) in about the same time or faster as with any other search engine or digital library. It should be shown that DAFFODIL's more efficient searching is not only to its parallel searching in ten different digital libraries, but also caused by the fact that DAFFODIL allows for easier recognition of the relevant items. With this task, we establish a baseline, which can be used as a starting point for further evaluations. The following two tasks also refer to this baseline.

Task 2: Known Item. As in task one, a document should be found based on a title, in about the same time or faster as with any other search engine. This task differs from task one, since the title is ambiguous. It is expected that the user is irritated and becomes uncertain about the task and therefore needs more time.

Task 3: All Articles. Task three should be performed more efficiently with DAFFODIL than with any other digital library. This task is more complex, since a set of documents has to be retrieved. It is expected that the test person needs less time than with any other search engine or digital library. Another outcome could be that more relevant information is retrieved.

Task 4: Author. The test person should identify the scientific interest via scanning of the retrieved publications. In this case, a proactive service delivers a list of related terms, based on the query. It is expected that the proactive service speeds up completion time for this task.

Task 5: New Area. Starting an information search in an unknown area is the most complex task one can imagine. It is not expected that the test person finds a complete and relevant result-set, since the overall task can take days or weeks. We want to observe how the test person enters the new research area, what tactics are used and what comments are given during the search.

As described above, even without strategic support, DAFFODIL should be more efficient in information searching than other systems. We expect that the higher level search services and the user interface allow for easier and faster recognition of the relevant information. We hope that the user will be satisfied with the retrieval result, and that s/he gains confidence in DAFFODIL's ability to retrieve relevant information.

By combining both efficiency and effectiveness for the user, we want to verify that DAFFODIL is a user-oriented virtual digital library that integrates different services in a user-friendly way.

3.5   Results

The result presentation follows the order of the tasks, and then we combine the results. Timings are only given for phase two. All test persons used Google as search engine, and did not consider any single digital library. The overall session time ranged from 60 minutes up to 90 minutes, including the introduction.

Task 1: Known Item. The test persons found the requested document in 72 seconds on average, whereas with Google, they needed only 44 seconds. Table 2 lists all timings of phase two. Although the overall time for DAFFODIL is higher, the user effort is about the same: on average, DAFFODIL needs 30 seconds for the online search in 10 digital libraries, whereas Google needs less than one second on this task. So the recognition of the requested information seems to be the major time factor in this task.

Task 2: Known Item. The second task confirmed the results from task one. The test persons needed even less time with DAFFODIL (avg. 54 seconds), although the complexity is higher. In contrast, the test persons needed about three times longer with Google (avg. 113 seconds) to fulfil this task. Two subjects did not find the document at all. Overall, with Google the test persons needed more steps to reach the requested document and seemed uncertain and irritated.

Task 3: All Articles. For task three, the test persons found with DAFFODIL 12 to 19 relevant documents, based on very similar queries[4]; the average time was four minutes. With Google, the test persons tried to use the advanced search form for searching, but most of them had trouble entering the year selection. One test person used the "file-type" filter for restricting the search to PDF documents (83 documents). Another test person found the publication list (more than 50 documents in that period) of "Norbert Fuhr" on the WWW and gave this list as answer. All other test persons aborted working on the task with Google. Most of them said: "It takes too much time to find the relevant documents", and they showed signs of frustration. Our expectation on this task is more than fulfilled.

Task 4: Author. The test users completed this task in about three minutes, by scanning the documents in the result list. The proactive tool, which already gives an overview via related terms to the given query, was not used by any test person. This outcome was due to the fact that the tool was misplaced on the DAFFODIL desktop or hidden by other tools. Thus, our expectation was not fulfilled in this case. But when the supervisor asked the test persons about the tool, the answer found before was confirmed. The users started to trust the tool and looked at it more often in the following task.

Task 5: New Area. As the subject matter of this task was unknown to all test users, they had to start searching from scratch, by using the given terms. Since the complete task can take days or weeks, we expected that the test persons would find at least some relevant objects for the requested subjects.

---

[4] "Author=Norbert Fuhr AND YEAR=2000-2003 AND Title=DL" or "Author=Norbert Fuhr AND YEAR=2000-2003 AND Full-Text=DL".

Test person	t1 DAFF.	WWW	t3 DAFF.	WWW	t3 DAFF.	WWW	Relevant
U1	50	39	50	45	355	0	X
U2	90	30	40	150	145	155	LS Pub
U3	70	70	80	125	545	305	X
U4	60	20	40	100	110	185	X
U5	86	52	55	110	134	110	PDF
U6	90	55	58	110	303	190	X
U7	64	42	58	155	330	270	X
U8	77	42	50	150	90	100	X
Avg.	73	44	54	118	251	164	

Fig. 2. Timings (in seconds) for the different tasks and test persons in phase 2.

The subjects started an explorative search as tactic, in order to find an entry point, like an author name or better search terms. For that they scanned large result lists and the related terms. Most of the test persons found at least 2 to 3 relevant documents for a further search. When asked about functions, to view the result-list on a higher level, related to *Multi-Level-Hypertext* [12], [13], like ranked authors, journals or conferences, test persons gave positive feedback.

In the first evaluation phase, efficiency was only a minor issue, since several program errors caused a high delay during search operations. The errors that occurred in this phase were identified and resolved before phase two started. The other observations, e. g. the found documents or attitudes of the users, are mostly the same as in phase two. But even with the high response times, some of the students found interest on DAFFODIL and it was shown that, as the work task becomes more complex, the WWW or any other digital library could not perform as well as DAFFODIL.

Effectiveness. In order to evaluate effectiveness, we analysed the videos. The comments and attitudes towards quality of the tools as well as the satisfaction of the users show that the expectations are fulfilled.

The quality of the search-tool, the corresponding result list and the detail view are very positive. Some comments are:

- The query term highlighting helps me to find the relevant information in the result list and detail view.
- The structure of the result list is very clear.
- The duplicate elimination really saves time.
- The integration of details, along with abstract and full-text link, is the ideal case.

Also the personal library was well judged, mainly because different object types can be stored together (like documents, authors, terms, journals or web-links).

Overall, all test persons concentrated on the tasks and intuitively used the tools. They started to trust DAFFODIL and used it to verify the tasks done with the WWW search engine. All results found with DAFFODIL were relevant to the specific task.

Concluding, we observed a high user satisfaction, based on the results from the two evaluation phases with DAFFODIL.

Phase Three: Search Experts. In this phase, three computer science professors and three librarians served as test persons. We assumed that these test persons know and use a variety of search tactics in there daily work, and that they know several other digital library systems. Therefore, we expected that the experts can make profound comments.

The experts could use all tools of DAFFODIL and had the same introduction as all other test persons. The topics of the task were chosen individually by the test subjects and should reflect a current interest. During the evaluation (time ranged from 30 minutes up to two hours) all experts concentrated on the task and intuitively used the tools. The librarians were positively surprised by the rich functionality and that most tactics they know are available. Asked about missing services, two named the combination of result-lists, one missed categorisation by general keywords, associated with documents. Some positive comments made are, "DAFFODIL *is an expert-system, since it not only retrieves information, but also mediates the knowledge on the tactics to the user*", "DAFFODIL*'s functionality goes beyond today's systems*", or "DAFFODIL *is useful; I would use it additionally to my usual system*". The professors, more associated to science, searched for a current personal work task. They tested the tools, according to their background, starting from known items. Finding, what was expected, they started to trust the system. Comments made are, "*Very interesting; I will propose the system to my research assistants*", or "DAFFODIL *seems in a state, where it can be really used*".

4   Summary and Outlook

DAFFODIL focuses on strategic support for searching digital libraries. In this paper we presented a first evaluation of this system. Based on a guideline by Saracevic and Covi a scheme is used to structure the evaluation. The evaluation was performed in three phases with 28 participants, ranging from information seeking novices to experts (more than 11 hour video material). The foundation and models used in DAFFODIL yield a high efficiency and effectiveness in the information retrieval process. Regarding efficiency, only very simple tasks can be solved faster with other systems, whereas DAFFODIL clearly beats competing systems on more complex tasks. For effectiveness, we could show, that DAFFODIL's high quality visualisation and the integration of different services provide a useful toolbox and lead to a high user satisfaction.

Based on the current DAFFODIL system, we will go further and do research on more complex scientific questions. One example is the concept of personalisation, since DAFFODIL offers a rich user profile based on the personal library and the event log.

Since this is the first evaluation of DAFFODIL, further evaluations will follow focusing e. g. on pro-activity, support of complete strategies or different visualisations for specific tools.

Currently we are developing an online-form for a long-term evaluation, where all interested DAFFODIL users will take part. The focus is on user satisfaction based on longer information needs (like task five).

The current DAFFODIL system can be accessed from anywhere on the Internet via the URL http://www.daffodil.de.

References

1. Bates, M.J.: Where should the person stop and the information search interface start? Information Processing and Management **26** (1990) 575–591
2. Steinerova, J.: In search for patterns of user interaction for digital libraries. In: Research and Advanced Technology for Digital Libraries. 7th European Conference, ECDL 2003, Heidelberg et al., Springer (2003) 13–21
3. Bates, M.J.: Idea tactics. Journal of the American Society for Information Science **30** (1979) 280–289
4. Fuhr, N., Gövert, N., Klas, C.P.: An agent-based architecture for supporting high-level search activities in federated digital libraries. In: Proceedings 3rd International Conference of Asian Digital Library, Taejon, Korea, KAIST (2000) 247–254
5. Fuhr, N., Klas, C.P., Schaefer, A., Mutschke, P.: Daffodil: An integrated desktop for supporting high-level search activities in federated digital libraries. In: Research and Advanced Technology for Digital Libraries. 6th European Conference, ECDL 2002, Heidelberg et al., Springer (2002) 597–612
6. Gövert, N., Fuhr, N., Klas, C.P.: Daffodil: Distributed agents for user-friendly access of digital libraries. In Borbinha, J., Baker, T., eds.: Research and Advanced Technology for Digital Libraries: ECDL 2000. Volume 1923 of Lecture Notes in Computer Science., Heidelberg et al., Springer (2000) 352–355
7. Weibel, S., Miller, E.: A summary of the CNI/OCLC image metadata workshop. D-Lib Magazine **3** (1997)
8. Paepcke, A.: Digital libraries: Searching is not enough - what we learned on-site. D-Lib Magazine **2** (1996)
9. Krause, J.: Graphische oberflächen für das textretrieval im rahmen des WOB-modells. Skriptum, Universität Koblenz, Institut für Informatik (1997)
10. Saracevic, T., Covi, L.: Challenges for digital library evaluation. In: Proceedings of the American Society for Information Science. Volume 37. (2000) 341–350
11. Ingwerswen, P.: Users in context. Lectures on information retrieval (2001) 157–178
12. Agosti, M., Gradenigo, G., Marchetti, P.G.: Architecture and functions for a conceptual interface to very large online bibliograhic collections. In: Proceedings RIAO 91, Paris, France, Centre de Hautes Etudes Internationales d'Informatique Documentaire (CID) (1991) 2–24
13. Fuhr, N.: Information retrieval in digitalen bibliotheken. In: 21. DGI-Online-Tagung – Aufbruch ins Wissensmanagement., Frankfurt, DGI (1999)

Using Digital Library Techniques –
Registration of Scientific Primary Data

Jan Brase

L3S Research Center
Deutscher Pavillon, Expo Plaza 1
30539 Hannover, Germany

Abstract. Registration of scientific primary data, to make these data citable as a unique piece of work and not only a part of a publication, has always been an important issue. With the new digital library techniques, it is finally made possible. In the context of the project "Publication and Citation of Scientific Primary Data" founded by the German research foundation (DFG) the German national library of science and technology (TIB) has become the first registration agency worldwide for scientific primary data. The datasets receive unique DOIs and URNs as citable identifiers and all relevant metadata information is stored at the online library cataloque. Registration has started for the field of earth science, but will be widened for other subjects in 2005.

In this paper we will give you a quick overview about the project and the registration of primary data.

1   Introduction

In principle, scientists are prepared to provide data, but for the time being it is unusual to appreciate the necessary extra work for processing, context documentation and quality assurance. The classical mode of distributing scientific results is their publication in professional journals. These articles in journals are recorded in the "citation index". The index is used for a performance evaluation of scientists. Data publications have not been taken into account until now.

Project data is widely spread among research institutes and is collected and governed by scientists. Due to the lack of acknowledgement of this extra work, project data is often poorly documented, therefore badly accessible and not maintainable over long time periods. Large amounts of data are unused as they are only known and accessible to a small group of scientists.

Lately discussion about falsification in scientific results resulted in the introduction of new rules of good scientific practice in the German scientific institutions. The rules also include guidelines for data access. Primary data of a publication has to be stored and made accessible for at least 10 years to allow a verification of the results.

In existing scientific journals, there is no room for repeating data work, like use of existing methods to complete a data basis and by this making it usable for later scientific applications. Repeating data work is no original scientific effort but is necessary as support of science.

R. Heery and L. Lyon (Eds.): ECDL 2004, LNCS 3232, pp. 488–494, 2004.
© Springer-Verlag Berlin Heidelberg 2004

2   The Project "Publication and Citation of Scientific Primary Data"

2.1   Background

On an initiative from a coData (see [1]) working group, the German research foundation (see [2]) has started the project *Publication and Citation of Scientific Primary Data* as part of the program *Information-infrastructure of network-based scientific-cooperation and digital publication* in 2004. Starting with the field of earth science the *German national library of science and technology (TIB)* is established as a registration agency for scientific primary data. The data is still stored at the local research institutions, where the responsibility for valuating and maintaining of the data still lies.

2.2   Describing Primary Data

In addition to the local data preparation the research institutions transmit the URL where the data can be accessed to the *TIB*, together with a XML-file containing all relevant metadata. This metadata includes all information obligatory for the citing of electronic media (ISO 690-2):

- author
- title
- size
- edition
- language
- publisher
- publishing date
- publishing place

The TIB is saving this information about the primary data and awards the primary data with a *DOI* as unique identifier for registration (See section 3.1 for details). Any scientist working with this data is now able to cite the data in his work by its DOI. By this, scientific primary data is not exclusively understood as part of a scientific publication, but has its own identity. All information about the data is now accessible through the online library catalogue of the *TIB*. The data itself is accessible through resolving the *DOI* in any web browser.

2.3   Citing and Searching for Primary Data

If a scientist reads a publication where the registered data is used, he might be interested in analysing the data under different aspects. After gaining permission to do so by the research institution maintaining the data, he can cite the data in his own publications using its DOI, referring to the uniqueness and own identity of the original data.

If furthermore a scientist is interested in certain data, he can use the online library catalogue of the *TIB* to search for scientific primary data. A metadata search might result in a certain data set the scientist might want to use for his own publications. Resolving the DOI gives him access to the data, to find it sufficient or not. The metadata also reveals the copyright holders of the data. Gaining permission to use this data by the research institution maintaining the data, he can also cite the data in his own publications using its DOI.

3   Technical Aspects

3.1   Using Unique Identifiers

DOI. To register the data, the *TIB* awards it with a *DOI* as a unique identifier. *DOI (Digital Object Identifier)* is a system for persistent and actionable identification and interoperable exchange of intellectual property on digital networks, it is coordinated by the *International DOI foundation (IDF)* (see [3] for more details). The *TIB* has become a member of the *IDF* in 2003 and serves as the official Registration agency for scientific primary data. A DOI consists of two parts: a prefix and a suffix. For scientific primary data a DOI looks like this:

```
10.1594/WDCC/EH4_OPYC_SRES_A2
```

The structure is as follows:

10.1594 (Prefix) stands for the *TIB* as the registration agency who awarded this DOI.
WDCC stands for the respective research institution. In our example the *World Data Center for Climate (WDCC)*
EH4_OPYC_SRES_A2 is the internal name of the Data at the research institution.

This DOI can be resolved (and the data can be cited) in every web browser worldwide using the *Handle system* from the *Cooperation for National Research Initiatives (CNRI)*. The Handle system is a free java based comprehensive system for assigning, managing, and resolving persistent identifiers, known as "handles," for digital objects and other resources on the Internet (for more information see [4]). A Handle server is installed at the *IDF* homepage but also at the *TIB*, so every available DOI can by resolved via:

```
http://dx.doi.org/10.1594/WDCC/EH4_OPYC_SRES_A2
```

or

```
http://doi.tib-hannover.de:8000/10.1594/WDCC/EH4_OPYC_SRES_A2
```

There even is a browser plug-in available for the Internet Explorer via the Handle homepage [4] to identify DOI as a protocol and resolve DOIs by simple writing

```
doi:10.1594/WDCC/EH4_OPYC_SRES_A2
```

in the address bar.

URN. Another common identifier in the publication world is the *URN (Uniform resource name)*. We will not go into much detail about the differences between URN and DOI, we refer to [5] for this discussion. Although we have decided to use DOIs for our registration, every registered dataset is also awarded by a unique URN. The *TIB* has registered the URN namespace **URN:tib**. For best interoperability each awarded URN follows our DOI structure. For our example above the URN would look like:

```
URN:tib:10.1594/WDCC/EH4_OPYC_SRES_A2
```

To resolve this URNs the *TIB* has started a cooperation with the *German Library (DDB)* (see [6]) in Frankfurt. In the project *Epicur* (see [7]) the *DDB* has started to register online dissertations with unique URNs. The *DDB* will also register our URNs for scientific primary data and provide resolving of the URNs through the *DDB* infrastructure. There is however no metadata connected with this URNs.

3.2 Metadata Schema

The main reason we have decided to use DOIs for our registration is the possibility to create so called *DOI Application profiles (AP)*. APs, are abstractions used to group DOIs into sets in which all DOIs of the given set, or AP, share a metadata schema. We therefore designed a first set of metadata elements to describe our scientific primary data. Whenever possible, we have tried to use Dublin Core (DC) (see [8]) equivalent metadata elements.

Attribute	DC-mapping
1. DOI	none
2. identifier	*dc:identifier*
3. creator	*dc:creator*
4. publisher	*dc:publisher*
5. title	*dc:title*
6. language	*dc:language*
7. StructuralType (**digital**)	none
8. mode (**abstract**)	none
9. resourceType (**dataset**)	none
10. registrationAgency (**10.1594**)	none
11. issueDate	none
12. issueNumber	none
13. creationDate	*dcterms:created*
14. publicationDate	*dc:date*
15. description	*dc:description*
16. publicationPlace	none
17. size	*dcterms:extend*
18. format	*dc:format*
19. edition	none
20. relatedDOIs	*dc:source* (and others)

The elements *3,4,5,6,14,16,17,19* are obligatory for the citing of electronic media (ISO 690-2), the elements *7-12* give technical information and are required from the DOI metadata Kernel. Some of them have in our case default values, given in bold fonts. Element *11* is the date of the first registration of the metadata, element *12* allows a versioning if the metadata description for a given DOI changes. Element *13* is only required if there is a significant difference between the harvesting and the publication of the data. Element *20* is used to model relations between datasets that are versions of one another (e.g. temperature measuring at the same place over the years, when every year has its own dataset). This metadata set provides some basic information about the data, sufficient for citing, but not sufficient for comfortable metadata queries via the library catalogue. We are currently working on extending the set for this issues, based on initiatives like *Learning Objects Metadata (LOM)* by the *LTSC/IEEE* (see [9]) or the *CLRC Scientific Metadata Model* (see [10]).

3.3 Primary Data in the Online Library Catalogue

As mentioned before, every dataset is available via the online library catalogue of the *TIB*. The entry is displayed with all relevant metadata and the DOI as a link to access the dataset itself (see Fig. 1).

4 Conclusion and Further Work

Registration of scientific primary data has always been an important issue. With the new digital library techniques, it is finally made possible.

In cooperation with

- World Data Center for Climate (WDCC) (see [11])
- Geoforschungszentrum Potsdam (GFZ) (see [12])
- Alfred Wegener Institute (Marum/AWI) (see [13])
- Deutsches Klima Rechenzentrum (DKRZ) (see [14])
- Max Plank Institute for Meteorology (MPIM) (see [15])

The *German national library of science and technology (TIB)* now is the world's first registration agency for primary data in the field of earth sciences.

We expect an amount of approximately 150,000 datasets to be registered by the *TIB* until the end of this year. The registration of primary data will be widened to other science fields in 2005. The possibility of citing primary data as a unique piece of work and not only a part of a publication opens new frontiers to the publication of scientific work itself and to the work of the *TIB*. For a medium amount of time, the availability of high-class data respectively content can be assured and may therefore significantly contribute to the success of "eScience".

Acknowledgements

We gratefully acknowledge important input and discussion from all partners in this project, especially from Mrs. Irina Sens from the *TIB*.

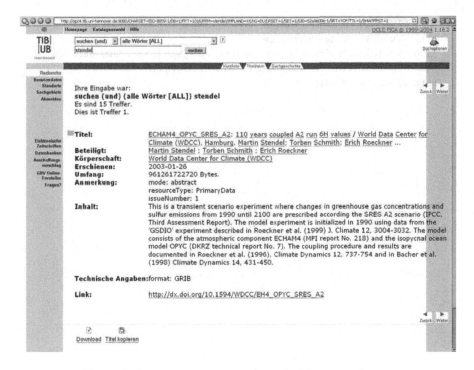

Fig. 1. A dataset as a query result in the library catalogue.

References

1. Committee on Data for Science and Technology http://www.codata.org
2. Deutsche Forschungsgemeinschaft (German research foundation) homepage http://www.dfg.de
3. *International DOI foundation website* http://www.doi.org
4. *The Handle System homepage* http://www.handle.net
5. C. Plott, R. Ball *Mit Sicherheit zum Dokument - Die Identifizierung von Online-Publikationen* in B.I.T. journal **1** (2004) 11–20
6. Die Deutsche Bibliothek (German library) homepage http://www.ddb.de
7. *Project "Enhancement of Persistent Identifier Services - Comprehensive Method for unequivocal Resource Identification" homepage* http://www.persistent-identifier.de/
8. *The Dublin Core Metadata Initiative* http://dublincore.org/
9. Learning Technology Standards Comittee of the IEEE: *Draft Standard for Learning Objects Metadata IEEE P1484.12.1/D6.4*12. June 2002). http://ltsc.ieee.org/doc/wg12/LOM_1484_12_1_v1_Final_Draft.pdf/
10. Council for the Central Laboratory of the Research Councils *CLRC Scientific Metadata Model* http://www-dienst.rl.ac.uk/library/2002/tr/dltr-2002001.pdf
11. World data center climate (WDCC) homepage http://www.mad.zmaw.de/wdcc/
12. Geoforschungszentrum Potsdam (GFZ) homepage http://www.gfz-potsdam.de

13. Alfred Wegener Institute (Marum/AWI) homepage
    `http://www.awi-bremerhaven.de`
14. Deutsches Klima Rechenzentrum (DKRZ) homepage `http://www.dkrz.de`
15. Max Plank Institute for Meteorology (MPIM) homepage
    `http://www.mpimet.mpg.de/`

Towards Topic Driven Access
to Full Text Documents

Caterina Caracciolo, Willem van Hage, and Maarten de Rijke

Informatics Institute, University of Amsterdam
Kruislaan 403, 1098 SJ Amsterdam, The Netherlands
{caterina,wrvhage,mdr}@science.uva.nl

Abstract. We address the issue of providing topic driven access to full text documents. The methodology we propose is a combination of topic segmentation and information retrieval techniques. By segmenting the text into topic driven segments, we obtain small and coherent documents that can be used in two ways: as a basis for automatically generating hypertext links, and as a visualization aid for the reader who is presented with a small set of focused and restricted text snippets. In the presence of a concept hierarchy, or ontology, information retrieval techniques can be used to connect the segments obtained to concepts in the ontology. In this paper we concentrate on the text segmentation phase: we describe our approach to segmentation, discuss issues related to evaluation, and report on preliminary results.

1 Introduction

The full text documents accessible in a digital library can be rather long, potentially with a loose structure or no structure at all. In such a context, a search system that would provide the user with a document relevant to a given information need, and then leave it up to the user to navigate within the document through a combination of "control F" and scrolling, would be very unsatisfactory. We address the issue of providing focused access to full text (scientific) documents in a digital environment, so as to enhance readability and minimize the browsing and scrolling effort. Specifically, we work in the setting of a collection of an electronic handbook consisting of "authoritative" (and usually lengthy) survey chapters. To provide access to the collection, a concept hierarchy (or "ontology") has been developed, consisting of concepts, and lexical relations (e.g., parent-child) and navigational relations (e.g., "see also") between those concepts. The concept hierarchy serves as a map of the handbook's domain, and, after browsing around the map, users jump from a concept to highly relevant text snippets, not complete chapters, in our collection.

We propose to use topic segmentation techniques as a way to subdivide documents into smaller documents (sub-documents), that are homogeneous in topic. Used as link *targets*, these sub-documents should provide readers with a highly relevant document whose coverage of a given topic is as exact as possible: shrinking the subdocument would cause relevant information to be left, and expand-

R. Heery and L. Lyon (Eds.): ECDL 2004, LNCS 3232, pp. 495–500, 2004.

ing the subdocument would bring in too much non-relevant information. As the *sources* of the links we use the concepts in our concept hierarchy.

In this paper we focus on the task of topic segmentation: in Section 2 we discuss previous work on topic segmentation and present our own approach; in Section 3 we discuss the issue of evaluation for this task and present current results. In Section 4 we draw preliminary conclusions and discuss future work.

2 Topic Segmentation

Previous work on text segmentation has focused on improving retrieval [7], and on topic tracking of broadcast speech data [10]. Text segmentation algorithms are often based on an underlying theory of discourse, or discourse structure. This theory can hypothesize that the text is linear [9] or hierarchical [14]. Skorochod'ko's seminal work [12] has influenced many approaches to topic segmentation; according to Skorochod'ko's topologies, the overlap of words in sentences is an indicator of the semantic structure of the text. One of the methods influenced by Skorochod'ko's works is Hearst's TextTiling algorithm [7], which we take as the basis for our own work. TextTiling performs a linear segmentation by using patterns of lexical connectivity (i.e., repetition of words through the text). The algorithm first compares adjacent *blocks* of text (real paragraphs are not considered because of their variability in length) and assigns them a similarity value. The resulting sequence of similarity values is smoothed. Then the smoothed values are examined and each gap is given a score computed by averaging the difference between the smoothed similarity value at the gap and the peak to the left and to the right. Segment brakes are placed at a gap whose score is lower than a certain threshold. Then, for the sake of the reader, the segment break is rounded to the end of the next paragraph.

The tunable parameters in the algorithm are the size of the blocks, in "sentence", used for comparison, and the number of words forming a sentence. Hearst found that for newspaper corpora a block of 6 sentences, each consisting of 20 words, is optimal. Similarity among two blocks is computed with a cosine similarity. Note that the actual value of similarity is not used for computing a breaks: the algorithm only looks at relative differences.

In this paper we also consider C99, an algorithm for linear topic segmentation described in [5, 6]. It differs from TextTiling in that it takes real sentences as the basic unit and uses a combination of similarity (computed among sentences) and clustering. After a phase of standard preprocessing steps (stop-words removal, stemming), the algorithm computes a matrix of similarity in a sentence by sentence manner, where the adopted similarity measure is the usual cosine similarity. Then, a ranking scheme is applied to the similarity matrix, in order to make more visible the differences in similarity among the sentences. Finally, a hierarchical divisive clustering is applied.

We applied C99[1] to (real) paragraphs, so as to prevent the algorithm from splitting paragraphs, and to be able to compare results with TextTiling. Finally,

---

[1] We used the implementation of C99 and TextTiling made available by Choi at http://www.cs.man.ac.uk/~mary/choif/software.html.

we did not specify a number of expected segments (as is standard practice when applying divisive clustering), but used the defaults described in [5, 6].

Creation of a manually segmented corpus. The experiments on which we report below take place in the setting of a digital library project. Specifically, the *Logic and Language Links* (LoLaLi) project [3] explores methods to extend the traditional form of scientific handbooks with electronic tools. These tools should help the reader explore the content of the handbook and make it easier to locate relevant information. As a case study the project focuses on the *Handbook of Logic and Language* [13] (20 chapters, 1200 pages), and uses a WordNet-like concept hierarchy to provide access to (an electronic version of) the handbook [1]. For the work on which we report in this paper, we use the LaTeX sources of the book as our corpus, which amounted to about 4.5MB of text.

To develop a gold standard to be used for assessing our segments, we selected two chapters from the collection of 20, and annotated the topic segmentation manually. The two chapters were chosen on the basis of the coverage in the LoLaLi concept hierarchy [4, 3] and of the differences in style. Two annotators annotated the text independently, then discussed critical cases to agree on a unique annotation. The annotators were given indications about minimal and maximal size of a segment (respectively a paragraph, and the entire section). No other references to the layout structure of the text were made.

One of the two chapters had a rather formal style, with many tables, figures and formulas, either in-line or as separate objects: here the difficulty was in the treatment of those objects. The second chapter was written in a more narrative style, with fewer tables and pictures: here the annotators had difficulties with the rhetorical style of writing, as almost all paragraphs referred to previous ones.

The annotators agreed on a large number of breaks, that we therefore consider more fundamental or evident than others. We found that within these breaks one of the two annotators would mark additional breaks, while the other would mark fewer breaks, displaying typical "splitter" and "lumper" behavior, respectively [8]. While this is hard to quantify, the resulting gold standard is more of a splitter than a lumper.

3   Evaluation Issues

The evaluation of a topic segmentation system can be either task independent or task dependent. If task independent, the evaluation is done by comparing the result of the system against an annotated corpus, a 'gold standard,' while a task dependent evaluation would look at how the segmentation improves other computational tasks. Here, we concentrate on a task independent evaluation, performed on the basis of our manually annotated corpus. The most commonly used measures are precision and recall, applied to topic breaks or entire segments. Precision (P) gives the proportion of hypothesized topic breaks (segments) that are correct, recall (R) gives the proportion of correct topic breaks (segments) that are hypothesized. The two measure are often combined by using the F-measure, which can be tuned so as to weigth precision and recall equally, or to privilege one of the two over the other. In Table 1 we report F values when P and R are equally treated, and when precision is twice as important as recall.

When applied to paragraph breaks, precision and recall can be interpreted as measuring how good the system is at recognizing topic shifts; when applied to entire segments, as measuring how good the system is at recognizing homogeneity in topic. Although crude measures (they do not give a measure of how distant the hypothesized segment break is from the real break), precision and recall are well understood measures. Reynar [11] suggests judging a boundary correct if it appeared within a fixed-sized window of words of an actual boundary. The disadvantage of this measure is that it does not distinguish between correct and incorrect boundaries within the window. Beeferman et al. [2] introduce the P_k precision measure, giving the probability that a randomly chosen pair of units (i.e., paragraphs or sentences) are classified accordingly in the gold standard and by the system being evaluated. The disadvantage is that P_k depends on the length of the document, in the sense that in case of non-trivial segmentation, it is likely that two distant units are not hypothesized as belonging to the same segments – i.e., provided that the whole document is not a single segment. For these reasons, we decided not to use the P_k measure. Finally, we remark that none of these measures say anything about how "reader-friendly" is the segmentation.

In our experiments, we compared three segmentation methods: a naive baseline that simply takes every paragraph break to be a segment break, TextTiling, and C99. The algorithms were applied to two chapters from the *Handbook of Logic and Language*, simply called A and B below, for which a gold standard was developed in the manner described previously. Chapter A consists of 13 sections (no subsections), organized into 179 paragraphs spanning 35 pages in the printed version[2]. It contains many tables, examples, explicit definitions and theorems, and many in-line formulas. The manual annotation results in 102 segments, on average 1.6 paragraphs long. Chapter B consists of 3 sections organized into respectively 0, 4 and 5 sub sections, spanning 54 pages in the printed version; the text is distributed into 221 paragraphs. Chapter B does not contain examples and theorems distinguished as such, nor tables and only a few figures, but it does contain many in-line formulas and lists of formulas (axioms or properties). Paragraphs in Chapter B can be quite long, up to the entire length of a subsection (ca. 300 words), on average ca. 80 words long. The annotation distinguishes 90 segments, on average ca. 2.5 paragraphs long.

The results of the evaluation are listed in Table 1. Let us briefly discuss them, starting with Chapter A. The recall value for the baseline is obviously the highest, since by placing a segment break at each paragraph breaks all breaks will be found. Precision is also high (more than 50% of the hypothesized breaks are correct), because there are almost twice as many paragraphs as segments in the manual annotation. For the same reason, TextTiling achieves a high recall (it hypothesizes 134 segments), while precision is not substantially different from the baseline. C99 returns only 15 segments, therefore recall is very low, but about half of the hypothesized breaks agree with the gold standard. For

---

[2] Bibliographic items are never considered.

Table 1. Evaluation results.

	Baseline	TextTiling	C99
chapter A	$P = .614, R = 1$	$P = .602, R = .803$	$P = .571, R = .078$
	$F_{P=R} = .760$	$F_{P=R} = .683$	$F_{P=R} = .137$
	$F_{P=2R} = .665$	$F_{P=2R} = .630$	$F_{P=2R} = .253$
chapter B	$P = .408, R = 1$	$P = .344, R = .681$	$P = .565, R = .142$
	$F_{P=R} = .579$	$F_{P=R} = .445$	$F_{P=2R} = .228$
	$F_{P=2R} = .462$	$F_{P=2R} = .370$	$F_{P=2R} = .167$

Chapter B, noticeably different scores are obtained, across the board. Again the baseline shows a total recall, but a lower precision than in the case of Chapter A. TextTiling scores worse than in the case of Chapter B, because it returns 168 segments, against the 90 distinguished by the annotators, and over a total of 221 paragraphs. C99 returns 23 segments, and recall score has doubled, while precision is stable.

4   Conclusions and Future Work

We reported on work in progress on the application of text segmentation techniques in a digital library environment. The overall aim of our work is to apply these techniques for the automatic generation of hypertext links to full text documents. In particular, we are interested in the application of these techniques for generating links from ontologies to corpora of full text documents. The work presented here concentrated on a task independent evaluation of the topic segmentation phase: we applied two well-known algorithms to a domain specific corpus, and evaluated the results against a previously manually annotated segmentation. As a baseline we used the system the identifies a segment break at each paragraph break. Our finding is that the baseline performs well when evaluated in terms of precision and recall, though more investigation should be done to assess such a segmentation in a more reader-oriented evaluation. In case of highly structured documents (Chapter A), TextTiling gives the best balance between precision and recall; however, scores degrade when the text has a more narrative style (Chapter B). C99 turns out to be the worse algorithm to use for such a task, mainly because it returns to few segments, too long.

Future work includes an analysis of the results that take into account the agreement of the human assessors, and the evaluation of the text segmentation algorithms within a larger task, viz. link generation. We plan to use the documents resulting from the topic segmentation as sub-documents to be retrieved by an IR system, where the concepts in the LoLaLi ontology [1] will serve as queries. Within this setting we also plan to compare the structure provided by our topic segmentation system with the layout structure of the underlying LaTeX documents.

Acknowledgements

We thank Joost Kircz and David Ahn for interesting discussions. Caterina Caracciolo was supported by Elsevier Science Publishers. Maarten de Rijke was supported by grants from the Netherlands Organization for Scientific Research (NWO) under project numbers 220- 80-001, 365-20-005, 612.069.006, 612.000.106, 612.000.207 and 612.066.302.

References

1. Logic and language links project. http://lolali.net.
2. Doug Beeferman, Adam Berger, and John D. Lafferty. Statistical models for text segmentation. *Machine Learning*, 34(1-3):177–210, 1999.
3. Caterina Caracciolo. Towards modular access to electronic handbooks. *JODI - Journal of Digital Information*, 3(4), 2003. http://jodi.ecs.soton.ac.uk/Articles/v03/i04/Caracciolo/.
4. Caterina Caracciolo and Maarten de Rijke. Structured access to scientific information. In *Proceeding of First Global WordNet Conference*, 2002.
5. Freddy Choi. Advances in independent linear text segmentation. In *Proc. of the 1st Meeting of the North American Chapter of the Association for Computational Linguistics (ANLP-NAACL-00)*, pages 26–33, 2000.
6. Freddy Choi. Linear text segmentation: approaches, advances and applications. In *Proc. of CLUK3*, 2000.
7. Marti A. Hearst. *Context and Structure in Automated Full-text Information Access*. PhD thesis, 1994.
8. Judith L. Klavans, Kathleen McKeown, Min-Yen Kan, and S. Lee. Resources for the evaluation of summarization techniques. In *Proceedings of the 1st International Conference on Language Resources and Evaluation, Grenada, Spain*, May 1998.
9. Judith L. Klavans Min-Yen Kan and Kathleen R. McKeown. Linear segmentation and segment relevence. In *Proceedings of 6th International Workshop of Very Large Corpora (WVLC-6)*, pages 197–205, 1998.
10. Jay M. Ponte and W. Bruce Croft. Text segmentation by topic. In *European Conference on Digital Libraries*, pages 113–125, 1997.
11. Jeffrey C. Reynar. *Topic Segmentation: Algorithms and Applications*. PhD thesis, University of Pennsylvania, 1998.
12. E. Skorochod'ko. Adaptive method of automatic abstracting and indexing. *Information processing*, 71:1179–1182, 1092.
13. Johan van Benthem and Alice ter Meulen, editors. *Handbook of Logic and Language*. Elsevier, 1997.
14. Y. Yaari. Segmentation of expository text by hierarchical agglomerative clustering. In *Proceeding of the Conference on Recent Advances in Natural Language Processing*, pages 59–65, 1997.

Bibliographic Component Extraction Using Support Vector Machines and Hidden Markov Models

Takashi Okada[1,*], Atsuhiro Takasu[2], and Jun Adachi[2]

[1] The University of Tokyo, Information Science and Technology,
Information and Communication Engineering, 7-3-1 Bunkyo-ku Tokyo, Japan
takashi@nii.ac.jp
[2] National Institute of Informatics, 2-1-2, Hitotsubashi, Chiyoda-ku, Tokyo, Japan
{takasu,adachi}@nii.ac.jp

Abstract. Article citations are composed of subfields such as 'author', 'title', 'journal', and 'year'. It is useful to automatically identify attributes of these subfields, since they are used for linking a citation with the actual cited article. In this article, we employ a Support Vector Machine (SVM), a method of machine learning, to automatically identify subfields. We then employ a Hidden Markov Model (HMM) to improve the identification accuracy. Information from the subfields identified by the SVM, and syntactic information analyzed by the HMM, are integrated to make an accurate identification.

1 Introduction

Citation analysis of articles in scholarly journals is a very effective method for the evaluation of journals, and citation-based links between journal articles are helpful for users of electronic journals.

Several hurdles must be overcome in order to link citations to articles across these various resources. Current citation linkage methods concentrate on articles in English. However, links between articles written in various languages would allow users to access articles across several languages. In order to realize this, a linkage method is needed that is robust to the language of the paper.

Citations are represented in various ways, depending on the source of the article. In order to handle citations from various sources, the linkage method should be customizable. Citation linkage usually uses rules, so rule-learning ability is important.

Many researchers have tackled the problem of linking citations [1]. Citeseer [2] realized citation linkage for articles on websites, which enables to provide functions such as 'most cited documents' and 'most cited authors', in addition to other functions such as autonomous citation indexing. Itoh and his colleagues proposed a citation linkage method and applied it to citations obtained via OCR [3].

---

[*] He is currently working for NTT DATA CORPORATION, Kayabacho Tower Bldg., 21-2, Shinkawa 1-chome, Chuo-ku, Tokyo 104-0033, Japan, e-mail: okadatk@nttdata.co.jp

R. Heery and L. Lyon (Eds.): ECDL 2004, LNCS 3232, pp. 501–512, 2004.

We have developed a page layout analysis method that extracted reference strings from scanned article images based on the layout of page images [4]. We have also studied an effective method for matching citations with records in large bibliographic databases [5]. In this study, we propose an indexing method for efficient matching. And we have previously studied a bibliographic component extraction method based on approximate string matching [6], where bibliographic components such as titles and names of author(s) are extracted from citations.

In this paper, we propose a new method for extracting bibliographic components and labeling the parts of citations by using machine learning methods. The proposed method improves upon our previous method by using two types of information: term frequency, and syntactic information.

2 Problem Definition

Citation matching is the most important requirement for citation linkage. Since citations are usually represented as a string, approximate string matching is the basic technique used for citation linkage. Several types of approximate string matching methods are proposed, based on N-gram similarity and edit distance. In most approximate string matching methods, users must define the similarity function for the problem. Recent studies enable similarity functions to be determined from training data [7][8][6]. Accordingly, the cost of constructing similarity functions for approximate matching is reduced, and the approach can then be applied to citations from various sources.

Citations are usually composed of subfields, such as 'author' and 'title'. There are two options when defining similarity functions. The first is to apply approximate matching to the citation string. The second is to apply it to each subfield with a different similarity function, and then to combine the similarities across subfields. The latter approach can achieve higher matching accuracy; however, subfields must be extracted from the citation. In this paper, we propose a subfield extraction method where the citation is decomposed into subfields, and each segment is labeled with a type such as 'author' or 'title'. For example, suppose the following citation is given:

T. Okada, "Identification of citation data," Masters Thesis, Univ. of Tokyo, 2004.
The problem is to generate the following labeled data:

<Author>T. Okada</Author>
<Title>Identification of citation data</Title>
<Other>Masters Thesis</Other>
<Other>Univ. of Tokyo</Other>
<Year>2004</Year>.

After subfield extraction, citation matching is reduced to a problem similar to that of duplicate record detection in bibliographic databases, which has been studied in the fields of library and information sciences. In this detection problem, the author, title, or other subfields are used to calculate a similarity function. For example, Ayres proposed a method to detect a duplicate record using a code based on a substring that appears in a subfield (such as 'author' or 'title') [9].

Two types of information are available for labeling subfields. For example, term frequency can be used if a subfield contains numerical data such as 2004; the subfield is most likely a year or page number. Syntactic structure can also be used, because subfields in the citation are usually placed in a fixed order. For example, authors are usually located at the head of a citation, and the title follows the authors.

We can apply text categorization techniques to extract subfields. Recently, several types of classification methods have been applied to text categorization [1], and SVMs [3] perform very well. SVMs are binary classifiers, that is, an SVM can determine whether an object does or does not belong to a class. In the subfield extraction problem, we must also solve the multi-class classification problem, because each subfield must be classified into one of the bibliographic categories. Recently, some researchers have extended SVMs to handle multi-class classifications, such as 1-vs-rest, 1-vs-1, and DAG-SVM [10].

For syntactic information, we may apply grammatical approaches such as finite automata and context-free grammars. For the citation, regular grammars and finite automata have sufficient expressive power for the syntactic structure. When applying these techniques to subfield extraction, the key component is the rule-learning algorithm. A Hidden Markov Model (HMM) is an automaton that has both probabilistic state transitions and symbol outputs [11]. This model is effective when modeling the hidden structure behind a language phenomenon, based on observed language data, so the HMM is often adopted as a word segmenting model, an acoustic model for voice recognition, or as a probabilistic language model for tagging English parts of speech. Efficient learning algorithms for HMM also exist.

In this paper, we combine several SVMs with an HMM for handling both term frequency and syntactic information within the citation. The resulting method reflects the high performance and learning algorithm of these approaches, so it meets the above conditions for citation matching.

3   Citation Parser Using SVMs and the HMM

3.1   Overview of the Proposed Method

The purpose of this method is to decompose a citation into subfields, and associate each subfield with labels such as the author or title. Figure 1 shows the flow of this method. A citation, which is a normal sentence, is decomposed into subfields based on predefined delimiters, and a feature vector is then constructed using words appearing in the subfield. An SVM is applied to the feature vector to calculate the likelihood of the subfield for each bibliographic component. Finally, the HMM is applied to the subfield sequence and a tagged citation is generated. We describe each step in the following subsections.

3.2   Citation Segmentation

Citations are segmented into subfields using delimiters. We use the following rules for segmentation.

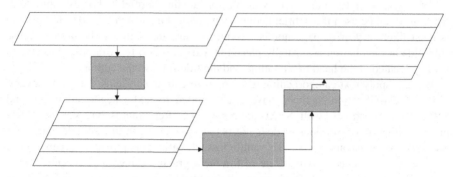

Fig. 1. Data flow of the method

1. Decompose the citation by ',' delimiters.
2. Decompose the citation before the terms 'vol.', 'no.', 'pp.' and 'ed.'.
3. Extract a substring surrounded by double-quotation marks as a subfield.
4. Decompose citations before prepositions.
5. Extract substrings that contain a digit as a subfield.
6. Decompose citations by symbols such as parentheses or colons.

This method sometimes causes over-segmentation. During the final step of the algorithm, subfields decomposed into more than two parts are merged.

3.3   Feature Vector Construction

In order to apply classification, subfields are represented with feature vectors. We use the vector space model for information retrieval, where words appearing in citations are used as a feature. The feature value for a word is calculated based on the frequency of the word in the subfield.

In order to construct a feature vector, we enumerate all words that appear in the learning dataset in advance, and then create a table of the words with their ID (called the *feature number*). Accordingly, the number of dimensions of the feature vector is equal to the number of words existing in the table. Some languages such as Japanese have no word boundaries, and in this case we first apply a lexical analyzer to the citation to extract words from the citation, and then apply the same procedure to construct the word table.

Usually the size of the training data is limited, and some words do not appear in the training data. In order to handle this problem, three heuristic procedures are applied in the feature vector construction. The first is a 'word pattern', where words that match a pattern are regarded as the same feature. The second improves the segmentation of words, while the last deletes symbolic characters. The following will explain these three methods in detail.

3.3.1   The Integration of Features. Let us consider digits such as 1, 5 and 9. They usually represent the volume number, or the number or year of a journal or a conference. In bibliographic component classification, it is meaningless to handle this number as is, and we must therefore consider patterns. For example, a four-digit number is likely to represent a year, whereas one- or two-digit numbers are likely to represent a volume or issue number. Therefore, we introduce patterns as features for numbers, and any word that matches the pattern is regarded as the same feature. Suppose "1997" appears in the learning dataset. Using this pattern, "1992" is regarded as the same feature as "1997" even if "1992" does not appear in the training data.

3.3.2 The Improvement of Word Segmentation.
Sometimes characters other than a space are used as a word separator in citations, when they are not used as separators in other contexts. For example, let us consider two words connected by a hyphen. The hyphen is used for representing compound terms in some cases, and it is used for hyphenating words in other cases. In order to deal with this, we extract two types of features. First, we extract the entire term, and then add words that are obtained by regarding the character as a separator within the term. For example, we extract three feature words, "multi-task", "multi", and "task", from the term "multi-task". This method is also applied to words separated by a slash or colon.

3.3.3 The Deletion of Symbolic Characters.
We remove symbolic characters, such as single quotes, from words.

3.4 Syntactic Analysis by Combining SVMs with an HMM

At this stage, segmented subfields are represented as a feature vector, so an SVM can be applied to the feature vector. In order to handle the multi-class classification, we have adopted the 1-vs-rest method. In this method, one SVM is constructed for each type of bibliographic component in the training data. When provided with a subfield represented by a feature vector, each SVM calculates a score indicating how likely the given vector is to be the corresponding bibliographic component. For example, an SVM for the author component calculates a score indicating how likely the vector is to hold the author. The substring is then classified into the type whose SVM holds the highest score. We have adopted the 1-vs-rest method because it achieved the highest accuracy in the preliminary experiment. When applying the SVM, the kernel function must be determined in advance. In the preliminary experiment, we observed any differences in accuracy among the kernel functions, and adopted the linear kernel because it requires fewer parameters.

The SVMs utilize term frequency only from the feature vector. Therefore, it is difficult to determine whether "1998", for example, represents a page or a year. In addition, some terms such as 'Neural Networks' can be used as either a title or a journal name. Consequently, it appears impossible to estimate the type of the subfield, which may be matched to two or more fields, using the SVMs. This ambiguity can be reduced by using syntactic information. For this example, 'year' is usually located after 'page' and we are able to determine this subfield as a 'year' if there is a page number before this subfield. In order to utilize this kind of syntactic information, we have developed the combined method of using SVMs with the HMM.

Suppose a sequence $\mathbf{f}_1, \mathbf{f}_2, \ldots, \mathbf{f}_n$ of subfields is given, where each subfield is represented with a feature vector. We apply a 1-vs-rest SVM to each subfield independently. For this step, we generate a vector of scores calculated by the SVMs, instead of determining the type of the bibliographic components. Assume, for example, that the types of bibliographic components are author, title, journal, volume, day, month, year, publisher, and other. Then, for a given feature vector, nine SVMs calculate the corresponding scores, and we obtain a nine-dimensional vector that consists of scores of bibliographic components, as shown in (1).

$$\vec{} = \tag{1}$$

The score vector represents a distribution of the likelihood of the bibliographic components. A sequence $\mathbf{f}_1, \mathbf{f}_2, \ldots, \mathbf{f}_n$ of feature vectors is converted into the sequence $\mathbf{v}_1, \mathbf{v}_2, \ldots, \mathbf{v}_n$ of score vectors by the corresponding SVM.

We may, however, construct an HMM whose states corresponds to the types of bibliographic components. The graphical structure of an HMM corresponds to that of a finite state automaton comprising the syntactic structure of the citation. However, the graphical structure of our HMM is a complete graph, i.e., there is a transition from any one state to any other state. Figure 2 depicts an example of the graphical structure for extracting four types of bibliographic components. Syntactic information is represented with transition probabilities. For example, if the transition probability from an author node to a title node is high, that title is likely to be located after the author in the citation. Note that this type of HMM enables us to omit the model structure learning process required for a regular HMM.

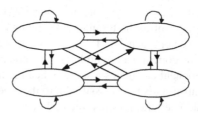

Fig. 2. An example of the graphical structure for extracting

Each state of the HMM produces a score vector, with the output probability representing the likelihood of a score vector at each state. For example, a score vector with a high author score has a high output probability at the state for the author, whereas it has low probabilities for the other states. Since the score vector is in continuous space, we must assign a density function to the output probability. Currently we use a Gaussian density function.

When given a sequence of score vectors, we may obtain the most likely state transition, as is the case with probabilistic finite state automata. For this transition, each score vector is associated with a state in the HMM, and each state is associated with a type of bibliographic component. Therefore, the most likely state transition determines the type of the score vector in the sequence, and consequently, the type of the subfields.

This classification method tends to classify the subfields according to the results of the SVMs due to the output probability. However, if the location of the subfields is unusual, the transition probability tends to correct the scores of the SVMs. For example, suppose a subfield located at the end of a citation obtains a score vector from the SVM having a high score for the author component. As authors are usually located at the head of the citation, the state transition probability for the case of authors located at the end of the citation is very low. Therefore, this state transition is not selected by the HMM. In this way, the SVMs' scores are corrected by the state transition.

As another example, assume that fields "1989" and "1990" appear in this order in a citation. The SVMs give the same score to both subfields, and it is impossible to determine whether they are page numbers or years. Using the transition probability, the proposed method will determine "1989" and "1990" to be a page number and a year, respectively. Therefore, both term frequency and syntactic information are used together in the proposed method.

Although we have omitted the learning methods for the SVMs and the HMM, we may obtain them from training data. Therefore, the proposed method can be applied to citations obtained from various resources by preparing training data specific to the resource. Furthermore, the proposed method is language independent, except for the feature vector construction, making it suitable for citation linkage.

3.5 Improved Method to Handle OCR Recognition Errors

In order to handle OCR-processed citations, we must handle OCR recognition errors. We handle these errors when constructing feature vectors. As mentioned in the previous section, we create the word table from clean training data. When given the citation via OCR, we calculate the edit distance between a word in the citation and words in the table, and regard the word as one whose edit distance is less than a predefined threshold.

4 Experimental Results

In this section, we discuss the results of five experiments we have conducted. The first was a preliminary experiment, where we compared methods for creating feature vectors (both with and without heuristics) described in section 3.3. The second experiment was to identify the attributes of subfields. The third was a complementary experiment, in which we compared the segmentation methods. In the fourth, we dealt with OCR data, and in the fifth, we dealt with citations that contain information in both English and Japanese. We used citations extracted from the IEICE Transactions on Fundamentals of Electronics, Communications and Computer Science, which was published in 2000. There are 371 articles and they contain 4651 citations. All citations are written in English. We executed 5-fold cross validation, using 75 percent of these citations as learning data and the remainder as test data. For this experiment, we set nine subfields as targets of classification, as shown in Table 1. In this table, the upper row shows the name of the subfields, while the lower row shows the range of objects that are synonymous with those subfields.

Table 1. Classification of Subfields

author	title	journal	volume	publisher	day	month	year	other
author	title	journal	volume	publisher	day	month	year	other
editor	booktitle	conference	number					
			page					

4.1 Experiment on Feature Vector Construction

An experiment was performed using the SVM^{light} method [12], which we have extended to deal with the multi-class problem. As a preliminary experiment, we first show in Figure 3 a comparison between a simple method and an improved one using heuristics described in section 3.3. This figure shows the recall, which will be reported for all following experimental results. The recall is defined as the proportion of the number of correctly extracted bibliographic components against all components. It is clear from these results that the improvement is significant. It is also clear that the improved method generates longer feature vectors than the simple method, as shown in Table 2. The longer feature vectors mean the increase of information used in the classification. And as a result of this, the accuracy of classification is improved.

Table 2. The length of feature vectors

	set 1	set 2	set 3	set 4	set 5
Simple Method	1.896	1.888	1.889	1.916	1.930
Improved Method	2.222	2.225	2.224	2.242	2.258

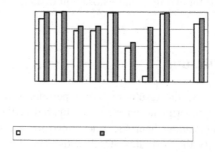

Fig. 3. Comparison of the methods for creating feature vectors

4.2 Experiments on the Combination of SVMs and an HMM

This section discusses the experiment results of dividing one citation into subfields and identifying their attributes, which is the main purpose of this study. First, we will compare the result of identification using the SVMs only, with the result of identification using both the SVMs and the HMM. From Figure 4, the accuracy of the experiment is higher for 'title', 'journal', 'publisher', and 'day' components when the HMM is applied. Comparing the totaled results (the bar labeled 'ALL' in Figure 4), the result when using SVMs and the HMM is 0.988, whereas the result when using the SVMs only is 0.974, showing that the experimental accuracy is higher when using both the SVMs and the HMM together.

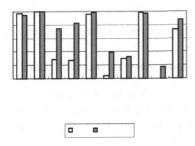

Fig. 4. Comparison of the methods for identification of the attributes of subfields

4.3   Comparison of the Segmentation Methods

In addition, in order to assure the superiority of the segmentation method described in section 3.2, we compared segmentation by the delimiter with the simpler approach of dividing into words. The results of this comparison are shown in Figure 5. The accuracy of the simple method for the totaled results is down to 0.874, so it is clear that dividing by the delimiter is the superior method. Looking at each field of the same figure, the accuracy of both methods is almost identical if the subfield consists of a single word, such as 'year', 'volume', 'month', or 'day'. However, the method of dividing by the delimiter is superior for the other, multi-word, subfields, suggesting that decreasing the information content by dividing a citation into very small parts results in misidentification of the attributes of the subfields.

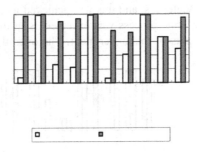

Fig. 5. Comparison of the dividing methods

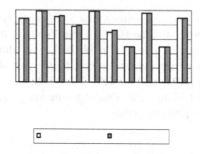

Fig. 6. Comparison between using and not using the edit distance

4.4 Experiments on Robustness Against OCR Data

We applied the proposed method to OCR data containing recognition errors. The OCR data used for this experiment originated from a section of the journal that was used in the above experiment. There are 371 citations, and the recognition accuracy of the OCR is 0.992.

In Figure 6, we compare results when creating feature vectors with and without using the edit distance. Little difference was recorded, due probably to the high recognition accuracy of the OCR, but using the edit distance provided slightly better results. As there are few cases where two or more words were recognized incorrectly in one subfield, it can be said that we can classify accurately for words that are correctly recognized by OCR. The accuracy for the totaled results is 0.978, suggesting that the extraction was highly accurate.

4.5 Experiment with Multi-language Citations

This section discusses results of experiments on a journal containing citations in both English and Japanese. The journal from which we have extracted citations is the Transactions of the Institute of Electronics, Information and Communication Engineers, published in 2000. There are 312 articles, containing 4814 citations in total. A space is inserted between words in Japanese citations, because there is no word boundary in Japanese sentences, and this was achieved using the Mecab morphological analyzer [13]. The same process was executed as in the above experiments, and Figure 7 shows the results of this experiment. The overall accuracy is 0.976 for the

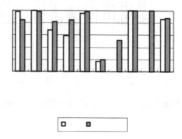

Fig. 7. Comparison of the identification methods (for multi-language citations)

method using both the SVMs and the HMM, showing that the proposed method gives valid results that are almost independent of the language of the citation.

5 Conclusions

In this paper, we have proposed a method to automatically extract bibliographic components, such as 'author' and 'title', in a citation by using SVMs and the HMM. It is possible to improve the accuracy of this extraction by additionally using heuristics. Moreover, we have also proposed an improved method that is robust to OCR data with some recognition errors. We also showed that our method does not depend on languages experimentally. For these experiments, we have used English-based heuristics but have not used Japanese-based ones, suggesting that we will be able to improve the accuracy of this experiment for Japanese citations.

We would like to point out future problems with the practical use of the proposed method in a digital library. It is necessary to handle many types of citations across different fields of study, yet only citations from two journals were used for these experiments. Citations referring to URLs or to software have different formats to citations referring to an article, but citations referring to articles are presented in similar formats. However, it is common that the citation format varies between fields of study. For example, in the Physical Society of Japan, the title is normally omitted from article citations, and accordingly, it will be assumed that the order of the components of the citations differ according to the type of journal. To solve this problem, it may be effective to construct correct HMM models for each field of study first, and then identify attributes of the subfields of the citation using the HMM model based on that journal. We believe that the proposed method can be customized to various types of citations easily due to its learning ability.

As an aside, it is often useful to correct OCR recognition errors. To achieve this, when registering the bibliographic data that are created by our method, we first examine the bibliographic database in a digital library. If a record exists that already has the same subfield data, it is possible to correct the errors.

References

1. Aizawa, A., Takasu, A., Oyama, K., Adachi, J.: Record Linkage of Multi-source Databases: Research Trends. NII Journal, No. 8 (2004) 43-51 (in Japanese)
2. Lawrence, S., Giles, C. L., Bollacker, K.: Digital Libraries and Autonomous Citation Indexing. IEEE Computer, 32(6) (1999) 67-71
3. Itho, T., Horibe, S., Shimbo, M., Matsumoto, Y.: Citation Indexing using Many Similarity Measures. IPSJ SIG Technical Report, 2003-DBS-130 (2003) 181-188 (in Japanese)
4. Takasu, A.: Probabilistic Interpage Analysis for Article Extraction from Document Images. Proc. of International Conference on Pattern Recognition (1998) 932-935
5. Takasu, A., et al: Approximate Matching for OCR-processed Bibliographic Data. Proc. Intl. Conf. on Pattern Recognition (13th ICPR) (1996) 175-179

6. Takasu, A.: Bibliographic Attribute Extraction from Erroneous References Based on Statistical Model. Proc. of 3rd ACM & IEEE Joint Conference on Digital Libraries (JCDL03) (2003) 49-60
7. Ristad, E.S., Yianilos, P.N.: Learning String Edit Distance. IEEE Trans., Patt. Anal. and Mach. Intellig., 20(2) (1998) 522–532
8. Bilenko, M., Mooney, R.J.: Adaptive Duplicate Detection Using Learnable String Similarity Measures. Proc. 9th ACM Intl. Conf. on Knowledge Discovery and Data Mining (2003) 39–48
9. Ayres, F. H., Huggill, J. A. W., Yannakoudakis, E. J.: The universal standard bibliographic code (USBC): its use for clearing, merging and controlling large databases. Program - Automated Library and Information Systems, 22(2) (1988) 117-132
10. Hsu, C., Lin, C.: A comparison on methods for multi-class support vector machines. Technical report, National Taiwan University, Taiwan (2001)
11. Kita, K.: Computation and Language, Volume 4: Probabilistic Language Model. University of Tokyo Press (1999)
12. Joachims, T.: Making large-scale SVM learning practical. Support Vector Learning, Schölkopf, B., Burges, C., Smola, A. (ed.), MIT-Press (1999)
13. Mecab: http://chasen.org/~taku/software/mecab/

Towards a Policy Language for Humans and Computers

Vicky Weissman[1] and Carl Lagoze[2]

[1] Department of Computer Science, Cornell University Ithaca, NY 14853
`vickyw@cs.cornell.edu`
[2] Department of Information Science, Cornell University Ithaca, NY 14853
`lagoze@cs.cornell.edu`

Abstract. A policy is a statement that an action is permitted or forbidden if certain conditions hold. We introduce a language for reasoning about policies called Rosetta. What makes Rosetta different from existing approaches is that its syntax is essentially a fragment of English. The language also has formal semantics, and we can prove whether a permission follows from a set of Rosetta policies in polynomial time. These features make it fairly easy for policy language developers to provide translations between their languages and ours. As a result, policy writers and (human) readers can create and access policies via the interface of their choice; these policies can be translated to Rosetta; and once in Rosetta can be translated to an appropriate language for enforcement.

1 Introduction

A policy describes the conditions under which an action, such as copying, modifying, or distributing digital content, is permitted or forbidden. Digital content providers write policies to govern the use of their works. For example, the ACM (Association for Computing Machinery) has a set of policies that regulate access to their digital library. These policies include statements such as 'members of the ACM are permitted to access the articles in the library for personal use' and 'members may not republish the articles without explicit permission from the ACM' [2]. Providers and managers of digital content want the task of writing policies to be as easy as possible. In addition, they want their policies to be intelligible to human readers and enforceable by computers.

Existing policy languages fail to meet these requirements. Although the details are deferred to the next section, the key points are as follows. Natural language is fairly intuitive for (human) readers and writers, but policies written in a natural language cannot be readily enforced by computers. XML-based languages, such as ODRL[9] and XrML [14], make progress towards enforceability, but have syntax that is too complex for non-expert users. Logic-based languages, such as the tractable fragments of first-order logic considered in [7] and Binder [4], are enforceable, but require policy writers and readers to be logicians and, thus, are not appropriate for many digital content creators and managers.

One solution is to create a new policy management system. The system would have a user interface to facilitate the writing and reading of policies, and would have a formal foundation so that policies written via the interface could be enforced in a provably correct manner. Unfortunately, this approach has two fundamental problems. First, it

R. Heery and L. Lyon (Eds.): ECDL 2004, LNCS 3232, pp. 513–525, 2004.

is unlikely that a single user interface will meet the needs of every community that is involved in right's management. Second, it will be difficult to convince industry to provide support for the language (e.g., build operating systems and media players that enforce the policies). Therefore, we are not proposing a new system. Instead, we are introducing a policy language that provides the glue between the different approaches.

We call our language the Rosetta Policy Language, because it is a gateway from one policy language to the next. The key features of Rosetta are:

- Statements in the language are constructed from a set of templates for English sentences. This makes the language well-suited to be the foundation for a variety of user interfaces, each tailored for specific communities (e.g., librarians, repository managers, content creators).
- The language is unambiguous and tractable. More precisely, we give the language formal semantics by providing a translation from expressions in the syntax to formulas in many-sorted first-order logic. It is this formal foundation that makes the language unambiguous, allows us to *prove* whether a permission or prohibition follows from a set of policies, and lets us show that determining if a permission or prohibition follows from a set of policies takes polynomial time.
- The language can serve as a front-end for existing policy language that are inaccessible to non-experts. Because several of the current policy languages in the formal methods community are fragments of many-sorted first-order logic, our translation amounts to one from our syntax to their languages. Furthermore, the translation from our language to ODRL and XrML is straightforward (although the details are left to the full paper).

In short, we believe that Rosetta's English-like syntax and formal semantics allow policy language developers to give translations between their approaches and ours. If this is done, then people can write and read policies via the interface of their choice and those policies can be translated through Rosetta to an appropriate reasoning engine (to answer questions such as what is and is not permitted) and to an appropriate enforcement mechanism (namely the one supported by the relevant industry).

The rest of this paper is organized as follows. In the next section we place our work in a broader context by briefly reviewing various policy languages. In Section 3, we introduce the basic syntax of our language, and in Section 4, we give formal semantics by translating expressions in the language to formulas in many-sorted first-order logic. Roughly speaking, any expression written in this core language can be translated to any of the popular languages discussed in Section 2. In Section 5 we discuss how the core language can be extended to match some of the unique capabilities of other policy languages, including ODRL, XrML, and the formal approaches, and we consider how these changes effect the language's usability and tractability. We conclude in Section 6.

2   Existing Approaches

Policies are traditionally written in a natural language, such as English. Using a natural language makes the policy writing task relatively easy, because the languages are usually well-known to the writer and are highly expressive. However, the meaning of statements in natural language can be ambiguous. For example, suppose that the ACM has two policies 'only authors may edit their works in the ACM digital library' and 'anyone who is not permitted to edit a work in the ACM digital library may submit a request for edits'. If Alice is the author of some work in the library, then the first policy might allow her to edit that work, or it might simply prevent other people from editing it. Furthermore, if the first policy does not permit authors to edit their works, then the second policy might allow Alice to submit a request for changes to her work (since she is not explicitly permitted to edit it) or it might not (since Alice is not forbidden from editing). Lacking precise meaning, such policies are confusing for human readers and unenforceable by computers.

The ODRL (Open Digital Rights Language) [9] and the XrML (eXtensible rights Markup Language) [14] were designed to capture policies in a way that could be readily manipulated by humans and enforced by computer programs. For many policy writers and readers; however, the languages are unintuitive. If a policy writer is not familiar with XML conventions, which is often the case, then she will find it difficult to write policies in any XML-based language, including ODRL and XrML. This is true despite XML toolkits such as XMLSpy [1] and Oxygen [16]. Moreover, even if the policy reader is conversant with XML-conventions, she will probably find policies written in an XML-based language difficult to read, because their meaning is buried in verbose XML syntax.

Not only does ODRL and XrML fail to meet the usability goal, they also fail to meet the enforceability goal. As with natural languages, ODRL is unenforceable because it is ambiguous. For example, a computer program cannot correctly enforce the policy 'anyone who is not permitted to edit a work may submit a request for edits' when written in ODRL, because the ambiguity that exists in the English version exists in the ODRL version as well. It also seems unlikely that an efficient enforcement algorithm exists for XrML, because determining if a permission follows from a set of XrML policies is an NP-hard problem [8] (i.e., the time needed to answer an arbitrary query is at least exponential in the size of the query).

While ODRL and XrML were under development, the formal methods community was creating its own policy languages. Most of the recent proposals are an extension of Datalog (function-free negation-free horn clauses) [6]. Perhaps the most popular choice is safe, stratified Datalog, which supports a limited use of negation (see for example, Delegation Logic[11], the RT (Role-based Trust-management) framework [13], Binder [4], and Sd3 [10]). Another option is Datalog with Constraints, which supports a limited use of functions (see for example [12] and [3]). Because these languages have formal semantics, they are unambiguous. Moreover, the languages are tractable; we can prove whether a permission follows from the policies written in one of these languages in polynomial time.

One problem with the Datalog languages is that they do not include policies that forbid actions if certain conditions hold. Instead, these languages assume that any action that is not explicitly permitted is forbidden. To see why this is a problem, suppose that Alice and Bob are collaborating on a multimedia project. Alice wants to show the work in progress to her friends and Bob does not care whether anyone sees the work before it is finished. Intuitively, Alice and Bob's policies do not contradict each other. However, if the policies are in one of the Datalog languages, then Bob's policy is that no one may view the unfinished work (since he does not explicitly allow the viewing) and, thus, Bob's policies do contradict Alice's. It is not hard to see that any two policy sets will contradict one another, unless they are identical. So, the Datalog approaches are not well-suited to environments in which multiple policy sets regulate the same resource.

To address this deficiency, we considered various fragments of first-order logic [7]. We refer to the most expressive tractable fragment discussed in [7] as the Lithium language. Lithium includes policies that forbid actions, although some restrictions on negation are needed to get tractability; the language also fully supports the use of functions. In many cases, the policies that people want to discuss can be written in Lithium and we can determine if those policies imply a permission or prohibition in polynomial time (see [7] for details).

Although the formal languages meet the enforceability goal and are sufficiently expressive for a number of applications, they are not appropriate for many policy writers or (human) readers. Policy writers are not typically logicians; therefore, expecting them to write policies in a fragment of first-order logic is unrealistic. Similarly, since policy readers are not usually logicians, they are not likely to understand the formulas (even though they are both succinct and unambiguous).

We have created Rosetta as a first step towards solving the usability and enforceability problems seen in the other languages. As discussed in the introduction, it is unlikely that a single interface will meet the usability goal for everyone involved in policy management. However, we believe that Rosetta provides a solid foundation for a family of intuitive interfaces, primarily because it has an English-like syntax and formal semantics. To make languages such as ODRL and XrML enforceable, we need to give them formal semantics (thereby removing ambiguity) and, if necessary, to find tractable fragments. We propose a formal semantics for ODRL in [15], and for XrML in [8]. (More specifically, we give a translation from policies written in a representative fragment of ODRL and XrML to formulas in many-sorted first-order logic and modal many-sorted first-order logic, respectively.) We have also found a tractable fragment of XrML that is fairly expressive [8] and are currently investigating the complexity of ODRL. While this work addresses key problems with both ODRL and XrML, the same problems are likely to exist in the next generation of policy languages (unless, of course, they are created by the formal methods community). Since we cannot rely on logicians retrofitting formal semantics to every new language, we need a way for the language developer to provide semantics without being a logician. This can be done through Rosetta. More specifically, language developers can guarantee that their policies are enforceable by translating them to the English-like (and, thus, fairly intuitive) Rosetta language. Of course, logicians are needed to extend Rosetta to suit more expressive languages; however, we expect that it will be much easier to extend Rosetta as needed than to give formal semantics to every new language directly.

3   Syntax

In this section, we introduce the basic syntax for our policy language, which we extend in Section 5. The language is a fragment of English with two exceptions. First, it supports a notion of labeling that is not commonly seen in English. We discuss the benefits of using labels later in the section. Second, for simplicity we relax the formal definitions of compound nominals and prepositions. Specifically, we include compound nominals such as 'ACM member' and 'library stacks' in our set of common nouns, and include 'than' in our set of prepositions even though it is sometimes used as a conjunction. The language is, admittedly, stilted; however, we believe that it provides a solid foundation for more natural user interfaces. Before presenting the language, we motivate our work with a few examples.

Example 1. Consider the simple sentence 'Alice's file is confidential'. While this sentence is not in our language, we can write the similar sentence 'if f is a file and Alice owns f, then f is confidential', where f is a label. Notice that the two sentences are not exactly equivalent; the first sentence, 'Alice's file is confidential', is ambiguous if Alice has zero files, or if she has more than one. The sentence in our language does not have this ambiguity because it says that every file that Alice has is confidential. ∎

Example 2. Consider the policy 'if a professor knows a student, then he is permitted to enter the library stacks'. This policy could mean that a student may enter the library stacks if the student has been vouched for by the professor, or it could mean that professors who socialize with students may enter the stacks. To determine the meaning of the policy, we need to know who is referred to by the pronoun 'he'. In our language, we avoid this ambiguity by using labels in place of pronouns. Specifically, we associate the common nouns professor and student with the labels p and s respectively. Then, we write the policy as 'if a professor p knows a student s, then s is permitted to enter the library stacks' or as 'if a professor p knows a student s, then p is permitted to enter the library stacks', depending on the policy's intended meaning. ∎

Example 3. Consider the policy 'ACM members may republish articles if they have permission from the ACM.' We could write this policy in our language as 'if an ACM member m has p and p is a permission and p is from ACM and a is an article, then m is permitted to republish a.' ∎

The syntax for our language is described by the grammar in Figure 1. To define the grammar, we use the abbreviations given in Figure 2 as well as the following notation. Elements in parenthesis are optional; s^+ denotes one or more occurences of s; and $[s \mid s']$ means s or s'. The start symbols are SS, CxP, and CxF. We note that basic facts such as 'Alice is a student' can be encoded in the language. Although these statements are not policies, they provide information that is often needed to determine the implications of policies. For example, to determine if Alice may download the syllabus, given the policy 'every student s may download the syllabus', we need to know if Alice is a student. We also remark that the language given below does not include a number of interesting features, including negation; however, the language is extended in Section 5.

We restrict the syntax so that the articles 'a' and 'an' appear in only if clauses, and the word 'every' never appears in an if clause. As a result, sentences such as 'Bob borrowed a book' and 'if every student s finishes the exam, then the teacher is permitted to post solutions' are not in Rosetta. It turns out that if we did not make this restriction, then determining if a permission follows from a set of statements in the language would

$SP \rightarrow NP$ is permitted to V_t NP	
$SF \rightarrow NP$ VP	
$SS \rightarrow SP \mid SF$	
$CdF \rightarrow SF$ (and SF)$^+$	
$CdS \rightarrow SS$ (and SS)$^+$	
$CxP \rightarrow$ if $[SS \mid CdS]$, then SP	
$CxF \rightarrow$ if $[SF \mid CdF]$, then SF	
$NP \rightarrow PN \mid$ the $CN \mid (a \mid an)$ CN $L \mid$	
every CN $L \mid L$	
$VP \rightarrow (V_{aux}) V_t$ $NP \mid$	
is $[Adj \mid (a \mid an) CN \mid (Adj) Prep NP]$	
$CN \rightarrow$ employee $\mid$ book $\mid$ collection $\mid$ ...	
$PN \rightarrow$ Alice $\mid$ University of Bath $\mid$ ...	
$L \rightarrow$ x $\mid$ y $\mid$ ...	
$V_t \rightarrow$ download $\mid$ edit $\mid$ distribute $\mid$ ...	
$V_{aux} \rightarrow$ is $\mid$ was $\mid$ does $\mid$ have $\mid$ ...	
$Adj \rightarrow$ trusted $\mid$ hi-res $\mid$ corrupt $\mid$ ...	
$Prep \rightarrow$ to $\mid$ of $\mid$ about $\mid$ with $\mid$ in $\mid$ ...	

SP	simple policy
SF	simple fact
SS	simple sentence
CdF	compound fact
CdS	compound sentence
CxP	complex policy
CxF	complex fact
NP	noun phrase
VP	verb phrase
CN	common noun
PN	proper noun
L	label
V_t	transitive verb
V_{aux}	auxiliary verb
Art	article
Adj	adjective
$Prep$	preposition

Fig. 1. The Grammar   **Fig. 2.** Abbreviations

be an undecidable problem. We discuss the technical details and their implications in the full paper. Also in the full paper, we extend the syntax so that common nouns do not need to be followed by labels. For example, in the full paper the sentence 'if every student finishes the exam, then the teacher is permitted to post solutions' is in the language, as is 'if a teacher vouches for a student s then s is permitted to enter the library stacks.' A preprocessing step adds a label after 'every student' and 'a teacher' before the translation (as described here) is done.

In practice, the set of terminal symbols (e.g., the adjectives, common nouns, and transitive verbs) will depend on the application. For example, the terminal symbols defined in a digital library application might include a proper noun for each employee, the common nouns 'adult' and 'child', the adjective 'hearing impaired', and the transitive verb 'download'. The symbols could be defined by the system before any policies are written; however, we expect that some of the terms will be imported from other applications or languages (XrML and ODRL both define a set of terms that are appropriate for various policies) and others will be created by policy writers 'as they go'. As an aside, the interface designer does not have to create a text-based application to use Rosetta; she simply has to provide a translation from the user's input (in whatever form it is given) to statements in our language.

In this section we have presented a simple grammar that is sufficiently expressive to capture a number of policies that are of practical interest. In Section 5, we consider various extensions to increase the language's expressivity. First, however, we give formal semantics to the language defined thus far.

4   Semantics

In this section we give a translation from statements in the grammar to formulas in many-sorted first-order logic. For the rest of this discussion, we assume knowledge of first-order logic at the level of Enderton [5]. More specifically, we assume familiarity with the syntax of first-order logic, including constants, variables, predicate symbols, function symbols, and quantification, with the semantics of first-order logic, including relational models and valuations, and with the notions of satisfiability and validity of first-order formulas.

We assume that the application provides a set *properNouns* of proper nouns, a set *commonNouns* of common nouns, a set *adjectives* of adjectives, a set *prepositions* of prepositions, a set *transitive Verbs* of transitive verbs, and a set *auxilliary Verbs* of auxiliary verbs. In addition, we define the set $verbs = \{transitive Verbs\} \cup \{v_{aux}v_t \mid v_{aux} \in auxilliary Verbs$ and $v_t \in transitive Verbs\}$. The vocabulary includes two sorts *ProperNouns* (e.g., Alice, University of Bath) and *Actions* (e.g., downloading 'Finding Nemo', editing a budget report). The vocabulary also includes the following symbols:

- a constant *pn* of sort *ProperNouns* for each $pn \in properNouns$;
- a constant *theCn* of sort *ProperNouns* and a unary predicate *Cn* that takes an argument of sort *ProperNouns* for each $Cn \in commonNouns$;
- a unary predicate *Adj* that takes an argument of sort *ProperNouns* for each adjective $Adj \in adjectives$;
- a binary predicate *Prep* that takes two arguments of sort *ProperNouns* for each preposition $Prep \in prepositions$;
- a binary predicate *AdjPrep* that takes two arguments of sort *ProperNouns* for each pair $(Adj, Prep)$, where $Adj \in adjectives$ and $Prep \in prepositions$;
- a binary predicate that takes two arguments of sort *ProperNouns* and a unary function with signature $ProperNouns \longrightarrow Actions$ for each $v \in verbs$; and
- a binary predicate **Permitted** that takes arguments of sort *ProperNouns* and *Actions*.

We remark that a common noun preceeded by the article 'the' refers to a specific object in much the same way that a proper noun does. For this reason, we associate each common noun in the syntax with a proper one in the translated language. We also associate each common noun with a predicate. Intuitively, $Cn(n)$ means the proper noun n is a Cn. For example, **Book**('*Moby Dick*') means that 'Moby Dick' is a book. The other predicates have a similar meaning. It is worth noting that if *verb* is a predicate, then $verb(n_1, n_2)$ means n_1 did *verb* to n_2. On the other hand, if *verb* is a function, then $verb(n_1, n_2)$ refers to the action of n_1 doing *verb* to n_2. For example, **Edits**(*Alice, the report*) is the statement 'Alice edits the report' if **Edits** is a predicate, and it is the action of Alice editing the report if **Edits** is a function. Also, **Permitted**(n, a) means n is permitted to do a. For example, **Permitted**(*Alice, edits*(*Alice, the report*)) means Alice is permitted to edit the report. The translation is given below.

- For every simple sentence, complex policy, and complex fact s in the language $[\![s]\!]^T = \forall x_1, \ldots, \forall x_n (\bigwedge_{(c,x) \in C_s} c(x) \Rightarrow ([\![s_L]\!]^I))$, where $x_1, \ldots, x_n$ are the labels in s and $C_s = \{(c, x) \mid$ the common noun c and the label x are in the same noun phrase in $s\}$.
- If $s = $ ' if S, then T' is a complex policy or a complex fact, then $[\![s]\!]^I = [\![S]\!]^I \Rightarrow [\![T]\!]^I$.

- If $s = S_1$ and ... and S_n is a compound sentence, then $[\![s]\!]^I = [\![S_1]\!]^I \wedge \ldots \wedge [\![S_n]\!]^I$.
- $[\![NP_1 \text{ is permitted to } V_t \ NP_2]\!]^I = \textbf{Permitted}([\![NP_1]\!]^O, [\![V_t]\!]^F([\![NP_2]\!]^O))$.
- $[\![NP_1 \ (V_{aux}) \ V_t \ NP_2]\!]^I = [\![V_{aux} \ V_t]\!]^P([\![NP_1]\!]^O, [\![NP_2]\!]^O)$.
- $[\![NP \text{ is } Adj]\!]^I = Adj([\![NP]\!]^O)$.
- $[\![NP \text{ is } (Art) CN]\!]^I = CN([\![NP]\!]^O)$.
- $[\![NP_1 \text{ is } Prep \ NP_2]\!]^I = Prep([\![NP_1]\!]^O, [\![NP_2]\!]^O)$.
- $[\![NP_1 \text{ is } Adj \ Prep \ NP_2]\!]^I = Adj Prep([\![NP_1]\!]^O, [\![NP_2]\!]^O)$, where $Adj Prep$ is the predicate associated with the pair $(Adj, Prep)$.
- $[\![PN]\!]^O = PN$, $[\![the \ CN]\!]^O = the \, CN$, which is the constant associated with CN, $[\![(a \mid an) CN \ L]\!]^O = L$, $[\![every \ CN \ L]\!]^O = L$, $[\![L]\!]^O = L$, $[\![verb]\!]^P$ is the predicate associated with $verb$, and $[\![verb]\!]^F$ is the function associated with $verb$.

To illustrate how the translation works, we revisit each of the examples in Section 3. For ease of exposition, we change the fonts and capitalization to match standard conventions For example, the common noun boy is associated with the predicate **Boy** and the constant *theBoy*.

Example 4. The translation of 'if f is a file and Alice owns f, then f is confidential' is $\forall f(\textbf{File}(f) \wedge \textbf{Owns}(Alice, f) \Rightarrow \textbf{Confidential}(f))$. ∎

Example 5. The translation of the complex policy 'if a professor p knows a student s, then s is permitted to enter the library stacks' is $\forall p \forall s(\textbf{Professor}(p) \wedge \textbf{Student}(s) \Rightarrow (\textbf{Knows}(p, s) \Rightarrow \textbf{Permitted}(s, \textbf{Enter}(the \ library \ stacks))))$, which is logically equivalent to $\forall p \forall s(\textbf{Professor}(p) \wedge \textbf{Student}(s) \wedge \textbf{Knows}(p, s) \Rightarrow \textbf{Permitted}(s, \textbf{Enter}(the \ library \ stacks)))$. ∎

Example 6. The translation of 'if an ACM member m has p and p is a permission and p is from ACM and a is an article, then m is permitted to republish a' is $\forall m \forall p \forall a(\textbf{ACMmember}(m) \Rightarrow (\textbf{Has}(m, p) \wedge \textbf{Permission}(p) \wedge \textbf{From}(p, ACM) \wedge \textbf{Article}(a) \Rightarrow \textbf{Permitted}(p, republish(a))))$, which is logically equivalent to $\forall m \forall p \forall a(\textbf{ACMmember}(m) \wedge \textbf{Has}(m, p) \wedge \textbf{Permission}(p) \wedge \textbf{From}(p, ACM) \wedge \textbf{Article}(a) \Rightarrow \textbf{Permitted}(p, republish(a)))$. ∎

We now formally define when a permission follows from a set of statements written in Rosetta, where a permission is a simple label-free policy, such as 'Alice is permitted to enter the library stacks'.

Definition 1. *Let $\{s_1, \ldots, s_n\}$ be a set of simple sentences, complex facts, and complex policies. A permission p follows from $\{s_1, \ldots, s_n\}$ iff the formula $[\![s_1]\!]^T \wedge \ldots \wedge [\![s_n]\!]^T \Rightarrow [\![p]\!]^T$ is valid.* ∎

Theorem 1. *Let $\mathcal{L}_0$ be the set of formulas of the form $[\![s_1]\!]^T \wedge \ldots \wedge [\![s_n]\!]^T \Rightarrow [\![p]\!]^T$, where each s_i is a simple sentence, complex sentence, or complex policy, and p is a permission. The validity problem for $\mathcal{L}_0$ is decidable in polynomial time.*

This result is immediate from the fact that every statement in the language translates to a formula that is essentially in Datalog. (Datalog does not include functions; however, the function symbols in our language cannot be nested. Including function symbols in this way does not effect tractability.) In fact, every statement in our language translates to a formula in Lithium and to an XrML policy (called a license in the XrML literature). Also, every policy in our language translates to a policy in ODRL. (ODRL does not include simple statements or complex facts.) This is not surprising; the language presented thus far arguably has the core features of any policy language. Thus, it is likely that every Rosetta policy can be translated to every language of interest. Of course, a policy that can be translated to a particular language of interest might not be expressible in Rosetta. Therefore, we consider various extensions to Rosetta in the next section.

5 Extensions

In this section, we consider key features of ODRL, XrML, Lithium, and the Datalog approaches that are not in our language, and we discuss the consequences of adding them.

5.1 Simple Extensions

There are a number of straightforward ways in which we can extend the language.

– Consider the sentence 'Bob is department chair from August, 1, 2002 to July 31, 2005'. Although this statement is not in our language, it is easy to modify our approach to include it. To do this, we extend the definition of verb phrases in the grammar to include strings of the form $is\ CN(PrepNP)^+$; we add an $(n+1)ary$ predicate $CN\,Prep_1\ldots Prep_n$ to the vocabulary for each sequence of a common noun and n prepositional symbols; and we add the following to the translation:

$$[\![NP_0\ is\ CN\,Prep_1 NP_1\ldots Prep_n NP_n]\!]^I = \mathbf{CnPreps}([\![NP_0]\!]^O,\ldots,[\![NP_n]\!]^O),$$

where $\mathbf{CnPreps}$ is the predicate associated with the sequence $CN, Prep_1,\ldots, Prep_n$. We remark that, as expected, $[\![NP_0\ is\ CN\,Prep_1 NP_1\ldots Prep_n NP_n]\!]^I = [\![NP_0\ is\ CN]\!]^I$ if $n = 0$ (i.e., if there are no prepositions following the common noun). Also, the sentence 'Bob is department chair from August, 1, 2002 to July 31, 2005' is in the extended language, and translates to

$$\mathbf{DepartmentChairFromTo}(Bob, August, 1, 2002, July31, 2005).$$

We can further extend the language to support an even wider range of statements by allowing sequences of prepositions to appear in noun phrases, at the end of every verb phrase, etc. These modifications are straightforward. Moreover, the additional predicates do not effect the language's tractability; we can still determine if a permission follows from a set of sentences in polynomial time. The only problem is that the translation does not attach any intrinsic meaning to words such as 'from' and 'to'. Therefore, it is up to the policy creator to include statements such as 'if x is department chair from t_i to t_f and t is greater than t_i and t is less than t_f then x is department chair at time t'. We discuss this in the full paper.

– ODRL, among other languages, supports a notion of action sequences. For example, Alice might be permitted to do the action sequence 'play 'Finding Nemo' and then pay five dollars'. We could extend our language to capture this idea by allowing verb phrases to have the form $(V_{aux}) V_t NP(and then (V_{aux}) V_t NP)^+$. The translation is analogous to our treatment for sequences of prepositional phrases; the extension does not effect tractability.

– Instead of having the sort *ProperNouns*, policy languages typically have a sort for principals (i.e., agents such as Alice) and resources (i.e., items such as the book 'Moby Dick'). Some languages have additional sorts for times, roles, and other useful categories. It is not difficult to mimic their approaches. To illustrate how this could be done, suppose that we wanted to replace our sort *ProperNouns* with two sorts *Princ* (for principals) and *Rsrc* (for resources). To do this, we would change the grammar so that $PN \rightarrow PN_P \mid PN_R$, where PN_P are proper nouns that are principals (e.g., Alice) and PN_R are proper nouns that are resources (e.g. 'Moby Dick'). We would need to make a similar split between common nouns, labels, adjectives, and prepositions; otherwise we would not be able to translate these to predicates that took arguments of the appropriate sort and, in the case of labels, to variables of the appropriate sort. In short, we can adapt our language to accommodate a variety of sorts in place of *ProperNouns*, but the result will be a language that is larger and, thus, less easy to use.

We believe that a better approach is to define common nouns such as 'principal' and 'resource' in our (unaltered) language. Then instead of defining an entity to be one sort or the other, we could make the same distinction, more or less, by adding sentences such as 'Alice is a principal' and '"Moby Dick' is a resource' to our set of statements. This approach does not have quite the same effect as multiple sorts because a proper noun can be described by several adjectives. As a result, a proper noun can be both a principal and a resource, or neither. Nevertheless, we feel that this approach strikes a better balance between expressivity and usability.

– ODRL classifies simple sentences based on whether or not a user has the ability to make the sentence true. For example, Alice can make the sentence 'Alice paid five dollars' true by paying five dollars, but if she is five years old, then there is little that she can do to make the sentence 'Alice is an adult' true. We can add this distinction to our language by splitting simple sentences into those that are within the user's control and those that are not. (Essentially, this is the same technique that we use to replace the sort *ProperNouns* with the sorts *Princ* and *Rsrc*.)

– XrML and ODRL allow an entity (principal, resource, etc.) to be a set of entities. We capture these groups in our language, by assuming that each one corresponds to a proper noun in *properNouns*. The relationship between a group and its members can be captured as policies and facts in the extended language. For example, to say that a group knows a password if a member of the group knows it, we could include the following complex fact in the set of statements: 'if a principal p knows a password w and p is a member of a group g, then g knows w'.

– ODRL supports statements such as 'at least one of the following policies hold: $p_1, \ldots, p_n$', 'exactly one of the following policies hold: $p_1, \ldots, p_n$', and 'all of the following policies hold: $p_1, \ldots, p_n$'. The last statement can be captured by simply including p_1 through p_n in the set of statements. To capture the other statements, we need to extend our language to support negation. To see this, notice that the statement 'at least one of the following policies hold: p_1, p_2' means 'if p_1 does not hold, then p_2 holds and if p_2 does not hold, then p_1 holds'. Similarly, 'exactly one of the following policies hold: p_1, p_2' means 'if p_1 does not hold, then p_2 holds, if p_2 does not hold, then p_1 holds, if p_1 holds, then p_2 does not hold, and if p_2 holds, then p_1 does not hold.' Adding negation to our language is not straightforward. We discuss it in some detail below.

5.2 Negation

Our language does not include sentences such as 'if Alice is not on disciplinary probation, then she is permitted to join the swim team' and 'Alice is not permitted to impersonate the professor'. It is easy to extend the language to include negation by replaying the definition of simple policies and verb phrases given in Section 3 to be, respectively,

$$SP \to NP \text{ is permitted to } V_t \ NP \mid NP \text{ is not permitted to } V_t \ NP$$
$$VP \to (V_{aux})(\text{not}) V_t \ NP \mid \text{is(not) } S,$$

where $S \to [Adj \mid (a \mid an)CN \mid (Adj)PrepNP]$. Accordingly, the translation could be extended to include the following definitions:

$$[\![NP_1 \text{ is not permitted to } V_t \ NP_2]\!]^I = \neg[\![NP_1 \text{ is permitted to } V_t \ NP_2]\!]^I$$
$$[\![(V_{aux}) \text{ not } V_t \ NP]\!]^I = \neg[\![(V_{aux})V_t \ NP]\!]^I$$
$$[\![\text{is not } S]\!]^I = \neg[\![\text{is } S]\!]^I,$$

where S is again $[Adj \mid (a \mid an)CN \mid (Adj)PrepNP]$.

Unfortunately, this solution leads to a language that is decidable, but not tractable.

Theorem 2. *Let $\mathcal{L}_1$ be the set of formulas of the form*

$$[\![s_1]\!]^T \wedge \ldots \wedge [\![s_n]\!]^T \Rightarrow [\![p]\!]^T,$$

where $\{s_1, \ldots, s_n\}$ is a set of statements (simple sentences, complex facts, and complex policies) and p is a permission in the language given in Section 3 extended to include negation. The validity problem for $\mathcal{L}_1$ is decidable; it is NP-hard.

The main reason for the NP-hardness result is that sentences can combine to imply new sentences without forming a chain. For example, consider the policies 'an employee e is permitted to enter the library stacks' and 'a student s is not permitted to enter the library stacks'. Together, these policies imply that employees are not students, because no one can be both permitted and not permitted to enter the stacks. Similarly, the policies 'if s is a good student, then s is permitted to watch 'Finding Nemo'' and 'if p is not a student, then p is permitted to watch 'Finding Nemo'' together imply that anyone who is good may watch the movie (since both a good student and a good non-student have permission). Determining the consequences of all these interactions is what leads to intractability.

By restricting the language appropriately, we can limit the ways in which statements interact and, thus, we can obtain a tractable fragment of the language that is still quite expressive. In [7] we give precise conditions under which a first-order policy language is tractable; these conditions readily apply to the language given here. We can restrict the language beyond what is strictly needed for tractability to create one that is still reasonably expressive and is also fairly easy to explain to users. (Details are given in the full paper.) In addition, if the set of statements include only simple facts and complex policies of the form ' if $[SF \mid CdF]$, then SP', then it is likely that we can determine if the statements imply a permission in a reasonable period of time. (See [7] for the empirical argument.)

Alternatively, we could tailor our support for negation according to how it is used in the Datalog languages or in ODRL. (XrML does not support negation; so, we cannot base our work on theirs.) However, as mentioned in Section 2, the Datalog approaches do not support negation in simple sentences or in the then clauses of complex policies or complex facts. Therefore, the languages might not support enough negation to be useful. Also, it is not clear how we could explain when negation could be used in the if clauses of complex sentences (the only place in which negation can appear), even if we were willing to restrict the language to make the task easier. As for negation in ODRL, we do believe that we could explain the ODRL restrictions on negation to a general audience. However, complexity results for ODRL are not available yet; so, we cannot rely on previous work to ensure that our language, extended to handle negation in the ODRL way, is tractable.

6   Conclusion

In this paper, we have introduced Rosetta, a policy language that is well-suited to be both the back-end for user interfaces and the front-end for policy languages that are otherwise inaccessible to non-experts. In the near future, we hope to work with our colleagues in human-computer interaction to design prototypes that exploit Rosetta's capabilities.

Acknowledgments

We would like to thank Joseph Halpern and Riccardo Pucella for giving helpful comments on earlier drafts. Authors supported in part by NSF under grants CTC-0208535 and IIS-9817416, by ONR under grants N00014-00-1-03-41 and N00014-01-10-511, by the DoD Multidisciplinary University Research Initiative (MURI) program administered by the ONR under grant N00014-01-1-0795, and by AFOSR under grant F49620-02-1-0101.

References

1. Altova. Xmlspy. http://www.xmlspy.com/products_ide.html, 2004.
2. Association for Computing Machinery. The ACM guide: Terms of usage. at http://portal.acm.org/info/usage.cfm, 2004.

3. E. Bertino, C. Bettini, E. Ferrari, and P. Samarati. An access control model supporting periodicity constraints and temporal reasoning. *ACM Transactions on Database Systems*, 23(3):231–285, 1998.

4. J. DeTreville. Binder, a logic-based security language. In *Proceedings 2002 IEEE Symposium on Security and Privacy*, pages 95–103, 2002.

5. H. B. Enderton. *A Mathematical Introduction to Logic*. Academic Press, New York, 1972.

6. H. Garcia-Molina, J. D. Ullman, and J. Widom. *Database Systems: The Complete Book*. Prentice Hall, New Jersey, 2002.

7. Joseph Halpern and Vicky Weissman. Using first-order logic to reason about policies. In *Proc. 16th IEEE Computer Security Foundations Workshop*, pages 187–201, 2003.

8. Joseph Halpern and Vicky Weissman. A formal foundation for XrML. In *Proc. 17th IEEE Computer Security Foundations Workshop*, 2004.

9. R. Iannella. ODRL: The open digital rights language initiative. `http://odrl.net/`, 2001.

10. T. Jim. SD3: A trust management system with certified evaluation. In *Proceedings 2001 IEEE Symposium on Security and Privacy*, pages 106–115, 2001.

11. N. Li, B. N. Grosof, and J. Feigenbaum. Delegation Logic: A logic-based approach to distributed authorization. *ACM Transaction on Information and System Security (TISSEC)*, February 2003. To appear.

12. N. Li and J. C. Mitchell. Datalog with constraints: A foundation for trust management languages. In *Proceedings of the Fifth International Symposium on Practical Aspects of Declarative Languages*, January 2003. To appear.

13. N. Li, J. C. Mitchell, and W. H. Winsborough. Design of a role-based trust-management framework. In *Proceedings 2002 IEEE Symposium on Security and Privacy*, pages 114–130, 2002.

14. MPEG. Information technology—Multimedia framework (MPEG-21) – Part 5: Rights expression language (ISO/IEC 21000-5:2004). `http://www.iso.ch/iso/en/`, 2004.

15. R. Pucella and V. Weissman. A formal foundation for ODRL rights. In *Workshop on Issues in the Theory of Security (WITS)*, 2004.

16. Ltd SyncRo Soft. Oxygen. `http://www.oxygenxml.com/javawebstart`, 2004.

Author Index

Lecture Notes in Computer Science

For information about Vols. 1–3092

please contact your bookseller or Springer

Vol. 3142: J. Diaz, J. Karhumäki, A. Lepistö, D. Sannella (Eds.), Automata, Languages and Programming. XIX, 1253 pages. 2004.

Vol. 3140: N. Koch, P. Fraternali, M. Wirsing (Eds.), Web Engineering. XXI, 623 pages. 2004.

Vol. 3139: F. Iida, R. Pfeifer, L. Steels, Y. Kuniyoshi (Eds.), Embodied Artificial Intelligence. IX, 331 pages. 2004. (Subseries LNAI).

Vol. 3138: A. Fred, T. Caelli, R.P.W. Duin, A. Campilho, D.d. Ridder (Eds.), Structural, Syntactic, and Statistical Pattern Recognition. XXII, 1168 pages. 2004.

Vol. 3137: P. De Bra, W. Nejdl (Eds.), Adaptive Hypermedia and Adaptive Web-Based Systems. XIV, 442 pages. 2004.

Vol. 3136: F. Meziane, E. Métais (Eds.), Natural Language Processing and Information Systems. XII, 436 pages. 2004.

Vol. 3134: C. Zannier, H. Erdogmus, L. Lindstrom (Eds.), Extreme Programming and Agile Methods - XP/Agile Universe 2004. XIV, 233 pages. 2004.

Vol. 3133: A.D. Pimentel, S. Vassiliadis (Eds.), Computer Systems: Architectures, Modeling, and Simulation. XIII, 562 pages. 2004.

Vol. 3132: B. Demoen, V. Lifschitz (Eds.), Logic Programming. XII, 480 pages. 2004.

Vol. 3131: V. Torra, Y. Narukawa (Eds.), Modeling Decisions for Artificial Intelligence. XI, 327 pages. 2004. (Subseries LNAI).

Vol. 3130: A. Syropoulos, K. Berry, Y. Haralambous, B. Hughes, S. Peter, J. Plaice (Eds.), TeX, XML, and Digital Typography. VIII, 265 pages. 2004.

Vol. 3129: Q. Li, G. Wang, L. Feng (Eds.), Advances in Web-Age Information Management. XVII, 753 pages. 2004.

Vol. 3128: D. Asonov (Ed.), Querying Databases Privately. IX, 115 pages. 2004.

Vol. 3127: K.E. Wolff, H.D. Pfeiffer, H.S. Delugach (Eds.), Conceptual Structures at Work. XI, 403 pages. 2004. (Subseries LNAI).

Vol. 3126: P. Dini, P. Lorenz, J.N.d. Souza (Eds.), Service Assurance with Partial and Intermittent Resources. XI, 312 pages. 2004.

Vol. 3125: D. Kozen (Ed.), Mathematics of Program Construction. X, 401 pages. 2004.

Vol. 3124: J.N. de Souza, P. Dini, P. Lorenz (Eds.), Telecommunications and Networking - ICT 2004. XXVI, 1390 pages. 2004.

Vol. 3123: A. Belz, R. Evans, P. Piwek (Eds.), Natural Language Generation. X, 219 pages. 2004. (Subseries LNAI).

Vol. 3122: K. Jansen, S. Khanna, J.D.P. Rolim, D. Ron (Eds.), Approximation, Randomization, and Combinatorial Optimization. IX, 428 pages. 2004.

Vol. 3121: S. Nikoletseas, J.D.P. Rolim (Eds.), Algorithmic Aspects of Wireless Sensor Networks. X, 201 pages. 2004.

Vol. 3120: J. Shawe-Taylor, Y. Singer (Eds.), Learning Theory. X, 648 pages. 2004. (Subseries LNAI).

Vol. 3118: K. Miesenberger, J. Klaus, W. Zagler, D. Burger (Eds.), Computer Helping People with Special Needs. XXIII, 1191 pages. 2004.

Vol. 3116: C. Rattray, S. Maharaj, C. Shankland (Eds.), Algebraic Methodology and Software Technology. XI, 569 pages. 2004.

Vol. 3114: R. Alur, D.A. Peled (Eds.), Computer Aided Verification. XII, 536 pages. 2004.

Vol. 3113: J. Karhumäki, H. Maurer, G. Paun, G. Rozenberg (Eds.), Theory Is Forever. X, 283 pages. 2004.

Vol. 3112: H. Williams, L. MacKinnon (Eds.), Key Technologies for Data Management. XII, 265 pages. 2004.

Vol. 3111: T. Hagerup, J. Katajainen (Eds.), Algorithm Theory - SWAT 2004. XI, 506 pages. 2004.

Vol. 3110: A. Juels (Ed.), Financial Cryptography. XI, 281 pages. 2004.

Vol. 3109: S.C. Sahinalp, S. Muthukrishnan, U. Dogrusoz (Eds.), Combinatorial Pattern Matching. XII, 486 pages. 2004.

Vol. 3108: H. Wang, J. Pieprzyk, V. Varadharajan (Eds.), Information Security and Privacy. XII, 494 pages. 2004.

Vol. 3107: J. Bosch, C. Krueger (Eds.), Software Reuse: Methods, Techniques and Tools. XI, 339 pages. 2004.

Vol. 3106: K.-Y. Chwa, J.I. Munro (Eds.), Computing and Combinatorics. XIII, 474 pages. 2004.

Vol. 3105: S. Göbel, U. Spierling, A. Hoffmann, I. Iurgel, O. Schneider, J. Dechau, A. Feix (Eds.), Technologies for Interactive Digital Storytelling and Entertainment. XVI, 304 pages. 2004.

Vol. 3104: R. Kralovic, O. Sykora (Eds.), Structural Information and Communication Complexity. X, 303 pages. 2004.

Vol. 3103: K. Deb, e. al. (Eds.), Genetic and Evolutionary Computation - GECCO 2004. XLIX, 1439 pages. 2004.

Vol. 3102: K. Deb, e. al. (Eds.), Genetic and Evolutionary Computation - GECCO 2004. L, 1445 pages. 2004.

Vol. 3101: M. Masoodian, S. Jones, B. Rogers (Eds.), Computer Human Interaction. XIV, 694 pages. 2004.

Vol. 3100: J.F. Peters, A. Skowron, J.W. Grzymała-Busse, B. Kostek, R.W. Świniarski, M.S. Szczuka (Eds.), Transactions on Rough Sets I. X, 405 pages. 2004.

Vol. 3099: J. Cortadella, W. Reisig (Eds.), Applications and Theory of Petri Nets 2004. XI, 505 pages. 2004.

Vol. 3098: J. Desel, W. Reisig, G. Rozenberg (Eds.), Lectures on Concurrency and Petri Nets. VIII, 849 pages. 2004.

Vol. 3097: D. Basin, M. Rusinowitch (Eds.), Automated Reasoning. XII, 493 pages. 2004. (Subseries LNAI).

Vol. 3096: G. Melnik, H. Holz (Eds.), Advances in Learning Software Organizations. X, 173 pages. 2004.

Vol. 3095: C. Bussler, D. Fensel, M.E. Orlowska, J. Yang (Eds.), Web Services, E-Business, and the Semantic Web. X, 147 pages. 2004.

Vol. 3094: A. Nürnberger, M. Detyniecki (Eds.), Adaptive Multimedia Retrieval. VIII, 229 pages. 2004.

Vol. 3093: S. Katsikas, S. Gritzalis, J. Lopez (Eds.), Public Key Infrastructure. XIII, 380 pages. 2004.